A CENTURY OF POETRY IN

THE NEW YORKER

A CENTURY OF POETRY IN

THE NEW YORKER

1925–2025

EDITED BY

Kevin Young

ALFRED A. KNOPF
NEW YORK
2025

All pieces in this anthology, except for the introduction, were originally published in *The New Yorker*.

Library of Congress Cataloging-in-Publication Data
Names: Young, Kevin, 1970– editor.
Title: A century of poetry in the New Yorker : 1925–2025 / edited by Kevin Young.
Other titles: New Yorker (New York, N.Y. : 1925)
Description: First edition. | New York : Alfred A. Knopf, 2025. | Includes index.
Identifiers: LCCN 2024030315 (print) | LCCN 2024030316 (ebook) | ISBN 9780593801932 (hardcover) | ISBN 9780593801949 (ebook)
Subjects: LCSH: American poetry. | LCGFT: Poetry.
Classification: LCC PS586 .C44 2025 (print) | LCC PS586 (ebook) | DDC 811.008—dc23/eng/20240711
LC record available at https://lccn.loc.gov/2024030315
LC ebook record available at https://lccn.loc.gov/2024030316

Jacket illustration by R. Kikuo Johnson
Jacket art direction and design by Chip Kidd

Manufactured in Canada
First Edition

CONTENTS

1920s & 1930s

LUNCH BREAK

1940s & 1950s

AFTER-WORK DRINK

1960s & 1970s

EVENING WALK

THE EIGHTIES

LAST TRAIN HOME

THE NINETIES

LATE SHIFT

THE AUGHTS (2000s TO EARLY 2010s)

NIGHT SONG

THE TEENS & TWENTIES

DAWNING

INTRODUCTION

I must have found it in a bookstore in Topeka, that yellow paperback, when I was a teenager there, new to poetry. Or not in a bookstore exactly, for there were no quirky independents—the Kansas capital saved that for record stores—or secondhand shops carrying old editions, at least that I knew of then. Rather, I bought my beloved copy of *The New Yorker Book of Poems*, the 1969 edition, in a B. Dalton or Town Crier, which was more a cigar and tobacco shop than a bookstore. Back then I took up whatever poetry made its way to my local shelves, which is how I read across a wide array—from Lawrence Ferlinghetti to Laura Riding—that has served me well. I still have my teenage copy of the 1969 selection, graced with neat little ink underlines beneath poems I must have admired. Many I recall loving, and others don't make the same impression now. I especially remember reading Anne Sexton's "Flee on Your Donkey," W. S. Merwin's "When You Go Away," and James Dickey's epic "Falling," which takes up more pages than one might manage in today's magazine. For me and many others, that anthology served as a time capsule of one of the most important magazines and poetry publications we have—and a kind of escape hatch for my imagination landlocked on the plains.

The New Yorker has published poetry from the start. Since the magazine's founding in 1925, poems have appeared alongside—and often among—its fiction, advertisements, and famous cartoons. The early verse helped define the frothy 1920s and 1930s—despite the

Great Depression—with rhyming wit by Ogden Nash, Dorothy Parker, and E. B. White, including some blues of Langston Hughes, down to the more serious 1940s and 1950s, where we find some of the more enduring names of contemporary poetry, including Elizabeth Bishop, Adrienne Rich, W. S. Merwin, and Sylvia Plath. This fruitful period was followed by the more political 1960s and 1970s, the lyrical 1980s and narrative 1990s, leading into those moments since the turn of the millennium that may be harder to characterize, if only because we find ourselves closer to them. The magazine's century of publishing has seen more than 13,500 poems squeezed in and spread out—poems by turns humorous and serious, epic and short, visionary and tactile, formal and experimental, topical and tireless.

We can say that the poems of our time aren't afraid to use humor or heartbreak, to abandon or include rhyme, to write about events small and cataclysmic, from 9/11 to the recent pandemic, engaging the world as it is and inventing worlds that may or may not be more enjoyable to inhabit. Much like the intrepid fiction that fills each issue—as well as a companion centenary anthology of *New Yorker* short fiction published alongside this one—the poems in the *New Yorker* take us on a journey, often through a writer's own evolving styles, themes, losses, and lessons. A poet like the late Merwin appeared in the pages of *The New Yorker* for more than six decades—and over two hundred times, not counting a decent amount of prose work. It is hard to picture any other such longstanding, ever-changing relationship with a publication, though others like Nobel laureates Louise Glück and Seamus Heaney come close, appearing regularly in the magazine from their earliest successes to after their deaths.

Decades after I first read the anthology and subscribed to the magazine—and after first appearing in the magazine myself in 1999—being named poetry editor in 2017 was an incredible full-circle moment and an honor. I knew the submissions, then clocking around forty thousand a year, were daunting but doable with the help of a lone reader and an intrepid assistant. But it was the memorial function of editor I hadn't anticipated—when prominent poets die, many of them past contributors, I have been moved or asked to write about them, to survey their careers, for *The New Yorker*. The experience is often uncanny: the Irish poet Ciaran Carson wrote me in the spring of 2019

to let me know he was dying from cancer; and that, after his diagnosis, he had created new poems, enough to fill a book. Or was it the poems had bid him to write them? Some of these he enclosed; I took two. His final poem appeared the week he died, the very week his book was published. In turn, the Irish poet Eavan Boland, whom I knew rather better, died suddenly in 2020; a new poem by her appeared, unplanned, the day after she died. There is a way that poetry must include the unexpected, the necessary, and the prescient.

So when the magazine's longtime editor David Remnick asked whether I was interested in editing this centenary anthology you have in your hands, I answered: only since I was fifteen years old.

Imagine my surprise when I pulled down the 1969 edition from my Zoom-ready bookshelf and found that in its 900 poems and 835 pages, no people of color appear—unless you count Jorge Luis Borges and one-fourth of William Carlos Williams. It is a striking absence, though many I have since mentioned it to have not found it surprising. For me such an absence conjures up Marianne Moore and her famous declaration about her radically revised collected poems: "Omissions are not accidents." (Moore did appear in the magazine as well as the 1969 anthology.) It isn't enough to say that the magazine merely overlooked or ignored Black and brown poets for decades; one has to try hard to miss nearly the entirety of Black poetry and its vibrancy across much of the twentieth century.

Nonetheless, knowing that the magazine did publish at least three Langston Hughes poems not considered worthy of the 1969 edition, I went back to the archive, hunting via spotty Internet searches and, with the help of deputy poetry editor Hannah Aizenman, spot-checking bound volumes of past issues from a time when the magazine's table of contents inexplicably included names of poems but no page numbers, so that we had to flip through issues page by page. Without a full database yet before us, I was holding out hope that we might locate a clutch of fantastic lost Black women poets of the past, say, who the magazine somehow published but didn't gather; or a bevy of experimentalists of any background that reflected the breadth and strength of American poetry over this past century, not to mention the ancient traditions of Native, African, and Asian poetry.

It was not to be. Having personally gone through a full database of all 13,500 poems published over the past hundred years, I can

safely say that with a few exceptions, *The New Yorker* didn't publish any poet who wasn't white for nearly the first seventy-five years of its history. On gender diversity it was better, if not actually fairly good, especially early on, when verse and humor were not seen—at least then—as male-only domains. Dorothy Parker, Elinor Wylie—and a host of other names (and pseudonyms) lost to time—graced our pages from the magazine's inception. But after Langston Hughes, no Black, brown, Asian, or Native poets appeared in *The New Yorker*. Indeed, after the last representation of Hughes in 1942, I could not locate any Black poets again until three decades later, in 1972, when Derek Walcott first appears; Michael S. Harper and Audre Lorde were allowed one poem each a few years later. *The New Yorker* didn't publish any Asian or Asian American poets to speak of until the 1980s, and Native voices had to wait even longer.

While I knew that Hughes was my literary ancestor, and had also lived in Kansas, I hadn't known he was the first Black writer in the magazine's history. And only in editing this anthology did I realize that, depending on how you count, I was only the sixth Black poet to appear in *The New Yorker*, exactly sixty years later. Such a legacy includes the important "Black in America" double issue of April 29 and May 6, 1996—that issue, with an Afro-deco Eustace Tilley on the cover rather than the iconic one complete with monocle, featured poems by Rita Dove and selections from *The Bounty* by Walcott, as well as a "memoir" by Anna Deavere Smith that reads as a poem (which is how you'll find it here). I have interleaved some of Walcott's "Bounty" poems throughout, and he is one of the several Nobel laureates in Literature who often appeared well before they were as revered as they came to be, including Glück and Heaney, Joseph Brodsky, Czesław Miłosz, Wisława Szymborska, and Tomas Tranströmer.

To say the magazine for decades didn't include a wide array of voices is not to say it wasn't without race. It can be startling to learn that from the start white poets, often notable ones, invoked (or mocked) those who were different, whether that's going uptown to Harlem, as does Alfred Kreymborg's cringey "Crossing the Color Line" from 1931, or James Dickey's "Slave Quarters" from 1965. Such poems have not aged well, and rather than devoting space to them, I have included works across time, often by white writers, that

do consider the complications of race, however uneasily, whether it is "At the Nordic Native American Society" or an ode "To Cab Calloway" from the 1920s; Marianne Moore's "Tom Fool at Jamaica" (1953) or Eudora Welty's "A Flock of Guinea Hens Seen from a Car" with its question, "Do you ever wonder where Africa has fled?" To be sure, we also have the powerful protests of Merwin's "The Asians Dying" (1966), William Stafford's "Slave on the Headland" (1977), and more recent work wrestling with questions found regularly in *The New Yorker* news stories and award-winning features.

The difficult truth is that *The New Yorker* missed out on decades of fine work—including, in African American poetry alone, all but ignoring the Harlem Renaissance of the 1920s and 1930s, which had work as lively (and rhyming) as the rest of what it did publish, and the Black Arts poets of the 1960s, who rejected *The New Yorker* long before it rejected them. Such omissions or metaphoric redlining are not only not accidental but look more and more like a systemic failing of the imagination, reminding us that any recent broadening of poetry is both welcome and awfully late to the party. We are fortunate that such lack of breadth is as unimaginable today as are the kind of silly questions, once posed so often in academic conferences and literary screeds as late as the early aughts, on whether poetry can be political. The answer of course is that leaving out large parts of the literary population, much less the populace, is a political act, however unacknowledged its legislators, to riff off Shelley. The fact of these omissions may remain, but so does the poetry—which, in its strength and singing, survives in our breath and our bodies.

A Century of Poetry in The New Yorker is arranged in alternating sections by both decades and times of day. The sections organized by eras are meant to represent the history of the work but also the times that shaped it. These sections group the generations, allowing Dorothy Parker to talk back to Ogden Nash or F. Scott Fitzgerald (and anyone else who'll listen) and featuring poets not read as widely today, such as Marjorie Allen Seiffert, who wrote as herself but also using a pseudonym, "Angela Cypher." Cypher acts less as a pen name than as what Portuguese poet Fernando Pessoa called a "heteronym": another entire persona complete with biographical backstory. Seiffert is all the more interesting for being part of the Spectra Hoax, the

notorious creation of poets Witter Bynner and Arthur Davison Ficke, who expanded their hoax to other poets before being exposed. (Yet not before, in a funny twist, Bynner wrote a credulous review of his own hoax poetry in the unsuspecting *New Republic*.) Even, or especially, after the exposure of her Spectra persona, Elijah Hay, Seiffert used Cypher as a mask and metaphor, its echo of her name conjuring a voice by turns wry, sly, and mysterious. In the end, Cypher is a better poet than Seiffert.

Such discoveries continue, with the 1920s and 1930s selections including more popular bohemians, from Joseph Moncure March (best known now for *The Wild Party*) to Maxwell Bodenheim. Satire and playful verse predominate, yet the 1930s end with some of the more poignant poems of any era: W. B. Yeats's "Death"; Louise Bogan's "To My Brother," a heartbreaking elegy for her sibling lost in World War I, which she was only able to write years later; and W. H. Auden's "Song," better known as "Refugee Blues," which appeared in 1939. The first of several decades of appearances by Auden in the magazine, "Song" remains an empathic use of the blues, recognizing the ways this music made in the Mississippi Delta gives voice to those who have less than a little.

Poems like Auden's usher in the 1940s and 1950s, riven by war, with poets who should be better known, like Karl Shapiro, Dilys Bennett Laing, and even Dorothy Parker, writing directly of conflict. Yet the entire era was inarguably shaped by it—take Malcolm Cowley's "The End of the World," which must have seemed near, or cult figures like Weldon Kees, whose portrait of "Robinson" represents a Crusoe lost in the modern world. "The dog stops barking after Robinson has gone. / His act is over. The world is a gray world, / Not without violence." Kees's car was found beside the Golden Gate Bridge and his body never recovered. Many a poem and plot have him escaped somewhere, resurrected like Jim Morrison or Tupac before their time.

It is at midcentury that the poets who began deepening the magazine's poetic reach and relevance began appearing. By the 1950s and 1960s, *The New Yorker* had right-of-first-refusal contracts with the likes of Elizabeth Bishop and Sylvia Plath, bringing out some of their most famous poems, some even after their deaths. Bishop's now-published letters to her *New Yorker* editor reveal the depth of the

editor-poet relationship and also describe no doubt boozy lunches and long vacations that anyone today would envy. (I will be gone till October and out of contact so please send to such and so in my stead as I'll be beyond reach. . . .) Merwin and Adrienne Rich began publishing, soon followed by other poets of the 1960s such as Mark Strand, Anne Sexton, and C. K. Williams, their poems embracing unrest much as their times did. Protest was in the air and in the magazine's pages.

Still, the record remains spotty in places. Now-popular poets like Denise Levertov and Frank O'Hara, to name just two, didn't appear in the magazine during their lifetimes; I leave it to another scholar to discover whether these omissions were rejections or the result of the writers' choosing not to submit. Rich, too, quit publishing in *The New Yorker*—or it quit publishing her—well before her more radical work (and while she still used her middle name, Cecile). Even a poet as beloved as E. E. Cummings, for many emblematic of the 1920s, doesn't appear until 1963, after his death—with ten poems, from which all his work included here is drawn.

This is not to say that there aren't unexpected revolutionary inclusions. Allen Ginsberg appeared in 1968 at the height of if not his powers, then his fame, and not again till the 1990s. Auden continued to appear, penning a moon-landing poem in 1969 and marveling at human foibles until his death in 1973. Indeed, Auden's passing might mark a turning in the work found in the magazine. During the 1970s into the 1980s, a period characterized by frequently longer poems and expansive poetry, *The New Yorker* began welcoming the lively and experimental work of Audre Lorde and Michael Harper, Glück and Heaney, Walcott and John Ashbery, to the delight of readers and critics alike. While Merwin, Bishop, Mark Strand, Sylvia Plath, and many others speak at length and say what only they can, there are many poets whose names might be new to us, offering up surprising work that tells us news we still need. There are also a number of songwriters who beautifully blur the lines, from Patti Smith and Joni Mitchell to Leonard Cohen and Johnny Cash.

There's a sense of discovery in these pages, reflected especially in the "times of day" sections of this anthology. These thematic sections move from "Morning Bell" to "Lunch Break" to "After-Work Drink" and on through the afternoon and evening, when "Night Song" at last gives way to "Dawning." Such sections mean to capture not only the movement of poetry across the past century but also the process of finding poems in the magazine as they jostle for attention beside stellar prose and those ever-popular cartoons; they show us how poems speak intimately and naturally to one another across the decades. In reading and rereading, I was constantly struck by the ways in which poets talk to one another, penning elegies (James Merrill's for Bishop; John Berryman's "Note to Wang Wei"), echoing styles, confiding their love. James Laughlin remembers his troubled author Ezra Pound in a poem that quickly turns to consider a private, failed romance; a clutch of poems from *Birthday Letters* by Ted Hughes gives a wrenching account of his courtship and marriage to the poet Sylvia Plath long after her suicide. Or, appearing decades apart, single poems by disparate writers about mules or drinking or sunrise, moose or mushrooms or hermit crabs, connect across the ether.

This book's daylong journey also allows a nod to the seasonal structure of the little-known *New Yorker Book of Verse* from 1936, which captures the first full decade of the magazine, but most especially it reinforces my core belief: that good poems make the everyday extraordinary and turn the extraordinary into a daily occurrence. Let's call them *refrigerator poems*—the kind of thing people cut out of the physical magazine and once put on their fridge, and now click as "likes" and send around the Internet and social media, sharing those words and the music that moved them. This readership is intimate, deep, and daring to care. I've had people come up to me at readings and show me *New Yorker* poems they carry folded in a wallet or purse, keepsakes always found on their person—the ultimate compliment, whose spirit is meant to be reflected in all of the selections here.

Given the scope of the book, those who wish to see all of one poet are encouraged to use the index by author, or if there's that one poem you cannot recall or wish to know the date of publication for, the title index should help. But in the main, the experience of reading the poems is meant to mirror that of the magazine—you go looking for something but also find more than you sought. Given the space constraints of even a generous book, there are poets once widely published who don't appear here at all; there are others who seem to speak all the more urgently now, who have bigger selections than in the past. Poets that the magazine missed but included later—not just Cummings but also Robert Hayden, Gertrude Stein, Robert Frost, Günter Grass, Hilda Morley, and others who appeared posthumously—are generally included when their poems first appeared, rather than when they wrote. This allows us to discover poets in an approximation of how and when the *New Yorker*'s readers did.

Above all, there is no way to re-create the entirety of the vast explosion of poetry and newer, essential poets over the last thirty years. This expansion of poetry was hard-won and shouldn't be taken for granted, and was ushered in by my two prior poetry editors, Alice Quinn (who served from the late 1980s to the mid-aughts) and Paul Muldoon (editor from 2007 to 2017). It is Alice who tells of finding Adam Zagajewski's poem "Try to Praise the Mutilated World" across the transom in those hazy days after the 9/11 attacks. This certainly was a redefining moment, which begins this book. The poem, originally published in the immediate wake of September 11, 2001, is bookended at the volume's close by Ada Limón's equally era-defining "The End of Poetry," published in 2020 right after the onset of the global Covid pandemic. These profound poems spoke to their moments and still speak to ours; their power is all the more notable in that they are both about and associated with profound junctures in our recent history but were written and submitted before such events occurred. Their echoes and effects only reinforce the notion that poetry is not only present but prescient. Great poems remain both timely and timeless.

In reading thousands of poems a year, and all the more for this anthology, those poems that make an impression do so because they uncover something for a reader, through language and music, form and freedom, something that we might not anticipate or know we need. A poetry of necessity is what drives me as a writer, reader, and editor. Because *The New Yorker* is a weekly magazine, we are able to run pieces almost immediately that speak to the fire in Notre-Dame, the onset of a global pandemic, or the murder of George Floyd, just to name some events my tenure has witnessed. By any measure this has been a time of societal change, even upheaval, as well as man-made and natural disasters—often commemorated in the poems themselves, not to mention the *New Yorker*'s iconic covers. Poems about 9/11 like Galway Kinnell's "When the Towers Fell" or Deborah Garrison's "I Saw You Walking" and Merwin's "To the Words," or those I've been able to publish more recently—from Terrance Hayes's "George Floyd" to Erika Meitner's "To Gather Together"—remind us that if people do not get the news from poems, they do find in them some comfort from the news, whether escape, investigation, or testimony, often in the same breath.

Then there are those celebrations of life in the face of it all— indeed you could say that this *Century of Poetry in The New Yorker* is framed by that very idea of going beyond survival into celebration, whether by Zagajewski and Limón, by Gabrielle Calvocoressi's "Hammond B3 Organ Cistern" or Saeed Jones's "Alive at the End of the World." "The End of the World was a nightclub," he writes. "The End of the World leaked music / like radiation, and we loved the neon echo, even / though it taunted us or maybe because it taunted us." The world is always about to end—might as well go on ahead and dance awhile.

—*Kevin Young*

A CENTURY OF POETRY IN

THE NEW YORKER

ADAM ZAGAJEWSKI

TRY TO PRAISE THE MUTILATED WORLD

Try to praise the mutilated world.
Remember June's long days,
and wild strawberries, drops of wine, the dew.
The nettles that methodically overgrow
the abandoned homesteads of exiles.
You must praise the mutilated world.
You watched the stylish yachts and ships;
one of them had a long trip ahead of it,
while salty oblivion awaited others.
You've seen the refugees heading nowhere,
you've heard the executioners sing joyfully.
You should praise the mutilated world.
Remember the moments when we were together
in a white room and the curtain fluttered.
Return in thought to the concert where music flared.
You gathered acorns in the park in autumn
and leaves eddied over the earth's scars.
Praise the mutilated world
and the gray feather a thrush lost,
and the gentle light that strays and vanishes
and returns.

(Translated, from the Polish, by Clare Cavanagh.)

(2001)

MORNING BELL

W. S. MERWIN

ANOTHER YEAR COME

I have nothing to ask of you,
Future, heaven of the poor.
I am still wearing the same things.

I am still begging the same question
By the same light,
Eating the same stone,

And the hands of the clock still knock without entering.

MAY SWENSON

SNOW BY MORNING

Some for everyone,
plenty,
and more coming—

fresh, dainty, airily arriving
everywhere at once,

transparent at first,
each faint slice—
slow, soundlessly tumbling;

then quickly, thickly, a gracious fleece
will spread like youth, like wheat,
over the city.

Each building will be a hill,
all sharps made round—

dark, worn, noisy narrows made still
wide, flat, clean spaces;

streets will be fields,
cars be fumbling sheep;

a deep, bright harvest will be seeded
in a night.

By morning we'll be children
feeding on manna,
a new loaf on every doorsill.

JANE COOPER
THE WEATHER OF SIX MORNINGS

I
Sunlight lies along my table
like abandoned pages.

I try to speak
of what is so hard for me—

this clutter of a life—
puritanical signature!

In the prolonged heat insects,
pine needles, birch leaves

make a ground bass of silence
that never quite dies.

II
Treetops are shuddering
in uneasy clusters

like rocking water
whirpooled before a storm.

Words knock at my breast,
heave and struggle to get out.

A black-capped bird
pecks on, unafraid.

Yield then, yield
to the invading rustle of the rain.

III
All is closed in
by an air so rain-drenched

the distant barking of tied-up dogs
ripples to the heart of the woods.

Only a man's voice
refuses to be absorbed.

Hearing of your death
by a distant roadside

I wanted to erect some marker
though your ashes float out to sea.

IV
If the weather breaks
I can speak of your dying,

if the weather breaks,
if the crows stop calling

and flying low
(again today there is thunder

outlying . . .),
I can speak of your living,

the lightning-flash of meeting,
the green leaves waving at our windows.

V
Yesterday a letter
spoke of our parting—

a kind of dissolution
so unlike this sudden stoppage.

Now all the years in between
flutter away like lost poems.

And the morning light is so delicate,
so utterly empty . . .

at high altitude, after long illness,
breathing in mote by mote a vanished world. . . .

VI
Rest,
a violin bow, a breeze

just touches the birches.
Cheep—a new flute

tunes up in a birch top.
A chipmunk's warning skirrs. . . .

Whose foot disturbs these twigs?
To the sea of received silence

why should I sign
my name?

CHARLES SIMIC

THIS MORNING

Enter without knocking, hardworking ant.
I'm just sitting here debating
What to do this cold, rainy day?
It was a night of the radio turned down low,
Fitful sleep, vague, troubling dreams.
I woke up lovesick and confused.
I thought I heard Estella in the garden singing
And some bird answering her,
But it was the rain. Dark treetops swaying
And whispering. "Come to me, my desire,"
I said. And she hurried to me,
Her breath smelling of mint, her tongue
Wetting my cheek, and then she vanished.
Slowly day came, a gray streak of daylight
To wash my hands and face in.
Hours passed, and then you crawled suddenly
Under the door, and stopped before me.
You visit the same tailors the mourners do,
Mr. Ant. I like the long silence between us.
Quiet, that holy state even the rain
Knows about. Listen to her begin to fall,
As if with eyes closed,
Muting each drop in her wild-beating heart.

DELMORE SCHWARTZ

A LITTLE MORNING MUSIC

The birds in the first light twitter and whistle,
Chirp and seek, sipping and chortling; weakly, meekly, they speak and
    bubble
As cheerful as the cherry would, if it could speak when it is cherry ripe or
    cherry ripening.

And all of them are melodious, erratic, and gratuitous,
Singing solely to heighten the sense of morning's beginning.

How soon the heart's cup overflows, how soon it is excited to delight and
    elation!

And in the first light the cock's chant, roaring,
Bursts like rockets, rising and breaking into fragments of brilliance;
As the fields arise, cock after cock catches on fire,
And the pastures loom out of vague blue shadow,
The red barn and the red sheds rise and redden, blocks and boxes of
    slowly blooming wet redness;
Then the great awe and splendor of the sun comes nearer,
Kindling all things, consuming the forest of darkness, lifting and lighting up
All the darkling ones who slept and grew
Beneath the petals, the frost, the mystery and mockery of the stars.

The darkened ones turn slightly in the faint light of the small morning,
Grow gray or glow green—
        They are gray and green at once
        In the pale cool of blue light;
They dream of that other life and that otherness
        Which is the darkness going over
Maple and oak, leafy and rooted in the ancient and famous light,
In the bondage of the soil of the past and radiance of the future.

But now the morning is growing, the sun is soaring, all
That lights up shows, quickly and slowly, the showering plenitude of
    fountains,
And soon an overflowing radiance, actual and dazzling, will blaze and
    brim over all of us;
Discovering and uncovering all color and all kinds, all forms and all
    distances, rising and rising higher
        and higher, like a stupendous bonfire of consciousness,
        Gazing and blazing, blessing and possessing all vividness and
        darkness.

ELLEN BASS

THE MORNING AFTER

You stand at the counter, pouring boiling water
over the French roast, oily perfume rising in smoke.
And when I enter, you don't look up.
You're hurrying to pack your lunch, snapping
the lids on little plastic boxes while you call your mother
to tell her you'll take her to the doctor.
I can't see a trace of the little slice of heaven
we slipped into last night—a silk kimono
floating satin ponds and copper koi, stars falling
to the water. Didn't we shoulder
our way through the cleft in the rock of the everyday
and tear up the grass in the pasture of pleasure?
If the soul isn't a separate vessel
we carry from form to form
but more like Aristotle's breath of life—
the work of the body that keeps it whole—
then last night, darling, our souls were busy.
But this morning it's like you're wearing a bad wig,
disguised so I won't recognize you
or maybe so you won't know yourself
as that animal burned down
to pure desire. I don't know
how you do it. I want to throw myself
onto the kitchen tile and bare my throat.
I want to slick back my hair
and tap-dance up the wall. I want to do it all
all over again—dive back into that brawl,
that raw and radiant free-for-all.
But you are scribbling a shopping list
because the kids are coming for the weekend
and you're going to make your special crab-cakes
that have ruined me for all other crab-cakes
forever.

ROBIN COSTE LEWIS

AUBADE

All night, my psyche comforts itself
with you. It delights in watching your body

travel through landscapes so lush even the bidet
is painted with twisting gouache flowers.

They frame a lady who rides an elephant,
while a gentleman stands holding up a lotus

toward her saddle. Then we are in a city, climbing
up a brownstone into the home of people you love.

I step behind you, smiling quietly into our bodies'
clement warmth. Except, instead of the usual deflecting

skirt, in my dream I've dressed you in mildly tailored
pants. Next, we are in a building, in a bazaar, in

a city inhabited by people subtle and endless
shades of a dark cinnamon. We walk through

room after room, then stop when we come
across two leather chairs with frames

carved from mangrove and mahogany.
The goatskin is dyed so red the color sprints

back and forth across that thin, thin line
between very elegant and exquisitely tacky.

We take both. Caramel and beige,
we are the whitest things around.

The shopkeepers greet us with a fondness
and familiarity that is also historical apology.

But we look back through our bodies completely
pleased by what—for millennia—the cell has seen

and done—and sustained. Something between us
refuses pity, because, of all the ancient masks

hanging from these walls, we are
the only two still walking and talking.

STEPHEN VINCENT BENÉT

METROPOLITAN NIGHTMARE

It rained quite a lot, that spring. You woke in the morning
And saw the sky still clouded, the streets still wet,
But nobody noticed so much, except the taxis
And the people who parade. You don't, in a city.
The parks got very green. All the trees were green
Far into July and August, heavy with leaf,
Heavy with leaf and the long roots boring and spreading,
But nobody noticed that but the city gardeners,
And they don't talk.
                              Oh, on Sundays perhaps, you'd notice:
Walking through certain blocks, by the shut, proud houses
With the windows boarded, the people gone away,
You'd suddenly seen the queerest small shoots of green
Poking through cracks and crevices in the stone
And a bird-sown flower, red on a balcony,
But then you made jokes about grass growing in the streets
And the end of the depression—and there were songs
And gags and a musical show called "Hot and Wet."
It all made a good box for the papers. When the flamingo
Flew into a meeting of the Board of Estimate,
Mayor O'Brien acted at once and called the photographers.
When the first green creeper crawled upon Brooklyn Bridge,
They thought it was ornamental. They let it stay.

That was the year the termites came to New York
And they don't do well in cold climates—but listen, Joe,
They're only ants and ants are nothing but insects.
It was funny and yet rather wistful, in a way
(As Heywood Broun pointed out in the *World-Telegram*),
To think of them looking for wood in a steel city.
It made you feel about life. It was too divine.
There were funny pictures by Steig and Peter Arno
And Macy's ran a terribly clever ad:
"The Widow's Termite" or something.

         There was no
Disturbance. Even the Communists didn't protest
And say they were Morgan hirelings. It was too hot,
Too hot to protest, too hot to get excited,
An even, African heat, lush, fertile, and steamy,
That soaked into bone and mind and never once broke.
The warm rain fell in fierce showers and ceased and fell.
Pretty soon you got used to its always being that way.

You got used to the changed rhythm, the altered bear,
To people walking slower, to the whole bright
Fierce pulse of the city slowing, to men in shorts,
The new sun helmets from Best's and cops' white uniforms
And the long noon rest in the offices, everywhere.

It wasn't a plan or anything. It just happened.
The fingers tapped the keys slower, the office boys
Dozed on their benches, the bookkeeper yawned at his desk.
The A.T. & T. was the first to change the shifts
And establish an official siesta-room,
But they were always efficient. Mostly it just
Happened like sleep itself, like a tropic sleep,
Till even the Thirties were deserted at noon
Except for a few tourists and one damp cop.
They ran boats to see the lilies on the North River,
But it was only the tourists who really noticed
The flocks of rose-and-green parrots and parakeets

Nesting in the stone crannies of the Cathedral.
The rest of us had forgotten when they first came.

There wasn't any real change, it was just a heat spell,
A rain spell, a funny summer, a weatherman's joke
In spite of the geraniums three feet high
In the tin-can gardens of Hester and Desbrosses.
New York was New York. It couldn't turn inside out.
When they got the news from Woods Hole about the Gulf Stream,
The *Times* ran an adequate story,
But nobody reads those stories but science cranks.

Until, one day, a somnolent city editor
Gave a new cub the termite yarn to break his teeth on.
The cub was just down from Vermont, so he took the time.
He was serious about it. He went around.
He read all about termites in the Public Library
And it made him sore when they fired him.
                                     So, one evening,
Talking with an old watchman, beside the first
Raw girders of the new Planetopolis Building
(Ten thousand brine-cooled offices, each with shower),
He saw a dark line creeping across the rubble
And turned a flashlight on it.
                            "Say, buddy," he said.
"You better look out for those ants. They eat wood, you know.
They'll have your shack down in no time."
                            The watchman spat.
"Oh, they've quit eating wood," he said, in a casual voice,
"I thought everybody knew that"
                          —and, reaching down,
He pried from the insect jaws the bright crumb of steel.

WILLIAM MEREDITH

POEM ABOUT MORNING

Whether it's sunny or not, it's sure
To be enormously complex:
Trees or streets outdoors, indoors whoever you share,
And yourself, thirsty, hungry, washing,
An attitude toward sex.
No wonder half of you wants to stay
With your head dark and wishing
Rather than take it all on again—
Weren't you duped yesterday?
Things are not orderly here, no matter what they say.

But the clock goes off, if you have a dog,
It wags, if you get up now, you'll be less
Late. Life is some kind of loathsome hag
Who is forever threatening to turn beautiful.
Now she gives you a quick toothpaste kiss
And puts a glass of cold cranberry juice,
Like a big fake garnet, in your hand.
Cranberry juice! You're lucky, on the whole,
But there is a great deal about it you don't understand.

EDWARD HIRSCH

BLUNT MORNING

It's almost unbearable to remember
so I scarcely ever think about it anymore,

that last summer morning when my mother-in-law floated
in a netherworld of morphine-induced sleep,

those lingering hours of an otherwise ordinary Sunday
when she entered into a country that wasn't sleep

so much as a blue comatose state of semi-
consciousness that she inhabited to avoid the pain.

All that blunt sunlit morning we signalled each other
and talked over and around her emaciated shape

propped up on the pillows for what were obviously
her final hours of life on this earth.

She was breathing heavily, she was laboring
in her non-sleep, in her state of drifting

to wherever it was she was going—and suddenly
I couldn't stand it any longer. I moved next to her

and began talking, I didn't ask any questions,
I didn't know what I was saying I was speaking so quickly.

I said that we were all there, all of us, Janet and Sophie
and Susan, who was playing the piano in the living room,

that we loved her intensely, fiercely,
that we missed her *already*—where *was* she?—

we wished we could *do* something, anything,
that we each have tasks to fulfill on this planet

and her job now was to die, which she was doing
so well, so courageously, so gracefully,

we were just amazed at her courage.
I know she could hear me—

and that's when she opened her eyes and fixed me
with her stare. She wasn't moving

but she was looking me precisely in the eyes.
I'll never forget that look—haunted, inquisitive, regal—

and she was speaking,
except her voice was too weak

and the sounds didn't rise beyond her throat,
but she was speaking,

and that's when Janet and Sophie started singing
Hebrew songs—not prayers or psalms but celebratory

songs from Gertrude's childhood in Detroit,
and she was singing, too, she remembered the words,

except we couldn't hear any words, nothing
was coming out of her mouth, but she was tapping

two fingers on the side of the rented hospital bed—
and her lips were moving, she was singing.

That's when Sophie started telling stories
about their childhood, which seemed so far away

and so near, like yesterday, and Gertrude was nodding,
except her head didn't move, but anyone

could see that she was nodding yes,
and then Janet started talking about *her* childhood

in this very room
where sunlight burned through the curtains,

and then suddenly Gertrude jolted forward
and started waving her arms—

What is it? What is it? What is it?—
because she was choking on her own phlegm

and then she fell back against her pillows,
and stopped breathing.

MARIE PONSOT

I'VE BEEN AROUND; IT GETS ME NOWHERE

Cuncta fui; conducit nihil.
　　　—V. Aurelius.

I am the woman always too young to be
holding the diamond the baby exulting.

I am the worker afraid of the rules & the boss; my
salary heats the house where I feed many children.

I am packing my bags for coming & going
& going much further than ever before.

> Though elsewhere gets me nowhere
> place is not a problem.
> Feet keep me going,
> the impressive exporters
> of what place is about. Maps—
> gold on parchment or printed
> Mobil travel ads—lay it all out.

> But over every place, time goes
> remote, a cloud-cover question.
> You, in love with your castle, your jet,
> your well-invested dollars,
> and I with my moving
> dictionaries & binoculars
> are both almost out of it,
> too far gone to find a bin
> with stores of more time in.
> A decade, a week, a second, then
> time shrugs and shudders out of touch
> into a perfect fit,
> and that's it.

I am the dog I let out in the morning
wagging & panting at the open door.

I am the foresworn child in the swing
arching & pumping, practicing: "More, more!"

I'm the crossword puzzle time & place
bound at the end by their loose embrace.

W. H. AUDEN

EARLY MORNING BATHING

What! are you still asleep in bed
The sky is such a brilliant blue
And dappled sunlight overhead
Throws down its dancing beams on you

What colors there are in the wood
Green hues I cannot count; and birds
Are busy singing in that wood
Too full of happiness for words

Hullo! so you are also here
O did you see; that dive was fine—
Lord! how the sun shines over there
You blasted fool! That towel is mine!

The bell sends forth its welcome chimes
Five minutes more to food I see
This world is far too good sometimes
For foolish folk like you and me.

JANE KENYON

PRIVATE BEACH

It is always the dispossessed—
someone driving a huge rusted Dodge

that's burning oil and must cost
twenty-five dollars to fill.

Today before seven I saw, through
the morning fog, his car leave the road,
turning into the field. It must be
his day off, I thought, or he's out
of work and drinking, or getting stoned.
Or maybe as much as anything
he wanted to see
where the lane through the hay goes.

It goes to the bluff overlooking
the lake, where we've cleared
brush, swept the slippery oak
leaves from the path, and tried to destroy
the poison ivy that runs
over the scrubby, sandy knolls.

Sometimes in the evening I'll hear
gunshots or firecrackers. Later a car
needing a new muffler backs out
to the road, headlights withdrawing
from the lowest branches of the pines.

Next day I find beer cans, usually
crushed; sometimes a few fish, too small
to bother cleaning, and left
on the moss to die; or the leaking
latex trace of outdoor love. . . .
Once I found the canvas sling chairs
broken up and burned.

Whoever laid the fire gathered stones
to contain it, like a boy pursuing
a merit badge, who has a dream of work,
and proper reward for work.

ALASTAIR REID

MAINE COAST

These islands are all anchored deep dark down.
Pines pitch-thick, gnarled green, and rich of root,
logs lying, lopped boughs, branches, broken rock,
the bow of a boat, the length of a life, weed-water.
I am an island, this is nearest home.

Time is called morning, clinging moist, mist-ridden.
Days are disguised, the houses are half trees—
wind in the attic, sea in the cellar, words
all alien. Though sun burns books, blinds eyes,
I see through to the bone and the beginning.

Tomorrow waits for the net; today tells
time in circles on the trunks, in tides.
Boats are lucky, love is lucky, children
are kings—and we must listen to the wise
wind saying all our other lives are lies.

RUTH STONE

WILD ASTERS

I am here to worship the blue
Asters along the brook,
Not to carry pollen on my legs
Or rub strutted wings in mindless sucking
But to feel with my eyes
The loss of you and me,
Not in the powdered mildew
That spreads from leaf to leaf
But in the glorious absence of grief
To see what was not meant to be seen:
The clusters, the aggregate,
The undenying multiplicity.

SAMUEL MENASHE

SHEEN

Sun splinters
In water's skin
Quivers hundreds
Of lines to rim
One radiance
You within

WINTER

I am entrenched
Against the snow,
Visor lowered
To blunt its blow

I am where I go

WILLIAM STAFFORD

A BABY TEN MONTHS OLD LOOKS AT THE PUBLIC DOMAIN

Somewhere near the end of a snowshoe trail
In a craggy waste where Standard Oil,
Even, won't stake its claim
To a rocky part of the public domain,
This latest baby of ours gets a last portion
Of the national parks belonging to everyone.

There where early snowflakes visit,
And government rules prohibit
The shooting of dwindling herds,
Our baby says "Mine!" for his first word.
One surviving part of a divided world
Belongs, in a vague way, to our child.

A few fought-over acres on the surface—
And, I suppose, a vast cone of space
Stretching up forever—are his by birth.
He sits in our front yard and gazes
Out where his little herd grazes,
Northwest in the direction
Of his cosmic section.

JOSHUA BENNETT

DAD POEM X

You can't have apples with everything,
we say to our son over breakfast, but that's
not technically true. He knows this, I suspect,
though his face reflects a certain understanding,
as if he's willing to negotiate. Before we moved here,
I knew so little of apples, their untamed array
of shapes & names: Ginger Gold, Honeycrisp, Crisp
-in, Cortland, Cameo. Both Rome & Empire,
somehow, which feels like it must be an inside joke
between members of the committee. Fuji, Winesap. Ruby
-Frost, which could be either a miracle or a plague,
I can't decide which. Paula Red is a Soviet secret
agent. Envy is a deadly sin. Holstein & Ambrosia
have skin like a storm on a televised map. On the ride
upstate to the orchard, I recount all the types to myself
in a private game. Select my prize in advance. Bags filled
with Liberty & Jazz will be my aims, like any good
American. Two months earlier, it is not yet my birthday.
I am in an office in Brighton. The doctor has never seen
a case quite like mine. During the tests, I make every task
a language game, even the ones with semicircles & blocks.
This part of my mind is *hypercharged,* he says, like a quasar,
or loving dispute. That morning, I cut a Braeburn into eighths
and cast the pieces into a small blue bowl: a handful of rowboats
swaying. At the orchard, we are stars set loose across the mind

of a boy in a field on his back, dreaming with both eyes open.
We run for hours. We gather enough apples to sate ourselves
for weeks on nothing but their cold red wealth. What marvels:
this most metaphorical of fruits, Newtonian, Edenic, pure
delight. Mighty & bright. And the orchard like a coliseum
of planets you could hold in your hand.

MONICA FERRELL

INFANCY

The gear in this jaw does nothing.
The muscle in her tongue unlooses only
Raw noise, but the machinery hasn't broken;
It's never been used. The baby doesn't even
Know yet how to sit. She just lies there,
Folded in herself, a scroll whose sutra is written
With still-invisible ink, portent no one can read
About some portion of sun I'll never see.
—But who smithed you, baby?
Who sewed this skin and found your name?
Who labored in dirt till it took the shape of a word?
Who walked the whole way to the orchard's end tree
And shook till you dropped to the earth?
I was the one who blew the trumpet when you came.

SHARON OLDS

I CANNOT SAY I DID NOT

I cannot say I did not ask
to be born. I asked with my mother's beauty,
and her money. I asked with my father's desire
for his orgasms and for my mother's money.
I asked with the cradle my sister had grown out of.
I asked with my mother's longing for a son,

I asked with patriarchy. I asked
with the milk that would well in her breasts, needing to be
drained by a little, living pump.
I asked with my sister's hand-me-downs, lying
folded. I asked with geometry, with
origami, with swimming, with sewing, with
what my mind would thirst to learn.
Before I existed, I asked, with the love of my
children, to exist, and with the love of their children.
Did I ask with my tiny flat lungs
for a long portion of breaths? Did I ask
with the space in the ground, like a portion of breath,
where my body will rest, when it is motionless,
when its elements move back into the earth?
I asked, with everything I did not
have, to be born. And nowhere in any
of it was there meaning, there was only the asking
for being, and then the being, the turn
taken. I want to say that love
is the meaning, but I think that love may be
the means, what we ask with.

DONALD JUSTICE

TO WAKEN A SMALL PERSON

You sleep at the top of streets
Up which workmen each morning
Go wheeling their bicycles

Your eyes are like the windows
Of some high attic the one
The very one you sleep in

They're shut it's raining the rain
Falls on the streets of the town
As it falls falls through your sleep

You must be dreaming these tears
Wake up please open yourself
Like a little umbrella

Hurry the sidewalks need you
The awnings not one is up
And the patient bicycles

Halted at intersections
They need you they are confused
The colors of traffic lights

Are bleeding bleeding wake up
The puddles of parking lots
Cannot contain such rainbows

JOHN BERRYMAN

A SYMPATHY, A WELCOME

Feel for your bad fall how could I fail,
poor Paul, who had it so good.
I can offer you only this world like a knife.
Yet you'll get to know your mother,
and, humorless as you do look, you will laugh,
and *all* the others
will not be fierce to you, and loverhood
will swing your soul like a broken bell
deep in a forsaken wood, poor Paul,
whose wild bad father loves you well.

TO-DO LIST

- Sharpen all pencils.
- Check off-side rear tire pressure.
- Defrag hard drive.
- Consider life and times of Donald Campbell, CBE.
- Shampoo billiard-room carpet.
- Learn one new word per day.
- Make circumnavigation of Coniston Water by foot, visit Coniston Cemetery to pay respects.
- Achieve Grade 5 Piano by Easter.
- Go to fancy-dress party as Donald Campbell complete with crash helmet and life jacket.
- Draft pro-forma apology letter during meditation session.
- Check world ranking.
- Skim duckweed from ornamental pond.
- Make fewer "apples to apples" comparisons.
- Consider father's achievements only as barriers to be broken.
- Dredge Coniston Water for sections of wreckage/macabre souvenirs.
- Lobby service provider to unbundle local loop network.
- Remove all invasive species from British countryside.
- Build 1/25 scale model of Bluebird K7 from toothpicks and spent matches.
- Compare own personality with traits of those less successful but more popular.
- Eat (optional).
- Breathe (optional).
- Petition for high-speed fibre-optic broadband to this postcode.
- Order by express delivery DVD copy of "Across the Lake" starring Anthony Hopkins as "speed king Donald Campbell."
- Gain a pecuniary advantage.
- Initiate painstaking reconstruction of Donald Campbell's final seconds using archive film footage and forensic material not previously released into public domain.
- Polyfilla all surface cracking to Bonneville Salt Flats, Utah.
- Levitate.

- Develop up to four thousand five hundred pounds/force of thrust.
- Carry on regardless despite suspected skull fracture.
- Attempt return run before allowing backwash ripples to completely subside.
- Open her up.
- Subscribe to convenient one-a-day formulation of omega-oil capsules for a balanced and healthy diet.
- Reserve full throttle for performance over "measured mile."
- Relocate to dynamic urban hub.
- Eat standing up to avoid time-consuming table manners and other nonessential mealtime rituals.
- Remain mindful of engine cutout caused by fuel starvation.
- Exceed upper limits.
- Make extensive observations during timeless moments of somersaulting prior to impact.
- Disintegrate.

RAYMOND ANTROBUS

SIGNS, MUSIC

The first word my son signed
was *music*: both hands, fingers conducting
music for everything—even hunger,
open mouth for the choo-chew spoon
squealing mmm—*music*. We'd play
a record while he ate *music* when
he wanted milk so I pour and hum
a lullaby or "I Just Don't Know"
by Bill Withers because it's O.K.
not to know what you want
and I want him to know that. *Music*
is wiping the table after the plates *music*
is feel my forehead for fever is whatever
occurs in the center of the body, whatever
makes arms raise up, up.

The second word my son signed
was *bird*—beaked finger to thumb, bird
for everything outside—window, sky, tree,
roof, chimney, aerial, airplane—birds. I saw
I had given him a sign name. Fingers
to eyes raising from thumbs—wide
eye meaning *watchful of the earth*
in three different roots—Hebrew, Arabic,
Latin—I love how he clings
to my shoulders and turns
his head to point at the soft body
of a caterpillar sliding across the counter,
and *signs*, music.

ERICA JONG

BREASTS

I always thought
they were small—
my breasts.

But they filled
my baby's mouth.
& my lover's tongue
loves them,
& my memory is
filled with all
the pleasure they gave
over the years,

while my mother's
100-year-old breasts
still hang
waiting.

For what?
For the tongue
of God?
For the spinning Fates
to release them
into the clouds
so she can remember
how to paint
again?

The sky awaits,
& earth itself.

She used to say,
we all
go back to earth
& become
beautiful tomatoes,
peas, carrots.

She was an
ecologist
before the term
was invented.

O Mother
I love you
despite
everything.

Peas, carrots,
cauliflower.
Even cabbage.

CARRIE FOUNTAIN

YOU BELONG TO THE WORLD

as do your children, as does your husband.
It's strange even now to understand that
you are a mother and a wife, that these gifts
were given to you and that you received them,
fond as you've always been of declining
invitations. You belong to the world. The hands
that put a peach tree into the earth exactly
where the last one died in the freeze belong
to the world and will someday feed it again,
differently, your body will become food again
for something, just as it did so humorously
when you became a mother, hungry beings
clamoring at your breast, born as they'd been
with the bodily passion for survival that is
our kind's one common feature. You belong
to the world, animal. Deal with it. Even as
the great abstractions come to take you away,
the regrets, the distractions, you can at any second
come back to the world to which you belong,
the world you never left, won't ever leave, cells
forever, forever going through their changes,
as they have been since you were less than
anything, simple information born inside
your own mother's newborn body, itself made
from the stuff your grandmother carried within hers
when at twelve she packed her belongings
and left the Scottish island she'd known—all
she'd ever known—on a ship bound for Ellis Island,
carrying within her your mother, you, the great
human future that dwells now inside the bodies
of your children, the young, who, like you,
belong to the world.

JOYCE CAROL OATES

EDWARD HOPPER'S "11 A.M.," 1926

She's naked yet wearing shoes.
Wants to think *nude*. And happy in her body.

Though it's a fleshy aging body. And her posture
in the chair—leaning forward, arms on knees,
staring out the window—makes her belly bulge,
but what the hell.

What the hell, *he* isn't here.

Lived in this damn drab apartment at Third Avenue,
Twenty-third Street, Manhattan, how many
damn years, has to be at least fifteen. Moved to the city
from Hackensack, needing to breathe.

She'd never looked back. Sure they called her selfish,
cruel. What the hell, the use they'd have made of her,
she'd be sucked dry like bone marrow.

First job was file clerk at Trinity Trust. Wasted
three years of her young life waiting
for R.B. to leave his wife and wouldn't you think
a smart girl like her would know better?

Second job also file clerk but then she'd been promoted
to Mr. Castle's secretarial staff at Lyman Typewriters. The
least the old bastard could do for her and she'd
have done a lot better except for fat-face Stella Czechi.

Third job, Tvek Realtors & Insurance and she's
Mr. Tvek's private secretary: *What would I do
without you, my dear one?*

As long as Tvek pays her decent. And *he* doesn't
let her down like last Christmas, she'd wanted to die.

This damn room she hates. Dim-lit like a region of the soul
into which light doesn't penetrate. Soft-shabby old furniture
and sagging mattress like those bodies in dreams we feel
but don't see. But she keeps her bed made
every God-damned day, visitors or not.

He doesn't like disorder. *He*'d told her how he'd learned
to make a proper bed in the U.S. Army in 1917.

The trick is, *he* says, you make the bed as soon as you get up.

Detaches himself from her as soon as it's over. Sticky skin,
hairy legs, patches of scratchy hair on his shoulders, chest,
belly. She'd like him to hold her and they could drift into
sleep together but rarely this happens. Crazy wanting her, then
abruptly it's over—*he's* inside his head,
and *she's* inside hers.

Now this morning she's thinking God-damned bastard, this has
got to be the last time. Waiting for him to call to explain
why he hadn't come last night. And there's the chance
he might come here before calling, which he has done more than once.
Couldn't keep away. God, I'm crazy for you.

She's thinking she will give the bastard ten more minutes.

She's Jo Hopper with her plain redhead's face stretched
on this fleshy female's face and *he's* the artist but also
the lover and last week he came to take her
out to Delmonico's but in this dim-lit room they'd made love
in her bed and never got out until too late and she'd overheard
him on the phone *explaining*—there's the sound of a man's voice
explaining to a wife that is so callow, so craven, she's sick
with contempt recalling. Yet *he* says he has left his family, he
loves *her*.

Runs his hands over her body like a blind man trying to see. And
the radiance in his face that's pitted and scarred, he needs her in

the way a starving man needs food. *Die without you. Don't
leave me.*

He'd told her it wasn't what she thought. Wasn't his family
that kept him from loving her all he could but his life
he'd never told anyone about in the war, in the infantry,
in France. What crept like paralysis through him.
Things that had happened to him, and things
that he'd witnessed, and things that he'd perpetrated himself
with his own hands. And she'd taken his hands and kissed them,
and brought them against her breasts that were aching like the
breasts of a young mother ravenous to give suck,
and sustenance. And she said *No. That is your old life.
I am your new life.*

She will give her new life five more minutes.

DEBORA GREGER

THE MAN ON THE BED

*In late September 1958, I visited his South Truro studio and saw on the easel not
an unfinished painting, nor even a stretched canvas, but a large empty stretcher.
"He's been looking at that all summer," Jo Hopper said.*
                                        —Lloyd Goodrich, on Edward Hopper

He lay on the bed, thinking
of what he could see from the window
as a little landscape of failure,
glittering after the rain,
the roses within reach but rusted,
a red bird lost in the thick
wet leaves of the oak,
the tree, caught in mirrors, shaking.
He lay on the bed,
his shirt turning blue with evening,
thinking that in the dark a red bird
might as well be black.

He slept then
and dreamt of a man
who slept with his glasses on,
the easier to find them when he woke.
The room seemed smaller,
the wind against the corner
of the house stronger.
If the heart is a house, he thought,
it is rented to strangers
who leave it empty.
If the heart is a house,
it is also the darkness around it
through which a black bird flies, unseen,
and unseeing, into the window,
beating and beating its wings
against the glass.

CAMONGHNE FELIX

WHY I LOVED HIM

I can't tell you
Why I loved him or
What it meant. When you
Are a child, you know only
The kind of love your little
Life lacked, so every
Blooming flower is a field. What I know
Is that there were two skies
And under one, I was a shadow. His
Sky was as blue as his eyes. Some
Of that is my doing and the rest of it
Is time. These days, he traces the shape of
The curds above him and I lay out under
A separate sun. Both of us are fine
With this. We picked our place
Under the lid of god and we shut

Our eyes to it every night. That's what it means
To have loved goodly—to meet
Fate in a lavender hall and walk
Right past it, the white train quivering,
Nostalgia in your wake.

NINA CASSIAN

SEPTEMBER

See, September is here. I used to address him
when, much stronger than he,
I would stretch out in the landscape
with my sparkling skin
like an enormous lizard, mistress
of her piece of sand.
"Pale offspring," I would call him.
"Bachelor September," I would laugh,
because I was always getting married,
the eternal spouse of summer, my glorious bridegroom.

See, September is here. "The tender month of fall"—
once upon a time.
His honey—today—is fermenting.
No more silence. Birdfolk clamor in the sky.
Cats full of kittens caterwaul.
The donkey hee-haws. The sheep uproots the grass
from the arid earth with a snap.

Without my bridegroom
I no longer exist.

> (*Translated, from the Romanian, by Ruth Whitman.*)

PAUL BLACKBURN

THE STONE

The stone found me in bright sunlight
around 9th and Stuyvesant Streets and
found, if not a friend, at
least a travelling companion.
Kicking, we crossed
Third Avenue, then Cooper Square, a-
voiding the traffic in our oblique and
random way, a cab almost got him, and I had
to wait a few seconds, crowding
in from the triangular portion edged about
with signs, safety island, crossed
Lafayette, him catching between the cobbles, then
with a judicious blow
from the toes of my foot (right), well, a
soccer kick aiming for height, we cleared
the curb and turned left down Lafayette,
that long block,
with a wide sidewalk and plenty of room to maneuver
in over metal cellar doorways or swinging
out toward the curb edge. The low worn
curb at 4th was a cinch to make, and
at Great Jones Street the driveway into a
gas station promised no impediment. But
then he rolled suddenly to the right
as though following an old gentleman in a long
coat, and at the same time I was addressed
by a painter I know and his girl on their way
to Washington Square, and as I looked up to
answer,
I heard the small sound. He had fallen
in his run, into water gathered in a sunken
plate which they lift to tighten or loosen
something to do with the city water supply I think,
and sank out of sight.
I spoke to Simeon and Dee

about a loft it turned out he hadn't gotten, but
felt so desolate at having lost him they didn't
stay long, I looked at the puddle, explained
we'd come all the way from beyond Cooper Square,
they hurried away.
I suppose I could have used my hands, picked him
out and continued, he'd have been dry by the time
we got home, but just as I decided to abandon him
the sun disappeared.
I continued on down Bleecker finally,
a warm front moving in from the west, the
cirrus clotting into alto-cumulus, sun seeping through
as the front thickened, but not shining, the air turned
cool, and there were pigeons
circling
over the buildings at
West Broadway, and over them a gull, a
young man with a beard and torn army jacket walked
a big mutt on a short leash teaching him to heel.
The mutt was fine, trotting alongside, nuzzling
lightly at his master's chino pants, the young
man smiled, the dog smiled too, and on they went.
They had each other.
I had left him there in the puddle, our game
over, no fair using hands I had told myself.
Not that he could have smiled.
The sun gone in.
He had been shaped like a drunken pyramid, ir-
regularly triangular.
I liked him.

FRED D'AGUIAR

A CLEAN SLATE

Each morning I worked up spit
Aimed at my slate and wiped
Shirttail from corner to corner

Each day was a clean start
Born again and born *big-so*
As grownups loved to say

The day before disappeared
Somewhere between
My saliva and Terylene shirt

The new day promised
Something hitherto not
Seen or guessed about

A cobweb not there
The previous twenty-four hours
That overnight dew reveals

"A" for aubergine
Known to us as *balanjay*
"B" for bat for playing cricket

Until I filled the slate
With slant text my left hand
Told my right-side brain was new

Coins on the sea pressed by light
This morning sky wiped of stars
Chalk off my shirt climbing sun

DEREK WALCOTT
THE BOUNTY I

New creatures ease from earth, nostrils nibbling air,
squirrels abound and repeat themselves like questions,
worms keep inquiring till leaves repeat who they are,
but here we have merely a steadiness without seasons,
and no history, which is boredom interrupted by war.

Civilization is impatience, a frenzy of termites
round the anthills of Babel, signalling antennae
and messages; but here the hermit crab cowers when it meets
a shadow and stops even that of the hermit.
A dark fear of my lengthened shadow, to that I admit,
for this crab to write "Europe" is to see that crouching child
by a dirty canal in Rimbaud, chimneys and butterflies, old bridges
and the dark smudges of resignation around the coal eyes
of children who all look like Kafka. Treblinka and Auschwitz
passing downriver with the smoke of industrial barges
and the prose of a page from which I brush off the ashes,
the tumuli of the crab holes, the sand hourglass of ages
carried over this bay like the dust of the Harmattan
of our blown tribes dispersing over the islands,
and the moon rising in its search like Diogenes' lantern
over the headland's sphinx, for balance and justice.

BILLY COLLINS

COSMOLOGY

I never put much stock in that image of the earth
resting on the backs of four elephants
who are standing on the back of a sea turtle,
who is in turn supported by an infinite regression
of turtles disappearing into a bottomless forever.
I mean how could you get them all to stay still?

Now that we are on the subject,
my substitute picture would have the earth
with its entire population of people and things
resting on the head of Keith Richards,
who is holding a Marlboro in one hand
and a bottle of Jack Daniel's in the other.

As long as Keith keeps talking about
the influence of the blues on the Rolling Stones,

the earth will continue to spin merrily
and revolve in a timely manner around the sun.
But if he changes the subject or even pauses
too long, it's pretty much curtains for us all.

Unless, of course, one person somehow survives
being hurtled into the frigidity of outer space;
then we would have a movie on our hands—
but wait, there wouldn't be any hands
to write the script or make the movie,
and no theatres, either, no buttered popcorn, no giant Pepsi.

Putting that aside, let's imagine Keith
standing on the other Rolling Stones,
who are standing on the shoulders of Muddy Waters,
and, were it not for that endless stack of turtles,
one on top of the other all the way down,
Muddy Waters would be standing on nothing at all.

JIM MOORE

MORNING SONG

It's a lucky day for me
if they are burning on the hill
the cut and fallen branches.
Fire consumes wood, smoke
consumes air. Lucky day
to see what burns and smokes
inside me. If I sit at the window
long enough, I know the moon
will come back. Is that enough then?
I don't mean is the moon enough,
but is the waiting for the moon enough?
I'm asking is the blue enough in Mary's robe
as she cradles her dead son in her lap.
It is Bellini's blue in the Accademia.

I stood for so long in front of it
that the guard, sitting on his little stool,
stopped whistling "Bridge
Over Troubled Water" and stared at me
in silence. But I stayed right where I was.
I had fallen in love with her,
that feeling of being nowhere
and everywhere at once, the way
they say the gods felt
when there were still gods. Meanwhile,
it's 6 a.m., and there is smoky light
on the mountain, the hill, the olive trees,
those two birds hiding under the neighbor's red tiles.
Serve us, they sing, us and us alone.
Are they swallows or swifts?
After all these years, I still don't know.

1920s & 1930s

SPRING COMES TO MURRAY HILL

I sit in an office at 244 Madison Avenue
And say to myself you have a responsible job, havenue?
Why then do you fritter away your time on this doggerel?
If you have a sore throat you can cure it by using a good goggeral,
If you have a sore foot you can get it fixed by a chiropodist
And you can get your original sin removed by St. John the Bopodist,
Why then should this flocculent lassitude be incurable?
Kansas City, Kansas, proves that even Kansas City needn't always be
    Missourible
Up up my soul! This inaction is abominable.
Perhaps it is the result of disturbances abdominable.
The pilgrims settled Massachusetts in 1620 when they landed on a
    stone hummock.
Maybe if they were here now they would settle my stomach.
Oh, if I only had the wings of a bird
Instead of being confined on Madison Avenue I could soar in a jiffy
    to Second or Third.

RANDOM REFLECTIONS

REMINISCENT

When I consider how my life is spent,
I hardly ever repent.

ON ICE-BREAKING

Candy
Is dandy
But liquor
Is quicker.

VERACIOUS

Purity
Is obscurity.

HELPFUL

A good way to forget today's sorrows
Is by thinking hard about tomorrow's.

CONRAD AIKEN

PRELUDE

We need a theme? then let that be our theme:
that we, poor grovellers between faith and doubt,
the sun and north star lost, and compass out,
the heart's weak engine all but stopped, the time
grown timeless in this chaos of our wills—
that we must ask a theme, something to think,
something to say, between dawn and dark,
something to hold to, something to love—

Medusa of the northern sky, shine upon us,
and if we fear to think, then turn that fear to stone,
that we may learn unconsciousness alone;
but freeze not the uplifted prayer of hands
that hope for the unknown.

Give us this day our daily death, that we
may learn to live;
teach us that we trespass; that we may learn,
in wisdom, not in kindness, to forgive;
and in the granite of our own bones seal us daily.

O neighbors, in this world of dooms and omens,
participators in the crime of god,
seekers of self amid the ruins of space:
jurors and guilty men, who, face to face,
discover you but judge yourselves to death,
and for such guilt as god himself prepared,
dreamed in the atom, and so brought to birth
between one zero and another,—

to the cold violet that braves the snow,
the murder in the tiger's eye, the pure
indifference in the star. Why, we are come
at last to that bright verge where god himself
dares for the first time, with unfaltering foot.
And shall we falter, who ourselves are god?

PRELUDE

Mysticism, but let us have no words,
angels, but let us have no fantasies,
churches, but let us have no creeds,
no dead gods hung on crosses in a shop,
nor beads nor prayers nor faith nor sin nor penance:
and yet, let us believe, let us believe.

Let it be the flower
seen by the child for the first time, plucked without thought
broken for love and as soon forgotten:

and the angels, let them be our friends,
used for our needs with selfish simplicity,
broken for love and as soon forgotten;

and let the churches be our houses
defiled daily, loud with discord,
where the dead gods that were our selves may hang:
our outgrown gods on every wall;
Christ on the mantelpiece, with downcast eyes;
Buddha above the stove;
the Holy Ghost by the hatrack, and god himself
staring like Narcissus from the mirror,
clad in a raincoat, and with hat and gloves.

Mysticism, but let it be a flower,
let it be the hand that reaches for the flower,
let it be the flower that imagined the first hand,

let it be the space that removed itself to give place
for the hand that reaches, the flower to be reached—

let it be self displacing self
as quietly as a child lifts a gray pebble,
as softly as a flower decides to fall—
self replacing self
as seed follows flower to earth.

HELENE MULLINS

THE PRODIGAL

O silver city, though you be in truth
My spirit's home, the temple of my youth,
Yet I have ever tried in vain to love
You with a splendid and a perfect love.
Your strength I boast, your unassailable pride,
The countless spears in your unwounded side,
Your cruelty and your magnificence,
Your barbarism and your ignorance.
Yet for the things you lack, the gallantry,
The erudition and philosophy,
I have renounced you time on time, and fled,
Only to hasten back with lowered head.
Having so longed to love you to excess,
And failed and failed, I thought to love you less,
And tore your gaudy colors from my breast,
Saying, "The lands of long ago were best.
I will go back, and I will find again
The ancient haunts of gods and hero-men,
Take counsel of the Delphian oracle,
Learn how to make life wise and beautiful."
You know the places, Athens, Astolat,
Carthage and Ulster, Troy and Camelot.
But you were with me like a clinging ghost;
Seeking more worthy loves, I loved you most.

Yours was the will I did, in singing chains,
Yours the consuming fever in my veins.
Far off and underneath enchanted moons,
My feet kept pace to your impetuous tunes.
Be friend to me a little; for the rest,
Withhold your trust from one who has confessed
A thousand nights of infidelities;
But I am done with sailing shadowed seas,
And am come home with breast torn wide apart,
To press my heart against your furious heart.

BABETTE DEUTSCH

ON LEARNING THAT THE RESERVOIR IS TO BE OBLITERATED

(With Apologies to Ella)

I knew a city once, I knew Manhattan,
In my days of childhood, in my joyful schooldays—
All, all are gone, the old familiar landmarks.

I have been laughing, I have been coquetting,
Primping late, preening late, in Peacock Alley—
All, all are gone, the old familiar landmarks.

I knew a square once, jolliest of plazas:
Rapt is its glory hence, the Garden brick-dust;
All, all are gone, the old familiar landmarks.

I have a friend, a kinder friend has no one:
Like an ingrate, I left my friend abruptly;
Left him, to muse on the old familiar landmarks.

Ghostlike I paced round the haunts of my childhood,
Paused at the reservoir, soon to be earth-choked,
Soon to be lost with the old familiar landmarks.

Friend of my bosom, thou more than brother,
Why wert not thou born in my old Manhattan?
So might we talk of the old familiar landmarks—

How some have changed, some been erased forever,
Some been disfigured; all are departed—
All, all are gone, the old familiar landmarks.

MARK VAN DOREN

THE ESCAPE

Going from us at last,
He gave himself forever
Unto the mudded nest,
Unto the dog and the beaver.

Sick of the way we stood,
He pondered upon flying,
Or envied the triple thud
Of horses' hooves; whose neighing

Came to him sweeter than talk,
Whereof he too was tired.
No silences now he broke,
No emptiness explored.

Going from us, he never
Sent one syllable home.
We called him wild; but the plover
Watched him, and was tame.

DOROTHY BELLE FLANAGAN
LIZ

Her mouth is a penny
Smudged with paint;
She isn't any
Like a saint.

Her eyes are beads
Of shiny black;
Her legs, slim steeds
That canter and clack.

She wears her thumbs
Inside her pockets;
She feasts on crumbs
And rides skyrockets.

Her conscience is tied
With scarlet bows;
She points with pride
To her button nose.

She clutters her days
With tinkling things;
Each night she prays
And feels for wings.

Her voice is a fiddle
Tuned more or less;
Her heart is a riddle
No priest may guess.

ANGELA CYPHER

ON EXCHANGING CONFIDENCES

Since you, my dear, have scads of charm
You might tell me (what's the harm,

Since in jealousy I rate zero?)
Many a story where you were the hero.

I am a woman of sweet personality,
I could relate you with true geniality

Many an episode you'd find marrow in
Where to another man I played heroine.

Many a problem that now perplexes
You and me, about our own sexes,

We could explain by clear illustration
Just for our mutual coëducation.

Yet I am warned by sheer intuition
We would embark upon keen competition

And matching stories would soon grow boring
With nobody umpire, and nobody scoring.

So let's retain with our wonted discretion
Our personal data in our own possession.

CONJUGATION

I sleep, thou sleepest
   It sleeps—
A dream that nobody
   Keeps.

We wake, you wake
   They wake;
A desperate
   Mistake.

A dream is pure
   And mural,
While living life
   Is plural,

And three or four-
   Dimensional,
With number and tense
   Declensional.

So then I try
   To live
In the
   Infinitive,

To love, to learn
   To die.
No heroine
   Am I,

But the subjunctive
   Mood
Still offers something
   Good—

So, might I, if I,
   Should I
By chance, perhaps,
   And could I,

Dispense with "if"
   And "maybe"—

I'd have a black-eyed
　　Baby.

STOP AND GO

People cannot
　　Learn in schools
The truth about
　　The traffic rules,

Or gauge the temper
　　Of a cop
And when to steal
　　A light, or stop,

Or swiftly shift
　　From gear to gear
To save collision
　　In the rear.

My chassis was
　　Designed for speed,
My engine does
　　Its stuff at need,

My brakes are new
　　And working fine,
I could skid close
　　To the danger line,

But with safe margins
　　I'm content—
I hate to get
　　My mudguard bent!

ARTHUR GUITERMAN

BACK HOME

Returned from where I now have no
    Excuse to be,
I find the town the same old show
    It used to be—
Each soul with some mirage in view
    Pursuing it,
And those with not a thing to do
    Still doing it;
The stage, with nothing much to play,
    Still playing it,
And writers having less to say
    Still saying it.

ELINOR WYLIE

DEFINITION OF NEW YORK

Next door to me, it now appears,
Is a bar where Masefield served up beers,
But I didn't find it out for years.

HUGHIE AT THE INN OR, ADVICE FROM A TAPSTER

Is it not fine to fling against loaded dice
Yet to win once or twice?
To bear a rusty sword without an edge
Yet wound the thief in the hedge?
To be unhorsed, and drown in horrid muck,
And in at the death, by luck?
To meet a masked assassin in a cape,
And kill him, and escape?
To have the usurers all your fortune take,
And a bare living make
By industry, and your brow's personal sweat?
To be caught in the bird-net

Of a bad marriage; then to be trepanned
And stranded on foreign land?
To be cast into a prison damp and vile,
And break bars with a blunt file?
To be cut down from gallows while you breathe
And live, by the skin of your teeth
To defy the tyrant world, and at a pinch
To wrest from it an inch?
To engage the stars in combat, and therefrom
Pluck a hair's breadth of room?
Is it not fine, worthy of Titans or gods,
To challenge such heavy odds?
But no, but no, my lad;
'Tis cruel chance gone mad;
A stab in the back; a serpent in the breast;
And worst that murders best.
Such broad and open affronts to fear and pain
Breed maggots in the brain:
They are not valour, but the merest rash
Rubbish and balderdash.
Fortune's a drab, and vice her native soil,
And the button's off her foil.
Season your ale, now these long nights draw in,
With thought to save your skin:
Be provident, and pray for cowardice
And the loaded pair of dice.

ANTI-FEMINIST SONG, FOR MY SISTER

Each of us, born every minute,
    Still wears fern-seed in her shoes;
Love of man, we always win it;
    Peace of mind, we always lose.

Drawing cheques is still our pastime;
    Paying checks our private hell;
No good swearing it's the last time
    While we know ourselves so well!

I am I, and you, my darling,
  Someone very like myself;
Hear the back-door wolf a-snarling
  For bread and cheese upon the shelf!

Well, and let him lick our platters!
  Let him drain our loving-cups!
Do we really think it matters
  Save as Cerberus his sops?

Ah, from such the rats have scampered
  Who give all, but not a damn!
How the wind remains ill-tempered
  To the thoroughly-shorn lamb!

Yes, we've had our fairly thick times
  Paying for the cakes and beers:
It's more fun to be the victims
  Than the bloody conquerors.

MUNA LEE

ATAVIAN

And I, a woman of the twentieth century, am well aware
That all my love for you is an anachronism,
Something Byronic, Tennysonian, with even a dash of Felicia Hemans,
And something of "Friendship's Garland" and something of the
      Napoleonic wars.
  It is an anachronism, my love for you; it might be worked into
      mournful willow wreaths of hair, or expressed by a
      sonnet sequence in feminine rhymes and couplet ending;
  It might mold its desires chastely into a garland of waxen fruit,
      perfect in form and color, lifeless, ornamental, useless;
  It might be built into a pseudo-Gothic castle, turrets and ghost
      and drawbridge all complete;

It might be Elizabethan-Arcadian or Victorian-Olympian; any sad,
     foolish, extravagant thing
Of an age that took its sentimental folly seriously.
But you, a product of this century,
Your mind a by-product of its mad towns, of New York and Madrid,
     London and Paris,
What, in the name of the four cities, could you ever do with my love?
And why cannot I follow the mode of my great-grandmother closer
     still
     And lay the silly thing away
     With a silly tear in its folds,
     And in the riband neatly clasping it,
     One little, pompous, declarative immortelle?

E. B. WHITE

HYMN TO THE DARK

Time, says the historian, thumbing the pages,
Maketh an end of light. It has before,
And will again. The prophet
Echoes the words, speaks of the Dark Ages,
Those that are past, those that are imminent,
On whose bright threshold in the blinding
Dusk of the world we stand
Like children, hand in hand,
Our eyeballs blistered with the unbearable brightness,
The neon hemorrhaging, trickling from the tubes,
Spilled on the earth like blood from a serpent,
The earth absorbent, the dusk tangible,
Culture, with one thread loose, at last unwinding.

Oh Christ, if darkness comes, let the dark be
Velvet and cool, and kind to the eyes
And to the unseated mind. Let the slowed wheel
In the great hour

With the light's thinning
Be through at last with its improbable spinning;
The reserves of oil, slowly refining,
Never more yield
Strength to the engines in the declining
Light, yield no more power
To the high whining
Plow in the long unprofitable field.

This is the prelude to darkness, this great time
Of light and war and youths who follow Hate
Shaped like a swastika, sadist economies,

The dominance of steel and the sword stainless,
The dissenting tongues cleft at the root and bleeding,
Singers with their throats cut, trying
(While yet there's time) to point out where the venom is,
Ink never drying
On the insatiable presses,
Science triumphant, soy beans more than edible,
And the stud chemist, with his lusty pestle,
Serving the broodmares of hysteria,
Getting the gases and the incredible
Sharp substances of our enlightened dying.

Life moves in an orb. We end at last
Where we began. The egg, if you recall,
Is a streamlined object. The first pap we ate,
The first digestible grain, the first cereal,
Was the bland granum which in dreams of conquest
Men called Imperial.

This is the light that failed. Oh Christ,
Make us an end of light if this be light,
Make us an end of sound if this ethereal
Babble, caught in the glowing tubes, translated into waves,
Be sound. If darkness comes, let the dark be
Velvet and cool . . . kind to the eyes, to the hands

Opened to the dust, and to the heart pressed
To the rediscovered earth, the heart reclaimed
For the millionth time by the slow sanity
Of the recurring tides.

A GENERAL SURVEY OF EARLY SUMMER IN TOWN AND COUNTRY

Oh, here we sit at summer's brink,
  With art and music at a standstill,
    So hail the clink
    Of sidewalk drink,
  And Junish weather seeming grand still.

In Summit, Stockbridge, Dennis (Mass.),
  The little-theatre groups assemble;
    Bright chiffons pass
    In the cool grass,
  And newborn actors all a-tremble.

In town, the drama groweth lean,
  An intimate and somewhat coarse show.
    Smart folks are seen
    On Armonk's green
  When Jack & Charlie stage a horse show.

At Greenwich depot and at Rye
  Descends at eve the homing broker;
    His wife sits by
    With welcoming eye
  In sport coupé of yellow ochre.

Observe the scene through country gates,
  The North Shore section, for example:
    Charity fêtes
    On large estates,
  And beds of foxglove deep in trample,

Where matrons vaunt the garden's crop,
    And debutantes the summer knees,
        And Scouts pick up
        The Lily cup,
    And men get sick in back of trees.

Sky-blue the stands of Meadow Brook
    O'er Hitchcock (Tom) and Cowdin (Chever).
        The subway's nook
        Betrays the look
    Of those who suffer from hay fever.

Now Mrs. Stanwood Menken haunts
    The shingle of her favorite beach club,
        Yet nothing daunts
        The crowd that wants
    The middle-class, not-hard-to-reach club.

Oh, fierce the highway's gaseous deck,
    The Sunday traveler returning;
        The steaming check
        Of bottleneck,
    And idle engine idly churning.

Apartment life grows unafraid
    For those whom heat has got a grip on,
        And pretty maid
        With undrawn shade
    Doth loll about with just her slip on.

So wind the merry hunting horn
    O'er penthouse roof and dale a-blooming,
        Dewy the thorn
        In park at morn—
    The swan-boat trade again is booming.

And pause with me at summer's brink;
    The days are long, the nights are stifling;
        All hail the clink

Of sidewalk drink:
    Life is a glorious show, though trifling.

K. C. SAPPINGTON
BOSTON BABY

Selma went to the Winsor School,
Bryn Mawr College, her Ultima Thule.
She took her junior year abroad,
Adopted "Sapristi" and dropped "Migawd."
Selma belongs to the Vincent Club.
She never bathes, she takes a tub.
Selma summers in Lancaster South.
Selma's laugh never reaches her mouth.
She's a love on water-color trips,
Her best gouache was the last eclipse.
Selma's posture shows she fences.
She unbends at Consequences.
Her conception of the pace that kills
Is a *tour d'Espagne* in espadrilles.
Born not for toil in life's colosseum,
She works for fun in the Fogg Museum.

TED ROBINSON
AT THE NORDIC NATIVE AMERICAN SOCIETY

Said Mr. Albert Wiggam to Mr. Lothrop Stoddard,
When they had finished dining, quite thoroughly befoddered:
"Now let us fill our glasses and drink to Racial Purity,
And may the Nordic rule supreme today and in futurity!"
"Religiously we raise our cups, and heartily we swig 'em!"
Said Mr. Lothrop Stoddard to Mr. Albert Wiggam.
Said Mr. Albert Wiggam to Mr. Lothrop Stoddard:
"In coddling swarthy Foreigners, not only Man but God erred.

I've proved by science that we must breed faster or be stung—
The future of the Nordic race depends on lots of young."
"Here's to the Young—especially that Young whose name was Brigham!"
Said Mr. Lothrop Stoddard to Mr. Albert Wiggam.
Said Mr. Albert Wiggam to Mr. Lothrop Stoddard:
"Of Freedom and Equality too long the books have doddered;
My Science shows Democracy to be unscientific,
Your Figures show that Black Folks are too terribly prolific."
"Statistics are our one best bet, if we can only rig 'em,"
Said Mr. Lothrop Stoddard to Mr. Albert Wiggam.

D. B. WYNDHAM LEWIS

SARABAND

M. Papanastasiou, agrarian candidate, has announced his intention of not contesting a seat in the Arcadian district.
                                        —News item from Greece.

Hog-Face! Flap-Ear!
Here!
Snouty and Rump and Flick,
Quick!
Gallop and chatter,
Every satyr,
Snicker and wheeze
As you plunge through the trees—
Hahay! Hist!
This way, where the forest noon swims in a quivering mist,
By the rocks
Where the fountain's cool irony flatters and mocks
The birds, the sky,
And the laugh and the shriek of the girls as they scatter and fly—
Hai! Hai!
Cheeks aflame, legs wine-splashed, long strangled cry—
Hai! Yai!
As we run like the wind and leap hard on the prey—
Ohé!

Not today.
Hairy ones, cock your ears, listen now, for I say
Not today.
Not now.
Wow!
Let 'em fly, let 'em go,
Hairy ones, stand your ground in a grimacing row,
Pipe your eyes,
Clash hoofs, bite the earth, shake the trees with your stampings and
    sighs,
Hou! Hou!
Papanastasiou
Comes no more, comes no more, comes no more . . .
Hairy ones, bellow and roar,
Oi! Oi!
Otototoi . . . oi!
Hairy ones, what a boy!
Remember his Hat? Remember his Boots?
And the tempest of hoots
As we sped him each day on his way to the neighboring town
(Bob down!),
While the dark forest rang with our yells and our jeers
(Twig his ears!),
And the dolphins from here to Propontis leaped sniggering out of
    the blue?
Hou!
Fled, fled is our joy,
(*Ototoroi, . . . oi!*)
Nevermore
Shall the sea-blue bird of the spring and the wave crashing green on
    the desolate Thracian shore
Hear that scream
Like a cry in a dream
And tremble and waver and flee in terror afar—
(Har! Har!)
Hou!
Papanastasiou
Comes no more, comes no more . . .

Sore
Is our harsh hairy grief as we posture and prance,
Pirouette and advance,
And grinning retreat, as our shadows perform a grotesque
Arabesque
And we twirl and leap thrice, hoof to hoof, hand in hand,
In our sad saraband:
'Tototoi! Nevermore shall the—*Hark!*
Who goes there in the dark?
Who treads soft, snapping twigs?
Oh, figs!
A shadow. A bird. A gust in the trees . . .
Cocytus! What gray hairy terror swoops down on the breeze?
Look! Look! *Sauve qui peut!* On the left! On the lfffffffft!
Whrrrrrrrrrft!
Prrrrft!

> (*The forest is silent.*)

VINCENT McHUGH

TO CAB CALLOWAY

On Hearing Him Sing "Sylvia"

No more. No more. Take Chloë, Dinah, bring
The red-headed woman with her store-bought hair,
Minnie the Moocher quavering at the fair
Of intimate apes and shadows—anything
Anesthetized, hunting the morgue, aghast
At its own life. Show us our natural face
In its extreme confounding beauty. Trace
The visible noble emblems of our past.

But who is Sylvia? Leave her. She's not ours.
Another age construed her with its sleight
Of pouring air like water, braiding light
Into a garland of tumultuous flowers.
Some women are more alive than silk and bone.
Leave her. She will find her way alone.

AN UNFINISHED HISTORY

We have loved each other in this time twenty years
And with such love as few men have in them even for
One or for the marriage month or the hearing of

Three nights' carts in the street but it will leave them:
We have been lovers the twentieth year now:
Our bed has been made in many houses and evenings:

The apple tree moves at the window in this house:
There were palms rattled the night through in one:
In one there were red tiles and the sea's hours:

We have made our bed in the changes of many months—and the
Light of the day is still overlong in the windows
Till night shall bring us the lamp and one another:

Those that have seen her have no thought what she is:
Her face is clear in the sun as a palmful of water:
Only by night and in love are the dark winds on it. . . .

     I wrote this poem that day when I thought
     Since we have loved we two so long together
     Shall we have done together—all love gone?

     Or how then will it change with us when the breath
     Is no more able for such joy and the blood is
     Thin in the throat and the time not come—
          the time not come to us for death. . . .

ALFRED KREYMBORG

MANHATTAN EPITAPHS

BROKER

This Wall Street
broker is broken
at last
and no more
need he moan:
his callers
and calls
and all
are past:
he can't hear
the telephone.

LAWYER

He sent so many
to jail for life,
so many
to sudden death,
he finally lost
his own private case
because he was out of
breath.

ACCEPTED

This was once
an editor
who rejected
the young unknowns.
When his very last breath
rejected Life,
Death
got into print
on his bones.

DOROTHY PARKER

BOHEMIA

Authors and actors and artists and such
Never know nothing, and never know much.
Sculptors and singers and those of their kidney
Tell their affairs from Seattle to Sydney.
Playwrights and poets and such horses' necks
Start off from anywhere, end up at sex.
Diarists, critics, and similar roe
Never say nothing, and never say no.
People Who Do Things exceed my endurance;
God, for a man who solicits insurance!

SONGS NOT ENCUMBERED BY RETICENCE

TO A FAVORITE GRANDDAUGHTER

Never love a simple lad;
    Guard against the wise;
Shun a timid youth, and sad;
    Hide from haunted eyes.

Never hold your heart in pain
    For an evil-doer;
Never flip it down the lane
    To a gifted wooer.

Never love a loving son;
    Nor a sheep astray;
Gather up your skirts and run
    From a wistful way.

Never give away a tear;
    Never toss and pine . . .
Should you heed my words, my dear,
    You're no blood of mine!

HEALED

Oh, when I threw my heart away
   The year was at its fall.
I saw my dear, the other day,
   Beside a flowering wall.
And this was all I had to say:
   "I thought that he was tall!"

SUPERFLUOUS ADVICE

Should they whisper false of you,
   Never trouble to deny;
Should the words they speak be true,
   Weep and storm and swear they lie.

AFTERNOON

When I am old and comforted
   And done with this desire,
With Memory to share my bed,
   And Peace to share my fire.

I'll fold my hair in scalloped bands
   Beneath my laundered cap;
And watch my cool and fragile hands
   Lie light upon my lap.

And I will wear a spriggéd gown
   With lace to kiss my throat.
I'll draw my curtains to the town,
   And him a purring note.

And I'll forget the way of tears,
   And rock, and stir my tea.
But oh, I wish those blesséd years
   Were further than they be!

SWAN SONG

First you are hot,
   Then you are cold;
And the best you have got
   Is the fact you're old.
Labor and hoard,
   Worry and wed;
And the biggest reward
   Is to die in bed.
A long time to sweat,
   A little while to shiver
Is all you will get—
   Where's the nearest river?

JAMES THURBER

STREET SONG

In Paris town the carts go down
   Rain-gray byways to the Seine,
And many little brazen bells
   Jingle in each horse's mane,
   Jingle in the rain.

In New York town but once I found
   Such a gray and rainy street,
And then I heard a teamster shout:
   "Pick up your god damn feet!
   "Pick up your feet!"

VILLANELLE OF HORATIO STREET, MANHATTAN

Rusted bed-springs in the street
   And rowdy kids that fight and yell,
All in a clutter at your feet.

No matter what the hour, you meet
    Brawling children and, as well,
Rusted bed-springs in the street;

Nothing here is clean and neat,
    What you'll find you can't foretell
All in a clutter at your feet—

Tawdry signs of life's defeat:
    Irate voices, supper smell,
Rusted bed-springs in the street,

A broken keg, a buggy seat—
    Stuff that junkmen buy and sell—
All in a clutter at your feet.

If your eyes lift up to greet
    The stars you fall on, sure as hell,
Rusted bed-springs in the street,
    All in a clutter at your feet.

ROSALIE MOORE

WHAT FUN TO BE, ETC.

What fun to be Picasso and landscape an oh so
Formal torso! What fun to be Picasso!

What fun to be Gris and—seated vis-à-vis—
Draw, quarter, and cube some noted portraitee,
Put a fluttering nose, an eye in the midst of him,
Interlocking jaws, and a double chin
(One, that is, that besides coming out goes in),
A tie, and limbs with a synonym!

What fun to be Braque, to shock, to paint bric-a-brac
Like bottles and guitars that say A B C!
Or Klee. What fun to be Klee, Gris, Picasso, or Braque!

MAXWELL BODENHEIM

RHYMES FROM A COQUETTE'S DIARY

1

Somehow he was a rarity
In collars, ties, and panties,
But he had one vulgarity—
He *would* sing sailor's chanties.

2

He always spoke of Joyce and Freud
As though they were his brothers.
But finally I grew annoyed—
I found he knew no others.

3

This boy had won a Ph.D.—
Just crammed with facts and learnings—
But one night he revealed to me
More ordinary yearnings.

PATIENCE EDEN

FOOT-NOTE ON A FLAPPER

Drinda's slippers kick the stars
   Round in great abandon,
She scarcely leaves one in the sky
   An angel-ette could stand on.
Drinda's slippers use my heart
   As a stone to rest on,
As she climbs to greater heights—
   She is just a guest on
All its throbbing valves and veins;
   Little that girl cares
That I sometimes need my heart
   For personal affairs!

LANGSTON HUGHES

HEY-HEY BLUES

I can HEY on water
Same as I can HEY-HEY on beer.
HEY on water
Same as I can HEY-HEY on beer.
But if you gimme good corn whiskey,
I can HEY-HEY-HEY—and cheer!

If you can whip de blues, boy,
Then whip 'em all night long.
Boy, if you can whip de blues,
Then whip 'em all night long.
Just play 'em, Perfesser,
Till I don't know right from wrong.

And while you play 'em,
I will sing 'em, too.
While you play 'em,
I will sing 'em, too.
I don't care how you play 'em, I'll
Keep right up with you.

'Cause I can HEY on water,
I said HEY-HEY on beer,
HEY on water
And HEY-HEY on beer,
But gimme good corn whiskey
And I'll HEY-HEY-HEY—and cheer!

Yee-ee-e-who-ooo-oo-o!

JOSEPH MONCURE MARCH

DIRGE

Poor little Matilda!
Nobody knows what killed her.
Some say l'amour,
Some aren't sure,
And the rest blame the hootch that filled her.

BELMONT PARK OPENS

Ah, me! what a rare and exceeding-
Ly splendid collection of breeding!
Ankle and limb
Silk-covered and slim;
Elegant hips;
Exquisite lips—
Flowers of womanhood, regal and glorious,
Registered, patented,
Famous, notorious:
Nodding to equals and social superiors;
Cutting the bounders and other inferiors—

And the talk is of benefits, bridge, and divorces:
But the reason they've come there of course is
The horses.

WILLIAM ROSE BENÉT

ODE FOR AN EPOCH

When at our history men stand amazed,
When there is light to see
The nature of such things as are to be,
And shall be—then—
When some, our captains, may have grown as quaint
And crazed as any mediæval saint
To marveling eyes of a new order of men . . .

When all that so involves our baffled day
Is passed away,
And these our cities, like Carthage or like Tyre,
Grow strange with alien arrogance and power,
That seemed the unfolding flower
And deepest utterance of Mankind's desire . . .

When our concerns, our tyrannous machines
That were the means
To no sure end, but turned against their masters—
Our intricate finance that would not fit
For all our wit
In any pattern save foretold disaster's—
When all these singular things,
Even our wings
That hummed and drummed, a locust-cloud, through heaven,
Are gathered to the ingurgitating past,
And men at last, steadfast
In flesh and blood, are for new sins forgiven . . .

Then even the Jeremiahs of our time,
Or those whose minds can climb
The clear, cold air of reason, or those others
Of hot head and hot heart—
Inveighing, for their part,
In the belief that all men may be brothers—
Even the words of these
Like leaves from autumn trees
May flutter to dust, or start mere bright surprise
Mixed, it may be, with laughter,
In minds that, after
An age, confute our cleverest surmise—
Mixed, it may be, with sighs
To think that on this wise
Our world-in-space, incredible to Time
For its swift power to move,
Crawls slower in the groove
Of progress than a snail its trail of slime . . .

Then the historian
Poring upon some plan
He draughts, with dates, with gazetteer and chart,
And burnishing fine prose
To explicate our woes,
Though still confounded by the human heart,
Will with a sage disdain
Make our confusion plain,
Precisely point the errors of all schools,
And, through the zodiac,
Show on a crazy tack
Our barque of souls, our precious ship of fools . . .

Meanwhile, the wintry tree
Cased in glare ice will be
A palace of blossom to the soft south air;
Meanwhile, rivers run
Under moon, under sun;
Mountains their flamboyant sunsets wear;
And deserts lie as still
As fields that men may till,
And stars to wondering lovers sparkle near,
Though far, cold worlds of light
To aging sight—
And poets are drunken with the atmosphere . . .

And rhythms fall and rise
In the earth, in the skies,
And fugitive, fortunate moments stand always;
And men contrive a god
From cloud or clod;
And night we know . . . and day . . .

Meanwhile, the hurried blood
Whirls us through myriad mood,
And instants are immortal in our breath,
And deeds are blowing grain,
And love we know, and pain . . .
And life . . . and death . . .

F. SCOTT FITZGERALD

OBIT ON PARNASSUS

Death before forty's no bar. Lo!
    These had accomplished their feats:
Chatterton, Burns, and Kit Marlowe,
    Byron and Shelley and Keats.

Death, the eventual censor,
    Lays for the forties, and so
Took off Jane Austen and Spenser,
    Stevenson, Hood, and poor Poe.

You'll leave a better-lined wallet
    By reaching the end of your rope
After fifty, like Shakespeare and Smollett,
    Thackeray, Dickens, and Pope.

Try for the sixties—but say, boy,
    That's when the tombstones were built on
Butler and Sheridan, the play boy,
    Arnold and Coleridge and Milton.

Three score and ten—the tides rippling
    Over the bar; slip the hawser.
Godspeed to Clemens and Kipling,
    Swinburne and Browning and Chaucer.

Some staved the debt off but paid it
    At eighty—that's after the law.
Wordsworth and Tennyson made it,
    And Meredith, Hardy, and Shaw.

But, Death, while you make up your quota,
    Please note this confession of candor—
That I wouldn't give an iota
    To linger till ninety, like Landor.

MIRIAM VEDDER

WARNING

When the universe began
God, they say, created man.

Later, with a mocking nod,
Man annihilated God.

Watch your worlds, or they may do
Something of the kind to you.

KENNETH FEARING

YES, THE SERIAL WILL BE CONTINUED

You recommend that the motive, in Installment 8, should be
        changed from ambition to a desire, on the heroine's part,
        for doing good; yes, that can be done.
Installment 9 could be more optimistic, as you point out, and it will
        not be hard to add a heartbreak to the class reunion in
        Installment 10.
The script for 11 may have, as you say, too much political intrigue
        of the sordid type; perhaps a diamond-in-the-rough
        approach would take care of this. And 12 has a reference
        to war that, as you suggest, had better be removed; yes.
This brings us to the holidays that coincide with our prison
        sequence. With the convicts' Christmas supper, if you
        approve, we can go to town.

Yes, this should not be difficult. It can be done. Why not?

And script 600 brings us to the millennium, with all the fiends of
        hell singing Bach chorales.
And in 601 we explore the Valleys of the Moon (why not?), finding
        in each of them fresh Fountains of Youth.

And there is no mortal ill that cannot be cured by a little money, or
        lots of love, or by a friendly smile; no.
And human hopes have never gone unrealized; no.
And the rain does not ever, anywhere, fall upon corroded
        monuments and the neglected graves of the dead.

OPERATIVE NO. 174 RESIGNS

The subject was put to bed at midnight, and I picked him up
    again at 8 A.M.
I followed, as usual, while he made his morning rounds.
After him, and like him, I stepped into taxis, pressed elevator
    buttons, fed nickels into subway turnstiles, kept him
    under close surveillance as he dodged through heavy
    traffic and pushed through revolving doors.

We lunched very pleasantly (though separately) for $1.50,
    plus a quarter tip. (Unavoidable expense.)
Then out again. For twenty minutes on the corner the
    subject watched two shoeshine boys fish for a dime
    dropped through a subway grating. (No dice.)
And then on. We had a good stare into a window made
    of invisible glass.
Another hour in a newsreel movie—the usual famine, fashions,
    Long Beach bathing and butchery. Then out again.
I realized, presently, that the subject was following a blonde
    dish in blue he had seen somewhere around.
(Nothing, ultimately, came of this.)
And shortly after that a small black pooch, obviously lost,
    attached himself to your operative's heels.
(Does he fit into this picture anywhere at all?
It doesn't matter. In any case, I resign.)

Because the situation, awkward to begin with, swiftly
    developed angles altogether too involved.
Our close-knit atomic world (to be dispersed by night)
    became a social structure, and then a solar system
    with dictates of its own.

We had our own World's Fair in a pinball arcade. The
    blonde had her picture taken in a Photomat.
And so (whether by law or magnetism) did we.
But still there was nothing, in any of this, essentially new
    to report.

Except I began to think of all the things the subject could
    have done but did not do.
All the exciting scenes he might have visited but failed
    to visit.
All the money I might have watched him make or helped
    him spend, the murders he might have committed,
    but somehow he abstained.
What if he met a visiting star from the Coast (and she had
    a friend)?
Or went to Paris, or the South Sea Islands? Did my
    instructions (with expenses) cover the case?
But none of this happened. Therefore, I resign.

I resign, because I do not think this fellow knew what he
    was doing.
I do not believe the subject knew at all clearly what he was
    looking for, or from what escaping.
Whether from a poor man's destiny (relief and the Bellevue
    morgue), or a middle class fate (always the same
    job with a different firm), or from a Kreuger-
    Musica denouement.
And then, whose life am I really leading? Mine or his? His
    or the blonde's?

And finally, because this was his business, all of it, not mine.
Whatever vices or virtues were his, whatever conscience,
    boredom, or penal justice he sought to escape,
    it was his business, not mine in the least. I
    want no part of it.
I have no open or concealed passion for those buttons we
    pressed together, those doors we opened, those levers,
    slots, handles, knobs.

Nor for the shadow of a bathing beauty on a screen. Nor
    any interest in possible defects shown by invisible glass.

I mean, for instance, I do not (often) feel drawn toward that
    particular type of blonde in that particular shade of blue.
And I have no room to keep a dog.

Therefore, this resignation.
Whether signed in a Turkish bath with a quart of rye, or in
    a good hotel, sealed with a bullet, is none of your
    business. None at all.
(There is no law compelling any man on earth to do the same,
    second-hand.)
I am tired of following invisible lives down to intangible avenues
    to fathomless ends.
Is this clear?
Herewith, therefore, to take effect at once, I resign.

WILLIAM CARLOS WILLIAMS

SPARROWS AMONG DRY LEAVES

The sparrows
by the iron fence post—
hardly seen

for the dry leaves
that half
cover them—

stirring up
the leaves, fight
and chirp

stridently,
search
and

peck the sharp
gravel to
good digestion

and love's
obscure and insatiable
appetite.

THEODORE ROETHKE
MEDITATION IN HYDROTHERAPY

Six hours each day I lay me down
Within this tub, but cannot drown.

The ice cap at my rigid neck
Has served to keep me with the quick.

This water, heated like my blood,
Refits me for the true and good.

Within this primal element
The flesh is willing to repent.

I do not laugh, I do not cry;
I'm sweating out the will to die.

My past is sliding down the drain;
I soon will be myself again.

LINES UPON LEAVING A SANITARIUM

Self-contemplation is a curse
That makes an old confusion worse.

Recumbency is unrefined
And leads to errors in the mind.

Long gazing at the ceiling will
In time induce a mental ill.

The mirror tells some truth, but not
Enough to merit constant thought.

He who himself begins to loathe
Grows sick in flesh and spirit both.

Dissection is a virtue when
It operates on other men.

MORRIS BISHOP

WHAT HATH MAN WROUGHT EXCLAMATION POINT

(Poem Suitable for Transmission by Western Union)

Amid Tibetan snows the ancient lama
Mutters his lifelong intercessions comma
Turns the unresting wheel of prayer a myriad
Times in its sacred circling period period
But hold comma what omen strange and dark
Is this on high interrogation mark
A giant bird has out of India stolen
To ravish holy Tibet semicolon
The plane soars upward comma tops the crest
Of the inviolate God of Everest
Period and the lama smote his wheel
Asunder semicolon with a peal
Of dreadful laughter he arose and cried
Colon quotation marks the God has died
Comma so worship man who dared and smote
Exclamation line of dots close quote

LOUISE BOGAN

TO MY BROTHER

Killed: Chaumont Wood, October, 1918

O you so long dead,
You masked and obscure,
I can tell you, all things endure:
The wine and the bread;

The marble quarried for the arch;
The iron become steel;
The spoke broken from the wheel;
The sweat of the long march;

The haystacks cut through like loaves,
And the hundred flowers from the seed.
All things indeed,
Though struck by the hooves

Of disaster, of time due,
Of fell loss and gain,
All things indeed,
I can tell you, this is true,

Though burned down to stone,
Though lost from the eye,
I can tell you, and not lie—
Save of peace alone.

W. B. YEATS

DEATH

Nor dread nor hope attend
   A dying animal;
A man awaits his end
   Dreading and hoping all;
Many times he died,
   Many times rose again.
A great man in his pride
   Confronting murderous men
Casts derision upon
   Supersession of breath;
He knows death to the bone—
   Man has created death.

W. H. AUDEN

SONG [REFUGEE BLUES]

Say this city has ten million souls;
Some are living in mansions, some are living in holes,
Yet there's no place for us, my dear, yet there's no place for us.

Once we had a country and we thought it fair;
Look in the atlas and you'll find it there.
We cannot go there now, my dear, we cannot go there now.

In the village churchyard there grows an old yew;
Every spring it flowers anew.
Old passports can't do that, my dear, old passports can't do that.

The Consul banged the table and said,
"If you've got no passport, you're officially dead."
But we are still alive, my dear, but we are still alive.

Went to a Committee; they offered me a chair,
Asked me politely to return next year.
But where shall we go today, my dear, where shall we go today?

Came to a public meeting; the speaker stood up and said,
"If we let them in, they will steal our daily bread."
He was talking of you and me, my dear, he was talking of you and me.

Thought I heard the thunder, rumbling in the sky.
It was Hitler over Europe, saying, "They must die."
O we were in his mind, my dear, O we were in his mind.

Saw a poodle wearing a jacket, fastened with a pin;
Saw a door open and a cat let in.
But they weren't German Jews, my dear, but they weren't German Jews.

Went down to the harbor and stood upon the quay;
Saw the fish swimming as if they were free,
Only ten feet away, my dear, only ten feet away.

Walked into a wood; saw the birds in the trees,
They had no politicians and sang at their ease.
They weren't the human race, my dear, they weren't the human race.

Dreamt I saw a building with a thousand floors,
A thousand windows, and a thousand doors.
Not one of them was ours, my dear, not one of them was ours.

Ran down to the station to catch the express;
Asked for two tickets to Happiness,
But every coach was full, my dear, but every coach was full.

Stood on a great plain in the falling snow;
Ten thousand soldiers marched to and fro
Looking for you and me, my dear, looking for you and me.

LUNCH BREAK

LOUISE GLÜCK

NOON

They're not grown up—more like a boy and girl, really.
School's over. It's the best part of the summer, when it's still beginning—
the sun's shining, but the heat isn't intense yet.
And freedom hasn't gotten boring.
So you can spend the whole day, all of it, wandering in the meadow.
The meadow goes on indefinitely, and the village keeps getting more and
        more faint—
It seems a strange position, being very young.
They have this thing everyone wants and they *don't* want—
but they want to keep it anyway; it's all they can trade on.
When they're by themselves like this, these are the things they talk about.
How time for them doesn't race.
It's like the reel breaking at the movie theater. They stay anyway—
mainly, they just don't want to leave. But till the reel is fixed
the old one just gets popped back in,
and all of a sudden you're back to long ago in the movie—
the hero hasn't even met the heroine. He's still at the factory,
he hasn't begun to go bad. And she's wandering around the docks, already bad.
But she never meant it to happen. She was good, then it happened to her,
like a bag pulled over her head.
The sky's completely blue, so the grass is dry.
They'll be able to sit with no trouble.
They sit, they talk about everything—then they eat their picnic.
They put the food on the blanket, so it stays clean.
They've always done it this way; they take the grass themselves.
The rest—how two people can lie down on the blanket—
they know about it but they're not ready for it.
They know people who've done it, as a kind of game or trial—
then you say, no, wrong time, I think I'll just keep being a child.
But your body doesn't listen. It knows everything now,
it says you're not a child, you haven't been a child for a long time.
Their thinking is, stay away from change. It's an avalanche—
all the rocks sliding down the mountain, and the child standing underneath
just gets killed.
They sit in the best place, under the poplars.

And they talk—it must be hours now, the sun's in a different place.
About school, about people they both know,
about being adult, about how you knew what your dreams were.
They used to play games, but that's stopped now—too much touching.
They only touch each other when they fold the blanket.
They know this in each other.
That's why it isn't talked about.
Before they do anything like that, they'll need to know more—
in fact, everything that can happen. Until then, they'll just watch
and stay children.
Today she's folding the blanket alone, to be safe.
And he looks away—he pretends to be too lost in thought to help out.
They know that at some point you stop being children, and at that point
you become strangers. It seems unbearably lonely.
When they get home to the village, it's nearly twilight.
It's been a perfect day; they talk about this,
about when they'll have a chance to have a picnic again.
They walk through the summer dusk,
not holding hands but still telling each other everything.

WALKER GIBSON

ESSAY ON LUNCH

Quick lunch! Quick lunch! the neon cries, and I,
Dismayed by any eating on the fly,
As you perhaps anticipate, reply:
Slow lunch! With beer, meat, gravy, pudding, pie.
Who is it that, for lunch, could really wish
A little salad, on a little dish?
Or cup of soup, lukewarm for gulping quick?
Or candy bar? Or ice cream on a stick?
Or hot dog gobbled at a hot-dog stand?
Or Coke, or Pepsi, or some other brand?
Our lunches, like our jets, designed for speed,
Hardly begin to meet the nation's need.

Not so the workingman, whose noon repast
Is seldom eaten light, and never fast.
The foreman's whistle calls him from his spade
To one full hour recumbent in the shade,
Where, as the sweat cools on his honest brow,
He leisurely attacks his honest chow.
His back against a tree in perfect ease,
He takes enormous bites of bread and cheese—
A clear reproof to that white-collar class
That will not trust its pants to God's green grass.
    The mighty sandwiches of beef and ham,
Of peanut butter, apple butter, jam,
Three hard-boiled eggs, six pickles, followed by
A huge and oozing slab of lemon pie,
Prepare the workingman to undertake,
Refreshed and braced, a chunk of chocolate cake.
We'll leave him here as he removes his shoes
And curls up underneath his tree, to snooze.
    Our drugstore fare must all the more displease
When we reflect on lunches overseas,
Where every Frenchman is a skilled gourmet,
And Spaniards take siestas every day.
The German waitress, seeing one sit down,
Makes for one's table, not with pad and frown
And tiny glass of water (as done here)
But with a stalwart, smiling stein of beer,
Assuming—and why not?—that anyone
Would gladly have his *Mahlzeit* thus begun.
She brings then loads of heavy German food,
Promoting heavy German lassitude,
And many a German, after such a snack,
Spends many an afternoon flat on his back.
    Far as we are, a long and liquid span,
From lunch by such a European plan,
Far as we are, as well, from workingmen,
By habit, on a bourgeois regimen,
This is the best advice you'll get from me:
Pack heavy lunch pails—or pack two or three—

And take them to your offices, and eat
In quantity and leisure. Prop your feet
(Shoeless, of course) against the window sill,
And let the hasty hustle, if they will.

ELISE PASCHEN
TAXI

Why don't we cruise
Times Square at noon
enjoy the jam
I'm not immune
to your deft charm
in one stalled car
I'd like to take
you as you are

CZESŁAW MIŁOSZ
GATHERING APRICOTS

In the sun, while there, below, over the bay
Only clouds of white mist wander, fleeting,
And the range of hills is grayish on the blue,
Apricots, the whole tree full of them, in the dark leaves,
Glimmer, yellow and red, bringing to mind
The garden of the Hesperides and apples of Paradise.
I reach for a fruit and suddenly feel the presence
And put aside the basket and say: "It's a pity
That you died and cannot see these apricots,
While I celebrate this undeserved life."

COMMENTARY
Alas, I did not say what I should have.
I submitted fog and chaos to a distillation.

That other kingdom of being or non-being
Is always with me and makes itself heard
With thousands of calls, screams, complaints,
And she, the one to whom I turned,
Is perhaps but a leader of a chorus.
What happened only once does not stay in words.
Countries disappeared and towns and circumstances.
Nobody will be able to see her face.
And form itself as always is a betrayal.

(Translated, from the Polish, by the author and Robert Hass.)

SYLVIA PLATH

BLACKBERRYING

Nobody in the lane, and nothing, nothing but blackberries,
Blackberries on either side, though on the right mainly,
A blackberry alley, going down in hooks, and a sea
Somewhere at the end of it, heaving. Blackberries
Big as the ball of my thumb, and dumb as eyes
Ebon in the hedges, fat
With blue-red juices. These they squander on my fingers.
I had not asked for such a blood sisterhood; they must love me.
They accommodate themselves to my milk bottle, flattening their sides.

Overhead go the choughs in black, cacophonous flocks—
Bits of burnt paper wheeling in a blown sky.
Theirs is the only voice, protesting, protesting.
I do not think the sea will appear at all.
The high green meadows are glowing, as if lit from within.
I come to one bush of berries so ripe it is a bush of flies
Hanging their blue-green bellies and their wing panes in a Chinese screen.
The honey feast of the berries has stunned them; they believe in Heaven.
One more hook, and the berries and bushes end.

The only thing to come now is the sea.
From between two hills a sudden wind funnels at me,

Slapping its phantom laundry in my face.
These hills are too green and sweet to have tasted salt.
I follow the sheep path between them. A last hook brings me
To the hills' northern face, and the face is orange rock
That looks out on nothing, nothing but a great space
Of white and pewter lights, and a din like silversmiths
Beating and beating at an intractable metal.

MARY JO SALTER

ARGUMENT

Lunch finished and pushed aside, lost
in a book, I hadn't registered
for some time what was going on
not ten feet from my table. But then
flew out one pointed, poisoned word—
"*You*"—and before I turned my head
I knew what I'd been hearing: the urgent,
stifled tones of an argument.

He (hunched in a black coat against
the backdrop of the window, one
fist jammed deep in a pocket) hissed
so near her face I couldn't view
either of them clearly. But
surely they were married, and to
each other. Had they been lovers, met
for an hour, she would have left *that* skirt

home in the closet. She had some suffering
under her belt, in the telltale bulge
of her belly. Yes—she'd borne him children.
Oh, she'd borne so much from him,
and what gave him the right to berate
her now, especially here? He had

a secret to lie about, or divulge,
and no wonder she was crying . . . But wait;

women tend to side with women.
She could be a devil, and he a saint
she'd driven to the breaking point—
No again. The truth, whatever it was,
was (as always) a mess. They were too close
to see it, I was too far away,
and when he sprang up, scraping his chair
behind him (Really leaving her

for good? Or was this the daily spat?
Little comfort to think of that),
I saw them both reduced, or heightened,
to something other than themselves,
cartoonish, tragic, archetypal:
Man rises, Woman dissolves.
Man rises and, having risen, has
to go through with it, through the door,

Woman stays, in her place to be hurt,
faced by her just dessert.
Striped like a flag, a three-layered piece
of cake she never should have ordered,
and no solace now; it promised only
the taste of tears and calories.
My lunch, too, sat less well. A spell
of solitude was what I'd had;

but the terror of being truly alone!
The pain we'll put up with, not to learn
how it feels . . . I heard her fork
clink on the plate, and couldn't look.
And, turning to the window, I thought
I saw the flapping tails of that black
coat tug at the man, as if to say,
You must go back to her, go back.

KATE BAER

MIXUP

In a cosmic mixup,
the wife switches bodies with her husband.
Nothing like this has happened before, she cries
as she pulls on his pants, minds the crotch,
barrels down the long staircase to an office where they call her
Bud & How About Those Steelers.
It's upsetting, the whole charade,
except at lunch when she orders fries and no one says,
We're so bad,
or at the meeting when she gives the room all her best ideas
and they say, *Man, where have you been?*

We have to fix this, her husband begs
when the wife returns for dinner.
Come here, she says, slipping off her shoes
and drawing the curtains
before she makes love to another life.

CLARENCE MAJOR

HAIR

In the old days
hair was magical.
If hair was cut
you had to make sure it didn't end up
in the wrong hands.

Bad people could mix it
with, say, the spit of a frog.
Or with the urine of a rat!
And certain words
might be spoken.

Then horrible things
might happen to you.

A woman with a husband
in the Navy
could not comb her hair after dark.
His ship might go down.

But good things
could happen, too.
My grandmother
threw a lock of her hair
into the fireplace.
It burned brightly.
That is why she lived
to be a hundred and one.

My uncle had red hair.
One day it started falling out.
A few days later
his infant son died.

Some women let their hair grow long.
If it fell below the knees
that meant
they would never find a husband.

Braiding hair into cornrows
was a safety measure.
It would keep hair
from falling out.

My aunt dropped a hairpin.
It meant somebody
was talking about her.

Birds gathered human hair
to build their nests.

They wove it around sticks.
And nothing happened to the birds.

They were lucky.
But people?

MATTHEW ZAPRUDER
MY GRANDMOTHER'S DICTIONARY

It must have arrived in the hands
of a salesman whose name
shall remain unrecorded. Let's
call him the handsome stranger.
She saw him through the little
window next to the door
and knew although she did not
believe she believed in such
things she had loved him
in a former life. She gave him
a glass of her legendary tea
and let him go. My grandfather
was upstairs in the immaculate
attic where after they died
I found this typewriter
sleeping among old blueprints.
During the war he diagrammed
routes so trucks of soldiers
could arrive precisely in time
to wait for their orders. Or
he worked in parts. I don't
remember. I can only picture
that afternoon he told me
exactly who he had been,
I hear the resigned
tone but not what he said,
I was as is my nature staring
out the kitchen window

thinking some great hypothesis
that could easily be disproved,
that day now lost in the book
no one can ever turn
around and read. This was
in a little town that was a harbor,
its restaurant a windmill
replica turning in no wind.
We never asked her why she
always stood in the darkest
part of any room. Once
she looked up from her
eternal soup long enough to say
to me you really must remove
that terrible beard. What
is the name of that sort
of love? I want to look it up,
I think it comes from the latin
for not knowing the greek
for the particular quiet
of that afternoon I finally
gave in and picked up
the forbidden ceramic lion
from the shelf, it slipped
from my hands which already
as they do today trembled
and hit the very thick carpet
with a silent thud, exploding
into so many tiny pieces.
Out of the kitchen she came
with a broom and we both
pretended it was never there.
What is that sort of love?
The dictionary knows. I opened
it and found dust. I remember
it had a solitary gold stripe
across blue gray fabric like a dress
you wear only once, by the sea.

TOI DERRICOTTE
FOR MY LIGHT SKIN

I can only be forgiven by Black people
for the million times I walked down a street
and no one knew I was there—
as if I were tiptoeing,
as if I took my self back from existence.
For the hundreds of times my mother and I
walked the galleries at Hudson's—
not a dark soul to be found!—
the furniture behind red ropes, untouchable.
For all the places she and I
kept eating our sandwiches.
My mother liked minestrone soup
on the thirteenth floor where the white
waitresses wore dull green dresses & caps.
I always enjoyed a hot-fudge sundae.
Only Black people can judge me. Only they know
the anguish inserted in history when some
ancestor of mine took the place of one
who went to the back. What was done
made me. Only Black people can know—
who I loved most;
for whom I have done good.

ELISA GONZALEZ
VISITATION

My grandmother died the day
the missionaries came for our souls.
To save them, I mean.

They cycled up the drive
as my mother and I carried her to the van,
on our way to the hospital.

We didn't hear their rattling till they dismounted,
we were so bent on moving her
without pain.

Their hands waved hello.
There was nothing
for the bicycles to do,

so I looked at the wheels
not the missionaries, who asked,
Do you have a source of happiness in your life?

What was my answer, what is it now?
My grandmother swayed
like a hammock between us, then stilled.

They sprang to help.
Bicycles clattered on asphalt—
Did we use dogwood switches? Did we use stones?

DONIKA KELLY

FISHING IN THE BLOOD

T Baby my mama third or fourth cousin.
T Baby got pretty skin and a mouth
like a old grave. T Baby living
on his cousins' land, been taking care
of my great grandma, his cousin Juel.
We standing on her front porch,
me and T, and I'm watching a ant drag
a mud dauber up the wall. Maybe I gotta tell you
we in Arkansas, that I'm twenty, that it's my
homeless summer, that I'm living
with my great grandma for a minute. Maybe
I gotta tell you T a man long grown but shiftless,
that he got the same sick my mama got—drink

and too much and all day—that sweet stink
coming off him where we standing
on the front porch. T say *if we wasn't cousins,*
we'd be married. He fishing in the blood
that bind us, the statement slurry
in the water. I say *would we* and cut my eyes
to the field next door where T live
with his wife and three kids.
I make a noise in my throat. I mean
    I ain't ready for the grave.

REED WHITTEMORE

CLAMMING

I go digging for clams every two or three years
Just to keep my hand in (I usually cut it),
And whenever I do so I tell the same story: how,
At the age of four,
I was trapped by the tide as I clammed a vanishing sandbar.
It's really no story at all, but I keep telling it
(Seldom adding the end, the commonplace rescue).
It serves my small lust to be thought of as someone who's lived.

I've a war, too, to fall back on, and some years of flying,
As well as a staggering quota of drunken parties,
A wife and children; but somehow the clamming thing
Gives me an image of me that soothes my psyche
As none of the louder events—me helpless,
Alone with my sand pail,
As fate in the form of soupy Long Island Sound
Comes stalking me.

My youngest son is that age now.
He's spoiled. He's been sickly.
He's handsome and bright, affectionate and demanding.

I think of the tides when I look at him.
I'd have him alone and seagirt, poor little boy:

The self, what a brute it is. It wants, wants.
It will not let go of its even most fictional grandeur,
But must grope, grope down in the muck of its past
For some little squirting life and bring it up tenderly
To the lo and behold of death, that it may weep
And pass on the weeping, keep it all going.

                  Son, when you clam,
Watch out for the tides, take care of yourself,
Yet no great care,
Lest you care too much and talk too much of the caring
And bore your best friends and inhibit your children and sicken
At last into opera on somebody's sandbar.
                  When you clam, Son,
Clam.

TIANA CLARK

NASHVILLE

is hot chicken on sopping white bread with green pickle
chips—sour to balance prismatic, flame-colored spice
for white people. Or, rather, white people now curate hot
chicken for $16 and two farm-to-table sides, or maybe

they've hungered fried heat and grease from black food
and milk—but didn't want to drive to Jefferson Street or
don't know about the history of Jefferson Street or Hell's
Half Acre, north of downtown. Where freed slaves lived

on the fringe of Union camps, built their own new country.
Where its golden age brought the Silver Streak, a ballroom
bringing Basie, Ellington, and Fitzgerald. First-run movies
at the Ritz and no one had to climb to the balcony. 1968,

they built the interstate. I-40 bisected the black community
like a tourniquet of concrete. There were no highway exits.
120 businesses closed. Ambulance siren driving over
the house that called 911, diminishing howl in the distance,

black bodies going straight to the morgue. At the downtown
library, a continuous loop flashes SNCC videos with black
and white kids training for spit and circular cigarette burns
as the video toggles from coaching to counters covered

in pillars of salt and pie and soda—magma of the movement.
On 1-65, there is a two-tone Confederate statue I flick off
daily on my morning commute. Walking down Second Avenue,
past neon honky-tonks playing bro-country and Cash

and herds of squealing pink bachelorette parties—someone
yelled *Nigger-lover* at my husband. Again. Walking down
Second Avenue, I thought I heard someone yelling at the back
of my husband. I turned around to find the voice and saw

myself as someone who didn't give a damn. Again. I turned
around to find that it was I who lived inside the lovely word
made flesh by white mouths masticating mashed sweet potatoes
from my mother's mother's mother—Freelove was her name,

a slave from Warrior, North Carolina, with twelve children
with names like Pansy, Viola, Oscar, Stella, and Toy—my
grandmother. There is always a word I'm chasing inside and
outside of my body, a word inside another word, scanning

the O.E.D. for soot-covered roots: 1577, 1584, 1608 . . . Tracing my
finger along the boomerang shape of the Niger River for my blood.
1856, 1866, 1889 . . . *Who said it?* A hyphen—crackles and bites,
burns the body to a spray of white wisps, like when the hot comb,

with its metal teeth, cut close to petroleum jelly edging the scalp—
sizzling. Southern Babel, smoking the hive of epithets hung fat

above bustling crowds like black-and-white lynching photographs,
mute faces, red finger pointing up at my dead, some smiling,

some with hats and ties—all business, as one needlelike lady
is looking at the camera, as if looking through the camera, at me,
in the way I am looking at my lover now—halcyon and constant.
Once my mother-in-law said *Watch your back*, and I knew exactly

what she meant. Again. I turned around to find I am the breath
of Apollo panting at the back of Daphne's wild hair, chasing words
like arrows inside the knotted meat between my shoulder blades—
four violent syllables stabbing my skin, enamored with pain.

I am kissing all the trees—searching the mob, mumbling to myself:
Who said it?
Who said it?
Who said it?

TIMOTHY DONNELLY

DIET MOUNTAIN DEW

I have built my ship of death
and when a wind kicks up
I'll cut it loose to do its thing
across an unnamed lake of you,
a firefly sent pulsing through
the non-stop estivation of
the verses of our South, who in
its larval phase would feast
on bitter worms and snails, who
emerges from its mud chamber
our planet's most efficient
luminescence, who turns
chemical energy into radiant
energy shedding very little heat,
so will I sail the compass of
you pleased with my cold light.

I have built my ship of death
aglow in sturdy chemicals
and powered up at night like
American Express, I'm all
customer service only minus
the customer, no service to speak
of other than death, you will
know my logo by its absence
and slogan from the past
ad for the sugared style of you
on TV in my youth, it goes
like this: "When my thirst
is at its worst . . ." and then I
let it trail off into the unsayable
or is it just unsaid because
my mouth is full of you again.

A green like no other green
in the dale, indelicate green or
green indecent, surpassing
the fern and sprout and April's
optimistic leaflet some stop
to admire in nature, they take
photographs noncognizant
of other vehicles, you are too
green for pasture, you are
my green oncoming vehicle,
usurper of green, assassin
to the grasshopper and its plan,
I put me in your path which is
the path a planet takes when it
means to destroy another I think
you know I'm O.K. with that.

A green like no other green
resplending in production since
1940 when brothers Barney
and Ally Hartman cooked it up

in Tennessee qua private
mixer named after moonshine,
its formula then revised by
Bill Bridgforth of the Tri-City
Beverage Corp. in 1958, year
Linwood Burton, chemically
inclined entrepreneur and ship
cleaning service owner, sold
his formula for a relatively safe
maritime solvent to Procter
& Gamble of Ohio, who went on
to market it under the name

of Mr. Clean, whose green
approaches yours then at the
last second swerves into
a joke yellow plays on green
to make blue jealous till it
blows up in its face but I can't
not love the smell of it, citrus
reimagined by an extra-
terrestrial lizard which is to say
inhuman in the way you say
inhuman to me, a compliment
unravelled in the drawl: "Hey
you, over there, you look
so unaccustomed to temporality
I would've sworn you were
inhuman," and time for it after

time I fall, further evidence
of my humanity: I am at heart
no less susceptible to rot
than the felt hat on the head
of the rifle-toting barefoot
hillbilly, your mascot until he
disappeared in 1969. Instinct
says he must have shot his

self in the woods in the mouth
one sunrise when a frost
was at hand and the apples
fell thick and he was way
too awake when he did so not to
think there would be another
waiting like a can of you in
the 12-pack in my refrigerator.

I have built my ship of death
and enough already, every
toxic sip of you preparing for
the journey to bloviation:
I leave to return and return
to depart again the stronger
for a satisfaction being bound
to no port has afforded me:
I have built my ship of death
so that even when I crawl
back down into the hold of it
alive as what unnaturalness
in you can keep me, it's only
to emerge from the other
end of it intact, and perfectly
prepared to be your grasshopper.

JANE KENYON

HEAVY SUMMER RAIN

The grasses in the field have toppled,
and in places it seems that a large, now
absent, animal must have passed the night.
The hay will right itself if the day

turns dry. I miss you steadily, painfully.
None of your blustering entrances

or exits, doors swinging wildly
on their hinges, or your huge unconscious
sighs when you read something sad,
like Henry Adams' letters from Japan
where he travelled after Clover died.

Everything blooming bows down in the rain:
white irises, red peonies, and the poppies
with their black and secret centers
lie shattered on the lawn.

JENNIFER CHAPIS

RAIN AT THE BEACH

This light makes me think of a house underwater.
Because the ocean has corners

I cannot stop looking for you.
Careful, the red jellyfish

washed up onshore
sting after they're dead. My mother said

a soul mate is
problematic. I imagine a mother and daughter

with dripping wet hair
running down the beach

holding hands. Left out in the rain,
a painting of a beach house

with a boat parked inside
is still a painting of a house.

Whoever said it's difficult for artists
to be original

probably wasn't an artist.
My new vegetarian lover

ate snails
off the house as a kid.

DEREK WALCOTT

THE BOUNTY II

The feel of the village in the afternoon heat, a torpor
that stuns chickens, that makes stones wish they could hide
from the sun at two, when to cross from door to door
is an expedition, when palm tree and almond hang their head
in dusty weariness, and the drunk old women sit on old canoes
from a county in Ireland you think you remember, where you felt
too tired to beg, and the young men have that dull stare
that says nothing, neither "Keep going" nor "Welcome." No noise
from the sea, the horizon dazzles; you are used to
this but sometimes something else pierces and the shallows sigh it:
Ici pas ni un rien? they say, here there's nothing. *Nada*
is the street with its sharp shadows and the venders quiet
as their yams, and strange to think the turrets of Granada
are *nada* compared to this hot emptiness, or all the white
stone castles in summer, or pigeons exploding into flocks
over St. Mark's, *nada* next to the stride-measuring egret,
compared to the leisurely patrolling of the frigate
over the stunned bay, and the crash of surf on the rocks.
It is only your imagination that cools or ignites it
at sunset in that half hour the color of regret,
when a truth older than your hand writes: "It
is nothing, and it this nothingness that makes it great."

WENDELL BERRY

A SPEECH TO THE GARDEN CLUB OF AMERICA

Thank you. I'm glad to know we're friends, of course;
There are so many outcomes that are worse.
But I must add I'm sorry for getting here
By a sustained explosion through the air,
Burning the world in fact to rise much higher
Than we should go. The world may end in fire
As prophesied—*our* world! We speak of it
As "fuel" while we burn it in our fit
Of temporary progress, digging up
An antique dark-held luster to corrupt
The present light with smokes and smudges, poison
To outlast time and shatter comprehension.
Burning the world to live in it is wrong,
As wrong as to make war to get along
And be at peace, to falsify the land
By sciences of greed, or by demand
For food that's fast or cheap to falsify
The body's health and pleasure—don't ask why.
But why not play it cool? Why not survive
By Nature's laws that still keep us alive?
Let us enlighten, then, our earthly burdens
By going back to school, this time in gardens
That burn no hotter than the summer day.
By birth and growth, ripeness, death and decay,
By goods that bind us to all living things,
Life of our life, the garden lives and sings.
The Wheel of Life, delight, the fact of wonder,
Contemporary light, work, sweat, and hunger
Bring food to table, food to cellar shelves.
A creature of the surface, like ourselves,
The garden lives by the immortal Wheel
That turns in place, year after year, to heal
It whole. Unlike our economic pyre
That draws from ancient rock a fossil fire,

An anti-life of radiance and fume
That burns as power and remains as doom,
The garden delves no deeper than its roots
And lifts no higher than its leaves and fruits.

NANCY WILLARD

THE EXODUS OF PEACHES

The new peach trees are bandaged
like the legs of stallions.

You can read the bark
over the tape's white lip

where its russet Braille
is peeling. The peaches hang

in their green cupolas,
cheeks stained with twilight,

the wind stencilled on velvet
livery. What a traffic

of coaches without wheels,
of bells without tongues!

Far off the barn doors
open, close,

open, close.
An argument,

both sides swinging.
The blue tractor zippers the field

and disappears behind slatted boxes
like weathered shingles, stained

with peach juice.
I stood under peaches

clumped close as barnacles,
loyal as bees,

and picked one
from the only life it knew.

STANLEY KUNITZ

MY MOTHER'S PEARS

Plump, green-gold, Worcester's pride,
transported through autumn skies
in a box marked "Handle With Care"

sleep eighteen Bartlett pears,
hand-picked and polished and packed
for deposit at my door,

each in its crinkled nest
with a stub of stem attached
and a single bright leaf like a flag.

A smaller than usual crop,
but still enough to share with me,
as always at harvest time.

Those strangers are my friends
whose kindness blesses the house
my mother built at the edge of town

beyond the last trolley-stop
when the century was young, and she
proposed, for her children's sake,

to marry again, not knowing how soon
the windows would grow dark
and the velvet drapes come down.

Rubble accumulates in the yard,
workmen are hammering on the roof,
I am standing knee-deep in dirt

with a shovel in my hand.
Mother has wrapped a kerchief round her head,
her glasses glint in the sun.

When my sisters appear on the scene,
gangly and softly tittering,
she waves them back into the house

to fetch us pails of water,
and they skip out of our sight
in their matching middy blouses.

I summon up all my strength
to set the pear tree in the ground,
unwinding its burlap shroud.

It is taller than I. "Make room
for the roots!" my mother cries,
"Dig the hole deeper."

IDEA VILARIÑO

ALMS

Open the hand and give me
the sweet sweet crumb
as if a god as if the wind
as if the burning dew
as if never
hear
open the hand and give me
the sweet dirty crumb
or give me perhaps the tender
heart that sustains you.
Not the skin or the disordered
hair or the breath
or the saliva or
everything that slips unconnected
past the skin.
No if it is possible
if you hear
if you are here if I am someone
if it is not an illusion
a crazy lens
a grim mockery
open the hand and give me
the dirty dirty crumb
as if a god as if the wind
as if the hand that opens
that distracts destiny
were granting us a day.

(*Translated, from the Spanish, by Jesse Lee Kercheval.*)

DAVID LEHMAN

IT COULD HAPPEN TO YOU

It's June 15, 2017, a Thursday,
fortieth anniversary of the infamous day
the Mets traded Tom Seaver to Cincinnati
and they're still losing

I mean we are

7 to 1 to the Washington Nationals
a team that didn't exist in 1977
the summer of a little tour in France
with Henry James
in a yellow Renault douze

the light a lovely gray
the rain a violin
concerto (Prokofiev's No. 2 in D Major)
and I had books to read

Huxley Woolf Forster and their enemy F. R. Leavis
Empson a little dull for my taste
also Freud on errors, Norman Mailer on orgasms,
James Baldwin in Paris
Dostoyevsky's "Notes from Underground" Part 1

and John Ashbery tells me he is reading "The Possessed"
translated as "The Demons" in the newfangled translation
while Ron and I stay faithful to Constance Garnett

I went upstairs stood on the terrace ate some cherries
admired the outline of trees in the dark

and Rosemary Clooney
sang "It Could Happen to You"

and I was a healthy human being, not a sick man
for the first summer in three years.

ADRIENNE SU

AN HOUR LATER, YOU'RE HUNGRY AGAIN

For the table to be round.
For the teapot to be bottomless.
For your elders to compose the menu.

For the waiter to recite the order back.
For the fish-maw soup to be ladled at the table.
For red vinegar to bloom in it, a submerged flower.

For the bright lights and immaculate tablecloth.
For the extra order of Singapore noodles.
For the white blossoms on Chinese broccoli.

For your mother to warn you which sauces are hot.
For your brother to turn the lazy Susan just when you need it.
For the cloth napkin to slide to the floor.

For rice in a hexagonal lacquered box.
For the hill of bones on your tiny plate.
For the Wash 'n Dri packet after the lobster.

For the sea bass to give up its spine without resistance.
For your aunt to serve you nameless meats you love.
For your grandfather to assign everyone a favorite dish, incorrectly.

For the shrimp to have expressionless eyes.
For your grandmother to murmur "thank you" as everyone serves her.
For the owner to insist on calling your father "professor."

For the ice water you requested but forgot to drink.
For the film of oil on your last grains of rice.
For the gift of red-bean soup with the oranges.

For the numbers on the check, in Chinese penmanship.
For the leftovers in their cartons, in tied plastic bags.
For the Chinese-newspaper rack in the vestibule.

For night to have fallen while you were eating.
For ginger and scallions to infiltrate the dreams
from which you will wake in the only home you know.

TYREE DAYE

WHAT THE ANGELS EAT

as children we ate watermelons over trash bags in my aunt's back yard
filled with so many black & blue-eyed crows
it stopped being an omen & they'd eat what fell to the ground
& our skin stayed on

we'd get yelled at for spitting seeds at each other
        saliva thick with red
we made a war from the sweetest things
the flies made a mess of our dancing
the flies made a dance in our messes

our mothers thanked god it was not the blood feared
a watermelon's vine would wrap itself around you
if you fell asleep under them watching meteors
melons make magic under midnight moons

i once grew watermelons that flowers could sing
if i sat there singing
the way my aunts break out into song   i mean beautiful
like that the flowers would start moving

i'm so free i make a river on both sides of my mouth
a fruit full of kinship
it once grew wild & bitter
        in the kalahari desert

the grandmother of all the watermelons   the first water
my grandmothers share a bowl every sunday

and drip juice on the floor
but never stain a sole
the only fruit the dead can eat

DIANE MEHTA

PLUM CAKE

I'd make a plum cake when she died,
a lamentation grief-bake, Kaddish through blood-recipe,
all of its colors shrieking at me; a sweet take on her love.
I gaze at the street. Tree branches out front are tangled,
my floor is slanted, my house-cage is so small and dark
for all the summits, slopes, and swamps of feeling.

I am not to be purple-plum-decided in any still-life of grief
or reminiscence, no waferlike religious feeling, never—
she will never be human again. I knew I wouldn't make it.

Italian plums are sweetest. I should find them in a market
when days are longer; fruit-of-aging, gift-of-goodness.
A friend who lost a friend and made the cake said *plum*
six times in one paragraph, so full of yearning are our phrases.
Snow-bright is her hair on the bed, knobby knuckle-skin
folded on her chest. She'd be delighted to celebrate her death.

I love that, she'd say happily about the plum-cake wake.
Plums pooled around the cake-slab in the photograph,
bloody and marvellous. Skylight took her in. I couldn't make it.

PHILLIP B. WILLIAMS

FINAL POEM FOR MY FATHER MISNAMED IN MY MOUTH

Sunlight still holds you and gives
your shapelessness to every room.
By noon, the kitchen catches your hands,
misshapen sun rays. The windows
have your eyes. Taken from me,
your body. I reorder my life with
absence. You are everywhere now
where once I could not find you
even in your own body. Death means
everything has become
possible. I've been told I have
your ways, your laughter haunts my mother
from my mouth. Everything
is possible. Fatherlight
washes over the kitchen floor.
I try to hold a bit of kindness
for the dead and make of memory
a sponge to wash your corpse.
Your name is not *addict* or *sir*.
This is not a dream: you died
and were buried three times. Once,
after my birth. Again, against
your hellos shedding into closing doors,
your face a mask I placed over my face.
The final time, you beneath my feet. Was I
buried with you then? I will not call
what you had left anything
other than *gone* and *sweet perhaps*. I am
not your junior, but I
survived. I fell in love with being
your son. Now what? Possibility
was a bird I once knew. It had one wing.

MAHMOUD DARWISH

REMAINDER OF A LIFE

If I were told:
By evening you will die,
so what will you do until then?
I would look at my wristwatch,
I'd drink a glass of juice,
bite an apple,
contemplate at length an ant that has found its food,
then look at my wristwatch.
There'd be time left to shave my beard
and dive in a bath, obsess:
"There must be an adornment for writing,
so let it be a blue garment."
I'd sit until noon alive at my desk
but wouldn't see the trace of color in the words,
white, white, white . . .
I'd prepare my last lunch,
pour wine in two glasses: one for me
and one for the one who will come without appointment,
then I'd take a nap between two dreams.
But my snoring would wake me . . .
so I'd look at my wristwatch:
and there'd be time left for reading.
I'd read a chapter in Dante and half of a mu'allaqah
and see how my life goes from me
to the others, but I wouldn't ask who
would fill what's missing in it.
That's it, then?
That's it, that's it.
Then what?
Then I'd comb my hair and throw away the poem . . .
this poem, in the trash,
and put on the latest fashion in Italian shirts,
parade myself in an entourage of Spanish violins,
and walk to the grave!

(Translated, from the Arabic, by Fady Joudah.)

PETER BALAKIAN

ZUCCHINI

My grandmother cored them
with a serrated knife

with her hands that had come
through the slaughter—

So many hours I stared at the blotch
marks on her knuckles,

her strong fingers around the
long green gourd—

In a glass bowl the stuffing was setting—
chopped lamb, tomato pulp, raw rice, lemon juice,

a sand brew of spices—
from the riverbank of her birth—

Can holding on to this image
help me make sense of time?

the temporal waves,
waves smashing and lipping

the pulverized stone; a bird dissolving
into a cloud bank in late day;

the happy and sad steps we walked

along the plaster walls and steel bridges,
the glass façades, highways of glistening money

the objects we caress in dreams
from which we wake to find the hallway dark,

the small light at the bottom of the stairs,
the kitchen waiting with a scent

of zucchini sautéed in olive oil
onions and oregano,

a waft of last night's red wine—a gulp
of cold water to bring on the day.

PAISLEY REKDAL

WHAT IS THE SMELL OF A CIRCLE?

Breast milk, yes, and tomato soup, fresh
algae blooming on the pond with one
carp quickening its surface. The egg-
colored rug on which snow slowly melted
from our boots. I remember
the slowness of the hour in which
we answered all the questions
our marriage counsellor put to us.
Imagine one of you has gotten sick.
Imagine the schools
you want your children educated in.
And you and I, healthy
but with no children, would spend the rest
of an afternoon arguing about
private schools and cancer treatments,
until rage had pared your face
to an acid set of lines and planes,
so that at restaurants the waitresses
would fill only your glass
with water, and the female students
at your law school, hearing
of our troubles, delivered pies
for you with notes expressing
sympathy, which I devoured alone,

tossing the notes they'd taped on the tins
for you into the trash. I gained
five pounds that winter, lost fifteen
the spring you moved out. Perhaps,
I remember telling the counsellor,
there are worse crimes than falling
out of love with one's own husband or falling
into some worse version of it
with someone else, though at the time
I couldn't imagine what those were.
Outside, in the counsellor's
parking lot, we would stand by the doors
of our separate cars, sullen and flushed,
as if each of us had contracted a specific
fever that began at the same hour
of the same day each week,
in the same location, even, the radiator
throwing off its blister
of heat, the rag rug, the counsellor's
window slowly filling up with snow. Only
after a week would the fever break, cooled
into half-hearted jokes,
or a stumbling embrace in our frozen yard:
some new understanding of what
we each could accept marriage to be—
not the same relationship but something
different, stranger, hard. I remember
walking past the bathroom door one night
and seeing you hunched there
over the sink, the wide, white
porcelain sides gripped in your palms, you
panting like a deer that had been struck
by a car. How much more pain
were we willing to endure to prove
we loved each other? Months
before we'd married, I remember we talked
about a child. It was Sunday, hot,
we'd been walking past the shut doors

of glass-fronted restaurants until we stopped
at a corner filled with shocking pink streaks
of bougainvillea. It's the one thing,
you told me, I really want. You were talking
about a child. Heady vanilla scent, and bees.
The sudden sense, as you touched your hand
to the back of my neck, that I hated
this embrace. Was it cruel
I never told you no? Was it cruel
you kept demanding it of me? The longer
we argued, the harder it became
to decipher what cruelty finally was: Was it cruel,
for instance, if one of us chose to sleep
on the couch, was it cruel if I fantasized
about living in Europe, or you kept a portrait
of a former wife on your bookshelf?
On the last day of therapy together,
you interrupted the counsellor
to say that in order for you to remain in any way
in my life, we would have to end the marriage
now. Do you understand? you asked me.
I touched my hand to the couch's
fraying comforter. There was,
I understood, no unlimited care
anyone should endure for another;
that, in the end, it was indeed love
that could make a reasonable person
leave a marriage. When I'm asked
to describe you to strangers now, I tell people
the truth: you were kind, you were curious,
we never hated each other, even
on our worst night when I came
into the kitchen to tell you
what you already knew, I'd done something
terrible, not naming it because
you begged me not to. It was the one
kindness I ever offered. I remember

how you screamed and flung
all the dishes in our cupboard
to the floor, one by one until I stood
inside a ring of white and blue and green porcelain
that bloomed around me. Every dish
we ever owned you threw, but even then,
in our worst sorrow, making sure
not one shard would touch me.

ANNE SEXTON

LETTER WRITTEN ON A FERRY CROSSING LONG ISLAND SOUND

I am surprised to see
that the ocean is still going on.
Now I am going back
and I have ripped my hand
from your hand as I said I would
and I have made it this far
as I said I would
and I am on the top deck now,
holding my wallet, my cigarettes,
and my car keys
at two o'clock on a Tuesday
in August of 1960.

Dearest,
although everything has happened,
nothing has happened.
The sea is very old.
The sea is the face of Mary,
without miracles or rage
or unusual hope,
grown rough and wrinkled
with incurable age.

Still,
I have eyes.
These are my eyes:
the orange letters that spell
"ORIENT" on the life preserver
that hangs by my knees,
the cement lifeboat that wears
its dirty canvas coat,
the faded sign that sits on its shelf
saying "KEEP OFF."
Oh, all right, I say,
I'll save myself.

Over my right shoulder
I see four nuns
who sit like a bridge club,
their faces poked out
from under their habits,
as good as good babies who
have sunk into their carriages.
Without discrimination
the wind pulls the skirts
of their arms.
Almost undressed,
I see what remains:
that holy wrist,
that ankle,
that chain.

Oh, God,
although I am very sad,
could you please
let these four nuns
loosen from their leather boots
and their wooden chairs
to rise out
over this greasy deck,

out over this iron rail,
nodding their pink heads to one side,
flying four abreast
in the old-fashioned side stroke,
each mouth open and round,
breathing together
as fish do,
singing without sound.

Dearest,
see how my dark girls sally forth,
over the passing lighthouse of Plum Gut,
its shell as rusty
as a camp dish,
as fragile as a pagoda
on a stone,
out over the little lighthouse
that warns me of drowning winds
that rub over its blind bottom
and its blue cover—
winds that will take the toes
and the ears of the rider
or the lover.

There go my dark girls;
their dresses puff
in the leeward air.
Oh, they are lighter than flying dogs
or the breath of dolphins;
each mouth opens gratefully,
wider than a milk cup.
My dark girls sing for this:
They are going up.

Here are my four dark girls.
See them rise
on black wings, drinking

the sky, without smiles
or hands
or shoes.
They call back to us
from the gauzy edge of paradise,
good news, good news.

COREY VAN LANDINGHAM

ADULT SWIM

Let them eat corn dogs. Let them
peel from its sack a freezer-burnt popsicle,
lime, green as an alien gem.

Let them pluck from the strung garland of chips.

Sugaring their lips with the fine grit
of Sour Patch Kids, these strange children
lift to their mouths those soft little bodies
and chew. They forget, for just a moment, the water
from which they've been banished.
Then a pause in the guard station's country radio—
they pirouette back and begin,
again, to sulk. Gawk. Let them.

It's nearly time to reclaim
their pool. Each day, each hour,
they have dragged their soaking bodies
from its coolness and allowed their mothers
the reapplication of lotion and the petting
of their wet, tender heads.

No agony is greater
than theirs. Never have I felt so powerful.

Aren't I magnificent,
floating on my back dead center? Aren't I
a kingdom of one?
I could grow new gods.
Small princes.

(My grandmother's voice—*if you own nothing,*
you are nothing—as she handed me, at Christmas,
a fresh certificate of stock. But she was an unhappy woman
and is dead.)

A whinny of pain
from a skinned knee, quick flash
of white before the blood. Not my wound
to treat. Another boy explaining to his mother's magazine
how every day, every single day,
God puts out the sun by dunking it in the ocean.
Like a match dropped
into a glass.

Where does the next one come from,
he wants to know.

One up to his thighs already
until the strict whistle, the chorus
of booing beside him,
a leap back.
Lined on the plastic rim, the boys stare differently
than the men they will become.

Where are the wild things?

The boy worries.
Who promises tomorrows to a whole needful planet,
restrikes that match?

Who bears that next fiery sphere?

Who will remind this woman
she's not some queen
acquiring a country estate—ruby brooches, oiled leaves
of topiaries glistening in midday sun—
while the real rural citizens starve. Fountains
upon fountains and a small pond
to reflect back her dais. Crystal plates
of petit fours. For which,
history admonishes, she was beheaded.

BRENDA HILLMAN

EARLY SEX

The one-celled creature brought to class
in the drop of pond water
took its main hunger around on the slide,

it had yes for a skin and a thousand
little hairs for feet
to help it decide. . . . You wanted to love the others

no matter what,
swam over the edge of yourself, swam
in the place that seemed like forever,

you loved when they visited you,
you changed shape for them, and when they left
you were the same as the water

MICHAEL TORRES

PORTRAIT OF MY BROTHER AT THIRTEEN AND 5'2"

Outside, my little brother presses his hands
into the window A.C. unit's aluminum grille
like a film star at the Grauman's Chinese Theatre

of the hood. It's summer. Sort of. School began
last week, but it takes all of August for us
to remember the boys our mother wants us to be.

My father has just tossed a glass bottle
into the street. Its pop and scatter against
concrete is what I'll remember; his laughter.

The car he tried to crack is up the block
and anonymous again. By this time
next year he will no longer be taller

than me or my brother. I grow impatient
for this evening, his eventual quiet and closing
of doors. It will take a decade before I begin

to wonder if each afternoon were actually
a lesson for my older self to use. My father
yells at us from across the driveway. I know

he will ask why I didn't stop my brother
from ruining the cooler. He's a puzzle
I've completed and stepped back from

without seeing much there. I want to watch
my brother be young for the last time, watch him
watch the impressions the metal has made

before his palms call back the blood.

DONALD JUSTICE

SCHOOL LETTING OUT

(Fourth or Fifth Grade)

The afternoons of going home from school
Past the young fruit trees and the winter flowers,
The schoolyard cries fading behind you then,
And small boys running to catch up, as though
It were an honor somehow to be near—
And all forgiven now, even the dog
Who, straining at his tether, starts to bark,
Not from anger but some secret joy.

MICHAEL DICKMAN

ALL SAINTS

I made the mask
from scratch
also the wings
all by myself
in the shape of a sick child
or newly cut
grass

It was hard to stand up at first because the wings were so heavy but
        I'm getting more and more used to them

More and more ready
Dripping
waves of silver paint
they shine like
the blind
But the beak is real

A real beak

Instead of a mouth

•

I brought the new
body to school
wrapped in tinfoil
but left it in the coat closet
in a backpack with
my brain

It was dark in there and scary and there were woods that no one had
     ever mentioned before and probably never would again

I was called on all the time
despite looking out the window
as if the playground were
burning

No one cared

The flames licked the blades

Stand closer

Stand a little closer

•

Later we will hold hands like children and sit on the floor in a large
     circle with our legs crossed in the late style of deathlessness

Waiting for
satori

What I wanted to show you
has disappeared
through a hole
in the back of my
head

What I wanted to tell you

If you pee your pants on the floor
you still have to sit there
on the spot where
you peed

A halo

seeping into the rug

SASKIA HAMILTON

ALL SOULS

Out of the window of the Committee
on Preschool Special Education,
a triangular intersection
of traffic at the uptown crossing.
The parents, here without their children,
to petition on their behalf, are lonely
only in this passageway, the unaccompanied
shelter of the twelfth floor where they are signed in
by a kindly woman to spend some hours
waiting for a supervisor always
late with the correspondent gates of paperwork
but who has primary authority to accede
or deny in many languages, for
there is no loneliness in the company
of children. With an air of apology,
the young woman calls out *Miss, Sir*,
not knowing the names, and they try to catch
in her glance to whom she wishes to speak,
but the optic axes of her eyes
coincide divergently, catching
two families simultaneously, every face
responds with apology to the summons,
the clerk's oblique eyes calling each of them,
none of them, all of them, generally beheld.

•

She is dying, said the nurse. It was a Tuesday
in the new century. But not then—
she found strength again, her sturdy legs
kept their footing in the beige laced shoes.
A greenwood of beeches outside her window.
A Wednesday, Thursday, Friday.
A Saturday. A Sunday.

•

How strange—but then '*strange* should be dried out
for a millennium,' Ricks says. *Journey*,
too. Poor old words. Even so, how *out
of the way*—? to be the subject.
To whom would it be otherwise?
Who becomes familiar with mortal
illness for very long. I was a stranger, &c.
Not everyone appreciates it, no
one finds being the third person
becoming, it's never accurate,
and then one is headed for the past tense.
Futurity that was once a lark, a gamble,
a chance messenger, traffic and trade, under sail.
The boy touches your arm in his sleep
for ballast. It's warm in the hold. Between
ship and sky, the bounds of sight
alone, sphere so bounded.

•

1955

Alone in the mountains one day
she felt, she heard, a half step behind her,
someone, who, the multitude, a sole
companion? Joining her at the left turn
of the road, and she did not break
her stride, her grandson from years hence,
or was it her dead brother from years past,
from childhood, from infancy,
keeping her company for now.

•

At a distance, a small wood islanded
in the meadows. Paths innumerable
through beech and growth, ferns and decay,
shifting light raising the dry scent of
summer sun from the ground.

The quarter hour abided, it had no
cessation while I stood there astride
the bicycle—what is not bounded
by the limits of perception but looks on,
a door unlatched, ajar—restless
irregular light and shadow, awakened,
having arrived at a turn—

then pushing off. At play with instability,
worthy of mastery, tires going at speed
along the packed sand of a road that ran
from field to field without discernible end
in all of Europe.

The child moved through the hour
from fridge to table to fridge again
with sure command, small strength and purpose,
all his might against the magnetic
door gasket. Consented to being dressed,
consented to the descent of stairs,
step over step, to meet the bus,
moving torso, hips, this way and that
in an early dance to the tune
of protest, clutching a black train as he boarded
and the driver swung the doors shut
and I waved at the children pressing their faces
to the windows as it drove towards the river.
May they all be covered by feathers.

THOMAS LUX

REFRIGERATOR, 1957

More like a vault: you pull the handle out
and on the shelves not a lot,
and what there is (a boiled potato
in a bag, a chicken carcass
under foil) looking dispirited,
drained, mugged. This is not
a place to go in hope or hunger.
But, just to the right of the middle
of the middle door shelf, on fire, a lit-from-within red,
heart-red, sexual-red, wet neon-red,
shining red in their liquid, exotic,
aloof, slumming
in such company: a jar
of maraschino cherries. Three-quarters
full, fiery globes, like strippers
at a church social. Maraschino cherries, "maraschino"
the only foreign word I knew. Not once
did I see these cherries employed: not
in a drink, nor on top
of a glob of ice cream,
or just pop one in your mouth. Not once.
The same jar there through an entire
childhood of dull dinners—bald meat,
pocked peas, and, see above,
boiled potatoes. Maybe
they came over from the old country,
family heirlooms, or were status symbols
bought with a piece of the first paycheck
from a sweatshop,
which beat the pig farm in Bohemia,
handed down from my grandparents
to my parents
to be someday mine,
then my child's?
They were beautiful

and if I never ate one
it was because I knew it might be missed
or because I knew it would not be replaced
and because you do not eat
that which rips your heart with joy.

1940s & 1950s

AWAKING

After night, the waking knowledge—
The gravel path searching the Way;
The cobweb crystal on the hedge,
The empty station of the day.

So I remember each new morning
From childhood, when pebbles amaze.
Outside my window, with each dawning,
The whiteness of those days.

The sense felt behind darkened walls
Of a sun-drenched world, a lake
Of light, through which light falls—
It is this to which I wake.

Then the sun shifts the trees around,
And overtops the sky, and throws
House, horse, and rider to the ground,
With knock-out shadows.

The whole day opens to an O,
The cobweb dries, the petals spread,
The clocks grow long, the people go
Walking over themselves, the dead.

The world's a circle, where all moves
Before after, after before,
And my aware awaking loves
The day—until I start to care.

LANGSTON HUGHES

WAKE

Tell all my mourners
To mourn in red—
'Cause there ain't no sense
In my bein' dead.

SUNDAY-MORNING PROPHECY

An old Negro minister concludes
his sermon in his
loudest voice, having previously
pointed out the
sins of this world.

The minister switches
his hips like a voluptuous
woman. He takes
two steps backward and
one forward.

His knees sway beneath him.

He comes up in a crouch.

He rears back and rocks
and he
rears back and sways.

His knees give way again.
They go way down, but
he rises tall
and smiles
at the triumph of God.

He turns,
smiles,
and steps forward.

He crouches and comes up.
Screams.
Frowns terribly.

His voice falls
ten octaves.

Softly.

Afterthought.

Organ music.

. . . Now,
When the rumble of death
Rushes down the drainpipe of eternity,
And hell breaks out
Into a thousand smiles,
And the devil licks his chops,
Preparing to feast on life,
And all the little devils

Get out their bibs
To devour the corrupt bones
Of this world—
Oh-ooo-oo-o! Then, my friends!
Oh, then! Oh, then!
What will you do?
You will turn back and look toward
The mountains.
You will turn back and grasp
For a straw.
You will holler, "Lord-d-d-d-d-d-ah!
Save me, Lord!
Save me!"
And the Lord will say,
"In the days of your greatness
I did not hear your voice!"
The Lord will say,
"In the days of your richness
I did not see your face!"
The Lord will say,
"No-oooo-ooo-oo-o!
I will not save you now!"

And your soul
Will be lost!

Come into the church this morning,
Brothers and sisters,
And be saved.

And give freely
In the collection basket
That I, who am thy shepherd,
Might live.
Amen!

ANNE RIDLER

RIVER GOD'S SONG

My eyes are white stones
That shine through water
As the moon shines
Through a glistening mist,
My limbs the supple ripples
That part like a fan
Or fuse into one,
Wrinkle and fade
As lines erased
On a carbon pad.
The racing weed
Is my green hair.
Stare in the pool—
My wraith is there
In a wreath of water
Around a rock;
Look for long,
It will disappear.

My name is Evenlode,
Windrush, or Dove;
Or else Alpheus,
Ladon, Leucyanias:
Water as dark
As a night with glittering
Stars of the frogbit;
Water so clear
That the peering fish
Fear their own shadows;
As sleek as oil,
Or boiling down
In white cascades
And braids of glass.
Choose my name
And paint my scene

After your choice,
I am still the river.
You passers by
Who share my journey,
You move and change,
I move and am the same;
You move and are gone,
I move and remain.

ROBERT GRAVES

MY NAME AND I

The impartial Law enrolled a name
  For my especial use;
My rights in it would rest the same
Whether I puffed it into fame
  Or drowned it in abuse.

Robert was what my parents guessed
  When first they peered at me,
And *Graves* an honorable bequest,
  With Georgian silver and the rest,
  From my male ancestry.

They taught me: "You are *Robert Graves*
  (Which you must learn to spell),
But see that *Robert Graves* behaves,
Whether with honest men or knaves,
  Exemplarily well."

Then, though my I was always I,
  Illegal and unknown,
With nothing to arrest it by—
As will be obvious when I die
  And *Robert Graves* lives on—

I cannot well repudiate
  This noun, this natal star,
This gentlemanly self, this mate
So kindly forced on me by fate,
  Time, and the registrar;

And therefore hurry him ahead
  As an ambassador
To fetch me home my beer and bread
Or commandeer the best green bed,
  As he has done before.

Yet, understand, I am not he
  Either in mind or limb;
My name will take less thought for me,
In worlds of men I cannot see,
  Than ever I for him.

THE NAKED AND THE NUDE

For me, the naked and the nude
(By lexicographers construed
As synonyms that should express
The same deficiency of dress
Or shelter) stand as wide apart
As love from lies, or truth from art.

Lovers without reproach will gaze
On bodies naked and ablaze;
The Hippocratic eye will see
In nakedness, anatomy;
And naked shines the Goddess when
She mounts her lion among men.

The nude are bold, the nude are sly
To hold each treasonable eye,
While draping, by a showman's trick,

Their dishabille in rhetoric,
They grin a mock-religious grin
Of scorn at those of naked skin.

The naked, therefore, who compete
Against the nude may know defeat,
Yet when they both together tread
The briary pastures of the dead,
By Gorgons with long whips pursued,
How naked go the sometime nude!

MILDRED WESTON

EAST RIVER NUDES

They stand,
As if to take a dare,
At water's edge,
Boy bathers,
Bare,
Drawn up
To meet a city stare:

Long legs,
Round heads,
The span between
As spare as wood
And whittled clean,
They make
A river-bank design
As lewd
As clothespins
On a line.

LOWER MANHATTAN

The windowed walls
By early light
Look waffled
But become at night
Great combs
Of what cannot be honey,
For these are hives
For making money.

PUBLIC LIBRARY

Tonight
By quiet pools of light
The opposites have met—
Those reading to remember,
Those reading to forget.

CONRAD AIKEN

THE HABEAS CORPUS BLUES

In the cathedral the acolytes are praying;
in the tavern the teamsters are drinking booze;
in his attic at dusk the poet is playing,
the poet is playing the Habeas Corpus Blues.

The poet prefers the black keys to the white,
he weaves himself a shroud of simple harmonics;
across the street a house burns; in its light
he skeins more skillfully his bland ironics.

All down the block the windows bloom with faces,
the paired eyes glisten in the turning glare;

and the engines throb, and up the ladder races
an angel, with a helmet on his hair.

He breaks the window in with a golden axe,
crawls through the smoke, and disappears forever;
the roof slumps in, and the whole city shakes,
the faces at the windows say *Ah!* and *Never!*

And then the hour; and near and far are striking
the belfry clocks; and from the harbor mourn
the tugboat whistles, much to the poet's liking,
smoke rings of bronze to the fevered heavens borne.

And the hydrants are turned off, the hose rewound;
no longer now are the dirty engines drumming;
the fireman's broken body at last is found,
the fire is out, the insurance man is coming.

And in the cathedral the acolytes are praying,
and in the tavern the teamsters are drinking booze;
while, in his attic, the poet is still playing,
the poet is playing the Habeas Corpus Blues.

DILYS BENNETT LAING

TEN LEAGUES BEYOND THE WIDE WORLD'S END

I pursue him, the loved one all unsolved,
through mines of mercury, salt caves, and folded stone,
down decimal steps of dream and sleep and death,
through flowering, breaking rocket-head of war
and long, anxious ferment of peace.

I pursue him whom I might catch if ever
only by sitting still.

I know, I have taken with sliding rule and wavering scale
his height and shape not fixed but leaping and falling
like fire and shadow forever between child and man.
I know his voice, treble and bass, infantile and mature.
I know the chords of his changes from god to demon
within the scale of his humanity.

I think he is my lover or my child.
When I attempt to take him in my arms
he pulls away from me with a boy's pride
and walks to the edge of the burning world with a gun in his hand.

SONG FOR DECEMBER

Gladly I saw the windy chute
of Autumn's furious avalanches.
The leafless crab tree, thick with fruit
struck dark by frost on iron branches,

stands like a tree of Chinese art,
an abstract on a silken void.
You may choose Summer. For my part
I quicken to the lean, uncloyed,

and celibate Winter. Then the cold
bodies the breath before the eye;
platinum twilights, drained of gold,
lie wide and clean in the freezing sky;

safe in the seed is Spring, packed little;
beech leaves flicker like fire gone low;
and cricket corpses, scattered and brittle,
are ruined fiddles under the snow.

DAVID DAICHES

TO KATE, SKATING BETTER THAN HER DATE

Wait, Kate! You skate at such a rate
You leave behind your skating mate.
Your splendid speed won't you abate?
He's lagging far behind you, Kate.
He brought you on this skating date
His shy affection thus to state,
But you on skating concentrate
And leave him with a woeful weight
Pressed on his heart. Oh, what a state
A man gets into, how irate
He's bound to be with life and fate
If, when he tries to promulgate
His love, the loved one turns to skate
Far, far ahead to demonstrate
Superior speed and skill. Oh, hate
Is sure to come of love, dear Kate,
If you so treat your skating mate.
Turn again, Kate, or simply wait
Until he comes, then him berate
(Coyly) for catching up so late.
For, Kate, he *knows* your skating's great,
He's *seen* your splendid figure eight,
He is not here to contemplate
Your supersonic skating rate—
That is not why he made the date.
He's anxious to expatiate
On how he wants you for his mate.
And don't you want to hear him, Kate?

DOROTHY PARKER
WAR SONG

Soldier, in a curious land
  All across a swaying sea,
Take her smile and lift her hand—
  Have no guilt of me.

Soldier, when were soldiers true?
  If she's kind and sweet and gay,
Use the wish I send to you—
  Lie not lone till day!

Only, for the nights that were,
  Soldier, and the dawns that came,
When in sleep you turn to her
  Call her by my name.

ARTHUR BARTLETT
LINES SCRIBBLED ON AN AUCTION CATALOGUE

Lord, how I hate coming out into the cold, sane light of day
And suddenly realizing that I now possess a framed Victorian
      wreath, a colored print called "Sleigh Ride in Russia," a
      wrought-iron fire grate, and a miscellaneous lot of wood
      candlesticks, metal busts, brass dishes, and a silver-plated
      breakfast tray!
The only thing I really wanted was a leather chair,
And here I am with an iron model-coach doorstop, an East Indian
      teakwood three-fold screen, an old mahogany shaving mirror,
      and an ebonized *étagère*.
Webster's Universal Dictionary, though old, I don't regret,
But what in heaven's name will I do with a terra-cotta bust of
      Marie-Antoinette?
As for that Jersey-glass carboy,
Oi!

Obviously, I was somewhat off my mental balance
When I bought a decorated Limoges luncheon set of forty-eight
      pieces, to say nothing of a pair of brocade damask portières and
      valance,
And what inner devil made me raise my hand
To bid on that mahogany Sheraton muffin stand?
I wouldn't feel quite such a fool
If I had a piano to go with the carved mahogany piano stool.
Ah, well! And so home, to look my long-suffering spouse boldly in
      the face
And tell her of my gift for her Early American bedroom: a carved
      and gilt Victorian pier glass, with marble top and console base.

ISABELLA GARDNER

IN THE MUSEUM

Small and emptied woman, you lie here a thousand years dead,
your hands on your diminished loins, flat in this final bed,
teeth jutting from your unwound head, your spiced bones black and dried.
Who knew you and kissed you and kept you and wept when you died?
Died you young? Had you grace? *Risus sardonicus* replied.
Then quick I seized my husband's hand while he stared at his bride.

KARL SHAPIRO

HOMAGE TO CALDER

To raise an iron tree
Is a wooden irony,
But to cause it to sail
In a clean perpetual way
Is to play
Upon the spaces of the scale.
Climbing the stairs, we say,
Is it work or is it play?

Alexander Calder made it
Work and play:
Leaves that will never burn
But were fired to be born,
Twigs that are stiff with life
And bend as to the magnet's breath,
Each segment back to back,
The whole a hanging burst of flak.

Still the base metals,
Touched by autumnal paint,
Fall through no autumn
But, turning, feint
In a fall beyond trees,
Where forests are not wooded,
There is no killing breeze,
And iron is blooded.

MARIANNE MOORE

LEONARDO DA VINCI'S

Saint Jerome and his lion,
            in that hermitage
of walls half gone,
            share sanctuary for a sage—
joint frame for impassioned, ingenious
            Jerome versed in language,
and for a lion like one on the skin of which
            Hercules's club made no impression.

The beast, received as a guest—
            although some monks fled—
with its paw dressed
            that a desert thorn had made red,
stayed as guard of the monastery ass,
            which vanished, having fed

its guard, Jerome assumed. The guest, then, like an ass,
        was made carry wood and did not resist,

        but, before long, recognized
                the ass and consigned
        its terrorized
                thieves' whole camel train to chagrined
Saint Jerome. The vindicated beast and
                saint somehow became twinned;
and now, since they behaved and also looked alike,
        their lionship seems officialized.

        Pacific yet passionate—
                for if not both, how
        could he be great?—
                Jerome, reduced by what he'd been through,
with tapering waist no matter what he ate,
        left us the Vulgate. That in Leo
the Nile's rise grew food, checking famine, made
        lion's-mouth fountains appropriate,

        if not universally
                at least not obscure.
        And here, though hardly a summary, astronomy—
                or pale paint—makes the golden pair
in Leonardo da Vinci's sketch seem
                sun-dyed. Blaze on, picture,
saint, beast—and Lion Haile Selassie, with household
        lions as symbol of sovereignty.

TOM FOOL AT JAMAICA

    Look at Jonah embarking from Joppa, deterred by
the whale; hard going for a statesman whom nothing could detain,
    although one who would not rather die than repent
        Be infallible at your peril, for your system will fail,
and select as a model the schoolboy in Spain
    who, at the age of six, portrayed a mule and jockey
        who had pulled up for a snail.

"'There is submerged magnificence,' as Victor Hugo
said." *Sentir avec Ardeur:* that's it; magnetized by feeling.
    Tom Fool "makes an effort and makes it oftener
        than the rest"—out on April 1st, a day of some significance
in the ambiguous sense—the smiling
    Master Atkinson's choice, with that mark of the champion,
        the extra
        spurt when needed. Yes, yes. Chance

    is "a regrettable impurity;" like Tom Fool's
left white hind foot—an unconformity; although judging by
    results, a kind of cottontail to give him confidence.
        Up in the cupola comparing speeds, Signor Capossela keeps
        his head.
"It's tough," he said, "but I get 'em, and why shouldn't I?
    I'm relaxed, I'm confident, and I don't bet." Sensational. He
        does not
        bet on his animated

    valentines—his pink-and-black striped, sashed, or dotted silks.
Tom Fool is "a handy horse," with a chiselled foot. You've the beat
    of a dancer to a measure—the harmonious rush
of a porpoise at the prow where the racers all win easily—
        like centaurs' legs in tune, as when kettledrums compete;
    nose rigid and suede nostrils spread, a light left hand on the
        rein, till
        well—this is a rhapsody.

    Of course, speaking of champions, there was Fats Waller
with the feather touch, giraffe eyes, and that hand alighting in
    "Ain't Misbehavin'." Ozzie Smith and Eubie Blake
        ennoble the atmosphere; you recall the Lipizzan school;
the time Ted Atkinson charged by on Tiger Skin—
    no pursuers in sight—cat-loping along. And you may have
        seen a monkey
        on a greyhound. "But Tom Fool . . ."

THE ARCTIC OX

(Derived from "Golden Fleece of the Arctic," an article in the "Atlantic Monthly,"
by John J. Teal, Jr., who rears musk oxen on his farm in Vermont)

To wear the arctic fox
you have to kill it. Wear
    qiviut—the underwool of the arctic ox—
pulled off it like a sweater;
your coat is warm, your conscience better.

I would like a suit of
qiviut, so light I did not
    know I had it on, and in the
course of time another,
since I had not had to murder

the "goat" that grew the fleece
that grew the first. The musk ox
    has no musk and it is not an ox—
illiterate epithet.
Bury your nose in one when wet.

It smells of water, nothing else,
and browses goatlike on
    hind legs. Its great distinction
is not egocentric scent
but that it is intelligent.

Chinchillas, otters, water rats,
and beavers keep us warm.
    But think! A "musk ox" grows six pounds
of *qiviut*; the cashmere ram,
three ounces—that is all—of *pashm*.

Lying in an exposed spot,
basking in the blizzard,
    these ponderosos could dominate

the rare-hairs market in Kashan, and yet
you could not have a choicer pet.

They join you as you work,
love jumping in and out of holes,
　　play in water with the children,
learn fast, know their names,
will open gates and invent games.

While not incapable
of courtship, they may find its
　　servitude and flutter too much
like Procrustes' bed,
so some decide to stay unwed.

Camels are snobbish
and sheep unintelligent,
　　water buffaloes neurasthenic,
even murderous,
reindeer seem overserious.

Whereas these scarce *qivies*,
with golden fleece and winning ways,
　　outstripping every fur bearer—
there in Vermont quiet—
could demand Bold Ruler's diet:

Mountain Valley water,
dandelions, carrots, oats;
　　encouraged as well, by bed
made fresh three times a day,
to roll and revel in the hay.

Insatiable for willow
leaves alone, our goatlike
　　qivi-curvi-capricornus
sheds down ideal for a nest.
Songbirds find *qiviut* best.

Suppose you had a bag
of it; you could spin a pound
    into a twenty-four- or five-
mile thread—one, forty-ply,
that will not shrink in any dye.

If you fear that you are
reading an advertisement,
    you are. If we can't be cordial
to these creatures' fleece,
I think that we deserve to freeze.

TED HUGHES

THE THOUGHT-FOX

I imagine this midnight moment's forest:
Something else is alive
Beside the clock's loneliness
And this blank page where my fingers move.

Through the window I see no star;
Something more near,
Though deeper within darkness,
Is entering the loneliness:

Cold, delicately as the dark snow,
A fox's nose touches twig, leaf;
Two eyes serve a movement that now,
And again now, and now, and now,

Sets neat prints into the snow
Between trees, and warily a lame
Shadow lags, by stump and in hollow,
Of a body that is bold to come

Across clearings, an eye,
A widening deepening greenness,

Brilliantly, concentratedly,
Coming about its own business

Till, with a sudden sharp hot stink of fox,
It enters the dark hole of the head.
The window is starless still; the clock ticks;
The page is printed.

RICHARD WILBUR

OCTOBER MAPLES

The leaves, though little time they have to live,
Were never so unfallen as today,
And seem to yield us through a rustled sieve
The very light from which time fell away.

A showered fire we thought forever lost
Redeems the air. Where friends in passing meet,
They parley in the tongues of Pentecost.
Gold ranks of temples flank the dazzled street.

It is a light of maples, and will go;
But not before it washes eye and brain
With such a tincture, such a sanguine glow
As cannot fail to leave a lasting stain.

So Mary's laundered mantle (in the tale
Which, like all pretty tales, may still be true),
Spread on the rosemary-bush, so drenched the pale
Slight blooms in its irradiated hue,

They could not choose but to return in blue.

GRASSE: THE OLIVE TREES

Here luxury's the common lot. The light
Lies on the rain-pocked rocks like yellow wool
And around the rocks the soil is rusty bright
From too much wealth of water, so that the grass
Mashes under the foot, and all is full
Of heat and juice and a heavy jammed excess.

Whatever moves moves with the slow complete
Gestures of statuary. Flower smells
Are set in the golden day, and shelled in heat,
Pine and columnar cypress stand. The palm
Sinks its combs in the sky. This whole South swells
To a soft rigor, a rich and crowded calm.

Only the olive contradicts. My eye,
Travelling slopes of rust and green, arrests
And rests from plenitude where olives lie
Like clouds of doubt against the earth's array.
Their faint dishevelled foliage divests
The sunlight of its color and its sway.

Not that the olive spurns the sun; its leaves
Scatter and point to every part of the sky,
Like famished fingers waving. Brilliance weaves
And sombres down among them, and among
The anxious silver branches, down to the dry
And twisted trunk, by rooted hunger wrung.

Even when seen from near, the olive shows
A hue of far away. Perhaps for this
The dove brought olive back, a tree which grows
Unearthly pale, which ever dims and dries,
And whose great thirst, exceeding all excess,
Teaches the South it is not paradise.

VIRGINIA BRASIER

OCTOBER HARVEST

The summer tourists all drift home.
The air's like nectar.
And miles of travel film are ripe
For the projector.

VLADIMIR NABOKOV

ON DISCOVERING A BUTTERFLY

I found it in a legendary land
all rocks and lavender and tufted grass,
where it was settled on some sodden sand
hard by the torrent of a mountain pass.

The features it combines mark it as new
to science: shape and shade—the special tinge,
akin to moonlight, tempering its blue,
the dingy underside, the checkered fringe.

My needles have teased out its sculptured sex;
corroded tissues could no longer hide
that priceless mote now dimpling the convex
and limpid teardrop on a lighted slide.

Smoothly a screw is turned; out of the mist
two ambered hooks symmetrically slope,
or scales like battledores of amethyst
cross the charmed circle of the microscope.

I found it and I named it, being versed
in taxonomic Latin; thus became
godfather to an insect and its first
describer—and I want no other fame.

Wide open on its pin (though fast asleep)
and safe from creeping relatives and rust,
in the secluded stronghold where we keep
type specimens it will transcend its dust.

Dark pictures, thrones, the stones that pilgrims kiss,
poems that take a thousand years to die
but ape the immortality of this
red label on a little butterfly.

WILLIAM CARLOS WILLIAMS
PUERTO RICO SONG

Well, God is
love,
so love me.

God
is love, so
love me. God

is
love, so love
me well.

Love, the sun
comes
up in

the morning,
and
in

the evening—
zippe, zappe!—
it goes.

MICHAEL KYRIAKIS

CICADAS

Bright
Bright
Bright day,
Drinking up the groves and the transparent sea,
Drinking up the valley and the tree,
Unseen cicadas sing of thee:

Bright
Bright
Bright day.

Offbeat
In the acacia retreat,
In the gray seat
Of the olive tree,
The leader anticipates the offbeat,
And echo is chorus
Of the off
Offbeat.

Bright
Bright
Bright day,
Full noon is in the trees
And the black bays.
High is the crown of the ebbing pine;
Your kingdom burns,
And green turns silver dust in time,
Hoarded by the olive and the vine.

Bright
Bright
Bright day,
Rocks resist, the sea

Opposes your holocaust decree;
Only cicadas are jubilant
In chorus and key,
Singing uncontrollably
Acclaiming thee:

Bright
Bright
Bright day.

EUDORA WELTY

A FLOCK OF GUINEA HENS SEEN FROM A CAR

The lute and the pear are your half sisters,
The mackerel moon a full first cousin,
And you were born to appear seemly, even when running on
       guinea legs,
As maiden-formed, as single-minded as raindrops,
Ellipses, small homebodies of great orbits (little knots
       at the back like apron strings),
Perfected, sealed off, engraved like a dozen perfect
       consciences,
As egglike as the eggs you know best, triumphantly
       speckled . . .
But fast!
Side-eyed with emancipation, no more lost than a string
       of pearls are lost from one another,
You cross the road in the teeth of Pontiacs
As over a threshold, into waving, gregarious grasses,
Welcome wherever you go—the Guinea Sisters.

Bobbins with the threads of innumerable visits behind you,
As light on your feet
As the daughters of Mr. Barrett of Wimpole Street,
Do you ever wonder where Africa has fled?

Is the strangeness of your origins packed tight in those
        little nutmeg heads, so ceremonious,
                        partly naked?
Is there time to ask each other what became of the family
                wings?
Do you dream?
Princess of Dapple,
Princess of Moonlight,
Princess of Conch,
Princess of Guinealand.
Though you roost in the care of S. Thomas Truly, Rt. 1
(There went his mailbox flying by),
The whole world knows you've never yet given up the secret
        of where you've hidden your nests.

WELDON KEES

ROBINSON

The dog stops barking after Robinson has gone.
His act is over. The world is a gray world,
Not without violence, and he kicks under the grand piano,
The nightmare chase well under way.

The mirror from Mexico, stuck to the wall,
Reflects nothing at all. The glass is black.
Robinson alone provides the image Robinsonian.

Which is all of the room—walls, curtains,
Shelves, bed, the tinted photograph of Robinson's first wife,
Rugs, vases, panatelas in a humidor.
They would fill the room if Robinson came in.

The pages in the books are blank,
The books that Robinson has read. That is his favorite chair,
Or where the chair would be if Robinson were here.

All day the phone rings. It could be Robinson
Calling. It never rings when he is here.

Outside, white buildings yellow in the sun.
Outside, the birds circle continuously
Where trees are actual and take no holiday.

ASPECTS OF ROBINSON

Robinson at cards at the Algonquin; a thin
Blue light comes down once more outside the blinds.
Gray men in overcoats are ghosts blown past the door.
The taxis streak the avenues with yellow, orange, and red.
This is Grand Central, Mr. Robinson.

Robinson on a roof above the Heights; the boats
Mourn like the lost. Water is slate, far down.
Through sounds of ice cubes dropped in glass, an osteopath,
Dressed for the links, recounts an old Intourist tour.
—Here's where old Gibbons jumped from, Robinson.

Robinson walking in the Park, admiring the elephant.
Robinson buying the *Tribune*, Robinson buying the *Times*, Robinson
Saying, "Hello. Yes, this is Robinson. Sunday
At five? I'd love to. Pretty well. And you?"
Robinson alone at Longchamps, staring at the wall.

Robinson afraid, drunk, sobbing. Robinson
In bed with a Mrs. Morse. Robinson at home;
Decisions: Toynbee or luminal? Where the sun
Shines, Robinson in flowered trunks, eyes toward
The breakers. Where the night ends, Robinson in East Side bars.

Robinson in Glen-plaid jacket, Scotch-gram shoes,
Black four-in-hand, and oxford button-down,
The jewelled and silent watch that winds itself, the brief-
Case, covert topcoat, clothes for spring, all covering
His sad and usual heart, dry as a winter leaf.

ROBINSON AT HOME

Curtains drawn back. The door ajar.
All winter long it seemed a darkening
Began. But now the moonlight and the odors of the street
Conspire and combine toward one community.

These are the rooms of Robinson.
Bleached, wan, and colorless this light, as though
All the blurred daybreaks of the spring
Found an asylum here, perhaps for Robinson alone,

Who sleeps. Were there more music sifted through the floors
And moonlight of a different kind,
He might awake to hear the news at ten,
Which will be shocking, moderately.

This sleep is from exhaustion, but his old desire
To die like this has known a lessening.
Now there is only this coldness that he has to wear.
But not in sleep. Observant scholar, traveller,

Or uncouth bearded figure squatting in a cave,
A keen-eyed sniper on the barricades,
A heretic in catacombs, a famed roué,
A beggar on the streets, the confidant of popes—

All these are Robinson in sleep, who mumbles as he turns,
"There is something in this madhouse that I symbolize—
This city—nightmare—black—"

                               He wakes in sweat
To the terrible moonlight and what might be
Silence. It drones like wires far beyond the roofs,
And the long curtains blow into the room.

RUTH STONE

THE WATCHER

The dog who knew the winter felt no spleen
And sat indoors; the birds made tracks all day
Across the blue-white crust; he watched the branches sway
Like grasping fingers mirrored on the snow.
The house was warm, and long ago the grass was green;
And all day long bones rattled in his head,
While seven withered apples swung like time,
So quick, so short the pendulum. The tree,
Cursing with wind, prayed mercy on its knee.
He saw the snow toward evening flush to red,
Stepped on his bowl of milk, licked up his crime,
Rolled on his cozy self and smelled his skin,
And snuffed the nighttime out around the bed.

ADRIENNE RICH

LIVING IN SIN

She had thought the studio would keep itself—
No dust upon the furniture of love.
Half heresy, to wish the taps less vocal,
The panes relieved of grime. A plate of pears,
A piano with a Persian shawl, a cat
Stalking the picturesque, amusing mouse
Had been her vision when he pleaded "Come."
Not that, at five, each separate stair would writhe
Under the milkman's tramp; that morning light
So coldly would delineate the scraps
Of last night's cheese and blank, sepulchral bottles;
That on the kitchen shelf among the saucers
A pair of beetle eyes would fix her own—
Envoy from some black village in the moldings. . . .
Meanwhile her night's companion, with a yawn,
Sounded a dozen notes upon the keyboard,

Declared it out of tune, inspected, whistling,
A twelve hours' beard, went out for cigarettes,
While she, contending with a woman's demons,
Pulled back the sheets and made the bed and found
A fallen towel to dust the tabletop,
And wondered how it was a man could wake
From night to day and take the day for granted.
By evening she was back in love again,
Though not so wholly but throughout the night
She woke sometimes to feel the daylight coming
Like a relentless milkman up the stairs.

A PIECE OF HAPPINESS

In the kitchen's light were our friends, with their faulty faces,
Among the broken nutshells, the ill-aimed ashes
Strewing the table where supper, two hours past,
Was somehow finished and the dishes tossed
Long ago to one side; in that light I was content
To let the voices carry me where they went.
A piece of happiness, not to need to speak
Or even agree in silence, but let break
The unruly wave of discourse over the mind,
Thinking that these were our own people, our kind.

How out of patience, too, how irritable we've grown
With them, as with ourselves. And how alone
We are, as without ourselves, now they are gone!

THE SURVIVORS

Quite rightly, we remained among the living;
Managed to hoard our strength; kept our five wits;
So far as possible, withheld our eyes
From sights that loosen keystones in the brain.
We suffered, where we had to, thriftily,
And wasted nothing on the hopeless causes,
Foredoomed escapes, symbolic insurrections.

So it is we, not you, who walk today
Under the rebuilt city's raw façades,
Who sit upon committees of selection
For the commemorative plaque. Your throats
Are dumb beneath the plow that must drive on
To turn the fields of wire to fields of wheat.
Our speeches turn your names like precious stone,

Yet we can pay our tax and see the sun.
What else could we, what else could you, have done?

KINGSLEY TUFTS

LIFE WITHOUT FATHER

My mother married my father during the season
For some unpublished, though probably natural, reason;
Then, learning to loathe each other, beak, bone, and feather,
They began splitting worms and quit flying together.

My father, I hear, was a bit of a singer and spender,
Up with the sunrise and off on a cherry-juice bender,
But Mother was close, saving string and always complaining
Even on days when there wasn't a chance of it raining.

Our nest grew shabby, the tree where we lived unbearable;
Life without Father was bad; in fact, it was terrible.
Mother grew hard, and one morning, asking God's pardon,
She booted me over, head foremost, into the garden.

I've never been back, and I've never been homesick a minute;
The tree of my birth, I loathe it, and every bird in it.
The world's full of cats, and my mother, I hear, has remarried;
They live, so I'm told, just above where my father is buried.

PHYLLIS McGINLEY

BALLADE OF LOST OBJECTS

Where are the ribbons I bind my hair with?
  Where is my lipstick? Where are my hose—
The sheer ones hoarded these weeks to wear with
  Frocks the closets do not disclose?
Perfumes, petticoats, sports chapeaux,
  The blouse Parisian, the earring Spanish—
Everything suddenly ups and goes.
  And where in the world did the children vanish?

This is the house I used to share with
  Girls in pinafores, shier than does.
I can recall how they climbed my stair with
  Gales of giggles, on their tiptoes.
Last seen wearing both braids and bows
  (But looking rather Raggedy-Annish),
When they departed nobody knows—
  Where in the world did the children vanish?

Two tall strangers, now, I must bear with,
  Decked in my personal furbelows,
Who raid the larder, who rend the air with
  Gossip and terrible radios.
Neither my friends nor quite my foes,
  Alien, beautiful, stern, and clannish,
Here they dwell, while the wonder grows:
  Where in the world did the children vanish?

Prince, I warn you, under the rose,
  Time is the thief you cannot banish.
These are my daughters, I suppose.
  But where in the world did the children vanish?

PUBLISHER'S PARTY

At tea in cocktail weather,
 The lady authors gather.
Their hats are made of feather.
 They talk of Willa Cather.

They talk of Proust and Cather,
 And how we drift, and whither.
Where wends the lady author,
 Martinis do not wither.

Their cocktails do not wither
 Nor does a silence hover.
That critic who comes hither
 Is perilled like a lover;

Is set on like a lover.
 Alert and full of power,
They flush him from his cover,
 No matter where he cower.

And Honor Guest must cower
 When they, descending rather
Like bees upon a flower,
 Demand his views on Cather—

On Wharton, James, or Cather,
 Or Eliot or Luther,
Or Joyce or Cotton Mather,
 Or even Walter Reuther.

In fact, the tracts of Reuther
 They will dispute together
For hours, gladly, soother
 Than fall on silent weather.

From teas in any weather
Where lady authors gather,
Whose hats are largely feather,
Whose cocktails do not wither,
Who quote from Proust and Cather
(With penitence toward neither),
Away in haste I slither
Feeling I need a breather.

EDMUND WILSON

ON EDITING SCOTT FITZGERALD'S PAPERS

Scott, your last fragments I arrange tonight,
Assigning commas, setting accents right,
As once I punctuated, spelled, and trimmed
When, passing in a Princeton spring, now dimmed—
A quarter-century ago and more—
You left your "Shadow Laurels" at my door.
That was the tale of one who sang and shone,
Lived for applause but had his life alone,
In some beglamoured, shimmering, bluish-green,
Imagined Paris wineshop of nineteen;
Who fed on drink for weeks, forgot to eat,
"Worked feverishly," nourished on defeat
A lyric pride, and lent a lyric voice
To all the tongueless, knavish tavern boys,
The liquor-ridden, the illiterate;
Got stabbed one midnight by a tavern mate—
Betrayed, but self-betrayed by stealthy sins—
And faded to the sound of violins.

Tonight, in this dark, long Atlantic gale,
I set in order such another tale,
While tons of wind that take the world for scope
Rock blackened fathoms where marauders grope
Our blue and bathed-in Massachusetts ocean;

The Cape shakes to the depth bomb's dumbed concussion;
And guns can interrupt me in these rooms,
Where now I seek to breathe again the fumes
Of iridescent drinking dens, retrace
The bright hotels, regain the eager pace
You tell of. . . . Scott, the bright hotels turn pale;
The pace limps or stamps; the fumes are stale;
The horns and violins blow faint tonight.
A rim of darkness that devours light
Runs like the wall of flame that eats the land;
Blood, brain, and labor pour into the sand;
And here among our comrades of the trade
Some buzz like husks, some stammer, much afraid,
Some mellowly give tongue and join the drag
Like hounds that bay the bounding anise bag,
Some swallow darkness and sit hunched and dull,
The stunned beast's stupor in the monkey skull.

I climbed, a quarter-century ago and more
Played out, the college steps, unlatched my door,
And, creature strange to college, found you there—
The pale skin, hard green eyes, and yellow hair—
Intently cleaning up before a glass
Some ravage wrought by evenings at the Nass;
Nor did you stop abashed, thus pocked and blotched,
But kept on peering while I stopped and watched.
Tonight, from days more distant now, we find,
Than holidays in France were, left behind,
Than spring of graduation from the fall
That found us grubbing below City Hall,
Through storm and darkness, time's contrary stream,
There gleams surprisingly your mirror's beam
To bring before me still, in graver guise,
The glitter of the hard and emerald eyes;
The cornea tough, the aqueous chamber cold,
Those glassy optic bulbs that globe and hold,
They pass their image on to what they mint,
Suffuse your tales of summer with their tint,

And leave us to turn over, iris-fired,
Not the great, Ritz-sized diamond you desired
But jewels in a handful, lying loose:
The opal's green chartreuses, shifting blues,
Its shadowy-vivid vein of red that flickers,
Tight phials of the spirit's light mixed liquors;
Some zircons livid, tinsel rhinestones; but
Two emeralds, green and lucid, one half cut,
One cut consummately—and both take place
In Letters' most expensive Cartier case.

And there I have set them out for final show,
And come to the task's dead end, and dread to know
The eyes struck dark, dissolving in the wrecked
And darkened world, the light of intellect
That spilled into the spectrum of tune, taste,
Scent, color, living speech is gone, is lost;
And we must dwell among the jagged stumps,
With owls digesting mice to gruesome lumps
Of skin and gristle, monkeys scared by thunder,
Great buzzards that descend to grab the plunder.
And I, your scraps and sketches sorting yet,
Can never thus relight one sapphire jet,
However close I look, however late,
But only spell and point and punctuate.

JOHN BERRYMAN

NOTE TO WANG WEI

How could you be so happy, now some thousand years
dishevelled, puffs of dust?
It leaves me uneasy at last,
your poems tease me to the verge of tears,
and your fate. It makes me think.
It makes me long for mountains & blue waters.
Makes me wonder how much to allow.

(I'm reconfirming, God of bolts & bangs,
of fugues & bucks, whose rocket burns & sings.)
I wish we could meet for a drink
in a "freedom from ten thousand matters."
Be dust myself pretty soon; not now.

THOMAS WHITBREAD

THE CCC

CCC campers near West Cummington
In the middle thirties built a sensible dam,
Considering the river—three strong piles
Of squarish field stones, rescued from old walls,
Held solid by concrete; between these piers,
Two slabs of tightly banded logs, let down
To make a pool in summer, taken up
In October when the after-swimming air
Would be too cold even if the water wasn't,
Then dropped back into place in middle June
When the ice-floed floods from springs of melting snow
Had reached the larger rivers and the sea.
I swam there seldom as a boy; the place
Seemed tame and dull compared to other parts
Of the same river, natural, undammed.
I liked much what the CCC
Had done upcountry: stands of spruce and fir
Planted in rambling patterns, some my height,
Some more, some less, all young and growing,
Handsome and sturdy in the midsummer air.
But I thanked the CCC boys most of all
For what they did at Windsor Jambs, a gorge
Of rapids and waterfalls—they let it be
Essentially as it was, as today it is,
Neither cutting nor planting trees atop its sides,
Sweeping no needles up, breaking no rocks,
Letting the waters fall as waters will.

They took away nothing. All they thought to add
Was a series of sturdy posts along the edge
Of its cliffs, above sheer drop-offs—thick brown posts
Connected by three strands of stout steel rope,
Which, as I walked, I could run my hand along
Like an electric train, adding my game
To the natural beauty into which I gazed.
When I went back, at twenty, after the war,
I found the tent floors rotting, the dam unused,
The pines far taller than I, growing on,
But the Jambs the same, and every post still strong.
Only the rust on the ropes, which stopped my hands
From feeling extended echoes, showed that here,
Even here, in time, like all things, time would change
And make forgotten the works of the CCC.

LAURIE LEE

BOY IN ICE

O river, green and still,
By frost and memory stayed,
Your dumb and stiffened glass divides
A shadow and a shade.

In air, my shadow's face
Its winter gaze lets fall
To see beneath the stream's bright bars
That other shade in thrall.

A boy, time-fixed in ice,
His cheeks with summer dyed,
His mouth a rose-devouring rose,
His bird throat petrified.

O fabulous and lost,
More distant to me now

Than rock-drawn mammoth, painted stag,
Or tigers in the snow,

You stare into my face,
Dead as ten thousand years,
Your sparrow tongue sealed in my mouth,
Your world about my ears.

And till our shadows meet,
Till time burns through the ice,
Thus frozen shall we ever stay
Locked in this paradise.

MALCOLM COWLEY

THE END OF THE WORLD

Not the harsh voice in the microphone,
Not broken covenants or hate in armor,
    But the smile like a cocktail gone flat,
    The stifled yawn.

Not havoc from the skies, death underfoot,
The farmhouse gutted, or the massacred city,
    But the very nice couple retired on their savings,
    The weeded garden, the loveless bed.

House warm in winter, city free of vice,
Tree that outstood the equinoctial gales:
    Dry at the heart, they crashed
    On a windless day.

GILBERT HIGHET

INSOMNIA

Midnight:
kill the light.

One:
thoughts still run.

Two:
what can I do, what can I do?

Three:
all asleep but me.

Four:
something breathing under the door.

Five:
the window comes alive.

Six:
sleep and waking mix.

Seven:
at least, still living.

Eight:
up, a little late.

Nine:
fine, thanks, fine.

REED WHITTEMORE

THE RADIO UNDER THE BED

Why was a radio sinful? Lord knows. But it was.
So I had one
That I kept locked in a strongbox under my bed
And brought forth, turned on, tuned, and fondled at night,
When the sneaky housemaster slept and vice was all right.

The music played in my ear from the Steel Pier,
Knob Hill, the Astor, and other housemasterless
Hebrides where (I heard) the loved lived it up.
I listened myself to sleep, the sweet saxes
Filtering into my future, filling my cup.

All prohibitions have vanished. Radios bore me,
As do the two-step debauches I used to crave.
But the songs still remain, the old vulgar songs, and will play me,
Tum-te-tum, tum-te-tum, tum-te-tum, into my grave.

H. D.

THE MOON IN YOUR HANDS

If you take the moon in your hands
and turn it round
(heavy, slightly tarnished platter),
you're there;

if you pull dry seaweed from the sand
and turn it round
and wonder at the underside's bright amber,
your eyes

look out as they did here
(you don't remember)
when my soul turned round,

perceiving the other side of everything,
mullein leaf, dogwood leaf, moth wing,
and dandelion seed under the ground.

ELIZABETH BISHOP

LARGE BAD PICTURE

Remembering the Strait of Belle Isle or
some northerly harbor of Labrador,
before he became a schoolteacher
a great-uncle painted a big picture.

Receding for miles on either side
into a flushed, still sky
are overhanging pale-blue cliffs
hundreds of feet high,

their bases fretted by little arches,
the entrances to caves
running in along the level of a bay
masked by perfect waves.

On the middle of that quiet floor
sits a fleet of small black ships,
square-rigged, sails furled, motionless,
their spars like burned matchsticks.

And high above them, over the tall cliffs'
semitranslucent ranks,
are scribbled hundreds of fine black birds
hanging in "n"s, in banks.

One can hear their crying, crying,
the only sound there is
except for occasional sighing
as a large aquatic animal breathes.

In the pink light
the small red sun goes rolling, rolling,
round and round and round at the same height
in perpetual sunset, comprehensive, consoling,

while the ships consider it.
Apparently they have reached their destination.
It would be hard to say what brought them there,
commerce or contemplation.

AT THE FISHHOUSES

Although it is a cold evening,
down by one of the fishhouses
an old man sits netting,
his net, in the gloaming almost invisible,
a dark purple-brown,
and his shuttle worn and polished.
The air smells so strong of codfish
it makes one's nose run and one's eyes water.
The five fishhouses have steeply peaked roofs
and narrow, cleated gangplanks slant up
to storerooms in the gables
for the wheelbarrows to be pushed up and down on.
All is silver: the heavy surface of the sea,
swelling slowly as if considering spilling over,
is opaque, but the silver of the benches,
the lobster pots, and masts, scattered
among the wild jagged rocks,
is of an apparent translucence
like the small old buildings with an emerald moss
growing on their shoreward walls.
The big fish tubs are completely lined
with layers of beautiful herring scales
and the wheelbarrows are similarly plastered
with creamy iridescent flies crawling on them.
Up on the little slope behind the houses,
set in the sparse bright sprinkle of grass,

is an ancient wooden capstan,
cracked, with two long bleached handles
and some melancholy stains, like dried blood,
where the ironwork has rusted.

The old man accepts a Lucky Strike.
He was a friend of my grandfather.
We talk of the decline in the population
and of codfish and herring
while he waits for a herring boat to come in.
There are sequins on his vest and on his thumb.
He has scraped the scales, the principal beauty,
from unnumbered fish with that black old knife,
the blade of which is almost worn away.

Down at the water's edge, at the place
where they haul up the boats, up the long ramp
descending into the water, thin silver
tree trunks are laid horizontally
across the gray stones, down and down
at intervals of four or five feet.

Cold dark deep and absolutely clear,
element bearable to no mortal,
to fish and to seals . . . One seal particularly
I have seen here evening after evening.
He was curious about me. He was interested in music;
like me a believer in total immersion,
so I used to sing him Baptist hymns.
I sang him "A mighty fortress is our God."
He stood up in the water and regarded me
steadily, moving his head a little.
Then he would disappear, then suddenly emerge
almost in the same spot, with a sort of shrug
as if it were against his better judgment.
Cold dark deep and absolutely clear,
the clear gray icy water . . . Back, behind us,
the dignified tall firs begin.

Bluish, associating with their shadows,
a million Christmas trees stand
waiting for Christmas. The water seems suspended
above the rounded gray and blue-gray stones.
I have seen it over and over, the same sea, the same,
slightly, indifferently swinging above the stones,
icily free above the stones,
above the stones and then the world.
If you should dip your hand in,
your wrist would ache immediately,
your bones would begin to ache and your hand would burn
as if the water were a transmutation of fire
that feeds on stones and burns with a dark-gray flame.
If you tasted it, it would first taste bitter,
then briny, then surely burn your tongue.
It is like what we imagine knowledge to be:
dark, salt, clear, moving, utterly free,
drawn from the cold hard mouth
of the world, derived from the rocky breasts
forever, flowing and drawn, and since
our knowledge is historical, flowing, and flown.

FILLING STATION

Oh, but it is dirty!
—this little filling station,
oil-soaked, oil-permeated
to a surprising, over-all
black translucency.
Be careful with that match!

Father wears a dirty,
oil-soaked monkey suit
that cuts him under the arms,
and several quick and saucy
and greasy sons assist him
(it's a family filling station),
all quite thoroughly dirty.

Do they live in the station?
It has a cement porch
behind the pumps, and on it
a set of crushed and grease-
impregnated wickerwork;
on the wicker sofa
a dirty dog, quite comfy.

Some comic books provide
the only note of color—
of certain color. They lie
upon a big dim doily
draping a taboret
(part of the set), beside
a big hirsute begonia.

Why the extraneous plant?
Why, oh why, the table?
Why, oh why, the doily?
(Embroidered in daisy stitch
with marguerites, I think,
and heavy with gray crochet.)

Somebody embroidered the doily.
Somebody waters the plant,
or oils it, maybe. Somebody
arranges the rows of cans
so that they softly say:
ESSO—SO—SO—SO
to high-strung automobiles.
Somebody loves us all.

AFTER-WORK DRINK

KENNETH KOCH

YOU WANT A SOCIAL LIFE, WITH FRIENDS

You want a social life, with friends,
A passionate love life and as well
To work hard every day. What's true
Is of these three you may have two
And two can pay you dividends
But never may have three.

There isn't time enough, my friends—
Though dawn begins, yet midnight ends—
To find the time to have love, work, and friends.
Michelangelo had feeling
For Vittoria and the Ceiling
But did he go to parties at day's end?

Homer nightly went to banquets
Wrote all day but had no lockets
Bright with pictures of his Girl.
I know one who loves and parties
And has done so since his thirties
But writes hardly anything at all.

DEBORAH GARRISON

SAYING YES TO A DRINK

What would a grown woman do?
She'd tug off an earring
when the phone rang, drop it to the desk

for the clatter and roll. You'd hear
in this the ice, tangling in the glass;
in her voice, low on the line, the drink

being poured. All night awake,
I heard its fruity murmur of disease
and cure. I heard the sweet word "sleep,"

which made me thirstier. Did I say it,
or did you? And will I learn
to wave the drink with a goodbye wrist

in conversation, toss it off all bracelet-bare
like more small talk about a small affair?
To begin, I'll claim what I want

is small: the childish hand
of a dream to smooth me over,
a cold sip of water in bed,

your one kiss, never again.
I'll claim I was a girl before this gin,
then beg you for another.

BURKE BOYCE
DOWN-TOWN LYRICS

FIVE O'CLOCK

When crisp commuters fill the streets
And window lights are lit,
When newsstands flash with colored sheets,
And doorways clog a bit—

When deeper shadows cross the "L,"
And fruit stalls have a richer smell,
And men come out with toys to sell,
And pushcart peddlers quit—

When all the cars by Bowling Green
    Have left their parking block,
When Nassau Street's a hectic scene,
And Wall's not any too serene,
There's only one thing this can mean—
    It's almost five o'clock.

WASHINGTON MARKET

The Washington Market takes personal care
    Of "things every city should eat";
It furnishes foodstuffs near Telegram Square,
    And it's named after Washington Street.

It has butter, and cheeses, elliptical eggs,
    There are baskets and boxes of greens,
With veal and mutton aloft (by the legs)
    And lobsters in nautical scenes.

It smacks of the silo, it smells of the shore,
    It is bumpily full, and it bulges;
And it gives the impression of knowing much more
    About food than it ever divulges.

MATTHEW DICKMAN

MINIMUM WAGE

My mother and I are on the front porch lighting
each other's cigarettes
as if we were on a ten-minute break from our jobs
at being a mother and son,
just ten minutes to steal a moment
of freedom before clocking back in,
before putting the aprons back on, the paper hats,
washing our hands twice and then standing

behind the counter again,
hoping for tips, hoping the customers
will be nice, will say some kind word, the cool
front yard before us and the dogs
in the back yard shitting on everything.
We are hunched over, two extras
on the set of "The Night of the Hunter." I am pulling
a second cigarette out of the pack,
a swimmer rising from a pool of other swimmers.
Soon we will go back inside and sit
in the yellow kitchen and drink the rest of the coffee
and what is coming to kill us will pour milk into mine
and sugar into hers. Some kitchens
are full of mothers and sons with no mouths, no eyes,
and no hands, but our mouths are like the mouths of fire-
eaters and our eyes are like the million
eyes of flies. Our hands are like the hands of the living.

LEONARD COHEN
DRANK A LOT

i drank a lot. i lost my job.
i lived like nothing mattered.
then you stopped, and came across
my little bridge of fallen answers.

i don't recall what happened next.
i kept you at a distance.
but tangled in the knot of sex
my punishment was lifted.

and lifted on a single breath—
no coming and no going—
o G-d, you are the only friend
i never thought of knowing.

your remedies beneath my hand
your fingers in my hair
the kisses on our lips began
that ended everywhere.

and now our sins are all confessed
our strategies forgiven
it's written that the law must rest
before the law is written.

and not because of what i'd lost
and not for what i'd mastered
you stopped for me, and came across
the bridge of fallen answers.

tho' mercy has no point of view
and no one's here to suffer
we cry aloud, as humans do:
we cry to one another.

And now it's one, and now it's two,
And now the whole disaster.
We cry for help, as humans do—
Before the truth, and after.

And Every Guiding Light Was Gone
And Every Teacher Lying—
There Was No Truth In Moving On—
There Was No Truth In Dying.

And Then The Night Commanded Me
To Enter In Her Side—
And Be As Adam Was To Eve
Before The Great Divide.

her remedies beneath my hand
her fingers in my hair—

and every mouth of hunger glad—
and deeply unaware.

and here i cannot lift a hand
to trace the lines of beauty,
but lines are traced, and beauty's glad
to come and go so freely.

and from the wall a grazing wind,
weightless and routine—
it wounds us as i part your lips
it wounds us in between.

and every guiding light was gone
and every sweet direction—
the book of love i read was wrong
it had a happy ending.

And Now There Is No Point Of View—
And Now There Is No Other—
We Spread And Drown As Lilies Do—
We Spread And Drown Forever.

You are my tongue, you are my eye,
My coming and my going.
O G-d, you let your sailor die
So he could be the ocean.

And when I'm at my hungriest
She takes away my tongue
And holds me here where hungers rest
Before the world is born.

And fastened here we cannot move
We cannot move forever
We spread and drown as lilies do—
From nowhere to the center.

Escaping through a secret gate
I made it to the border
And call it luck—or call it fate—
I left my house in order.

And now there is no point of view—
And now there is no other—
We spread and drown as lilies do—
We spread and drown forever.

Disguised as one who lived in peace
I made it to the border
Though every atom of my heart
Was burning with desire.

WILLIAM MATTHEWS

SAD STORIES TOLD IN BARS: THE "READER'S DIGEST" VERSION

First I was born and it was tough on Mom.
Dad felt left out. There's much I can't recall.
I seethed my way to speech and said a lot
of things: some were deemed cute. I was so small
my likely chance was growth, and so I grew.
Long days in school I filled, like a spring creek,
with boredom. Sex I discovered soon
enough, I now think. Sweet misery!

There's not enough room in a poem so curt
to get me out of adolescence, yet
I'm nearing fifty with a limp, and dread
the way the dead get tacked up like a cord
of wood. Not much of a story, is it?
The life that matter's not the one I've led.

JULIA KASDORF

AT THE ACME BAR & GRILL

In dim light Manhattanites sip Margaritas
and suck their fingertips. Who else is wondering
where Buffalo chicken wings come from?
I can't be alone in my memory of calico
bonnets to keep the gray air and stench
of chicken off your hair, or the heavy cart
pushed down dim aisles of hens
cramped into slots like tenements.
How they squawk and peck when you reach
for the eggs that drop without cracking
into wire troughs because of oyster shells
slipped in their feed. The eggs stack
on cardboard flats, a dozen square
and higher than your head. If one drops
you kick it in the gutter, where rats run
at night. Some eggs come smeared with shit
or blood, some huge with double yolks, and once
or twice a week you find one tiny as a robin's.
These I named lucky eggs—rare as luck,
small as luck—I sucked their insides
and saved shells. Who at the bar will admit
he knows how hot a henhouse becomes
under a corrugated tin roof like the restaurant's
ceiling? Or how you blink in the sunlight,
when you finally emerge, your shoes ancient
with dust, your clothes reeking, your ears
full of the dull din of thousands of chickens,
distant as the noise outside a night club.

MALCOLM LOWRY

THE DRUNKARDS

I

Notions of freedom are tied up with drink.
Our ideal life contains a tavern
Where man may sit and talk or just think,
All without fear of the nighted wyvern;
Or yet another tavern where it appears
There are no No Trust signs, no No Credit,
And, apart from the unlimited beers,
We sit unhackled, drunk, and mad to edit
Tracts of a really better land where man
May drink a finer, ah, an undistilled wine
That subtly intoxicates without pain,
Weaving the vision of the unassimilable inn
Where we may drink forever without owing,
With the door open, and the wind blowing.

II

The noise of death is in this desolate bar,
Where tranquillity sits bowed over its prayer
And music shells the dream of the lover,
But when no nickel brings this harsh despair
Into this loneliest of homes,
And of all dooms the loneliest yet,
When no electric music breaks the heat
Of hearts to be doubly broken but now set
By the surgeon of peace in the splint of woe,
Pierces more deeply than trumpets do
The motion of the mind into that web
Where disorders are as simple as the tomb
And the spider of life sits, sleep.

RACHEL WETZSTEON
LOVE AND WORK

In an uncurtained room across the way
a woman in a tight dress paints her lips
a deeper red, and sizes up her hips
for signs of ounces gained since yesterday.

She has a thoughtful and a clever face,
but she is also smart enough to know
the truth: however large the brain may grow,
the lashes and the earrings must keep pace.

Although I've spread my books in front of me
with a majestic air of I'll show her,
I'm much less confident than I'd prefer,
and now I've started pacing nervously.

I'm poring over theorems, tomes and tracts.
I'm getting ready for a heavy date
by staying up ridiculously late.
But a small voice advises, Face the facts:

go on this way and you'll soon come to harm.
The world's most famous scholars wander down
the most appalling alleyways in town,
a blond and busty airhead on each arm.

There is an inner motor known as lust
that makes a man of learning walk a mile
to gratify his raging senses, while
the woman he can talk to gathers dust.

A chilling vision of the years ahead
invades my thoughts and widens like a stain:
a barren dance card and a teeming brain,
a crowded bookcase and an empty bed . . .

what if I compromised? I'd stay up late
to hone my elocutionary skills,
and at the crack of dawn I'd swallow pills
to calm my temper and control my weight,

but I just can't. Romantics, so far gone
they think their lovers live for wisdom, woo
by growing wiser; when I think of you
I find the nearest lamp and turn it on.

Great gods of longing, watch me as I work,
and if I sprout a martyr's smarmy grin
please find some violent way to do me in;
I'm burning all these candles not to shirk

a night of passion, but to give that night
a richly textured backdrop when it comes.
The girl who gets up from her desk and dumbs
her discourse down has never seen the flight

of wide-eyed starlings from their shabby cage;
the fool whose love is truest is the one
who knows a lover's work is never done.
I'll call you when I've finished one more page.

STEPHEN DUNN

THE PARTY TO WHICH YOU ARE NOT INVITED

You walk in, your clothes dark
and strangely appropriate, an arrogance
about you as if you had a ramrod
for a spine. You feel posture-perfect.

When you speak, women move away.
You smile, and men see tombstones.

They think they know who you are,
that they could throw you out

as they could one man. But today you are
every man who has been omitted
from any list: how quickly they see
they would have no chance.

You pour yourself a drink,
as if ready to become one of them.
Under your skin, nerve endings, loose
wires, almost perceivable. Something

somewhere is burning. You tell them
you've dreamed of moments like this,
to be in their lovely house,
to have everyone's attention. You ask

of the children, are they napping?
You extend your hand to the host,
who won't take it, reminds you
you were not invited, never will be.

You have things in your pockets
for everybody. House gifts.
Soon you'll give them out.
If only they could understand

how you could be ruined
by kindness, how much
you could love them
if they knew how to stop you.

ANONYMOUS
PILGRIMAGE

Presently on all the trees
Leaves will flame in brilliancies
Of every hue.

And after work, before it's dark,
I'll stroll up past Central Park
To see a few.

MARIE HOWE
THE LETTER, 1968

That he wrote it with his hand and folded the paper

and slipped it into the envelope and sealed it with his tongue

and pressed it closed so I might open it with my fingers.

That he brought it to the box and slipped it through the slot

so that it might be carried through time and weather to where

I waited on the front-porch step.

      (We knew how to wait then—it was what life was,

much of it.) So, when the mailman came up the walk and didn't have it,

he might have it the next day or the next, when it bore the mark

of his hand who had written my name, so I might open it and read

and read it again, and then again and look at the envelope he'd sealed,

and press my mouth to where his mouth had been.

KIMIKO HAHN

THE LIGHT

After you leave the office
I turn off the overhead so the secretary
will think I've left.
I sit looking at the white paper on my graying desk
and recall being an adolescent
in the same light: not
being able to move into the world
that wants you to do everything
the way it wants. The backstroke.
Touch-typing.
Cutting a dress from a pattern.
An A-line: Cotton.
A pink daisy print
spread smooth on the Home Ec. table,
pins between my lips.
Later hemmed at home. This was when
we had to wear dresses to school.
This was when I knew I would marry one day
but first have my own office.
This office is light, or dark really,
the way my room was always dark
so I could avoid being the daughter
in the rooms with lamps.
How I wish you would turn your car
away from your wife and child
and return to this square of dark light
so familiar, as I've already said,
it fails to pulse with grief.

JOSÉ ANTONIO RODRÍGUEZ

TENDER

Thinking of how much my father loved flowering plants
And how much my mother still does.

And of how unfathomably hard it must have been
To clothe and feed ten children

With the most meagre of salaries for tending to citrus orchards—
For shovelling and irrigating and shovelling again.

How he groaned when I removed his work boots
At day's end, an exhaustion deeper than any well.

Mom says his boss was a jerk, nothing ever good enough.
On top of everything, that empathy of her for him

Who'd never listened to her pleas because the priest said
All the children God will allow, the priest

Who never saw her afternoons slumped by the kitchen table,
A blank stare into somewhere

My voice could never reach.
Nothing to do but walk away. I swear

This is not about the unwanted child,
Or what a therapist called embodiment of the violation,

But about the strength and will to cradle the plants
Outside—the pruning, the watering, the sheltering

In found tarps and twine against the coldest nights.
To lean into the day's hard edge,

And still find that reserve of tenderness
For the bougainvillea, the hibiscus, the blue morning.

RITA DOVE

HATTIE McDANIEL ARRIVES AT THE COCONUT GROVE

late, in aqua and ermine, gardenias
scaling her left sleeve in a spasm of scent,
her gloves white, her smile chastened, purse giddy
with stars and rhinestones clipped to her brilliantined hair,
on her free arm that fine Negro
Mr. Wonderful Smith.

It's the day that isn't, February 29th,
at the end of the shortest month of the year—
and the shittiest, too, everywhere
except Hollywood, California,
where the maid can wear mink and still be a maid,
bobbing her bandaged head and cursing
the white folks under her breath as she smiles
and shoos their silly daughters
in from the night dew . . . What can she be
thinking of, striding into the ballroom
where no black face has ever showed itself
except above a serving tray?

Hi-Hat Hattie, Mama Mac, Her Haughtiness,
the "little lady" from Showboat whose name
Bing forgot, Beulah & Bertha & Malena
& Carrie & Violet & Cynthia & Fidelia,
one half of the Dark Barrymores—
dear Mammy we can't help but hug you crawl into
your generous lap tease you
with arch innuendo so we can feel that
much more wicked and youthful
and sleek but oh what

we forgot: the four husbands, the phantom
pregnancy, your famous parties, your celebrated
ice box cake. Your giggle above the red petticoat's rustle,

black girl and white girl walking hand in hand
down the railroad tracks
in Kansas City, six years old.
The man who advised you, now
that you were famous, to "begin eliminating"
your more "common" acquaintances
and your reply (catching him square
in the eye): "That's a good idea.
I'll start right now by eliminating you."

Is she or isn't she? Three million dishes,
a truckload of aprons and headrags later, and here
you are: poised, between husbands
and factions, no corset wide enough
to hold you in, your huge face a dark moon split
by that spontaneous smile—your trademark,
your curse. No matter, Hattie: it's a long, beautiful walk
into that flower-smothered standing ovation,
so go on
and make them wait.

ANTHONY WALTON

GWENDOLYN BROOKS

(1917–2000)

Sometimes I see in my mind's eye a four- or five-
year-old boy, coatless and wandering
a windblown and vacant lot or street in Chicago
on the windblown South Side. He disappears
but stays with me, staring and pronouncing
me guilty of an indifference more callous
than neglect, condescension as self-pity.

Then I see him again, at ten or fifteen, on the corner,
say, 47th and Martin Luther King, or in a group
of men surrounding a burning barrel off Lawndale,

everything surrounding vacant or for sale.
Sometimes I trace him on the train to Joliet
or Menard, such towns quickly becoming native
ground to these boys who seem to be nobody's
sons, these boys who are so hard to love, so hard
to see, except as case studies.

Poverty, pain, shame, one and a half million
dreams deemed fit only for the most internal
of exiles. That four-year-old wandering
the wind tunnels of Robert Taylor, of Cabrini
Green, wind chill of an as yet unplumbed degree—
a young boy she did not have to know to love.

PHYLLIS McGINLEY

JOURNEY TOWARD EVENING

Fifty, not having expected to arrive here,
Makes a bad traveller; grows dull, complains,
Suspects the local wine, dislikes the service,
Is petulant on trains,
And thinks the climate overestimated.
Fifty is homesick, plagued by memories
Of more luxurious inns and expeditions,
Calls all lakes cold, all seas
Too tide-beset (for Fifty is no swimmer),
Nor, moving inland, likes the country more,
Believes the hills are full of snakes and brigands.
The scenery is a bore,
Like the plump, camera-hung, and garrulous trippers
Whose company henceforward he must keep.
Fifty writes letters, dines, yawns, goes up early
But not to sleep. He finds it hard to sleep.

ANTHONY LOMBARDY

FOR THE WAITRESS BRINGING WATER

She brings us water, not intending harm,
And now a drier throat cannot confess
My praises for the motions of this waitress
And for the oneness of her uniform.
I know already that I lack the charm
For that; with her, there's nothing counts for less
Than thoughts which fall as readily as a dress
And yet as finally as a severed arm.
The truckers at the other table try
A CB raunchy line to make her stay,
But I can only smile and order pie
To slow her in the cession of her tray,
Until I've tasted all that I could say
And swinging doors have swallowed our goodbye.

RICHARD F. HUGO

THE ONLY BAR IN DIXON

Home. Home. I knew it entering.
Green cheap plaster and the stores
across the street toward the river
failed. One Indian depressed
on Thunderbird. Another buying
Thunderbird to go. This air
is fat with gangsters I imagine
on the run. If they ran here
they would be running from
imaginary cars. No one cares
about the wanted posters
in the brand new concrete block P.O.

This is home because some people
go to Perma and come back

from Perma saying Perma
is no fun. To revive, you take 382
to Hot Springs, your life savings
ready for a choice of bars, your hotel
glamorous with neon up the hill.
Is home because the Jocko
dies into the Flathead. Home because
the Flathead goes home north northwest.

I want home full of grim permission.
You can go as out of business here
as rivers or the railroad station.
I knew it entering.
                    Five bourbons
and I'm in some other home.

TANEUM BAMBRICK
SEPARATING

At twenty-nine I drink strawberry cider with an ex in the mist

outside a pizza restaurant. He painted off a ladder this summer.

Asks if I've smelled the difference between fear and regular sweat.

Down the road, there's a church with a tall wooden door where we
        once kissed

so fast the earrings fell off my head. Today he lives with a beautiful
        artist.

I often think of him holding my thighs beside a river after we
        finished a bottle of Malbec.

Mosquitos pulling little blankets above the grass. I know if I sit here
        long enough

he will say the thing he forgets he always says: *You're a planet. I never want*

you to leave. I know I am not the only woman he keeps

wrapped in the same story. Because I've been hurt, I order another
    drink.

Wait for him to say what men say before getting married: *Loving you*

is its own time. A place that always exists but cannot in this life.

MONICA YOUN

BROWNACRE

We were sitting, leaning back against the house,
on the stone patio, or terrace, looking out over a steep drop

at the mountains arrayed in a semicircle around us,
all expectant angles, like the music stands

of an absent orchestra—summer colors, orangey golds
and dim blues and there must have been greens as well—

I wasn't paying attention: I was watching the thing
you had just said to me still hanging in the air between us,

its surfaces beading up with a shiny liquid like contempt
that might have been seeping from the words themselves

or else condensing from the air, its inscrutable humidity—
the droplets rounding themselves in their fall,

etching a darker patch on the patio tiles, a deepening
concavity, and, above it, a roughness in the air,

the molecules of concrete coalescing grain by grain
into a corrugated pillar topped by a cloud—a tree form:

not a sapling or a mountain tree, but a tree
that would look at home in a farmyard or meadow,

sheltered from winds, branches stretching out,
with all confidence, toward the horizon—

a shape that should have been an emblem
of sufficiency, of calm, but whose surfaces

were teeming with a turbulent rush of particles
like the inner workings of a throat exposed, and

whose dimensions were expanding with shocking speed,
accumulating mass, accumulating coherence

and righteousness, pulling more and more
of the disintegrating terrace into its form, taller than us,

then shadowing us, and doubtlessly, underground,
a root system of corresponding complexity and spread

was funnelling down displaced nothingness
from a hole in the upper air, and then it was time,

and I stood up and went inside and shut the door,
unsure what still anchored us to the mountainside.

SHARON OLDS

THE PROMISE

With the second drink, at the restaurant,
holding hands on the bare table
we are at it again, renewing our promise
to kill each other. You are drinking gin,
night-blue juniper berry
dissolving in your body, I am drinking Fumé,
chewing its fragrant dirt and smoke, we are
taking on earth, we are part soil already,
and always, wherever we are, we are also in our
bed, fitted naked closely
along each other, half passed out
after love, drifting back and
forth across the border of consciousness, our
bodies buoyant, clasped. Your hand
tightens on the table. You're a little afraid
I'll chicken out. What you do not want
is to lie in a hospital bed for a year
after a stroke, without being able to
think or die, you do not want
to be tied to a chair like my prim grandmother,
cursing. The room is dim around us,
ivory globes, pink curtains
bound at the waist, and outside
a weightless bright lifted-up
summer twilight. I tell you you don't
know me if you think I will not
kill you. Think how we have floated together
eye to eye, nipple to nipple,
sex to sex, the halves of a single creature
drifting up to the lip of matter
and over it—you know me from the bright, blood-
flecked delivery room, if a beast
had you in its jaws I would attack it, if the ropes
binding your soul are your own wrists I will cut them.

SUSAN MINOT

THE TOAST

After I've made it stumbling through the day
And liquid light surrounds the window sill,
After paper buds have furled their wrinkled way
And, tired, I've relaxed my will,
I think of you and of your warm embrace
And recall the disturbed calmness of your face
In repose. And all the sorrow I've contained
This brilliant Tuesday in this lonely place
Vanishes. It topples down the hours strained
Till memory leaves another trace:
The time you smiled and covered me with kisses
And clicked your teeth to mine in a brisk toast,
And I think, At least I have that clinking ghost.

BARBARA HAMBY

ODE ON WORDS FOR PARTIES (AMERICAN EDITION)

Why do we have so many words for parties, a slew
    of them once you start looking: shindig, bash,
meet-and-greets, raves, blowouts, barbecues,
    and more tepid functions, receptions, luncheons, and do's
of all kinds, though, let's face it, most people have no clue
    about how to throw a party, like the friend who was complaining
because her husband wanted to have lots of food at the brunch
    they were planning, but she knew people didn't go
to parties to eat, and Marsha and I had to break it to her
    that brunch was the combination of two meals,
so her guests were expecting to eat double, and you can't believe
    the shock on her face, but her husband put out a great spread
and everyone ate and talked, though we've all been to those parties
    with the bowl of dead chips and the onion dip
that looks like cat vomit on the driveway, actually not that good,
    but my sister throws a fabulous party, because she's a great cook

and has an army of wine bottles that never stops marching,
    and her garden is verdant, and she has a pool,
which some people end up in at the end of the night. What
    would be the word for that kind of party—Vinocoolpool
Party? And the other one might be a Kittydip Party. And guests!
    They can ruin a party, too. Think of the Music Nazis
who make their way through the world with their one-upmanship,
    and your collection of Van Morrison and Jimi Hendrix
is so uncool compared with the Mud Stumps and Echo Park,
    but only before they caved and became famous
and were no longer cool. Then there are the couples
    who are glued at the hip, twins conjoined
by church and state, or the bloviators, or the drunks who can turn
    a party into a Godzilla-stomps-Tokyo apocalypse,
like the time the guy with the Ponderosa belt buckle slid chest first
    in a dance move and put a gouge three feet long
in my hardwood floor, and I hadn't even invited him; he was
    my hairdresser's friend. That party was over. I wanted
everyone out of my house. Or what about the people who live
    in the middle of nowhere, and you know
that on the way home you'll end up in Hades or a ditch,
    if you're lucky, what would you call those?
Suburban-Hell Parties? Hansel-and-Gretel-Lost-Weekend Parties?
    I often try to talk my husband into pulling over
so we don't crash, but he reminds me that we're just setting
    ourselves up for the serial killers who roam lonesome
highways looking for poets, and what would you call
    that concatenation of events? Zodiac-After-Party-Stab-Fest?
Post-Bash-Head-Bash? You can see that when I'm not
    going to parties I'm watching too many true-crime shows,
which make you mistrust your fellow human beings
    in the most basic way, and yet we continue to throw parties,
which is an interesting choice of verbs, and English
    is full of them—throw a party, pitch a fit, pitch a tent, pitch
a no-hitter, pitch in, pitch-black, and that's what the road
    is like now, and I'd give anything to be at that Kittydip Party
two blocks from my house, with the Einstein Brains
    blaring on the sound system so I can't hear the guy talking

about how he prepares petri dishes for his research
    or the woman who is describing an airline-ticket fiasco
that wouldn't even be interesting if it had happened
    to me, but I guess that's life—a continuum between darkness
and *mala folla*, a Spanish phrase that describes an indifference
    so profound it can't be bothered with scorn,
but I remember one of the best parties ever was a wine tasting
    put together by an Australian father and son
and by the end everyone was dancing to "Tutti Frutti"
    and screaming drunk and in love with the world and I danced
with a roly-poly lawyer named Booter, whom I never saw
    again, and the hangover the next day was a small price to pay
for that crazy mix of Little Richard and Cabernet,
    and there was food, yeah, but who remembers what.

STAV POLEG

AFTER-PARTY

Yes, there was the abundance of nightfall—
the sky with a parachute scar,
the spoon clinking

on glass.
But no one could trace, like a hymn,
the blue-vanishing

trail of an apple-throw
arc. Things like this
happen—

a hula-hoop pivoting
beauty, a wonder thrown
like a firework into

the crowd.
Some say it was only
an arrow, meaning—

an error.
Others swear they could hunt down
the deepest

of sighs.
That the transformation
from an apple into

a question
was inevitable—
that the answer was no more

than a boy
offsetting fire with sci-fi
animation—I mean—what

would you choose?
The possession of Europe and
Asia / the greatest of warriors' rivers

and tongues—the green in their night-vision
maps / a doorbell and how it rings
night.

TERRANCE HAYES

ANTEBELLUM HOUSE PARTY

To make the servant in the corner unobjectionable
Furniture, we must first make her a bundle of tree parts
Axed and worked to confidence. Oak-jawed, birch-backed,

Cedar-skinned, a pillowy bosom for the boss infants,
A fine patterned cushion the boss can fall upon.
Furniture does not pine for a future wherein the boss

Plantation house will be ransacked by cavalries or Calvary.
A kitchen table can, in the throes of a yellow-fever outbreak,
Become a cooling board holding the boss wife's body.

It can on ordinary days also be an ironing board holding
Boss garments in need of ironing. Tonight it is simply a place
For a white cup of coffee, a tin of white cream. Boss calls

For sugar and the furniture bears it sweetly. Let us fill the mouth
Of the boss with something stored in the pantry of a house
War, decency, nor bedevilled storms can wipe from the past.

Furniture's presence should be little more than a warm feeling
In the den. The dog staring into the fireplace imagines each log
Is a bone that would taste like a spiritual wafer on his tongue.

Let us imagine the servant ordered down on all fours
In the manner of an ottoman whereupon the boss volume
Of John James Audubon's "Birds of America" can be placed.

Antebellum residents who possessed the most encyclopedic
Bookcases, luxurious armoires, and beds with ornate cotton
Canopies often threw the most photogenic dinner parties.

Long after they have burned to ash, the hound dog sits there
Mourning the succulent bones he believes the logs used to be.
Imagination is often the boss of memory. Let us imagine

Music is radiating through the fields as if music were reward
For suffering. A few of the birds Audubon drew are now extinct.
The Carolina parakeet, passenger pigeon, and Labrador duck

No longer nuisance the boss property. With so much
Furniture about, there are far fewer woods. Is furniture's fate
As tragic as the fate of an axe, the part of a tree that helps

Bring down more upstanding trees? The best furniture
Can stand so quietly in a room that the room appears empty.
If it remains unbroken, it lives long enough to become antique.

TAYI TIBBLE
CREATION STORY

You can never live the same party twice & that makes me want to cry.
That makes me want to get so high that even the stars start trying it on.

Searching for Te Kore until I'm fully gone. Now we can start again.
Kick the night up from the earth, in our platform boots, & let the light in.

This is what made me tender like a pork bone boiling in every situation
I could barely sit in. On the flax mat going at god for hours & hours.

On the whenua calming Ruaumoko, while the police lasso the land.
In the car outside the station, my mother dependent on his rib. I had

my hands out the window, weighing the air to see if it felt like a Saturday
    night
or a Sunday, wondering if Dad would be let out of his cage in time

to see god today. I see atua today in everything. This is what made me.
    Watching
their descendants drop it lower than their expectations. They could never

sit in our situations which is why they can't get up & break it down like
    we do
& this song made from Polynesian mystics, deceptive transformers,
    delivers us

back to when we were down on ourselves doing ugly little things. Rolling
our eyes at the singing. Avoiding the sun. Just as our mothers had done

when their mothers spent generations powdering themselves pretty
in the image of the father, ignoring both her mother & the whenua in her.

I should have held my fist up then, a palmful of protest, but that's why
    I keep
my hands up, my hands up in the air now & this fresh set of fire
    reminds me

of how Nanny Pearl had nails so long it used to freak me out & now
I'm like wtf was I even on about & every time I see my nail tech

it's an homage & an apology for every time I didn't listen, bit the apple &
felt abandoned, & then abandoned me & me & me. But here we are now

created, & on fire like Mahuika. This is what made me. Trying to weave
perfect sentences, forming mountains I don't have the answers for. I'd ask

my ancestors, but I'm not sure they know. All we have ever done is our best
with the materials on hand: heat, water, soil. A smattering of words &

this is what made me drag myself upward from the ocean like Pania.
Fresh-faced & curious. This is what made me worshipful & marvellous,
        able to

stand upright, & some of that time I was dancing. This is what
        made me.
A duplicate of Hineahuone, our blood of red sand. No matter how hard we

sculpt ourselves, in the end we will always collapse back, & in the
        meantime
it is my friends who make me bow. Get on my hands & knees for

mop their drink up from the floor, kiss their beautiful ankles.
My god, you are so talented, embodied & creative. This is what

made me let down my ancestral knot, let my hips rock with all the rhythm
of the wind, this party beating & cultured in the space between

the sky & the land. Get high while you can. You have travelled
very far. I saw you coming in my mind born from the last burst star.

EMERGENCY MANAGEMENT

The sun eats away at the earth, or the earth eats away
at itself and burning up,

I sip at punch.
So well practiced at this
living. I have a way of seeing

things as they are: it's history
that's done this to me.
It's the year I'm told

my body will turn rotten,
my money talks but not enough,
I feel my body turn
against me.

Some days I want to spit
me out, the whole mess of me,
but mostly I am good

and quiet.
How much silence buys me

mercy, how much
silence covers all the lives it takes to make me.

In the event of every day and its newness
of disaster, find me sunning on the rooftop, please
don't ask anything of me.

If I could be anything
I would be the wind,

if I could be nothing
I would be.

TOI DERRICOTTE

WEEKEND GUESTS FROM CHICAGO, 1945

In their brand-new caramel Cadillac,
Julia and Walter arrived at four,
Trunk stuffed with leather suitcases,
Steaks, champagne, and oysters in a cooler,
And Walter's only drink—Johnnie Walker Blue.
Julia, hands flaring, in the clunky music
Of a pound of real gold charms,
Walter in a tan linen jacket
And shoes soft as old money.

Sweet-tempered, sweet-tongued,
He'd tease the women to blushing,
And let his wife reign queen
In a diamond ring to knock your eyes out.

She was known from New York to L.A.
For her fried chicken and greens,
And didn't hesitate, after hours of driving,
To throw an apron over a French cotton dress
And slap the flour on thirty or more pieces.

Oh, the chicken breasts and thighs
Spattering, juicy, in just the right degree of heat,
As she told stories, hilarious and true,
To a kitchen full of steamy women
That made them double over and pee themselves.

Saturday morning, men to golf,
And women in floral robes
With cups of a New Orleans blend
So strong they said
It stained the rim and turned you black;
Me, in a high chair, straining
For language, my bottle
Stirred with a spoon of coffee
And half a pint of cream.

At fifteen,
My first trip cross-country on a train,
I stopped to spend the night.
We took the El to Marshall Field's,
Where Julia bought my first expensive cold creams
And hose the shades of which—for the first time—
Dared the colors of our colored skin.

She told me she had lovers,
One a handsome Pullman porter.
My last nights onboard,
I, myself, enjoyed a notable service:
A café-au-lait gentleman
Woke me for breakfast
By slipping his hand through the sealed drapes
And gently shaking my rump.
I waited all night,
damp with wonder.

She had a wart on her chin or nose—
I can't remember which—
She wore it
Like exquisite jewelry,
The way Marilyn Monroe wore her beauty mark,
With unforgettable style.

ALICE OSWALD

EVENING POEM

Old scrap-iron foxgloves
rusty rods of the broken woods

what a faded knocked-out stiffness
as if you'd sprung from the horsehair
            of a whole Victorian sofa buried in the mud down there

or at any rate something dropped from a great height
straight through flesh and out the other side
has left your casing pale and loose and finally

just a heap of shoes

they say the gods being so uplifted
can't really walk on feet but take tottering steps
and lean like this closer and closer to the ground

                              which gods?

it is the hours on bird-thin legs
the same old choirs of hours
returning their summer clothes to the earth

with the night now
as if dropped from a great height

falling

L. E. *SISSMAN*

DYING: AN INTRODUCTION

Always too eager for future, we
Pick up bad habits of expectancy.
                    —Philip Larkin

I. RING AND WALK IN
Summer still plays across the street,
An ad-hoc band
In red, white, blue, and green
Old uniforms
And rented instruments;
Fall fills the street
From shore to shore with leaves,

A jaundiced mass
Protest against the cold;
I slip on ice
Slicks under powder snow and stamp my feet
Upon the doctor's rubber mat,
Ring and Walk In
To Dr. Sharon's waiting room—
For once, with an appointment,
To nonplus
Ugly Miss Erberus.
Across from other candidates—
A blue-rinsed dam
In Davidows, a husk
Of an old man,
A one-eyed boy—I sit
And share their pervigilium.
One *Punch* and two
Times later comes the call.

II. PROBABLY NOTHING
Head cocked like Art, the *Crimson* linotype
Operator, Dr. Sharon plays
Taps on my game leg, spelling out the name,
With his palpating fingers, of my pain.
The letters he types are not visible
To him or me; back up the melting pot
Of the machine, the matrix dents the hot
Lead with a letter and another; soon a word,
Tinkling and cooling, silver, will descend
To be imposed upon my record in
Black-looking ink. "My boy, I think," he says,
In the most masterly of schoolish ways,
In the most quiet of all trumps in A
Flat, "this lump is probably nothing, but"—
A but, a buzz of omen resonates—
"I'd check it anyway. Let's see when I
Can take a specimen." Quiet business
With the black phone's bright buttons. Sst, ssst, st:

An inside call. In whispers. Over. Out.
"Can you come Friday noon? We'll do it then."
I nod I can, and pass the world of men
In waiting, one *Life* further on.

III. O.P.O.R.

Undressing in the locker room
Like any high school's, full of shades
In jockstraps and the smell of steam,
Which comes, I guess, from autoclaves,
And not from showers, I am struck
By the immutability,
The long, unchanging, childish look
Of my pale legs propped under me,
Which, nonetheless, now harbor my
Nemesis, or, conceivably,
Do not. My narcissistic eye
Is intercepted deftly by
A square nurse in a gas-green gown
And aqua mask—a dodo's beak—
Who hands me a suit to put on
In matching green, and for my feet
Two paper slippers, mantis green:
My invitation to the dance.
I shuffle to the table, where
A shining bank of instruments—
Service for twelve—awaits my flesh
To dine. Two nurses pull my pants
Down and start shaving. With a splash,
The Doctor stops his scrubbing-up
And walks in with a quiet "Hi."
Like hummingbirds, syringes tap
The Novocain and sting my thigh
To sleep, and the swordplay begins.
The stainless-modern knife digs in—
Meticulous trencherman—and twangs
A tendon faintly. Coward, I groan.
Soon he says, "Sutures," and explains

To me he has his specimen
And will stitch up, with boundless pains,
Each severed layer, till again
He surfaces and sews with steel
Wire. "Stainless." Look how thin it is,
Held in his forceps. "It should heal
Without a mark." These verities
Escort me to the tiring room,
Where, as I dress, the Doctor says,
"We'll have an answer Monday noon."
I leave to live out my three days,
Reprieved from findings and their pain.

IV. PATH. REPORT
Bruisingly cradled in a Harvard chair
Whose orange arms cramp my pink ones, and whose black
Back stamps my back with splat marks, I receive
The brunt of the pathology report,
Bitingly couched in critical terms of my
Tissue of fabrications, which is bad.
That Tyrian specimen on the limelit stage
Surveyed by Dr. Cyclops, magnified
Countless diameters on its thick slide,
Turns out to end in -oma. "But be glad
These things are treatable today," I'm told.
"Why, fifteen years ago—" a dark and grave-
Shaped pause. "But now, a course of radiation, and—"
Sun rays break through. "And if you want X-ray,
You've come to the right place." A history,
A half-life of the hospital. Marie
Curie must have endowed it. Cyclotrons,
Like missile silos, lurk within its walls.
It's reassuring, anyway. But bland
And middle-classic as these environs are,
And sanguine as his measured words may be,
And soft his handshake, the webbed, inky hand
Locked on the sill and the unshaven face

Biding outside the window still appall
Me as I leave the assignation place.

V. OUTBOUND
Outside, although November by the clock,
Has a thick smell of spring,
And everything—
The low clouds lit
Fluorescent green by city lights;
The molten, hissing stream
Of white car lights cooling
To red and vanishing;
The leaves,
Still running from last summer, chattering
Across the pocked concrete;
The wind in trees;
The ones and twos,
The twos and threes
Of college girls,
Each shining in the dark,
Each carrying
A book or books,
Each laughing to her friend
At such a night in fall;
The two-and-twos
Of boys and girls who lean
Together in an A and softly walk
Slowly from lamp to lamp,
Alternatively lit
And nighted; Autumn Street,
Astonishingly named, a rivulet
Of asphalt twisting up and back
To some spring out of sight—and everything
Recalls one fall
Twenty-one years ago, when I,
A freshman, opening
A green door just across the river,

Found the source
Of spring in that warm night,
Surprised the force
That sent me on my way
And set me down
Today. Tonight. Through my
Invisible new veil
Of finity, I see
November's world—
Low scud, slick street, three giggling girls—
As, oddly, not as sombre
As December,
But as green
As anything:
As spring.

BILLY COLLINS

DOWNPOUR

Last night we ended up on the couch
trying to remember
all of the friends who had died so far,

and this morning I wrote them down
in alphabetical order
on the flip side of a shopping list
you had left on the kitchen table.

So many of them had been swept away
as if by a hand from the sky,
it was good to recall them,
I was thinking
under the cold lights of a supermarket
as I guided a cart with a wobbly wheel
up and down the long strident aisles.

I was on the lookout for blueberries,
English muffins, linguini, heavy cream,
light bulbs, apples, Canadian bacon,
and whatever else was on the list,
which I managed to keep grocery side up,

until I had passed through the electric doors,
where I stopped to realize,
as I turned the list over,
that I had forgotten Terry O'Shea
as well as the bananas and the bread.

It was pouring by then,
spilling, as they say in Ireland,
people splashing across the lot to their cars.
And that is when I set out,
walking slowly and precisely,
a soaking-wet man
bearing bags of groceries,
walking as if in a procession honoring the dead.

I felt I owed this to Terry,
who was such a strong painter,
for almost forgetting him
and to all the others who had formed
a circle around him on the screen in my head.

I was walking more slowly now
in the presence of the compassion
the dead were extending to a comrade,

plus I was in no hurry to return
to the kitchen, where I would have to tell you
all about Terry and the bananas and the bread.

VICTORIA CHANG

FROM THE TREES WITNESS EVERYTHING

DISTANT MORNING

Another morning.
The trees always look the same.
I am different.
Each day, I am greedier.
How do trees refuse evening?

THAT MUSIC

Once, I fell in love
with the music, not the man.
When the music played,
my heart moved like paper boats.
When it stopped, I was eighty.

IN A CLEARING

My whole life, I thought
to mourn leaves falling. Now I
marvel at all the splitting.

TO THE HAND

Someone is turning
the earth with wrenches, each turn
a bit closer to the end.
The earth is warmer.
The crickets are still singing,
rehearsing for the last day.

TOOL

We make tools to fix
everything—hammers, nails, wires

that we twist to hold
down or bend into beauty.
We make a small tree
into the shape we want, to
be slanted, silent.
The wire on my wrists cut in,
I take the shape of desire.

JASWINDER BOLINA

ANCESTRAL POEM

And so we settled upon the shore
of a nasally Midwestern sea
governed by a moon that hung
like a medal we'd won above
the subdivision. Evenings,
the starlings made an ecstatic
calligraphy against the gloam,
landed upon the slack, black
wires, our antique telephony
rippling between their toes.
From my vantage in a second-story
window of the split-level ranch
where we kept our things,
I could see some moths mistake
the neon heat of a Blockbuster
Video sign to the west for home,
your babaji watering the impatiens
in their beds beneath a local cosmos.
Crisscross of the pinkening contrails,
your bibiji nursing her twilight
chai in a patio chair. She said a thing
then that made them laugh, the clouds
like painted bulls tumbling across a cave wall
in this, the only known record of these events.

HAFIZAH GETER

THE BREAK-IN

When I close my eyes I see my mother running
from one house to another, throwing her fist
at the doors of neighbors, begging anyone
to call the police.
There are times when every spectator is hungry,
times a thief takes nothing, leaves you a fool
in your inventory.
How one trespass could make all others
suddenly visible. My mother counted
her jewelry and called
overseas. My father counted women
afraid one of us would go
missing. When I close my eyes
I hear my mother saying, "*A'aha*, this new country,"
my cousins exclaiming "Auntie!"
between the clicking line and their tongues.
Tonight the distance between me, my mother, and Nigeria
is like a jaw splashed against a wall.
I close my eyes and see my father
sulking like a pile of ashes,
his hair jet black and kinky,
his silence entering a thousand rooms.
Then outside, trimming hedges as if home
were a land just beyond the meadow,
the leaves suddenly back.
When I close my eyes
I see my mother, mean for the rest of the day,
rawing my back in the tub
like she's still doing dishes.

JANE HUFFMAN

ODE

Andrea taught me to ride sidesaddle. I rode
in small and dizzying circles around her.
I rode around her in small and dizzying
circles. Past the mirror and past the mirror
where, one summer, she was reared off
by a stallion attacking his own flaring
reflection. One summer, she was reared
off, or almost. I rode into the acres
of our sunflowers. In the acres, the fields,
I overindulged in beauty. In the fields,
I rode. Andrea leaned on a rail, her body
a rail. Andrea leaned on the shadow
of a rail. My shadow rode around her,
the small bells of my intuition. She rang
the small bells of the saddle. I was
small and dizzying. I was dizzy. I rode
in small and dizzying circles. Andrea
taught me to ride, no stirrups. Nothing
suspending my body but intuition, the small
and dizzying circles of my body.
My intuition rode around me in small
and dizzying circles, her shadow riding
circles around me. I called her Andrea.

LARRY LEVIS

PICKING GRAPES IN AN ABANDONED VINEYARD

Picking grapes alone in the late-autumn sun,
A short, curved knife in my hand,
Its blade silver from so many sharpenings,
Its handle black.
I still have a scar where a friend
Sliced open my right index finger once

In a cutting shed—
The same kind of knife.
The grapes drop into the pan
And the gnats swarm over them as always.
Fifteen years ago
I worked this row of vines beside a dozen
Families up from Mexico.
No one spoke English, or wanted to.
One woman, who made an omelette with a sheet of tin
And five spotted quail eggs,
Had a voice full of dusk, and jail cells,
And birdcalls. She spoke
In Spanish to no one, as they all did.
Their swearing was specific
And polite.
I remember two of them clearly:
A man named Tea, six feet nine inches tall
At the age of sixty-two,
Who wore white spats into downtown Fresno
Each Saturday night,
An alcoholic giant whom the women loved.
One chilled morning they found him dead outside
Rose's Café. . . .
And Ángel Dominguez,
Who came to work for my grandfather in 1910.
And who saved for years to buy
Twenty acres of rotting Thompson Seedless vines.
While the sun flared all one August
He decided he was dying of a rare disease
And spent his money and his last years
On specialists,
Who found nothing wrong.
Tea laughed and, tipping back
A bottle of muscatel, said, "Nothing's wrong.
You're just dying."
At seventeen, I discovered
Parlier, California, with its sad topless bar,

And its one main street, and its opium.
I would stand still and chalk my cue stick
In Johnny Palore's East Front Pool Hall and watch
The room filling with tobacco smoke as the sun set
Through one window.
Now all I hear are the vines rustling as I go
From one to the next,
The long canes holding up dry leaves, reddening
So late in the year.
What the vines want must be this silence spreading
Over each town, over the dance halls and the dying parks,
And the police drowsing in their cruisers
Under the stars.
What the men who worked here wanted was
A drink strong enough
To let out what laughter they had.
I can still see the two of them:
Tea smiles and lets his yellow teeth shine,
While Angel, the serious one, for whom
Death was a rare disease,
Purses his lips and looks down, as if
He is already mourning himself,
A soft gray hat between his hands.
Today, in honor of them,
I press my thumb against the flat part of this blade
And steady a bunch of Red Malaga grapes
With one hand,
The way they showed me, and cut—
And close my eyes to hear them laugh at me again,
And then, hearing nothing, no one,
Carry the grapes up into the solemn house
Where I was born.

TRACY K. SMITH

I SIT OUTSIDE IN LOW LATE-AFTERNOON LIGHT TO FEEL EARTH CALL TO ME

I wish it would grab me by the ankles and pull.
I wish its shadow would dance up close, closing in.

When I close my eyes a presence forms, backs away.
I float above a lake, am dragged back

from a portion of sky. Down, down, the falling doesn't end.
Every marked body must descend.

Is the world intended for me? Not just me but
the we that fills me? Our shadows reel and dart.

Our blood simmers, stirred back. What if
the world has never had—will never have—our backs?

The world has never had—will never have—our backs.
Our blood simmers, stirred back. What if

the we that fills me, our shadows real and dark,
is the world intended for me? Not just me but

every marked body must descend
from a portion of sky. Down, down, the falling doesn't end.

I float above a lake, am dragged back
when I close my eyes. A presence forms, backs away.

I wish its shadow would dance up close, closing in.
I wish it would grab me by the ankles and pull.

JAMES SCHUYLER

SONG

The light lies layered in the leaves.
Trees, and trees, more trees.
A cloud boy brings the evening paper:
The Evening Sun. It sets.
Not sharply or at once
a stately progress down the sky
(it's gilt and pink and faintly green)
above, beyond, behind the evening leaves
of trees. Traffic sounds and
bells resound in silver clangs
the hour, a tune, my friend
Pierrot. The violet hour:
the grass is violent green.
A weeping beech is gray,
a copper beech is copper red.
Tennis nets hang
unused in unused stillness.
A car starts up and
whispers into what will soon be night.
A tennis ball is served.
A horsefly vanishes.
A smoking cigarette.
A day (so many and so few)
dies down a hardened sky
and leaves are lap-held notebook leaves
discriminated barely
in light no longer layered.

ELIZABETH BISHOP

THE MOOSE

From narrow provinces
of fish and bread and tea,
home of the long tides
where the bay leaves the sea
twice a day and takes
the herrings long rides,

where if the river
enters or retreats
in a wall of brown foam
depends on if it meets
the bay coming in,
the bay not at home;

where, silted red,
sometimes the sun sets
facing a Red Sea,
and others, veins the flats'
lavender, rich mud
in burning rivulets;

on red, gravelly roads,
down rows of sugar maples,
past clapboard farmhouses
and neat, clapboard churches,
bleached, ridged as clamshells,
past twin silver birches,

through late afternoon
a bus journeys west,
the windshield flashing pink,
pink glancing off of metal,
brushing the dented flank
of blue, beat-up enamel;

down hollows, up rises,
and waits, patient, while
a lone traveller gives
kisses and embraces
to seven relatives
and a collie supervises.

Goodbye to the elms,
to the farm, to the dog.
The bus starts. The light
is deepening; the fog,
shifting, salty, thin,
comes closing in.

Its cold, round crystals
form and slide and settle
in the white hens' feathers,
in gray glazed cabbages,
on the cabbage roses
and lupins like apostles;

the sweet peas cling
to wet white string
on the whitewashed fences;
bumblebees creep
inside the foxgloves,
and evening commences.

One stop at Bass River.
Then the Economies—
Lower, Middle, Upper;
Five Islands, Five Houses,
where a woman shakes a tablecloth
out after supper.

A pale flickering. Gone.
The Tantramar marshes
and the smell of salt hay.

An iron bridge trembles
and a loose plank rattles
but doesn't give way.

On the left, a red light
swims through the dark:
a ship's port lantern.
Two rubber boots show,
illuminated, solemn.
A dog gives one bark.

A woman climbs in
with two market bags,
brisk, freckled, elderly.
"It's a grand night. Yes, sir,
all the way to Boston,"
regarding us amicably.

Moonlight as we enter
the New Brunswick woods,
hairy, scratchy, splintery;
moonlight and mist
caught in them like lamb's wool
on bushes in a pasture.

The passengers lie back.
Snores. Some long sighs.
A dreamy divagation
begins in the night,
a gentle, auditory,
slow hallucination. . . .

In the creakings and noises,
an old conversation
—not concerning us,
but recognizable, somewhere,
back in the bus:
Grandparents' voices

uninterruptedly
talking, in Eternity:
names being mentioned,
things cleared up finally;
what he said, what she said,
who got pensioned;

deaths, deaths and sicknesses;
the year he re-married;
the year (something) happened.
She died in childbirth.
That was the son lost
when the schooner foundered.

He took to drink. Yes.
She went to the bad.
When Amos began to pray
even in the store and
finally the family had
to put him away.

"Yes . . ." that peculiar
affirmative. "Yes . . ."
A sharp, indrawn breath,
half-groan, half-acceptance,
that means "Life's like that.
We know *it* (also death)."

Talking the way they talked
in the old featherbed,
peacefully, on and on,
dim lamplight in the hall,
down in the kitchen, the dog
tucked in her shawl.

Now, it's all right now
even to fall asleep
just as on all those nights.

—Suddenly the bus driver
stops with a jolt,
turns off his lights.

A moose has come out of
the impenetrable wood
and stands there, looms, rather,
in the middle of the road.
It approaches; it sniffs at
the bus's hot hood.

Towering, antlerless,
high as a church,
homely as a house
(or, safe as houses).
A man's voice assures us
"Perfectly harmless. . . ."

Some of the passengers
exclaim in whispers,
childishly, softly,
"Sure are big creatures."
"It's awful plain."
"Look! It's a she!"

Taking her time,
she looks the bus over,
grand, otherworldly.
Why, why do we feel
(we all feel) this sweet
sensation of joy?

"Curious creatures,"
says our quiet driver,
rolling his R's.
"Look at that, would you."
Then he shifts gears.
For a moment longer,

by craning backward,
the moose can be seen
on the moonlit macadam;
then there's a dim
smell of moose, an acrid
smell of gasoline.

1960s & 1970s

LESLIE NORRIS

BURNING THE BRACKEN

When summer stopped, and the last
Lit cloud blazed tawny cumulus
Above the hills, it was the bracken

Answered; its still crests
Contained an autumn's burning.
Then, on an afternoon of promised

Cold, true flames ripped
The ferns. Hurrying fire, low
And pale in the sun, ran

Glittering through them. As
Night fell, the brindle
Flambeaux, full of chattering

We were too far to hear, leapt
To the children's singing.
"Fire on the mountain," we

Chanted, who went to bed warmed
By joy. But I would know that fires
Die, that the cold sky holds

Uneasily the fronds and floating
Twigs of broken soot, letting
Them fall, fall now, soft

As darkness on this white page.

W. H. AUDEN

FAIRGROUND

Thumping old tunes give a voice to its whereabouts
long before one can see the dazzling archway
of colored lights, beyond which household proverbs
cease to be valid,

a ground sacred to the god of vertigo
and his cult of disarray: here jeopardy,
panic, shock are dispensed in measured doses
by foolproof engines.

As passive objects, packed tightly together
on roller coaster or ferris wheel, mortals
taste in their solid flesh the volitional
joys of a seraph.

Soon the roundabout ends the clumsy conflict
of Right and Left: the riding mob melts into
one spinning sphere, the perfect shape performing
the perfect motion.

Mopped and mowed at, as their train worms through a tunnel,
by ancestral spooks, caressed by clammy cobwebs,
grinning initiates emerge into daylight
as tribal heroes.

Fun for Youth who knows his libertine spirit
is not a copy of Father's, but has yet to
learn that the tissues which lend it stamina,
like Mum's, are bourgeois.

Those with their wander-years behind them, who are rather
relieved that all routes of escape are spied on,
all hours of amusement counted, requiring
caution, agenda,

keep away:—to be found in coigns where, sitting
in silent synods, they play chess or cribbage,
games that call for patience, foresight, maneuver,
like war, like marriage.

A CURSE

Dark was that day when Diesel
conceived his grim engine that
begot you, vile invention,
more vicious, more criminal
than the camera even,
metallic monstrosity,
bale and bane of our Culture,
chief woe of our Commonweal.

How dare the Law prohibit
hashish and heroin yet
licence your use, who inflate
all weak inferior egos?
Their addicts only do harm
to their own lives: you poison
the lungs of the innocent,
your din dithers the peaceful,
and on choked roads hundreds must
daily die by chance-medley.

Nimble technicians, surely
you should hang your heads in shame.
Your wit works mighty wonders,
has landed men on the Moon,
replaced brains by computers,
and can smithy a "smart" bomb.
It is a crying scandal
that you cannot take the time
or be bothered to build us,
what sanity knows we need,

an odorless and noiseless
staid little electric brougham.

JAMES WRIGHT

LIGHTING A CANDLE FOR W. H. AUDEN

(In the Church of Maria am Gestade, Vienna)

The poet kept his promise
To the earth before he died.
He sleeps now in Kirchstetten
Some twenty miles from here.
I did not go to mourn him,
Although I could have gone
And found him among beeches.
Best to leave him alone.

Maria am Gestade,
Mary on the shore,
The loud gouge of the subway
Scuttles my silences.
If I come here to laud a
Wise shadow, I restore
The first light in my hallway,
A strange, forgiving grace.

Twenty miles east, Vienna
Scrambles to keep its trees.
Since 1957
The poet, shragged and wise,
Sang in an Austrian choir,
A sudden holiness
Behind the crag-faced fire,
The prayer, the good man's prayers.

I happen now to be
Within his twenty miles.

Kindly as Thomas Hardy,
Whose dream the towpath fills.
The poet Auden lies down
His twenty miles from here.
His perfect love is limestone,
Maria on the shore.

What have I got to do
With a kind poet's death?
One day he wrote to me
I had a book to give.
I gave my book, Maria,
While Auden was awake.
I give you my small candle
For the large Master's sake.

BEFORE THE CASHIER'S WINDOW IN A DEPARTMENT STORE

1

The beautiful cashier's white face has risen once more
Behind a young manager's shoulder.
They whisper together, and stare
Straight into my face.
I feel like grabbing a stray child
Or a skinny old woman
And diving into a cellar, crouching
Under a stone bridge, praying myself sick,
Till the troops pass.

2

Why should he care? He goes.
I slump deeper.
In my frayed coat, I am pinned down
By debt. He nods,
Commending my flesh to the pity of the daws of God.

3

Am I dead? And, if not, why not?
For she sails there, alone, looming in the heaven of the beautiful
She knows
The bulldozers will scrape me up
After dark, behind
The officers' club.
Beneath her terrible blaze, my skeleton
Glitters out. I am the dark. I am the dark
Bone I was born to be.

4

Tu Fu woke shuddering on a battlefield
Once, in the dead of night, and made out
The mangled women, sorting
The haggard slant-eyes.
The moon was up.

5

I am hungry. In two more days
It will be Spring. So: this
Is what it feels like.

WITH THE SHELL OF A HERMIT CRAB

Lugete, O Veneres Cupidinesque . . .
　　　　　　　—Catullus

This lovely little life whose toes
Touched the white sand from side to side
How delicately no one knows
Crept from his loneliness, and died.

From deep waters long miles away
He wandered, looking for his name,
And all he found was you and me,
A quick life and a candle flame.

Today, you happen to be gone.
I sit here in the raging hell,
The city of the dead, alone,
Holding a little empty shell.

I peer into his tiny face.
It looms too huge for me to bear.
Two blocks away the sea gives place
To river. Both are everywhere.

I reach out and flick out the light.
Darkly I touch his fragile scars
So far away, so delicate,
Stars in a wilderness of stars.

MICHAEL DENNIS BROWNE

THE DELTA

There are men making death together in the wood

We have not deserved this undergrowth
We have not merited this mud
O Jesus this mud

There are men making death together in the wood

My sergeant lies in a poisoned shadow
My friend has choked on a flower
The birds are incontinent in their terror

There are men making death together in the wood

They have taken my hands away
And they have hidden me from the moon
Pain makes decisions all around me

There are men making death together in the wood

The fish are puzzled among darkening knots of water
The ancient stairways of light sway and spill
The ferns are stained with the yellow blood of stones

There are men making death together in the wood

We have hidden the children for safety beneath the water
And the children are crying to us through the roots of the trees
They are soft pebbles without number
And they fill the streams

And the moon appears to watch now white with grief

See them now
Pilgrimming unwilling into dying
Unburdened now of blood
Their hurt bodies soaked with the dusk
See the reluctant file

In a line he leads them
In a long slow line

They leave us over the hill
They are grass
They are dust
They are shed stone
Cold as the moon

And the widow moon above
Is cold and white
And will let no lovers in tonight

NEWS FROM THE HOUSE

Love, I have warmed the car,
the snow between us lies

shaking at the sound of my wheels
pawing the ground, my radio

snorting through its shimmering
nostrils.
                    I

have command of the seats,
the trunk has been blessed

by Eskimos, and the hood
(or British Bonnet) anointed
with a stern steam.
                              There

is no time like the present,
send for me.

                    Love, over
what dark miles do I come, shall I,
dark

as the wind round the house
I lie in,

the great bed, the long
night draining me,
                              Love,
in what season may it, tell me
the green date mice may

swear by, and the vast
branches spread dizzy those
distances my eyes too well

see through this winter. What
I have done that you

weep, what you have
worked that I
pace continually

this most sad house, meals
of its emptiness in every
corner, that the wind
                              sounds,

the house refusing to be musical,

in the sheerest dark. Tell me
the previous times, hear my

greed for you. Under it all
and the cold ground
                              we
sleeping you said, and ending,
the April waking, that trap
sprung.
              Love, in my
solitude my hands
garrisoned, hear them

nightly beside me muttering
of freedoms they were

warm in. How
on these nights the house
refusing to be musical
                              I

lie stone, seed-
cold, kernel of this

husked house, the white
miles between us

coiled soft as roads inside
me, my walls the blood
of rabbits, the bathroom
                    a lodge for hunters,
the bath

of fur and stained.
                    Love,

in what season, tell
me, I may unwrap this house
from me, these walls

remove, from my pockets
these stairs, drink

such dark no more
            nor wear ever

this most sad hat of shadows. Tell

me, make me instructions,
send them like news
from a dairy.
            I will feed

no more on this print and milk,
wait, crouch, mad in the sad house

refusing to be musical,
though I sing it each night the notes
my longest body is learning.

E. E. CUMMINGS

"NOW DOES OUR WORLD DESCEND"

now does our world descend
the path to nothingness
(cruel now cancels kind;
friends turn to enemies)
therefore lament, my dream
and don a doer's doom

create is now contrive;
imagined, merely known
(freedom: what makes a slave)
therefore, my life, lie down
and more by most endure
all that you never were

hide, poor dishonoured mind
who thought yourself so wise;
and much could understand
concerning no and yes:
if they've become the same
it's time you unbecame

where climbing was and bright
is darkness and to fall
(now wrong's the only right
since brave are cowards all)
therefore despair, my heart
and die into the dirt

but from this endless end
of briefer each our bliss—
where seeing eyes go blind
(where lips forget to kiss)
where everything's nothing
—arise, my soul; and sing

T. H. WHITE

TO MYSELF, AFTER FORTY YEARS

Terence, if I could return
My drear tideway to your bright burn,
If we could meet where I once strayed,
The betrayer and the betrayed,
If we could win back in time's defiance,
Would you be afraid of me, ten-year-old Terence?

No, you would not fear.
You would love, trust,
Cherish, admire
This tedious dust.

For, oh, we were all brimming once
With the sun-sparkled dew.
One heart could have loved this hulk—
The ignorant heart of you.

DJUNA BARNES

THE WALKING-MORT

Call her walking-mort; say where she goes
She squalls her bush with blood. I slam a gate.
Report her axis bone it gigs the rose.
What say of mine? It turns a grinning grate.
Impugn her that she baits time with an awl.
What do my sessions then? They task a grave.
So, shall we stand, or shall we tread and wait
The mantled lumber of the buzzard's fall
(That maiden resurrection and the freight),
Or shall we freeze and wrangle by the wall?

YEHUDA AMICHAI

SONG OF RESIGNATION

I

I resign!

My son has my father's eyes,
My mother's hands,
And my own mouth.
There is no further need of me. Many thanks.
The refrigerator is beginning to hum toward a long journey.
An unknown dog sobs over the loss of a stranger.

I resign!

II

I paid my dues to so many funds.
I am fully insured.
Let the world care for me now;
I am knotted and tied with it and all of them.
Every change in my life will cost them cash.
Every movement of mine will hurt them.
My death will dispossess them.
My voice passes with clouds.
My hand, stretched out, has turned into paper. Yet another contract.
I see the world through the yellow roses
Someone has forgotten
On the table near my window.

III

Bankruptcy!
I declare the whole world to be a womb.
And as of this moment
I appoint myself,
Order myself
At its mercy.
Let it adopt me. Let it care for me.

I declare the President of the United States to be my father,
The Chairman of the Soviet Union to have my power of attorney,
The British Cabinet to be my family,
And Mao Tse-tung to be my grandmother.

I resign!
I declare the heavens to be God.
They all together go ahead and do those things
That I never believed they would.

(*Translated, from the Hebrew, by Assia Gutmann.*)

KEITH WALDROP

TO ROSMARIE IN BAD KISSINGEN

I just squashed a fat
fly who was buzzing me, but he's
more disgusting dead.

If we go by numbers, my old
zoology prof used to say, this
is the age of insects,
more specifically, of beetles.

This is also the age of information.

I hope the church bells
of Bad Kissingen aren't
keeping you awake—though it's
nice, hearing tones decay. You
won't let the bells chase you to church.

Somebody, just the other day, claimed
that you and I haven't
any roots (he thinks that's bad). It's
true enough that we've fallen between

two generations—one drunk, the other
stoned. The one has
inhibitions to get rid of (you know
what that means—liquor and
analysis); the other, a great
blank space to fill.

The wars of the young I
think will be wars of religion.

But all this letter is really
meant to say is that you should
leave those kraut Quasimodos at their
glockenspiels and
hurry back here, because whatever we
don't see together has for me always
a dead spot somewhere,

even though I know that one
place is much the same as another,

and all the air we could
breathe anywhere in the world
has already, numberless times, been the
breath of a fern and
a marigold
and an oak.

YANNIS RITSOS

THE DISTANT

O distant, distant; deep unapproachable; receive always
the silent ones in their absence, in the absence of the others,
when the danger from the near ones, from the near itself, burdens
during nights of promise with many-colored lights in the gardens,
when the half-closed eyes of lions and tigers scintillate

with flashing green omissions in their cages
and the old jester in front of the dark mirror
washes off his painted tears so that he can weep—
O quiet ungrantable, you with the long, damp hand,
quiet invisible, without borrowing and lending, without obligations,
nailing nails on the air, shoring up the world
in that deep inaction where music reigns.

PREPARING THE CEREMONY

Something has gone wrong with the celebration they're preparing for me.
They go up and down stairs, jostle each other in the corridors.
The three chandeliers in the large hall have come on.
Up on the podium the glass of water glows. They announce me.
I urge my feet; search myself with my hands; I'm missing.
And if I try to go down the stairs, the usher will arrest me.

(Translated, from the Greek, by Edmund Keeley.)

GEORGE OPPEN

BAHAMAS

Where are we,
Mary, where are we?
They screen us and themselves
With tree-lined lanes

And the gardens of hotels though we have travelled
Into the affluent tropics. The harbors
Pierce all that. There are these islands

Breaking the surface
Of the sea. They are the sandy peaks
Of hills in an ocean

Streaked green by their shoals. The fishermen
And the crews from Haiti
Tide their wooden boats out

In the harbors. Not even the guitarists,
Singing the island songs
To the diners,

Tell of the Haitian boats,
Which bear their masts, the tall
Stripped trunks of trees

(Perhaps a sailor,
Barefoot on the ragged deckload
Of coconuts and mats, leans

On the worn mast) across the miles
Of the Atlantic, and the blinding glitter
Of the sea.

DEREK WALCOTT

THE MUSE OF HISTORY AT RAMPANALGAS
(Trinidad)

I

Miasma, acedia, the enervations of damp,
as the teeth of the mold gnaw, greening the carious stump
of the beaten, corrugated silver of the marsh light,
where the red heron hides, without a secret,
as the cordage of mangrove tightens
bland water to bland sky
heavy and sodden as canvas,
where the pirogue foundered with its caved-in stomach
(a hulk, trying hard to look like
a paleolithic, half-gnawed memory of pre-history)
as the too-green acid grasses set the salt teeth on edge,
acids and russets and water-colored water,
let the historian go mad there
from thirst. Slowly the water rat takes up its reed pen
and scribbles. Leisurely, the egret
on the mud tablet stamps its hieroglyph.

The explorer stumbles out of the bush crying out for myth.
The tired slave vomits his past.
The Mediterranean accountant, with the nose of the water rat,
ideograph of the egret's foot,
calculates his tables,
his eyes reddening like evening in the glare of the brass lamp;
the Chinese grocer's smile is leaden with boredom:
so many lbs. of cod,
                          so many bales of biscuits,
on spiked shop paper,
the mummified odor of onions,
spikenard, and old Pharaohs peeling like onionskin
to the archeologist's finger—all that
is the muse of history, Potsherds,
and the crusted amphora of cutthroats.

Like old leather,
tannic, stinking, peeling in a self-contemptuous
curl away from itself,
the yellowing poems, the spiked brown paper,
the myth of the golden Carib,
like a worn-out film,
the lyrical arrow in the writhing Arawak maiden
broken under the leaf-light.
                          The astigmatic geologist
stoops, with the crouch of the heron,
deciphering—not a sign.
All of the epics are blown away with the leaves,
blown with the careful calculations on brown paper;
these were the only epics: the leaves.

No horsemen here, no cuirasses
crashing, no fork-bearded Castilians,
only the narrow, silvery creeks of sadness
like the snail's trail,
only the historian deciphering, in invisible ink,
its patient slime,

no cataracts abounding down gorges
like bolts of lace,
while the lizards are taking a million years to change,
and the lobbed head of the coconut rolls to gasp on the sand,
its mouth open at the very moment
of forgetting its name.

That child who sets his half shell afloat
in the brown creek that is Rampanalgas River—
my son first, then two daughters—
toward the roar of waters,
toward the Atlantic with a dead almond leaf for a sail,
with a twig for a mast,
was, like his father, this child,
a child without history, without knowledge of its pre-world,
only the knowledge of water runnelling rocks,
and the desperate whelk that grips the rock's outcrop
like a man whom the waves can never wash overboard;
that child who puts the shell's howl to his ear,
hears nothing, hears everything
that the historian cannot hear, the howls
of all the races that crossed the water,
the howls of grandfathers drowned
in that intricately swivelled Babel,
hears the fellahin, the Madrasi, the Mandingo, the Ashanti,
yes, and hears also the echoing green fissures of Canton,
and thousands without longing for this other shore
by the mud tablets of the Indian Provinces,
robed ghostly white and brown, the twigs of uplifted hands,
of manacles, mantras, of a thousand kaddishes,
whorled, drilling into the shell,
see, in the evening light by the saffron, sacred Benares,
how they are lifting like herons,
robed ghostly white and brown,
and the crossing of water has erased their memories.
And the sea, which is always the same,
accepts them.

And the shore, which is always the same,
accepts them.

In the shallop of the shell,
in the round prayer,
in the palate of the conch,
in the dead sail of the almond leaf
are all of the voyages.

II
And those who gild cruelty,
who read from the entrails of disembowelled Aztecs
the colors of Hispanic glory
greater than Greece,
greater than Rome,
than the purple of Christ's blood,
the golden excrement on barbarous altars
of their beaked and feathered king,
and the feasts of human flesh,
those who remain fascinated,
in attitudes of prayer,
by the festering roses made from their fathers' manacles,
or upraise their silver chalices flecked with vomit,
who see a golden, cruel, hawk-bright glory
in the conquistador's malarial eye,
crying, *at least here*
something happened—
they will absolve us, perhaps, if we begin again,
from what we have always known, nothing,
from that carnal slime of the garden,
from the incarnate subtlety of the shake,
from the Egyptian moment of the heron's foot
on the mud's entablature,
by this augury of ibises
flying at evening from the melting trees,
while the silver-hammered charger of the marsh light
brings toward us, again and again, in beaten scrolls,

nothing, then nothing,
and then nothing.

III

                    Here, rest. Rest, heaven. Rest, hell.
Patchwork, sunfloor, seafloor of pebbles at Resthaven,
      Rampanalgas.
Sick of black angst.
Too many penitential histories passing
for poems. Avoid:
                  1857 Lucknow and Cawnpore.
The process of history machined through fact,
for the poet's cheap alcohol,
lines like the sugarcane factory's mechanization of myth
ground into rubbish.
                  1834 Slavery abolished.
A century later slavishly revived
for the nose of the water rat, for the literature of the factory,
in the masochistic veneration of
chains, and the broken rum jugs of cutthroats.
Exegesis, exegesis, writers
giving their own sons homework.

Ratoon, ratoon,
immigrant hordes downed soughing,
sickled by fever, *mal d'estomac*,
earth-eating slaves fitted with masks against despair,
not mental despondence but helminthiasis.
Pour la dernière fois, nommez! Nommez!

Abouberika Torre commonly called Joseph Samson.
Hammadi Torrouke commonly called Louis Modeste.
Mandingo sergeants offered Africa back,
the boring process of repatriation,
while to the indentured Indians
the plains of Caroni seemed like the Gangetic plain,
our fathers' bones. Which father?

Burned in the pyre of the sun.
On the ashpit of the sand.
Also you, Grandfather. Rest, heaven, rest, hell.
I sit in the roar of that sun
like a lotus yogi folded on his bed of coals,
my head is circled with a ring of fire.

IV

O sun, on that morning,
did I not mutter toward your
holy, repetitive resurrection, "Hare,
hare Krishna," and then, politely,
"Thank you, life"? Not
to enter the knowledge of God
but to know that His name
had lain too familiar on my tongue,
as this one would say "bread,"
or "sun," or "wine," I staggered,
shaken at my remorse, as one
would say "bride," or "bread,"
or "sun," or "wine," to believe—
and that you would rise again,
when I am not here, to catch
the air afire, that you need not
look for me, or need this prayer.

V

So, I shall repeat myself,
prayer, same prayer, toward fire, same fire,
as the sun repeats itself and the thundering waters

for what else is there
but books, books and the sea,
verandas and the pages of the sea,
to write of the wind and the memory of wind-whipped hair
in the sun, the color of fire?

I was eighteen then, now I am forty-one,
I have had a serpent for companion,
I was a heart full of knives,
but, my son, my sun,

holy is Rampanalgas and its high-circling hawks,
holy are the rusted, tortured, rust-caked, blind almond trees,
your great-grandfather's, and your father's torturing limbs,
holy the small, almond-leaf-shadowed bridge
by the small red shop, where everything smells of salt,
and holiest the break of the blue sea below the trees,
and the rock that takes blows on its back
and is more rock,
and the tireless hoarse anger of the waters
by which I can walk calm, a renewed, exhausted man,
balanced at its edge by the weight of two dear daughters.

VI

> Holy were you, Margaret,
> and holy our calm.
> What can I do now
>
> but sit in the sun to burn
> with an aging mirror that blinds,
> combing, uncombing my hair—
>
> escape? No, I am inured
> only to the real, which
> burns. Like the flesh
>
> of my children afire.
> Inured. Inward. As rock,
> I wish, as the real
>
> rock I make real,
> to have burnt out desire,
> lust, except for the sun

with her corona of fire.
Anna, I wanted to grow white-haired
as the wave, with a wrinkled

brown rock's face, salted,
seamed, an old poet,
facing the wind

and nothing, which is,
the loud world in his mind.

CESARE PAVESE

PRISON: POGGIO REALE

A small window on the sky
calms the heart; someone died here, at peace.
Outside are trees and clouds and earth
and sky. Up here only a whisper comes:
the blurred sounds of all of life.

                        The empty window
doesn't show the hills beneath the trees
and the river winding clearly in the distance.
The water is as clear as the breath of wind,
but nobody notices.

               A cloud appears,
compact and white, and lingers in the square of sky.
It sees stunned hills and houses, everything
shining in the transparent air, sees lost birds
sailing in the sky. People pass quietly
along the river and no one even notices
the little cloud.

              In the small window
the blue is empty now: into it falls the cry

of a bird, breaking the whisper. Maybe
that cloud is touching the tree or sinking into the river.
The man lying in the meadow ought to feel it
in the breathing of the grass. But he doesn't move his eyes,
only the grass moves. He must be dead.

(Translated, from the Italian, by William Arrowsmith.)

DAVID ANTIN
THE PASSENGERS

Who are they
they come by train by car
they won't stand still
we see them underground
through windows
by lamplight
they read they speak they eat
they move their hands
their breath is on the glass
is moving

       toward a fruit tree
beside a river
beside a stone lion on the steps
       toward a field of white stones

sit on the floor
eat fish place salt upon your tongue
throw in pine cones and pieces of cedar
throw in kleenex and coffee grounds
and the remnants of shoes
raise a lament of white scarves

in a field of white stones
cultivated by the wind

among white pebbles in a light rain
        we cast
                a shadow
that moves over the ground
like the shadow of a bird

every single thing contains all things

the pebble in your mouth its blue flame
the feather its blood
your hand falling releases the light
that your hand rising encloses
the shadow of pain in your eyes
the shadows of clouds over water
in principle your eyes
could annihilate the earth
with their shadow

the fruit tree moves its branches beside the river
the stone lion licks salt from its eyes
a building at the bottom of a lake
between me and the sun
gives back the light
particulate petals of the flower
a window an orange a shadow of an odor.

RANDALL JARRELL

NEXT DAY

Moving from Cheer to Joy, from Joy to All,
I take a box
And add it to my wild rice, my Cornish game hens.
The slacked or shorted, basketed, identical
Food-gathering flocks
Are selves I overlook. Wisdom, said William James,

Is learning what to overlook. And I am wise
If that is wisdom.
Yet somehow, as I buy All from these shelves
And the boy takes it to my station wagon,
What I've become
Troubles me even if I shut my eyes.

When I was young and miserable and pretty
And poor, I'd wish
What all girls wish: to have a husband,
A house and children. Now that I'm old, my wish
Is womanish:
That the boy putting groceries in my car

See me. It bewilders me he doesn't see me.
For so many years
I was good enough to eat: the world looked at me
And its mouth watered. How often they have undressed me,
The eyes of strangers!
And, holding their flesh within my flesh, their vile

Imaginings within my imagining,
I too have taken
The chance of life. Now the boy pats my dog
And we start home. Now I am good.
The last mistaken,
Ecstatic, accidental bliss, the blind

Happiness that, bursting, leaves upon the palm
Some soap and water—
It was so long age, back in some Gay
Twenties, Nineties, I don't know. . . . Today I miss
My lovely daughter
Away at school, my sons away at school,

My husband away at work—I wish for them.
The dog, the maid,

And I go through the sure unvarying days
At home in them. As I look at my life,
I am afraid
Only that it will change, as I am changing:

I am afraid, this morning, of my face.
It looks at me.
From the rearview mirror with the eyes I hate,
The smile I hate. Its plain, lined look
Of gray discovery
Repeats to me, "You're old." That's all, I'm old.

And yet I'm afraid, as I was at the funeral
I went to yesterday.
My friend's cold made-up face, granite among its flowers,
Her undressed, operated-on, dressed body
Were my face and body.
As I think of her I hear her telling me

How young I seem; I *am* exceptional;
I think of all I have.
But really no one is exceptional,
No one has anything, I'm anybody,
I stand beside my grave
Confused with my life, that is commonplace and solitary.

ANTHONY TOWNE
DEAD OF WINTER

The city shuffles through the snow, the whirling snow, and I, indifferent
To cold, remember how he looked, the casket much too small, the grief a
Discomfort buried under triumphs of survival—memories
Of snowdrifts hollowed out, as I am hollowed out, a snowman
Dissolving into frozen sunlight, caving into dust,
A drift of words, iambic flights of migratory
Goodbyes, a dead-of-winter funeral, the earth
Too stiff to weep, the open grave a trenchant
Disclosure. Nothing lasts and nothing lives
Forever; even now the city
Disintegrates in gusts of snow,
The words revolve like poems
Around a solitude
Of empty feelings,
Around myself,
Until, dead,
Alone,
I,
Alive,
Begin to
Feel tears run down
My face, the plowed-up
Drifts melting into slush.
An alley cat, emerging,
Shakes off paralysis, accepts
The warm, triumphant sun; the pigeons,
A flock in flight, discover crusts of bread
Among old ladies blinking through the park, as
Regrets give way to tremblings underground, murmurings,
And I, delivered from despair, rejoice, remember
How, snowbound, schools were closed, toboggans hurtled down the street,
A snowball slowly rolled across the yard became a beach ball—
Bright colors spinning into golden suns, reflective moons, as words
That whirl become a warm embrace, a dance of birds across an open
Astonishment of sky, and I, I think of you, I think that you know why.

MARK STRAND

MOONTAN

The bluish, pale
face of the house
rises above me
like a wall of ice

and the distant
solitary
barking of an owl
floats toward me.

I half close my eyes.

Over the damp
dark of the garden,
flowers swing
back and forth
like small balloons.

The solemn trees,
each buried
in a cloud of leaves,
seem lost in sleep.

It is late.
I lie in the grass,
smoking,
feeling at ease,
pretending the end
will be like this.

Moonlight
falls on my flesh.
A breeze
circles my wrist.

I drift.
I shiver.
I know that soon
the day will come
to wash away the moon's
white stain,

that I shall walk
in the morning sun
invisible
as anyone.

THE REMAINS

I empty myself of the names of others.
I empty my pockets. I empty my shoes and leave them beside
the road. At night I turn back the clocks; I open the family
album and look at myself as a boy.

What good does it do? The hours have done their job.
I say my own name. I say goodbye.
The words follow each other downwind.
I love my wife but send her away.

My parents rise out of their thrones
into the milky rooms of clouds. How can I sing?
Time tells me what I am. I change and I am the same.
I empty myself of my life and my life remains.

ELIZABETH BISHOP

SANDPIPER

The roaring alongside he takes for granted,
and that every so often the world is bound to shake,
He runs, he runs to the south, finical, awkward,
in a state of controlled panic, a student of Blake.

The beach hisses like fat. On his left, a sheet
of interrupting water comes and goes
and glazes over his dark and brittle feet.
He runs, he runs straight through it, watching his toes.

—Watching, rather, the spaces of sand between them,
where (no detail too small) the ocean drains
rapidly backwards and downwards. As he runs,
he stares the dragging grains.

The world is a mist. The world is marvellously
minute and vast and clear. The tide
is higher or lower. He couldn't tell you which.
His beak is focussed; he is preoccupied,

looking for something, something, something.
Poor bird, he is obsessed!
The millions of grains are black, white, tan, and gray,
and mixed with quartz grains, rose and amethyst.

IN THE WAITING ROOM

In Worcester, Massachusetts,
I went with Aunt Consuelo
to keep her dentist's appointment
and sat and waited for her
in the dentist's waiting room.
It was winter. It got dark
early. The waiting room
was full of grown-up people,
arctics and overcoats,
lamps and magazines,
My aunt was inside
what seemed like a long time
and while I waited I read
the *National Geographic*
(I could read) and carefully
studied the photographs:

The inside of a volcano,
black, and full of ashes;
then it was spilling over
in rivulets of fire.
Osa and Martin Johnson
dressed in riding breeches,
laced boots, and pith helmets.
A dead man slung on a pole
—"Long Pig," the caption said.
Babies with pointed heads
wound round and round with string;
black, naked women with necks
wound round and round with wire
like the necks of light bulbs.
Their breasts were horrifying.
I read it right straight through.
I was too shy to stop.
And then I looked at the cover:
the yellow margins, the date.

Suddenly, from inside,
came an *oh!* of pain
—Aunt Consuelo's voice—
not very loud or long.
I wasn't at all surprised;
even then I knew she was
a foolish, timid woman.
I might have been embarrassed,
but wasn't. What took me
completely by surprise
was that it was *me:*
my voice, in my mouth.
Without thinking at all
I was my foolish aunt,
I—we—were falling, falling,
our eyes glued to the cover
of the *National Geographic*,
February, 1918.

I said to myself: three days
and you'll be seven years old.
I was saying it to stop
the sensation of falling off
the round, turning world
into cold, blue-black space.
But I felt: you are an *I*,
you are an *Elizabeth*,
you are one of *them*.
Why should you be one, too?
I scarcely dared to look
to see what it was I was.
I gave a sidelong glance
—I couldn't look any higher—
at shadowy gray knees,
trousers and skirts and boots
and different pairs of hands
lying under the lamps.
I knew that nothing stranger
had ever happened, that nothing
stranger could ever happen.
Why should I be my aunt,
or me, or anyone?
What similarities—
boots, hands, the family voice
I felt in my throat, or even
the *National Geographic*
and those awful hanging breasts—
held us all together
or made us all just one?
How—I didn't know any
word for it—how "unlikely" . . .
How had I come to be here,
like them, and overhear
a cry of pain that could have
got loud and worse but hadn't?

The waiting room was bright
and too hot. It was sliding
beneath a big black wave,
another, and another.

Then I was back in it.
The War was on. Outside,
in Worcester, Massachusetts,
were night and slush and cold,
and it was still the fifth
of February, 1918.

JAMES MERRILL
THE BROKEN HOME

Crossing the street,
I saw the parents and the child
At their window, gleaming like fruit
With evening's mild gold leaf.

In a room on the floor below,
Sunless, cooler—a brimming
Saucer of wax, marbly and dim—
I have lit what's left of my life.

I have thrown out yesterday's milk
And opened a book of maxims.
The flame quickens. The word stirs.

Tell me, tongue of fire,
That you and I are as real
At least as the people upstairs.

My father, who had flown in World War I,
Might have continued to invest his life

In cloud banks well above Wall Street and wife.
But the race was run below, and the point was to win.

Too late now, I make out in his blue gaze
(Through the smoked glass of being thirty-six)
The soul eclipsed by twin black pupils, sex
And business; time was money in those days.

Each thirteenth year he married. When he died
There were already several chilled wives
In sable orbit—rings, cars, permanent waves.
We'd felt him warming up for a green bride.

He could afford it. He was "in his prime"
At three score ten. But money was not time.

When my parents were younger this was a popular act:
A veiled woman would leap from an electric, wine-dark car
To the steps of no matter what—the Senate or the Ritz Bar—
And bodily, at newsreel speed, attack

No matter whom—Al Smith or José Maria Sert
Or Clemenceau—veins standing out on her throat
As she yelled *War mongerer! Pig! Give us the vote!*,
And would have to be hauled away in her hobble skirt.

What had the man done? Oh, made history.
Her business (he had implied) was giving birth,
Tending the house, mending the socks.

Always that same old story—
Father Time and Mother Earth,
A marriage on the rocks.

One afternoon, red, satyr-thighed
Michael, the Irish setter, head

Passionately lowered, led
The child I was to a shut door. Inside,

Blinds beat sun from the bed.
The green-gold room throbbed like a bruise.
Under a sheet, clad in taboos,
Lay whom we sought, her hair undone, outspread,

And of a blackness found, if ever now, in old
Engravings where the acid bit.
I must have needed to touch it
Or the whiteness—was she dead?
Her eyes flew open, startled strange and cold.
The dog slumped to the floor. She reached for me. I fled.

Tonight they have stepped out onto the gravel.
The party is over. It's the fall
Of 1931. They love each other still.

SHE: Charlie, I can't stand the pace.
HE : Come on, honey—why, you'll bury us all!

A lead soldier guards my windowsill:
Khaki rifle, uniform, and face.
Something in me grows heavy, silvery, pliable.

How intensely people used to feel!
Like metal poured at the close of a proletarian novel,
Refined and glowing from the crucible,
I see those two hearts, I'm afraid,
Still. Cool here in the graveyard of good and evil,
They are even so to be honored and obeyed.

. . . Obeyed, at least, inversely. Thus
I rarely buy a newspaper, or vote.
To do so, I have learned, is to invite
The tread of a stone guest within my house.

Shooting this rusted bolt, though, against him,
I trust I am no less time's child than some
Who on the heath impersonate Poor Tom
Or on the barricades risk life and limb.

Nor do I try to keep a garden, only
An avocado in a glass of water—
Roots pallid, gemmed with air. And later,

When the small gilt leaves have grown
Fleshy and green, I let them die, yes, yes,
And start another. I am earth's no less.

A child, a red dog roam the corridors,
Still, of the broken home. No sound. The brilliant
Rag runners halt before wide-open doors.
My old room! Its wallpaper—cream, medallioned
With pink and brown—brings back the first nightmares,
Long summer colds, and Emma, sepia-faced,
Perspiring over broth carried upstairs
Aswim with golden fats I could not taste.

The real house became a boarding school.
Under the ballroom ceiling's allegory,
Someone at last may actually be allowed
To learn something; or, from my window, cool
With the unstiflement of the entire story,
Watch a red setter stretch and sink in cloud.

JAMES REISS

SUEÑOS

In my dreams I always speak Spanish.
The cemetery may be in Brooklyn,
and I may be kneeling on a rise

looking out at the skyline of the city,
but I will whisper, *Mira el sol.*

And it is true the late morning
sun will turn that bank of skyscrapers
the color of bleached bone in Sonora,
and all the window washers of Manhattan
will white-out like a TV screen

in Venezuela turning to snow.
But the gray face on the headstone photograph
has a nose like my father's,
and his voice had the lilt of the ghettos
of central Europe.

So I should kneel lower and say something
in Yiddish about fathers, grandfathers,
the hacked limbs of a family tree
that reaches as high as Manhattan.
I should say, *Grampa, I loved those times*

we ran through the underpasses in Central
Park, you with your cane, I with my ice
cream cones, shouting for echoes,
bursting out into sunlight—
if I only knew the language to say it in.

DIANE WAKOSKI

INSIDE OUT

I walk the purple carpet into your eye,
carrying the silver butter server,
but a truck rumbles by,
                    leaving its black tire prints on my foot,
and old images—
          the sound of banging screen doors an hot afternoons

and a fly buzzing over Kool-Aid spilled on the sink—
flicker, as reflections on the metal surface.

Come in, you said,
inside your paintings, inside the blood factory, inside the
old songs that line your hands, inside
eyes that change like a snowflake every second,

inside spinach leaves holding that one piece of gravel,

inside the whiskers of a cat,

inside your old hat, and most of all inside your mouth where you
grind the pigments with your teeth, painting
with a broken bottle on the floor, and painting
with an ostrich feather on the moon that rolls out of my mouth.

You cannot let me walk inside you too long
inside the veins where my small feet touch
bottom.
You must reach inside and pull me
like a silver bullet
from your arm.

THEODORE ROETHKE

THE TREE, THE BIRD

Uprose, uprose, the stony fields uprose,
And every snail dipped toward me its pure horn.
The sweet light met me as I walked toward
A small voice calling from a drifting cloud.
I was a finger pointing at the moon,
At ease with joy, a self-enchanted man;
Yet when I sighed, I stood outside my life,
A leaf unaltered by the midnight scene,
Part of a tree still dark, still, deathly still,

Riding the air, a willow with its kind,
Bearing its life and more, a double sound,
Kin to the wind, and the bleak whistling rain.

The willow with its bird grew loud, grew louder still.
I could not bear its song, that altering
With every shift of air, those beating wings,
The lonely buzz behind my midnight eyes;
How deep the mother-root of that still cry!

The present falls, the present falls away.
How pure the motion of the rising day,
The white sea widening on a farther shore.
The bird, the beating bird, extending wings.
Thus I endure this last pure stretch of joy,
The dire dimension of a final thing.

SYLVIA PLATH

AMNESIAC

No use, no use, now, begging Recognize!
There is nothing to do with such a beautiful blank but smooth it.
Name, house, car keys,

The little toy wife—
Erased, sigh, sigh.
Four babies and a cocker!

Nurses, the size of worms, and a minute doctor
Tuck him in.
Old happenings

Peel from his skin.
Down the drain with all of it!
Hugging his pillow

Like the red-headed sister he never dared to touch,
He dreams of a new one—
Barren, the lot are barren!

And of another color.
How they'll travel, travel, travel, scenery
Sparking off their brother-sister rears

A comet tail!
And money the sperm fluid of it all.
One nurse brings in

A green drink, one a blue.
They rise on either side of him like stars.
The two drinks flame and foam.

O, sister, mother, wife,
Sweet Lethe is my life.
I am never, never, never coming home!

MIRROR

I am silver and exact. I have no preconceptions.
Whatever I see I swallow immediately
Just as it is, unmisted by love or dislike.
I am not cruel, only truthful—
The eye of a little god, four-cornered.
Most of the time I meditate on the opposite wall.
It is pink, with speckles. I have looked at it so long
I think it is a part of my heart. But it flickers.
Faces and darkness separate us over and over.
Now I am a lake. A woman bends over me,
Searching my reaches for what she really is.
Then she turns to those liars, the candles or the moon.
I see her back, and reflect it faithfully.
She rewards me with tears and an agitation of hands.
I am important to her. She comes and goes.
Each morning it is her face that replaces the darkness.

In me she has drowned a young girl, and in me an old woman
Rises toward her day after day, like a terrible fish.

GALWAY KINNELL

WAIT

Wait, for now.
Distrust everything, if you have to.
But trust the hours. Haven't they
carried you everywhere, up to now?
Personal events will become interesting again.
Hair will become interesting.
Pain will become interesting.
Buds that open out of season will become interesting.
Secondhand gloves will become lovely again;
their memories are what give them
the need for other hands. And the desolation
of lovers is the same; that enormous emptiness
carved out of such tiny beings as we are
asks to be filled;
the need for the new love is faithfulness to the old.

Wait.
Don't go too early.
You're tired. But everyone's tired.
But no one is tired enough.

Only wait a little, and listen—
music of hair,
music of pain,
music of looms weaving all our loves again.

Be there to hear it, it will be the only time,
most of all to hear
the flute of your whole existence,
rehearsed by the sorrows, play itself into total exhaustion.

SAINT FRANCIS AND THE SOW

The bud
stands for all things,
even for those things that don't flower,
because everything flowers from within, of self-blessing.
Though sometimes it's necessary
to reteach a thing its loveliness,
to put a hand on its brow
of the flower
and retell it in words and in touch
it is lovely
until it flowers again from within, of self-blessing.
As Saint Francis
put his hand on the creased forehead
of the sow, and told her in words and in touch
blessings of earth on the sow, and the sow
began remembering all down her thick length,
from the earthen snout all the way through the fodder and slops
to the spiritual curl of the tail,
from the hard spininess spiked out from the spine
down through the great, unbreakable heart
to the sheer blue milken dreaminess shuddering and squirting
from the fourteen teats into the fourteen mouths sucking and
blowing beneath them;
the long, perfect loveliness of sow.

TESS GALLAGHER

ZERO

Stupid tranquillity, to be most sure
in the abstract, the zebra
raising its head from the river, the clock
wound to the usual multitude, the junco bird
appearing as a miracle on the blind magician's
balcony. A thing among things,
the magician is there as an absolute, his

long sleeves an attitude of sight
that amounts to seeing, the morning steady

in the orange grove. To sit with him
is to sense the luminous sides
of objects making a finite path
to an infinite doorway. See how he multiplies
himself like the doves in his hat
not flying away into the village
but resting in the white brocade
on the crook of his arm.

He walks the promenade, a procession
of explicit consequences, the funeral
climbing the hill with its tub
of roses. Magic powder clings
to his tongue, alum and ginger. A mild
contraction in the landscape, his reticence
to prove himself. Doesn't the sun

look as if it got there again
over the handkerchief snake
in his palm? This knot could make you cry,
how it slips past itself, now a
bracelet, now a white stem
drawn in the serious air of your breath,
letting itself down, the careful
ballerina closing the halo
of her partner's arms.

IRA SADOFF

GOYA

It is night so you can shoot me.
I'm no rich man, what difference could it make?
Yet there are certain things I'm aware of:
the grief of my friends, my enemies'

indifference, the king's palace, its dull
shine against this cloudless night.
And the blood of my father by my side.
The crops and the cicadas go on perfectly well
without me; I am of no importance, a man
with a family, enough children to make me weep.
Go ahead and shoot. Relieve me of my misery.
I'd kill you if I had the chance.
All I ask for is a little music, a small
ceremony for my death: the orchestration
of the king's militia, the silver instruments,
the guns' voices before the chorus of wounds.

JAMES DICKEY

FALLING

*A 29-year-old stewardess fell . . . to her death tonight when she was swept through
an emergency door that suddenly sprang open. . . . The body . . . was found . . .
three hours after the accident.*

—The Times.

The states when they black out and lie there rolling   when they turn
To something transcontinental   move by   drawing moonlight out of
    the great
One-sided stone hung off the starboard wing tip.   Some sleeper next to
An engine is groaning for coffee   and there is faintly coming in
Somewhere the vast beast-whistle of space. In the galley with its racks
Of trays   she rummages for a blanket   and moves in her slim tailored
Uniform to pin it over the cry at the top of the door.   As though she blew

The door down with a silent blast from her lungs   frozen   she is black
Out finding herself   with the plane nowhere and her body taking by the
    throat
The undying cry of the void   falling   living   beginning to be
    something

That no one has ever been and lived through   screaming without
       enough air
Still neat   lipsticked   stockinged   girdled by regulation   her hat
Still on   her arms and legs in no world   and yet spaced also strangely
With utter placid rightness on thin air   taking her time   she holds it
In many places   and now, still thousands of feet from her death   she
       seems
To slow   she develops interest   she turns in her maneuverable body

To watch it. She is hung high up in the overwhelming middle of
       things   in her
Self   in low body-whistling wrapped intensely   in all her dark
       dance-weight
Coming down from a marvellous leap   with the delaying, dumfounding
       ease
Of a dream of being drawn   like endless moonlight to the harvest soil
Of a central state of one's country   with a great gradual warmth coming
Over her   floating   finding more and more breath in what she has
       been using
For breath   as the levels become more human   seeing clouds placed
       honestly
Below her left and right   riding slowly toward them   she clasps it all
To her and can hang her hands and feet in it in peculiar ways   and,
Her eyes opened wide by wind, can open her mouth as wide   wider
       and suck
All the heat from the cornfields   can go down on her back with a feeling
Of stupendous pillows stacked under her   and can turn   turn as to
       someone
In bed   smile, understood in darkness   can go away   slant   slide
Off tumbling   into the emblem of a bird with its wings half-spread
Or whirl madly on herself   in endless gymnastics in the growing warmth
Of wheatfields rising toward the harvest moon. There is time to live
In superhuman health   seeing mortal unreachable lights far down
       seeing
An ultimate highway with one late priceless car probing it   arriving
In a square town   and off her starboard arm the glitter of water catches

The moon by its one shaken side   scaled, roaming silver   My God it
     is good
And evil   lying in one after another of all the positions for love
Making   dancing   sleeping   and now cloud wisps at her   no
Raincoat   no matter   all small towns brokenly brighter from inside
Cloud   she walks over them like rain   bursts out to behold a
     Greyhound
Bus shooting light through its sides   it is the signal to go straight
Down like a glorious diver   then feet first   her skirt stripped
     beautifully
Up   her face in fear-scented cloths   her legs deliriously bare   then
Arms out   she slow-rolls over   steadies out   waits for something
     great
To take control of her   trembles near feathers   planes head-down
The quick movements of bird-necks turning her head   gold eyes
     the insight-
eyesight of owls blazing into the hencoops   a taste for chicken
     overwhelming
Her   the long-range vision of hawks enlarging all human lights   of
     cars
Freight trains   looped bridges   enlarging the moon racing slowly
Through all the curves of a river   all the darks of the Midwest blazing
From within. A rabbit in bush turns white   the smothering chickens
Huddle   for over them there is still time for something to live
With the streaming half-idea of a long stoop   a hurtling   a fall
That is controlled   that plummets as it wills   turns gravity
Into a new condition, showing its other side like a moon   shining
New Powers   there is still time to live on a breath made of nothing

But the whole night   time for her to remember to arrange her skirt
Like a diagram of a bat   tightly it guides her   she has this flying-skin
Made of garments   and there are also those sky-divers on TV   sailing
In sunlight   smiling under their goggles   swapping batons back and
     forth
And He who jumped without a chute and was handed one by a diving
Buddy. She looks for her grinning companion   white teeth   nowhere
She is screaming   singing hymns   her thin human wings spread out
From her neat shoulders   the air beast-crooning to her   warbling

And she can no longer behold the huge partial form of the world   now
She is watching her country lose its evoked master shape   watching it
      lose
And gain   get back its houses and peoples   watching it bring up
Its local lights   single homes   lamps on barn roofs   if she fell
Into water she might live   like a diver   cleaving   perfect
      plunge

Into another   heavy silver   unbreathable   slowing   saving
Element: there is water   there is time to perfect all the fine
Points of diving   feet together   toes pointed   hands shaped right
To insert her into water like a needle   to come out healthily dripping
And be handed a Coca-Cola   there they are   there are the waters
Of life   the moon packed and coiled in a reservoir   *so let me begin*
To plane across the night air of Kansas   opening my eyes superhumanly
Bright   to the dammed moon   opening the natural wings of my jacket
By Don Loper   moving like a hunting owl toward the glitter of water
One cannot just *fall   just tumble screaming all that time   one must* use
It   she is now through with all   through all   clouds   damp
      hair
Straightened   the last wisp of fog pulled apart on her face like wool
      revealing
New darks   new progressions of headlights along dirt roads   from
      chaos

And night   a gradual warming   a new-made, inevitable world of
      one's own
Country   a great stone of light in its waiting waters   hold   hold out
For water: who knows when what correct young woman must take up her
      body
And fly   and head for the moon-crazed inner eye of Midwest
      imprisoned
Water   stored up for her for years   the arms of her jacket slipping
Air up her sleeves to go   all over her? What final things can be said
Of one who starts out sheerly in her body in the high middle of night
Air   to track down water like a rabbit where it lies like life itself
Off to the right in Kansas? She goes toward   the blazing-bare lake
Her skirts neat   her hands and face warmed more and more by the air

Rising from pastures of beans   and under her   under chenille
      bedspreads
The farm girls are feeling the goddess in them struggle and rise
      brooding
On the scratch-shining posts of the bed   dreaming of female signs
Of the moon   male blood like iron   of what is really said by the moan
Of airliners passing over them at dead of Midwest midnight   passing
Over brush fires burning out in silence on little hills   and will wake
To see the woman they should be   struggling on the rooftree to become
Stars.   For her the ground is closer   water is nearer   she passes
It   then banks   turns   her sleeves fluttering differently as she rolls
Out to face the east, where the sun shall come up from wheatfields   she
      must
Do something with water   fly to it   fall in it   drink it   rise
From it   but there is none left upon earth   the clouds have drunk it
      back
The plants have sucked it down   there are standing toward her only
The common fields of death   she comes back from flying to falling
Returns to a powerful cry   the silent scream with which she blew down
The coupled door of the airliner   nearly   nearly losing hold
Of what she has done   remembers   remembers the shape at the heart
Of cloud   fashionably swirling   remembers she still has time to die
Beyond explanation. Let her now take off her hat in summer air the contour
Of cornfields   and have enough time to kick off her one remaining
Shoe with the toes   of the other foot   to unhook her stockings
With calm fingers, noting how fatally easy it is to undress in midair
Near death   when the body will assume without effort any position
Except the one that will sustain it   enable it to rise   live
Not die   nine farms hover close   widen   eight of them separate,
      leaving

One in the middle   then the fields of that farm do the same   there
      is no
Way to back off   from her chosen ground   but she sheds the jacket
With its silver sad impotent wings   sheds the bat's guiding tailpiece
Of her skirt   the lightning-charged clinging of her blouse   the
      intimate
Inner flying-garment of her slip in which she rides like the holy ghost

Of a virgin   sheds the long wind-socks of her stockings   absurd
Brassière   then feels the girdle required by regulations squirming
Off her: no longer monobuttocked   she feels the girdle flutter   shake
In her hand   and float   upward   her clothes rising off her
     ascending
Into cloud   and fights away from her head the last sharp dangerous shoe
Like a dumb bird   and now will drop in   SOON   now will drop

In like this   the greatest thing that ever came to Kansas   down
     from all
Heights   all levels of American breath   layered in the lungs   from
     the frail
Chill of space to the loam where extinction slumbers in corn tassels
     thickly
And breathes like rich farmers counting   will come among them after
Her last superhuman act   the last slow careful passing of her hands
All over her unharmed body   desired by every sleeper in his dream:
Boys finding for the first time their loins filled with heart's blood
Widowed farmers whose hands float under light covers to find themselves
Arisen at sunrise   the splendid position of blood unearthly drawn
Toward clouds   all feel something   pass over them as she passes
Her palms over *her* long legs   *her* small breasts   and deeply between
Her thighs   her hair shot loose from all pins   streaming in the wind
Of her body   let her come openly   trying at the last second to land
On her back   This is it   THIS
                                        All those who find her impressed
In the soft loam   gone down   driven well into the image of her body
The furrows for miles flowing in upon her where she lies very deep
In her mortal outline   in the earth as it is in cloud   can tell nothing
But that she is there   inexplicable   unquestionable   and
     remember
That something broke in them as well   and began to live and die more
When they walked for no reason into their fields to where the whole earth
Caught her   interrupted her maiden flight   told her how to lie
     she cannot
Turn   go away   cannot move   cannot slide off it and assume
     another

Position   no sky-diver with any grin could save her   hold her in his
     arms
Plummet with her   unfold above her his wedding silks   she can no
     longer
Mark the rain with whirling women that take the place of a dead wife
Or the goddess in Norwegian farm girls   or all the backbreaking whores
Of Wichita. All the known air above her is not giving up quite one
Breath   it is all gone   and yet not dead   not anywhere else
Quite   lying still in the field on her back   sensing the smells
Of incessant growth try to lift her   a little sight left in the corner
Of one eye   fading   seeing something wave   lies believing
That she could have made it   at the best part of her brief goddess
State   to water   gone in head first   come out smiling
     invulnerable
Girl in a bathing-suit ad   but she is lying like a sunbather at the last
Of moonlight   half-buried in her impact on the earth   not far
From a railroad trestle   a water tank   she could see if she could
Raise her head from her modest hole   with her clothes beginning
To come down all over Kansas   into bushes   on the dewy sixth
     green
Of a golf course   one shoe   her girdle coming down fantastically
On a clothesline, where it belongs   her blouse on a lightning rod:

Lies in the fields   in *this* field   on her broken back as though on
A cloud she cannot drop through   while farmers sleepwalk without
Their women from houses   a walk like falling toward the far waters
Of life   in moonlight   toward the dreamed eternal meaning of their
     farms
Toward the flowering of the harvest in their hands   that tragic cost

Feels herself go   go toward   go outward   breathes at last fully
Not   and tries   less   once   tries   tries   AH, GOD—

ANNE SEXTON

LITTLE GIRL, MY STRINGBEAN, MY LOVELY WOMAN

My daughter, at eleven
(almost twelve), is like a garden.

Oh, darling! Born in that sweet birthday suit
and having owned it and known it for so long,
now you must watch high noon enter—
noon, that ghost hour.
Oh, funny little girl—this one under a blueberry sky,
this one! How can I say that I've known
just what you know and just where you are?

It's not a strange place, this odd home
where your face sits in my hand
so full of distance,
so full of its immediate fever.
The summer has seized you,
as when, last month in Amalfi, I saw
lemons as large as your desk-side globe—
that miniature map of the world—
and I could mention, too,
the market stalls of mushrooms
and garlic buds all engorged.
Or I think even of the orchard next door,
where the berries are done
and the apples are beginning to swell.
And once, with our first back yard,
I remember I planted an acre of yellow beans
we couldn't eat.

Oh, little girl,
my stringbean,
how do you grow?
You grow this way.
You are too many to eat.

I hear
as in a dream
the conversation of the old wives
speaking of *womanhood*.
I remember that I heard nothing myself.
I was alone.
I waited like a target.

Let high noon enter—
the hour of the ghosts.
Once the Romans believed
that noon was the ghost hour,
and I can believe it, too,
under that startling sun,
and someday they will come to you,
someday, men bare to the waist, young **Romans**
at noon where they belong,
with ladders and hammers
while no one sleeps.

But before they enter
I will have said,
Your bones are lovely,
and before their strange hands
there was always this hand that formed.

Oh, darling, let your body in,
let it tie you in,
in comfort.
What I want to say, Linda,
is that women are born twice.

If I could have watched you grow
as a magical mother might,
if I could have seen through my magical transparent belly,
there would have been such ripening within:
your embryo,

the seed taking on its own,
life clapping the bedpost,
bones from the pond,
thumbs and two mysterious eyes,
the awfully human head,
the heart jumping like a puppy,
the important lungs,
the becoming—
while it becomes!
as it does now,
a world of its own,
a delicate place.

I say hello
to such shakes and knockings and high jinks,
such music, such sprouts,
such dancing-mad-bears of music,
such necessary sugar,
such goings on!

Oh, little girl,
my stringbean,
how do you grow?
You grow this way.
You are too many to eat.

What I want to say, Linda,
is that there is nothing in your body that lies.
All that is new is telling the truth.
I'm here, that somebody else,
an old tree in the background.
Darling,
stand still at your door,
sure of yourself, a white stone, a good stone—
as exceptional as laughter
you will strike fire,
that new thing!

FLEE ON YOUR DONKEY

Ma Faim, Anne, Anne, Fuis sur ton âne. . . .
                                    —Rimbaud.

(June, 1962)

Because there was no other place
to flee to,
I came back to the scene of the disordered senses,
came back last night at midnight,
arriving in the thick June night
without luggage or defenses,
giving up my car keys and my cash,
keeping only a pack of Salem cigarettes
the way a child holds on to a toy.
I signed myself in where a stranger
puts the inked-in X's—
for this is a mental hospital,
not a child's game.

Today an interne knocks my knees,
testing for reflexes.
Once I would have winked and begged for dope.
Today I am terribly patient.
Today crows play blackjack
on the stethoscope.

Everyone has left me
except my muse,
that good nurse.
She stays in my hand,
a mild white mouse.

The curtains, lazy and delicate,
billow and flutter and drop
like the Victorian skirts
of my two maiden aunts
who kept an antique shop.

Hornets have been sent.
They cluster like floral arrangements on the screen.
Hornets, dragging their thin stingers,
hover outside, all knowing,
hissing: *the hornet knows.*
I heard it as a child
but what was it that he meant?
The hornet knows!
What happened to Jack and Doc and Reggy?
Who remembers what lurks in the heart of man?
What did the Green Hornet mean, *he knows*?
Or have I got it wrong?
Is it the Shadow who had seen
me from my bedside radio?

Now it's *Dinn, Dinn, Dinn!*
while the ladies in the next room argue
and pick their teeth.
Upstairs a girl curls like a snail;
in another room someone tries to eat a shoe;
meanwhile an adolescent pads up and down
the hall in his white tennis socks.
A new doctor makes rounds
advertising tranquillizers, insulin, or shock
to the uninitiated.

Six years of such small preoccupations!
Six years of shuttling in and out of this place!
Oh, my hunger! My hunger!
I could have gone around the world twice
or had new children—all boys.

It was a long trip with little days in it
and no new places.

In here,
it's the same old crowd,

the same ruined scene.
The alcoholic arrives with his golf clubs.
The suicide arrives with extra pills sewn
into the lining of her dress.
The permanent guests have done nothing new.
Their faces are still small
like babies with jaundice.

Meanwhile,
they carried out my mother
wrapped like somebody's doll, in sheets,
bandaged her jaw and stuffed up her holes.
My father, too. He went out on the rotten blood
he used up on other women in the Middle West.
He went out, a cured old alcoholic
on crooked feet and useless hands.
He went out calling for his father
who died all by himself long ago—
that fat banker who got locked up,
his genes suspended like dollars,
wrapped up in his secret,
tied up securely in a strait jacket.

But you, my doctor, my enthusiast,
were better than Christ;
you promised me another world
to tell me who
I was.

I spent most of my time,
a stranger,
damned and in trance—that little hut,
that naked blue-veined place,
my eyes shut on the confusing office,
eyes circling into my childhood,
eyes newly cut.
Years of hints
strung out—a serialized case history—

thirty-three years of the same dull incest
that sustained us both.
You, my bachelor analyst,
who sat on Marlborough Street,
sharing your office with your mother
and giving up cigarettes each New Year,
were the new God,
the manager of the Gideon Bible.

I was your third-grader
with a blue star on my forehead.
In trance I could be any age,
voice, gesture—all turned backward
like a drugstore clock.
Awake, I memorized dreams.
Dreams came into the ring
like third-string fighters,
each one a bad bet
who might win
because there was no other.

I stared at them,
concentrating on the abyss
the way one looks down into a rock quarry,
uncountable miles down.
my hands swinging down like hooks
to pull dreams up out of their cage.
Oh, my hunger! My hunger!

Once,
outside your office,
I collapsed in the old-fashioned swoon
between the illegally parked cars.
I threw myself down,
pretending dead for eight hours.
I thought I had died
into a snowstorm.
Above my head

chains cracked along like teeth
digging their way through the snowy street.
I lay there
like an overcoat
that someone had thrown away.
You carried me back in,
awkwardly, tenderly,
with the help of the red-haired secretary
who was built like a lifeguard.
My shoes,
I remember,
were lost in the snowbank
as if I planned never to walk again.

That was the winter
that my mother died,
half mad on morphine,
blown up, at last,
like a pregnant pig.
I was her dreamy evil eye.
In fact,
I carried a knife in my pocketbook—
my husband's good L. L. Bean hunting knife.
I wasn't sure if I should slash a tire
or scrape the guts out of some dream.

You taught me
to believe in dreams;
thus I was the dredger.
I held them like an old woman with arthritic fingers,
carefully straining the water out—
sweet, dark playthings,
and above all mysterious
until they grew mournful and weak.
Oh, my hunger! My hunger!
I was the one
who opened the warm eyelid

like a surgeon
and brought forth young girls
to grunt like fish.
I told you,
I said—
but I was lying—
that the knife was for my mother . . .
and then I delivered her.

The curtains flutter out
and slump against the bars,
They are my two thin ladies
named Blanche and Rose.

The grounds outside
are pruned like an estate at Newport.
Far off, in the field,
something yellow grows.

Was it last month or last year
that the ambulance ran like a hearse
with its siren blowing on suicide—
Dinn, dinn, dinn!—
a noon whistle that kept insisting on life
all the way through the traffic lights?

I have come back
but disorder is not what it was.
I have lost the trick of it!
The innocence of it!
That fellow-patient in his stovepipe hat,
with his fiery joke, his manic smile—
even he seems blurred, small and pale.
I have come back,
recommitted,
fastened to the wall like a bathroom plunger,
held like a prisoner

who was so poor
he fell in love with jail.

I stand at this old window
complaining of the soup,
examining the grounds,
allowing myself the wasted life.
Soon I will raise my face for a white flag,
and, when God enters the fort,
I won't spit or gag on his finger.
I will eat it like a white flower.
Is this the old trick, the wasting away,
the skull that waits for its dose
of electric power?

This is madness
but a kind of hunger.
What good are my questions
in this hierarchy of death
where the earth and the stones go
Dinn! Dinn! Dinn!
It is hardly a feast.
It is my stomach that makes me suffer.

Turn, my hungers!
For once make a deliberate decision.
There are brains that rot here
like black bananas.
Hearts have grown as flat as dinner plates.
Anne, Anne,
flee on your donkey,
flee this sad hotel.
ride out on some hairy beast,
gallop backward pressing
your buttocks to his withers,
sit to his clumsy gait somehow.
Ride out
any old way you please!

In this place everyone talks to his own mouth.
That's what it means to be crazy.
Those I loved best died of it—
the fool's disease.

FOR MY LOVER, RETURNING TO HIS WIFE

She is all there.
She was melted carefully down for you
and cast up from your childhood,
cast up from your one hundred favorite aggies.

She has always been there, my darling.
She is, in fact, exquisite.
Fireworks in the dull middle of February
and as real as a cast-iron pot.

Let's face it, I have been momentary.
A luxury. A bright red sloop in the harbor.
My hair rising like smoke from the car window.
Littleneck clams out of season.

She is more than that. She is your have to have,
has grown you your practical, your tropical growth.
This is not an experiment. She is all harmony.
She sees to oars and oarlocks for the dinghy,

has placed wild flowers at the window at breakfast,
sat by the potter's wheel at midday,
set forth three children under the moon,
three cherubs drawn by Michelangelo,

done this with her legs spread out
in the terrible months in the chapel.
If you glance up, the children are there
like delicate balloons resting on the ceiling.

She has also carried each one down the hall
after supper, their heads privately bent,

two legs protesting, person to person,
her face flushed with a song and their little sleep.

I give you back your heart.
I give you permission—

for the fuse inside her, throbbing
angrily in the dirt, for the bitch in her
and the burying of her wound—
for the burying of her small red wound alive—

for the pale flickering flare under her ribs,
for the drunken sailor who waits in her left pulse,
for the mother's knee, for the stockings,
for the garter belt, for the call—

the curious call
when you will burrow in arms and breasts
and tug at the orange ribbon in her hair
and answer the call, the curious call.

She is so naked and singular.
She is the sum of yourself and your dream.
Climb her like a monument, step after step.
She is solid.

As for me, I am a watercolor.
I wash off.

MAXINE KUMIN

HOW IT IS

Shall I say how it is in your clothes?
A month after your death I wear your blue jacket.
The dog at the center of my life recognizes
you've come to visit, he's ecstatic.

In the left pocket, a hole.
In the right, a parking ticket
delivered up last August on Bay State Road.
In my heart, a scatter like milkweed,
a flinging from the pods of the soul.
My skin presses your old outline.
It is hot and dry inside.

I think of the last day of your life,
old friend, how I would rewind it, paste
it together in a different collage,
back from the death car idling in the garage,
back up the stairs, your praying hands unlaced,
reassembling the bites of bread and tuna fish
into a ceremony of sandwich,
running the home movie backward to a space
we could be easy in, a kitchen place
with vodka and ice, our words like living meat.

Dear friend, you have excited crowds
with your example. They swell
like wine bags, straining at your seams.
I will be years gathering up our words,
fishing out letters, snapshots, stains,
leaning my ribs against this durable cloth
to put on the dumb blue blazer of your death.

MAY SWENSON

THE LOWERING (ARLINGTON CEMETERY, JUNE 8, 1968)

The
flag
is folded
lengthwise,
and lengthwise
again,

folding toward the
open edge,
so that the union of stars
on the blue
field remains outward in full view;

a triangular folding is then begun
at the striped end,
by bringing the corner of the folded edge
to the open edge;
the outer point, turned inward

along the open edge,
forms the next triangular fold;
the folding continued so, until the end is reached,
the final corner tucked between
the folds of the blue union,
the form of the folded flag

   is found to resemble that
   of a 3-cornered pouch, or thick cocked hat.
   Take this flag, John Glenn, instead of a friend;

instead of a brother, Edward
Kennedy, take this flag;

instead of a father, Joe
Kennedy, take this flag;
this flag instead of a husband, Ethel
Kennedy, take this flag;

this 9-times-folded
red-white-striped, star-spotted-blue flag,
tucked and pocketed neatly, Nation,
instead of a leader, take

this folded flag. Robert
Kennedy, coffin without coverlet,

beside this hole in the grass,
beside your brother, John
Kennedy, in the grass,
take, instead of a country,
this folded flag;
Robert

Kennedy, take
this hole
in the
grass.

STAYING AT ED'S PLACE

I like being in your apartment, and not disturbing anything.
As in the woods I wouldn't want to move a tree,
or change the play of sun and shadow on the ground.

The yellow kitchen stool belongs right there
against white plaster. I haven't used your purple towel
because I like the accidental cleft of shade you left in it.

At your small six-sided table, covered with mysterious
dents in the wood like a dartboard, I drink my coffee
from your brown mug. I look into the clearing

of your high front room, where sunlight slopes through bare
window squares. Your Afghanistan hammock, a man-sized cocoon
slung from wall to wall, your narrow desk and typewriter

are the only furniture. Each morning your light from the east
douses me where, with folded legs, I sit in your meadow,
a casual spread of brilliant carpets. Like a cat or dog

I take a roll, then, stretched out flat
in the center of color and pattern, I listen
to the remote growl of trucks over cobbles on Bethune Street
         below.

When I open my eyes I discover the peaceful blank
of the ceiling. Its old paint-layered surface is moonwhite
and trackless, like the Sea—of Tranquillity.

HEATHER McHUGH

IT IS 70° IN LATE NOVEMBER. OPENING A WINDOW, YOU NEARLY KNOW

how certain
days filter themselves through screen, chain
saw, sundust, games of chance.
How certain as cliché
certain days are. You make a bed.
Sunlight runs in. The bed
reconciles everything. You know

how the far-off can surround
you, how things swim
here thousands of miles inland,
of their own accord, in the unknown
passage of your human ear.
You know now how the times
at times can lose their most acerbic
edge, and your planned child and your grand
mother rise as a sound
and single sweetness in the aural shell
you carry from amphibian history.
It is history

whose sharks sharpen the future.
You nearly know it. It
is softer carnivores, these days.
It is the small
time fisherman you are on shore, on edges
temporarily obscured,
of rising, sinking treasure.

It is the mooning
of the earth;
the measure of your catch, this life you have
to scale; this little
gross, and no net,
worth.
Momentarily
you will know
what you never have.

ALFRED CORN

PROMISED LAND VALLEY, JUNE, '73

The lake at nightfall is less a lake,
but more, with reflection added, so
this giant inkblot lies on its side,
a bristling zone of black pine and fir
at the dark fold of the revealed world.

Interpret this fallen symmetry,
scan this water and these water lights,
and follow a golden scribble toward
the lantern, the guessed boat, the voices
that skip across sky to where we stand.

You are vanishing and so am I
as everything surrenders color,
falling silent to vision. Darkness
rises to drown out the sky and silence
names us to the asking boat.

Who echoes who in the black mirror?
Riddles are answers here at the edge.
And still, we can imagine some clear call,
a spoken brilliance blazing a trail . . .
ourselves moving out across the sky.

TED WALKER

MULES

In warm war-sun they erupt
in frontier towns, hard-
hoofed in a dark, cobbled yard,
waiting for what is apt:
cartridge cases, cordite, shells.

Always the sight of them compels
the memory of what we are.
A newsreel of a distant war
that flickers in our room recalls
a savage, wasting sense in us;

eyes that stare from skirmishes
a continent away propound
the pith of life our lives have dulled.
A braying in the silences
beyond those Asian leaves betrays

some close, restless agency,
half detected, feared, unseen
in unfamiliar terrain,
marauding, like the lurking spy
that snipes us from the wilderness

of dreams. We know ourselves wise,
mastering violence; but sometimes,
dimly, we sense other wisdoms—
he totally lives who dies
imminently; those eyes

only that see with terror see.
We do not say we would have gone
gladly, scrabbling screes to melon-
smelling foothill towns to be
quickened with fear; nor would these

wide-eyed soldiers fail to lob
grenades at the sniper's nest.
It will be time enough to test
our doctrines when our cancers throb.
But, as we watch the mules trot past,

we muse on how, in time of peace,
their withers twitch to flies
as, listlessly, they laze
neglected in corrals, or pace
at tether, shabby and unkempt.

MURIEL RUKEYSER

ENDLESS

Under the tall black sky you look out of your body
lit by a white flare of the time between us
your body with its touch its weight smelling of new wood
as on the day the news of battle reached us
falls beside the endless river
flowing to the endless sea
whose waves come to this shore a world away.

Your body of new wood your eyes alive barkbrown of treetrunks
the leaves and flowers of trees stars all caught in crowns of trees
your life gone down, broken into endless earth
no longer a world away but under my feet and everywhere
I look down at the one earth under me,
through to you and all the fallen
the broken and their children born and unborn
of the endless war.

W. S. MERWIN

THE WIDOW

How easily the ripe grain
Leaves the husk
At the simple turning of the planet

There is no season
That requires us

Masters of forgetting
Threading the eyeless rocks with
A narrow light

In which ciphers wake and evil
Gets itself the face of the norm
And contrives cities

The Widow rises under our fingernails
In this sky we were born we are born

And you weep wishing you were numbers
You multiply you cannot be found
You grieve
Not that heaven does not exist but
That it exists without us

You confide
In images in things that can be
Represented which is their dimension you
Require them you say This
Is real and you do not fall down and moan

Not seeing the irony in the air

Everything that does not need you is real

The Widow does not
Hear you and your cry is numberless

This is the waking landscape
Dream after dream after dream walking away through it
Invisible invisible invisible

THE ASIANS DYING

When the forests have been destroyed their darkness remains
The ash the great walker follows the possessors
Forever
Nothing they will come to is real
Nor for long
Over the watercourses
Like ducks in the time of the ducks
The ghosts of the villages trail in the sky
Making a new twilight

Rain falls into the open eyes of the dead
Again again with its pointless sounds
When the moon finds them they are the color of everything

The nights disappear like bruises but nothing is healed
The dead go away like bruises
The blood vanishes into the poisoned farmlands
Pain the horizon
Remains
Overhead the seasons rock
They are paper bells
Calling to nothing living

The possessors move everywhere under Death their star
Like columns of smoke they advance into the shadows
Like thin flames with no light
They with no past
And fire their only future

COME BACK

You came back to us in a dream and we were not here
In a light dress laughing you ran down the slope
To the door
And knocked for a long time thinking it strange

Oh come back we were watching all the time
With the delight choking us and the piled
Grief scrambling like guilt to leave us
At the sight of you
Looking well
And besides our questions our news
All of it paralyzed until you were gone

Is it the same way there

AUDRE LORDE

CONIAGUI WOMEN

The Coniagui women wear their flesh like war
bear children
who have eight days to choose their mothers
the children must decide to stay
boys burst from raised loins
twisting and shouting
from the bush secret they run
beating the other women
avoiding the sweet flesh
hidden near their mother's fire
but they must take her blood as a token
the wild trees have warned them
"Beat her and you will be free"
on the third day
they creep up to her
cooking pot
bubbling over the evening's fire

she feeds them
yam soup and silence.

"Let us sleep in your bed," they whisper
"let us sleep in your bed," they whisper
"let us sleep in your bed."
But she has mothered
before them
she closes her door.

They become men.

ALASTAIR REID

MY FATHER, DYING

At summer's succulent end,
the house is green-stained.
I reach for my father's hand

and study his ancient nails.
Feeble-bodied, yet at intervals
a sweetness appears and prevails.

The heavy-scented night
seems to get at his throat.
It is as if the dark coughed.

In the other rooms of the house,
the furniture stands mumchance.
Age has engraved his face.

Cradling his wagged-out chin,
I shave him, feeling bone
stretching the waxed skin.

By his bed, the newspaper lies furled.
He has grown too old
to unfold the world

which has dwindled to the size of a sheet.
His room has a stillness to it.
I do not call it waiting, but I wait,

anxious in the dark, to see if
the butterfly of his breath
has fluttered clear of death.

There is so much might be said,
dear old man, before I find you dead,
but we have become too separate

now in human time
to unravel all the interim
as your memory goes numb.

But there is no need for you to tell—
no words, no wise counsel,
no talk of dying well.

We have become mostly hands
and voices in your understanding.
The whole household is pending.

I am not ready
to be without your frail and wasted body,
your miscellaneous mind-way,

the faltering vein of your life.
Each evening, I am loath
to leave you to your death.

Nor will I dwell on
the endless, cumulative question
I ask, being your son.

But on any one
of these nights soon,
for you, the dark will not crack with dawn,

and then I will begin
with you that hesitant conversation
going on and on and on.

PABLO NERUDA

FATHER

My blunt father comes back
from the trains.
We recognize
in the night
the whistle
of the locomotive
perforating the rain
with a wandering moan,
lament of the night,
and later
the door shivering open.
A rush of wind
came in with my father,
and between footsteps and drafts
the house
shook,
the surprised doors
banged with the dry
bark of pistols,
the staircase groaned,
and a loud voice,
complaining, grumbled
while the wild dark,
the waterfall rain
fell on the roofs
and, little by little,
drowned the world,
and all that could be heard was the wind
battling with the rain.

It was, however, a daily happening.
Captain of his train, of the cold dawn—
and scarcely had the sun
begun to show itself
than there he was with his beard,
his red and green
flags, his lamps prepared,
the engine coal in its little inferno,
the station with trains in the mist
and his geographical obligations.

The railway man is a sailor on the earth,
and in the small ports without a sea line—
the forest towns—the train runs, runs,
keeping a check on the natural world,
completing its navigation of the earth.
When the long train comes to rest,
friends come together,
come in, and the doors of my childhood open,
the table shakes
at the slam of a railway man's hand,
the thick glasses of companions jump,
and the fullness
flashes out
from the eyes of the wine.
My poor, hard father,
there he was at the axis of existence,
virile in friendship, his glass full.
His life was a running campaign,
and between his early risings and his travelling,
between arriving and rushing off,
one day, rainier than other days,
the railway man, José del Carmen Reyes,
climbed aboard the train of death, and so far has not come back.

(Translated, from the Spanish, by Alastair Reid.)

FALLING

Milk-rose, duplicate
dove of the water, I summon you—
come out of that spring,
give new life to our linens,
fire the sun's rutting day
on the other side of our winter.

I speak for myself; today
I'm a nude pilgrim
on his way to the church of the sea;
I've crossed the salt stones,
followed the discourse of rivers,
sat close to the fire
without guessing my destiny.

Having survived all that brine,
the bonfires, the boulders,
I kept crossing the zones
with only my grief to sustain me,
in love with my shadow.
For all my meandering, in this sign
alone I've come to outdistance myself.

This whole lying day,
furtive and false in its light,
I am drained of my strength;
I fall through *the time of the well*
paddling alone in the depths
of a spring's inexactitude
till a part of me breaks toward the light,
wearing my same old gray hat,
with a thumb on the selfsame guitar.

(Translated, from the Spanish, by Ben Belitt.)

TED HUGHES
CROW FROWNS

Is he his own strength?
What is its signature?
Or is he a key, cold-feeling,
To the fingers of prayer?

He is a prayer-wheel, his heart hums.
His eating is the wind—
Its patient power of appeal.
His footprints assail infinity

With signatures: We are here, we are here.
He is the long waiting for something
To use him for some everything
Having so carefully made him

Of nothing.

JOHN BERRYMAN
POSTHUMOUS DREAM SONGS

I'm reading my book backward. It sounds odd.
It came twenty minutes ago. The hell with god.
A student just called up
about a grade earlier in the year.
The hell with students. And my mother ("Mir")
did the indexes to this book.

There's madness in the book. And sanenesses,
he argued. Ha! It's all a matter of
control (& so forth) of the subject.
The subject? Henry House & his troubles, yes
with his wife & mother & baby, yes
we're now at the end, enough.

A human personality, that's impossible.
The lines of nature & of will, that's impossible.
I give the whole thing up.
Only there resides a living voice
which if we can make we make it out of choice
not giving the whole thing up.

.

Take that, old clown, & that & that & that,
who roost among my trousers:
at 65 do you plan to be browsers
among the young'uns? Let the young'uns have it.
Closer settled the sky, in rain not snow,
It's odd though,

odd the distance frantic between father & son,
  between the son & the father
who would have pickt him up & kissed him rather
but felt he had to die
so he went outside with a gun, gracefully.
I receive this information, I.

It's humanhood kept some of them along,
old pal, and I would not put that down.
Wind it up with a sorry song.
In a worthier end I'd meet you all downtown
and we'd have a ball, but that would be the end,
toward which we all depend.

.

Good words & irreplaceable: serenade, *Schadenfreude*,
angst & *malheur*, we need them, we bow to them:
what raving genius
in our past coined such wisdom? I cannot know.
Nor can you, my deep dear. You cannot know.
They were ineffable.

Who coined despair? I hope you never hear,
my lovely dear, of any such goddamned thing.

Set it up on a post
& ax the post down while the angels sing
& bury the stenchful body loud & clear
with an appropriate toast.

Who made you up? That was a thin disguise:
the soul shows through. You are my honey dear.
Come, come & live with me.
I can deal with everything but your eyes
in tears—tears I invented & put there,
during our mystery.

HOWARD NEMEROV

WOLVES IN THE ZOO

They look like shaggy dogs, but wrongly drawn,
And a legend on their cage tells us there is
No evidence that any of their kind
Has ever attacked man, woman, or child.

Now it turns out there were no babies dropped
In sacrifice, delaying tactics, from
Siberian sleds; now it turns out, so late,
That Little Red Ridinghood and her Gran

Were the aggressors with the slavering fangs
And telltale tails; now it turns out, at last,
That gray wolf and timber wolf are nearly gone,
Done out of being by the tales we tell

Told us by Nanny in the nursery—
Young sparks we were, to set such forest fires
As blazed from story into history,
And put such bounty on their wolfish heads

As brought the few survivors to our terms,
Surrendered in happy Babylon among
The peacock dusting off the path of dust,
The tiger pacing in the striped shade.

JOSEPH BRODSKY

ELEGY: FOR ROBERT LOWELL

I
In the autumnal blue
of your church-hooded New
England, the porcupine
sharpens its golden needles
against Bostonian bricks
to a point of needless
blinding shine.

White foam kneels and breaks
on the altar. People's
eyes glitter inside
the church like pebbles
splashed by the tide.

What is Salvation, since
a tear magnifies like glass
a future perfect tense?
The choir, time and again,
sings in the key of the Cross
of Our Father's gain,
which is but our loss.

There will be a lot,
a lot of Almighty Lord,
but not so much as a shred

of your flesh. When man dies
the wardrobe gapes instead.
We acquire the idle state
of your jackets and ties.

II

On the Charles's bank
dark, crowding, printed letters
surround their sealed tongue.

A child, commalike, loiters
among dresses and pants
of vowels and consonants

that don't make a word. The lack
of pen spells
their uselessness. And the black

Cadillac sails
through the screaming police sirens
like a new Odysseus keeping silence.

III

Planes at Logan thunder
off from the brown mass
of industrial tundra
with its bureaucratic moss.

Huge autoherds graze
on gray, convoluted, flat
stripes shining with grease
like an updated flag.

Shoals of cod and eel
that discovered this land before
Vikings or Spaniards still
beset the shore.

In the republic of ends
and means that counts each deed
poetry represents
the minority of the dead.

Now you become a part
of the inanimate, plain
terra of disregard
of the common pain.

IV
You knew far more
of death than he ever will
learn about you or
dare to reveal.

It might feel like an old
dark place with no match
to strike, where each word
is trying a latch.

Under this roof
flesh adopts all
the invisibility of
lingering soul.

In the sky with the false
song of the weathercock
your bell tolls
—a ceaseless alarm clock.

TO A TYRANT

He used to come here till he donned gold braid,
a good topcoat on, self-controlled, stoop-shouldered.
Arresting these café habitués—
he started snuffing out world culture somewhat later—
seemed sweet revenge (on Time, that is, not them)

for all the lack of cash, the sneers and insults,
the lousy coffee, boredom, and the battles
at twenty-one he lost time and again.

And Time has had to stomach that revenge.
The place is now quite crowded; bursts of laughter,
records boom out. But just before you sit
you seem to feel an urge to turn your head around.
Plastic and chrome are everywhere—not right;
the pastries have an aftertaste of bromide.
Sometimes before the place shuts down he'll enter
straight from a theatre, anonymous, no fuss.

When he comes in, the lot of them stand up.
Some out of duty, the rest in unfeigned joy.
Limp-wristed, with a languid sweep of palm,
he gives the evening back its cozy feel.
He drinks his coffee—better, nowadays—
and bites a roll, while perching on his chair,
so tasty that the very dead would cry
"Oh, yes!" if only they could rise and be there.

(*Translated, from the Russian, by Alan Myers.*)

JOHN ASHBERY

FEAR OF DEATH

What is it now with me
And is it as I have become?
Is there no state free from the boundary lines
Of before and after? The window is open today

And the air pours in with piano notes
In its skirts, as though to say, "Look, John,
I've brought these and these"—that is,
A few Beethovens, some Brahmses,

A few choice Poulenc notes. . . . Yes,
It is being free again, the air, it has to keep coming back
Because that's all it's good for.
I want to stay with it out of fear

That keeps me from walking up certain steps,
Knocking at certain doors, fear of growing old
Alone, and of finding no one at the evening end
Of the path except another myself

Nodding a curt greeting: "Well, you've been awhile
But now we're back together, which is what counts."
Air in my path, you could shorten this,
But the breeze has dropped, and silence is the last word.

THE WRONG KIND OF INSURANCE

I teach in a high school
And see the nurses in some of the hospitals,
And if all teachers are like that
Maybe I can give you a buzz some day,
Maybe we can get together for lunch or coffee or something.

The white marble statues in the auditorium
Are colder to the touch than the rain that falls
Past the post-office inscription about rain or snow
Or gloom of night. I think
About what these archaic meanings mean
That unfurl like a rope ladder down through history
To fall at our feet like crocuses.

All of our lives is a rebus
Of little wooden animals painted shy,
Terrific colors, magnificent and horrible,
Close together. The message is learned
The way light at the edge of a beach in autumn is learned.
The seasons are superimposed.
In New York we have winter in August

As they do in Argentina and Australia.
Spring is leafy and cold, autumn pale and dry.
And changes build up
Forever, like birds released into the light
Of an August sky, falling away forever
To define the handful of things we know for sure,
Followed by musical evenings.

Yes, friends, these clouds pulled along on invisible ropes
Are, as you have guessed, merely stage machinery,
And the funny thing is it knows we know
About it and still wants us to go on believing
In what it so unskillfully imitates, and wants
To be loved not for that but for itself:
The murky atmosphere of a park, tattered
Foliage, wise old tree trunks, rainbow-tissue-paper wadded
Clouds down near where the perspective
Intersects the sunset so we may know
We too are somehow impossible, formed of so many different things,
Too many to make sense to anybody.
We straggle on as quotients, hard-to-combine
Ingredients, and what continues
Does so with our participation and consent.

Try milk of tears, but it is not the same.
The dandelions will have to know why, and your comic
Dirge routine will be lost on the unfolding sheaves
Of the wind, a lucky one, though it will carry you
Too far, to some manageable, cold, open
Shore of sorrows you expected to reach,
Then leave behind.
                        Thus, friend, this distilled,
Dispersed musk of moving around, the product
Of leaf after transparent leaf, of too many
Comings and goings, visitors at all hours.
                                        Each night
Is trifoliate, strange to the touch.

CITY AFTERNOON

A veil of haze protects this
Long-ago afternoon forgotten by everybody
In this photograph, most of them now
Sucked screaming through old age and death.

If one could seize America
Or at least a fine forgetfulness
That seeps into our outline
Defining our volumes with a stain
That is fleeting too,

But commemorates
Because it does define, after all;
Gray garlands, that threesome
Waiting for the light to change,
Air lifting the hair of one
Upside down in the reflecting pool.

PAUL BLACKBURN

THE CROSSING

The stream
piles out of the pile-
up of earth—
we call them mountains.

It
runs west to east,
roughly, or
from where it starts in the
pileup of earth, it runs
ESE
        to be very exact. &

in spring the birds cross it
                                heading north.

Thousands and thousands of birds
heading north cross it heading
north   .
                  Singing   .   It makes everyone
                  very happy. The
stream is reasonably happy by itself
                         running ESE
                                        as it does
                  & is basically unaffected
         by all those migrations
of thousands and thousands of birds.

ANNE HUSSEY

THE WHEELCHAIRS

in the sun they glint they spin
until the spokes blur like twin batons
they race downhill against their shadows
and uphill against the drag of the land
they circle or pivot around one still wheel
their tracks thin ropes or chains
we follow these indentations like the
lines and montes of the hand
as they cross paths and roll on through
the wet grass we think we are coming to
know their hesitations and their obstacles
we think we are coming to know their routines
whether they will assemble at the slow fountain
where brown furred leaves have settled
on the bottom under the resin-colored water
or behind the big rock where an oak tree
has grown up like a whale's spout
or on the bluff overlooking the sea

we follow them only to have them disappear
in the grape arbor or the tan grass
only to have them disappear within the house
where their wheels having picked up tiny white pebbles
and held them in their treads now
deposit them on the green rug
like ants' eggs only to have them
sneak up behind us and roll away
empty and silent until the
next time when they may come at us
in an unexpected place where not even
god as a fat-cheeked cloud
or the waves marching toward the shore
in policemen's uniforms
can stop them

J. D. REED

ORGAN TRANSPLANT

I drank,
my arteries filled with fat;
the ventricle went lax
and a clot stopped my heart.

Now I sit
in St. Petersburg sunshine.
No whiskey;
wearing a girl's heart.

My blood has adopted a child
who shuffles through my chest
carrying a doll.

SEAMUS HEANEY

CASUALTY

I

He would drink by himself
And raise a weathered thumb
Towards the high shelf,
Calling another rum
And black currant, without
Having to raise his voice,
Or order a quick stout
By a lifting of the eyes
And a discreet dumb show
Of pulling off the top;
At closing time would go
In waders and peaked cap
Into the showery dark,
A dole-kept breadwinner
But a natural for work.
I loved his whole manner,
Sure-footed but too sly,
His deadpan, sidling tact,
His fisherman's quick eye
And turned observant back.

Incomprehensible
To him, my other life.
Sometimes, on his high stool,
Too busy with his knife
At a tobacco plug
And not meeting my eye,
In the pause after a slug,
He mentioned poetry.
We would be on our own
And, always politic
And shy of condescension,
I would manage by some trick
To switch the talk to eels

Or lore of the horse and cart
Or the Provisionals.

But my tentative art
His turned back watches, too:
He was blown to bits
Out drinking in a curfew
Others obeyed, three nights
After they shot dead
The thirteen men in Derry.
PARAS THIRTEEN, the walls said,
BOGSIDE NIL. That Wednesday
Everybody held
His breath and trembled.

II
It was a day of cold
Raw silence, windblown
Surplice and soutane:
Rained-on, flower-laden
Coffin after coffin
Seemed to float from the door
Of the packed cathedral
Like blossoms on slow water.
The common funeral
Unrolled its swaddling band,
Lapping, tightening
Till we were braced and bound
Like brothers in a ring.

But he would not be held
At home by his own crowd
Whatever threats were phoned,
Whatever black flags waved.
I see him as he turned
In that bombed, offending place,
Remorse fused with terror
In his still knowable face,

His cornered, outfaced stare
Blinding in the flash.

He had gone miles away
For he drank like a fish
Nightly, naturally
Swimming towards the lure
Of warm lit-up places,
The blurred mesh and murmur
Drifting among glasses
In the gregarious smoke.
How culpable was he
That last night when he broke
Our tribe's complicity?
"Now you're supposed to be
An educated man,"
I hear him say. "Puzzle me
The right answer to that one."

III
I missed his funeral,
Those quiet walkers
And sideways talkers
Shoaling out of his lane
To the respectable
Purring of the hearse . . .
The move in equal pace
With the habitual,
Slow consolation
Of a dawdling engine,
The line lifted, hand
Over fist, cold sunshine
On the water, the land
Banked under fog: that morning
I was taken in his boat,
The screw purling, turning
Indolent fathoms white,
I tasted freedom with him.

To get out early, haul
Steadily off the bottom,
Dispraise the catch, and smile
As you find a rhythm
Working you, slow mile by mile,
Into your proper haunt
Somewhere, well out, beyond . . .

Dawn-sniffing revenant,
Plodder through midnight rain,
Question me again.

OSIP MANDELSTAM
FOUR POEMS

I

At the hour when the moon appears in its city
and the wide avenues slowly fill with its light,
then the night swells with bronze and sadness,
time the barbarian smashes the wax songs,

then the cuckoo counts her griefs on the stone tower
and the pale woman with the sickle steps down
through the dead, scattering straw on the board floor,
rolling huge spokes of shadow slowly across it.

II

How dark it gets along the Kama.
The cities kneel by the river on oaken knees.

Draped in cobwebs, beard with beard,
black firs and their reflections run back into their childhood.

The water leaned into fifty-two pairs of oars,
pushed them upstream, downstream, to Kazan and Cherdyn.

There I floated with a curtain across the window,
a curtain across the window, and the flame inside was my head

And my wife was with me there five nights without sleeping,
five nights awake keeping an eye on the guards.

III
Now I lodge in the cabbage patches of the important.
A servant might come walking here out of an old song.
The factory winds work for nothing.
The road paved with brushwood runs into the distance

At the edge of the steppe the plow has turned up night
bristling with a frost of tiny lights.
In the next room, in big boots,
the peeved landlord stomps and stomps

over the floor, the deck, the coffin lids
warped into crusts.
Not much sleep under strange roofs
with my life far away.

IV
Through Kiev, through the streets of the monster,
some wife's trying to find her husband.
One time we knew that wife,
the wax cheeks, dry eyes.

Gypsies won't tell fortunes for beauties.
Here the concert hall has forgotten the instruments.
Dead horses along the main street.
The morgue smells in the nice part of town.

The Red Army trundled its wounded
out of town on the last streetcar,
one blood-stained overcoat calling,
"Don't worry, we'll be back!"

(*Translated, from the Russian, by W. S. Merwin.*)

GERALD STERN

LITTLE WHITE SISTER

It was in Philadelphia that I first lived a life of deferment,
putting everything off until I could be at ease.
There, more than in New York and more than in Paris,
I lay for hours in bed, forgetting to eat, forgetting
to swim, dying of imperfection and loneliness.
It was in Vienna that I learned what it would be like
to live in two lives, and learned to wander between them;
and it was in the rotten underbelly
of western Pennsylvania that I was saved twice by a pear tree,
one time living and one time dead, and enslaved
once and for all by a patented iron grate
carrying words of terror through the yellow air.
    My ear betrayed me, my little white sister
glued to the side of my head, a shiny snail
twisted everywhere to catch the slightest
murmur of love, the smallest sobbing and breathing.
It wasn't the heart, stuck inside the chest
like a bloody bird, and it wasn't the brain,
dying itself from love; it was that messenger,
laughing as she whispered the soft words,
making kissing sounds with her red lips,
moaning with pleasure for the last indignity.

MARY OLIVER

MUSHROOMS

Rain, and then
the cool pursed
lips of the wind
draw them
out of the ground—
red and yellow skulls
pummelling upward

through leaves,
through grasses,
through sand; astonishing
in their suddenness,
their quietude,
their wetness, they appear
on fall mornings, some
balancing in the earth
on one hoof
packed with poison,
others billowing
chunkily, and delicious;
those who know
walk out to gather, choosing
the benign from flocks
of glitterers, sorcerers,
russulas,
panther caps,
shark-white death angels
in their torn veils
looking innocent as sugar
but full of paralysis—
to eat
is to stagger down
fast as mushrooms themselves
when they are done being perfect
and, overnight,
slide back under the shining
fields of rain.

GARY SOTO

THE LITTLE ONES

When fog
Stands weed-high
And sky
Is the color

Of old bedsheets,
Molina and I
Squat under an oak
On a bench of roots,
Burning paper
And leaves
To keep warm.
We blow into
Our hands
And the white
That comes out
Drifts upward
Where heat
Does not reach.
Our eyes glow
Before the fire.
And Molina says
The sparrows
In this tree,
The little ones,
Find their heaven
Where the sky
Meets the earth.
For days
They will point
Far into coldness
Until that cold
Becomes the dark
Blowing across
Their eyes.
They will know
The south
When a bundle
Of smoke moves
Against the wind
And fields
Lift the rains
Of a thousand years.

WILLIAM HEYEN

MUSHROOMS

A dark sky blowing over
our backyard maples,
the air already cool,
Brockport begins its autumn.
My mower's drone and power
drift past the first leaves fallen
curled into red and yellow fists.
In a corner of lawn against
an old wire fence against the older woods,
a grove of mushrooms the kids
already hacked umbrellaless with golfclubs
rots into a mush of lumped columns,
pleats, and fans.

These are the suburbs
where I loved that tree, our one elm.
Now, an inch under the loam,
its stump is a candle
of slow decay, lighting, above it,
thousands of perfect pearls
tiered like anteggs,
and these, by nature, growing so low
my mower's blades will never touch them.

WILLIAM JAY SMITH

MORELS

A wet gray day—rain falling slowly, mist over the
    valley, mountains dark circumflex smudges in the distance—

Apple blossoms just gone by, the branches feathery still
    as if fluttering with half-visible antennae—

A day in May like so many in these green mountains, and
    I went out just as I had last year

At the same time, and found them there under the big maples—
    by the bend in the road—right where they had stood

Last year and the year before that, risen from the dark duff
    of the woods, emerging at odd angles

From spores hidden by curled and matted leaves, a fringe of
    rain on the grass around them,

Beads of rain on the mounded leaves and mosses round them,

Not in a ring themselves but ringed by jack-in-the-pulpits
    with deep eggplant-colored stripes;

Not ringed but rare, not gilled but polyp-like, having
    sprung up overnight—

These mushrooms of the gods, resembling human organs
    uprooted, rooted only on the air,

Looking like lungs wrenched from the human body, lungs
    reversed, not breathing internally

But being the externalization of breath itself, these
    spicy, twisted cones,

These perforated brown-white asparagus tips—these morels,
    smelling of wet graham crackers mixed with maple leaves;

And, reaching down by the pale green fern shoots, I nipped
    their pulpy stems at the base

And dropped them into a paper bag—a damp brown bag (their
    color)—and carried

Them (weighing absolutely nothing) down the hill and into
      the house; you held them

Under cold bubbling water and sliced them with a surgeon's
      stroke clean through,

And sautéed them over a low flame, butter-brown; and we ate
      them then and there—

Tasting of the sweet damp woods and of the rain one inch
      above the meadow:

It was like feasting upon air.

CHARLES SIMIC

SUNFLOWERS

Kings, here are your jewellers,
the crows. The blue sky is a scale.
We'll weigh each seed's dark half.

They hover. The shade of the oak
is damp and heavy. At its rim—
wick of the cricket
against the noon sun.

Farther off, the hidden brook,
meandering. Its ripples,
peas shaken from a pod,
a shy sound, barely audible . . .

I came to touch you.
You've fallen asleep in the grass.
You'll think it's a leaf
drifting down on your face.

The door of our house is the entrance
of a church on a day of wedding
and the glow inside is the ring
in the hand of the bridegroom.

Sunflowers,
my greed is not for gold.

BEN BELITT
LATE DANDELIONS

The dandelions, wrecked on their stems
in a carnage of tentacles, conduits, and hoses,
clock-faces timed for a morning's explosion
that triggers the wire in the crabweed with its dynamite charges,
and detonates roses,

are a judgment. Crowding the clover and fern,
something demoniac, a gross Babylonian brass
hammered in sunburst and pentacle, Medusan or Coptic by turns,
a puffball of plumage on its way to a savage transfiguration,
is struck down in the grass

and time is made human again. Oh, angel
of process, who arranges the sequences
and interprets the seasons, how you wrestled
that night with the dandelion's changes, the wormwood
and work of mutation no watcher has followed,

the fiend in the bag of the mushroom, the corolla's
untimely unreason that forces its ores into feathers,
ravaged the tuft in the bubble, blew a planet away,
leaving only a space where seed after seed gathered,
and a scarab aloft on the stem revelation had hollowed!

ALLEN GINSBERG

WALES VISITATION

White fog lifting & falling on mountain-brow
       Trees moving in rivers of wind
                    The clouds arise
   as on a wave, gigantic eddy lifting mist
      above teeming ferns exquisitely swayed
                  along a green crag
      glimpsed thru mullioned glass in valley raine—

Bardic, O Self, Visitacione, tell naught
   but what seen by one man in a vale in Albion,
      of the folk, whose physical sciences end in Ecology,
         the wisdom of earthly relations,
   of mouths & eyes interknit ten centuries visible,
         orchards of mind language manifest human,
   of the satanic thistle that raises its horned symmetry
   flowering above sister grass-daisies' small pink
             bloomlets angelic as lightbulbs—

Remember 160 miles from London's symmetrical thorned tower
      & network of TV pictures flashing bearded your Self
   the Lambs on the tree-nooked hillside this day bleating
      heard in Blake's old ear, & the silent thought of Wordsworth in
             eld Stillness
   clouds passing through skeleton arches of Tintern Abbey—
      Bard Nameless as the Vast, babble to Vastness!

All the Valley quivered, one extended motion, wind
          undulating on mossy hills
  a giant wash that sank white fog delicately down red runnels
          on the mountainside
  whose leaf-branch tendrils moved asway
          in granitic undertow down—
and lifted the floating Nebulous upward, and lifted the arms of the trees
   and lifted the grasses an instant in balance

and lifted the lambs to hold still
and lifted the green of the hill, in one solemn wave.

A solid mass of Heaven, mist-infused, ebbs thru the vale,
a wavelet of Immensity, lapping gigantic through Llanthony Valley,
the length of all England, valley upon valley under Heaven's ocean
tonned with cloud-hang,
Heaven balanced on a grassblade,
Roar of the mountain wind slow, sigh of the body,
One Being on the mountainside stirring gently
Exquisite scales trembling everywhere in balance, one motion
on the cloudy sky-floor shifting through a million
footed daisies,
pheasant croaking up steep meadows,
one Majesty the motion that stirred wet grass quivering
to the farthest tendril of white fog poured down
through shivering flowers on the mountain's
head—

No imperfection in the budded mountain,
Valleys breathe, heaven and earth move together,
daisies push inches of yellow air, vegetables tremble,
green atoms shimmer in grassy mandalas,
sheep speckle the mountainside, revolving their jaws with empty eyes,
horses dance in the warm rain,
tree-lined canals network through live farmland,

blueberries fringe house walls
on hills nippled with white rock,
meadow-bellies haired with fern—

Out, out on the hillside, in to the ocean sound, delicate
gusts of wet air,
Fall on the ground, O great Wetness, O mother, No harm on your body!
Stare close, no imperfection in the grass,
each flower Buddha-eye, repeating the story,
the myriad-formed soul—

Kneel before the foxglove raising green buds, mauve bells drooped
        doubled down the stem trembling antennae,
     look in the eyes of the branded lambs that stare
        breathing stockstill under dripping hawthorn—
I lay down mixing my beard with the wet hair of the mountainside,
        smelling the brown vagina-moist ground, harmless,
            tasting the violet thistle-hair, sweetness—
One being so balanced, so vast, that its softest breath
        moves every floweret in stillness on the valley floor,
     trembles lamb-hair hung gossamer rain-beaded in the grass,
  lifts trees on their roots, birds in the great draught
        hiding their strength in the rain, bearing same weight,

Groan thru breast and neck, a great Oh! to earth heart
                Calling our Presence together
        The great secret is no secret
            Senses fit the winds,
                Visible is visible,
     rain-mist curtains wave through the bearded vale,
            gray atoms wet the wind's Kaballah
Crosslegged on a rock in dusk rain,
        rubber-booted in soft grass, mind moveless,
     breath trembles in white daisies by the roadside,
            Heaven breath and my own symmetric
        Airs wavering thru antlered green fern
  drawn in my navel, same breath as breathes thru Capel-y-Ffn,
        Sounds of Aleph and Aum
                through forests of gristle,
     my skull and Lord Hereford's Knob equal,
                All Albion one.

What did I notice? Particulars! The
        vision of the great One is myriad—
     smoke curls upward from ash tray,
            house fire burned low,
The night, still wet & moody black heaven
            starless
  upward in motion with wet wind.

CAROLYN FORCHÉ

FOR THE STRANGER

We are *not.*
We were *this or that.*
    —Rafael Alberti.

Although you mention Venice,
keeping it on your tongue
like a fruit pit, and I say, "Yes,
perhaps Bucharest," neither of us
really knows. There is only this train
slipping through pastures
of snow, a sleigh reaching down
to touch its buried runners.
We meet on the shaking platform,
the wind's broken teeth sinking into us.
You unwrap your fist of dark bread
and share with me the coffee
sloshing into your gloves.
Telegraph posts chop the winter fields
into white blocks—in each window
the crude painting of a small farm.
We listen to mothers scolding
children in English as if
we do not understand a word of it:
sit still, sit still.

There are few clues as to where
we are: The baled wheat scattered
everywhere like missing coffins.
The distant yellow kitchen lights
wiped with oil.
Everywhere the black dipping wires
stretching messages from one side
of a country to the other.
The men who stand on every border
waving to us.

Wiping ovals of breath from the windows
in order to see ourselves, you touch
the glass tenderly wherever it holds
my face. Days later, you are showing me
photographs of a woman and children
smiling from the windows of your wallet.

Each time the train slows, a man
with our faces in the gold buttons
of his coat passes through the cars
muttering the name of a city. Each time
we lose people. Each time I find you
again between the cars, holding out
a scrap of bread for me, something
hot to drink until there are
no more cities, and you pull me
toward you, sliding your hands
into my coat, telling me
your name over and over, hurrying
your mouth into mine.
We have, each of us, nothing.
We will give it to each other.

C. K. WILLIAMS
TOIL

After the argument—argument? battle, war, harrowing—you need
     shrieks, moans from the pit;
after that woman and I anyway stop raking each other with the
     meat-hooks we've become with each other
I fit my forehead into the smudge I've already sweated onto the
     window with a thousand other exhaustions
and watch an old man having breakfast out of a pile of bags on my
     front step.
Peas from a can, bread with the day-old price scrawled over the label
     in big letters,

and then a bottle that looks so delectable, the way he carefully
    unsheathes it
so the neck just lips out of the wrinkled foreskin of the paper and
    closes his eyes and tilts,
long and hard, that if there were one lie left in me to forgive a last
    rapture of cowardice,
I'd go down there, too, and sprawl and let the whole miserable rest
    of it go to pieces.
Does anyone still want to hear how love can turn rotten?
How you can get so desperate that even going adrift like that
    wouldn't do it—
you want to scour yourself out, get rid of all the needs you've still
    got in yourself
that keep you endlessly tearing against yourself in rages of guilt and
    frustration?
I don't. I'd rather talk about other things. . . . Anything. Beauty.
    How do you learn to believe there's beauty?
The kids going by on their way to school with their fat little lunch
    bags: beauty!
My old drunk with his bags, bottle bags, ragbags, shoe bags: beauty!
    beauty!
He lies there like the goddess of wombs and first fruits, asleep in the
    riches,
one hand still hooked in mid-flight over the intricacies of the iron
    railing.
Old father, wouldn't it be a good ending if you and I could just walk
    away together?
Or that you were the king who reveals himself, who folds back the
    barbed, secret wings,
and we're all so in love now, one spirit, one flesh, one generation,
    that the truces don't matter?
Or maybe a better ending would be that there is no ending.
Maybe the Master of Endings is wandering down through his herds
    to find it,
and the cave-cow who tells truth and the death-cow who holds the
    sea in her eyes are all there
but all that he hears are the same old, irresistible slaughter-pen
    bawlings.

So maybe there is no end to the story and maybe there's no story.
Maybe the last calf just ambles up to the trough through the clearing
and nudges aside the things that swarm on the water and her mouth
      dips in among them and drinks.
Then she lifts, and it pours, everything, gushes, and we're lost in
      both waters.

STEVIE SMITH

TO CARRY THE CHILD

To carry the child into adult life
Is good? I say it is not.
To carry the child into adult life
Is to be handicapped.

The child in adult life is defenseless
And, if he is grown up, knows it,
And the grownup looks at the childish part
And despises it.

The child, too, despises the clever grownup,
The man-of-the-world, the frozen,
For the child has the tears alive on his cheeks,
And the man has none of them,

As the child has colors, and the man sees no
Colors or anything,
Being easy only in things of the mind;
The child is easy in feeling—

Easy in feeling, easily excessive,
And, in excess, powerful,
For instance, if you do not speak to the child,
He will make trouble.

You would say the man had the upper hand
Of the child (if a child survive),
But I say the child has fingers of strength
To strangle the man alive.

Oh, it is not happy, it is never happy,
To carry the child into adulthood.
Let children lie down before full growth
And die in their infanthood,
And be guilty of no one's blood.

EZRA POUND

FROM CANTO CXIII

Then a partridge-shaped cloud over dust storm.
The hells move in cycles,
                  No man can see his own end.
The Gods have not returned. "They have never left us."
                  They have not returned.
Cloud's processional and the air moves with their living.
Pride, jealousy, and possessiveness
             3 pains of hell
and a clear wind over garofani
            over Portofino 3 lights in triangulation
Or apples from Hesperides fall in their lap
            from phantom tress.
The old Countess remembered (say 1928)
            that ball in St. Petersburg
and as to how Stef got out of Poland. . . .
           Sir Ian told 'em help
              would come via the sea
(the black one, the Black Sea)
              Pétain warned 'em.
And the road under apple-boughs
           mostly grass-covered

And the olives to windward
                Kalenda Maja.
Li Sao, Li Sao, for sorrow

      but there is something intelligent in the cherry-stone
Canals, bridges, and house walls
                      orange in sunlight
But to hitch sensibility to efficiency?
            grass versus granite,
For the little light and more harmony
Oh God of all men, none excluded
and howls for Schwundgeld in the Convention
                   (our Constitutional
                17 . . . whichwhat)
Nothing new but their ignorance,
               ever perennial
Parsley used in the sacrifice
     and (calling Paul Peter) 12%
     does not mean one, oh, four, 104%

Error of chaos. Justification is from kindness of heart
     and from her hands floweth mercy.
As for who demand belief rather than justice.
And the host of Egypt, the pyramid builder,
          waiting there to be born.

No more the pseudo-gothic sprawled house
             out over the bridge there
                  (Washington Bridge, N.Y.C.)
              but everything boxed for economy.
That the body is inside the soul—
          the lifting and folding brightness
            the darkness shattered,
              the fragment.
That Yeats noted the symbol over that portico
                (Paris).
And the bull by the force that is in him—
      not lord of it,
        mastered.

And to know interest from usura
(Sac. Cairoli, prezzo giusto)
      In this sphere is giustizia.
In mountain air the grass frozen emerald
       and with the mind set on that light
          saffron, emerald,
              seeping.
"but that kind of ignorance" said the old priest to Yeats
  (in a railway train) "is spreading every day from the schools"—
  to say nothing of other varieties.
Article X for example—put over, and 100 years to get back
                     to the awareness of
            (what's his name in that Convention).
And in thy mind beauty,
         O Artemis.
As to sin, they invented it—eh?
        to implement domination
eh? largely.
     There remains grumpiness,
     malvagità
Sea, over roofs, but still the sea and the headland.
And in every woman, somewhere in the snarl is a tenderness,
        A blue light under stars.
The ruined orchards, trees rotting. Empty frames at Limone.
And for a little magnanimity somewhere,
And to know the share from the charge
       (scala altrui)
Gal's eye art 'ou, do not surrender perception.

And in thy mind beauty, O Artemis
     Daphne afoot in vain speed.
When the Syrian onyx is broken.
   Out of dark, thou, Father Helios, leadest,
but the mind as Ixion, unstill, ever turning.

OCTAVIO PAZ

OBJECTS & APPARITIONS

(For Joseph Cornell)

Hexagons of wood and glass,
scarcely bigger than a shoebox,
with room in them for night and all its lights.

Monuments to every moment,
refuse of every moment, used:
cages for infinity.

Marbles, buttons, thimbles, dice,
pins, stamps, and glass beads:
tales of the time.

Memory weaves, unweaves the echoes:
in the four corners of the box
shadowless ladies play at hide-and-seek.

Fire buried in the mirror,
water sleeping in the agate:
solos of Jenny Colonne and Jenny Lind.

"One has to commit a painting," said Degas,
"the way one commits a crime." But you constructed
boxes where things hurry away from their names.

Slot machine of visions,
condensation flask for conversations,
hotel of crickets and constellations.

Minimal, incoherent fragments:
the opposite of History, creator of ruins,
out of your ruins you have made creations.

Theatre of the spirits:
objects putting the laws
of identity through hoops.

"Grand Hotel de la Couronne": in a vial,
the three of clubs and, very surprised,
Thumbelina in gardens of reflection.

A comb is a harp strummed by the glance
of a little girl
born dumb.

The reflector of the inner eye
scatters the spectacle:
God all alone above an extinct world.

The apparitions are manifest,
their bodies weigh less than light,
lasting as long as this phrase lasts.

Joseph Cornell: inside your boxes
my words became visible for a moment.

(Translated, from the Spanish, by Elizabeth Bishop.)

BETWEEN LEAVING AND STAYING

A solid transparence, the day
is caught between leaving and staying,

all of it seen but elusive,
the horizon an untouchable nearness.

Papers on the table, a book, a glass—
things rest in the shadow of their names.

The blood in my veins rises more and more slowly
and repeats its obstinate syllable within my temples.

The light makes no choices, now changing a wall
that merely exists in time without history.

The afternoon spreads, is already a bay;
its quiet motions are rocking the world.

We are neither asleep nor awake:
we merely are, merely stay.

The moment is falling from itself, pausing,
becoming the passage through which we continue.

(Translated, from the Spanish, by Mark Strand.)

ROBERT PENN WARREN

AUDUBON: A VISION AND A QUESTION FOR YOU

I
Was not the lost dauphin, though handsome was only
Baseborn and not even able
To make a decent living, was only
Himself, Jean Jacques, and his passion—what
Is man but his passion?

     Saw,
Eastward and over the cypress swamp, the dawn,
Redder than meat, break;
And the large bird,
Long neck outthrust, wings crooked to scull air, moved
In a slow calligraphy, crank, flat, and black against
The color of God's blood spilt, as though
Pulled by a string. Saw
It proceed across the inflamed distance.

Moccasins set in hoarfrost, eyes fixed on the bird,
Thought: "On that sky it is black."
Thought: "In my mind it is white."
Thinking: "*Casmerodius albus*, heron, white."

Dawn: his heart shook in the tension of the world.

Dawn: and what is your passion?

II
(a)
His life, at the end, seemed—even the anguish—simple.
Simple, at least, in that it had to be,
Simply, what it was, as he was,
In the end, himself and not what
He had known he ought to be. The blessedness!

To wake in some dawn and see,
As though down a rifle barrel, lined up
Like sights, the self that was, the self that is, and there,
Far off but in range, completing that alignment, your fate.

Hold your breath, let the trigger squeeze be slow and steady.

The quarry lifts, in the halo of gold leaves, its noble head.

This is not a dimension of Time.

(b)
Keep store, dandle babies, and at night nuzzle
The hazel-nut-shaped sweet tits of Lucy, and
With the piratical markup of the frontier, get rich.

But you did not, being of weak character.

You saw, from the forest pond, already dark, the great trumpeter swan
Rise, in clangor, and fight up the steep air where,
In the height of last light, it glimmered, like white flame.

The definition of love being, as we know, complex,
We may say that he, after all, loved his wife.

The letter, from campfire, keelboat, or slum room in New Orleans,
Always ended, "God bless you, dear Lucy." After sunset,

Alone, he played his flute in the forest.

(c)
The world declares itself. That voice
Is vaulted in—oh, arch on arch—redundancy of joy, its end
Is its beginning, necessity
Blooms like a rose. Why,

Therefore, is truth the only thing that cannot
Be spoken?

It can only be enacted, and that in dream,
Or in the dream become, as though unconsciously, action, and he
        stood,

At dusk, in the street of the raw settlement, and saw
The first lamp lit behind a window, and did not know
What he was. Thought: "I do not know my own name."

He walked in the world. He was sometimes seen to stand
In perfect stillness, when no leaf stirred.

Tell us, dear God—tell us the sign
Whereby we may know the time has come.

III
(a)
He walked in the world.   Knew the lust of the eye.

Wrote: "Ever since a Boy I have had an astonishing desire
                    to see Much of the World and particularly
                    to acquire a true knowledge of the Birds of
                    North America."

He dreamed of hunting with Boone, from imagination painted his
    portrait.
He knew that the buzzard does not scent its repast, but sights it.
He looked in the eye of the wounded White-headed Eagle.

Wrote: ". . . the Noble Fellow looked at his Ennemies
                       with a Contemptible Eye."

At dusk he stood on a bluff, and the bellowing of buffalo
Was like distant ocean. He saw
Bones whiten the plain in the hot daylight.

He saw the Indian, and felt the splendor of God.

Wrote: ". . . for there I see the Man Naked from his
                       hand and yet free from acquired Sorrow."

Below the salt, in rich houses, he sat, and knew insult.
In the lobbies and *couloirs* of greatness he dangled,
And was not unacquainted with contumely.

Wrote: "My Lovely Miss Pirrie of Oackley Passed by Me
                       this Morning, but did not remember how
                       beautifull I had rendered her face once by
                       Painting it at her Request with Pastelles."

Wrote: ". . . but thanks to My humble talents I can run
                       the gantlet throu this World without her help."

And ran it, and ran undistracted by promise of ease,
Or even the kind condescension of Daniel Webster.

Wrote: ". . . would give me a fat place was I willing to
                       have one; but I love indepenn and piece more
                       than humbug and money."

And proved same, but in the end, entered
On honor.   Far, over the ocean, in the silken salons,

With hair worn long like a hunter's, eyes shining,
He whistled the birdcalls of his distant forest.

Wrote: "... in my sleep I continually dream of birds."

And in the end entered into his earned house,
And slept in a bed, and with Lacy.

                         But the fiddle
Soon lay on the shelf untouched, the mouthpiece
Of the flute was dry, and his brushes.

                           His mind
Was darkened, and his last joy
Was in the lullaby they sang him, in Spanish, at sunset.

He died, and was mourned, who had loved the world.

Who had written: "... a world which though wicked enough
                   in all conscience is *perhaps* as good
                   as worlds unknown."

(b)
Night leaned, and now leans,
Off the Atlantic, and is on schedule.
Grass does not bend beneath that enormous weight
That with no sound sweeps westward. In the Mississippi,
On a mudbank, the wreck of a great tree, left
By flood, lies, the root system and now stubbed boughs
Lifting in darkness. It
Is white as bone. That whiteness
Is reflected in dark water, and a star
Thereby.

     Later,
In the shack of a sheepherder, high above the Bitterroot,
The light goes out. No other
Light is visible.

The Northwest Orient plane, New York to Seattle,
    has passed, winking westward.

IV
Their footless dance
Is of the beautiful liability of their nature.
Their eyes are round, boldly convex, bright as a jewel,
And merciless. They do not know
Compassion, and if they did,
We should not be worthy of it. They fly
In air that glitters like fluent crystal
And is hard as perfectly transparent iron; they cleave it
With no effort. They cry
In a tongue multitudinous, often like music.

He slew them, at surprising distances, with his gun.
Over a body held in his hand, his head was bowed low,
But not in grief.

He put them where they are, and there we see them:
In our imagination.

What is love?

One name for it is knowledge.

V
Tell me a story.

In this century, and moment, of mania,
Tell me a story.

Make it a story of great distances, and starlight.

The name of the story will be Time,
But you must not pronounce its name.

Tell me a story of deep delight.

MONA VAN DUYN

AT PÈRE LACHAISE

What began as death's avenue
becomes, as we go on,
death's village, then metropolis,
and the four of us,
reading our rain-blistered Michelin
map of graves, keep looking back,
but cafés, tabacs,
boulangeries are gone.
It is a long way yet
to where we are going to please me,
and the bunch of muguets
I am holding too tightly is frayed
already. On either side
of the cobbles we slip on,
darkly arched over by dripping chestnuts,
the ten-foot high deathhouses
stand, and we can see
at hilltop intersections
only further suburbs of
the imposing dead.
For a while we are lost
in this silent city—
the map is not detailed
and the avenues curve.
It is cold here. I am very cold.
My friend begins to cry.
We find a Kleenex for her
and a tranquilizer.
Head bent, hand clenched
to her mouth, her black bob
spattered with chestnut petals,
she stumbles and turns her ankle.
I am to blame.
A whole afternoon in Paris spent

on this spooky pilgrimage,
and we are too far in to go back.

The rain has stopped.
"Look, my God, *look!*"
Anything awful can happen here,
but I look where she points.
Ahead, at a break in the trees
where a weak ray of sun shines through,
two of the great dun tombs
are dappled with color, with cats,
more cats than I can believe,
two dozen at least,
sitting or lying on doorsills,
window ledges, pedestals, roofs,
and a yellow one, high in the air,
curled round at rest on the bar
of a towering cross.
Grimalkins, grandpas,
lithe rakes, plump dowagers,
princes, peasants, old warriors, hoydens,
gray, white, black, cream, orange,
spotted, striped, and plain—
a complete society of cats,
posed while we stand and stare.
My heart is thumping.
"Are we dreaming?
Oh, aren't they beautiful!"
my friend whispers.
We smile at the cats for a long time
before we go on past.
We are almost there.

Off to the side,
behind the grand monuments,
we find a flat slab marked MARCEL PROUST,
and, feeling a little foolish,

I lay my fist-sized white bouquet
on his black marble.

We go back another way
where the street widens,
opening out to gardens,
and we run down broad steps,
laughing at nothing.
A few people appear,
arranging gladioli in urns,
and far down the hill we can see
an exit to the boulevard.
We find Colette's grave
on the way out and call to her,
"You should have seen the cats!"

MICHAEL S. HARPER

KIN

When news came that your mother'd
smashed her hip, both feet caught
in rungs of the banquet table,
our wedding rebroken on the memory
of the long lake of silence
when the stones of her body
broke as an Irish fence of stones,
I see your wet dugs drag
with the weight of our daughter
in the quick of her sleep
to another feeding.

I pick you up from the floor
of your ringing fears, the floor
where the photographs you have worked
cool into the sky of the gray you love,

and you are back at the compost pile
where the vegetables burn,
or swim in the storm of your childhood
when your father egged you on with his
open machinery, the exhaust choking your sisters,
and your sisters choked still.

Now the years pile up on themselves,
and his voice stops you in accusation,
in the eggs of your stretched sons,
one born on his birthday, both dead.
I pull you off into the sanctuary
of conciliation, of quiet tactics,
the uttered question, the referral,
which will quiet the condition you have seen
in your mother's shadow, the crutches
inching in the uncut grass,
and the worn body you will carry
as your own birthmark of his scream.

WILLIAM STAFFORD

SLAVE ON THE HEADLAND

When they brought me here from the north island
my mother stayed alive but I didn't tell
where she lay hidden, headland of spray
waiting for canoes farther north that would come.
For years in gull voices I heard echoes
of dying that day, and my father spoke then,
wind counselling where to turn my eyes
when captors talked about returning to the island.
Gradually I learned this wasn't to be.
Now they call me "The Silent." My work
takes me where gulls wander all day,
and wind. I bend over, listening far,

but also at home here: this island is one
of the mountains connected with all the earth
my father told me about, and he still wanders
calling together the scattered pieces
over my bent head and the wide sea.

ASK ME

Some time when the river is ice ask me
mistakes I have made. Ask me whether
what I have done is my life. Others
have come in their slow way into
my thought, and some have tried to help
or to hurt—ask me what difference
their strongest love or hate has made.

I will listen to what you say.
You and I can turn and look
at the silent river and wait. We know
the current is there, hidden; and there
are comings and goings from miles away
that hold the stillness exactly before us.
What the river says, that is what I say.

EVENING WALK

LOUISE GLÜCK

BIRCHES

Already the hills are being delivered to moonlight.
The rest follows: the labored
green of the fields, the little garden
darned with green thread—

They vanish.
The trees also, whose shadows were blue spokes.

But some the light chooses.
How they tremble
as the moon mounts them, brutal and sisterly—

And then they become the birches.

I used to watch them,
all night absorbed
in the moon's neutral silver until
they were finally blurred, disfigured,

and it was my mother moving in the house
fixing this and that, her small things
no longer needing to be visible.

MEGAN FERNANDES

ON YOUR DEPARTURE TO CALIFORNIA

Prayer for you out west.
Where night falls only after mine.
The second curtain. That enigmatic dark,
and daylight so clarifying, it hurts.
Prayer for the headless deer in Saratoga
and the thirty lobster shells we buried
in a small Connecticut town.

For the elementary-school kids rushing headfirst
into the Brooklyn twilight. For the poets who came before
and saw the purple northeast, blizzard-full
but no quakes, and wanted for nothing else.
For the gold shops of Jackson Heights
and the dead soldiers in Mt. Auburn.
For the dead who just want to remain dead
and not dance into the speech of men.
For the tiny churches and their sullied bells.
For every gas station. For the tri-states.
Yes, even for Jersey's ease. For Café Paulette,
our last meal, before the city fell.
Prayer for our Hart Crane. For our bridge.
The blue one. For your return to Prospect Park,
where I'll be waiting, smug, dripping in city bees.
Prayer for you, queen of the wide air,
and your happy flights and scraped-up knees
and the young fields behind you.
Prayer for the sand-whipped Rockaway Beach,
where we spent a birthday and fought the wind.
You ran into the cold May ocean,
and I thought, *am I going to have to go in
if she gets caught?* just as you rose
from the water and waved.

THOMAS SNAPP

JULY AND THE BOAT

July
and the boat
ninety feet from shore—
we dove and came up splashing
August
around us. When we could stand,
September
trembled, was still, and ran down our backs

with the river; as we climbed the high banks.
October
clung until we dried and kissed,
then slid away with our footprints.
November
crumbled in color under us
as we rolled. When we stood apart at the top, small
lines formed around your eyes
and under my fingers your skin turned rough—
December
strung the sky with bells, clouds, and the smell
of snow. When we looked out, the moon was
fat over the river, and, half a year below,
summer
drifted bow-down, darkened amber—
so we ran, sliding and falling, to
shore and dove with momentum enough
to come up close, and climb into
the boat and
July.

SHARON OLDS

SUMMER SOLSTICE, NEW YORK CITY

By the end of the longest day of the year he could not stand it,
he went up the iron stairs through the roof of the building
and over the soft, tarry surface
to the edge, put one leg over the complex green tin cornice
and said if they came a step closer that was it.
Then the huge machinery of the earth began to work for his life,
the cops came in their suits blue-gray as the sky on a cloudy evening,
and one put on a bulletproof vest, a
black shell around his own life,
life of his children's father, in case
the man was armed, and one, slung with a
rope like the sign of his bounden duty,

came up out of a hole in the top of the neighboring building,
like the gold hole they say is in the top of the head,
and began to lurk toward the man who wanted to die.
The tallest cop approached him directly,
softly, slowly, talking to him, talking, talking,
while the man's leg hung over the lip of the next world,
and the crowd gathered in the street, silent, and the
dark hairy net with its implacable grid was
unfolded near the curb and spread out and
stretched as the sheet is prepared to receive at a birth.
Then they all came a little closer
where he squatted next to his death, his shirt
glowing its milky glow like something
growing in a dish at night in the dark in a lab, and then
everything stopped
as his body jerked and he
stepped down from the parapet and went toward them
and they closed on him, I thought they were going to
beat him up, as a mother whose child has been
lost will scream at the child when it's found, they
took him by the arms and held him up and
leaned him against the wall of the chimney and the
tall cop lit a cigarette
in his own mouth, and gave it to him, and
then they all lit cigarettes, and the
red glowing ends burned like the
tiny campfires we lit at night
back at the beginning of the world.

ROBERT PINSKY

AT MT. AUBURN CEMETERY

Walking among the graves for exercise
Where do you get your ideas how do I stop them
Looking for Mike Mazur's marker I looked
Down at the grass and saw Stanislaw Baranczak

Our Solidarity poetry reading in Poznan
Years later in Newton now he said I'm a U.S.
Liberal with a car like everybody else
When I held Bobo dying in my arms
His green eyes told me *I am not done yet*
Then he was gone when he was young he enjoyed
Leaping up onto the copy machine to press
A button and hear it hum to life and rustle
A blank page then another out onto its tray
Sometimes he batted the pages down to the floor
I used to call it his hobby here's a marble
Wicker bassinet marking a baby's grave
To sever the good fellowship of dust the vet's
Needle first a sedative then death now Willie
Paces the house mowling his elegy for Bobo
They never meow to one another just to people
Or to their nursing mother when they're small I
Marvel at this massive labelled American elm
Spreading above a cluster of newer names
Chang, Ohanessian, Kondakis joining Howells,
Emerson, Parkinson and here's a six-foot sphere
Of polished granite perfect and inscribed *Walker*
Should I have let him die his own cat way
Bruce Lee spends less on a stone than Schwarzenegger
The cemetery official confided what will mark
The markers when like mourners they bow and kneel
And topple down flat to kiss the very heaps
They have in trust under the splendid elm
Also marked with its tag a noble survivor
Civilization lifted my cat from the street gave him
A name and all his shots and determined his death
Now Willie howls the loss from room to room
When people say I'm ashamed of being German
Said Arendt I want to say I'm ashamed of being
Human sometimes when Bobo made the machine
Shoot copies of nothing I crumpled one he could chase
And combat practicing the game of being himself.

LUCILLE CLIFTON

HERE RESTS

my sister Josephine,
born july in '29
and dead these 15 years,
who carried a book
on every stroll.

when daddy was dying
she left the streets
and moved back home
to tend him.

her pimp came too,
her Diamond Dick,
and they would take turns
reading

the bible aloud through the house.
when you poem this,
and you will, she would say,
remember the Book of Job.

happy birthday and hope
to you Josephine,
one of the east's
most wanted.

may heaven be filled
with literate men,
may they bed you
with respect.

JOSÉ ANTONIO RODRÍGUEZ

SHELTER

Don't misunderstand me, I love a good poem
Like half my Facebook friends, one that transports you
To a corner of the soul you didn't know was there
Because you couldn't find the precise metaphor,
Even if you felt it, like that time my parents saw
A local news story of an older woman asking for help
With an ailing husband, and I volunteered to drive them
To the address onscreen, a neighborhood
I'd never driven through, though it looked familiar
With its usual poverty: a few leaning boards called a house
And inside the woman from the news in half-light
Thanking us for the comforters in our hands and pointing
To a foldout chair where we could place them
Before introducing us to her husband, a scraggly beard
Beneath a crinkled blanket on a cot right there
In what would have been the living room, groaning
In the muted manner of those who know this is
As good as it'll get, the woman's non-stop small talk
About "So it is, life's a struggle" and "Please stay awhile"
And "Take a seat," as if we were long-missed relatives,
All this in Spanish, though I translate it here
Because I want to reach the widest audience
And not burden the monolingual English reader
When they've already gifted me their time by reading this,
Which I'll call a poem, one that my parents can't read,
As they only speak Spanish with that poor Mexican lilt of apology
Which kept them from interrupting the woman, a Spanish
I've kept but rarely use, though I did that moment
When I kept telling my mother "We have to go"
With an almost impolite urgency, because I couldn't bear
One more minute in that near-replica of the room of my childhood,
Even as the woman said "He seems to be in such a hurry"
And my mother smiled, making excuses as we turned to leave,
While I bemoaned my parents' passive politeness
So common in the Mexican in America, though by then

I was already a grad student in upstate New York
And down in South Texas for the winter break
Between semesters of reading Adichie and Alexie
And risking words together to find something
Like the point of this, some search for the reason
For the speaker's love of poems, that pull
Of the written word as artifact, as a kind of tool
Against the sometimes overwhelming sadness about all of it—
Including the fact that some of us it seems will never be allowed
The time and energy to sit with a poem, like them
In that illusion of shelter, though perhaps
They were closer to poetry's pursuit, that edge of oblivion
Where words begin becoming insufficient—the woman
With her frantic speech beseeching us and the man
Extending his bony hand out, as if from the cot itself,
The tremor of it trying to say something that sounded
Like a greeting, that sounded like a plea.

HARRISON DOWD
WATCH THE LEAF

This is the slumber of man,
The gray leaf and the tan.
This is sleep to him
Of the tired limb.

Not in the summer sun,
Sweating, undone
By the thought of time—
The hours that climb and climb—

Does man remember this,
And how good it is,
How good it is to stand,
Dropping the calloused hand,

Lifting the sleepy eye
To the darkening sky
And watching how
The dry leaf breaks from the bough.

GERALD STERN

BEE BALM

Today I'm sticking a shovel in the ground
and digging up the little green patch
between the hosta and the fringe bleeding heart.
I am going to plant bee balm there
and a few little pansies till the roots take
and the leaves spread out in both directions.

This is so the hummingbird will rage
outside my fireplace window; this is so
I can watch him standing in the sun
and hold him a little above my straining back,
so I can reach my own face up to his
and let him drink the sugar from my lips.

This is so I can lie down on the couch
beside the sea horse and the glass elephant,
so I can touch the cold wall above me
and let the yellow light go through me,
so I can last the rest of the summer on thought,
so I can live by secrecy and sorrow.

JULIA STORY

TOAD CIRCUS

The day after my toad circus the toads were all dead, crunchy and
silent in their window well. I wanted to draw a doorway to walk

through to get to the world of lilacs: purple, contagious green leaves and no movement but the steady invisible breathing of flowers. I knew I had to tell someone what I had done so I first walked to the park and stayed there until dusk, sitting on the glider or in the middle of the rusty and dangerous merry-go-round; I can't remember which. When it was nearly dark I walked home, certain that they were worried and maybe even out looking for me. When I got there I saw them busy in the kitchen through the window, so I hid in the back yard until it was good and dark, a living thing on a swing set in the gloom, the attic in my head cracking open for the first time and I went in.

SIMON ARMITAGE

BEACH WEDDING

Being just a stone's throw from the pretty church
they often tumble out onto the beach,
unworldly creatures, the bride herself
an apparition of satins or silks
among stripy towels and inflatable sharks,
the groom in a morning suit, walking the sand
in bare feet, wearing his shoes on his hands.

She'll hitch her dress as far as her garter,
he'll carry her some way into the water.
Setting out for Atlantis they pause here
on the point of departure; her long train
floats on the surface and drifts and darkens.

Each empty evening a figure arrives
in a shooting jacket and combat trousers,
combing the shore with a metal detector,
grubbing for coins or keys, sweeping for mines.
The shovel hooked to the back of his belt
drags behind him like a devil's tail,
plowing a furrow, marking a lone trail.

Before first light a spring tide does its work,
panning for gold, resetting the sand,
while under a thin sheet husband and wife
lie badly wounded after the first fight.

TRACI BRIMHALL

LOVE POEM WITHOUT A DROP OF HYPERBOLE IN IT

I love you like ladybugs love windowsills, love you
like sperm whales love squid. There's no depth
I wouldn't follow you through. I love you like
the pawns in chess love aristocratic horses.
I'll throw myself in front of a bishop or a queen
for you. Even a sentient castle. My love is crazy
like that. I like that sweet little hothouse mouth
you have. I like to kiss you with tongue, with gusto,
with socks still on. I love you like a vulture loves
the careless deer at the roadside. I want to get
all up in you. I love you like Isis loved Osiris,
but her devotion came up a few inches short.
I'd train my breath and learn to read sonar until
I retrieved every lost blood vessel of you. I swear
this love is ungodly, not an ounce of suffering in it.
Like salmon and its upstream itch, I'll dodge grizzlies
for you. Like hawks and skyscraper rooftops,
I'll keep coming back. Maddened. A little hopeless.
Embarrassingly in love. And that's why I'm on
the couch kissing pictures on my phone instead of
calling you in from the kitchen where you are
undoubtedly making dinner too spicy, but when
you hold the spoon to my lips and ask if it's ready
I'll say it is, always, but never, there is never enough.

EDWARD HIRSCH

MAN ON A FIRE ESCAPE

He couldn't remember what propelled him
out of the bedroom window onto the fire escape
of his fifth-floor walkup on the river,

so that he could see, as if for the first time,
sunset settling down on the dazed cityscape
and tugboats pulling barges up the river.

There were barred windows glaring at him
from the other side of the street
while the sun deepened into a smoky flare

that scalded the clouds gold-vermillion.
It was just an ordinary autumn twilight—
the kind he had witnessed often before—

but then the day brightened almost unnaturally
into a rusting, burnished, purplish-red haze
and everything burst into flame:

the factories pouring smoke into the sky,
the trees and shrubs, the shadows
of pedestrians scorched and rushing home. . . .

There were storefronts going blind and cars
burning on the parkway and steel girders
collapsing into the polluted waves.

Even the latticed fretwork of stairs
where he was standing, even the first stars
climbing out of their sunlit graves

were branded and lifted up, consumed by fire.
It was like watching the start of Armageddon,
like seeing his mother dipped in flame. . . .

And then he closed his eyes and it was over.
Just like that. When he opened them again
the world had reassembled beyond harm.

So where had he crossed to? Nowhere.
And what had he seen? Nothing. No foghorns
called out to each other, as if in a dream,

and no moon rose over the dark river
like a warning—icy, long forgotten—
while he turned back to an empty room.

MARILYN NELSON

PIGEON AND HAWK

A new grad student far away from home,
I took every step on trembling ground.
I knew no one. Who were my friends?
The other black student in the program
ducked and rushed away when our eyes met.
Seminar rooms were full of hungry dogs
snapping up scraps of nodding approval.
At the end of a campus reception
I accepted the offer of a ride
from campus to my downtown room-with-bath.

October. Evenings were getting cool.
The walk over the bridge downtown
felt dangerously long when it was dark.
Did the young man who offered me a ride
tell me his name? What was it about him
that made me say Yes thanks, like a damn fool?
When we were in his car and he said oops,
he had forgotten something at his place
he had to pick up, and asked if I'd mind
if we stopped there, why did I say O.K.?

Did we talk during the drive? Was the radio on?
Did I just watch the businesses,
in thinning traffic, become a suburb
where his apartment complex was in a woods
already splendid in autumn colors
so beautiful they took my words away?
When he pulled up and said I should come in,
it would only take a minute, why did I go
upstairs with him, wait as the key unlocked
his apartment, and go inside?

The building was silent. A big window
in the living room looked at parking lots
with a few parked cars, and the glowing trees.
He said I'll be right back, and disappeared
into the bedroom. I turned to the view,
thinking of nothing, my mind a blank page
that grew emptier as the minutes passed.
What was he doing during those minutes,
as I stood dreaming like a fat pigeon
in the keen purview of a circling hawk?

What could he have needed to go home for,
that was so important he had to go
there first, before he drove me home? Was he
wrestling with opportunity?
       Human horrors
are not inevitable. Some people stop
themselves, before they cross moral divides.
A drinking buddy might say Cool it, bro.
A cop might take his knee off a black man's throat.
A young man might come out and say O.K.,
let's go, and drive you home. What was his name?

CAROL MUSKE-DUKES

DAPHNE, AFTER

So Spring blossomed in spite of itself.
Uniform skirts up-rolled high by wild girls
curbside, smoking. Still, two of us, heads

together, translating. Our selves as Stoic
teens, thinking Marcus, Marcus A.!
So: month of rose pagodas, of lilacs

impetuous, blue. Twigs spill from
her dropped text, as she flees
translation class, the nun's query.

He demanded her name first. Just
steps from the bus stop. Sunset:
shade before ancient dark. Blossoms

beneath her, beneath the shock-light of
staggered street lamps coming on. Leda's
Zeus, his suit & tie, swan's hiss in her ear.

She told me only. The great wings of
aloneness closed in us, we learned how
the passive voice was magnified: "The soul

is dyed with the color of its thoughts."
Powerless to move, she became past
tense of strength once standing tall

at her father's grave. His name in brass
florets. But Latin offhand—"to seize or
abduct." Ovid's shudder: Vos mos non

sit sponsa . . . Once we might have found it
funny: *You will not be a bride, you will be
a tree.* At each ring where her flesh became

bark, a path opened: root split. Some
believe that anger can take the place of
love. She found the verb for it. Having to

do with the forest & a young girl running fast,
calling out—then silence. Becoming as she
had, one of them, reaching skyward. Their

witness, bowing. Those wings hidden in
the tree, meaning she was not ready to be
cut down, not ready to be chopped into little

sticks & tossed into fire's assumed supremacy—
all that smoke, her ashes refusing to fly.

WILLIAM STAFFORD

AN EVENING WALK

All the animals are looking over
their shoulders. They come toward us, but
they look away. We try to see what
is frightening them—nothing. Why?

At the summit, a rock we had left
is gone. Our breath hangs in the air—
we see it after we start for home.
What happens to it, along about sundown?

Somebody calls us and calls us, "You there!"
But we can't make them hear our call
in return. Then we know we have
invented the world and are walking on it.

Animals, rocks, breath, people:
Listen to us! Listen! Like you, we are alone.

ALEX DIMITROV

JUNE

There will never be more of summer
than there is now. Walking alone
through Union Square I am carrying flowers
and the first rosé to a party where I'm expected.
It's Sunday and the trains run on time
but today death feels so far, it's impossible
to go underground. I would like to say
something to everyone I see (an entire
city) but I'm unsure what it is yet.
Each time I leave my apartment
there's at least one person crying,
reading, or shouting after a stranger
anywhere along my commute.
It's possible to be happy alone,
I say out loud and to no one
so it's obvious, and now here
in the middle of this poem.
Rarely have I felt more charmed
than on Ninth Street, watching a woman
stop in the middle of the sidewalk
to pull up her hair like it's
an emergency—and it is.
People do know they're alive.
They hardly know what to do with themselves.
I almost want to invite her with me
but I've passed and yes it'd be crazy
like trying to be a poet, trying to be anyone here.
How do you continue to love New York,
my friend who left for California asks me.
It's awful in the summer and winter,
and spring and fall last maybe two weeks.
This is true. It's all true, of course,
like my preference for difficult men
which I had until recently
because at last, for one summer

the only difficulty I'm willing to imagine
is walking through this first humid day
with my hands full, not at all peaceful
but entirely possible and real.

ALBERT GOLDBARTH
THE WAY

The sky is random. Even calling it "sky"
is an attempt to make a meaning, say,
a shape, from the humanly visible part
of shapelessness in endlessness. It's what
we do, in some ways it's entirely what
we do—and so the devastating rose

of a galaxy's being born, the fatal lamé
of another's being torn and dying, we frame
in the lenses of our super-duper telescopes the way
we would those other completely incomprehensible
fecund and dying subjects at a family picnic.
Making them "subjects." "Rose." "Lamé." The way

our language scissors the enormity to scales
we can tolerate. The way we gild and rubricate
in memory, or edit out selectively.
An infant's gentle snoring, even, apportions
the eternal. When they moved to the boonies,
Dorothy Wordsworth measured their walk

to Crewkerne—then the nearest town—
by pushing a device invented especially
for such a project, a "perambulator": seven miles.
Her brother William pottered at his daffodils poem.
Ten thousand saw I at a glance: by which he meant
too many to count, but could only say it in counting.

THE DOLLS' MUSEUM IN DUBLIN

The wounds are terrible. The paint is old.
The cracks along the lips and on the cheeks
cannot be fixed. The cotton lawn is soiled.
The arms are ivory dissolved to wax.

Recall the Quadrille. Hum the waltz.
Promenade on the yacht-club terraces.
Put back the lamps in their copper holders,
the carriage wheels on the cobbled quays.

Re-create Easter in Dublin.
Booted officers. Their mistresses.
Sunlight crisscrossing College Green.
Steam hissing from the flanks of horses.

Here they are. Cradled and cleaned,
Held close in the arms of their owners.
Their cold hands clasped by warm hands,
Their faces memorized like perfect manners.

The altars are mannerly with linen.
The lilies are whiter than surplices.
The candles are burning and warning:
Rejoice, they whisper. After sacrifice.

Horse chestnuts hold up their candles.
The Green is vivid with parasols.
Sunlight is pastel and windless.
The bar of the Shelbourne is full.

Laughter and gossip on the terraces.
Rumor and alarm at the barracks.
The Empire is summoning its officers.
The carriages are turning: they are turning back.

Past children walking with governesses,
looking down and cosseting their dolls,
then looking up as the carriage passes,
the shadow chilling them. Twilight falls.

It is twilight in the dolls' museum. Shadows
remain on the parchment-colored waists,
are bruises on the stitched cotton clothes,
are hidden in the dimples on the wrists.

The eyes are wide. They cannot address
a helplessness, which has lingered in
the airless peace of each glass case:
To have survived. To have been stronger than

a moment. To be the hostages ignorance
takes from time and ornament from destiny. Both.
To be the present of the past. To infer the difference
with a terrible stare. But not feel it. And not know it.

HALA ALYAN

HALF-LIFE IN EXILE

I'm forever living between Aprils.
The air here smells of jacarandas and lime;
it's sunset before I know it. I'm supposed
to rest, but that's where the children live.
In the hot mist of sleep. Dream after dream.
Instead, I obsess. I draw stars on receipts.
Everybody loves the poem.
It's embroidered on a pillow in Milwaukee.
It's done nothing for Palestine.
There are plants out West that emerge only after fires.
They listen for smoke. I wrote the poem
after weeks of despair, hauling myself
like a rock. Everyone loves the poem.

The plants are called fire-followers,
but sometimes it's after the rains. At night,
I am a zombie feeding on the comments.
Is it compulsive to watch videos?
Is it compulsive to memorize names?
Rafif and Ammar and Mahmoud.
Poppies and snapdragons and calandrinias:
I can't hear you. I can't hear you under the missiles.
A plant waits for fire to grow.
A child waits for a siren. It must be a child.
Never a man. Never a man without a child.
There is nothing more terrible
than waiting for the terrible. I promise.
Was the grief worth the poem? No,
but you don't interrogate a weed
for what it does with wreckage.
For what it's done to get here.

SYLVIA PLATH

THE ELM SPEAKS

I know the bottom, she says. I know it with my great tap root.
It is what you fear.
I do not fear it; I have been there.

Is it the sea you hear in me,
Its dissatisfactions?
Or the voice of nothing that was your madness?

Love is a shadow.
How you lie and cry after it!
Listen. These are its hooves. It has gone off, like a horse.

All night I shall gallop thus, impetuously,
Till your head is a stone, your pillow a little turf,
Echoing, echoing.

Or shall I bring you the sound of poisons?
This is rain now, this big hush.
And this is the fruit of it: tin-white, like arsenic.

I have suffered the atrocity of sunsets.
Scorched to the root,
My red filaments burn and stand, a hand of wires.

Now I break up in pieces that fly about like clubs.
A wind of such violence
Will tolerate no bystanding; I must shriek.

The moon, also, is merciless; she would drag me
Cruelly, being barren.
Her radiance scathes me. Or perhaps I have caught her.

I let her go. I let her go,
Diminished and flat, as after radical surgery.
How your bad dreams possess and endow me!

I am inhabited by a cry.
Nightly it flaps out,
Looking, with its hooks, for something to love.

I am terrified by this dark thing
That sleeps in me;
All day I feel its soft, feathery turnings, its malignity.

Clouds pass and disperse.
Are those the faces of love, those pale irretrievables?
Is it for such I agitate my heart?

I am incapable of more knowledge.
What is this, this face
So murderous in its strangle of branches?

Its snaky acids hiss.
It petrifies the will. These are the isolate, slow faults
That kill, that kill, that kill.

DELMORE SCHWARTZ

DURING DECEMBER'S DEATH

The afternoon turned dark early;
The light suddenly faded;
The dusk was black although elsewhere the first star in the cold sky
     whistled;
And I thought I heard the fresh scraping of the flying steel of boys
     on roller skates
Rollicking over the asphalt in 1926,
And I thought I heard the dusk and silence raided
By a calm voice commanding consciousness:
Wait: wait: wait as if you had always waited
And as if it had always been dark
And as if the world had been from the beginning
A lost and drunken ark in which the only light
Was the dread and white of the terrified animals' eyes.
And then, turning on the light, I took a book
That I might gaze upon another's vision of the abyss of
     consciousness—
The hope, and the pain of hope, and the patience of hope, and its
     torment, its astonishment, its endlessness.

PATTI SMITH

TARA

She stood by the door
of her Virginia farm
pulling a sweater on
the branches
of the dogwood
she had tended
were bowed
blossoms loosened
tossed in sudden snow
the deer stood

in mute wonder
by her garden's edge
she slipped the phone
in her pocket
her daughter
unharmed
among
petals gone
she snapped
a branch
a tempest stalled
she felt the boy
she felt the dead
she felt the families
she felt the wind
the deer don't do that
she said
the deer don't do that

COLIN CHANNER

SPUMANTE

Weeks diffuse into each other like
they're sprayed; jetted, they shoot certain:
days, times, doodles, kept appointments,
next is lull, pool, fading, flash-disperse.

I was shook and shocked by death,
chanced upon it on a winter walk,
proof of plod for miles behind me
swept in fog, a wet so thick

it blended with the snow that
settled plenty on the sand. It
was not yet daybreak, and I'd driven
miles to walk and think,

find peace in sweat and sea racket,
that ancient wise asthmatic sound.
The light took its lazy time for lifting.
In the shift I saw a darker shaping

than the gray—at two miles a boat
of some proportion, at quarter mile a whale.
Since then I've been lamenting,
moving as if held in gel.

At night I dream it, see it stretched
across the wrack of high tide,
belly to the stars—flung shells and gravel—
throat-part grooved, fins unflappable,

balletic flukes symmetric
in their pointing, how they fused:
all this in half-light, all this in sea dirge,
wet air matte, toned silver,

and I hunched in the hood of my parka,
God-awed before shavasana,
stilled as if the glassy eye that looked to me
had fixed me in a century of tintype.

Ah-gah-pay. I've only recently discovered
love of animals—well, Kili, Nan, and Rebus,
three dogs. Now I've partly taken leave
of language, have given incoherence due.

I know what it's like to be mammal
filled with deepest ocean sounds:
oblivion, solitude, stillness
intermitted by quake roar,

tectonic slipping, lava fissures,
ship propellers drilling,
the human croons of whales.
There is slave in me, fat heritage,

no fluke I'm invested with hurt,
echo of the hunted, located, natural
rights redacted, meagered to resource.
All is flux as I'm collapsing

love and distance, moving through the gel,
my life, edging the canals of my city,
clomping up its hills, memory aerosol,
head in self cloud, getting Melville

as I should have, watching at him
contemplate the vista from a landlocked house,
hills becoming pods of transmigrating giants:
Greylock. Berkshire range.

There's thirst for music in this less than solid
state. Ampless back in my office,
I knee-prop my Fender, ancient black thing.
Strum it casual, weep;

suck salt in darkness, fingers guessy,
lazing up the sound. Still, something
brusque runs up me: shuddered
wood, that deep flesh shook

that makes string music fuse to you.
The thumbing further breaks the thing in me.
I know what now love is,
know tentative for sure its

incoherence, jelly analog, is mine for life.
The windows stay black and phlegmatic
as the air outside begins to heave with rain.
I hum, thumbing, fashion something of a home,

some succor, pulse quick but steady as I deep dive
to dub. With it comes the baleen
wheeze of mouth organs, plangent blue whoop.
I am dub and dub is water.

Exile, I wish you could have lived in me,
plunging, life *spumante*. I'd slip my hold
on you like magma shot for islands
every single time you breach.

NINA RUBINSTEIN ALONSO

CROSBY POND

Broken fire, corrupted air,
Earth crazy and the water dying,
Yet small dark birds still fly to this pond
And seem to build nests around the edges
Somewhere high in the gash-marked trees;
I hear them singing as I walk
And count all the half-submerged tires,
Mud-heavy, coated with fall algae;
Somebody flung them in the muck,
Perhaps boys at night, I can picture them.

How long does the water take,
I wonder, to reclaim these enemies?
Or maybe a spring is not strong enough
To devour metal, rubber, glass,
The machines that men pick up and throw
In full absurdity into a pond.
Nevertheless this fall continues
Aging the leaves, bringing red to them,
And time, for a moment, comforts me,
Being guiltless and unalterable,

Taking everything in its turn
But itself not changing to another thing.
Fernando is running in the woods
Scouting for the camp of a friend
Who said he was settling in here,
And I walk slowly looking for signs
Of all that is not easy to kill:

Could it go on then, under the water,
Some sort of fish find its life
In the round silent mirror of the pond?

ELLEN BRYANT VOIGT
GROUNDHOG

not unlike otters which we love frolicking
floating on their backs like truant boys unwrapping lunch
same sleek brown pelt some overtones of gray and rust
though groundhogs have no swimming hole and lunch
is rooted in the ground beneath short legs small feet
like a fat man's odd diminutive loafers not

frolicking but scurrying layers of fat his coat
gleams as though wet shines chestnut sable darker
head and muzzle lower into the grass
a dark triangular face like the hog-nosed skunk another delicate
nose and not a snout doesn't it matter what they're called I like swine

which are smart and prefer to be clean using their snouts
to push their excrement to the side of the pen
but they have hairy skin not fur his fur
shimmers and ripples he never uproots the mother plant his teeth
I think are blunt squared off like a sheep's if cornered does he
cower like sheep or bite like a sow with a litter is he ever

attacked he looks to me inedible he shares his acreage

with moles voles ravenous crows someone
thought up the names his other name is botched Algonquin
but yes he burrows beneath the barn where once a farmer

dried cordwood he scuttles there at speech cough laugh
at lawnmower swollen brook high wind he lifts his head
as Gandhi did small tilt to the side or stands erect
like a prairie dog or a circus dog but dogs don't waddle like Mao

with a tiny tail he seems asexual like Gandhi like Jesus if Jesus
came back would he be vegetarian also pinko freako homo

in Vermont natives scornful of greyhounds from the city
self-appoint themselves woodchucks unkempt hairy macho
who would shoot on sight an actual fatso shy mild marmot radiant
as the hog-nosed skunk in the squirrel trap both cleaner than sheep
fur fluffy like a girl's maybe he is a she it matters
what we're called words shape the thought don't say
rodent and ruin everything

HENRI COLE

TWILIGHT

There's a black bear
in the apple tree
and he won't come down.
I can hear him panting,
like an athlete.
I can smell the stink
of his body.

Come down, black bear.
Can you hear me?

The mind is the most interesting thing to me;
like the sudden death of the sun,
it seems implausible that darkness will swallow it
or that anything is lost forever there,
like a black bear in a fruit tree,
gulping up sour apples
with dry sucking sounds,

or like us at the pier, sombre and tired,
making food from sunlight,
you saying a word, me saying a word, trying hard,
though things were disintegrating.

Still, I wanted you,
your lips on my neck,
your postmodern sexuality.
Forlorn and anonymous:
I didn't want to be that. I could hear
the great barking monsters of the lower waters
calling me forward.

You see, my mind takes me far,
but my heart dreams of return.

Black bear,
with pale-pink tongue
at the center of his face,
is turning his head,
like the face of Christ from life.
Shaking the apple boughs,
he is stronger than I am
and seems so free of passion—
no fear, no pain, no tenderness. I want to be that.

Come down, black bear,
I want to learn the faith of the indifferent.

CIARAN CARSON

CLAUDE MONET, "THE ARTIST'S GARDEN AT VÉTHEUIL," 1880

Today I thought I'd just take a lie-down, and drift. So here I am
    listening
To the tick of my mechanical aortic valve—overhearing, rather, the way
    it flits
In and out of consciousness. It's a wonder what goes on below the
    threshold.
It's quiet up here, just the muted swoosh of the cars on the Antrim Road,
And every so often the shrill of a far-off alarm or the squeal of brakes;
But yesterday some vandal upended the terra-cotta pot of daffodils

In our little front garden, that's not even as big, when I consider it,
As the double bed I'm lying on. Behind the privet hedge, besides the
    daffodils
There's pansies, thyme, and rosemary. A Hebe bush. A laurel. Ruefully
I scuffed the spilled earth and pebbles with my shoe and thought of
    Poussin—
Was it Poussin?—and his habit of bringing back bits of wood, stones,
    moss,
Lumps of earth from his rambles by the Tiber; and the story of him
Reaching among the ruins for a handful of porphyry and marble chips
And saying to a tourist, "Here's ancient Rome." So, here's Glandore
    Avenue.

So different now from thirty years ago, the corner shop at the interface
Torched and the roadway strewn with broken glass and rubble.

There was something beautiful about the tossed daffodils all the same.
I'd never really taken them under my notice these past few difficult weeks.
It's late March, some of them beginning to turn and wilt and fade, heads
Drooping, papery at the tips, desiccated, or completely gone, reduced
    to calyx.
So many shades of yellow when you look at them. Gorse. Lemon.
    Mustard.
Honey. Saffron. Ochre. But then any word you care to mention has so
    many
Shades of meaning, and the flower itself goes by different names.
    Narcissus.
Daffadowndilly. Lent lily. So we wander down the road of what it is we
    think
We want to say. Etymologies present themselves, like daffodil from
    asphodel—
Who knows where the "d" came from?—the flower of the underworld.
They say it grows profusely in the meadows of the dead, like a
    buttercup
On its branching stem. And I see a galaxy of buttercups in a green field,
And the yellow of the tall sunflowers in Monet's "Garden at Vétheuil"
    that flank
The path where the woman and the two children stand commemorated.

Strange how a smear of color, like a perfume, resurrects the memory
Of another, that which I meant to begin with. "Asphodel, that greeny
    flower."

I'd just found the book I had in mind—"What Painting Is," by James
    Elkins—
When the vandal struck. *Thud*. What the . . . ? The gate clanged. I
    looked out
The bay window to see a figure scarpering off down the street to the
    interface . . .
What a book, though. I have it before me, open at this color plate, jotting
Notes into a jotter, which I'll work up later into what you're reading now.
"The detail I'm reproducing here is a graveyard of scattered brush hairs
And other detritus," says Elkins. "At the centre left, glazed over by
    Malachite Green,
Are two crossed brush hairs, one of them bent almost at a right angle.
Just below them are two of Monet's own hairs, fallen into the wet paint."
Brushstrokes laid down every which way. Jiggles. Jabs. Impulsive
Twists and turns. Gestures that "depend on the inner feelings of the body"
And "the fleeting momentary awareness of what the hand might do next."
You listen to the body talking, exfoliating itself cell after cell. I saw it
Happening just now in the dust motes drifting through this ray of sunlight.

So everything gets into the painting, wood smoke from the studio stove,
The high pollen count of a high summer's day *en plein air* by the Seine.

The detail is so magnified it is impossible to tell what it is of, if you didn't,
Like Elkins, know. The visual field looks like a field. Shades of umber,
    khaki, mud,
And other greens beside the Malachite. It could stand for anything, it
    seems,
In Monet's garden—or "Garden," rather—as Poussin's handful of porphyry
Is Rome and of the days of the fall of Rome. I want it to go to the stately
    tune
Of a Poussin painting, "Landscape with a Man Washing His Feet at a
    Fountain,"
Say, where a woman sweeps by, balancing a basket on her head, and an
    old man

In blue dreams full-length on the grass. There are milestones and tombs,
And puddles on the road, and you can just imagine the whispering of the
    cistern.
A line of blue hills in the distance is contoured like a monumental
    sentence.
It's beautiful weather, the 30th of March, and tomorrow the clocks go
    forward.
How strange it is to be lying here listening to whatever it is is going on.
The days are getting longer now, however many of them I have left.
And the pencil I am writing this with, old as it is, will easily outlast
    their end.

ANNE SEXTON

THE ROAD BACK

The car is heavy with children
tugged back from summer,
swept out of their laughing beach,
swept out while a persistent rumor
tells them nothing ends.
Today, we fret and pull
on wheels, ignore our regular loss
of time, count cows and others,
while the sun moves over
like an old albatross
we must not count or kill.

There is no word for time.
Today, we will not think
to number another summer
or watch its white bird into the ground.
Today, all cars,
all fathers, all mothers, all
children and lovers will
have to forget
about that thing in the sky

going around
like a persistent rumor
that will get us yet.

MICHAEL RYAN

SWITCHBLADE

Most of the past is lost,
and I'm glad mine has vanished
into blackness or space or whatever nowhere
what we feel and do goes,
but there were a few cool Sunday afternoons
when my father wasn't sick with hangover
and the air in the house wasn't foul with anger
and the best china had been cleared after the week's best meal
so he could place on the table his violins
to polish with their special cloth and oil.
Three violins he'd arrange
side by side in their velvet-lined cases
with enough room between for the lids to lie open.
They looked like children in coffins,
three infant sisters whose hearts had stopped for no reason,
but after he rubbed up their scrolls and waists
along the lines of the grain to the highest sheen,
they took on the knowing posture of women in silk gowns
in magazine ads for big cars and ocean voyages,
and, as if a violin were a car in storage
that needed a spin around the block every so often,
for fifteen minutes he would play each one—
though not until each horsehair bow was precisely tightened
and coated with rosin, and we had undergone an eon of tuning.
When he played no one was allowed to speak to him.
He seemed to see something drastic across the room
or feel it through his handkerchief padding the chinboard.
So we'd hop in front of him waving or making pig-noses
the way kids do to guards at Buckingham Palace,

and after he finished playing and had returned to himself
he'd softly curse the idiocy of his children
beneath my mother's voice yelling to him from the kitchen
That was beautiful, Paul, play it again.

He never did, and I always hoped he wouldn't,
because the whole time I was waiting for his switchblade
to appear, and the new stories he'd tell me
for the scar thin as a seam
up the white underside of his forearm,
for the chunks of proud flesh on his back and belly,
scarlet souvenirs of East St. Louis dance halls in the twenties,
cornered in men's rooms, ganged in blind alleys,
always slashing out alone with this knife.
First the violins had to be snug again
inside their black cases
for who knew how many months or years or lifetimes;
then he had to pretend to have forgotten
why I was sitting there wide-eyed across from him
long after my sister and brother had gone off with friends.
Every time, as if only an afterthought,
he'd sneak into his pocket and ease the switchblade
onto the bare table between us,
its thumb-button jutting from the pearl-and-silver plating
like the eye of some sleek prehistoric fish.
I must have known it wouldn't come to life
and slither toward me by itself,
but when he'd finally nod to me to take it
its touch was still warm with his body heat
and I could feel the blade inside aching
to flash open with the terrible click
that sounds now like just a *tsk* of disappointment,
it has become so sweet and quiet.

CLOUDS

To those worried about the future,
You bring tidings,
Shapes that may recall things
Without ever shedding
Their troubling ambiguity.

Like a troupe of illusionists
Travelling in circus wagons
You play hide-and-seek with the light
In country fairgrounds
Until overtaken by night.

Taking a break from prophecy
Over small prairie towns
In company of dark trees,
Courthouse statues, crickets,
And other amateur ventriloquists.

SALLY THOMAS
REUNION

My grandfather stands on the front porch
watching the dogs come back, reassembled

from hair and grit and eyeteeth. Now
the twin mares browse by the fence

in their coats of dust. Nobody asks
what they mean, appearing so suddenly

when nobody needed them, or called.
In the back yard, the buried people—

great-grandmothers in spectator pumps,
the great-grandfather who died of sneezing,

the first baby, never named—
stay buried. It's not their overshoes

lost in the grass behind the smokehouse,
not their faces alive in anyone's

memory. But my mother waits
in the pecan tree's fingered shadow,

holding a broken milk jug full
of daylilies, waiting as if

she wanted someone to tell her again
it's all right to be born now,

now is as good a time as any.
In a month we'll find my grandfather's glasses

in their case under the front seat
of his car. "Oh goodness," my aunt will say,

as if it were a matter of his
forgetting them. As if we could

give them back. We're all convinced
we've missed the moment. We forget

that pause while a soul undoes
its buttons, the world falls away,

and one by one we step out
into this death, to be remembered.

DON PATERSON

RAIN

I love all films that start with rain:
rain, braiding a windowpane
or darkening a hung-out dress
or streaming down her upturned face;

one long thundering downpour
right through the empty script and score
before the act, before the blame,
before the lens pulls through the frame

to where the woman sits alone
beside a silent telephone
or the dress lies ruined on the grass
or the girl walks off the overpass,

and all things flow out from that source
along their fatal watercourse.
However bad or overlong
such a film can do no wrong,

so when his native twang shows through
or when the boom dips into view
or when her speech starts to betray
its adaptation from the play,

I think to when we opened cold
on a rain-dark gutter, running gold
with the neon of a drugstore sign,
and I'd read into its blazing line:

forget the ink, the milk, the blood—
all was washed clean with the flood
we rose up from the falling waters
the fallen rain's own sons and daughters

and none of this, none of this matters.

ISHMAEL REED

INSPIRATION POINT, BERKELEY

"If you despise this state so
why did you move here?"
I come here to remind myself
The meadows are designed
by Thomas Hart Benton
Underneath the bridge
white sharks are preying
It is a golden door to Singapore
The freighters are bringing
rare mushrooms
The mountain lions are yawning
There are walkers, cyclists, and
runners on the trails
I never knew there were so
many shades of trees
The cows and I are black
I don't even mind the radio
towers
From here
you can see everything
but the faults

DOROTHEA LASKY

THE GREEN LAKE

What work will you leave behind
I ask the tailor
Who has sewn the button upon my shoe
I can walk again

Yesterday everything felt so hopeless
Now I have the energy to sit in the sun

All of the damned seething baths
Now I am finally on my own

When I go places I call her
And unload my fashionable happenstance
I used to stop in the street and pick up an acorn
There were so many things I used to do

In the middle of the fire
I went and thought to mention it to the ghost
I have already burned, it said
Its face was like my father's but was different

What work will you leave behind
I asked myself while in the rain
Oh, this and that, it answered me
And handed me the stars, then the moon

JESSAMYN WEST

GREEN TWILIGHT

Close the door quickly, before the green
eye of the twilight inserts itself,
shattering with spite the picture you've
made of tranquillity; lidlessly
stare at the fire and the flowers, at the
curtains adrift in the evening air.

Close the door quickly and shutter the
windows (else evil will enter, will
quietly smile at the pitiful room,
at the hopeful arrangement of
chairs and of books), as if time were thus
foiled—as if walls would not fall and the
books lie unread in the unending twilight.

CHARLES RAMOND

ON A PORCH NEAR THE SHORE

Its spring released, there hangs into the dusk
An old screen door, ajar to distant scenes
Of majesty and lassitude, and leans
Against the August wind, that velvet musk
Portending rain and autumn. We sit there
Summer evenings, fading silhouettes
Lit by orange stars of cigarettes.
The quiet tunes of insects stir the air.

But someone scrapes his shoe across the floor,
And then a chilly gust comes off the bay;
Someone wonders what's the date today,
And finally someone's up to fix the door.
Summer ends then with a fearful crack,
As, spring rehooked, the old screen door swings back.

RICHIE HOFMANN

FRENCH NOVEL

You were my second lover.
You had dark eyes and hair,
like a painting of a man.
We lay on our stomachs reading books in your bed.
I e-mailed my professor. I will be absent
from French Novel due to sickness. You put on
some piano music. Even though
it was winter, we had to keep
the window open day and night, the room was so hot, the air so dry
it made our noses bleed.
With boots we trekked through slush for a bottle of red wine
we weren't allowed to buy, our shirts unbuttoned
under our winter coats.

The French language distinguishes
between the second
of two and the second
of many. Of course
we'd have other lovers. Snow fell in our hair.
You were my second lover.
Another way of saying this:
you were the other,
not another.

SAFIYA SINCLAIR

GOSPEL OF THE MISUNDERSTOOD

I want to be the blade striking
        knotted brown, to kiss the nape of any hunger;
American beautyberry or rutted cane, warm branch
        of man pinning me here in mute study. To be an ache
in the breast of a burst jelly is what I wanted, vine-slick
        and torrid in summer's greed, pressing my fears against
the light of the lonely. Nameless, I haunt for god and love
        in extinct places, curve myself inside desire's eye and drink.
All peeled vermillion, all caught promise. Again all-seeing, and finally.
        To be seen. Is what I wanted. To trawl the sleep of his body.
To make a burning room of this mouth. Skinned eager
        with spiderbite and holy. Split-pink, drunken. Choked quiet,
as life unfolds its sticky wings in me. Snuffing me sweetly.

Isn't this love? To walk hand in hand toward the humid dark,
        enter the ghost web of the hungry, to consider some wants
were not meant to be understood. Some women.
        The way my brother prays I'll still find a man to divine me,
and my father tells me lazy women will never be loved.
        Like today's new trumpet pushing its bright flower
in my slutty way. The slow voice of its angel hissing breathless:
        No. He is not here. He is not here. He is nowhere.

DEREK WALCOTT

THE BOUNTY III

It depends on how you look at the cream house on the cliff
with the rusted roof and a stunted bell tower in the garden
off the road edged with white hard lilies, it could seem sad if
you were from another country, and your faith did not harden
into pity for the priest in boots and muddy clothes who comes
from a county in Ireland you think you remember, where you felt
perhaps the same sadness for a stone chapel and low walls
heavy with time, an iron sea, and the history of the Celt
told in an earlier time with bagpipes and drums
turned into a Catholic station, a peaked, brown vestry
and a bleating lamb in the grass. So the visitor believes
the rusted trunk in the shade of large almond leaves.
On a Saturday, shut, and a temperate sky, Blanchisseuse
closed and an elsewhere-remembering sea,
you, too, could succumb to a helpless shrug that says,
"God! the sad magic that is the hope of black people!"
All the drumming and dancing, the ceremonies, the chants.
The chantwell screeching like a brass cock on a steeple.
The intricate, unlit labyrinth of their ignorance.
Or walk out to a gray sea no stranger than Ireland's
to be swept by a peace not even the wind understands.

E. E. CUMMINGS

WHO ARE YOU, LITTLE I

who are you, little i

(five or six years old)
peering from some high

window; at the gold

of november sunset

(and feeling: that if day
has to become night

this is a beautiful way)

SARA LUDLOW HOLMES
DOG AT DUSK

Down the roadway, rutted, dusty,
Lolly takes her evening run;
Enters tall grass, ripened, rusty,
Misty pink with after-sun.

Cool beneath the bridge's timber,
Where I follow Lolly by,
Swims the dark trout, wary, limber;
Hangs in cloud the short-lived fly.

All about in quiet rises,
While I wait for Lolly there,
Spring of ground-green-scent surprises,
Mingling with the day-left air.

By the bobbing where she passes
I can guess where Lolly goes,
Lost to view in lush, lit grasses.
I can guess at what she knows.

GALWAY KINNELL
ASTONISHMENT

Oarlocks knock in the dusk, a rowboat rises
and settles, surges and slides.
Under a great eucalyptus,
a boy and girl feel around with their feet
for those small flattish stones so perfect
for scudding across the water.

A dog barks from deep in the silence.
A woodpecker, double-knocking,
keeps time. I have slept in so many arms.
Consolation? Probably. But too much
consolation may leave one inconsolable.

       •

The water before us has hardly moved
except in the shallowest breathing places.
For us back then, to live seemed almost to die.
One day a darkness fell between her and me.
When we woke, a hawthorn sprig
stood in the water glass at our bedside.

       •

There is a silence in the beginning.
The life within us grows quiet.
There is little fear. No matter
how all this comes out, from now on
it cannot not exist ever again.
We liked talking our nights away
in words close to the natural language,
which most other animals can still speak.

       •

The present pushes back the life of regret.
It draws forward the life of desire. Soon memory
will have started sticking itself all over us.
We were fashioned from clay in a hurry,
poor throwing may mean it didn't matter
to the makers if their pots cracked.

       •

On the mountain tonight the full moon
faces the full sun. Now could be the moment
when we fall apart or we become whole.
Our time seems to be up—I think I even hear it stopping.
Then why have we kept up the singing for so long?
Because that's the sort of determined creature we are.
Before us, our first task is to astonish,
and then, harder by far, to be astonished.

THE EIGHTIES

GARRETT HONGO

YELLOW LIGHT

One arm hooked around the frayed strap
of a tar-black patent-leather purse,
the other cradling something for dinner—
fresh bunches of spinach from a J-Town *yaoya*,
sides of split Spanish mackerel from Alviso's,
maybe a loaf of Langendorf—she steps
off the hissing bus at Olympic and Fig,
begins the three-block climb up the hill,
passing gangs of schoolboys playing war,
Japs against Japs, Chicanas chalking sidewalks
with the holy double-yoked crosses of hopscotch,
and the Korean grocer's wife out for a stroll
around this neighborhood of Hawaiian apartments
just starting to steam with cooking
and the anger of young couples coming home
from work, yelling at kids, flicking on
TV sets for the Wednesday Night Fights.

If it were May, hydrangeas and jacaranda
flowers in the streetside trees would be
blooming through the smog of late spring.
Wisteria in Masuda's front yard would be
shaking out the long tresses of its purple hair.
Maybe mosquitoes, moths, a few orange butterflies
settling on the lattice of monkey flowers
tangled in chain-link fences by the trash.

But this is October, and Los Angeles
seethes like a billboard under twilight.

From used-car lots and the movie houses uptown
long silver sticks of light probe the sky.
From the Miracle Mile, whole freeways away,
a brilliant fluorescence breaks out

and makes war with the dim squares
of yellow kitchen light winking on
in all the side streets of the Barrio.

She climbs up the two flights of flagstone
stairs to 201-B, the spikes of her high heels
clicking like kitchen knives on a cutting board,
props the groceries against the door,
fishes through memo pads, a compact,
empty packs of chewing gum, and finds her keys.

The moon then, cruising from behind
a screen of eucalyptus across the street,
covers everything, everything in sight,
in a heavy light like yellow onions.

MAUREEN HOWARD

PLAGIARISM

(For My Students in Writing 210)

On the arched bridge by the library
   he will come to me in mist.
Just as I am walking to class he will come,
   your steady boyfriend.
Choose morning mist or evening haze,
   but I will have him appear bit by bit,
   clear brow, heroic jaw, the sullen smile.
The blue eyes go. The build is frail now,
   romantic in my way, and I have given him a lisp.
Propped on his cane, he flirts with me—
   Claude Armande Count Amboy.
I have given him a mustache and a cough.
On the arched bridge over the Seine,
   he betrays you, your steady boyfriend.

I appropriate your mother gladly, from the prison of her home.
Woman without past or future, malingering in her bathrobe,
    on the phone.
I give her a blue suit and a big career.
She sits in a restaurant dealing with important men.
I will take pounds off her hips, the scales from her eyes.
At home in New Jersey, she waters the plants,
    though she is never to think of carpets or the tub.
All morning she eats mung beans with honey while you sleep.
Your mother is from Havana.
    I love the way she dances.
Your mother is from Trieste.
    The way she reads Italian is a dream.
I take your mother in her middle age,
    her record of miscarriages, her general good health,
    her memories of high school in Montclair.
She is burning her bathrobe.
She is buying lettuce, picking out a peach.
I place her on this kitchen chair so that she may speak.

Keep the endings.
I cannot use murder, abortion, rape,
    the disorder of your dormitory room.
I am too old to force violence or despair.
The course goes on:
Your lover comes back on the Turnpike.
Your mother is brushing her hair.

DENIS JOHNSON

THE MONK'S INSOMNIA

The monastery is quiet; Seconal
drifts down upon it from the moon.
I can see the lights
of the city I came from,
can remember how a boy sets out

like something thrown from the furnace
of a star. In the conflagration of memory
my people sit on green benches in the park,
terrified, evil, broken by love—
to sit with them inside that invisible fire
of hours day after day while the shadow of the milk
billboard crawled across the street
seemed impossible, but how
was it different from here,
where they have one day they play over
and over as if they think
it is our favorite, and we stay
for our natural lives,
a phrase that conjures up the sun's
dark ash adrift after ten billion years
of unconsolable burning? Brother Thomas's
schoolgirl obsession with the cheap
doings of TV starlets breaks
everybody's heart, and the yellow sap
of one particular race of cactus grows
tragic for the fascination in which
it imprisons Brother Toby—I can't witness
his slavering and relating how it can be changed
into some unprecedented kind of plastic—
and the monastery
refuses to say where it is taking us.
At night we hear the trainers from the base
down there, and see them blotting out the stars,
and I stand on the hill and listen, bone-white with desire.
It was love that set me on the journey,
love that called me home. But it's the terror
of being just one person—one chance, one set of days—
that keeps me absolutely still tonight and makes me listen
intently to those young men above us
flying in their airplanes in the dark.

ABRAHAM SUTZKEVER

PRAYER FOR A SICK FRIEND

The wicked have too much power,
it would be enough for them to have the strength of rabbits.
Feed the weak one with mercy,
for here he lies: half man, half bedsheet.

I'm his prayer. His lips
have already lost the words.
They're despoiled seashells
without echo, without salt, without pearls.

He still needs to light up a sentence
in the temple of his dark burrow.
He must accompany the young
queen of the bees to her be-starred dawn.

I've seen a fish leap
from the sea-heart to the clouds
and carry the clouds with him—
is my friend less than a fish?

Instead of little red circles
in his veins, red fiddles
are swimming, mastered by you—
no one else can play them.

He must still hear how his pulse
is spring-rain running in his body.
He must still sip dreams, keep faith,
and—in late fall—putty the windows.

(Translated, from the Yiddish, by Ruth Whitman.)

JAMES WRIGHT

YES, BUT

Even if it were true,
Even if I were dead and buried in Verona,
I believe I would come out and wash my face
In the chill spring.
I believe I would appear
Between noon and four, when nearly
Everybody else is asleep or making love,
And all the Germans turned down, the motorcycles
Muffled, chained, still.

Then the plump lizards along the Adige by San Giorgio
Come out and gaze,
Unpestered by temptation, across the water.
I would sit among them and join them in leaving
The golden mosquitoes alone.
Why should we sit by the Adige and destroy
Anything, even our enemies, even the prey
God caused to glitter for us
Defenseless in the sun?
We are not exhausted. We are not angry, or lonely,
Or sick at heart.
We are in love lightly, lightly. We know we are shining,
Though we cannot see one another.
The wind doesn't scatter us,
Because our very lungs have fallen and drifted
Away like leaves down the Adige,
Long ago.

We breathe light.

JACQUELINE OSHEROW

LOOKING FOR ANGELS IN NEW YORK

All this travelling around and I've learned
Nothing less obvious than this: that each
Piece of the world has something missing.
Home again, I have forgotten the stops of the trains,
My friends' phone numbers. I haven't even the heart
To take the maps out, to say, "Here I have been,
Here and here." I want to explain that there
Can be no adequate descriptions, but you will think
I mean the differences are insurmountable,
When it is this vast sameness over everything
I cannot name, the thing you wait for
And do not believe in when it's come and gone,
The words that will not stand still
Long enough for you to take a picture.

My friend asks questions and I answer.
He says he read the Metropolitan Life
Building is based on something Italian.
I look at it and shrug. "Not that I know."
And then I see the campanile of San Marco,
Squat, granite, white instead of red.
It will become my personal comfort
In the skyline, one of those public things
You have no right to but you say you own.

If Jacob had rested in New York, he
Would have seen angels on elevators,
And St. Mark, though an insurance salesman,
Would certainly have witnessed miracles.

I don't necessarily have to see
An angel, I just want to see some wings,
Even a flash of them, gliding, moving
Up and out, a balloon some child

Has let go of, smaller and smaller in
The sky, only wings, definite, white wings.

From the No. 7 train out to Queens,
A chance glimpse of the Unisphere brings
The future in its purest form, the whole
World connected by picture telephones
And cars that look like earthbound rocketships.
Odd that they should have left the silver globe
Still standing there, now the children it was
Built for have all grown. The space between the
Continents seems eerie now, foreboding,
And the dazzling modern sculpture weirdly
Archaic, almost shocking, like the face
Of a great movie star no longer young.

Who would have thought that people would reject
The picture telephone, the moving sidewalk,
That I would come home from all my travels
To New Jersey, to settle for a bit
Of quiet and some green, and the moment
On the hill before the Lincoln Tunnel
When I really do possess something extraordinary.
Loyal, I pick out my Metropolitan Life,
At night drenched in a white light almost blue.
Who can know that by day it is not brick
And red and surrounded by a great piazza
Opening on water, that, in the huge
White space we cannot see, there is no thick
Flock of cooing pigeons, taking off, alighting,
In a constant, dreamy fluttering of wings.

NICHOLAS CHRISTOPHER

WALT WHITMAN AT THE REBURIAL OF POE

. . . of the poets invited only Walt Whitman attended.

—Julian Symons.

They got him in the end, of course.
In a polling booth, dead-drunk.
Vagrant, ballot-stuffer . . .
Four Baltimore coppers to carry that meagre frame.
Our first detective of the broken heart,
he picked through its rubble
with his frenzied calculations,
his delirium of over-clarity,
until he found too many clues . . .
Once I dreamt of a man on a schooner,
compact and handsome, alone on the Sound,
thrilling to a violent storm,
threaded to this world by the silver
of a dying spider:
that man was Edgar.
He loved the moon, and the night torch,
the notion of blood sea-temperatured,
of the cold rush impelling him . . .
In life, in poetry, my antithesis:
detached from the true life,
of rivers and birds and swaying trees,
of soil red with tubers and pregnant clay,
detached from the wondrous release of sex,
his spleen beating heavier than his heart—
two or three men (at least)
packed in among a dozen demons.
He never much cared for my work.
I admired only a fraction of his.
But I happened to be in Washington
last night . . . and I'm old now, half wise,
too old not to have a sixth sense—
for the genuine article, anyway . . .
I marvel at all he accomplished

in such a hatcheted life,
electrifying his losses,
celebrating the deer park, the potter's field,
as I celebrated forest and plain . . .
But then to finish here,
another half-forgotten city,
wearing another man's rags—
a scene he might have written:
streets snaking around him,
steaming and sulphurous,
rain dirty as it left the sky—
one last maze before the foothills of hell . . .
And that polling booth . . .
the drinking pals who dumped him there,
frightened perhaps by that dying wolf's voice;
it strikes me now, the eulogies concluded
(I wouldn't give one and I wouldn't say why),
how appropriate he should go that way,
how perversely American in the end—
a man who had consumed himself with exotica,
green as the Republic itself,
poet of our bloodied ankles and ashen
bones, our cankers and lurid dreams:
I wonder who he voted for.
I wonder if he won.

ANDREW HUDGINS

AWAITING WINTER VISITORS: JONATHAN EDWARDS, 1749

When thunder fell in Tinsley's pasture
we recognized a sign from Heaven.
From that day on we have rejoiced
that God has not forsaken us:
A blast upon the wavering wheat
is God's lean son walking ghost-

colored through our bodies, saying
Yours is a famine of the soul.

On my advice the congregation met
six nights a week to pray and sing,
to burn the bushel off our flame,
Beneath a tired December sky
we looked for a descending light
to radiate from New England shores
to the almost mythic cusp of Asia.

Instead, the signs would not form
a prophecy. Attendance fell;
the fervor would not hold its bloom.
In March, hens in the cemetery
pecked up the younger Perkins boy,
who died the winter past.
And yesterday the family cat

ate a poison spider, sickened, died.
I shall miss Joshua. Asleep on my lap
while I composed sermons, he'd purr
like a bit of Satan almost controlled.
At home Sarah's held to the hard faith.
We've supped on vegetables and bones,
but mostly bones, those old friends

returning from other, more fleshy stews.
It built, it built to no climax
then passed to spring—with dandelions
and little purple weeds: the white
fields laced with merciless speedwell.
I shall retire and read St. Paul,
who called the human corpse a seed.

PATRICIA HAMPL

SUMMER SUBLET

All summer those books in a row,
at the window across the way, leaning
against each other like guys standing at a bar.
I'll remember that, how aimless books seemed.
And why read one? Just let them be
together, touching, at a window.
Everything arrives in its own way,
even China on the sweetish spume
of the restaurant ventilator—
even China arrives, and the first law
of the species, handed down
through the neon arteries, red and hot:
EAT EAT.

IRA SADOFF

AUTUMN ELEGY FOR THE GIANTS

For those of us who remember
the Alley at Coogan's Bluff,
the famous overhead catch, the home run
that left the Dodgers stunned
in '51, for those who can't forget
the dream outfield they gave away—
as if God asked for charity
from the poor—the present
seems a tiny scar above the eye
that hurts in the humidity,
that no one notices,
that gives us character
when character's not required.

How did it get there? The child
in us remembers. We recall the hour

and the day of every error,
the way we remember Willie's number,
the way we still wonder
how Joey Amalfitano
had even one good day.

So today, as we wrap ourselves
in the chilled and foggy air
of another era, another park,
it shouldn't bother us,
the complacent and the aging,
the newly lost, to watch
the hitless, to count the empty seats.
We think ourselves beyond defeat.

But each seat radiates
its ghostly presence: the fan
who gave it up for alcohol,
for TV, for the daily stroll
through Golden Gate Park,
where he hoped to be mugged. It hurts
like history, the way pleasure fades
so quickly—like the double play
that cut short a possibly wonderful inning.
It hurts like the strike they should have swung at
thirty years ago in a ballpark in Manhattan,
where thousands gather in their apartments now
not watching the Giants, enjoying themselves.

A. R. AMMONS

DAY GHOSTS

Spring thaw peels loose
the leaves snow caught
last fall before they
had really settled down:

now, windy Sunday, they
stir over dry lawn
and remnant windrows of
ice, as if looking

for the place they'd meant
to go: but it's not now
as it was then
settling-down time, and

everywhere the leaves go
greens are
breaking out
amid the funeral arrangements

and the eyes of jonquils
hold on to their morning
tears and demure snowdrops
try not to look so bright.

CHARLES SIMIC
RURAL DELIVERY

I never thought we'd end up
This far north, love.
Cold blue tinge in lieu of heavens.
Quarter moon like chalk on a slate.

This week it's subtraction
And the art of erasure we study.
Oh, the many blanks to ponder
Before the arctic night overtakes us
One more time on this lonely stretch of road
Unplowed since morning,
Snow mittens raised against the sudden
Blinding gust of wind,

But the mailbox empty.
I had to stick my bare hand
All the way to nothing and no one
To make absolutely sure
This is where we live.

The wonder of it! It seemed
We retraced our footsteps homeward
Lit up by the same fuel as the snow
Glinting in the gloom
Of the early nightfall.

VICKIE KARP

STILL-LIFE IN THE COAT-FACTORY OFFICE

   What did you think would happen
When you got on that pale boat and

Came to America, came here to Essex Street,
Where the vibrant machinery of your heart

Is rustic compared to the hiss and boom
Of this captainless ship?

   You speak to women you've never met
On the telephone, voices full of curls

And twangs thickened by the borderless
Hallucinations of long-distance wires.

Their laughter clicks and drones until
The women themselves become nothing

But another machine you've learned how to run,
A switchboard for the bodiless voices of Georgia.

In the beginning, they squealed at
Your accent and you clucked at theirs.

You've made up a game about it—you
Pretend it's all French and elegant as lace.

A still-life of the Café de la Paix
Hangs by one nail behind the Big Boss's desk.

In the perpetual rain, a woman sits
By a green table and stares at her leg.

She doesn't see the broad-chested waiter
Under the awning, but you do . . .

His face is a lunacy of fixed points
Painstakingly arranged in the name of art.

He's been looking straight at you for years,
Waiting to take your order.

AMY CLAMPITT

WHAT THE LIGHT WAS LIKE

Every year in June—up here, that's the month for lilacs—
        almost his whole front yard,
with lobster traps stacked out in back atop the rise
        that overlooks the inlet,
would be a Himalayan range of peaks of bloom,
        white and mauve-violet,

gusting a turbulence of perfume, and every year the same
        iridescent hummingbird,
or its descendant, would be at work among the mourning
        cloaks and swallowtails, its motor loud,

its burning gorget darkening at moments as though charred.
        He kept an eye out

for it, we learned one night, as for everything that flapped
        or hopped or hovered
crepuscular under the firs; he'd heard the legendary
        trilling of the woodcock,
and watched the eiders, once rare along these coasts,
        making their comeback,

so that now they're everywhere, in tribes, in families
        of aunts and cousins,
a knit-and-purl of irresistibly downy young behind them,
        riding every cove and inlet;
and yes, in answer to the question summer people always ask,
        he'd seen the puffins

that breed out on 'Tit Manan in summer, improbably
        clown-faced behind the striped scarlet
of commedia dell'arte masks we'll never see except in
        Roger Tory Peterson's
field guide, or childish wishful thinking. There was much
        else I meant to ask about

another summer. But in June, when we came limping up here
        again, looking forward
to easing up from a mean, hard, unaccommodating winter,
        we heard how he'd gone out
at dawn one morning in October, unmoored the dinghy,
        and rowed to his boat,

as usual (the harbor already chugging with half a dozen
        neighbors' revved-up craft,
wet decks stacked abaft with traps, the bait and kegs stowed
        forward, a lifting weft
of fog spooled off in pearl-pink fleeces overhead with the first
        daylight), and steered,

as usual, past first the inner and then the outer bar, where in
         whatever kind of weather
the red reef-bell yells, in its interminable treble, *Trouble*,
         out past where the Groaner
lolls, its tempo and forte changing with the chop, played on
         by every wind shift,

straight into the sunrise, a surge of burning turning the
         whole ocean iridescent
fool's gold over molten emerald, into the core of that
         quotidian astonishment—
a clue, one must suppose, to why lobstermen are often
         naturally gracious:

maybe, out there beside the wheel, the Baptist spire
         shrunk to a compass
point, the town an interrupted circlet, feeble as an
         apron string, for all the labor
it took to put it there, it's finding, out in that ungirdled
         wallowing and glitter,

finally, that what you love most is the same as what
         you're most afraid of—God,
in a word; whereas it seems they think they've got it
         licked (or used to) back there
in the Restricted Area, for instance, where that huge
         hush-hush thing they say is radar

sits sprawling on the heath like Stonehenge, belittling
         every other man-made thing
in view, even the gargantuan pods of the new boat
         hulls you now and then see lying
stark naked, crimson on the inside as a just-skinned
         carcass, in Young's boatyard,

even the gray Grange Hall, wood-heated by a yardarm
         of stovepipe across the ceiling.

Out there, from that wallowing perspective, all
           comparisons amount to nothing,
though once you've hauled your last trap, things tend
           to wander into shorter focus

as, around noon, you head back in: first 'Tit Manan
           lighthouse, a ghostly gimlet
on its ledge by day, but on clear nights expanding to a
           shout, to starboard,
the sunstruck rock pile of Cranberry Point to port;
           then you see the hamlet

rainbowed, above the blurring of the spray shield,
           by the hurrying herring gulls'
insatiable fandango of excitement—the spire first, then
           the crimson boat hulls,
the struts of the ill-natured gadget on the heath behind
           them as the face of things expands,

the hide-and-seek behind the velvet-shouldered, sparse
           tree-spined profiles,
as first the outer, then the inner bar appears, then
           the scree-beach under Crowley Island's
crowding firs and spruces, and you detect among
           the chimneys and the TV aerials

yours. But by midafternoon of that October day,
           when all his neighbors'
boats had chugged back through the inlet, his
           was still out; at evening,
with half the town out looking, and a hard frost
           settling in among the alders,

there'd been no sign of him. The next day, and
           the next, the search went on,
and widened, joined by planes and helicopters from as
           far away as Boston.

When, on the third day, his craft was sighted
        finally, it had drifted,

with its engine running, till the last gulp of fuel
        spluttered and ran out,
beyond the town's own speckled noose of buoys, past
        the furred crest of Schoodic,
vivid in a skirt of aspens, the boglands cranberry-
        crimson at its foot,

past the bald brow the sunrise always strikes first, of
        the hulk of Cadillac,
riding the current effortlessly as eiders tied to water
        by the summer molt,
for fifty miles southwestward to where, off Matinicus,
        out past the rock

that, like 'Tit Manan, is a restricted area, off limits
        for all purposes but puffins',
they spotted him, slumped against the kegs. I find it
        tempting to imagine what,
when the blood roared, overflowing its cerebral sluiceway,
        and the iridescence

of his last perception, charring, gave way to unreversed,
        irrevocable dark,
the light out there was like that's always shifting—from
        a nimbus gone berserk
to a single gorget, a cathedral train of blinking, or
        the fogbound shroud

that can turn anywhere into a nowhere. But it's useless.
        Among the mourning-cloak-
hovered-over lilac peaks, their whites and purples,
        when we pass his yard,
poignant to excess with fragrance, this year we haven't
        seen the hummingbird.

THE KINGFISHER

In a year the nightingales were said to be so loud
they drowned out slumber, and peafowl strolled screaming
beside the ruined nunnery, through the long evening
of a dazzled pub crawl, the halcyon color, portholed
by those eye-spots' stunning tapestry, unsettled
the pastoral nightfall with amazements opening.

Months later, intermission in a pub on Fifty-fifth Street
found one of them still breathless, the other quizzical,
acting the philistine, puncturing Stravinsky—"Tell
me, what *was* that racket in the orchestra about?"—
hauling down the Firebird, harum-scarum, like a kite,
a burnished, breathing wreck that didn't hurt at all.

Among the Bronx Zoo's exiled jungle fowl, they heard
through headphones of a separating panic the bellbird
reiterate its single *chong*, a scream nobody answered.
When he mourned, "The poetry is gone," she quailed,
seeing how his hands shook, sobered into feeling old.
By midnight, yet another fifth would have been killed.

A Sunday morning, the November of their cataclysm
(Dylan Thomas brought in *in extremis* to St. Vincent's
that same week, a symptomatic datum) found them
wandering a downtown churchyard. Among its headstones,
while from unruined choirs the noise of Christendom
poured over Wall Street, a benison in vestments,

a late thrush paused, in transit from some grizzled
spruce bog to the humid equatorial fireside: berry-
eyed, bark-brown above, with dark hints of trauma
in the stigmata of its underparts—or so, too bruised
just then to have invented anything so fancy,
later, reëmbroidering a retrospect, she had supposed.

In gray England, years of muted recrimination (then
dead silence) later, she could not have said how many

spoiled takeoffs, how many entanglements gone sodden,
how many gaudy evenings made frantic by just one
insomniac nightingale, how many liaisons gone down
screaming in a stroll beside the ruined nunnery;

a kingfisher's burnished plunge, the color
of felicity afire, came glancing like an arrow
through landscapes of untended memory—ardor
illuminating with its terrifying currency
now no mere glimpse, no porthole vista
but, down on down, the uninhabitable sorrow.

MAN FEEDING PIGEONS

It was the form of the thing, the unmanaged
symmetry of it, of whatever it was
he convoked as he knelt on the sidewalk
and laid out from his unfastened briefcase
a benefaction of breadcrumbs—this band

arriving of the unhoused and opportune
we have always with us, composing
as they fed, heads together, wing tip
and tail edge serrated like chicory
(that heavenly weed, that cerulean

commoner of waste places) but with a
glimmer in it, as though the winged
beings of all the mosaics of Ravenna
had gotten the message somehow and come
flying in to rejoin the living: plump-

contoured as the pomegranates and pears
in a Della Robbia holiday wreath that had
put on the bloom, once again, of the soon
to perish, to begin to decay, to reënter
that dance of freewheeling dervishes,

the breakdown of order: it was the form
of the thing, if a thing is what it was,
and not the merest wisp of a part of
a process—this unravelling inkling
of the envisioned, of states of being

past alteration, of all that we've
never quite imagined except by way of
the body: the winged proclamations,
the wheeling, the stairways, the
vast, concentric, paradisal rose.

CARLOS DRUMMOND DE ANDRADE

AN OX LOOKS AT MAN

They are more delicate even than shrubs and they run
and run from one side to the other, always forgetting
something. Surely they lack I don't know what
basic ingredient, though they present themselves
as noble or serious, at times. Oh, terribly serious,
even tragic. Poor things, one would say that they hear
neither the song of air nor the secrets of hay;
likewise they seem not to see what is visible
and common to each of us, in space. And they are sad,
and in the wake of sadness they come to cruelty.
All their expression lives in their eyes—and loses itself
to a simple lowering of lids, to a shadow.
And since there is little of the mountain about them—
nothing in the hair or in the terribly fragile limbs
but coldness and secrecy—it is impossible for them
to settle themselves into forms that are calm, lasting,
and necessary. They have, perhaps, a kind
of melancholy grace (one minute) and with this they allow
themselves to forget the problems and translucent
inner emptiness that make them so poor and so lacking

when it comes to uttering silly and painful sounds: desire, love,
    jealousy
(what do we know?)—sounds that scatter and fall in the field
like troubled stones and burn the herbs and the water,
and after this it is hard to keep chewing away at our truth.

(Translated, from the Portuguese, by Mark Strand.)

SHEROD SANTOS
THE DAIRY COWS OF MARÍA CRISTINA CORTÉS

Although they may be
the most mothering of all the animals,
the ones with the gentlest
complaint, the ones whose milk
has left on our tongues
the knowledge that life can be simple
and good, still,

in their pendulous,
earthbound, solitary ways, they remind me
of nothing quite so much
as those people we become after
the houselights rise
on a movie that finds us wiping back
a tear. And since

sadness, however
privately borne, secreted however far inside,
is a thing that finally
weighs us down, they are also
the ones most likely
in the end to inherit the earth; so wherever
they go, wandering

the mud lanes out
from the dairy, or wading into grasses
at a pond's edge, they
move the way a slow-forming storm
cloud moves, gathering
within it a heaviness drawn from deep
in the soil,

a heaviness it will
return there. And yet a cow jumped over
the moon, we're told, and
what in the world has ever been
more filled with light
than a glass of milk placed by the bed
of a child still struggling

from a nightmare?
But whatever it is we say about the cow,
it's the face we love,
a face that, in spite of what we do
with our fences and barbs
and electrically charged cattle prods,
shines equally on us

and on the grasses
of the world; and shines in a way that makes
us feel forgiven after all
for forgetting we, too, are animals—base-
born, landlocked, spattered
with mud, and filled with an ancient cow-
sorrow and -wonder.

CAROLYN KIZER

THE UNBELIEVERS

At first it was only a trickle
Of eminent men, with their astrolabes and armillae,
Who passed cautious notes to each other, obscurely worded.
Of course, the terrible news leaked out
And the peasants were agitated.
Moans arose from the windowless hovels.
Men, hardly human, shouldering crude farm implements,
Gathered in knots along the roads, and raved:
Storm the great houses! Smash the laboratory!
The retorts, the lenses—instruments of Satan.
But the minions of the manors
Lashed them back from the bronze gates,
Back to the fetid darkness, where they scoured their knees,
Praying for us.

The magnificent correspondence between Madame A.
And the more eminent, though less notorious,
Monsieur B. reveals a breathtaking indifference
To You—not even the target of a bilious epigram.
They move intently toward their prime concern:
Which voice, this time, will loose
Its thunderbolt? The straggling troops of revolution
Must be rallied yet again.
In perfect confidence of their powers,
As if they, who after all are people of flesh and bone
Despite their attainments, had replaced You,
Not by storming the throne room, or by those manifestos
They so supremely compose.
You were swept out, and they swept in, that's all.

Out there, on the edge of the familiar world,
Are knots of men burned dark as our own peasants
Used to be but better armed. We know;
We armed them.

From time to time they bang their heads on the sand,
And shout, unintelligibly, of You.
Their version of You, of course, quite different
From the blandness You metamorphosed into
Over the centuries, progressively edited.
Holy war! Can they be in earnest?
After all, this isn't the fourteenth century.
Is it the uneasiness we feel, or the remnants
Of ancestral superstition, which makes us ask ourselves,
Can this be Your planned revenge?

How can You be vengeful when You don't exist?
If only the weight of centuries
Wasn't on Your side.
If only unbelief was more like faith.

LAWRENCE RAAB

WHAT WE DON'T KNOW ABOUT EACH OTHER

In the next room my youngest daughter
is practicing the piano. I don't know why
that halting scale has made me think
of writing to you, after so many years.
Isn't it always the weather one begins with?
Here there is still a little color left,
the bronze of the oaks, pale yellows
of the lesser trees. Three or four
warm days in October are what we believe
we're entitled to, but that turned into a week,
then another, until we felt blessed
and disconcerted. Today the children and I
discovered a small patch of ice
and we were excited to have found it,
bright and brittle, full of shapes.
I walked them out to the bus stop;

they ran on ahead, and back to me.
It was one of those mornings
when you feel the season change, and you think
tomorrow you'll have it again
even more keenly. I remembered others.
I thought of how, looking a long way back,
I expect always to uncover some personal design
in everything. And so it's there,
by chance, by mistake, by necessity.
All the moments that might have gone differently
become the scraps of stories I run through
while falling asleep, so similar
in their melancholy heroism, their few
predictable cruelties. For all I know
you may have given up thinking about me.
For all you know I may have died,
a sudden, tragic illness, or perhaps
the time my car spun out of control on the ice.
What they say is true—everything slows down
to a long arc, and though you do the right
or the wrong thing with the wheel, whichever
way you're supposed to turn it, the car
goes on as if you'd been abandoned, or released.
So there was an odd disappointment
plowing into that snowbank, the snap
of the seat belts telling me I was safe,
then the stupid difficulties of getting out.
Later, I could afford to be afraid,
when it didn't matter. Then I just stood there,
looking around me at the fields
and a small grove of pine trees
where snow was sliding off the heavy branches
very quietly and very slowly. That whole scene
was so sharp and certain, so *new*, I thought
I should feel as if I'd been given a second life.
Then would I decide to write to you,
hoping to explain how often I'd wished this

or that day had gone differently, and you or I
had spoken as we never did?
Now she's moved on to a song, "Waltz"
or "The Three Boatmen." You'd laugh
to think it was a song at all,
but inside those stiff, hesitant repetitions
I can hear the melody she's after. What we know
or don't know about each other—it doesn't matter,
except that I've moved beyond these careful inventions,
beyond the glittery trash and souvenirs of memory.
And that young woman you saw this morning
hurrying out of the library, fastening her coat,
looked like me only for a moment. There was
ice on the pathway, the sweet possibility
of snow in the air, all of the necessary
appearances of change—and yet the life
you've taken up to make this letter
could not be my life, just as this voice
was never mine, nor even yours.

MOLLY PEACOCK

A GESTURE

Something kind done, something kind said
in spite of everything done and said, in spite
of a soreness of mind, is like being led
to a lawn edged with trees in partial light
where a cloth is spread out for a picnic
—or is it a towel? This is not a picture
but, surprised by sun, put together quick,
a meal of invention startled by nature
into being at all—a startled meal,
arrested on a beach towel, drumsticks,
a half-gone litre of wine: a gift of the real,
an imperfect, conscious attempt to fix
something wrong with something kind, beautiful

because the ragged haste of the gesture is full
of half-creation and suddenly wanting
to do something, since something was wanting.

JOSEPH BRODSKY
A SONG

I wish you were here, dear,
I wish you were here.
I wish you sat on the sofa
and I sat near.
The handkerchief could be yours,
the tear could be mine, chin-bound.
Though it could be, of course,
the other way around.

I wish you were here, dear,
I wish you were here.
I wish we were in my car,
and you'd shift the gear.
We'd find ourselves elsewhere,
on an unknown shore.
Or else we'd repair
to where we've been before.

I wish you were here, dear,
I wish you were here.
I wish I knew no astronomy
when stars appear,
when the moon skims the water
that sighs and shifts in its slumber.
I wish it were still a quarter
to dial your number.

I wish you were here, dear,
in this hemisphere,

as I sit on the porch
sipping a beer.
It's evening; the sun is setting,
boys shout and gulls are crying.
What's the point of forgetting
if it's followed by dying?

JAMES SCHUYLER

WHITE BOAT, BLUE BOAT

Two boats parked
and posing in
the sunstruck
winter landscape:
rough grass, bare
with green washes.
Against self-colored
bark, lithe twigs
end in red buds:
you can't see it,
the red, and when
you do, you can't
not see it, against
a scaling trunk that,
higher than three
men on each
other's shoulders,
becomes more trunks.
Beyond, marsh grass
and reeds scratched
swiftly in.
A woman goes by,
her dog, too,
in short lopes:
a mutt. The day
can't get brighter,

clearer, but it
brightens, brightens,
so much and so
much more under
infinite cloudlessness
and icy spaces
and endless mystery.

DEREK WALCOTT

THE SEASON OF PHANTASMAL PEACE

Then all the nations of birds lifted together
the huge net of the shadows of this earth
in multitudinous dialects, twittering tongues,
stitching and crossing it. They lifted up
the shadows of long pines down trackless slopes,
the shadows of glass-faced towers down evening streets,
the shadow of a frail plant on a city sill—
the net rising soundless as night, the birds' cries soundless, until
there was no longer dusk, or season, decline, or weather,
only this passage of phantasmal light
that not the narrowest shadow dared to sever.

And men could not see, looking up, what the wild geese drew,
what the ospreys trailed behind them in silvery ropes
that flashed in the icy sunlight; they could not hear
battalions of starlings waging peaceful cries,
bearing the net higher, covering this world
like the vines of an orchard, or a mother drawing
the trembling gauze over the trembling eyes
of a child fluttering to sleep;
                                  it was the light
that you will see at evening on the side of a hill
in quiet October, and no one hearing knew
what change had brought into the raven's cawing,
the killdeer's screech, the ember-circling chough

such an immense, soundless, and high concern
for the fields and cities where the birds belong,
except it was their seasonal passing, Love,
made seasonless, or, from the high privilege of their birth,
something brighter than pity for the wingless ones
below them who shared dark holes in windows and in houses,
and higher they lifted the net with soundless voices
above all change, betrayals of falling suns,
and this season lasted one moment, like the pause
between dusk and darkness, between fury and peace,
but, for such as our earth is now, it lasted long.

STEPHEN DOBYNS

THE DELICATE, PLUMMETING BODIES

A great cry went up from the stockyards and
slaughterhouses, and Death, tired of complaint
and constant abuse, withdrew to his underground garage.
He was still young and his work was a torment.
All over, their power cut, people stalled like streetcars.
Their gravity taken away, they began to float.
Without buoyancy, they began to sink. Each person
became a single darkened room. The small hand
pressed firmly against the small of their backs
was suddenly gone and people swirled to a halt
like petals fallen from a flower. Why hurry?
Why get out of bed? People got off subways,
on subways, off subways, all at the same stop.
Everywhere clocks languished in antique shops
as their hands composed themselves in sleep.
Without time and decay, people grew less beautiful.
They stopped eating and began to study their feet.
They stopped sleeping and spent weeks following stray dogs.
The first to react were remnants of the church.
They falsified miracles, displayed priests posing
as corpses until finally they sneezed or grew lonely.

Then governments called special elections to choose those
to join the ranks of the volunteer dead—unhappy people
forced to sit in straight chairs for weeks at a time.
Interest soon dwindled. Then the army seized power
and soldiers ran through the street dabbling the living
with red paint. You're dead, they said. Maybe
tomorrow, people answered, today we're just breathing;
look at the sky, look at the color of the grass.
For without Death each color had grown brighter.
At last a committee of businessmen met together,
because with Death gone money had no value.
They went to where Death was waiting in a white room,
and he sat on the floor and looked like a small boy
with pale blond hair and eyes the color of clear water.
In his lap was a red ball heavy with the absence of life.
The businessmen flattered him. We will make you king,
they said. I am king already, Death answered. We will
print your likeness on all the money of the world.
It is there already, Death answered. We adore you
and will not live without you, the businessmen said.
Death said, I will consider your offer.

How Death was restored to his people:

At first the smallest creatures began to die—
bacteria and certain insects. No one noticed. Then fish
began to float to the surface; lizards and tree toads
toppled from sun-warmed rocks. Still no one saw them.
Then birds began tumbling out of the air,
and as sunlight flickered on the blue feathers
of the jay, brown of the hawk, white of the dove,
then people lifted their heads and pointed to the sky
and from the thirsty streets cries of welcome rose up
like a net to catch the delicate and plummeting bodies.

CAROL MUSKE-DUKES

SKID

Where the snow effigies stood
hard-packed and hosed to ice
in front of the frat houses,
in the middle of the little bridge
over the stopped river,
my leased car spun three times

before the chainless tires caught.
Each time round I saw a face:
the man who imagined he loved me,
the woman who confided in me,
the child who cried "No" upon meeting me,
as if he saw at once to what use

we put those vanishing, invented selves.
The slurred tracks, ringed dark
on the outbound path, froze and unfroze
for weeks after the party to celebrate spring.
Down the road, the local museum
considered the Ice Age. The glacier

slid in and out of its lit shape
through a fan of color transparencies,
each ray labelled with an age, a thaw,
the gauged bed of the moraine. Showed how
the ice junk heap hauled the broken shapes
in which we live, cave and gully and flat.

And a further dissolution, part of
a shape we would not recognize for centuries,
like the coins that tumble down the dark slide
to the weighted spar that triggers the mechanism
that lifts the needle to the jukebox disk: "Blue Moon"—
you saw it standing like an atomic field

charged with particles: little "you"s and "me"s,
estranged suddenly from the vanity of their motion,
and the prefigured feel of it, music and moon,
turning full force into its mindless will,
then stopping, my foot on the accelerator.

ELIZABETH MACKLIN
ALL OVER

All of a sudden one year, we seemed to be dying
in droves, in whole or in part. This one lost a breast
as if it were a child. That one's head filled dark to bursting
like a stranger blackjacked, over and over. One simply died.
There were those of us forced to straitjacket maddened color,
or helpless desire. Twelve of us woke up
robbed, in varied ways. All of us watched our breath
blacken the air before us on cold days. All over,
we seemed to be dying.
The eyes of one of our own fell to tatters
and stopped reading, or seeing.
And drunks came down from the bars with their arms flung wide,
calling, *"This way—this way."* And held out their trousers
like children's nightclothes, for us to climb into
and sleep, or cry.

SURFACE TENSION

Desire restrained takes a long, cool bath,
indistinct at first in the blue water.

I make out a line of arm, a half-turned breast;
she slides down, runs the tap again, slides farther.

The bath is rippled porcelain, on cast iron,
with claws. A skylight catches sunlight. The room is bare.

This late-days hour was fired in a dry kiln.
Soap goes taut as boysenberries, around air.

No setting foot yet into the small room:
eyes only. Water any higher could do her harm,

or flood the checkered tiles too far beyond "eureka."
Still, scattered fruit gathers on her raised arm.

MARY OLIVER

WHITE OWL FLIES INTO AND OUT OF THE FIELD

Coming down
out of the freezing sky
with its depths of light,
like an angel,
or a Buddha with wings,
it was beautiful
and accurate,
striking the snow and whatever was there
with a force that left the imprint
of the tips of its wings—
five feet apart—and the grabbing
thrust of its feet,
and the indentation of what had been running
through the white valleys
of the snow—

and then it rose, gracefully,
and flew back to the frozen marshes,
to lurk there,
like a little lighthouse,
in the blue shadows—
so I thought:
maybe death
isn't darkness, after all,
but so much light
wrapping itself around us—

as soft as feathers—
that we are instantly weary
of looking, and looking, and shut our eyes,
not without amazement,
and let ourselves be carried,
as through the translucence of mica,
to the river
that is without the least dapple or shadow,
that is nothing but light—scalding, aortal light—
in which we are washed and washed
out of our bones.

DAVID BOTTOMS

UNDER THE BOATHOUSE

Out of my clothes, I ran past the boathouse
to the edge of the dock
and stood before the naked silence of the lake,
on the drive behind me my wife
rattling keys, calling for help with the grill,
the groceries wedged into the trunk.
Near the tail end of her voice, I sprang
from the homemade board, bent body
like a hinge, and speared the surface,
cut through water I would not open my eyes in,
to hear the junked depth pop in both ears
as my right hand dug into silt and mud,
my left clawed around a pain.
In a fog of rust I opened my eyes to see
what had me, and couldn't, but knew
the fire in my hand and the weight of the thing
holding me under, knew the shock of all
things caught by the unknown
as I kicked off the bottom like a frog,
my limbs doing fearfully strange strokes,

lungs collapsed in a confusion of bubbles,
all air rising back to its element.
I flailed after it, rose toward the bubbles
breaking on light, then felt down my arm
a tug running from a taut line.
Halfway between the bottom of the lake
and the bottom of the sky, I hung like a buoy
on a short rope, an effigy
flown in an underwater parade,
and imagined myself hanging there forever,
a curiosity among fishes, a bait hanging up
instead of down. In the lung-ache,
in the blue pulsing of temples, what gave first
was something in my head, a burst
of colors that the blind see, and I saw
against the surface a shadow like an angel
quivering in a dead man's float,
then a shower of plastic knives and forks
spilling past me in the lightened water, a can
of barbequed beans, a bottle of A.1., napkins
drifting down like white leaves,
heavenly litter from the world I struggled toward.
What gave then was something on the other end,
and my hand rose on its own and touched my face.
Into the splintered light under the boathouse,
the loved, suffocating air hovering over the lake,
the cry of my wife leaning dangerously
over the dock, an empty grocery bag at her feet,
I bobbed with a hook through the palm of my hand.

DANA GIOIA

IN CHANDLER COUNTRY

California night. The Devil's wind,
the Santa Ana, blows in from the east,
raging through the canyon like a drunk
screaming in a bar.

The air tastes like
a stubbed-out cigarette. But why complain?
The weather's fine as long as you don't breathe.
Just lean back on the sweat-stained furniture,
lights turned out, windows shut against the storm,
and count your blessings.

Another sleepless night,
when every wrinkle in the bedsheet scratches
like a dry razor on a sunburned cheek,
when even ten-year whiskey tastes like sand,
and quiet women in the kitchen run
their fingers on the edges of a knife
and eye their husbands' necks. I wish them luck.

Tonight it seems that if I took the coins
out of my pocket and tossed them in the air
they'd stay a moment glistening like a net
slowly falling through dark water.

I remember
the headlights of the cars parked on the beach,
the narrow beams dissolving on the dark
surface of the lake, voices arguing
about the forms, the crackling radio,
the sheeted body lying on the sand,
the trawling net still damp beside it. No,
she wasn't beautiful—but at that age
when youth itself becomes a kind of beauty—
"Taking good care of your clients, Marlowe?"

Relentlessly the wind blows on. Next door,
catching a scent, the dogs begin to howl.
Lean, furious, raw-eyed from the storm,
packs of coyotes come down from the hills
where there is nothing left to hunt.

PAMELA ALEXANDER

HOWARD HUGHES LEAVES MANAGUA: PEACETIME, 1972

The car is comfortable,
but people swarm in the headlights,
carrying kettles and babies. It's his birthday.
Sometimes the road shakes. Buildings drop
to rubble, and dust
dulls the hood of the Mercedes. Which
birthday? He tries to count. The dead lie
beside the road, looking surprised. He sings
a phrase, forgets to sing, curls
against cool leather. The car follows
whichever roads aren't blocked
with debris. This must be someone else's
movie. He takes another Valium.

Among the buildings flames stand up,
and then gray light connects them. He sees
small fires fall into line: an airfield.
When he leaves the car, heat
and Spanish assault him,
and smoke, and people coughing. He knows
the set: "Hell's Angels," his crews running
and stunt pilots carried away
on covered stretchers. He walks slowly,
but no one recognizes him. Which
birthday? He will ask.

Nothing is more elegant than the empty white jet
touching down. It will bring him codeine
and the sky, which is never busy.
He will ask someone how old he is,
and the answer will come quietly
on a piece of paper. People die
in movies. He will sleep
and wake up in a different country.

JAMES MERRILL

OVERDUE PILGRIMAGE TO NOVA SCOTIA

Elizabeth Bishop (1911–1979)

Your village touched us by not knowing how.
Even as we outdrove its clear stormlight
A shower of self-belittling brilliants fell.
Miles later, hours away, here are rooms full
Of things you would have known: pump organ, hymnal,
Small-as-life desks, old farm tools, charter, deed,
Schoolbooks (Greek grammar, "A Canadian Reader"),
Queen Mary in oleograph, a whole wall hung
With women's black straw hats, some rather smart
—All circa 1915, like the manners
Of the fair, soft-spoken girl who shows us through.
Although till now she hasn't heard of you
She knows these things you would have known by heart
And we, by knowing you by heart, foreknew.

The child whose mother had been put away
Might wake, climb to a window, feel the bay
Steel itself, bosom bared to the full moon,
Against the woebegone, cerebral Man;
Or by judicious squinting make noon's red
Monarch grappling foreground goldenrod
Seem to extract a further essence from
Houses it dwarfed. Grown up, the visitor
Could find her North by the green velvet map
Appliquéd upon this wharfside shack—
Its shingles (in the time her back was turned)
Silver-stitched to visionary grain
As by a tireless, deeply troubled inmate,
Were Nature not by definition sane.

In living as in poetry, your art
Refused to tip the scale of being human
By adding unearned weight. "New, tender, quick"—
Nice watchwords; yet how often they invited

The anguish coming only now to light
In letters like photographs from space, revealing
Your planet tremulously bright through veils
As swept, in fact, by inconceivable
Heat and turbulence—but there, I've done it,
Added the weight. What tribute could you bear
Without dismay? Well, facing where you lived
Somebody's been inspired (*can* he have read
"Filling Station"?) to put pumps, a sign:
ESSO—what else! We filled up at the shrine.

Wait, those were elms! Long vanished from *our* world.
Elms, by whose goblet stems distance itself
Once taken between two fingers could be twirled,
Its bouquet breathed. The trees looked cumbersome,
Sickly through mist, like old things on a shelf—
Astrolabes, pterodactyls. They must know.
The forest knows. Out from such melting backdrops
It's the rare conifer stands whole, one sharp
Uniquely tufted spoke of a dark snow crystal
Not breathed upon, as yet, by our exhaust.
Part of a scene that with its views and warblers,
And at its own grave pace, but in your footsteps
—Never more imminent the brink, more sheer—
Is making up its mind to disappear

. . . With many a dirty look. That waterfall
For instance, beating itself to grit-veined cream
"Like Roquefort through a grater"? Or the car!
So here we sit in the car wash, snug and dry
As the pent-up fury of the storm hits: streaming,
Foaming "emotions"—impersonal, cathartic,
Closer to both art and what we are
Than the gush of nothings one outpours to people
On the correspondence side of bay and steeple,
Whose dazzling whites we'll never see again,
Or failed to see in the first place. Still, as the last

Suds glide, slow protozoa, down the pane,
We're off—Excuse our dust! With warm regards,—
Gathering phrases for tomorrow's cards.

DAN EBALO
THE STAR STORY

I wait
for the stars
to emerge from their dark
canyons.

I know them well;
they rise
above me every evening
like balloons,

each one rising,
burning,
into the sky.
Clouds

part like smoke,
moving on
to something else,
but I stay

to watch the stars
go higher, deeper
into the night.
The dead,

I was told
and believed,

become stars.
They emerge

from behind
their smoky gauze
in clusters:
Christmas lights

moving across the sky.
Some nights they
are like young
Cassiopeia,

distant and solitary.
Tonight she sits in the sky
holding hands with war
dead, widow-makers,

and a man whose heart
medicine is still
in the kitchen cabinet—
my father.

KATHA POLLITT

FAILURE

You'd never set foot in this part of town before,
so how could the landlady wink as if she recognized you?
Still, it's uncanny, the way when you open the door
to your room the scratched Formica bureau and table
give off a gleam of welcome, the foldaway bed
sags happily into itself like an old friend,
and, look, the previous tenant has considerately
left you his whole library: "Ferns of the World"
and "How to Avoid Probate." Even the water stain
spreading on the ceiling has your profile.

Well, never mind. Unpack your suitcase, put
boric acid out for the roaches. Here,
too, there are plenty of tears for things, probably, but
don't think about that just now. Outside your window,
ailanthus trees, bringing you an important message
about the nutritive properties of garbage,
wave their arms for attention, Third World raiders,
scrawny, tough, your future if you're lucky.

ALICIA OSTRIKER

MOVE

Whether it's a turtle who drags herself
Slowly to the sandlot, where she digs
The sandy nest she was born to dig

And lay leathery eggs in, or whether it's salmon
Rocketing upstream
Toward pools that call *Bring your eggs here*,

And nowhere else in the world, whether it is turtle-green
Ugliness and awkwardness, or the seething
Grace and gild of silky salmon, we

Are envious, our wishes speak out right here,
Thirsty for a destiny like theirs,
An absolute right choice

To end all choices. Is it memory,
We ask, is it a smell
They remember,

Or just what is it—some kind of blueprint
That makes them move, hot grain by grain,
Cold cascade above icy cascade,

Slipping through
Water's fingers
A hundred miles

Inland from the easy, shiny sea?
And we also—in the company
Of our tribe

Or perhaps alone, like the turtle
On her wrinkled feet with the tapping nails—
We also are going to travel, we say let's be

Oblivious to all, save
That we travel, and we say
When we reach the place we'll know

We are in the right spot, somehow, like a breath
Entering a singer's chest, that shapes itself
For the song that is to follow.

WONG MAY

THE DIFFICULTY OF MOONLIGHT IN THE 6TH ARRONDISSEMENT

I've wanted to write about the recluse
in Paris who thought giving up the world
was easy. If one could die
from not leaving one's apartment—
it was a sickness—
& if one could not, why go out at all?
In stages it must have been easy,
difficult, not easy, not difficult.
What was it?
She did not leave a word.
In 1957 she was a *Vogue* mannequin

modelling hats & ball gowns,
$\qquad$ ball gowns & veils.
Givenchy put her in a green netting:
a wasp, waist up or down,
holding herself open & gathered.
A spike of lupine she was
$\qquad$ for another,
whom she married. Her face the formal perfection
of the fifties. Eyes closed
under the sculpted lids, or peeled back,
2 swallows, 2 swallow heads.
In the château, of which we saw only the hall
on the marble hall table
there was a basket of
$\qquad$ magnificent summer lilies.
She moved back to her arrondissement
when an apartment upstairs from her father's
barbershop became vacant.
Her father died in the seventies.
At what point she went out less & less
nobody would care to say. After all,
what did she think she was,
$\qquad$ or what did she see the world as?
$\qquad$ When the flesh formally withdraws
doesn't the world, too, in stages, with a bad odor?
She was strong enough to starve in her apartment.
Alternately weak & strong
& too weak & strong altogether. When
$\qquad$ discovered a year later—
i.e., approximately 6 months from her demise
—not by a neighbor,
$\qquad$ she was by herself.

$\qquad$ Who has not carried out
the formal nightmare of returning
to one's abode after 6 months/a year
pleading forgetfulness?

As though one had left.
The student now sitting in the kitchen
                        facing the same wall
using the old stove & fridge
sees nothing to complain of.
Easy enough to see stains everywhere, he said.
In stages it was easy,
difficult, then easy. It does not stop.

MARK JARMAN

THE SUPREMES

In Ball's Market, after surfing till noon,
we stand in wet trunks, shivering
as icing dissolves off our sweet rolls
inside the heat-blued counter oven,
when they appear on his portable TV,
riding a float of chiffon as frothy
as the peeling curl of a wave.
The parade m.c. talks up their hits
and their new houses outside of Detroit
and old Ball clicks his tongue.
Gloved up to their elbows, their hands raised
toward us palm out, they sing
"Stop! In the Name of Love" and don't stop
but slip into the lower foreground.

Every day of a summer can turn,
from one moment, into a single day.
I saw Diana Ross in her first film
play a brief scene by the Pacific—
and that was the summer it brought back.
Mornings we paddled out, the waves
would be little more than embellishments:
lathework and spun glass
gray-green with cold, but flawless.

When the sun burned through the light fog,
they would warm and swell,
wind-scaled and ragged,
and radios up and down the beach
would burst on with her voice.

She must remember that summer
somewhat differently, and so must the two
who sang with her in long matching gowns,
standing a step back on her left and right,
as the camera tracked them
into our eyes in Ball's Market.
But what could we know, tanned white boys,
wiping sugar and salt from our mouths
and leaning forward to feel their song?
Not much, except to feel it
ravel us up like a wave
in the silk of white water,
simply, sweetly, repeatedly,
and just as quickly let go.

We didn't stop, either, which is how
we vanished, too, blowing apart like spray—
Ball's Market, my friends, and I.
Dredgers ruined the waves,
those continuous dawn perfections,
and Ball sold high to the high rises
cresting over them. His flight out of L.A.,
heading for Vegas, would have banked
above the wavering lines of surf.
He may have seen them. I have,
leaving again for points north and east,
glancing down as the plane turns.
From that height they still look frail and frozen,
full of simple sweetness and repetition.

EAMON GRENNAN

SEA DOG

The sea has scrubbed him clean
as a deal table. Picked over, plucked
hairless, drawn tight as a drum,
an envelope of tallow jutting with
rib cage, hips, assorted bones. The once
precise pads of his feet are buttons
of bleached wood in a ring of stubble.
The skull—trimly tapered to a caul
of wrinkles; bonneted, gap-toothed—
wears an air faintly human, almost
ancestral.

                    Now the tide falls back
in whispers, leaving the two of us
alone a moment together. Almost loving
what I see, I see the lye-bright
parchment skin has been scabbed black
by a rack of flies
that rise up, a humming chorus,
at my approach, settle again when I
stop to stare. These must be
the finishing touch, I think,
until I see round the naked neck bone
a tightly knotted twist of rope, a frayed noose
that hung him up or held him under water
till the snapping and jerking stopped.
Such a neat knot: someone knelt safely
down to do it, pushing those ears back
with familiar fingers. The drag end
now a seaweed tangle round leg bones
stretched against their last leash. And

nothing more to this sad sack
of bones, these poor enduring remains
in their own body bag. Nothing more.

Death's head here holds its own peace
beyond the racket-world of feel and fragrance
where the live dog bent, throbbing
with habit, and where the quick children
now shriek by on sand—staring, averting.
I go in over my head in stillness, and see
behind the body and the barefoot children
how on the bent horizon to the west
a sudden flowering shaft of sunlight
picks out four pale haycocks
saddled in sackcloth
and makes of them a flared quartet
of gospel horses—rearing up; heading for us.

CYNTHIA MACDONALD

BY THE SEA

This is the day of the night it began to turn,
Like milk, slightly sour, still
So close to freshness one is not sure if
The tongue or the cream is at fault.

He, floundering back toward the bay
Like a suddenly beached fish, cannot see that
The water has changed, as if the dairy plant
Behind him had confused its flows, releasing
All its curds the way defective plants can.

He, lunging toward water, does not know,
Has never had to, that even with the ocean's
Grand dilution the balance of fluids has been
Slightly altered, like the shift of residue in
The ear's circular canals. I, experienced
In acute pain, too full of acuity, know
But do not know why milk
Spoils when it seems fresh.

"Your family has had bad luck," he said last night
Just before he found the clocks had stopped
And indicted the house again. Perhaps that is it.
The stroke of his hand makes time seamless but
The clock strikes, even if unheard, and blood poisoning
(Which killed my father's mother when she used
A knitting needle on the fetus, which killed
My uncle when, even with an open cut, he wore
Blue socks) moves through me into him as we come together.

Louis Pasteur, I beg you, seal us in a bottle,
Let us remain bacilli-free, save us from relative
Poisons and deaths, from what may prey on us.

It takes a while to read the ocean,
To see that the prayer is the agent of
What is prayed against. But we've caught it
Early. Let's stop stamping, like spoiled children,
Trying to seal the bargain. Instead
Let's clap our flippers (how I admire
The silvery gloss of sun on your body), spin
Bottles on our noses, beg for
Kippers, and kiss by the beautiful sea.

ALICE FULTON

SCUMBLING

Absolved, face to the wall, alive only
in fact. It was always evening
in my head, an evening of thoughts
cool as sheets. His skin
made its silk sound, no
two glissandos alike. A fine fear
streaked through. Let somebody else
sponge up those tremors.
My reserve circled, imperial

as the inside of a pearl. All night
I pretended night was an unruly
day. I pretended
my voice. I pretended my hair. I pretended
my friend. But there it was—"I"—
I couldn't get rid of that.
What could I do but let it learn
to tremble? So I watched feelings hover
over like the undersides
of water lilies: long serpentines
topped by nervous, almost
sunny undulations. I had to learn
largo. I had to trust
that two bodies scumbling
could soften
one another. I had to
let myself be gone
through, do it in the arbitrary light
tipping and flirting
with seldom-seen surfaces.

SHARON OLDS

POEM FOR MY SON, AGED 10, AFTER A HIGH FEVER

When you have a seizure and I call the doctor and I'm
waiting for her to call back,
I think of the greenish skin of your throat like the
ice at the center of the pond when it starts to melt,
and the dark skin at the base of your neck
rich as the moss you can scrape from the north side of trees.
I think of the insides of your wrists, their
filthy gold waxy glow like
saints' candles fallen in the dust
behind the altar, where the mice live and
propagate, feeding their young on the

crumbs of the host, like little pieces of light,
I think about the layer of grime all over your body,
as if you have been rubbed with the soil of this earth,
like a sacred object, I think of how light
catches on each facet of grit so you
gleam with a rubbed haze. I think of how they
caught you when you thrust from me in
slow pulses, one, two, three,
head, shoulders, body, your feet
like the pointed fins of a tail as they lifted you up,
glossy, glittering with blood clots like a
kid covered with cookie crumbs after a long journey,
fallen asleep next to the train window,
the green fields of ice going by in the evening,
the way your brain falls asleep twice a day now for four minutes
and everything seems to be going fast and loud.
I think of your brain, that red-gold cauliflower,
the leaves with their veins wrapped around the stem and the white
      heart,
I think of your navel, that dark rose
always folded, I think of your penis, its
candor and virtue, I think of your long
narrow feet and your bony chest and your
clever hands—you let them lie in your lap
when the seizure comes, you wait for it to be over,
I think of every part of your body,
thought being a form of prayer,
but it's hard to think of your face, the pale
globe forehead, the thin cheeks
freckled like wild birds' eggs, the
chapped dark lips, the mouth
slightly set, and especially the eyes—I can
hardly stand to see the courage there,
the calmness of the fear, you are prepared to bear
anything.

PERENNIALS

I don't remember the day I was born.
I ask my brother, the one born
on the same day. He says it was cold.
He shudders and puts on a sweater.
So long ago in January, the snow
collecting between the windowpanes
through which the sunlight of Detroit
smeared with the oils of exhaustion broke
into my untarnished deep-blue gaze
for the first time. And my brother's, too.

.

Out of duty to the war effort
I put in radishes, carrots, corn
in the sandy loam behind the garage
and got a dozen or so pale roots,
thin and damp, more earth than anything.
I waited a whole year. In the black soil
of the yard I tried again, and this time
added mock orange and lilac. I watered.
On a windy afternoon I knelt
to find a purple spike of wild flag
risen from nowhere and what proved to be
six thick stubs of a hand of rhubarb.

.

Each year I drive the coastal hills
in search of a place I must have seen
once in a dream. The highway rises
past fields of gnarled trees, Joshuas
and olives or perhaps the mythical
St. John's bread, spreading out hard arms.
I park and climb on foot. At this height
the air rings and my breathing struggles
until there is music in silence. The magpies
keep ahead or turn away to flash
their sudden white underwings. I follow,

but the land never crests, to slide down
into an ocean and begin again.

     •

Winter. The marketplace of the village
of Fuengirola. A tattered mongrel,
tan, brown, and black with a white muzzle.
The stubby, bowed forelegs set apart
in a stance suitable for a short advance
or a sudden retreat. I know this beast,
I think, I know this dirty, boxlike head
ringed with curls, this dry, foolish bark
that scares off nothing. "Marilyn," I say,
remembering one who scorned me years before.
Each day my son John calls out "Marilyn!"
as stamping we wait our turn in line
before the black oil drums of burning fat
where the *churros* fry. "Marilyn," he calls
until she comes to beg bread from his hand.

     •

Under the windows onto the gray yard
a green glass wine bottle with one branch
of blood-tipped bursting plum. The odor
of midsummer hanging in winter.
The room thickens around the living core
as I pass and stop. Where was I going
that I should ignore the heart of my house,
this new intruder come in another
dark season to tell me the year won't wait?
I was on the way to the kitchen
for a glass of water, and now I have wine.
I was looking for a brown paper sack
of sleep, an old pillow of forgetting,
a way out before the world got in,
and found the dining room in riot
from one black branch as arched as I.

ON THE LANGUAGE OF DUST

Though the wallflower is fidelity in adversity,
The broken straw the spoiling of a contract,
The sparrow sweeps the streets, the wren proclaims.
The neat and humble broom, bindweed, docile rush,
The cup of kindness spill through open hands,
The polestar is lost or shattered on the grass.

White poppy, sleep, my bane and antidote.
Pitch pine, you think you think too much.
For benevolence I peeled the squat potato,
For bluntness gathered borage; the oat hummed back.
The simple barn owl slept above my lintel
While the weekday came, the pale bride of no one.

When the Northern Lights go out the larks collide
And lupine takes their blood voraciously.
Indian jasmine, I attach myself to you.
The cabbage thrives and profits in its season,
But not the swallowwort that cured my heartache,
Nor lemon in its zest, nor solitary lichen.

Without the seven stars, without the moon,
Without the sun-drenched winds, without my care,
Birds pass above into the space where no birds are.
Rose, deep red, give me your bashful shame,
White rose, I am unworthy of you, rose,
Dog, thornless, full-blown, white and red together,

Blasted rose placed over two buds, rose of war,
White rosebud of girlhood, cluster and musk,
Ragged robin of wit, single, burned, bleached.
The silent days are one. Rose of endings,
Calm me now, night-blooming cereus, nettle,
Bravery of oak leaf, wingless, talk to me, foxglove.

LINDA GREGG

SAYING GOODBYE TO THE DEAD

I walk on the dirt roads being my father.
Between tobacco fields empty in February
except for the wooden stakes and the wires.
The earth is spongy after the rains
which washed the snow away. Dogs bark
near the houses around the fields.
Mountains beyond that. I clap my hands
in the air over my head, four times.
Turn on one foot around with my arms lifted.
Stop and look at the sky fast and hard.
Then walk to the bakery and buy day-old
sweet rolls to eat in my room at the hotel.

BILLY COLLINS

THE BROOKLYN MUSEUM OF ART

I will now step over the soft velvet rope
and walk directly into this massive Hudson River
painting and pick my way along the Palisades
with this stick I snapped off a dead tree.

I will skirt the smoky, nestled towns
and seek the path that leads always outward
until I become lost, without a hope
of ever finding the way back to the museum.

I will stand on the bluffs in nineteenth-century
clothes, a dwarf among rock, hills, and flowing water,
and I will fish from the banks in a straw hat,
which will feel like a brushstroke on my head.

And I will hide in the green covers of forests,
so no appreciator of Frederick Edwin Church,

leaning over the soft velvet rope,
will spot my tiny figure moving in the stillness
and cry out, pointing for the others to see,

and be thought mad and led away to a cell
where there is no vaulting landscape to explore,
none of this bird song that halts me in my tracks,
and no wide curving of this river that draws
my steps toward the misty vanishing point.

JOHN UPDIKE

GRADATIONS OF BLACK

(Third Floor, Whitney Museum)

Ad Reinhardt's black, in "Abstract Painting 33,"
    seems atmosphere, leading the eye into
that darkness where, self-awakened, we

grope for the bathroom switch; no light goes on,
    but we come to see that the corners of his square
black canvas are squares slightly, slightly brown.

Frank Stella, in "Die Fahne Hoch," aligns
    right-angled stripes, dark gray, upon black ground
lustrous and granular, like the shiny hide

of some hairless, geometrical reptile.
    The black of Mark Rothko's "Four Darks in Red"
holds grief; small lakes of sheen reflect the light,

and the eye, seeking to sink, is rebuffed
    by a much-worked dullness, the patina of a rag
that oily Vulcan uses, wiping up.

While Clyfford Still, in his tall "Untitled,"
    has laid on black in flakes of hardening tar,
a dragon's scales so slick the viewer's head

is mirrored, a murky helmet, as he stands
        waiting for the flame-shaped passion to clear.
With broad housepainter's brush and sweeping hands

Franz Kline's "Mahoning" barred radiance; now each
        black gobby girder has yielded cracks to time
and lets leak through the dead white underneath.

WILLIAM MATTHEWS

MOOD INDIGO

From the porch; from the hayrick where her prickled
brothers hid and chortled and slurped into their young pink
lungs the ash-blond dusty air that lay above the bales

like low clouds; and from the squeak and suck
of the well pump, and from the glove of rust it implied
on her hand; from the dress parade of clothes

in her mothproofed closet; from her tiny Philco
with its cracked speaker and Sunday litany
("Nick Carter," "The Shadow," "Sky King");

from the loosening bud of her body; from hunger,
as they say; and from reading; from the finger
she used to dial her own number; from the dark

loam of the harrowed fields and from the very sky—
it came from everywhere. Which is to say it was
always there, and that it came from nowhere.

It evaporated with the dew, and at dusk when dark
spread in the sky like water in a blotter it spread, too,
but it came back and curdled with milk and stung

with nettles. It was in the bleat of a lamb, the way
a clapper is in a bell, and in the raucous, scratchy
gossip of the crows. It walked with her to school and lay

with her to sleep and at last she was well pleased.
If she were to sew, she would prick her finger with it.
If she were to bake, it would linger in the kitchen

like an odor snarled in the deepest folds of childhood.
It became her dead pet, her lost love, the baby sister
blue and dead at birth, the chill headwaters of the river

that purled and meandered and ran and ran until
it issued into her, as into a sea, and then she was its
and it was wholly hers. She kept to her room, as we

learned to say, but now and then she'd come down
and pass through the kitchen, and the screen door
would close behind her with no more sound than

an envelope being sealed, and she'd walk for hours
in the fields like a lithe blue rain, and end up
in the barn, and one of us would go and bring her in.

LYNDA HULL

JACKSON HOTEL

Sometimes after hours of wine I can almost see
    the night gliding in low off the harbor
        down the long avenues of shopwindows

past mannequins, perfect in their gestures.
    I leave water steaming on the gas ring
        and sometimes I can slip from my body,

almost find the single word to prevent evenings
    that absolve nothing, a winter lived alone
      and cold. Rooms where you somehow marry

the losses of strangers that tremble
    on the walls, like the hands
      of the dancer next door luminous

with Methedrine; she taps walls for hours
    murmuring about the silver she swears
      lines the building, the hallways

where each night drunks stammer their
    usual Rosary until they come to rest
      beneath the tarnished numbers, the bulbs

that star each ceiling.
    I must tell you I am afraid to sit here
      losing myself to the hour's slow erasure

until I know myself only by this cold weight,
    this hand on my lap, palm up.
      I want to still the dancer's hands

in mine, to talk about forgiveness
    and what we leave behind—faces
      and cities, the small emergencies

of nights. I say nothing but,
    leaning on the sill, I watch her leave
      at that moment

when the first taxis start rolling
    to the lights of Chinatown, powered
      by sad and human desire. I watch her fade

down the street until she's a smudge,
    violet in the circle of my breath. A figure
      so small I can cup her in my hands.

CROSSINGS

On St. Brigid's Day the new life could be entered
By going through her girdle of straw rope.
The proper way for men was right leg first,

Then right arm and right shoulder, head, then left
Shoulder, arm, and leg. Women drew it down
Over the body and stepped out of it.

The open they came into by these moves
Stood opener, hoops came off the world,
They could feel the February air

Still soft above their heads and imagine
The limp rope fray and flare like windborne gleanings
Or an unhindered goldfinch over plowland.

　　•

Not an avenue and not a bower.
For a quarter mile or so, where the county road
Is running straight across North Antrim bog,

Tall old fir trees line it on both sides.
Scotch firs, that is. Calligraphic shocks
Bushed and tufted in prevailing winds.

You drive into a meaning made of trees.
Or not exactly trees. It is a sense
Of running through and under without let,

Of glimpse and dapple. A life all trace and skim
The car has vanished out of. A fanned nape
Sensitive to the millionth of a flicker.

　　•

Running water never disappointed.
Crossing water always furthered something.
Stepping stones were stations of the soul.

A kesh could mean the track some called a causey
Raised above the wetness of the bog,
Or the part of it that bridged old drains and streams.

It steadies me to tell these things. Also
I cannot mention keshes or the ford
Without my father's shade appearing to me

On a path toward sunset, eying spades and clothes
That turf-cutters stowed perhaps or souls cast off
Before they crossed the log that spans the burn.

     •

Be literal a moment. Recollect
Walking out on what had been emptied out
After he died, turning your back and leaving.

That morning tiles were harder, windows colder,
The raindrops on the pane more scourged, the grass
Barer to the sky, more wind-harrowed,

Or so it seemed. The house that he had planned—
"Plain, big, straight, ordinary, you know?"—
A paradigm of rigor and correction,

Rebuke to fanciness and shrine to limit,
Stood firmer than ever for its own idea,
Like a printed X-ray for the X-rayed body.

     •

To those who have seen spirits, human skin
For a long time afterward appears most coarse.
The face I see that all falls short of since

Passes down an aisle: I share the bus
From San Francisco airport into Berkeley
With one other passenger, who's dropped

At Treasure Island military base,
Halfway across Bay Bridge. Vietnam-bound,
He could have been one newly dead come back,

Unsurprisable but still disappointed,
Having to bear his farm-boy self again,
His shaving cuts, his otherworldly brow.

　　　　　·

Shaving cuts. The pallor of bad habits.
Sunday afternoons, when summer idled
And couples walked the road along the Foyle,

We brought a shaving mirror to our window
In the top story of the boarders' dorms:
Lovers in the happy valley, cars

Eager-backed and silent, the absolute river
Between us and it all. We tilted the glass up
Into the sun and found the range and shone

A flitting light on what we could not have.
Brightness played over them in chancy sweeps
Like flashes from a god's shield or the gene pool.

　　　　　·

And yes, my friend, we, too, walked through a valley.
Once. In darkness. With all the street lamps off.
When scaresome night made *valley* of that town.

Scene from Dante, made more memorable
By one of his head-clearing similes—
Fireflies, say, since the policemen's torches

Clustered and flicked and tempted us to trust
The unpredictable, attractive light.
We were like herded shades who had to cross

And did cross, in a panic, to the car
Parked as we'd left it, that gave when we got in
Like Charon's boat under the faring poets.

ROBERT PINSKY

SHIRT

The back, the yoke, the yardage. Lapped seams,
The nearly invisible stitches along the collar
Turned in a sweatshop by Koreans or Malaysians

Gossiping over tea and noodles on their break
Or talking money or politics while one fitted
This armpiece with its overseam to the band

Of cuff I button at my wrist. The presser, the cutter,
The wringer, the mangle. The needle, the union,
The treadle, the bobbin. The code. The infamous blaze

At the Triangle factory in 1911.
One hundred and forty-six died in the flames
On the ninth floor, no hydrants, no fire escapes—

The witness in a building across the street
Who watched how a young man helped a girl to step
Up to the windowsill, then held her out

Away from the masonry wall and let her drop.
And then another. As if he were helping them up
To enter a streetcar, and not eternity.

A third before he dropped her put her arms
Around his neck and kissed him. Then he held
Her into space, and dropped her. Almost at once

He stepped to the sill himself, his jacket flared
And fluttered up from his shirt as he came down,
Air filling up the legs of his gray trousers—

Like Hart Crane's Bedlamite, "shrill shirt ballooning."
Wonderful how the pattern matches perfectly
Across the placket and over the twin bar-tacked

Corners of both pockets, like a strict rhyme
Or a major chord. Prints, plaids, checks,
Houndstooth, Tattersall, Madras. The clan tartans

Invented by mill-owners inspired by the hoax of Ossian,
To control their savage Scottish workers, tamed
By a fabricated heraldry: MacGregor,

Bailey, MacMartin. The kilt, devised for workers
To wear among the dusty clattering looms.
Weavers, carders, spinners. The loader,

The docker, the navvy. The planter, the picker, the sorter
Sweating at her machine in a litter of cotton
As slaves in calico headrags sweated in fields:

George Herbert, your descendant is a Black
Lady in South Carolina, her name is Irma
And she inspected my shirt. Its color and fit

And feel and its clean smell have satisfied
Both her and me. We have culled its cost and quality
Down to the buttons of simulated bone,

The buttonholes, the sizing, the facing, the characters
Printed in black on neckband and tail. The shape,
The label, the labor, the color, the shade. The shirt.

LAST TRAIN HOME

JACOB TRAPP

THREE WAYS TO MANHATTAN FROM JERSEY

One, we dive down under the Hudson
River and come up dry on Broadway;
two, we're swung from steel cables
high above ships, and look
across, level, at blue shafts
and towers tapering to a dream;
three, and most miraculous,
we walk at dusk on flowing waters
gleaming with their own dark light,
ferryboats under our feet, toward
the immense black hull of one
gigantic, star-masted ship,
mystic, cargoed with night, yet gay
with how many spars, cabins,
castles and constellations of light!

DAVID BIESPIEL

MEN WAITING FOR A TRAIN

At first they stand, orphaned, like a line of birds,
First on one foot, then the other, in unison,
Like any other unnamed someones, as if poised
For a firing line, until someone thinks he knows
A train is coming in the sparrow-morning light,
And someone else taps a pack of cigarettes
Against his gloved hand, not exotic,
But it's as if he's slipped into captivity. One
Of those corner-of-the-eye, white-sky
Days, late winter a hammer against the
Platform, and gathered above the grave-
Line of the gap enough snow
To consider the blue clouds floating,

Like forgiveness, above us all. Only two
Are cresting at this moment, one a show
Of hands, an explosion of clapping, the
Other a mask of a baptismal face
Failing behind the city's blood-brown
Skyline. Whoever screamed just then,
Then quieted, then shouted, high, like a crow,
Leaves me filled with absence, listening
For silences, cupping my ears. For
A moment, nothing is being celebrated,
Nothing undone, or measured, nothing
Moves, or rings, in the air, and in the next
Moment sirens are continually dying in
The distance. In the time it takes the train's
Doors to open, and close, and for the train
To swirl us all off, half in, half out, of
Our own wills, underground, something
Like joy pours out of the cloudburst heart,
And whatever feelings each one of us has had
Goes off into the daylight without us.

CYNTHIA ZARIN

NOW

It's spring out, and the acrid
hiss of rain on Madison
heaves in the wake of the buses.

Such a long time we've been sitting here.
The dusty fronds are old green loden coats,
heavy around us, the crushed

clouds of tissue roses are
light-resistant, and a little torn.
Watery, thin, the daylight

is whittled down by the revolving door,
becoming another day
entirely, a scrimshaw of "Later on,

when things get better" that is always in front
and also behind us, junky and bleached,
like the word *now*, that small atom, that pearl.

JAMESON FITZPATRICK

WHITE GAYS

Privilege is a man
taking up two seats on the train.
Now four, putting his feet up.

It is also my not having
to describe his leather loafers for you
to fill in the white space of his body
straight and able

and also my body's proximity
to his, socially and physically,
on this train he is taking from
the Hamptons and I am taking
from the Pines. And how

my finding him handsome
keeps him handsome,
that if he were to look my way,
his would be worth more to me
than any other gaze.

What I'm trying to say is
proximity is the problem with White Gays.
I'm one of them, so I can say that.

Proximity, because it promises
the possibility of arriving
where all the room in the world
waits to be claimed.

Privilege is a tease, we forget,
what we learned in grade school.
Even spread in his lap,
everything for the taking
taken from someone.

LES MURRAY

THE HARLEYS

Blats booted to blatant
dubbin the avenue dire
with rubbings of Sveinn Forkbeard
leading a black squall of Harleys
with Moe Snow-Whitebeard and

Possum Brushbeard and their ladies
and, sphincter-lipped, gunning,
massed leather muscle on a run,
on a roll, Santas from Hell
like a whole shoal leaning

wide-wristed, their tautness stable
in fluency, fast streetscape dwindling,
all riding astride, on the outside
of sleek grunt vehicles, woman-clung,
forty years on from Marlon.

JOY HARJO

RUNNING

It's closing time. Violence is my boyfriend
With a cross to bear
                              Hoisted on by the church.
He wears it everywhere.
There are no female deities in the Trinity.
        I don't know how I'm going to get out of here,
Said the flying fish to the tree.
                              Last call.
We've had it with history, we who look for vision here
In the Indian and poetry bar, somewhere
To the left of Hell.
Now I have to find my way, when there's a river to cross and no
Boat to get me there, when there appears to be no home at all.
                              My father gone, chased
By the stepfather's gun. *Get out of here.*
I've found my father at the bar, his ghost at least, some piece
Of him in this sorry place. The boyfriend's convincing to a crowd.
Right now, he's the spell of attraction. What tales he tells.
In the fog of thin hope, I wander this sad world
We've made with the enemy's words.
The lights quiver,
        Like they do when the power's dwindling to a dangling string.
It is time to go home. We are herded like stoned cattle, like children
    for the bombing drill—
                              Out the door, into the dark street of this old Indian town
Where *there are no Indians anymore.*
I was afraid of the dark, because then I could see
                              Everything. The truth with its eyes staring
Back at me. The mouth of the dark with its shiny moon teeth,
No words, just a hiss and a snap.
                              I could hear my heart hurting
With my *in-the-dark* ears.
                              I thought I could take it. Where was the party?
It's been a century since we left home with the American soldiers at our
    backs.

The party had long started up in the parking lot.
                        He flew through the dark, broke my stride with a punch.
I went down then came up.
                    I thought I could take being a girl with her heart in her
Arms. I carried it for justice. For the rights of all Indians.
                                            We all had that cross to bear.
Those Old Ones followed me, the quiet girl with the long dark hair,
            The daughter of a warrior who wouldn't give up.
I wasn't ready yet, to fling free the cross
            I ran and I ran through the 2 A.M. streets.

It was my way of breaking free. I was anything but history.
I was the wind.

DAVID ST. JOHN

THE SHORE

So the tide forgets, as morning
Grows too far delivered, as the bowls
Of rock and wood run dry.
What is left seems pearled and lit,
As those cases
Of the museum stood lit
With milk jade, rows of opaque vases
Streaked with orange and yellow smoke.
You found a lavender boat, a single
Figure poling upstream, baskets
Of pale fish wedged between his legs.
Today, the debris of winter
Stands stacked against the walls,
The coils of kelp scattered
Across the floor. The oil fire
Smokes. You turn down the lantern
Hung on its nail. Outside,
The boats aligned like sentinels.
Here beside the blue depot, walking

The pier, you can see the way
The shore
Approximates the dream, how distances
Repeat their deaths,
Above these tables and panes of water.
As climbing the hills above
The harbor, up to the lupine drifting
Among the lichen-masked pines,
The night is pocked with lamps lit
On every boat offshore,
Galleries of floating stars. Below,
On its narrow tracks shelved
Into the cliff's face,
The train begins its slide down
To the harbor, the warehouses. Loaded
With diesel, coal, paychecks, whiskey,
Bedsheets, slabs of ice—for the fish,
For the men. You lean on my arm,
As once
I watched you lean at the window,
The bookstalls below stretched a mile
To the quay, the afternoon crowd
Picking over the novels, the histories.
You walked out, as you walked out last
Night, onto the stone porch. Dusk
Reddened the walls, the winds sliced
Off the reefs. The vines of the gourds
Shook on their lattice. You talked
About that night you stood
Behind the black pane of the French
Window, watching my father read some long
Passage
Of a famous voyager's book. You hated
That voice filling the room,
Its light. So tonight we make a soft
Parenthesis upon the sand's black bed.
In that dream we share, there is
One shore, where we look out upon nothing

And the sea our whole lives;
Until turning from those waves, our hair
The white sky, we find
One shore, where we look out upon nothing
And the earth our whole lives.
Where what is left between shore and sky
Is traced in the vague wake of
(The stars, the sandpipers whistling)
What we forgive. *If you wake soon, wake me.*

WILLIAM MATTHEWS

HOUSEWORK

How precise it seems, like a doll house,
and look: the tiniest socks ever knit
are crumpled on a chair in your bedroom.
And how still, like the air inside a church
or basketball. How you could have lived
your boyhood here is hard to know,

unless the blandishing lilacs
and slant rain stippling the lamplight
sustained you, and the friendship of dogs,
and the secrecy that flourishes in vacant lots.
For who would sleep, like a cat in a drawer,
in this house memory is always dusting,

unless it be you? I'd hear you on the stairs,
an avalanche of sneakers, and then the sift
of your absence, and then I'd begin to rub
the house like a lantern until you came back
and grew up to be me, wondering how to sleep
in this lie of memory, unless it be made clean.

JORGE LUIS BORGES

PLAINNESS

The garden's grillwork gate
opens with the ease of a page
in a much thumbed book,
and, once inside, our eyes
have no need to dwell on objects
already fixed and exact in memory.
Here habits and minds and the private language
all families invent
are everyday things to me.
What necessity is there to speak
or pretend to be someone else?
The whole house knows me,
they're aware of my worries and weakness.
This is the best that can happen—
what Heaven perhaps will grant us:
not to be wondered at or required to succeed
but simply to be let in
as part of an undeniable Reality,
like stones of the road, like trees.

(Translated, from the Spanish, by Norman Thomas di Giovanni.)

A. R. AMMONS

TREE LIMBS DOWN

The poverty of having everything is not
wanting anything: I trudge down the mall halls

and see nothing wanting which would pick me
up: I stop at a cheap $79 piece of jewelry,

a little necklace dangler, and it has a diamond
chip in it hardly big enough to sparkle, but it

sparkles: a piece of junk, symbolically vast;
imagine, a life with a little sparkle in it, a

little sparkle like wanting something, like
wanting a little piece of shining, maybe the

world's smallest ruby: but if you have everything
the big carats are merely heavy with price and

somebody, maybe, trying to take you over: the dull
game of the comers-on, waiting everywhere like

moray eels poked out of holes: what did Christ
say, sell everything and give to the poor, and

immediacy enters; daily bread is the freshest
kind: dates, even, laid up old in larders, are

they sweet: come off sheets of the golden
desert, knees weak and mouth dry, what would

you think of an oasis, a handful of dates, and
a clear spring breaking out from under some stones:

but suppose bread can't daily be found or no
oasis materializes among the shimmers: lining

the outside of immediacy, alas, is uncertainty:
so the costly part of the crust of morning

bread is not knowing it will be there: it has
been said by others, though few, that nothing

is got for nothing: so I am reconciled: I
traipse my dull self down the aisles of

desire and settle for nothing, nothing wanted,
nothing spent, nothing got.

JOSEPHINE DICKINSON

THERE WERE RAINBOWS EVERY DAY

There were rainbows every day
for three or four days afterward.
I sat in the large soft bed
with silence and stillness falling
around me like snow. Cross Fell
was icy white with a shock
of frozen cloud on its uppermost
tip. The carpet by the bed,
washed several times on the last
day you were home, took a week
to dry to a nubbly paperiness.
The henhouse filled with wind,
the roof was ripped away.
First one side of it split
open, then the other.
The garden shed blew apart,
the timbers of the frame rattled loose.
Rain lashed the windows.
The trees strained. The back door
blew open. Greenhouse glass
smashed. You were beautiful.
Your forehead smelled of powdered
millstone grits and moss.
Your ruby lips and throat
glistened. A red dot stood
on your eyebrow. (Did I nick
you slightly when I snipped
those troublesome hairs you'd swiped
me off from trimming?) Your Top
Man shirt and navy soft wool
waistcoat. A barely visible
smudge on your chin where the last
few mouthfuls of soup spooned in
had dribbled out again.

Your gray eyes dry and sinking,
like a Grünewald's overcome with wonder.

JAMES GALVIN

INDEPENDENCE DAY, 1956: A FAIRY TALE

I think this house's mouth is full of dirt.
                                    Smoke is nothing up its sleeve.
I think it could explode.
                    Where I am, in the dirt under the floor, I hear
them.
        They don't know.
                            My mother leaves each room my father enters.
                                                            Now
she is cleaning things that are already clean.
                                    My father is in the living
room.
        He's pouring.
                    Rum into a glass, gas into a lamp, kerosene into a can.

He pours capped fuses, matches, dynamite sticks into his pockets.
                                                            He pours
rounds into the .45 which he will point skyward and hold next to
        his ear
as if it were telling him things.
                            Where I am, the spider spins.
                                                    The broken
mouse drags a trap through lunar talc of dust.
                                        Where the bitch whelps is
where I wriggle on my belly, cowardly, ashamed, to escape the
        Fourth of
July.
        I think the house is very ready.
                                    It seems to hover like an "exploded
view" in a repair manual.

Parts suspended in disbelief.

                                     Nails pulled back,

aimed.

        My father goes out.

                    My mother whimpers.

                              There'll be no supper.

She opens the firebox and stuffs it full of forks.

JOSEPHINE SAUNDERS

A LION COME TO DINE

Name-dropper, huntress of lions,
veteran of countless safaris
into others' dinner parties,

a specimen you have brought back,
tonight embellishes your own party.
The evening is coming off perfectly—

all faces are scalloped with smiles;
the lion, carefully curried, becalmed,
is behaving for once as though tamed.

Just when it seems an evening like this
could make the game be worth the candle,
seizing on a conversational lull,

your guest of honor turns and growls at you,
and next you learn what ought to have been clear:
a lion come to dine may eat you for his supper.

Meanwhile, the appreciative lesser guests—
hyenas sitting out the kill—
wait their turn avid, if peripheral.

DAVE SMITH

RED DOG

We bought you for our son. Half-grown,
already your bag of skin sagged everywhere,
you fell to sleep like the dark in corners,
predictably where we wouldn't look: under
wash piled and waiting, in closets, the moan
and wheeze of your easy breathing pointed
with pips and starts of other sounds, cries
rising, a chain of woof-woof-woofs soon to
decline like cars down the hill's far glide
of night where we said he might never go.
Of course he went, as with him went also you.

You dragged, then lost a bright steel chain: two tags
hung like my dad's world war loudly declared
"Red Dog," your name, our place, and that year's
shots, identities you'd shake off to wander
the possible world. I'd hear you, coming back,
my son still out looking, afraid you'd got
worse than traveller's bite on your mopy flanks.
His shoes puffed up dirt like spurts of time. You
mostly don't expect to find the lost—and yet
fearful, I'd shout, then sleep, then shout. Gone.
You'd wait. You'd creep like sun across the lawn,

then, with him, leap up everywhere, dying splits
of rockets in the roses, crushing mulched shoots
faithfully planted year after year, and roots
whose volunteers you watered brown. When we knew
he'd leave, you'd chase God knows what twitch
of spoor, still, we took your balls. You slowed. Dirt
bedded you till you smelled. Your bones fouled floors.
Squirrels reclaimed their nuts. The awful spew
of what spoiled in you, lying by our fire,
comes back to me as the vet says you've worn
out the heart that banged to sleep beside my son.

What does it sound like, I ask? The vet listens.
Once you climbed a six-foot fence, barking, one leap,
a storm of breath we loved. Now you only eat,
ninety wheezing pounds, a processor of meat.
Like my dad, you face me, hesitate, then piss
blankets and floor. Deaf, eyes blank, the chain
slipped again, you're lost. You don't miss a boy's
games, nothing swells your interest, even the moon's
rattling tags I've hung above old yard rakes.
The vet claims it's time; he'd put you down.
Calling at last, I say "Son. It's Red. Come home."

HOWARD MOSS

GOING TO SLEEP IN THE COUNTRY

The terraces rise and fall
As the light strides up and rides over
The hill I see from my window.
The spring in the dogwood now,
Enlarging its small preconceptions,
Puts itself away for the night.
The mountains do nothing but sit,
Waiting for something to happen—
Perhaps for the sky to open.

In the distance, a waterfall,
More sound than vision from here,
Is weighing itself again,
A sound you can hardly hear.
The birds of the day disappear,
As if the darkness were final.
The harder it is to see,
The louder the waterfall.

And then the whippoorwill
Begins its tireless, cool,

Calm, and precise lament—
Again and again and again—
Its love replying in kind,
Or blindly sung to itself,
Waiting for something to happen.

In that rain-prickle of song,
The waterfall stays its sound,
Diminishing like a gong
Struck by the weakening hand
Of a walker walking away,
Who is farther away each time,

Until it is finally dumb.
Each star, at a different depth,
Shines down. The moon shines down.
The night comes into its own,
Waiting for nothing to happen.

PATRICIA GOEDICKE

MAHLER IN THE LIVING ROOM

Low to the ground, the windows are full of lake water.
Leaden, the pure slabs rise straight up into the air

From the summerhouse, where we sit watching them.
Shivering on the threshold of late fall,

The bronze hills in their shabby coats
Arch themselves over a cold radiator—

And Mahler in the living room like an earthquake. Behind the eyes
Sorrow heaves upward, the heavy planks of it gigantic

As armies at a distance, as oak trees, as the tar surface
Of a road giving way to frost, buckling under and over

To the white forces of winter: the underground tears bent
Like ribs cracking, hundreds of paralyzed veins

That are now, suddenly, released, in great silver floods.
Powerful as oceans, our whole lives rise up

Into a sky full of planets tumbling and shooting,
First lavender, then apricot, then plum-colored;

Hissing like skyrockets they streak
Over the slumberous oars in the depths voluptuously rowing,

Velvet as elephants, whose liquid footsteps wallow,
About to submerge everything: dock, landing place, lawn . . .

But there are jagged slashes, too,
Impertinent brass flourishes, horns that bite air

And bray at each other like gold rifles

Over the little pebbles, the quaint Chinese sparrows
Of the piccolos humorously yammering, trying not to listen

To the huge hesitation waltz beneath them,
The passionate kettledrums rolling

In the throbbing cradle of the gut,
Sighing over and over, "Let go,

Abandon yourself to the pain, the wild love of it that surges,
Resistless, through everyone's secret bowels,

Till the walls almost collapse, our clothes fall from us like leaves."
Trembling, helplessly tossed

In an uncontrollable windstorm, the branches weave and sob
As if they would never stop, unbearable the sky,

Unbearable the weight of it, the loss, solitude, suffering,
The hills staring at us blindly,

The house nothing but a shell, the bare floors
Relentless, our eyes welling over with such pain

It is all absolutely uncontainable; in a few minutes
Surely everything will dissolve. . . .

When the first duck of a new movement appears

In the middle distance, the bottle-green oboe bobs,
Blue-ringed, graceful, under the little rowboat;

The invisible red feet sturdily paddle
Like webbed spoons in the chill soup of the water

That turns into a flatness now,
The agonized surface lies down

In the glass eyes of the windows,
Those solid transparencies.

We orchestrate ourselves
To keep the world framed, at bay,

As the great lake of the symphony sways
Far down, far down

The violent sun sets
Over the wet shingles, the shining flanks of the house;

The threadbare arm of the hills sinks,
The wave of feeling rests.

MARY JO BANG

LANDSCAPE WITH THE FALL OF ICARUS

How could I have failed you like this?
The narrator asks
The object. The object is a box
Of ashes. How could I not have saved you,
A boy made of bone and blood. A boy
Made of a mind. Of years. A hand
And paint on canvas. A marble carving.
How can I not reach where you are
And pull you back. How can I be
And you not. You're forever on the platform
Seeing the pattern of the train door closing.
Then the silver streak of me leaving.
What train was it? The number six.
What day was it? Wednesday.
We had both admired the miniature mosaics
Stuck on the wall of the Met.
That car should be forever sealed in amber.
That dolorous day should be forever
Embedded in amber.
In garnet. In amber. In opal. In order
To keep going on. And how can it be
That this means nothing to anyone but me now.

DONALD FINKEL

NOT SO THE CHAIRS

The tables slept on their feet
like horses
could wait there
forever if commanded
no matter what men set on them
a strong back was all it took
and a little patience

the beds never got up at all
pampered in linens
sprawling in perfumed chambers
while on their breasts the gentry
shrieked and sweated
muffling from time to time a sigh
in a diffident pillow

once in a long while a mirror
might lift a negligent arm
or brush dust from a sleeve
merely to lapse in an absent smile
against the entry wall
a portrait of discretion

not so the chairs
no wonder at first so few appeared
only a king could afford one
set cross-legged on a stone
at the end of the hall
his master ground
the royal haunches in his lap
after an hour all circulation ceased

later in the dark he sat
unflinching as a tree
while silver straight-pins pierced
his meek upholstered thighs
through all of which he made not once out-cry
nor raised an arm in self-defense

little wonder now in the night
they bruise our shins with their bony knees
or drive a sinewy shoulder
in the corporate belly
one day they will turn the tables on us
the mirrors will begin to leer in our faces
there is no viper
like an insolent servant

LITTLE BLACK HEART OF THE TELEPHONE

That telephone keeps screaming its little black heart out:
Nobody there? Oh, nobody's there!—and the blank room bleeds
For the poor little black bleeding heart of the telephone.
I too have suffered. I know how it feels
When you scream and scream, and nobody's there.
I am feeling that way this goddam minute,
If for no particular reason.

Tell the goddam thing to shut up! Only
It's not ringing now at all, but I
Can scrutinize it and tell that it's thinking about
Ringing, and just any minute, I know.
So, you demand, the room's not empty, you're there?
Yes, I'm here, but it might start screaming just after
I've gone out the door, in my private silence.

Or if I stayed here I mightn't answer, might pretend
Not to be here at all, or just be part of the blankness
The room is, as the blankness
Bleeds for the little bleeding black heart
Of the telephone. If, in fact, it should scream,
My heart would bleed too, for I know how pain can't find words.
Or sometimes is afraid to find them.

I tell you because I know you will understand.
I know you have screamed: *Nobody there? Oh, nobody's there!*
You've looked up at stars lost in blankness that bleeds
Its metaphysical blood, but not of redemption.
Have you ever stopped by the roadside at night, and couldn't
Remember your name, and breath
Came short? Or at night waked up with a telephone screaming,
And covered your head, afraid to answer?

Anyway, now in broad daylight, I'm out in the street,
And no telephone anywhere near, or even

Thinking about me. But tonight, back in bed, I may dream
Of a telephone screaming its little black heart out,
In an empty room, toward sunset,
While a year-old newspaper, yellowing, lies on the floor, and velvety
Dust thick over everything, especially
On the black telephone, on which no thumbprint has,
For a long time now, been visible.

In my dream, I wonder why, long since, it's not been disconnected.

HOWARD NEMEROV

THE DIAL TONE

A moment of silence first, then there it is;
But not as though it only now began
Because of my attention; rather, this:
That I begin at one point on its span
Brief kinship with its endless going on.

Between society and self it poses
Neutrality perceptible to sense,
Being a no man's land the lawyer uses
Much as the lover does. Charged innocence,
It sits on its own electrified fence,

Is neither pleased nor hurt by race results,
Or by the nasty thing John said to Jane,
Is merely interrupted by insults,
Devotions, lecheries; after the sane
And mad hang up at once, it will remain.

Suppose that, in God, a black bumblebee
Or colorless hummingbird buzzed all night,
Dividing the abyss up equally,
And carried its neither sweetness nor its light
Across impossible eternity.

Now take this hummingbird, this bee, away;
And, like the Cheshire smile without its cat,
The remnant hum continues on its way,
Unwinged, able at once to move and wait,
An endless freight train on an endless flat.

Something like that, some loneliest of powers
That never has confessed its secret name.
I do not doubt that if you gave it hours,
And then lost patience, it would be the same
After you left that it was before you came.

KATHLEEN RAINE

MESSAGE FROM HOME

Do you remember, when you were first a child,
Nothing in the world seemed strange to you;
You perceived for the first time shapes already familiar,
And seeing, you knew that you had always known
The lichen on the rock, fern leaves, the flowers of thyme,
As if the elements newly met in your body,
Caught up into the momentary vortex of your living,
Still kept the knowledge of a former state—
In you retained recollection of cloud and ocean,
The branching tree, the dancing flame.

Now when nature's darkness seems strange to you,
And you walk, an alien, in the streets of cities,
Remember earth breathed you into her with the air, with the sun's
        rays,
Laid you in her waters asleep, to dream
With the brown trout among the milfoil roots—
From substance of star and ocean fashioned you,
At the same source conceived you
As sun and foliage, fish and stream.

Of all created things the source is one,
Simple, single as love; remember
The cell and seed of life, the sphere
That is, of child, white bird, and small blue dragonfly,
Green fern and the gold four-petalled tormentilla,
The ultimate memory.
Each latent cell puts forth a future,
Unfolds its differing complexity
As a tree puts forth leaves, and spins a fate
Fern-traced, bird-feathered, or fish-scaled;
Moss spreads its green film on the moist peat,
The germ of dragonfly pulses into animation and takes wing
As the water lily from the mud ascends on its ropy stem
To open a sweet white calyx to the sky.
Man, with farther to travel from his simplicity,
From the archaic moss, fish, and lily, parts
And into exile travels his long way.

As you leave Eden behind you, remember your home,
For, as you remember back into your own being,
You will not be alone; the first to greet you
Will be those children playing by the burn,
The otters will swim up to you in the bay,
The wild deer on the moor will run beside you.
Recollect more deeply and the birds will come,
Fish rise to meet you in their silver shoals,
And darker, stranger, more mysterious lives
Will throng about you at the source
Where the tree's deepest roots drink from the abyss.

Nothing in that abyss is alien to you.
Sleep at the tree's root, where the night is spun
Into the stuff of worlds, listen to the winds,
The tides, and the night's harmonies, and know
All that you knew before you began to forget,
Before you became estranged from your own being,
Before you had too long parted from those other
More simple children, who have stayed at home

In meadow and island and forest, in sea and river.
Earth sends a mother's love after her exiled son,
Entrusting her message to the light and air,
The winds and waves that carry your ship, the rain that falls,
The birds that call to you, and all the shoals
That swim in the natal waters of her ocean.

JUDITH BAUMEL

YOU WEREN'T CRAZY AND YOU WEREN'T DEAD

Four neat sonnets ago we were twenty.
You weren't crazy and you weren't dead.
We still counted ourselves four girlfriends
who'd gone to Radcliffe from the Bronx.

Later, nervous elegies, those four boxy
sonnets, emerged from my stunned hand.
I didn't have the courage to write them to you,
but to your parents, survivors again.

Your name in the synagogue's blue glass window
panel always makes me cry and in the film
over my eyes I collect square Polaroids
of Purim costumes, graduations, day camps,

the mean permutations of the cubic friendship:
who was whose best friend, who telling secrets
to whom, who prettiest, smartest, the showoff, the bore.
A story of small, sorry memories.

The year after you killed yourself
the rest of us took a four-bedroom apartment.
The fourth was always changing owners.
We mentioned your name from time to time.

Your brother named his baby girl for you.
He seemed to leave the names of those others lost

in the war in the war.
I try to find comfort in this birth, this life,

the odd fact of another child with this name.
And, astonished that we have grown up, become mothers
five times over among the three of us,
the old numbers jumbled somehow and you

somehow gone out, away, or stayed behind,
I find the image of another, still young
Emily toddling into warped rooms all wrong.
Who will forgive her for what you did?

CHRISTIAN WIMAN

FIVE HOUSES DOWN

I loved his ten demented chickens
and the hell-eyed dog, the mailbox
shaped like a huge green gun.
I loved the eyesore opulence
of his five partial cars, the wonder-cluttered porch
with its oilspill plumage, tools
cauled in oil, the dark
clockwork of disassembled engines
christened Sweet Baby and benedicted Old Bitch;
and down the steps into the yard the explosion
of mismatched parts and black scraps
amid which, like a bad sapper cloaked
in luck, he would look up stunned,
patting the gut that slopped out of his undershirt
and saying, *Son,*
you lookin' to make some scratch?
All afternoon we'd pile the flatbed high
with stacks of Exxon floormats
mysteriously stencilled with his name,
rain-rotted sheetrock or miles
of misfitted pipes, coil after coil

of rusted fencewire that stained for days
every crease of me, rollicking it all
to the dump where, while he called
every ragman and ravened junkdog by name,
he catpicked the avalanche of trash
and fished some always fixable thing
up from the depths. Something
about his endless aimless work
was not work, my father said.
Somehow his barklike earthquake curses
were not curses, for he could *goddam*
a slipped wrench and *shitfuck* a stuck latch,
but one bad word from me
made his whole being
twang like a nail mis-struck. *Aint no call for that,
son, no call at all.* Slipknot, whatknot, knot
from which no man escapes—
prestoed back to plain old rope;
whipsnake, blacksnake, deep in the wormdirt
worms like the clutch of mud:
I wanted to live forever
five houses down
in the womanless rooms a woman
sometimes seemed to move through, leaving him
twisting a hand-stitched dishtowel
or idly wiping the volcanic dust.
It seemed like heaven to me:
beans and weenies from paper plates,
black-fingered tinkerings on the back stoop
as the sun set, on an upturned fruitcrate
a little jamjar of rye like ancient light,
from which, once, I took a single, secret sip,
my eyes tearing and my throat on fire.

X. J. KENNEDY

GOLGOTHA

Gray fur collars on a steel limb,
The welders, keeping hands warm
Inside their sheet-plastic cocoon,
Weave the new dorm
Late into night. It's deadlined
For April. According to plan,
The chewed hill's to be redefined,
And seedlings, to a man,
Stood up in ranks against bright,
Green lawn unrolled,
Brick walls, adolescently bright,
Sprayed to look old.

In my locked childproof basement workroom,
Furnace vapors
Chase their own tails in the gloom,
I face ungraded papers,
An iron door in a brick wall
A kick could splinter
Diking the ashes of all
Our hearths of winter,
Half-hear a slow thrash of bedsheets,
A mouse scratch, taking chances
At the trap. Down the spine of my Keats
Mildew advances.

Cramped hand, an unrecognized name:
*How Youth Is Shafted
By Society* . . . now I know him,
They got him. Drafted.
Through vines in a gnarled neutral zone,
A locust nation,
With flamethrowers chewing, moves on
About slow defoliation.
Interesting idea, says my pen

To a John Bircher—liar, liar!
Shots rattle. No, the stuffed lion's
Brass eyeballs in the dryer.

I take out trash, not to read more.
Torn gift wraps, Christmas-tree rain.
Lift can cover on a white horde
Writhing. Lean rain
Blown to bits by the murderous wind
Has it in for you, finger and face,
Drives through every hole to your brain,
Taking over the place
As though it had been there before,
Had come back in its own hour,
Snow gaining ground in the dark yard,
The mad in absolute power.

RICHARD WILBUR

IN LIMBO

What rattles in the dark? The blinds at Brewster?
I am a boy then, sleeping by the sea,
Unless that clank and chittering proceed
From a bent fan blade somewhere in the room,
The air-conditioner of some hotel
To which I came too deadbeat to remember.
Let me, in any case, forget and sleep.
But listen: under my billet window, grinding
Through the shocked night of France, I surely hear
A convoy moving up, whose treads and wheels
Trouble the planking of a wooden bridge.

For a half-kindled mind that flares and sinks,
Damped by a slumber which may be a child's,
How to know when one is, or where? Just now
The hinged roof of the Cinema Vascello

Smokily opens, beaming to the stars
Crashed majors of a final panorama,
Or else that spume of music, wafted back
Like a girl's scarf or laughter, reaches me
In adolescence and the Jersey night,
Where a late car, tuned in to wild casinos,
Guns past the quiet house toward my desire.

Now I could dream that all my selves and ages,
Pretenders to the shadowed face I wear,
Might, in this clearing of the wits, forgetting
Deaths and successions, parley and atone.
It is my voice which prays it; mine replies
With stammered passion or the speaker's pause,
Rough banter, slogans, timid questionings—
Oh, all my broken dialects together;
And that slow tongue which mumbles to invent
The language of the mended soul is breathless,
Hearing an infant howl demand the world.

Someone is breathing. Is it I? Or is it
Darkness conspiring in the nursery corner?
Is there another lying here beside me?
Have I a cherished wife of thirty years?
Far overhead, a long susurrus, twisting
Clockwise or counterclockwise, plunges east—
Twin floods of air in which our flagellate cries,
Rising from love-bed, childbed, bed of death,
Swim toward recurrent day. And farther still,
Couched in the void, I hear what I have heard of,
The god who dreams us, breathing out and in.

Out of all that I fumble for the lamp chain,
A room condenses and at once is true—
Curtains, a clock, a mirror which will frame
This blinking mask the light has clapped upon me.
How quickly, when we choose to live again,
As Er once told, the cloudier knowledge passes!

I am a truant portion of the all
Misshaped by time, incorrigible desire,
And dear attachment to a sleeping hand,
Who lie here on a certain day and listen
To the first birdsong, homelessly at home.

ROBERT PACK

THE STONE WALL CIRCLING THE GARDEN

Instantly my fingers know surely
      where the stone will fit.
Its curved weight surges up my arms,
      humming in my blood:
I have waited now a hundred years, knowing
      I belong here.
A twist, a nudge, and there it is
      in its fixed place
in a destined design, balanced in the sun
      which says: *So be it,*
I adore all circles, I commend your work.
      I hear the bees arrive
and the earth revolve, tightening the grip
      of each stone, one
to the other, to the other, to the other,
      in the bronze heat,
ore of my bones, which says: *Breathe in*
      the bees' dark rose
and the dust of the air. And so I do
      as the circle grows
more still, gathering the garden in,
      while bees follow
the odor the wind-lanes waft away
      beyond my sight.
And there another circle tightens, made
      of the shape of stones,
as the bees revolve and the dust follows
      beyond in the wind-lanes,

each speck shaped like a star, where a circle
      tightens and holds
like a single stone—like the stone I grasp
      in the fixed clutch
of my hands, which says: *There is nothing*
      further for you to desire.

DEBORAH DIGGES

THE BIRTHING

Call out the names in the procession of the loved.
Call from the blood the ancestors here to bear witness
to the day he stopped the car,
we on our way to a great banquet in his honor.
In a field a cow groaned lowing, trying to give birth,
what he called *front leg presentation*,
the calf come out nose first, one front leg dangling from his mother.
A fatal sign he said while rolling up the sleeves
of his dress shirt, and climbed the fence.
I watched him thrust his arms entire
into the yet-to-be, where I imagined holy sparrows scattering
in the hall of souls for his big mortal hands just to make way,
With his whole weight he pushed the calf back in the mother
and grasped the other leg tucked up like a closed wing
against the new one's shoulder.
And found a way in the warm dark to bring both legs out
into the world together.
Then heaved and pulled, the cow arching her back,
until a bull calf, in a whoosh of blood and water,
came falling whole and still onto the meadow.
We rubbed his blackness, bloodying our hands.
The mother licked her newborn, of us oblivious,
until he moved a little, struggled.
I ran to get our coats, mine a green velvet cloak,
and his tuxedo jacket, and worked to rub the new one dry
while he set out to find the farmer.

When it was over, the new calf suckling his mother,
the farmer soon to lead them to the barn,
leaving our coats just where they lay
we huddled in the car.
And then made love toward eternity,
without a word drove slowly home. And loved some more.

AMY WOOLARD

WAGE

One by one as they burned out we
Triaged the light bulbs to priority slots

Around the house. The bedroom still
Held a candle for us. The walls stayed

Rented white. I can take almost
Anything at this point. The waking

Wince of morning, which is afternoon, which
Is like someone holding tightly your hand

While you're wearing a ring. The kitchen litigates
Our unreturned dishes. The birds have not yet

Learned to mimic our phones, but coolly master
Car alarms & the dog's longing. Baby, paradise

Will be a house without linoleum floors, edges
Puckered up like an open carton of milk,

Its origami lip. All I need to know is
The time of day & the names of

The regulars. Not their names, but what
They drank: *old-fashioned, car bomb, purple rain, dirty*

Skyy. Showing up is a full-time job where the
Paycheck is a paper ghost tendering the wrong

Kind of zeros. It was the year of the drought.
Our stacked cash never laid flat. We pulled

One bright twenty & kept it rolled like
A rumor. A season fleshed out by what fell:

Ice into a glass, a dress onto a floor, a girl
Into a grind. Once, a boy off a fourth-story roof.

What you get is to be changed. Nothing
From the sky for weeks & then—; I poured

Everyone & myself a drink. All of us were taken
With leaving town. By which I mean:

We were taken with not leaving. The town took
As fact we'd be back. It'd all be here waiting

To step into, like a dress, or a downpour: the house,
The glass, the time of day. Even the boy, come

Back as a bird, thin beak tilting at every
Wind-felled scrap: *what-was-That, what-was-That.*

The night downtown blacked out, we walked
Out of the bars, unbanked, as if it were the first

Snow, arms raised to catch—what—on our skin. I felt it
Melt into me anyway. I've trained my wrists to carry more

Than I can carry. A malfunction of lightning bugs, the tight
Fists of peonies demanding their rights, the delinquent

Quiet, the lip-bitten memory of when we first learned
To lie, brick by brick. What was the time. That hour

Slipping itself up under my shirt. I can take anything.
Our currency is we stood outside of everyone else.

I open all the windows & doors because I do, in fact,
Want to air-condition the whole neighborhood. I want

To bring it all down a dozen degrees until even the churches
Of our enfolded hands are cooled & congregationless & still

Possible. My sleep put each next day on layaway until
The once-too-many: I came back & you did not.

How could I even touch it. Your love like
An orange wedge breaking apart in my mouth.

The sky touches the birds & the birds keep
Their distance, faking thirst & emergency.

It's no stretch for us to see how anybody—in the right
Light—surely will confess to something they didn't do.

STANLEY PLUMLY

THE IRON LUNG

So this is the dust that passes through porcelain,
so this is the unwashed glass left over from supper,
so this is the air in the attic, in August,
and this the down on the breath of the sleeper . . .

If we could fold our arms, but we can't.
If we could cross our legs, but we can't.
If we could put the mind to rest . . .
But our fathers have set this task before us.

My face moons in the mirror, weightless,
without air, my head propped like a penny.

I'm dressed in a shoe, ready to walk out
of here. I'm wearing my father's body.

•

I remember my mother standing in the doorway
trying to tell me something. The day is thick
with the heat rising from the road. I am
too far away. She looks like my sister.

And I am dreaming of my mother in a doorway
telling my father to die or go away.
It is the front door, and my drunken father falls
to the porch on his knees like one of his children.

It is precisely at this moment I realize
I have polio and will never walk again.
And I am in the road on my knees, like my father,
but as if I were growing into the ground

I can neither move nor rise.
The neighborhood is gathering, and now
my father is lifting me into the ambulance
among the faces of my family. His face is

a blur or a bruise and he holds me
as if I had just been born. When I wake
I am breathing out of all proportion to myself.
My whole body is a lung; I am floating

above a doorway or a grave. And I know
I am in this breathing room as one
who understands how breath is passed
from father to son and passed back again.

•

At night, when my father comes to talk,
I tell him we have shared this body long enough.
He nods, like the speaker in a dream.
He knows that I know we're only talking.

Once there was a machine for breathing.
It would embrace the body and make a kind of love.
And when it was finished it would rise
like nothing at all above the earth

to drift through the daylight silence.
But at dark, in deep summer, if you thought you heard
something like your mother's voice calling you home,
you could lie down where you were and listen to the dead.

MARY RUEFLE

INGLENOOK

I live in the museum of
everyday life,
where the thimble is hidden
anew every week and often
takes five days to find.
Once it was simply lying
(laying?) on the floor
and I missed it,
looking inside my mouth.
A grease fire in the inglenook!
That took a lot of soda!
Free admission, but guests
are required to face-wash
before entering and
tooth-clean before leaving.
Open daily, the doorknobs
are covered with curated
fingerprints, and pass
on the latest news.

LAWRENCE RAAB

AFTER EDWARD HOPPER

Usually it is night
but always there are windows.
And the green shades
in the rooms of small hotels
drawn halfway.
The carafe of water
on a heavy bureau.
And the woman
taking off her clothes.

The letter on the bed
beneath a picture of the ocean.
The yellow windows of the buildings.
Halfway through the afternoon
trees are drawn
to the edge of a field, and the light
in the rooms of houses by the sea
is still
almost perfectly white.

JEAN GARRIGUE

YOU KNOW

You know those rose sherbets,
The gathering of evening around the leaves,
The suffusions of such tinctures of heavens
On the shorn meadows, the suèdes going gold,
And the delicious checkerboard squares
Taking on every strain of the light;
And you know how the shutters close,
How the rocks, wedged in between trees,
Turn rose,
And somebody blue in the grasses

Makes the gold leap, and how the washed skies
Glitter like scales.
So do checks, eyes, on fire
With the stilled clarity of the rose of air,
And we get on the bus,
Taking the last of it down with us.

JAMES LONGENBACH

112TH STREET

If only once, if ever you have the chance,
You should climb a volcano.
The hermitage at base camp, the glasses of brandy—
That's the past.
Who wants to think about the past?

You want to push forward, climb higher, while all around you,
Inches beneath your feet,
Earth is seething, a river of liquid rock.

Will you make it to the summit—
The flying slag, the potholes
Red as an open wound?
Of course you will, it's easy; everybody does.

So little behind you,
So much ahead—

Once, walking up Broadway
Late at night,
Both of us a little drunk, flurries in the air, Christmas trees
Lining the sidewalk, block after block—

At every corner
You kissed me.
Then the light would change.

MEGHAN O'ROURKE

APARTMENT LIVING

So those despotic loves have become known to you,
rubbing cold hands up your thighs, leaving oily trails,
whispering, *Just how you like it, right?*
Upstairs the sorority girls are playing charades
again, smoking cigarettes, wearing shifts, burning
pain into their synapses.
Life is a needle. And now it pricks you:
the silver light in which you realize
your attempts at decadence
tire the earth and tire you. The etymology
of "flag" as in "to signal to stop"
is unknown. It is time to sit and watch. Don't
call that one again, he's pitiless in his self-certainty.
You used to be so.
You laid your black dress on the bed.
You stepped in your heels over sidewalk cracks.
You licked mint and sugar from the cocktail mixer,
singing nonsense songs,
and the strangers, they sang along.

DONALD JUSTICE

THE SMALL WHITE CHURCHES OF THE SMALL WHITE TOWNS

The twangy, off-key hymn songs of the poor,
Not musical, but somehow beautiful.
And the paper fans in motion, like little wings.

CZESŁAW MIŁOSZ

THE THISTLE, THE NETTLE

The thistle, the nettle, the burdock, the belladonna
Have a future. Theirs are wastelands
And rusty railroad tracks, the sky, silence.

Who shall I be for men many generations later?
When, after the noise of languages, the award goes to silence?

I was to be redeemed by the gift of arranging words
But must be prepared for an earth without grammar,

For the thistle, the nettle, the burdock, the belladonna,
And a small wind above them, a sleepy cloud, silence.

(Translated, from the Polish, by the author and Robert Hass.)

MAY SARTON

THE HOUSE IN WINTER

The house in winter creaks like a ship;
Snow-locked to the sills, and harbored snug
In soft white meadows, it is not asleep.
When icicles pend on the low roof's lip,
The shifting weight of a slow-motion tug
May slide off sometimes in a crashing slip.
At zero I have heard a nail pop out
From clapboard like a pistol shot.

All day this ship is sailing out on light:
At dawn we wake to rose and amber meadows,
At noon plunge on across the waves of white,
And, later, when the world becomes too bright,
Tack in among the lengthening blue shadows
To anchor in black-silver pools of night.

Although we do not really come and go,
It feels a long way up and down from zero.

At night I am aware of life aboard.
The scampering presences are often kind,
Leaving, under a cushion, a seed hoard,
But I can never open any cupboard
Without a question: What shall I find?
A hard nut in my boot? An apple cored?
The house around me has become an ark,
As we go creaking on from dark to dark.

There is a wilder solitude in winter,
When every sense is pricked alive and keen
For what may pop or tumble down or splinter.
The light itself, as active as a painter,
Swashes bright flowing banners down
The flat white walls. I stand here like a hunter
On the *qui vive*, though all appears quite calm,
And feel the silence gather like a storm.

ELIZABETH MACKLIN

TREE WITH ORNAMENTS BY MY MOTHER

It could be a wintering bear this year,
long furred & yet unclassified fat fir, rearing
uncrouched by the couch, a bear cub, my first—
a Douglas?—first ever long-needle pine & name unknown.

So thickly fern-broom-, borzoi- or yak-feathered,
whisks under eaves, that ornaments disappear:
the forest of branches has made an interior,
all of her ornaments inside in, and not shown.

But let them try to remain hidden: glass-bird
light paint glows like a house in the woods at four,

snowbound-warm and excited given. It hides this year
but desires to be seen—makes no grief—to be spoken.

This year's tree makes its scent felt across the yards
in between; the past at last has remade the present. *Hark
not to the shining idols* but to their singular deity, inward
invisible bird fir fragrance, who says they could even be broken.

MUNA LEE
CHRISTMAS EVE

At this moment in Mississippi
Red leaves linger, chrysanthemums smolder,
Late roses clamber pale but fragrant
Right across the porch's shoulder.
At this moment in Oklahoma
Mistletoe weighs down great branches,
Sumach glows a frosty crimson,
Bittersweet wreathes broken fences.
At this moment in the New York subway
Package-laden melancholy
Bears poinsettia, crumbling pine-sprays,
Everywhere the brand of holly.
At this moment in Puerto Rico
Great waves smashing, bright and riven,
Fling spray to shore in salty garlands
Spattering spider lily and tree of heaven.

MURIEL SPARK
HOLIDAYS

The month of the holidays,
where is the . . . who can find
him . . . the electrician, there
is a water problem, the oil tank
leaks, do you know what
that means? It is the holidays, there are
no electricians, no shops, no tanks,
no cisterns. Nails
are breaking, blood does not gush.
Ring, ring, ring, dial 023
dial 576 and 999. Nothing
doing, my friend. All the machines
are dead. Money doesn't speak.
Nobody. The desert.
      And now come the floods.
Escape, escape quickly. Leave
everything. No point in locking
up.
      Go away, far far away. The
month of the holidays.

MARY JO SALTER
MOVING

Like planning one's own funeral:
papers finally in their file,
change-of-address cards like a will

showing where everything should be going;
shut windows and the billowing
curtains that caught the breath of spring

folded like shrouds in the spiritless
coffins of labelled cardboard boxes;
boxes and boxes and more boxes

lined up on the lawn like gravestones,
then lifted groaningly into vans—
how could we bear to make such plans

if we didn't believe that purgatory
is waiting for us precisely where
our cartons will next see the air,

the sealed flaps opening like a pair
of French windows on another story?

GARY SNYDER

WAITING FOR A RIDE

Standing at the baggage, passing time:
Austin, Texas, airport—my ride hasn't come yet.
My former wife is making Web sites from her home,
one son's seldom seen,
the other one and his wife have a boy and girl of their own.
My wife and stepdaughter are spending weekdays in town
so she can get to high school.
My mother, ninety-six, still lives alone and she's in town, too,
always gets her sanity back just barely in time.
My former former wife has become a unique poet;
most of my work,
such as it is, is done.
Full moon was October 2nd this year,
I ate a mooncake, slept out on the deck,
white light beaming through the black boughs of the pine,
owl hoots and rattling antlers,
Castor and Pollux rising strong—
it's good to know that the polestar drifts!
That even our present night sky slips away,

not that I'll see it.
Or maybe I will, much later,
some far time walking the spirit path in the sky,
that long walk of spirits—where you fall right back into the
"narrow painful passageway of the Bardo"
squeeze your little skull
and there you are again

waiting for your ride

CATHERINE BARNETT

SON IN AUGUST

Dignity, I said to myself
as he carried his last things into the dorm.
It was not a long goodbye,

nothing sad in it,
all I had to do was turn
and head up the hill.

All I had to do was balance
on two feet that seemed to belong
to a marionette who had no idea

what came next or who governed the strings.
There's no emergency, I told her,
just get back to your car,

that's it, that's all that's required.
I didn't mind accompanying her,
I myself had nowhere to go.

She drove east then farther east
under a river through a tunnel
until she found herself back at home,

with a purpose.
And the purpose was?
To recognize the green awning.

To find a key in a pocket.
To fit that key in the lock,
take off her shoes, drop them on the floor

with others left there like old coins
from a place she must have visited.
Worth something but what.

There were no clues in the medicine cabinet,
none in the cupboard, none in the freezer
where she found old licorice and Bit-O-Honey

shoved next to a ziplock of bluish breast milk,
all of it frozen solid over nineteen years
into some work of art, a sculpture,

an archaic something of something.
She looked at my hands reaching into the freezer.
Or I looked at hers.

They were strong, worn, spackled with age
as they removed the milk-ice
stashed like weed far in the back.

Do they even make this stuff anymore?
What's it good for?
What was it ever good for?

Repurposed, she thought,
isn't that the word the kids keep saying
these days? Hey sweetie,

she called to the unoccupied room,
hey love. It was so hot the air
from the freezer turned to steam

and she took the ice into her own hands,
held it, held it gently against the back
of my warm animal neck

until something began to melt and I was alone.

JOSEPH LANGLAND

GETTING READY TO REALLY LEAVE

Then, gathering in the dusk,
comes the strange long possibility of loneliness.
Some simple rolling tune invades the dark,
routing all that nostalgic poise
of half shadows.
He pauses,
alone in an open room,
listening.

A moth beats at the rusted back-door screen;
a stray car hums in another street.
Old songs, old songs:
someone is going; someone is going away. . . .
And then that tune, like a sentimental favorite
waltzing mindlessly around the years of young nights
and floating over the glamorous local stages
of county fairs,
trembles once more, follows
an echo further down the street,
falters, fades in again, and is gone.

We swing for an utter moment upon that hinge—
hello, Somebody—
hover, ever so briefly upon that porch,
impersonal as the summer air,
and move on out
info the perfect silence of the town.

CAMPBELL McGRATH

HUMMINGBIRDS

The moon, the ocean—some things never change.
At first the hummingbirds shared the feeder
but then some began to chase the others away,
keeping all the sugar water for themselves.
The baby calls the rainbow a *rainbow*
and the lighthouse a *nighthouse*.
Who could question the full moon
for seeking to guide us
across the ocean on a path of wavering golden light?
Some things never change. And then they do.

THE NINETIES

ALAIN BOSQUET
A FILM

Now that my life is coming to an end,
a director wants to turn it into a film,
an hour and forty minutes long.
Would I agree to play myself,
exaggerating my nervous tics
and suffering in some aesthetic fashion?
I should no longer bend over to write
poems on my knees;
instead, my forehead must shine
and my pen scrawl
my name with a flourish in the sky,
while my nostrils widen
and a thousand mirrors do me justice.
I insist:
no profiles, please, no flattering grins.
As for my books, whose fidelity I now find questionable,
they'd better be signed by some other poet.

(Translated, from the French, by William Jay Smith.)

LOUISE GLÜCK
VITA NOVA

You saved me, you should remember me.

The spring of the year, young men buying tickets for the ferryboats.
Laughter, because the air is full of apple blossoms.

When I woke up, I realized I was capable of the same feeling.

I remember sounds like that from my childhood,
laughter for no cause, simply because the world is beautiful,
something like that.

Lugano. Tables under the apple trees.
Deckhands raising and lowering the colored flags.
And by the lake's edge, a young man throws his hat into the water;
perhaps his sweetheart has accepted him.

Crucial
sounds or gestures like
a track laid down before the larger themes

and then unused, buried.

Islands in the distance. My mother
holding out a plate of little cakes—

as far as I remember, changed
in no detail, the moment
vivid, intact, having never been
exposed to light, so that I woke elated, at my age
hungry for life, utterly confident—

By the tables, patches of new grass, the pale green
pierced into the dark existing ground.

Surely spring has been returned to me, this time
not as a lover but a messenger of death, yet
it is still spring, it is still meant tenderly.

VESPERS

In your extended absence, you permit me
use of earth, anticipating
some return on investment. I must report
failure in my assignment, principally
regarding the tomato plants.
I think I should not be encouraged to grow
tomatoes. Or, if I am, you should withhold
the heavy rains, the cold nights that come
so often here, while other regions get

twelve weeks of summer. All this
belongs to you: on the other hand,
I planted the seeds, I watched the first shoots
like wings tearing the soil, and it was my heart
broken by the blight, the black spot so quickly
multiplying in the rows. I doubt
you have a heart, in our understanding of
that term. You who do not discriminate
between the dead and the living, who are, in consequence,
immune to foreshadowing, you may not know
how much terror we bear, the spotted leaf,
the red leaves of the maple falling
even in August, in early darkness: I am responsible
for these vines.

SANDRA CISNEROS

STILL-LIFE WITH POTATOES, PEARLS, RAW MEAT, RHINESTONES, LARD, AND HORSE HOOVES

In Spanish it's *naturaleza muerta* and not life at all.
But certainly not natural. What's natural?
You and me. I'll buy you a drink.
To a woman who doesn't act like a woman.
To a man who doesn't act like a man.
Death is natural, at least in Spanish, I think.
Life? I'm not so sure.
Consider the Contessa, who in her time was lovely
and now sports a wart the size of this diamond.
So, *ragazzo*, you're Venice.
To you. To Venice.
Not the one of Casanova.
The other one of cheap *pensiones* by the railway station.
I recommend a narrow bed stained with semen, pee, and sorrow
        facing the wall.
Stain and decay are romantic.

You're positively Pasolini.
Likely to dangle and fandango yourself to death.
If we let you. I won't let you!
Not to be outdone, I'm Piazzolla.
I'll tango for you in a lace G-string
stained with my first-day flow
and one sloppy tit leaping like a Niagara from my dress.
Did you say duress or dress?
Let's sing a Puccini duet—I like "La Traviesa."
I'll be your trained monkey.
I'll be sequin and bangle.
I'll be Mae, Joan, Bette, Marlene for you—
I'll be anything you ask. But ask me something glamorous.
Only make me laugh.
Another?
What I want to say, *querido*, is
hunger is not romantic to the hungry.
What I want to say is
fear is not so thrilling if you're the one afraid.
What I want to say is
poverty's not quaint when it's your house you can't escape from.
Decay's not beautiful to the decayed.
What's beauty?
Lipstick on a penis.
A kiss on a running sore.
A reptile stiletto that could puncture a heart.
A brick through the windshield that means I love you.
A hurt that bangs on the door.
Look, I hate to break this to you, but this isn't Venice or Buenos
    Aires.
This is San Antonio.
That mirror isn't a yard sale.
It's a fire. And these are remnants
of what could be carried out and saved.
The pearls? I bought them at the Winn's.
My mink? Genuine acrylic.
Thank God this isn't Berlin.

Another drink?
Bartender, another bottle, but—
¡Ay caray! and oh dear!
The pretty blond boy is no longer serving us.
To the death camps! To the death camps!
How rude! How vulgar!
Drink up, honey. I've got money.
Doesn't he know who we are?
Que vivan los de abajo de los de abajo,
los de rienda suelta, the witches, the women,
the dangerous, the queer.
Que vivan las perras.
"Que me sirvan otro trago . . ."
I know a bar where they'll buy us drinks
if I wear my skirt on my head and you come in wearing nothing
but my black brassiere.

RITA DOVE

INCARNATION IN PHOENIX

Into this paradise of pain she strides
on the slim tether of a nurse's bell,
her charcoal limbs emerging from crisp whites
unlikely as an envelope issuing smoke.
I've rung because my breasts have risen,
artesian: I'm not ready for this motherhood stuff.

Her name is Raven. And she swoops
across the tiled wilderness, hair boiling
thunder over the rampart of bobby pins
spoking her immaculate cap. She dips once
for the baby just waking, fists punching
in for work "right on schedule"—
bends again to investigate what
should be natural, milk sighing into

one tiny, vociferous mouth. "Ah,"
she whispers, "ambrosia,"

shaming me instantly. But
no nectar trickles forth, no manna
descends from the vault of heaven
to feed this pearly syllable, this
package of leafy persuasion
dropped on our doorstep and ripening
before us, a miniature United Nations.
"Just like me!" Raven says, citing

the name of her mother's village
somewhere in Norway, her father
a Buffalo soldier. Now,
of course, we can place her:
an African Valkyrie
who takes my breast in her fists,
grunting, "This hurts you more
than it does me"—then my laugh
squeezed to a whimper and the milk running out.

MICHAEL ONDAATJE

THE BROTHER THIEF

Four men rob the bronze
Buddha at Veheragale
and disappear from their families

The statue carried
along jungle pathways
its right arm raised
to the jerking sky
in the gesture of
"protection" "reassurance"

toward clouds and birdcall
to this quick terror
in the four men
moving under him

The Buddha with them
all night by a small
thorn fire, touching
the robe at his shoulder
ahvana mudra—"gesture
of calling for a discourse"

Three of the men asleep.
The youngest feeds the fire
beside the bronze
its dark-gemmed eyes,

allows himself honey
as night progresses
as sounds quieten and thicken

the shift during night hours
to lesser, more various animals.
Creatures like us, he thinks.

Beyond this pupil of heat
all geography is burned.

No mountain or star
no river noise,
                    nothing
to give him course.

His world is
a honey pot
a statue on its side
the gaze restless
from firelight

                He climbs
behind the bronze
slides his arm around
with the knife
and cuts the eyes

                chipped gems
fall into his hands

                then startles
wakes innocent
out of his nightmare

rubs his own eyes

He stands and
breathes night

air deep
into himself

swallows all
he can of

thorn-smoke
nine small sounds
a distant coolness

                Dark peace,
like a cave of water

CAROLINE FRASER

PASSES

WHITE PASS

For a real thrill, don't get gas
at Naches. Pass the abandoned
fruit stands, pass the shuttered fishing cabins,
pass the sign that says "White Pass," pass
Tieton Dam, pass the filling slit
of Rimrock Lake—not a lake,
really, but a vacuum sucking water
out of the William O. Douglas
Wilderness—pass the signs that say, "WATCH
FOR FALLING ROCK," pass walls
of rock wearing what look like hairnets
to keep their loose parts
in place, pass sheer air yawning open
to your left and sheer cliffs rising up
to your right, but, whatever you do, pass
no one before you pass over
the Pass. Shift. Then
start going down.

SNOQUALMIE PASS

The talk of chains always started somewhere
between Issaquah and North Bend, sometime
after we passed the Swiss chalet
that sold Rocky Road candy with milk chocolate
or dark chocolate and marshmallows
and nuts. Did we remember the chains, would we need
the chains, would we be required to stop the car
below the Pass and put the chains
on? The more the talk of chains,
the more certain it was that we would have to gun
the engine and go without stopping
for eating or sleeping or anyone

stipulating chains, or even for gas,
because the engine was so fuel-efficient,
it could run on fumes.

CASCADE PASS

You can't drive there. Drive,
if you want, to the trailhead, thirty-six hundred
feet up, one lane, pullouts, sand,
gravel, trees rearranged
for the convenience of the North Fork
of the Cascade River. Park
across the valley from the glaciers
hanging off Johannesburg, pick up a pack
that pulls your shoulders
into your back, climb thirty-three switch-
backs, two miles, a couple
of thousand feet. Stop only
if you can stand the flies. Above the tree line
there are no flies, there is just
moraine—fields of pebbles the size
of cars, scabs
of snow. The Pass is just sitting
up there, five thousand feet in the air,
a saddle of green grass and nodding
alpine flowers that seems
to say, *Doesn't this*
look safe? Don't
look now, but it doesn't care
how you got here. It is massively
indifferent, waiting, glacially
patient, for the mistake you must
make—given how you crawled
up here—waiting for you
to start to enjoy the view.

SPARROW

MY FATHER WAS A SNOWMAN

My father was a snowman, but he melted.

All that's left is his eyes—two pieces of coal—
that sit on my kitchen table
and watch me as I walk around the room.

I ate his nose a long time ago.

MARK LEVINE

WORK SONG

My name is Henri. Listen. It's morning.
I pull my head from my scissors, I pull
the light bulb from my mouth—Boss comes at me
while I'm still blinking.
Pastes the pink slip on my collarbone.
It's O.K., I say, I was a lazy worker, and I stole.
I wipe my feet on his skullcap on the way out.

I am Henri, mouth full of soda crackers.
I live in Toulouse, which is a piece of cardboard.
Summers the mayor paints it blue, we fish in it.
Winters we skate on it. Children are always
drowning or falling through cracks. Parents are distraught
but get over it. It's easy to replace a child.
Like my parents' child, Henri.

I stuff my hands in my shoes
and crawl through the snow on all fours.
Animals fear me. I smell so good.
I have two sets of footprints, I confuse the police.
When I reach the highway I unzip my head.

I am a zipper. A paper cut.
I fed myself so many times
through the shredder I am confetti,
I am a ticker-tape parade, I am an astronaut
waving from my convertible at Henri.

Henri from Toulouse, is that you?
Why the unhappy face? I should shoot you
for spoiling my parade. Come on, man,
glue yourself together! You want so much to die
that you don't want to die.

My name is Henri. I am Toulouse. I am scraps
of bleached parchment, I am the standing militia,
I am a quill, the Red Cross, I am the feather
in my cap, the Hebrew Testament, I am the World Court.
An electric fan blows
beneath my black robe. I am dignity itself.

I am an ice machine.
I am an alp.
I stuff myself in the refrigerator
wrapped in newsprint. With salt in my heart
I stay good for days.

HILDA MORLEY

YOUR COLOR

More in some ways than when you were alive, I try to
please you,
            to find I am of your way of
            thinking, as with these red carnations:
they're your color.
                    For myself I'd always
chosen white, saying—

that red's too strong for thinking
in a room, too much.
                              But now I love these flowers,
having grown, these years ("mourning" they said),
more into what you wished:
                                        a clearer form now, seeing
this redness (suspended) above green stems as
thumbprints of Mediterranean earth that
you belong to,   crop of a heart's blood on
this city's grayness,
this room's whiteness.

DEBORAH GARRISON

THE FIREMEN

God forgive me—

It's the firemen,
leaning in the firehouse garage
with their sleeves rolled up
on the hottest day of the year.

As usual, the darkest one is handsomest.
The oldest is handsomest.
The one with the thin, wiry arms is handsomest.
The young one already going bald is handsomest.

And so on.
Every day I pass them at their station:
The word sexy wouldn't do them justice.
Such idle men are divine—

especially in summer, when my hair
sticks to the back of my neck,
a dirty wind from the subway grate
blows my skirt up, and I feel vulgar,

lifting my hair, gathering it together,
tying it back while they watch
as a kind of relief.
Once one of them walked beside me

to the corner. Looked into my eyes.
He said, "Will I never see you again?"
Gutsy, I thought.
I'm afraid not, I thought.

What I said was *I'm sorry*.
But how could he look into my eyes
if I didn't look equally into his?
I'm sorry: as though he'd come close, as though

this really was a near miss.

MARK STRAND
FAREWELL

I

It is true, as someone has said, that in
A world without Heaven all is farewell.
Whether you wave your hand or not,

It is farewell, and if no tears come to your eyes
It is still farewell, and if you pretend not to notice,
Hating what passes, it is still farewell.

Farewell no matter what. And the palms as they lean
Over the green, bright lagoon, and the pelicans
Diving, and the glistening bodies of bathers resting

Are stages in an ultimate stillness, and the movement
Of sand, and of wind, and the secret moves of the body
Are part of the same, a simplicity that turns being

Into an occasion for mourning, or into an occasion
Worth celebrating, for what else does one do,
Feeling the weight of the pelicans' wings,

The density of the palms' shadows, the cells that darken
The backs of bathers? These are beyond the distortions
Of chance, beyond the evasions of music. The end

Is enacted again and again. And we feel it
In the temptations of sleep, in the moon's ripening,
In the wine as it waits in the glass.

II
The sickness of angels is nothing new.
We have seen them crawling like bees,
Flightless, chewing their tongues, not singing,

Down by the bus terminal, hanging out,
Showing their legs, hiding their wings,
Carrying on for their brief term on earth,

No longer smiling, asleep in the shade of each other,
They drift into the arms of strangers who step
Into their light, which is the mascara of Eden,

Offering more than invisible love,
Intangible comforts, offering the taste,
The pure erotic glory of darkness,

Of death without echoes, the feel of kisses
Blown out of Heaven, melting the moment they land.

III

Go in any direction and you will return to the main drag.
Something about the dull little shops, the useless items
That turn into necessity, a sense of direction,

Even the feel of becoming yourself on your return,
As you pass through the outskirts, the rows of houses
Aglow with an icy green from TVs, spreading

A sheen of familiarity, of deliverance, as you
Make your way back to the center, where, because of the hour,
The streets are deserted except for the slow passage of cars,

And here and there somebody standing for no reason,
Holding a letter in her hand or holding a leash
With no dog visible at the other end, casting a still shadow,

And you pass by unsure if this coming back is a failure
Or a sign of success, a sign that the time has come
To embrace your origins as you would yourself,

That staying away no longer makes sense, even if no one
Is shedding tears over the folly or wisdom of your decision.
The world has always gotten along without you,

Which is why you left home in the first place.
So what about those shops and the empty luminous cones
Of light that fall from the lamps, and the echo of your own steps?

From far away, life looked to be simpler back in the town
You started from . . . Look, there in the kitchen are Mom and Dad,
He's reading the paper, she's killing a fly.

RUTH PADEL

COLD

You're almost fifty. Nightlong
your stubble grows white
against my throat. We unwrap

in an attic that smells of tar.
When you push inside, you keep
your eyes closed
as if there's no through way.

These blue corridors, mazy
stairlets, have lost us. We run
from one carved pub to another,

sneezing under high ceilings,
talking magic wands: your father—
proud of you,
his voice a surprise through

a voice on a train. Plus
the dottiness of believing
your Church.

Talking? I listen.
I hold you, stare
at the bathroom strip-glow,
one aureole of hi-glisten ivory

up the half-shut door.
This is me adrift, spindrift,
in your sleep. Drowning in fog.

Learning the unearthly start of ferns,
their brittle browning back,
the many ways of leaving
your town. Where did we go?

BREYTEN BREYTENBACH

UNE VIE SANS AILLEURS

but why does the heart still stir
remembering its dark wings?
and where this wind, down from a hushed sky
bending the trees that silently quake?

and this choked scream unfurling
black as a bird shot up from the reeds
and all those blind houses
where the dying fasten their breath
to the steam on the windows
who cares about the color of the night watchman's coat
since when do feathers scud across the patio
what's the point in remembering,
in paraphrasing dusk?
or the sun behind a woman's eye in early morning
or the woman in the sun, under a weighted branch?
how many dead lie openmouthed in the mines?

the blood is dry and the embers' ash forgotten
in the cold earth—
out of a forest bristling with ice blue stars
the wind unfolds its dark wings:
but what does the heart have left to sing?

(Translated, from the Afrikaans, by Rita Dove.)

HEBERTO PADILLA

POSTCARD TO THE U.S.A.

How can one go on living
with two languages, two houses, two nostalgias,
two temptations, two kinds of melancholy?
Mother, put aside for me the Blake engravings
that are still on the shelf.

In the kitchen, next to the white bookshelf,
I used to amuse myself with Burns's epigrams and epitaphs.
Please keep that book for me.
Another year has passed
and your Communist here will not be able to visit you.

(Translated, from the Spanish, by Alastair Reid.)

CRAIG RAINE

FROM HISTORY: THE HOME MOVIE

1921: NEP AND NARKOMINDEL

His toupee was an open book
but his pallid hands
were guarded on the desk.

They gave nothing away,
not the tiniest gesture,
while his wet lips came and went,

explaining to Lydia
that there were no exit visas
for the family of Pasternak.

There is nothing he can do
and, as if to illustrate,
he takes his right hand

in his left, and shifts it slowly,
like a pointer, heavy, stiff,
to a brass bell by the in-tray.

He tings it carefully,
leaving his hand on the nipple
and curve of the brass.

Before the clerk arrives:
"Germany, you said? Parents and sister?
Yes. Your legs are very beautiful."

She has been observing his legs.
The desk is without a modesty board.
A caliper clamped to his boot

like the steel stirrup
of a bike's front brake.
Surprised, she looks up.

Has she heard what she heard?
The official shows her
the gap left by a canine.

"Our train is leaving tomorrow.
We must have the visas.
I was told they were ready."

The beige folder is on the desk,
unopened, left by the clerk.
Again, the missing eyetooth.

"As you can see for yourself,
there is no record of your application."
A pause prolongs itself

until, almost primly,
"I must ask you to leave.
People are queuing outside."

Shocked, she cannot speak.
Will she be able to walk
on her beautiful legs,

out through this ordinary door
and back into Russia for good?
Never to be abroad again?

Hammer and sickle. Forever.
Gilt on red. Cloisonné. Blurred
emblem of the ampersand.

She might be the North Star,
Sarah Bernhardt herself,
making an entrance:

everyone waiting watches the door,
as if the door were God,
as if the door were a loaded gun.

Descending the five flights
of gray stone stairs,
she is stopped by a shout:

it is an old man, breathless,
with trembling sticky brown lips,
who wants her to look at his papers.

"You have a kind face.
They won't look at my papers.
Wrong stamp. Should be a circle.

Not this what's-it triangle.
They gave me the wrong one.
See. So now I don't exist."

She cannot face his eyes
as he stands there in tears.
He is too old. He trembles too much.

She hands him her handkerchief
and then runs away
down the rest of the stairs.

At home on the Volkhonka,
they are roping the trunks
with their brass epaulettes.

"I will ask Lunacharsky.
Shush. God is good."
And Leonid unhooks the telephone.

hung in the hall,
an earwig of brass and Bakelite.
"There has been a mistake."

So, next morning the visas arrive,
stabbed all over with stamps,
smashed and smeared like flies.

1946: REUNION

Still stencilled with swastikas,
front-wheel casings like spats,
peristaltic, single prop,

a Focke-Wulf 190 at Luton
shimmies in the shock of heat,
waiting for Natasha Kroll:

priority flight to Paris,
arranged by Simpson's. Purpose:
fashions for the Christmas windows.

(And meeting her mother,
missed for almost ten years.)
Perfume and petrol

in the cockpit's blister.
The joke of being a Jew
in a German warplane. Laughter.

Petite. A touch of Tartar
in her sloping olive-stone eyes.
The mapping-pen exactness

of her eyebrows' India ink.
Features cleverly asymmetric.
Skin fine as Rizla papers.

She is wearing a Simpson's suit:
five-button, neat gray check.
And an overcoat with Astrakhan trim,

curly as walnut, slightly waisted,
gold glass rosebud buttons.
Her dark red hat is on her lap

so headphones can be worn
and the pilot proposition her
with dinner, dancing, drinking,

with offers to explain
in detail the etymologies
of jazz and joystick.

Offers she cannot refuse
because her mike switch is kaput.
Headphones in her lap,

two Bakelite bluebottles,
intermittent, indecent, over
and out, she thinks of England:

of hydrangeas in Hyde Park,
subtle shades of litmus,
of helter-skelter whelks at Brighton,

of taking her parents to Lords,
of a cricket ball in wet outfield
like a circular saw,

of anything English. *Novy mir.*
Aus der neuen Welt.
And when she holds her mother tight,

the fierce love she feels
exists with irritation. As of old.
Love has broken a rosebud button.

JESSICA GREENBAUM

THE YELLOW STAR THAT GOES WITH ME

Sometimes when I'm really thirsty, I mean really dying of thirst
For five minutes
Sometimes when I board a train
Sometimes in December when I'm *absolutely freezing*

For five minutes
Sometimes when I take a shower
Sometimes in December when I'm *absolutely freezing*
Sometimes when I reach from steam to towel, when the bed has soft,
    blue sheets

Sometimes when I take a shower
For twenty minutes, the white tiles dripping with water
Sometimes when I reach from steam to towel, when the bed has soft,
    blue sheets
Sometimes when I split an apple, or when I'm hungry, painfully
    hungry

For twenty minutes, the white tiles dripping with water
As the train passes Chambers Street. We're all crammed in like
    laundry
Sometimes when I split an apple, or when I'm hungry, painfully
    hungry
For half an hour, sometimes when I'm on a train

As it passes Chambers Street. We're all crammed in like laundry
It's August. The only thing to breathe is everybody's stains
For half an hour. Sometimes when I'm on a train
Or just stand along the empty platform

It's August. The only thing to breathe is everybody's stains
Sometimes when I board a train
Or just stand along the empty platform—
Sometimes when I'm thirsty, I mean really dying of thirst

ANNA DEAVERE SMITH

AUNT ESTHER (A MEMOIR)

verbatim excerpt from an interview of Esther Y. Blake

Long as I can remember
people always told me I was cute
but
I never felt that I was cute,
I never thought that I was an ugly child,
nor do I feel that I was a pretty child.
I just thought I was a child!
All my life,
people had told me that I was cute,
and I know when I was little
a white lady stole me.
You never heard that tale?
When we were on Biddle Street you had the
        Richmond Market up there
and you had people coming up
from Charles Street
from Cathedral Street
and whatnot
the Richmond Market was a very good market
you got gourmet foods up there and all like that.
I know Daddy,
your grandfather used to bring Miss Langral in from
        Roland Park to shop at the Richmond
Market
and all
along with going to Lexington Market
and you had the maids and the um butlers

and whatnot from the big houses over on Charles Street
coming over
to Richmond Market
getting things
and from what I understand
and Mother used to keep me looking real nice
I was out on the front and Argrel was supposed to be watching me
and Aunt Argrel wasn't too bright
and they looked and I wasn't on the front!
I was like between two and three
something like that.
And when I was little
I had these big blue eyes
and blond hair,
curly blond hair.
You can see my baby picture how I was.
Well they were all up and down looking for Esther.
I was like the pet on the block
I was very friendly very outgoing.
One man used to tell the story about how I came up to him and said
Aren't my shoes delicious?
And like the Germans who lived up the street
they went up to the Krauses
I wasn't up there—
Miss Robinson hadn't seen me—
Miss Patterson who loved me just like her own child
she didn't know where I was—
the barber nobody knew where I was.
Well I was one of those little friendly children.
Well the word got out that Esther was missing.
Well the story gets vague but the way I understand it—
somebody who worked down on Cathedral Street
realized that they had been lookin' for me
said
Well a white lady was taking Esther down to a house on Cathedral
     Street.
Well they went down there
and here I was with this white woman

and seemed like she asked me did I want some candy or some ice
    cream or something
maybe it was one of those women who wanted a child
and I just went right on with her.
What always puzzled me,
see I was light
like I met somebody not too long ago
said "you look different"
I said "yeah."
Like I told a fellow when I went to work in Washington
he said "what happened to your hair it used to be lighter, you dying
    it?"
And I'm wondering now—
Had they not found me and she kept me
and I started blossoming,
blossoming out
with all these Negroid features
what would have happened
she wouldn't have known
and I would have been one of those people who grew up without
    knowing their heritage.
It has happened.

JANE KENYON
PROGNOSIS

I walked alone in the chill of dawn
while my mind leapt, as the teachers

of detachment say, like a drunken
monkey. Then a gray shape, an owl,

passed overhead. An owl is not
like a crow. A crow makes convivial

chuckings as it flies,
but the owl flew well beyond me

before I heard it coming, and when it
settled, the bough did not sway.

THE SICK WIFE

The sick wife stayed in the car
while he bought a few groceries.
Not yet fifty,
she had learned what it's like
not to be able to button a button.

It was the middle of the day—
and so only mothers with small children
or retired couples
stepped through the muddy parking lot.

Dry cleaning swung and gleamed on hangers
in the cars of the prosperous.
How easily they moved—
with such freedom,
even the old and relatively infirm.

The windows began to steam up.
The cars on either side of her
pulled away so briskly
that it made her sick at heart.

DONALD HALL

THE SHIP POUNDING

Each morning I made my way
among gangways, elevators,
and nurses' pods to Jane's room
to interrogate grave helpers
who had tended her all night
like the ship's massive engines
kept its propellers turning.

Week after week, I sat by her bed
with black coffee and the *Globe*.
The passengers on this voyage
wore masks or cannulae
or dangled devices that dripped
chemicals into their wrists,
but I believed that the ship
travelled to a harbor
of breakfast, work, and love.
I wrote: "When the infusions
are infused entirely, bone
marrow restored and lymphoblasts
remitted, I will take my wife,
as bald as Michael Jordan,
home to our dog and day."
Months later these words turn up
among papers on my desk at home,
as I listen to hear Jane call
for help, or speak in delirium,
waiting to make the agitated
drive to Emergency again,
for re-admission to the huge
vessel that heaves water month
after month, without leaving
port, without moving a knot,
without arrival or destination,
its great engines pounding.

AFFIRMATION

To grow old is to lose everything.
Aging, everybody knows it.
Even when we are young,
we glimpse it sometimes, and nod our heads
when a grandfather dies.
Then we row for years on the midsummer
pond, ignorant and content. But a marriage,

that began without harm, scatters
into debris on the shore,
and a friend from school drops
cold on a rocky strand.
If a new love carries us
past middle age, our wife will die
at her strongest and most beautiful.
New women come and go. All go.
The pretty lover who announces
that she is temporary
is temporary. The bold woman,
middle-aged against our old age,
sinks under an anxiety she cannot withstand.
Another friend of decades estranges himself
in words that pollute thirty years.
Let us stifle under mud at the pond's edge
and affirm that it is fitting
and sweet to lose everything.

SUSAN WHEELER

SHANKED ON THE RED BED

The perch was on the roof, and the puck was in the air.
The diffident were driving, and the daunted didn't care.
When I came out to search for you the lauded hit the breeze
On detonated packages the bard had built to please.

The century was breaking and the blame was on default,
The smallest mammal redolent of what was in the vault,
The screeches shrill, the ink lines full of interbred regret—
When I walked out to look for you the toad had left his net.

The discourse flamed, the jurors sang, the lapdog strained its leash—
When I went forth to have you found the tenured took the beach
With dolloped hair and jangled nerves, without a jacking clue,
While all around the clacking sound of polished woodblocks blew.

When I went out to look for you the reductions had begun.
A demento took a shopgirl to a raisin dance for fun,
And f'r you, for me, for our quests ridiculous and chaste
The lead sky leered in every cloud its consummate distaste.

The mayors queued for mug shots while the banner rolled in the wind
That beat at bolted windows and bore down upon the thin,
And everywhere warped deliverers got bellicose and brave,
When I walked out to find you in the reconstructed rave.

The envelopes were in the slots and paperweights were flung.
When I came down to seek you out the torrents had begun
To rip the pan from handle and horizons from their shore,
To rip around your heady heart looking there for more.

DONALD JUSTICE

PANTOUM OF THE DEPRESSION YEARS

Our lives avoided tragedy
Simply by going on and on,
Without end and with little apparent meaning.
Oh, there were storms and small catastrophes.

Simply by going on and on
We managed. No need for the heroic.
Oh, there were storms and small catastrophes.
I don't remember all the particulars.

We managed. No need for the heroic.
There were the usual celebrations, the usual sorrows.
I don't remember all the particulars.
Across the fence, the neighbors were our chorus.

There were the usual celebrations, the usual sorrows.
Thank God no one said anything in verse.

The neighbors were our only chorus,
And if we suffered we kept quiet about it.

At no time did anyone say anything in verse.
It was the ordinary pities and fears consumed us,
And if we suffered we kept quiet about it.
No audience would ever know our story.

It was the ordinary pities and fears consumed us.
We gathered on porches; the moon rose; we were poor.
What audience would ever know our story?
Beyond our windows shone the actual world.

We gathered on porches; the moon rose; we were poor.
And time went by, drawn by slow horses.
Somewhere beyond our windows shone the world;
But the Great Depression had entered our souls like fog.

And time went by, drawn by slow horses.
We did not ourselves know what the end was.
The Great Depression had entered our souls like fog.
We had our flaws, perhaps a few private virtues.

But we did not ourselves know what the end was.
People like us simply go on.
We have our flaws, perhaps a few private virtues,
But it is by blind chance only that we avoid tragedy.

And there is no plot in that; it is devoid of poetry.

THERE IS A GOLD LIGHT IN CERTAIN OLD PAINTINGS

I
There is a gold light in certain old paintings
That represents a diffusion of sunlight.
It is like happiness, when we are happy.
It comes from everywhere and from nowhere at once, this light,
    And the poor soldiers sprawled at the foot of the cross
    Share in its charity equally with the cross.

II

Orpheus hesitated beside the black river.
With so much to look forward to, he looked back.
We think he sang then, but the song is lost.
At least he had seen once more the beloved back.
　　　I say the song went this way: *O prolong*
　　　Now the sorrow if that is all there is to prolong.

III

The world is very dusty, Uncle. Let us work.
One day the sickness shall pass from the earth for good.
The orchard will bloom; someone will play the guitar.
Our work will be seen as strong and clean and good.
　　　And all that we suffered from having existed
　　　Shall be forgotten as though it had never existed.

DAVID WOO

EDEN

Yellow-oatmeal flowers of the windmill palms
like brains lashed to fans—
even they think of cool paradise,

not this sterile air-conditioned chill
or the Arizona hell in which they sway becomingly.
Every time I return to Phoenix I see these palms

as a child's height marks on a kitchen wall,
taller now than the yuccas they were planted with,
taller than the Texas sage trimmed

to a perfect gray-green globe with pointillist
lavender blooms, taller than I,
who stopped growing years ago and commenced instead

my slow, almost imperceptible slouch
to my parents' old age:
Father's painful bend—really a bending of a bend—

to pick up the paper at the end of the sidewalk;
Mother, just released from Good Samaritan,
curled sideways on a sofa watching the soaps,

an unwanted tear inching down
at the plight of some hapless Hilary or Tiffany.
How she'd rail against television as a waste of time!

Now, with one arthritis-mangled hand,
she aims the remote control at the set
and flicks it off in triumph, turning to me

as I turn to the trees framed in the Arcadia door.
Her smile of affection melts into the back of my head,
a throb that presses me forward,

hand pressed to glass. I feel the desert heat
and see the beautiful shudders of the palms in the yard
and wonder why I despised this place so,

why I moved from city to temperate city, anywhere
without palms and cactus trees.
I found no paradise, as my parents know,

but neither did they, with their eager sprinklers
and scrawny desert plants pumped up to artificial splendor,
and their lives sighing away, exhaling slowly,

the man and woman
who teach me now as they could not before
to prefer real hell to any imaginary paradise.

TED HUGHES

FROM BIRTHDAY LETTERS

FULBRIGHT SCHOLARS

Where was it, in the Strand? A display
Of news items, in photographs.
For some reason I noticed it.
A picture of that year's intake
Of Fulbright Scholars. Just arriving—
Or arrived. Or some of them.
Were you among them? I studied it,
Not too minutely, wondering
Which of them I might meet.
I remember that thought. Not
Your face. No doubt I scanned particularly
The girls. Maybe I noticed you.
Maybe I weighed you up, feeling unlikely.
Noted your long hair, loose waves—
Your Veronica Lake bang. Not what it hid.
It would appear blond. And your grin.
Your exaggerated American
Grin for the cameras, the judges, the strangers, the frighteners.
Then I forgot. Yet I remember
The picture: the Fulbright Scholars.
With their luggage? It seems unlikely.
Could they have come as a team? I was walking
Sore-footed, under hot sun, hot pavements.
Was it then I bought a peach? That's as I remember.
From a stall near Charing Cross station.
It was the first fresh peach I had ever tasted.
I could hardly believe how delicious.
At twenty-five I was dumbfounded afresh
By my ignorance of the simplest things.

THE LITERARY LIFE

We climbed Marianne Moore's narrow stair
To her bower-bird bric-a-brac nest, in Brooklyn.

Daintiest curio relic of Americana.
Her talk, a needle
Unresting—darning incessantly
Chain-mail with crewelwork flowers,
Birds and fish of the reef
In phosphor-bronze wire.
Her face, tiny American treen bobbin
On a spindle,
Her voice the flickering hum of the old wheel.
Then the coin, compulsory,
For the subway
Back to our quotidian scramble.
Why shouldn't we cherish her?

You sent her carbon copies of some of your poems.
Everything about them—
The ghost gloom, the constriction,
The bell-jar air-conditioning—made her gasp
For oxygen and cheer. She sent them back.
(Whoever has her letter has her exact words.)
"Since these seem to be valuable carbon copies
(Somewhat smudged) I shall not engross them."
I took the point of that "engross"
Precisely, like a bristle of glass,
Snapped off deep in my thumb.
You wept
And hurled yourself down a floor or two
Further from the Empyrean.
I carried you back up.
And she, Marianne, tight, brisk,
Neat and hard as an ant,
Slid into the second or third circle
Of my Inferno.

A decade later, on her last visit to England,
Holding court at a party, she was sitting
Bowed over her knees, her face,
Under her great hat-brim's floppy petal,

Dainty and bright as a piece of confetti—
She wanted me to know, she insisted
(It was all she wanted to say)
With that Missouri needle, drawing each stitch
Tight in my ear,
That your little near-posthumous memoir
"OCEAN 1212"
Was "so wonderful, so lit, so wonderful"—

She bowed so low I had to kneel. I kneeled and
Bowed my face close to her upturned face
That seemed tinier than ever,
And studied, as through a grille,
Her lips that put me in mind of a child's purse
Made of the skin of a dormouse,
Her cheek, as if she had powdered the crumpled silk
Of a bat's wing.
And I listened, heavy as a graveyard
While she searched for the grave
Where she could lay down her little wreath.

FREEDOM OF SPEECH

At your sixtieth birthday, in the cake's glow,
Ariel sits on your knuckle.
You feed it grapes, a black one, then a green one,
From between your lips pursed like a kiss.
Why are you so solemn? Everybody laughs

As if grateful, the whole reunion—
Old friends and new friends,
Some famous authors, your court of brilliant minds,
And publishers and doctors and professors,
Their eyes creased in delighted laughter—even

The late poppies laugh, one loses a petal.
The candles tremble their tips

Trying to contain their joy: And your Mummy
Is laughing in her nursing home. Your children
Are laughing from opposite sides of the globe.
       Your Daddy

Laughs deep in his coffin. And the stars,
Surely the stars, too, shake with laughter.
And Ariel—
What about Ariel?
Ariel is happy to be here.

Only you and I do not smile.

CHANA BLOCH

MRS. DUMPTY

The last time the doctors gave up,
I put the pieces together
and bought him a blue wool jacket, a shirt,
and a tie with scribbles of magenta,
brown buckle shoes. I dressed him
and sat him down
with a hankie in his pocket, folded into points.
Then a shell knit slowly
over his sad starched heart.

He'd laugh and dangle his long legs and call out,
What a fall that was!
And I'd sing the refrain,
What a fall!

And now he's at my door again, begging
in that leaky voice,
and I start wiping the smear
from his broken face.

VIJAY SESHADRI

DIVINATION IN THE PARK

I

Under the bursting dogwoods et cetera,
having just finished a pear
for lunch, I lie over the earth
to feel it swim
inside my posture, and sleep,
while full-bellied women pole home
with small children,
and black waves fling
grappling hooks and grab by inches
the torn-off, uplifted rocks,
stranded offshore like apple trees in the fog.

2

Parts of the earth are slowly thawing.
Less than slowly, the groundwater
rises in the crevices
and exposed places
five strata down where the fossils are.
The winter was mild:
in the bulbs and empty hives
spring rubs the velvet
from its new brace of horn,
and around the drowning rocks
the feral light of equinox
sheds a pattern on the ocean.

3

To think that before this day,
of all the days,
I was less than a snake sunning
on a rock, but that now
I'm the lord of the serpents in the temple,
worshipped and adorned
in my eloquent lengths.

So what if I fail the test of time?
I cling to the earth as it
banks and glides. Miners
enter my abandoned skin
with strings of lights and diagrams;
gods on couches ring the horizon.

VIRGINIA HAMILTON ADAIR

THE DARK HOLE

Douglass the third is three.
He is digging a hole in the sand on the beach at Nags Head.
Nearby is Kitty Hawk, where our first plane
flew for a few hundred yards.
Another name is in the air: Hiroshima,
a bomb dropping. It sounds like the ocean wind;
but the voices are strange, triumphant and horrified.
He has no words yet for this mixture of tones.
"Does this mean the war has ended?" he asks.
"Yes." "Who won?"
"We did," his mother tells him. "We have the bomb."

Days later his mother is ironing.
She asks him, "Will you go up to the dark hole
and bring me three coat hangers?
They're in a box at the door."
The dark hole is their name for the windowless attic.
Douglass asks, "Do I have to go?"
"No, but you always like to be helpful."
"I'll go," he says.

Twenty years later they both recall the incident.
"When you said we had the atomic bomb," he tells her,
"I thought you meant our family did.
I thought it must be in the dark hole."
He had thought at first it must all be an accident,

like when you dropped something you didn't mean to:
you were ashamed, and sometimes punished.
Fifty years later we still have no words
for the confusion of jubilation and horror,
for the agony of bodies with flesh hanging in tatters
from their shoulder bones;
triumphant, the secret fruit of Oak Ridge
had ripened, falling from a single plane
on an unsuspecting town.
Pity for the three-year-old climbing the stairs
with silent courage
into the terror of catastrophe,
into the dark hole where, yes,
our entire nation owned and kept the fire-wind
of Hiroshima, Nagasaki, the atolls and islands,
the pasturelands of Utah, other remote and quiet
playing fields of a nonexistent war.

GERTRUDE SCHNACKENBERG

A MONUMENT IN UTOPIA

(Osip Mandelstam)

Five thousand miles east of *childless Petrograd*,
You! You, with your hair-raising tales,
Your coat without buttons, your raging fits,
Your history of poverty, your torn cigarettes!
You, with your heart still set
On impossible things,
Touching the top of your head absently
Like Pharaoh's baker trying to explain
His dream that there were birds
Devouring cakes from a basket on his head—
Then falling silent to feast upon a grain of sugar
That audibly melted on your tongue,
A crumb you lifted to your lips

With a delicate finger-and-thumb
In a trance of concentration,
The first grain from that half kilo of sugar,
Like a sack of diamonds finely ground,
For which you traded a shredded
Yellow leather overcoat in December,
Though God knows where you'd acquired
Such a coat,

Though granted that, in the old stories,
Garments are lavished on paupers,
Granted that, in one's childhood books,
The coat of the King
Always comes to rest around
The stooped shoulders of his poorest subject,
Albeit no longer lined with a flash of silk,
No longer even held together
With the precious stitches of silk thread

Inside the coat of Akaky Akakyevich,
Who, though he squandered all that he had
For his lofty dream of a new overcoat,
Though for months he went hungry at night,
Though he did without tea and candles,
Still had to skimp on the calico lining
And a collar of cat's fur.

Even at the Expulsion, God made
With His own hands garments of fur and skin
For the expelled—

But for you the sum of your inheritance,
Of which you were robbed anyway,
Was a veil of threads handed down
Through the generations, a veil descended
From that succession of stolen overcoats
Stuffed with paper shreds
From the nineteenth century.

Out there a giant scissors pursues
Little men, insignificant men, non-persons,
Up and down the lanes of Vtoraya Rechka,
Clacking and clacking behind them,
Cutting their overcoats into streamers,
Until all that is left is a bit to drape
Over the shoulders, but not enough
To cover the face with, when the time comes.

And who wouldn't want to press
His coat on you?
Who wouldn't exchange
Your bunk for his comfortable bed?

Who, then, that has lived such a life
Has escaped the Emperor's notice?
For each and every one of them
Was denounced.
What land and sea did he not thoroughly search,
What clefts in the rocks,
What secret holes in the earth,
That he might bring to the light of day
One who was hidden there? And once he had found
Such a one he would carry him away,
And not to his palace, either.

> •

You will be free to wander
In the metropolitan library,
Free to stare,
Without arousing suspicion,
At the statue voted by the senate
To honor Poetry,
Once a block of undifferentiated marble
Originally destined, in the old life,
For a grandiloquent hotel lobby
In the Empire style, hinting at transports
Of stone in wobbling wheelbarrows driven

Along filthy lanes by men whose fingernails
Are suitable for decapitating fleas
And scratching their beards as if
They sandpapered a shadow—
Once a block of marble,
Yet now a spirit glinting in the room,
With a starry hoard of words
Like tiny prisms on its lips.

Although the rhapsodes themselves
Will be banished from the reading rooms
To the public park, exiles
Even from the reconstructed life,
Framed in the library's windows,
They will reappear in bronze
Along the radiating paths,
Among the avenues of limes, for miles.
They will populate the gravel walks
In greatcoats, holding hats and books,
Although with interchangeable heads
In deference to changing tastes and styles.
Among the reveries of oval ponds
Like looking glasses with drifting swans,
None will be represented pushing a wheelbarrow,
No man, with his head between his knees,
Will be seated and puking between his feet,
No scarecrow with his hands
Fastened beneath his armpits,
Looking cautiously over his shoulder
From his gravel mound,
Will thus indicate the wind-chill factor
On the "date of death unknown."

Seated in the shade of your monument,
Where you will wear an absurd morning coat
Far above your station in life,
Schoolboys will read your lines:

Now I'm dead in the grave with my lips moving
And every schoolboy repeating the words by heart.
Although you are laid nowhere in a grave,
Although you speak without moving your lips,
Although your words shine by themselves.

Beyond the statues of Important Persons
Posthumously rehabilitated
Retired prison guards will be seated in the shade
In flocks along the banks of a green river,
As if a goosegirl had driven
Them to the edge of the pond.
Seated on stone benches,
They will be excused and pensioned off.
In their eighties now, they will snooze
And nurse their tea, and their frail shoulders
Will shake when they cough.
At night, for them, there will be
A tincture of valerian and teaspoon
Glimmering on the bedside table.

Even that one will have attained
A gentle expression,
Who stirred the gravel with a stick
And asked, *So now where is your poetry?*
Even his shadow will tower over nothing more
Than a board of dominoes,
His double chin propped on his fist,
His elbow crushing wadded headlines.

He will die in his own bed
Like an old woman, his head dropping down
Between his glass of tea and a needlepoint cushion
Where a tattered finch flutters,
Though it is stabbed to the heart,
Across a shallow autumnal stream,
Plush with once bright-red thread
Gone muddy brown;

For him, death will lie
Open like a newspaper in a dream,
A paper he ransacks his apartment for,
And when he lays his hands on it at last,
As he smooths the crinkled page to read,
He will simply spread before his face
Not a page but, oddly, a black comet,
Or rather a rococo ornament in empty space
Hanging intriguingly before his eyes,

And he will turn his face toward an evening
So thick with butterflies
Along a blurry road
That the convoy truck in which he is transported
Will lay two black tire stripes
Through the white, rustling millions . . .

It will have evaporated,
That whiff of the scaffold, the siege tower.
Of vaults sealed so long that no one
Would wish to break them,
That sense that a bone is being broken
Somewhere in the world,
That one's number is called out.

Even the dictator, the son of a devout
Washerwoman and a cobbler who savagely beat him,
Will be seated in the library among
Unsuspecting readers,
Including you, where you will be hidden
Behind your book, thumbing the last page
Of your life, still afraid to read it;

Even the dictator will leave off
Doodling wolves in red ink,
And will begin, tentatively, to explore
The vaults of white paper
With a sharpened pencil,

Where howls still will be trapped
In the gray zone of lead.
Even he will turn a sequence of the intricate
Misfortunes of other people
Into icy, twinkling, jagged metres
Until the page will be as blackened
As those black wells
Into which you were lowered
In a nightmare of the skull-piled woods
Outside of Novgorod.

GRACE SCHULMAN

NOTES FROM UNDERGROUND: W. H. AUDEN ON THE LEXINGTON AVENUE I.R.T.

Hunched in a corner seat, I'd watch him pass
riders who gaped at headlines—"300 DEAD"—
and, in their prized indifference to all
others, were unaware he was one who heard
metre in that clamor of wheels on rails.

Some days I took the local because he did:
he sank down into plastic, his bruised sandals
no longer straining with the weight of him;
there, with the frankness of the unacquainted,
I studied his face, a sycamore's bark,

with lichen poking out of crevices.
His eyes lifted over my tattered copy
of his "Selected Poems," then up to where
they drilled new windows in the car and found,
I guessed, tea roses and a healing fountain.

All memories are echoes: some whisper,
others roar, as this does. Dazed by war,
I, who winced at thunder, knew that train

screeched "DISASTER!" How it jolted and veered,
station after station, chanting "*Kyrie*

eleison," while metal clanged on metal
and bulbs went dim. Peering at tracks, I heard
"Still persuade us to rejoice." I glimpsed
a worn sandal, turned, and then my eyes
met his eyes that rayed my underworld.

KEVIN YOUNG

LANGSTON HUGHES

LANGSTON HUGHES
LANGSTON HUGHES
   O come now
   & sang
them weary blues—

Been tired here
feelin' low down
   Real
   tired here
since you quit town

Our ears no longer trumpets
Our mouths no more bells
   FAMOUS POET©—
   Busboy—Do tell
us of hell—

Mr. Shakespeare in Harlem
Mr. Theme for English B
   Preach on
   kind sir
of death, if it please—

We got no more promise
We only got ain't
       Let us in
       on how
you 'came a saint

LANGSTON
       LANGSTON HUGHES
       Won't you send
all heaven's news

ALBERTO RÍOS

THE INFLUENZAS

The last of the epidemics bore him
Specially away, a favorite
Son of their group
In that he had taken such care with them,
Always being sick;
The illnesses came as a knock
Regular at the door,
And his invitation,
Which might have seemed tired from another—
Please come in—
Was full of the ready enthusiasm
For which he was known in all things,
And always the wink of mischief in melodrama:
Always the big show,
Hunching his shoulders
That his wife should not see.
Keeping him quiet and in socks, illness
And its children over the years
Made a second home here,
In him,
At the dinner table

Behind his eyes, sitting
In the most comfortable chair
This withdrawing room in his face had to offer,
Filled drinks always in hand.
This man was a comfort in his manners—
Even disease could see this,
So that when he left he went
Voluntarily, all intentions honest:
Out there tonight the party for him was to be
Very good, and to be there without him now
Would be unbearable.
With his hat, his heavy coat,
Walking that way he walked
When he was quiet in his socks,
Hunching his shoulders so that his wife
Again should not see
Him, with his friends he went drinking
The hundred good glasses of very cold beer.

A. R. AMMONS

BIRTHDAY POEM TO MY WIFE

Have you considered how inconsequential we all
are: I mean, in the long term: but

anything getting closer to now—deaths, births,
marriages, murders—grows the consequence

till if you kissed me that would be a matter
of great consequence: large spaces also include

us into anonymity, but you beside me, as the
proximity heightens, declares myself, and you, to

the stars: not a galaxy refuses its part in
spelling our names: thus you understand if you

go out in the back yard or downtown to the
grocery store—or take a plane to Paris—

time pours in around me and space
devours me and like inconsequence I'm little and lost.

JEAN VALENTINE

THE BADLANDS SAID

I am the skull
under your hundred doubts. I, I
will be with you always.
Heart's-deprive.
Still numinous and alive.
Elephant's side.

Come lie down,
tooth and bone.

Ya, ya,
from a mile high
I crook you up warm,
rabbit-arm.

I am love's sorrow,
the desert's violet needle and gray star.

THE SUICIDES

The tractors at night,
the dimly lighted
kindly lobsters
with glass sides,
with men inside,
and at home wives,

and depression's black dogs
walking out of
the January hedges'
hacked-off sides.

CYNTHIA ZARIN

HAWK-WATCHING

So as the hawk flies over the ridge's beak
you sail over me, under me, wing, shoulder,
jib, sheet, breath material as air, bird shadow
the sky's quick fingerprint, as if the god
of wind had just begun to sing, after a long silence,
a mute wandering, and put his hands just there,
and there, to keep his balance. His hands

are the hawk's black wings, and the bereft
stars that in a dream now fall on those green
hills, absolved, recalled, are the river's upper
reaches talking back, about a summer's day,
a paper boat that didn't sink. Your hands linked
are those great wings—I fall upward as I drink—
my head a nest of feathers on your back.

AMY CLAMPITT

IN UMBRIA: A SNAPSHOT

The coldest, wettest spring within living memory
is the way they describe it. At Assisi
there have been six straight weeks of rain.
They blame it on the Gulf War, of which Melina
happily, for the time being, knows nothing.
A vehement "*Good*ness!" is her fiercest expletive.

Little runaway, forget-me-not-eyed, ringlet-
aureoled refugee from a fresco by Lorenzetti—
all those gold-leaf rigors, the theological
murk underneath—whom nobody can begin to
keep up with, or anyhow nobody human. *Her*
peers are the brown-faced saint's familiars:

he of the caninely grinning lope, they of
the barnyard strut and chuckle, the noon-hour
flurry, by the recycled temple of Minerva, of
brakings and hoverings, structure and function
of wingbeats she'd been gleefully part of
minutes before going romping off into a dark

she knows nothing about—or is one at a year
and eight months already prey to nightmares?—
that goes back to before the Gulf War. *"La bimba!"*—
the reverberation accused us along the catacomb
she stood crying in, consoled by who knows, by now,
how many strangers: Kodachromed all over Umbria

beaming, the crowd scene in the café or the square
perceived as benediction, one unendingly
extended family: or come to a halt, as now,
halfway up an impossible hill, aware of being
small and alone: incipience a spinning globe
(look! the sun's out), all is great spaces opening.

CZESŁAW MIŁOSZ

AMERICA

A tawny and lead-gray current of swift river
To which a man and a woman come, leading a yoke of oxen,
To found a city and to plant in the middle of it a tree.
Under this tree I used to sit at midday
And look at the low bank on the other side:

There, a marsh, rushes, a pond overgrown with duckweed
Shone as before, when the two, of unknown name, were alive.
I did not expect it would fall to me: the river, the city,
Here, nowhere else, the bench and the tree.

(Translated, from the Polish, by the author and Robert Hass.)

GUILLERMO CABRERA INFANTE

LA ISLA

marmarmarmarmarmarmarmarmarmarmarmarmarmarmarmarmarmarmarmarmarmarmarmarmarmarmarmarmarmarmarmarmar
marmarmarmarmarmarmarmarmarmarmarmarmarmarmarmarmarmarmarmarmarmarmarmarmarmarmarmarmarmarmarmarmar
marmarmarmarmarmarmarmarmarmarmarmarmarmarmarmarmarmarmarmarmarmarmarmarmarmarmarmarmarmarmarmarmar
marmarmarmarmarmarmarmarmarmarmarmarmarmarmarmarmarmarmarmarmarmarmarmarmarmarmarmarmarmarmarmarmar
marmarmarmarmarmarmarmarmarmarmarmarmarmarmarmarmarmarmarmarmarmarmarmarmarmarmarmarmarmarmarmarmar
marmarmarmarmarmarmar   ‸‸marmarmarmarmarmarmarmarmarmarmarmarmarmarmarmarmarmarmar
marmarmarr‸   ‸armarmarmarmarmarmarmarmarmarmarmarmarmarmarmar
marmarmar?   .narmarm   ‸‸marmarmarmarmarmarmarmarmarmarmarmar
marmarrr   ...marmarmarmc‸   ‸‸‸‸marmarmarmarmarmarmarmarmarmarmar
marrr   .narmarmarmarmarmarmarmarmarı.ı...   ‸armarmarmarmarmarmarmar
marmarmarmarmarmarmarmarmarmarmarmarmarn..   ‸armarmarmarmarmarmar
marmarmarmarmarmarmarmarmarmarmarmarmarmarmaı.   ‸‸armarmarmarmarmar
marmarmarmarmarmarmarmarmarmarmarmarmarmarmarm.   ‸‸‸armarmarmarmar
marmarmarmarmarmarmarmarmarmarmarmarmarmarmarmaı.   ‸rmarmarmarmar
marmarmarmarmarmarmarmarmarmarmarmarmarmarmarmarmıı. ‸‸narmarmar
marmarmarmarmarmarmarmarmarmarmarmarmarmarmarmarmarmıı ‸‸marmar
marmarmarmarmarmarmarmarmarmarmarmarmarmarmarmarmarmar‸ ..armarmar
marmarmarmarmarmarmarmarmarmarmarmarmarmarmarmaıı.ı.armarmarmarmarmarmarmar
marmarmarmarmarmarmarmarmarmarmarmarmarmarmarmarmarmarmarmarmarmarmarmarmarmar
marmarmarmarmarmarmarmarmarmarmarmarmarmarmarmarmarmarmarmarmarmarmarmarmarmar
marmarmarmarmarmarmarmarmarmarmarmarmarmarmarmarmarmarmarmarmarmarmarmarmarmar
marmarmarmarmarmarmarmarmarmarmarmarmarmarmarmarmarmarmarmarmarmarmarmarmarmar
marmarmarmarmarmarmarmarmarmarmarmarmarmarmarmarmarmarmarmarmarmarmarmarmarmar

PHILLIS LEVIN

PART

Of something, separate, not
Whole; a role, something to play
While one is separate or parting;

Also a piece, a section, as in
Part of me is here, part of me
Is missing, an essential portion,

Something falling to someone
In division; a particular voice
Or instrument (also the score

For it), or line of music;
The line where the hair
Is parted. A verb: to break

Or suffer the breaking of,
Become detached,
Broken; to go from, leave,

Take from, sever, as in
Lord, part me from him,
I cannot bear to ever

KENNETH KOCH

TO MY OLD ADDRESSES

Help! Get out of here! Go walking!
Forty-six (I think) Commerce Street, New York City
The Quai des Brumes nine thousand four hundred twenty-six,
    Paris
Georgia Tech University Department of Analogues
Jesus Freak Avenue No. 2, in Clattery, Michigan
George Washington Model Airplane School, Bisbee, Arizona
Wonderland, the stone font, Grimm's Fairy Tales
Forty-eight Greenwich Avenue the landlady has a dog
She lets run loose in the courtyard seven
Charles Street which Stefan Volpe sublet to me
Hotel de Fleurus in Paris, Via Convincularia in Rome
Where the motorcycles speed
Twelve Hamley Road in Southwest London O
My old addresses! O my addresses! Are you addresses still?
Or has the hand of Time roughed over you
And buffered and stuffed you with peels of lemons, limes, and
    shells

From old institutes? If I address you
It is mostly to know if you are well.
I am all right but I think I will never find
Sustenance as I found in you, oh old addresses
Numbers that sink into my soul
Forty-eight, nineteen, twenty-three, O worlds in which I was alive!

TO MY FIFTIES

I should say something to you
Now that you have departed over the mountains
Leaving me to my sixties and seventies, not hopeful of your return,
O you, who seemed to mark the end of life, who ever would have
     thought that you would burn
With such sexual fires as you did? I wound up in you
Some work I had started long before. You were
A time for completion and for destruction. My
Marriage had ended. In you I sensed trying to find
A way out of you actually that wasn't toward nonexistence.
I thought, "All over." You cried, "I'm here!" You were like travelling
In this sense, but on one's own
With no tour guide or even the train schedule.
As a "Prime of Life" I missed you. You seemed an incompletion
     made up of completions
Unacquainted with each other. How could this be happening? I
     thought. Or
What should it mean, exactly, that I am fifty-seven? I wanted to be
     always feeling desire.
Now you're a young age to me. And in you, as at every other time
I thought that one year would last forever.
"I did the best possible. I lasted my full ten years. Now I'm
     responsible
For someone else's decade and haven't time to talk to you, which is a
     shame
Since I can never come back." My Fifties! Answer me one question!
Were you the culmination or a phase? "Neither and both." Explain!
     "No time. Farewell!"

JULIA ALVAREZ

AUDITION

Porfirio drove Mami and me
to Cook's mountain village
to find a new pantry maid.
Cook had given Mami a tip
that her home town was girl-heavy,
the men lured away to the cities.
We drove to the interior,
climbing a steep, serpentine,
say-your-last-prayers road.
I leaned toward my mother
as if my weight could throw
the car's balance away
from the sheer drop below.
Late morning we entered
a dusty village of huts.
Mami rolled down her window
and queried an old woman,
Did she know of any girls
looking for work as maids?
Soon we were surrounded
by a dozen señoritas.
Under the thatched cantina
Mami conducted interviews—
a mix of personal questions
and Sphinx-like intelligence tests.
Do you have children, a novio?
Would you hit a child who hit you?
If I give you a quarter to buy
guineos at two for a nickel,
how many will you bring back?
As she interviewed I sat by,
looking the girls over;
one of them would soon
be telling me what to do,
reporting my misbehaviors.

Most seemed nice enough,
befriending me with smiles,
exclamations on my good hair,
my being such a darling.
Those were the ones I favored.
I'd fool them with sweet looks,
improve my bad reputation.
As we interviewed we heard
by the creek that flowed nearby
a high, clear voice singing
a plaintive lullaby . . .
as if the sunlight filling
the cups of the allamandas,
the turquoise sky dappled
with angel-feather clouds,
the creek trickling down
the emerald green of the mountain
had found a voice in her voice.
We listened. Mami's hard-line,
employer-to-be face
softened with quiet sweetness.
The voice came closer, louder—
a slender girl with a basket
of wrung rags on her head
passed by the cantina,
oblivious of our presence.
Who is she? my mother asked.
Gladys, the girls replied.
Gladys! my mother called
as she would for months to come.
Gladys, come clear the plates!
Gladys, answer the door!
Gladys! the young girl turned—
Abruptly, her singing stopped.

ALAN SHAPIRO

THE SINGER

The way you sang, half dozing as I drove,
the radio on—the way your hovering
so near sleep, unaware of me, appeared
to purify your shyness, not free you from it;
the way you needed even then to sing
without appearing to, your hushed voice lagging
with a furtive clumsiness behind the singer's,
each syllable only half formed on your lips
before the next one and the next arrived;
the way you happily seemed to falter after
what was always half a syllable beyond—
was not the least accomplished of your many
unknowingly disclosed when most disguised
most accidental flashing of a presence
that's not for yours but other people's eyes.

JOY WOSU

WORRYWART

Worrisome you

You worry for your mother, your father, your sister, your
brother, stepsister, stepbrother, stepmother, stepfather

You worry for your husband, daughters, sons, stepsons, stepdaughters

Now you're worrying for Tom
Worry for you
                    not Tom
Tom worries for Tom
                    as tomorrow worries for itself

No letters! No packages! Phone disconnected!

Parole board is approaching
       No home to go to!
         Halfway housing! No money but handouts!
Prison to bleak future?
          Lord help the homeless!

Now you're rocking,
          cannibalizing yourself
By the time you're finished
          nothing will be left of you
Body filled with cankers, ulcers,
         paranoia, hallucinations
         800 milligrams of Motrin
             four times a day
Wrinkles, gray hairs that dance their way through your skull

Worry not you!
        Health's too precious to swim with worries

NICHOLSON BAKER

FROM THE INDEX OF FIRST LINES

Ha! Small wonder joists are suspect here, 73
Habit, trial and error, jurisprudence, 161
Hack on, hack on, you specimen of waste, 80
Handel bites the bag, and Bach, 193
Happy the charmglow hostess she of late, 52
"Hardihood will see us through," said Chapman, 94
Harm's bordello is the op-ed page, 132
Has this been tried before? he asked the glass, 213
Hasn't your Philip written yet? Politely, 23
Haste hangs on every syllable, 136
He lost the rest on Thursday afternoon, 36

ZBIGNIEW HERBERT

MR. COGITO AND A POET OF A CERTAIN AGE

1
A poet after the prime of life
a peculiar phenomenon

2
he looks as himself in the mirror
he breaks the mirror

3
on a moonless night
he drowns his birth certificate
   in a black pond

4
he watches the young
imitates the way they swing their hips

5
he chairs a meeting
of independent Trotskyites
incites them to acts of arson

6
he writes letters
to the President of the Solar System
full of intimate confessions

7
the poet of a certain age
in the middle of an uncertain age

8
instead of cultivating
pansies and onomatopoeias
he plants prickly exclamations
invectives and treatises

9
he reads one after the other
Isaish and "Das Kapital"
then in the fervor of discussion
confuses his quotations

10
a poet at an unclear time of life
between departing Eros
and Thanatos who has not yet risen
    from his stone

11
he smokes hashish
but does not see
infinity
or flowers

or waterfalls
he sees a procession
of hooded monks
climbing a rocky mountain
with extinguished torches

12
the poet of a certain age
remembers his warm childhood
his exuberant youth
inglorious manhood

13
he plays
the game of Freud
he plays
the game of hope
he plays
at the red and black
he plays
at flesh and bones
he plays and loses
he bursts out with insincere laughter

14
only now does he understand his father
he cannot forgive his sister
who ran away with an actor
he envies his younger brother
bent over the photograph of his mother
he tries once more
to persuade her to conceive

15
his dreams
pubertal not serious
the priest from catechism

protruding objects
and the unattainable Jadzia

16
at dawn he looks
at his hand
he is surprised by his own skin
similar to bark

17
against the young blue sky
the white tree of his veins

(Translated, from the Polish, by John and Bogdana Carpenter.)

MR. COGITO LAMENTS THE PETTINESS OF DREAMS

Even dreams become smaller
                where are our grandmothers' and grandfathers'
                                entranced processions
when colorful as birds lighthearted as birds they mounted high
on an imperial staircase a thousand chandeliers were glowing
and grandfather familiar now only with the cane pressing to his side
a silver sword and unloved grandmother who was so kind
she put on for him the face of their first love

                to them
Isaiah spoke from clouds that looked like clouds of tobacco smoke
                and they saw how St. Teresa
white as a wafer carried a real basket with kindling

their terror was as great as the Tartar Horde
and their happiness in dream was like golden rain

my dream—a doorbell I am shaving in the bathroom I open the door
a collector hands me the bill for gas and electricity
I have no money return to the bathroom meditating

on the number 63.50
I raise my eyes and see in the mirror
my face that is so real I wake with a shout

if I dreamt at least once of an executioner's red jacket
or the necklace of a queen I would be grateful to dreams

(Translated, from the Polish, by John and Bogdana Carpenter.)

MICHAEL KRUGER

FOOTNOTE

We're coming back to fetch
what remains: pillow, pillowcase, pall,
a drawing which hung unprotected
above the stove—"Hermes, the Guide
of the Dead," who, for the space of four years,
added spice to our meals. God has still
not been born; the clock stays hanging there;
so, in the hall, does the mirror. How
the flat grows and grows the more it
empties, and how small is Time,
brooding away in the tomblike rooms.
All is now dark, we've
removed the lamps: everything
passes softly through us. From where
my writing desk once was,
I try to decipher a note
on the wall: Your Anger Is Love.
A footnote in the History
of Vanity, still to be written.

(Translated, from the German, by Richard Dove.)

THOMAS LUX

THE VOICE YOU HEAR WHEN YOU READ SILENTLY

is not silent, it is a speaking-
out-loud voice in your head: it is *spoken*,
a voice is *saying* it
as you read. It's the writer's words,
of course, in a literary sense
his or her "voice" but the sound
of that voice is the sound of *your* voice.
Not the sound your friends know
or the sound of a tape played back
but your voice
caught in the dark cathedral
of your skull, your voice heard
by an internal ear informed by internal abstracts
and what you know by feeling,
having felt. It is your voice
saying, for example, the word "barn"
that the writer wrote
but the "barn" you say
is a barn you know or knew. The voice
in your head, speaking as you read,
never says anything neutrally—some people
hated the barn they knew,
some people love the barn they know
so you hear the word loaded
and a sensory constellation
is lit: horse-gnawed stalls,
hayloft, black heat tape wrapping
a water pipe, a slippery
spilled *chirr* of oats from a split sack,
the bony, filthy haunches of cows . . .
And "barn" is only a noun—no verb
or subject has entered into the sentence yet!
The voice you hear when you read to yourself
is the clearest voice: you speak it
speaking to you.

PHILIP LEVINE
WHAT WORK IS

We stand in the rain in a long line
waiting at Ford Highland Park. For work.
You know what work is—if you're
old enough to read this you know what
work is, although you may not do it.
Forget you. This is about waiting,
shifting from one foot to another.
Feeling the light rain falling like mist
into your hair, blurring your vision
until you think you see your own brother
ahead of you, maybe ten places.
You rub your glasses with your fingers,
and of course it's someone else's brother,
narrower across the shoulders than
yours but with the same sad slouch, the grin
that does not hide the stubbornness,
the sad refusal to give in to
rain, to the hours wasted waiting,
to the knowledge that somewhere ahead
a man is waiting who will say, "No,
we're not hiring today," for any
reason he wants. You love your brother,
now suddenly you can hardly stand
the love flooding you for your brother,
who's not beside you or behind or
ahead because he's home trying to
sleep off a miserable night shift
at Cadillac so he can get up
before noon to study his German.
Works eight hours a night so he can sing
Wagner, the opera you hate most,
the worst music ever invented.
How long has it been since you told him
you loved him, held his wide shoulders,
opened your eyes wide and said those words,

and maybe kissed his cheek? You've never
done something so simple, so obvious,
not because you're too young or too dumb,
not because you're jealous or even mean
or incapable of crying in
the presence of another man, no,
just because you don't know what work is.

THE MERCY

The ship that took my mother to Ellis Island
eighty-three years ago was named the Mercy.
She remembers trying to eat a banana
without first peeling it and seeing her first orange
in the hands of a young Scot, a seaman
who gave her a bite and wiped her mouth for her
with a red bandanna and taught her the word
"orange," saying it patiently over and over.
A long autumn voyage, the days darkening
with the black waters calming as night came on;
then nothing as far as her eyes could see and space
without limit rushing off to the corners
of creation. She prayed in Russian and Yiddish
to find her family in New York, prayers
unheard or misunderstood or perhaps ignored
by all the powers that swept the waves of darkness
before she woke, that kept the Mercy afloat
while smallpox raged among the passengers
and crew until the dead were buried at sea
with strange prayers in a tongue she could not fathom.
The Mercy, I read on the yellowing pages of a book
I located in a windowless room of the library
on Forty-second Street, sat thirty-one days
offshore in quarantine before the passengers
disembarked. There a story ends. Other ships
arrived, Tancred out of Glasgow, the Neptune,
registered as Danish, Umberto IV,
the list goes on for pages, November gives

way to winter, the sea pounds this alien shore.
Italian miners from Piemonte dig
under towns in western Pennsylvania
only to rediscover the same nightmare
they left at home. A nine-year-old girl travels
all night by train with one suitcase and an orange.
She learns that mercy is something you can eat
again and again while the juice spills over
your chin, you can wipe it away with the back
of your hands and you can never get enough.

NIKKI GIOVANNI

LOVE IN PLACE

I really don't remember falling in love all that much
I remember wanting to bake corn bread and boil a ham and I
certainly remember making lemon pie and when I used to smoke I
stopped in the middle of my day to contemplate

I know I must have fallen in love once because I quit biting
my cuticles and my hair is gray and that must indicate
something and I all of a sudden had a deeper appreciation
for Billie Holiday and Billy Strayhorn so if it wasn't love I don't
know what it was

I see the old photographs and I am smiling and I'm sure quite
happy but what I mostly see is me
through your eyes
and I am still young and slim and very much committed to the
love we still have

GERTRUDE STEIN

"DO YOU REALLY THINK . . ."

As Alice B. Toklas typed out Gertrude Stein's notebooks each day, she often found love notes between the pages. Some of them—including the following, written around 1940—were turned over to Yale University Library, where they were rediscovered in 1981 and displayed for the first time in May 1996.

Do you really think I would yes I would and
I do love all you with all me.
Do you really think I could, yes I could
yes I would love all you with all me.
Do you really think I should yes I should
love all you with all me yes I should
yes I could yes I would.
Do you really think I do love all you
with all me yes I do love all you with all
me And bless my baby.

WILLIAM MATTHEWS

POEM ENDING WITH A LINE FROM DANTE

Snow coming in parallel to the street,
a cab spinning its tires (a rising whine
like a domestic argument, and then
the words get said that never get forgot),

slush and backed-up runoff waters at each
corner, clogged buses smelling of wet wool . . .
The acrid anger of the homeless swells
like wet rice. *This slop is where I live, bitch,*

a sogged panhandler shrieks to whom it may
concern. None who can hear him stall or turn,
there's someone's misery in all we earn.
But like a burr in a dog's coat his rage

has borrowed legs. We bring it home. It lives
like kin among the angers of the house,
and has the same sad zinc taste in the mouth:
And I have told you this to make you grieve.

RICHARD HOWARD

AMONG THE MISSING

Know me? I am the ghost of Gansevoort Pier.
     Out of the Trucks, beside the garbage scow
     where rotten pilings form a sort of prow,
I loom, your practiced shadow, waiting here

for celebrants who cease to come my way,
     though mine were limbs as versatile as theirs
     and eyes as vagrant. Odd that no one cares
to ogle me now where I, as ever, lay

myself out, all my assets and then some,
     weather permitting. Is my voice so faint?
     Can't you hear me over the river's complaint?
Too dark to see me? Have you all become

ghosts? What earthly good is that? I want
     incarnate lovers hungry for my parts,
     longing hands and long-since lonely hearts!
It is your living bodies I must haunt,

and while the Hudson lugs its burdens past,
     having no hosts to welcome or repel
     disclosures of the kind I do so well,
I with the other ghosts am laid at last.

WAYNE KOESTENBAUM
THE GARBO INDEX

My dead friend Vito praised Garbo's last scene in "Queen
    Christina"—
the closeup uncomprehended gays stared into, seeking dissolution.
I remember Vito eating pizza at my table in the Village, 1986.
He removed the sausage nuggets, placed them at plateside.

"I don't eat pork," he said: H.I.V.-positive precautions.
He was watching his system, as we were watching our own systems,
and are, to this day, watching. The last time I saw Vito entirely well
he was wearing pearls on his bare chest, high tea, the Pines—

never my scene. Who co-stars in "Romance"? Can't ask Vito.
When he was alive, I never helped him very much, and now he's
beyond telephone—waiting with Garbo
by the schoolyard's huddled ailanthus, waiting for the fire drill to end.

Four new Passover questions. Am I a child or an adult?
Am I a creature of memory or of action?
If I knew I were to die tomorrow, would I phrase this question
    differently?
Is it valedictory to write about Vito, or is it vanity?

My life is small, formal, and walled, and around every vista
I contain, imagine black shutters, the limits that Garbo
decreed must flank the lens filming her face in closeup,
so she could see only the camera's eye, without distracting leading
    man and crew.

Her life, if indexed, could yield surprises,
as could any life, if indexed, if reprieved.
Sea glass, Garbo's collection of. Camellias, Garbo's paradisiacal.
Grotto, Garbo's imaginary. Ghost, Garbo's.

Once, Garbo was whispering secrets of performance
in a bandaged voice, and I was listening, and no toxins in the field
of vision arose to violate the soliloquy, unfolding
with the tranquillity of all final compositions.

JORIE GRAHAM

NOTES ON THE REALITY OF THE SELF

Watching the river, each handful of it closing over the next,
brown and swollen. Oaklimbs,
gnawed at by waterfilm, lifted, relifted, lapped-at all day in
this dance of non-discovery. All things are
possible. Last year's leaves, coming unstuck from shore,
rippling suddenly again with the illusion,
and carried, twirling, suddenly shiny again and fat,
toward the quick throes of another tentative
conclusion, bobbing, circling in little suctions their stiff
                              presence
on the surface compels. Nothing is virtual.
The long brown throat of it sucking up from some faraway melt.
Expression pouring forth, all content no meaning.
The force of it and the thingness of it identical.
Spit forth, licked up, snapped where the force
exceeds the weight, clickings, pockets.
A long sigh through the land, an exhalation.
I let the dog loose in this stretch. Crocus
appear in the gassy dank leaves. Many
earth gases, rot gases.
I take them in, a breath at a time. I put my
breath back out
onto the scented immaterial. How the invisible
roils. I see it from here and then
I see it from here. Is there a new way of looking—
valences and little hooks—inevitabilities, proba-
bilities? It flaps and slaps. Is this body the one
I know as me? How private these words? And these? Can you

smell it, brown with little froths at the rot's lips,
meanwhiles and meanwhiles thawing then growing soggy then
the filaments where leaf-matter accrued round a
pattern, a law, slipping off, precariously, bit by bit,
sudden flicks, swiftnesses suddenly more water than not.
The nature of goodness the mind exhales.
I see myself. I am a widening angle of
and *nevertheless* and *this performance has rapidly*—
nailing each point and then each next right point, inter-
locking, correct, correct again, each rightness snapping loose,
floating, hook in the air, swirling, seed-down,
quick—*the evidence of the visual henceforth*—and henceforth,
    loosening—

C. K. WILLIAMS

THIRST

Here was my relation with the woman who lived all last autumn and
    winter day and night
on a bench in the 103rd Street subway station until finally one day
    she vanished:

we regarded each other, scrutinized one another: me shyly,
    obliquely, trying not to be furtive;
she boldly, unblinkingly, even pugnaciously; wrathfully even, when
    her bottle was empty.

I was frightened of her, I felt like a child, I was afraid some repressed
    part of myself
would go out of control and I'd be forever entrapped in the shocking
    seethe of her stench.

Not excrement, merely, not merely surface and orifice going
    unwashed, rediffusion of rum:
there was will in it, and intention, power and purpose; a social,
    ethical rage and rebellion.

. . . Despair, too, though, grief, loss: sometimes I'd think I should take her home with me,
bathe her, comfort her, dress her: she wouldn't have wanted me to, I would think

Instead I'd step into my train: how rich, I would think, is the lexicon of our self-absolving;
how insane our bland, fatal assurance that reflection is righteousness being accomplished.

The dance of our glances, the clash: pulling each other through our perceptual punctures;
then holocaust, holocaust: host on host of ill, injured presences squandered, consumed.

Her vigil, somewhere, I know, continues: her occupancy, her absolute, faithful attendance;
the dance of our glances: challenge, abdication, effacement; the perfume of our consternation.

TASLIMA NASRIN

THINGS CHEAPLY HAD

In the market nothing can be had as cheap as women.
If they get a small bottle of *alta* for their feet
          they spend three nights sleepless for sheer joy.
If they get a few bars of soap to scrub their skin
          and some scented oil for their hair
they become so submissive that they scoop out
          chunks of their flesh
to be sold in the flea market twice a week.
If they get a jewel for their nose
          they lick feet for seventy days or so,
a full three and a half months
          if it's a single striped sari.

Even the mangy cur of the house barks now and then,
and over the mouths of women cheaply had
                there's a lock
a golden lock.

     (Translated, from the Bengali, by Carolyne Wright, Mohammad Nurul
     Huda, and the author.)

PAUL MULDOON

HAY

This much I know. Just as I'm about to make that right turn
off Province Line Road
I meet another beat-up Volvo
carrying a load

of hay. (More accurately, a bale of lucerne
on the roof rack,
a bale of lucerne or fescue or alfalfa.)
My hands are raw. I'm itching to cut the twine, to unpack

that hay accordion, that hay concertina.
It must be ten o'clock. There's still enough light
(not least from the glow

of the bales themselves) for a body to ascertain
that when one bursts, as now, something takes flight
from those hot and heavy box pleats. This much, at least, I know.

ERRATA

For "Antrim" read "Armagh."
For "mother" read "other."
For "harm" read "farm."
For "feather" read "father."

For "Moncrieff" read "Monteith."
For "*Béal Fierste*" read "*Béal Feirste*."
For "brave" read "grave."
For "revered" read "reversed."

For "married" read "marred."
For "pull" read "pall."
For "ban" read "bar."
For "smell" read "small."

For "spike" read "spoke."
For "lost" read "last."
For "Steinbeck" read "Steenbeck."
For "ludic" read "lucid."

For "religion" read "region."
For "ode" read "code."
For "Jane" read "Jean."
For "rod" read "road."

For "pharoah" read "pharaoh."
For "*Fíor-Gael*" read "*Fíor-Ghael*."
For "Jeffrey" read "Jeffery."
For "vigil" read "Virgil."

For "flageolet" read "fava."
For "veto" read "vote."
For "Aiofe" read "Aoife."
For "anecdote" read "antidote."

For "Rosemont" read "Mount Rose."
For "plump" read "plumb."
For "hearse" read "hears."
For "loom" read "bloom."

MARIE HOWE

PRACTICING

I want to write a love poem for the girls I kissed in seventh grade,
a song for what we did on the floor in the basement

of somebody's parents' house, a hymn for what we didn't say but
    thought:
That feels good or *I like that*, when we learned how to open each
    other's mouths

how to move our tongues to make somebody moan. We called
    it practicing, and one
was the boy and we paired off—maybe 6 or 8 girls—and
    turned out

the lights and kissed and kissed until we were stoned on kisses, and
    lifted our
nightgowns or let the straps drop, and, Now you be the boy:

concrete floor, sleeping bag or couch, playroom, game room, train
    room, laundry.
Susan's basement was like a boat, with booths and portholes

instead of windows. Cynthia's father had a bar downstairs with stools
    that spun,
plush carpeting. We kissed each other's throats.

We sucked each other's breasts, and we left marks, and never spoke
    of it upstairs
outdoors, in daylight, not once. We did it, and it was

practicing, and slept, sprawled so our legs still locked or crossed, a
    hand still lost
in someone's hair . . . and we grew up and hardly mentioned who

the first kiss really was—a girl like us, still sticky with the
        moisturizer we'd
shared in the bathroom. I want to write a song

for that thick silence in the dark, and the first pure thrill of
        unreluctant desire
just before we made ourselves stop.

THOM GUNN

RAPALLO

Before the heavy hotel sink
I lost myself a minute.
I paused as people do who think,
And gazed at what was in it.

Rinsed from my swimming trunks, the sand
Wavered down, grain by grain,
To settle at the bottom, stunned,
Distinct on thick porcelain.

As if my happiness was tired
And sought that strange, mild pause,
It still observantly endured
And yet forgot its cause.

But then, from habit, I looked around
For what I thought it lacked.
Of course: for, without you as ground,
How could it stay intact?

Turned to miss you, amnesiac,
I was restored when you
Across the floor were given back—
Changing for dinner, too,

For those discoveries still ahead
To match those of our play
Upon the beach where we had led
All of a spacious day.

That summer I was twenty-three,
You about twenty-one,
We hoped to live together, as we
(Not to be smug) have done.

If, in four decades, matter-of-factly
Coming to be resigned
To separate beds was not exactly
What we then had in mind,

Something of our first impetus,
Something of what we planned,
Remains of what was given us
On the Rapallo sand.

Against our house of floors and beams
A mannerless wind strains
Down from the North, and cold rain streams
Across the windowpanes.

The structure creaks we hold together.
Water blurs all detail.
This wood will speak beneath worse weather
Yet than the Yukon's hail.

TO ANOTHER POET

You scratch my back, I like your taste it's true,
But Mister I won't do the same for you,
Though you have asked me twice. I have taste too.

TO CUPID

You make desire seem easy.
                     So it is:
Your service perfect freedom to enjoy
Fresh limitations. I've watched you in person
Wait for the light and relish the delay
Revving the engine up before you spurt
Out of the intersection.

                  How all your servants
Compose their amorous scripts—scripts of confinement,
Scripts of displacement, scripts of delay, and scripts
Of more delay. Your own Fabrice so hankered
After the distance of his prison cell
He managed to regain it, for the sake
Of viewing her, the jailer's daughter, daily—
But at a window, but among her birds.
Of course they could not touch. In later life
They touched, they did touch, but in darkness only.
When I switched off my light I was dog-tired
But for some minutes held off sleep: I heard
The pleasant sound of voices from next door
Through windows open to the element darkness.
A dinner for the couple one floor up,
Married today. I hardly had the time
Before falling away, to relish it,
The sociable human hum, easy and quiet
As the first raindrops in the yard, on bushes,
Heard similarly from bed. Chatting, the sounds
Of friendliness and feeding often broken
By laughter. It's consoling, Mr. Love,
That such conviviality is also
One more obedience to your behest,
The wedding bed held off by the wedding feast.

Good will within delay within good will.
And Cupid, devious master of our bodies,
You were the source then of my better rest.

MARK DOTY

COASTAL

Cold April and the neighbor girl
   —our plumber's daughter—
      comes up the wet street

from the harbor carrying,
   in a nest she's made
      of her pink parka,

a loon. *It's so sick*,
   she says when I ask.
      Foolish kid,

does she think she can keep
   this emissary of air?
      Is it trust or illness

that allows the head
   —sleek tulip—to bow
      on its bent stem

across her arm?
   Look at the steady,
      quiet eye. She is carrying

the bird back from indifference,
   from the coast
      of whatever rearrangement

the elements intend,
     and the loon allows her.
          She is going to call

the Center for Coastal Studies,
     and will swaddle the bird
          in her petal-bright coat

until they come.
     She cradles the wild form.
          Stubborn girl.

KAY RYAN

CRUSTACEAN ISLAND

There could be an island paradise
where crustaceans prevail.
Click, click, go the lobsters
with their china mitts and
articulated tails.
It would not be sad like whales
with their immense and patient sieving
and the sobering modesty
of their general way of living.
It would be an island blessed
with only cold-blooded residents
and no human angle.
It would echo with a thousand castanets
and no flamencos.

BLANDEUR

If it please God,
let less happen.
Even out Earth's

rondure, flatten
Eiger, blanden
the Grand Canyon.
Make valleys
slightly higher,
widen fissures
to arable land,
remand your
terrible glaciers
and silence
their calving,
halving or doubling
all geographical features
toward the mean.
Unlean against our hearts.
Withdraw your grandeur
from these parts.

WISŁAWA SZYMBORSKA

MAYBE ALL THIS

Maybe all this
is happening in some lab?
Under one lamp by day
and billions by night?

Maybe we're experimental generations?
Poured from one vial to the next,
shaken in test tubes,
not scrutinized by eyes alone,
each of us separately
plucked up by tweezers in the end?

Or maybe it's more like this:
No interference?

The changes occur on their own
according to plan?
The graph's needle slowly etches
its predictable zigzags?

Maybe thus far we aren't of much interest?
The control monitors aren't usually plugged in?
Only for wars, preferably large ones,
for the odd ascent above our clump of earth,
for major migrations frown Point A to Point B?

Maybe just the opposite:
They've got a taste for trivia up there?
Look, on the big screen a little girl
is sewing a button on her sleeve.
The radar shrieks,
the staff comes at a run.
What a darling little being
with its tiny heart beating inside it!
How sweet its solemn
threading of the needle!
Someone cries, enraptured,
Get the Boss,
tell him he's got to see this for himself!

(Translated, from the Polish, by Stanislaw Baranczak and Clare Cavanagh.)

SOME LIKE POETRY

Some—
that means not all.
Not even the majority of all but the minority.
Not counting school, where one must,
and poets themselves,
there will be perhaps two in a thousand.

Like—
but one also likes chicken-noodle soup,

one likes compliments and the color blue,
one likes an old scarf,
one likes to prove one's point,
one likes to pet a dog.

Poetry—
but what sort of thing is poetry?
More than one shaky answer
has been given to this question.
But I do not know and do not know and clutch on to it,
as to a saving bannister.

(Translated, from the Polish, by Joanna Trzeciak.)

I'M WORKING ON THE WORLD

I'm working on the world,
revised, improved edition,
featuring fun for fools,
blues for brooders,
combs for bald pates,
tricks for old dogs.

Here's one chapter: The Speech
of Animals and Plants.
Each species comes, of course,
with its own dictionary.
Even a simple "Hi, there,"
when traded with a fish,
makes both the fish and you
feel quite extraordinary.

The long-suspected meanings
of rustlings, chirps, and growls!
Soliloquies of forests!
The epic hoots of owls!
Those crafty hedgehogs drafting
aphorisms after dark,

while we blindly believe
they're sleeping in the park!

Time (Chapter Two) retains
its sacred right to meddle
in each earthly affair.
Still, time's unbounded power
that makes a mountain crumble,
moves seas, rotates a star,
won't be enough to tear
lovers apart: they are
too naked, too embraced,
too much like timid sparrows.

Old age is, in my book,
the price that felons pay,
so don't whine that it's steep:
you'll stay young if you're good.
Suffering (Chapter Three)
doesn't insult the body.
Death? It comes in your sleep,
exactly as it should.

When it comes, you'll be dreaming
that you don't need to breathe;
that breathless silence is
the music of the dark,
and it's part of the rhythm
to vanish like a spark.

Only a death like that. A rose
could prick you harder, I suppose;
you'd feel more terror at the sound
of petals falling to the ground.

Only a world like that. To die
just that much. And to live just so.

And all the rest is Bach's fugue, played
for the time being
on a saw.

(Translated, from the Polish, by Stanislaw Baranczak and Clare Cavanagh.)

STANLEY KUNITZ

HALLEY'S COMET

Miss Murphy in first grade
wrote its name in chalk
across the board and told us
it was roaring down the storm tracks
of the Milky Way at frightful speed
and if it wandered off its course
and smashed into the earth
there'd be no school tomorrow.
A red-bearded preacher from the hills
with a wild look in his eyes
stood in the public square
at the playground's edge
proclaiming he was sent by God
to save every one of us,
even the little children.
"Repent, ye sinners!" he shouted,
waving his hand-lettered sign.
At supper I felt sad to think
that it was probably
the last meal I'd share
with my mother and my sisters;
but I felt excited, too,
and scarcely touched my plate.
So Mother scolded me
and sent me early to my room.
The whole family's asleep now

except for me. They never heard me steal
into the stairwell hall and climb
the ladder to the fresh night air.

Look for me, Father, on the roof
of the red-brick building
at the foot of Green Street—
that's where we live, you know, on the top floor.
I'm the boy in the white flannel gown
sprawled on this coarse gravel bed
searching the starry sky,
waiting for the world to end.

LATE SHIFT

GERALD STERN
96 VANDAM

I am going to carry my bed into New York City tonight
complete with dangling sheets and ripped blankets;
I am going to push it across three dark highways
or coast along under six hundred thousand faint stars.
I want to have it with me so I don't have to beg
for too much shelter from my weak and exhausted friends.
I want to be as close as possible to my pillow
in case a dream or a fantasy should pass by.
I want to fall asleep on my own fire escape
and wake up dazed and hungry
to the sound of garbage grinding in the street below
and the smell of coffee cooking in the window above.

SEAMUS HEANEY
THE GUTTURAL MUSE

Late summer, and at midnight
I smelt the heat of the day:
At my window over the hotel car park
I breathed the muddied night airs off the lake
And watched a young crowd leave the discothèque.

Their voices rose up thick and comforting
As oily bubbles the feeding tench sent up
That evening at dusk—the slimy tench
Once called the doctor fish because his slime
Was said to heal the wounds of fish that touched it.

A girl in a white dress
Was being courted out among the cars:
As her voice swarmed and puddled into laughs
I felt like some old pike all badged with sores
Wanting to swim in touch with soft-mouthed life.

LOUISE BOGAN

SOLITARY OBSERVATION BROUGHT BACK FROM A SHORT SOJOURN IN HELL

At midnight tears
Run into your ears.

JAMES LAUGHLIN

LA TRISTESSE

And Pound in his despair in the Army prison camp at Pisa
Wrote, "*Tard, très lard je t'ai connue, la Tristesse.*"
And he said that the tears he had caused in his life were
    drowning him.
"*Les larmes que j'ai créées m'inondent.*"

I have been reading some pages in the Tristia of Ovid,
Who was exiled to Pontus on the Black Sea, the end of nowhere,
Because he had offended Augustus.
Ovid longs for Rome, for his homeland.
You are my homeland and I seek permission to return to you.

You are the solitary voyager, the bird of lone fight.
I was foolish; I tried to capture you, to bring you down from
    your sky.
I am rightly punished, but exile from you is a hard pain to bear.
My sadness is a dull ache, a wound that won't heal.
I have injured the one I love best.
She also has her wound, the one I gave her.
La tristesse, tard, très tard je t'ai connue.

RICHARD WILBUR

WALKING TO SLEEP

As a queen sits down, knowing that a chair will be there,
Or a general raises his hand and is given the field-glasses,
Step off assuredly into the blank of your mind.
Something will come to you. Although at first
You nod through nothing like a fogbound prow,
Gravel will breed in the margins of your gaze,
Perhaps with tussocks or a dusty flower,
And, humped like dolphins playing in the bow-wave,
Hills will suggest themselves. All such suggestions
Are yours to take or leave, but hear this warning:
Let them not be too velvet green, the fields
Which the deft needle of your eye appoints,
Nor the old farm past which you make your way
Too shady-lintelled, too instinct with home.
It is precisely from Potemkin barns,
With their fresh-painted hex-signs on the gables,
Their sparkling gloom within, their stanchion-rattle
And sweet breath of silage, that there comes
The trotting cat whose head is but a skull.
Try to remember this: what you project
Is what you will perceive; what you perceive
With any passion, be it love or terror,
May take on whims and powers of its own.
Therefore a numb and grudging circumspection
Will serve you best—unless you overdo it,
Watching your step too narrowly, refusing
To specify a world, shrinking your purview
To a tight vision of your inching shoes,
Which may, as soon you come to think, be crossing
An unseen gorge upon a rotten trestle.
What you must manage is to bring to mind
A landscape not worth looking at, some bleak
Champaign at dead November's end, its grass
As dry as lichen, and its lichens gray—
Such glumly simple country that a glance

Of flat indifference from time to time
Will stabilize it. Lifeless thus, and leafless,
The view should set at rest all thoughts of ambush.
Nevertheless, permit no roadside thickets
Which, as you pass, might shake with worse than wind;
Revoke all trees and other cover; blast
The upstart boulder which a flicking shape
Has stepped behind; above all, put a stop
To the known stranger up ahead, whose face
Half-turns to mark you with a creased expression.
Here let me interject that steady trudging
Can make you drowsy, so that without transition,
As when an old film jumps in the projector,
You will be wading a dun hallway, rounding
A newel post, and starting up the stairs.
Should that occur, adjust to circumstances
And carry on, taking these few precautions:
Detach some portion of your thought to guard
The outside of the building; as you wind
From room to room, leave nothing at your back,
But slough all memories at every threshold;
Nor must you dream of opening any door
Until you have foreseen what lies beyond it.
Regardless of its seeming size, or what
May first impress you as its style or function,
The abrupt structure which involves you now
Will improvise like vapor. Groping down
The gritty cellar steps and past the fuse-box,
Brushing through sheeted lawn-chairs, you emerge
In some cathedral's pillared crypt, and thence,
Your brow alight with carbide, pick your way
To the main shaft through stopes and rubbly tunnels.
Promptly the hoist, ascending toward the pit-head,
Rolls downward past your gaze a dinted rock-face
Peppered with hacks and drill-holes, which acquire
Insensibly the look of hieroglyphics.
Whether to surface now within the vast
Stone tent where Cheops lay secure, or take

The proffered shed of corrugated iron
Which gives at once upon a vacant barracks,
Is up to you. Need I, at this point, tell you
What to avoid? Avoid the pleasant room
Where someone, smiling to herself, has placed
A bowl of yellow freesias. Do not let
The thought of her in yellow, lithe and sleek
As lemonwood, mislead you where the curtains,
Romping like spinnakers which taste the wind,
Bellying out and lifting till the sill
Has shipped a drench of sunlight, then subsiding,
Both warm and cool the love-bed. Your concern
Is not to be detained by dread, or by
Such dear acceptances as would entail it,
But to pursue an ever-dimming course
Of pure transition, treading as in water
Past crumbling tufa, down cloacal halls
Of boarded-up hotels, through attics full
Of glassy taxidermy, moping on
Like a drugged fire-inspector. What you hope for
Is that at some point of the pointless journey,
Indoors or out, and when you least expect it,
Right in the middle of your stride, like that,
So neatly that you never feel a thing,
The kind assassin Sleep will draw a bead
And blow your brains out.

                  What, are you still awake?
Then you must risk another tack and footing.
Forget what I have said. Open your eyes
To the good blackness not of your room alone
But of the sky you trust is over it,
Whose stars, though foundering in the time to come,
Bequeath us constantly a jetsam beauty.
Now with your knuckles rub your eyelids, seeing
The phosphenes caper like St. Elmo's fire,
And let your head heel over on the pillow
Like a flung skiff on wild Gennesaret.

Let all things storm your thought with the moiled flocking
Of startled rookeries, or flak in air,
Or blossom-fall, and out of that come striding
In the strong dream by which you have been chosen.
Are you upon the roads again? If so,
Be led past honeyed meadows which might tempt
A wolf to graze, and groves which are not you
But answer to your suppler self, that nature
Able to bear the thrush's quirky glee
In stands of chuted light, yet praise as well,
All leaves aside, the barren bark of winter.
When, as you may, you find yourself approaching
A crossroads and its laden gallows tree,
Do not with hooded eyes allow the shadow
Of a man moored in air to stain your forehead,
But lift your gaze and stare your brother down,
Though the swart crows have pecked his sockets hollow.

As for what turn your travels then will take,
I cannot guess. Long errantry perhaps
Will arm you to be gentle, or the claws
Of nightmare flap you pathless God knows where,
As the crow flies, to meet your dearest horror.
Still, if you are in luck, you may be granted,
As, inland, one can sometimes smell the sea,

A moment's perfect carelessness, in which
To stumble a few steps and sink to sleep
In the same clearing where, in the old story,
A holy man discovered Vishnu sleeping,
Wrapped in his maya, dreaming by a pool
On whose calm face all images whatever
Lay clear, unfathomed, taken as they came.

SYLVIA PLATH

NIGHT WALK

    Flintlike, her feet struck
  such a racket of echoes from the steely street,
tacking in moon-blued crooks from the black
    stone-built town, that she heard the quick air ignite
      its tinder and shake

    a firework of echoes from wall
  to wall of the dark, dwarfed cottages.
But the echoes died at her back as the walls
    gave way to fields and the incessant seethe of grasses
      riding in the full

    of the moon, manes to the wind,
  tireless, tied, as a moon-bound sea
moves on its root. Though a mist-wraith wound
    up from the fissured valley and hung shoulder-high
      ahead, it fattened

    to no family-featured ghost,
  nor did any word body with a name
the blank mood she walked in. Once past
    the dream-peopled village, her eyes entertained no dream,
      and the sandman's dust

    lost lustre under her footsoles.
  The long wind, paring her person down
to a pinch of flame, blew its burdened whistle
    in the whorl of her ear, and, like a scooped-out pumpkin crown,
      her head cupped the babel.

    All the night gave her, in return
  for the paltry gift of her bulk and the beat
of her heart, was the humped, indifferent iron
    of its hills, and its pastures bordered by black stone set
      on black stone. Barns

guarded broods and litters
behind shut doors; the dairy herds
knelt in the meadow, mute as boulders;
sheep drowsed stoneward in their tussocks of wool; and birds,
twig-sleeping, wore

granite ruffs, their shadows
the guise of leaves. The whole landscape
loomed absolute, as the antique world was
once, in its earliest sway of lymph and sap,
unaltered by eyes,

enough to snuff the quick
of her small heat out. But before the weight
of stones and hills of stones could break
her down to mere quartz grit in that stony light,
she turned back.

B. H. FAIRCHILD

EARLY OCCULT MEMORY SYSTEMS OF THE LOWER MIDWEST

In his fifth year the son, deep in the back seat
of his father's Ford and the *mysterium*
of time, holds time in memory with words,
night, this night, on the way to a stalled rig south
of Kiowa Creek where the plains wind stacks
the skeletons of weeds on barbed-wire fences
and rattles the battered DeKalb sign to make
the child think of time in its passing, of death.

Cattle stare at flatbed haulers gunning clumps
of black smoke and lugging damaged drill pipe
up the gullied, mud-hollowed road. *Road, this
road*. Roustabouts shouting from the crow's nest
float like Ascension angels on a ring of lights.

Chokecherries gouge the purpled sky, cloud
swags running the moon under, and starlight
rains across the Ford's blue hood. *Blue, this blue.*

Later, where black flies haunt the mud tank,
the boy walks along the pipe rack dragging
a stick across the hollow ends to make a kind
of music, and the creek throbs with frog songs,
locusts, the rasp of tree limbs blown and scattered.
The great horse people, his father, these sounds,
these things saved from time's dark creek as the car
moves across the moving earth: *world, this world.*

QUAN BARRY

IF $\dfrac{dY}{dX} = \dfrac{4x^3 + x^2 - 12}{\sqrt{2x^2 - 9}}$, THEN

you are standing at the ocean,
in the moon's empirical light
each mercurial wave

like a parabola shifting on its axis,
the sea's dunes differentiated & graphed.
If this, then that. The poet

laughs. She wants to lie
in her own equation, the point slope
like a woman whispering *stay me*

with flagons. What is it to know the absolute value
of negative grace, to calculate
how the heart becomes the empty set

unintersectable, the first & the last?
But enough.
You are standing on the shore,

the parameters like wooden stakes.
Let x be the moon like a notary.
Let y be all things left unsaid.

Let the constant be the gold earth
waiting to envelop what remains,
the sieves of the lungs like two cones.

MAURA STANTON

LITTLE ODE FOR X

Sometimes I call X nostalgia.
My mother telephones her fear of snow
caving the roof in; she hired a man
who rakes it off every time, but today
he's sick & so my mother paces room
after room, watching the ceiling . . .
When she hangs up, I imagine
her face resembling the crisp fly wing
stuck on the storm window, or her raisins
heated in pans until they dry out,
although their bitterness ruins cakes.
Last night a child threw a stone
hard against my front door. That's X, too,
for I've no father to chase him away.
Now I find the stone on the step,
milk crystal so strange I wash
my hands over & over in the kitchen sink,
afraid the child soaked it for hours
in poison from his Christmas chemistry set.
X is the fifth time a friend says no
to dinner, preferring to polish heirloom
silverware until the garland handles gleam,
or my brother's letter from Florida
describing a fight with his third wife.
That feeling of ants in my father's chest,

red fighters circling his heart that night
he sat up in bed, sure of death;
that's X, the specific hum of blood
beating against a clot in my mother's leg.
I hold a mirror behind my own knees,
touching the blue tubes running like roots
into my body, finally an equation for X,
as it, too, now grows by subtraction.

ELLY BOOKMAN

DARK

Schools gone dark. On the last day
we told the children to take everything
home, supervised as they emptied dark
lockers of books, loose pages, mirrors.
I don't drive past the dark windows and
halls, missing it. I make dark the living
room and fill it back up with the light of
a movie. Something about creatures who
stalk in the dark, thrive on its blankness.
But I go to bed before the end, when
dark returns to the screen with its list
of names. I sleep in dark, but shove
voices in my ears that belong to bodies
who sat in lit rooms a good while ago
to discuss science, loss. Even sunrises—
I sleep through them now, can't stand
that semi-dark slide into the worsened
day. Dark soil in the garden beds, in
the houseplants, spilled on the kitchen
floor. The dark fur of the dog so soft
I'd skin her to make myself a coat if I
didn't love the rest of her so desperately.
Dark thoughts like that in my head
all day. Dark mode so the screens are

gentler on the eyes. Not that they feel
any strain—no dark itch in the pupil.
If anything I feel so much the same—
no new humid night sets its dark down
in my swallow (the sickness), nor does
any heart-wound turn rotten and raw.
I am the dark's pale rider, indifferent
and slow. By the time schools reopen,
dark won't be anything on which to
remark. A girl will open her locker and
out dark will pour and she'll think how
she's learned it. Dark homework. Dark
that has spent all these days staring
into a left-behind mirror at itself, stirred
to cloud at last, to a downpour about
to make the day cool and blue, make all
this a yesterday. Her shadowy backpack.

SUSAN MITCHELL

ELEGY FOR A CHILD'S SHADOW

Perhaps the moment included a bench, a tree with a bicycle
leaning against it, and a shadow.
From the position of the shadow, the mother
might know whether something
was entering or just leaving. And whether,
if it was leaving, it would be back.

                      If she had to describe
the shadow, she would say it is shaped like a sundial
in a park where all afternoon children have been playing.
Or she would say it is like a pool
where golden fish swim. When the sun is at a certain angle,
she can hear the water inside the water,
and what she thinks of is a life
dissolving slowly
like a wafer in the mouth of a child.

The fish swim in the pool without expectations.
She feeds them leaves and grass,
but they refuse to eat. Perhaps they feed on time.
Is it necessary to know whether leaves
which have been falling into the pool all afternoon
are floating face up or face down? Or whether
the fish are able to see through clouds
reflected in the water?

                    Sometimes death is humble,
merely a space
tempting a child to fill it with itself.
As the grass, so plush and blue,
tempts the mother. Lying there, she hears
the sound of rain exciting the leaves
to stillness, and later,
much later, she feels the dark
gliding gently as an eraser over her life.

ADRIENNE RICH

THE INSOMNIACS

The mystic finishes in Time,
The actor finds himself in Space,
And each, wherever he has been,
Must know his hand before his face,
Must crawl back into his own skin
As in the darkness after crime
The thief can hear his breath again,
Resume the knowledge of his limbs
And how the spasm goes and comes
Under the bones that cage his heart.

So, we are fairly met, grave friend—
The meeting of two wounds in man.

I, gesturing with practiced hand,
I, in my great brocaded gown,
And you, the fixed and patient one,
Enduring all the world can do;
I, with my shifting masks, the gold,
The awful scarlet, laughing blue,
Maker of many worlds, and you,
Worldless, the pure receptacle.

And yet your floating eyes reveal
What saint or mummer groans to feel:
That finite creatures finally know
The damp of stone beneath the knees,
The stiffness in the folded hands,
A duller ache than holy wounds,
The draught that never stirs the sleeve
Of glazed evangelists above
But drives men out from sacred calm
Into the violent, wayward sun.

My voice commands the formal stage;
A jungle thrives beyond the wings—
All formless and benighted things
That rhetoric cannot assuage.
I speak a dream and turn to see
The sleepless night outstaring me.
My pillow sweats; I wake in space;
This is my hand before my face;
This is the headboard of my bed
Whose splinters stuff my nightmare mouth;

This is the unconquerable drouth
I carry in my burning head.
Not my words nor your visions mend
Such infamous knowledge. We are split,
Done into bits, undone, pale friend,
As ecstasy begets its end.

As we are spun of rawest thread,
The flaw is in us; we will break.
O dare you of this fracture make
Hosannas plain and tragical,

Or dare I let each cadence fall
Awkward as learning newly learned,
Simple as children's cradle songs,
As untranslatable and true,
We someday might conceive a way
To do the thing we long to do:
To do what men have always done,
To live in time, to act in space,
Yet find a ritual to embrace
Raw towns of man, the pockmarked sun.

TENNESSEE WILLIAMS

BLUE SONG

I am tired.
I am tired of speech and of action.
If you should meet me upon the
street do not question me for
I can tell you only my name
and the name of the town I was
born in—but that is enough.
It does not matter whether tomorrow
arrives anymore. If there is
only this night and after it is
morning it will not matter now.
I am tired. I am tired of speech
and of action. In the heart of me
you will find a tiny handful of
dust. Take it and blow it out
upon the wind. Let the wind have
it and it will find its way home.

MURIEL SPARK

THAT BAD COLD

That hand, a tiny one, first at my throat;
That thump in the chest.
I know you of old, you're a bad cold
Come to stay for a few days,
Unwanted visitor—a week perhaps.

Nobody asked him to come. (Yes,
He is masculine, but otherwise
Don't try to parse the situation.)
Everything stops. Perhaps
He is providentially intended to
Make cease and desist an overworking
State of mind. Yes, there is a certain
Respite. Friends mean merely a bed
And a hot drink. Enemies and all
Paranoias, however justified, lose their way
In the fog. And the desk diary
Lies open with a vacant grin.

AMY WOOLARD

LATE SHIFT

Those days I could only love someone who was ashamed
Of their teeth. The way the dogs will always sleep in the spots

They know I'll need to step. The things we do so not to lose
Each other. So as to lose something every day. Church key,

Bar rag, the obscene puckered red of maraschino, the wrecked
Line cook in the walk-in. His chilled kiss. How it tastes like a future

Eviction. Thieves in the temple of our bodies. Years later I will
Still feel most at home when I eat standing up. When I settle up

In cash. When I barter for your attention. Fingernail of heat
Lightning tapping the tabled sky. A broken pint glass

In the ice bin. Every shift Sinéad sings This is the last day
Of our acquaintance. *There are nights I give up on the world*

But not my body. How in the Bruegel, if you didn't know
The title you might not look for Icarus at all, a paper lantern

Giving its wish back to ground long after we've left. Push
A fork into a fish & what you get is a meal. Push a knife into

A knuckle & what you get is to be changed. Like Icarus, what I want
Is to start over but not do it all again. Like Icarus, I wanted the light

To love me back. How in my lungs still nests the fur of every animal I
Ever kept. Years later the gods will have me cough up a snow leopard.

I thought the main selling point of breathing was we didn't have to
Be reminded to do it. I never wanted children but I always liked the one

About Athena pouring full-grown from Zeus' forehead. How did we survive
Before Advil, love. Before the armor of us glinting in the closed kitchen

Dark. The way a creaky floorboard's one job is to wait. Service means
The spoon appears before you know you need it. The water looks

To refill itself. The napkin calls a truce. When something is soft we believe
We deserve to touch it & so we do. When something is sharp we long to

Perfect it. Nothing belongs to us until last call: one more &
Then no more. The lights go on & it's time to cough up

What's owed. Build a cathedral in the dead of night & then give it
A shift meal, a smoking section, a cover charge, a swinging door, a till

To reckon. Those days we didn't have a prayer, separated our love
From each other like cupping a yolk between the cracked half

Shells back & again until it's perfect. Forgive ourselves. Give
Ourselves the tenderest title & call it a day. How could we ever

How could we not. Baby, draw the spoked sun in the corner
Of our afternoon sky. Wake us in its slow-cooked gaze.

BURKE BOYCE

PAVEMENT PORTRAITS: NIGHT WATCHMAN

The flame burns hot
In an iron pot,
   And leaps above the rim—
He sits beside,
Where the shadows slide,
   Flickering, mad, and dim.

He sits alone
With the planks and stone,
   The scaffoldings, beams, and floors;
The night winds shout,
And caper about,
   And push at the vacant doors.

The shadows stretch,
And creeping, etch
   A study of souls in grief—
The man is gray
Who waits for day,
   And parched like a winter's leaf.

He makes no sound,
And the frozen ground
   Is barren as the tomb;
Alone he stands
With ivory hands,
   And feeds the firelit gloom.

DAVID WAGONER

A VALEDICTORY TO STANDARD OIL OF INDIANA

In the darkness east of Chicago, the sky burns over the plumbers'
    nightmares
Red and blue, and my hometown lies there loaded with gasoline.
Registers ring like gas pumps, pumps like pinballs, pinballs like broken
    alarm clocks,
And it's time for morning, but nothing's going to work.
From cat-cracker to candle shop, from greaseworks along the pipeline,
Over storage tanks like kings on a checkerboard ready to jump the
    county,
The word goes out: With refined regrets,
We suggest you sleep all day in your houses shaped like lunch buckets
And don't show up at the automated gates.
Something else will tap the gauges without yawning
And check the valves at the feet of the cooling-towers without
    complaining.

Standard Oil is canning my high-school classmates
And the ones who fell out of junior high or slipped in the grades.
What should they do, gassed up in their Tempests and Comets, raring to go
Somewhere, with their wives scowling in front and kids stuffed in the back,
Past drive-ins jammed like car lots, trying to find the beaches
But blocked by freights for hours, stopped dead in their tracks
Where the rails, as thick as thieves along the lake front,
Lower their crossing gates to shut the frontier? What can they think about
As they stare at the sides of boxcars for a sign,
And Lake Michigan drains slowly into Lake Huron,
The mills level the Dunes, and the eels go sailing through the trout,
And mosquitoes inherit the evening while toads no bigger than horseflies
Hop crazily after them over the lawns and sidewalks, and the rainbows fall
Flat in the oil they came from? There are two towns now,
One dark, one going to be dark, divided by cyclone fences;
One pampered and cared for like pillboxes and cathedrals,
The other vanishing overnight in the dumps and swamps like a struck
    sideshow.
As the Laureate of the Class of '44—which doesn't know it has one—

I offer this poem, not from hustings or barricades
Or the rickety stage where George Rogers Clark stood glued to the wall,
But from another way out, like Barnum's "This Way to the Egress,"
Which moved the suckers when they'd seen enough. Get out of town.

JANE HAYMAN

THE MURDERED GIRL IS FOUND ON A BRIDGE

Hammerstroke and
hammerstroke and
hammerstroke de-
stroyed me—

that mallet
(or what you call it)
pounding away.
My thighs betrayed me.

The noise! The cries!
I cracked like a bell
forcing a chime
and came

or went.
At any rate I'm here
over streets that bear,
easily, giant trees;

here where the air's
absorbed my blood
into white light,
silence a bell,

an odor all about,
the smell of
oranges or
something growing.

THEODORE ROETHKE

IN A DARK TIME

I

In a dark time, the eye begins to see.
I meet my shadow in the deepening shade;
I hear my echo in the echoing wood—
A lord of nature weeping to a tree.
I live between the heron and the wren,
Beasts of the hill and serpents of the den.

II

What's madness but nobility of soul
At odds with circumstance? The day's on fire!
I know the purity of pure despair,
My shadow pinned against a sweating wall.
That place among the rocks—is it a cave,
Or winding path? The edge is what I have.

III

A steady storm of correspondences!
A night flowing with birds, a ragged moon,
And in broad day the midnight come again!
A man goes far to find out what he is—
Death of the self in a long, tearless night,
All natural shapes blazing unnatural light.

IV

Dark, dark my light, and darker my desire.
My soul, like some heat-maddened summer fly,
Keeps buzzing at the sill. Which I is *I*?
A fallen man, I climb out of my fear.
The mind enters itself, and God the mind,
And one is One, free in the tearing wind.

SHERMAN ALEXIE
THE FACEBOOK SONNET

Welcome to the endless high-school
Reunion. Welcome to past friends
And lovers, however kind or cruel.
Let's undervalue and unmend

The present. Why can't we pretend
Every stage of life is the same?
Let's exhume, resume, and extend
Childhood. Let's all play the games

That occupy the young. Let fame
And shame intertwine. Let one's search
For God become public domain.
Let church.com become our church.

Let's sign up, sign in, and confess
Here at the altar of loneliness.

CHARLES WRIGHT
HOMAGE TO PAUL CÉZANNE

At night, in the fish-light of the moon, the dead wear our white shirts
To stay warm, and litter the fields.
We pick them up in the mornings, dewy pieces of paper and scraps of
    cloth.

Like us, they refract themselves. Like us,
They keep on saying the same thing, trying to get it right.
Like us, the water unsettles their names.

Sometimes they lie like leaves in their little arks, and curl up at the edges.

Sometimes they come inside, wearing our shoes, and walk
From mirror to mirror.

Or lie down in our beds with their gloves off
And touch our bodies. Or talk
In a corner. Or wait like envelopes on a desk.

They reach up from the ice plant.
They shuttle their messengers through the oat grass.
Their answers rise like rust on the stalks and the spidery leaves.

We rub them off our hands.

Each year the dead grow less dead, and nudge
Close to the surface of all things.
They start to remember the silence that brought them there.
They start to recount the gain in their soiled hands.

Their glasses let loose, and grain by grain return to the river bank.
They point to their favorite words
Growing around them, revealed as themselves for the first time—
They stand close to the meanings and take them in.

They stand there, vague and without pain,
Under their fingernails an unreturnable dirt.
They stand there and it comes back,
The music of everything, syllable after syllable

Out of the burning chair, out of the beings of light.
It all comes back.
And what they repeat to themselves, and what they repeat to themselves,
Is the song that our fathers sing.

In steeps and sighs,
The ocean explains itself, backing and filling
What spaces it can't avoid, spaces
In black shoes, their hands clasped, their eyes teared at the edges:
We watch from the high hillside,
The ocean swelling and flattening, the spaces
Filling and emptying, horizon blade
Flashing the early afternoon sun.

The dead are constant in
The white lips of the sea.
Over and over, through clenched teeth, they tell

Their story, the story each knows by heart:
Remember me, speak my name.
When the moon tugs at my sleeve,
When the body of water is raised and becomes the body of light,
Remember me, speak my name.

The dead are a cadmium blue.
We spread them with palette knives in broad blocks and planes.

We layer them stroke by stroke
In steps and ascending mass, in verticals raised from the earth.

We choose, and layer them in,
Blue and a blue and a breath,

Circle and smudge, cross-beak and button hook,
We layer them in. We squint hard and terrace them line by line.

And so we are come between, and cry out,
And stare up at the sky and its cloudy panes,

And finger the cypress twists.
The dead understand all this, and keep in touch,

Rustle of hand to hand in the lemon trees,
Flags, and the great sifts of anger

To powder and nothingness.
The dead are a cadmium blue, and they understand.

The dead are with us to stay.
Their shadows rock in the back yard, so pure, so black,
Between the oak tree and the porch.

Over our heads they're huge in the night sky.
In the tall grass they turn with the zodiac.
Under our feet they're white with the snows of a thousand years.

They carry their colored threads and baskets of silk
To mend our clothes, making us look right,
Altering, stitching, replacing a button, closing a tear.
They lie like tucks in our loose sleeves, they hold us together.

They blow the last leaves away.
They slide like an overflow into the river of heaven.
Everywhere they are flying.

The dead are a sleight and a fade
We fall for, like flowering plums, like white coins from the rain.
Their sighs are gaps in the wind.

The dead are waiting for us in our rooms,
Little globules of light
In one of the far corners, and close to the ceiling, hovering, thinking
        our thoughts.

Often they'll reach a hand down,
Or offer a word, and ease us out of our bodies to join them in theirs.
We look back at our other selves on the bed.

We look back and we don't care and we go.

And thus we become what we've longed for,
                            past tense and otherwise,
A BB, a disc of light,
                    song without words.

And refer to ourselves
In the third person, seeing that other arm
Still raised from the bed, fingers like licks and flames in the boned air.

Only to hear that it's not time.
Only to hear that we must re-enter and lie still, our arms at rest at our
        sides,
The voices rising around us like mist

And dew, *it's all right, it's all right, it's all right* . . .

The dead fall around us like rain.
They come down from the last clouds in the late light for the last time
And slip through the sod.

They lean uphill and face north.
                              Like grass,
They bend toward the sea, they break toward the setting sun.

We filigree and we baste.
But what do the dead care for the fringe of words,

Safe in their suits of milk?
What do they care for the honk and flash of a new style?

And who is to say if the inch of snow in our hearts
Is rectitude enough?

Spring picks the locks of the wind.
High in the night sky the mirror is hauled up and unsheeted.
In it we twist like stars.

Ahead of us, through the dark, the dead
Are beating their drums and stirring the yellow leaves.

We're out here, our feet in the soil, our heads craned up to the sky,
The stars streaming and bursting behind the trees.

At dawn, as the clouds gather, we watch
The mountain glide from the east on the valley floor,
Coming together in starts and jumps.

Behind their curtain, the bears
Amble across the heavens, serene as black coffee . . .

Whose unction can intercede for the dead?
Whose tongue is toothless enough to speak their piece?

What we are given in dreams we write as blue paint,
Or messages to the clouds.
At evening we wait for the rain to fall and the sky to clear.
Our words are words for the clay, uttered in undertones,
Our gestures salve for the wind.

We sit out on the earth and stretch our limbs,
Hoarding the little mounds of sorrow laid up in our hearts.

SHARON OLDS

SELF-EXAM

They tell you it won't make much sense, at first,
you will have to learn the terrain. They tell you this
at thirty, and fifty, and some are late
beginners, at last lying down and walking
the old earth of the breasts—the small,
cobbled, plowed field of one,
with a listening walking, and then the other—
fingertip-stepping, divining, north
to south, east to west, sectioning
the little fallen hills, sweeping
for mines. And the matter feels primordial,
unimaginable—dense,
cystic, phthistic, each breast like the innards
of a cell, its contents shifting and changing,
streambed gravel under walking feet, it
seems almost unpicturable, not
immemorial, but nearly un-
memorizable, but one marches,

slowly, through grave or fatal danger,
or no danger, one feels around in the
two tack-room drawers, ribs and
knots like leather bridles and plaited
harnesses and bits and reins,
one runs one's hands through the mortal tackle
in a jumble, in the dark, indoors. Outside—
night, in which these glossy ones were
ridden to a froth of starlight, bareback.

SHAUNA BARBOSA

WHAT IS A DIAGNOSIS TO A DEMON

My Gods fast together. Nod in agreement
before relaying results. I stroll around on the verge
of an omg a gasp a wow a why don't the doctors
jazz it up a bit. Say it's a delayed overdose,
a *you been out here looking for what's been looking for you.*
Turn the heat up. Say there's something bigger waiting.
Say what doesn't drown you makes you taller.
Say every new wound is still a regular old wound.
Say you'll meet a man who's going to love you
while your body grows with nothing in it.
Tell me he'll have a voice deeper than demons.
Tell me he'll be tall like stacked milk crates.
That way he could also be a bedframe.
Could carry decaying vinyl. Tell me
I could shoot a ball straight through him.
Don't tell me a couple hours before morning break
that it's just a cyst. A li'l fibroid. A change in diet,
a birth-control pill, and come back next year. My God,
just break me to blood, let me bleed to abandon
on a white couch, from the same cancers
obsessed with all my fat aunties from the South.
I was taught to bring food up to my lips.
For quality assurance, I want all the salt.
I want to drop with the beat.

ROBERT POLITO

YOUR CALL

My mother worked the Tilt-A-Whirl
at the Jefferson County carnival—

or so someone said.
The rock-ribbed bass of generators
underneath the calliope
tooting "Goodbye Cruel World"
over carpet clowns, spec girls, and an armless
knife-thrower retreating to his tent between shows.

Let the people point at me and stare—

From home
to the edge of town
is a bike ride,
or the *Shoot me out of a cannon!* trip of a lifetime.
Your call.

TED KOOSER

THE FAN IN THE WINDOW

It is September, and a cool breeze
from somewhere ahead is turning the blades;
night, and the slow flash of the fan
the last light between us and the darkness.
Dust has begun to collect on the blades,
haymaker's dust from distant fields,
dust riding to town on the night-black wings
of the crows—a thin frost of dust,
which clings to the fan in just the way
we cling to the earth as it spins.
The fan has brought us through,
its shiny blades like the screw of a ship

that has pushed its way through summer—
cut flowers awash in its wake,
the stagnant Sargasso Sea of July
far behind us. For the moment, we rest;
we lie in the dark hull of the house,
we rock in the troughs off the shore
of October, the engine cooling,
the fan blades so lazily turning, yet turning.

SARAH HOLLAND-BATT

EPITHALAMIUM

Any wonder he tossed back Sazeracs & sidecars,
the one who always woke sullen
as the long blue light between buildings,
who slept with his back curled
like an accusation, who rocked
his weight onto his heels like an amateur
actor overdoing Stanley in "Streetcar"
when he hailed his cab in the morning.
Any wonder there were apologies
& bodega flowers wreathed with baby's breath,
any wonder there was another woman
I never met & then the wedding invitation,
no warning. He knew he was handsome—
his worst gift. In restaurants he ordered
without asking—steak tartare, dollop of yolk
glistening in raw meat. To love a narcissist
you have to believe, & reader, I did—
for a time, I loved him, I believed
in his cruelty & beauty—buds in silver
birch, sparrows scuffling
in the gravel by the basketball court
where I watched him play Sunday pickup—
his brute musculature twisting
beneath his T-shirt, the springtime

itch of him—O, I believed as he shoved
& dodged his way up to dunk, I believed
as he spun that pebbled orange leather
in his fingertips like a cartographer
turning the first terrestrial globe,
its oceans gathered at the poles
like the curtains of a diorama,
its continents warped & stretched—
I believed the swish I heard
was the susurrus of reeds
on the bank of a blessed body of water,
I believed in his first principles & precepts—
& what I remember best
is how the ball slipped over the lip
then hung there a second—
a midair moon in the shredded net.

T. R. HUMMER

MY MOTHER IN BARDO

I.

Dear Future: It's strange how much
     you resemble the past, all the houses
Gone dark, the rooms where we lived
     so many lives: the ruptured sofa
Groaning as we read the book about the rabbit,
     the kitchen table shattered with flour
For bread, all vanished into an emptiness
     thirsty as old iron, a plowshare
Left in a fallow field for decades beside
     a snakeskin wound through the eyehole
Of a steer's skull. Dear Future: I am still
     standing there, a shadow at the threshold.
My mother was the door through which
     I entered the light. Now she is gone
Alone through her own vanishing door.

2.

With the hands of my heart
    I would claw out a place
For her in the darkness beyond
    breath, I would break through
The silence after heartbeat
    with another rhythm hammered
On the hide drumhead of death.
    It would sound like the ghost
Of Professor Longhair raging
    for goat's blood from the bowl
I hold up in the underworld, that great
    New Orleans shuffle of hers, so she can
Dance again, with the hands of my heart.

3.

No one in the family thought I could do anything
    practical in this world, Mother, but look:
I have raised out of the core of the firmament
    of my being a great lighthouse made
Of what looks like gleaming obsidian but
    in fact, if there are facts anymore, is nothing
But the grief of my time on this earth. It stands
    on the edge of the valley of living fog
Where you have chosen to wander, flashing
    its warning: do not turn back, do not
Think of us here still going on, because
    life doesn't do that, we are here
On the wrecking stones of existence
    just like you. Its light goes on
As long as I go on. So go on. And there, look
    how solid it stands. Dear Future: See what I did?

NATASHA TRETHEWEY

REPENTANCE

After Vermeer's "Maid Asleep"

To make it right   Vermeer painted   then painted over

this scene   a woman alone at a table   the cloth pushed back

rough folds at the edge   as if   someone   had risen

in haste   abandoning the chair   beside her   a wineglass

nearly empty   just   in her reach   Though she's been called

idle and drunken   a woman drowsing   you might see

in her gesture   melancholia   Eyelids drawn

she rests   her head   in her hand   Beyond her   a still-life

white jug   bowl of fruit   a goblet overturned   Before this

a man stood   in the doorway   a dog lay   on the floor

Perhaps   to exchange   loyalty   for betrayal

Vermeer erased   the dog   and made   of the man

a mirror   framed   by the open door   *Pentimento*

the word   for a painter's change   of heart   revision

on canvas   means the same   as remorse   after sin

Were she to rise   a mirror   behind her   the woman

might see   herself   as I did   turning   to rise

from my table   then back as if   into   Vermeer's scene

It was after   the quarrel   after   you'd had   again

too much to drink   after the bottle   did not shatter   though

I'd brought it   down hard   on the table   and the dog

had crept   from the room to hide   Later   I found

a trace   of what   I'd done   bruise on the table   the size

of my thumb   Worrying it   I must have looked   as she does

eyes downcast   my head   on the heel   of my palm   In paint

a story can change   mistakes be   undone   Imagine

Still-Life   with Father   and Daughter   a moment so

far back   there's still time   to take the glass   from your hand

or mine

D. NURKSE
MOZART'S FINAL HOUR

I
My father is playing the B-Flat Sonata.
Hidden under the rented baby grand
I press one pedal or another,
"damper," "sustain"—

Mozart grows pompous, prissy,
or strangely tongue-tied.

You can watch the shadows come—
the elm in the French window
impenetrable as a score.
Rain is a diminished chord.

I press those huge slippers
that smell of fart and wax,
gently, and my father
adjusts his timing delicately.

It's late.

Mozart bloated with sepsis says:
Fetch me my quill. I have an idea
that will make me famous.

Now the room is entirely dark.
My father is playing by heart.
That stupid grief—he memorized it.

Our love is like nightfall
or a trill: you can see through it
but not *it.*

2
Then time shall be no more.

ROGER REEVES

GRENDEL

All lions must lean into something other than a roar:
James Baldwin, for instance, singing "Precious Lord,"
His voice as weary as water broken over his scalp
In a storefront Sanctified Church's baptismal pool
All those years ago when he wanted to be
Somebody's child and on fire in that being. Lord,
I want to be somebody's child and chosen
Water spilling over their scalp, water
Taking the shape of their longing, a deer
Diving into evening traffic and the furrow drawn
In the air over the hood of the car—power
And wanting to be something alive and open.
Lord, I want to be alive and open,

A glimpse of power: the shuffle of a mother's hand
Over a sleeping child's forehead
As if clearing the city's rust from its face,
Which we mostly are: a halo of rust,
A glimpse of power—James Baldwin leaning
Into the word *light*, his voice jostling that single grain
In his throat as if he might drop it or
Already has. I am calling to that grain
Of light, to that gap between his teeth
Where the many-of-us fatherless sleep
And bear and be whatever darkness or leaping
Thing we can be. In James Baldwin's mouth,
My difficult beauty, my weak and worn,
My future as any number of angels,
Which is not unlike the beast Grendel,
Coming out of the wild heaven into the hills
And halls of the mead house at the harpist's call
With absolute prophecy in his breast
And a desire for mercy, for a friend, an end
To drifting in loneliness, and in that coming
Down out of the hills, out of the trees, for once,
Bringing humans the best vision of themselves,
Which, of course, must be slaughtered.

CLIVE JAMES

SEASON TO SEASON

I have been fooled before, and just because
This summer seems so long, it might not be
My last. Winter could come again, and pause
The sky like a taped tactical descent
Of pocket paratroopers. Things to see
Could happen yet, and life prove not quite spent
But still abundant, still the main event.

The trick, I'm learning, is to stay in doubt,
Season to season, of what time might bring,

And patiently await how things turn out.
Eventually time tells you everything.
If it takes time to do so, no surprise
In that. You fold your arms, you scan the skies,
And tell yourself that life has made you wise,

If only by the way it ebbs away.
But still it takes an age, and after all,
Though nearly gone, life didn't end today,
And you might be here when the first leaves fall
Or even when the snow begins again,
If life that cast you, when this all began,
As a small boy, still needs a dying man.

COLM TÓIBÍN

VINEGAR HILL

The town reservoir on the hill
Was built in the twenties.
If you lifted a round metal covering
And dropped a stone, you could

Hear it plonk into the depths.
There were small hollows in the rocks
That, no matter how dry the weather,
Were filled with rainwater.

These rock pools must have been here
With different water in them
That summer when the rebels
Fled toward Needham's Gap.

From the hill, as the croppies did,
You can view the town, narrow
Streets even narrower, and more
Trees and gardens than you imagined.

It was burning then, of course,
But now it is quiet. There is,
In the Market Square, a monument
To Father Murphy and the Croppy Boy.

We can see the hill from our house.
It is solid rock in the mornings
As the sun appears from just behind it.
It changes as the day does.

My mother is taking art classes
And, thinking it natural to make
The hill her focal point,
Is trying to paint it.

What color is Vinegar Hill?
How does it rise above the town?
It is humped as much as round.
There is no point in invoking

History. The hill is above all that,
Intractable, unknowable, serene.
It is in shade, then in light,
And often caught between.

When the blue becomes gray
And fades more, the green glistens,
And then not so much. The rock also
Glints in the afternoon light,

Which dwindles, making the glint disappear.
Then there is the small matter of clouds,
Which make tracks over the hill in a smoke
Of white, as though instructed

By their superiors to break camp.
They change their shape, crouch down,
Stay still, all camouflage, dreamy,
Lost, with no strategy to speak of,

Yet resigned to the inevitable:
When the wind comes for them, they will retreat.
Until this time, they are surrounded by sky
And can, as yet, envisage no way out.

KWAME DAWES

BEFORE WINTER

I imagine there is a place of deep rest—not in the resting but after,
when the body has forgotten the weight of fatigue or of its many

betrayals—how unfair that once I thought it clever to blame my body
for the wounds in me: the ankle bulbous and aching, the heaviness

in the thigh, and the fat, the encroachment of flesh. It is hard to
    believe
that there are those who do not know that it is possible to let things

go, to then see the expansion of flesh—it is so easy, and that knowing
is a pathology. What is unknown to me is the clear day of rest—

I carry a brain of crushed paper, everything unfolds as if by magic,
every spot of understanding is a miracle, I cannot take any credit

for the revelations, they come and go as easily as the wind.
You must know that this is a preamble to an epiphany I will record—

the late-morning light of October, the damp soiled back yard,
the verdant green lawn, the bright elegance of leaves strewn

over it all, turning nonchalantly in the wind, and the Nebraska sky
blue as a kind of watery ease, a comfort, it is all I can say, the kind

one knows, even standing there waiting for the dog to squat;
one that I will remember for years but will never have the language

to speak of—one of those precious insignificances that we collect
and hoard. The moment lasts ten breaths, and in that silence

I imagine that I can see spirits, I can know myself, and I will not fear
the betrayals of body and love and earth, and the machinations

of self-made emperors and pontificates. It will be winter soon. I know
    my body
is collecting water in its nether regions, the weight of the hibernating

mammal, storing everything in drowsy, slow-moving preservation.
I mean I am losing myself to the shelter we build to beat back

sorrow and the weight of our fears. I have covered thousands of miles
in a few days, and I feel my parts flaking off, a shedding of yellow

pieces covering the turning earth, and I am helpless to this soft
disappearing that some call sleep. I will stretch out and breathe.

MAGGIE SMITH

BRIDE

How long have I been wed
to myself? Calling myself

darling, dressing for my own
pleasure, each morning

choosing perfume to turn
me on. How long have I been

alone in this house but not
alone? Married less

to the man than to the woman
silvering with the mirror.

I know the kind of wife
I need and I become her:

the one who will leave
this earth at the same instant

I do. I am my own bride,
lifting the veil to see

my face. Darling, I say,
I have waited for you all my life.

STEPHANIE BURT

HERMIT CRAB

That shell is pretty, but that shell is too small for me.

Each home is a hideout; each home is a secret; each home
is a getaway under the same hot lamp, a means
to a lateral move at low velocity.

I live in a room in the room
of a boy I barely see.

Sometimes the boy & his talkative friends raise
too-warm hands & try to set me free

& I retreat into myself, hoping they place
me back in my terrarium, & they
do, with disappointed alacrity.

Scatter patterns in sand, adnates, cancellates, gaping
whelk husks, a toy tractor-trailer, cracked
and dinged, beside the spine of a plastic tree,

the helmet-shaped shelter of a shadow cast
by a not-quite-buried wedge of pottery . . .

if I have a body that's wholly my own
then it isn't mine. For a while I was
protected by what I pretended to be.

A. E. STALLINGS

SWALLOWS

Every year the swallows come
And put their homestead in repair,
And raise another brood, and skim
And boomerang through summer air,
And reap mosquitoes from the hum
Of holidays. A handsome pair,
One on the nest, one on the wire,
Cheat-cheat-cheat, the two conspire

To murder half the insect race,
And feed them squirming to their chicks.
They work and fret at such a pace,
And natter in between, with clicks
And churrs, they lift the raftered place
(Seaside taverna) with their tricks
Of cursive loops and Morse-code call,
Both analog and digital.

They seem to us so coupled, married,
So flustered with their needful young,
So busy housekeeping, so harried,
It's hard to picture them among
The origins of myth—a buried
Secret, rape, a cut-out tongue,
Two sisters wronged, where there's no right,
Till transformation fledges flight.

But Ovid swapped them in the tale,
So that the sister who was forced

Becomes instead the nightingale,
Who sings as though her heart would burst.
It's Ovid's stories that prevail.
And so the swallow is divorced
Twice from her voice, her tuneless chatter,
And no one asks her what's the matter.

These swallows, though, don't have the knack
For sorrow—or we'd not have guessed—
Though smartly dressed in tailored black,
Spend no time mourning, do not rest.
One scissors forth, one zigzags back,
They take turns settled on the nest
Or waiting on a perch nearby
To zero in on wasp or fly.

They have no time for tragic song,
As dusk distills, they dart and flicker,
The days are long, but not as long
As yesterday. The night comes quicker,
And soon the season will be wrong.
Knackered, cross, they bitch and bicker,
Like you and me. They never learn.
And every summer, they return.

RICK BAROT

THE LOVERS

One of them is still there, in the smell of burnt toast
    and dirty clothes that was my twenties, always waiting
to be picked up outside some station, that tenderness
set against each building's law of metal and stone.

One of them is still on a slope of the Sandias,
jeans pushed down to his knees
    so I can pick out the cactus needles from his thigh.
    The sky is late, the color of grape soda. In weeks, he will go

to a war, write letters that now sleep in a box
in the basement, next to a box of Christmas ornaments.

I open a book I read in college
   and one of them is in the margins, his handwriting
an enthusiastic vine, like the vines at the edges
of medieval texts, each "O" of his cursive a tiny horse chestnut,
   the paperback's pages yellow as a smoker's fingers.

Another one is still on his motorcycle
between Connecticut and Manhattan, driving a cab on weekends
for his tuition. On the nights I rode behind him,
   my head against the black leather of his back, I knew
I would die many times before my death.

One death for the one walking down Iowa Avenue,
   brooding on the problem of wearing a jacket
over a Halloween costume. One death
for the one scorned by his parents and brothers.
One death for the one locked for days in his room, drawing lines
   in a notebook, over and over and over.

Standing in front of a glass case in a museum, he is beside me,
looking at the silver hand
   resting like a claw on the gray velvet.
Another one is in his grandfather's miles of orchards,
   a place more immense because he is a boy
   lost in it, even though everything he sees is his kingdom.

There is no logic in what we keep.
   The freckles on his forearms. The surgery scar
on his shoulder. The reliquary that outlasts the bone of the saint.

In the coffeehouse, I see them, the lovers,
   the two teen-age boys on a couch,
   cuddling into one fused shape, one boy holding a phone
they lean toward, their faces lit by the platinum glow.
I have been them, and whatever comes after,

and it has taken all my heart to contain both.
There is no logic in what we keep, even of ourselves.

I am near him on a winter beach, the sky above shining like coal.
    I am sitting with him on a sidewalk
and he is weeping. I am alone in a hotel room,
thinking of all the ice machines on every floor of every hotel
    in the world, the sad machines dreaming
    of each pure cube of light.

THOM GUNN

NEW YORK

It wasn't ringworm he
explained it was speed
made those blotches all
over his body
                On the catwalk
above the turning wheels, high
on risk
        his luck
and the resources of the body
kept him going we were
balancing
            up there
                    all night
grinning and panting
hands black with machine oil
grease monkeys of risk
and those wheels were turning *fast*

I return to the sixth floor
where I am staying: the sun
ordering the untidy kitchen,
even the terraced black circles
in the worn enamel are bright,

the faucet dripping,
the parakeets chirping quietly
domestic about their cage,
my dear host in the bed and
his Newfoundland on it, together
stretching, half-woken, as
I close the door.
                    I calm down,
undress, and slip
in between them and think
of household gods.

YI LEI

FLAME IN THE CLOUD AT MIDNIGHT

Flame in the cloud at midnight
Blankets my bed with light.
The scent of winter jasmine
Rises from a tomb to meet my eyes.

I watch you as if from my girlhood.
I watch as if from death, anonymous
Beneath a dim sky, holding aloft
The burden of my body. Death,

Bloodless and unfeeling, is familiar.
But what if we could live that way, too?
At the moment, darling,
At the moment I'm a woman without lust.

Moonlight, like new snow,
Covers the hands and feet of night.
Huge strange faces
Fade from my windows and doors.

(Translated, from the Chinese, by Tracy K. Smith and Changtai Bi.)

LOUIS SIMPSON

MY FATHER IN THE NIGHT COMMANDING NO

My father in the night commanding No
Has work to do. Smoke issues from his lips;
     He reads in silence.
The frogs are croaking and the street lamps glow.

And then my mother winds the gramophone—
The Bride of Lammermoor begins to shriek—
     Or reads a story
About a prince, a castle, and a dragon.

The moon is glittering above the hill.
I stand before the gateposts of the King—
     So runs the story—
Of Thule, at midnight when the mice are still.

And I have been in Thule! It has come true—
The journey and the danger of the world,
     All that there is
To bear and to enjoy, endure and do.

Landscapes, seascapes . . . Where have I been led?
The names of cities—Paris, Venice, Rome—
     Held out their arms.
A feathered god, seductive, went ahead.

Here is my house. Under a red rose tree
A child is swinging; another gravely plays.
     They are not surprised
That I am here; they were expecting me.

And yet my father sits and reads in silence,
My mother sheds a tear, the moon is still,
     And the dark wind
Is murmuring that nothing ever happens.

Beyond his jurisdiction as I move,
Do I not prove him wrong? And yet, it's true
          They will not change
There, on the stage of terror and of love.

The actors in that playhouse always sit
In fixed positions—father, mother, child
          With painted eyes.
How sad it is to be a little puppet!

Their heads are wooden. And you once pretended
To understand them! Shake them as you will,
          They cannot speak.
Do what you will, the comedy is ended.

Father, why did you work? Why did you weep,
Mother? Was the story so important?
          "*Listen!*" the wind
Said to the children, and they fell asleep.

ERICA JONG

HIS TUNING OF THE NIGHT

All night he lies awake tuning the sky,
tuning the night with its fat crackle of static,
with its melancholy love songs crooning
across the rainy air above Verdun
& the Autobahn's blue, suicidal dawn.

Wherever he lives, there is the same unwomaned bed,
the ashtrays overflowing their reproaches,
his stained fingers on the tuning bar, fishing
for her voice in a deep mirrorless pond,
for the tinsel & elusive fish,
glittering like pennies in water,
the copper-colored daughter of the pond god.

He casts for her, the tuning bar his rod,
but only long-dead lovers with their griefs
haunt him in Piaf's voice
(as if a voice could somehow only die
when it was sung out, utterly).

He finally lies down & drowns the light,
but the taste of her rises, brackish,
from the long dark water of her illness
& his grief is terrible as drowning
when he reaches for the radio again.

In the daytime, you hardly know him—
he walks in a borrowed calm.
You cannot sense
his desperation in the dawn
when the abracadabras of the birds
conjure another phantom day.

He favors cities which blaze all night,
hazy mushrooms of light under the blue
& blinking eyes of jets.
But when the lamps across the way go under,
& the floorboards settle,
& the pipes fret like old men gargling,
he is alone with his mouthful of ghosts,
his tongue bitter with her unmourned death . . .

I watch from my blue window
knowing he does not trust me,
though I know him as I know my ghosts,
though I know his drowning,
though, since that night when all harmony broke for me,
I have been trying to tune the sky.

DANIEL HALPERN

STILL

I hear callers in the trees
but I stay in one place,
knowing motion is nothing
if I can't stand like this,
hour after hour.

In this immobility a fire inflates,
and so much turbulence within the static—
the owls call, still in their trees.
They can see in the night, they don't need to move.
I don't move myself—the river moves

somewhere, the clouds without sound
move and move. They drift and disband.
The dogs are still, except for their jaws,
which click in the night.
They smell the darkness, they don't need to move.

My work is to stand still and see everything.
My work is to rethink the immobile,
the owl and dog, and without moving release them,
release myself, let everything live again,
recalled into movement and loved, wholly still.

JAMES TATE

ANCIENT STORY

    At midnight I went outside to look at the
full moon. Bats were feasting on mosquitoes.
Out in the field a coyote was howling. The field
was bathed in a soft yellow light, and I could
see him, his head thrown back, like a passionate
tenor in an eerie opera. I wanted to join him, but
my howling was rusty. I walked slowly and quietly

in his direction. Several times bats swooped within
an inch of my face. My blood was rushing. The coyote
saw me and went right on singing. I froze in my
tracks. It was beautiful. His song told some
ancient tale of grief and sorrow. I started to
whimper. And that turned into squealing. Then I
was bawling and weeping. Kind of blubbering, with
some yips and yelps thrown in. My head thrown back,
I began to wail. And I couldn't stop wailing, it
felt so good. I had wakened the whole neighborhood,
and now they, too, were wailing.

ADRIENNE SU
THE DAYS

If only I could live my life, not write it,
I'd have double the experience

and be better at nothingness, at being present.
The page, I once believed, offers permanence,

sanctifying time, making it longer,
but now I see my words as susceptible,

even if digital, to fire, flood, misplacement.
To misinterpretation. To accidental

download by enemy. I don't yet want them
to be lost, but I dread the possibility

that they won't self-destruct at the end
of my life, or the end of my lucidity.

Maybe I've been using paper all wrong,
committing to ink what should live in my head,

which is part of my body, which will not last.
Long ago, in college, a friend once said

he would never keep a journal; he preferred
to live in the moment. Back home in June,

I threw the lot of them, dating back to childhood,
into a rose-red shopping bag—we reused

every one—then put the bag out with the trash.
Thank the stars or our thrift for its luminosity:

my mother asked what was in it, then ran
down the driveway, hauled it back up. Her family

had once lost everything. She knew what I wanted
to be, what I already was. "You have to keep them!"

she yelled. She never yelled. Even my friend,
hearing it later, said the same. What worked for him

might not be right for me. He loved to argue
and was always there, vociferous, ready to engage,

while I was too receptive, too easily swayed,
though I often swatted back. That's what college

is for, the wisdom goes, late-night conversation
with challenging peers. A few years later,

we were no longer friends, not through conflict
but cliché: he had wanted more, I had demurred,

and then there was nothing to say. But maybe
I'd been partial to aspects of his attention—

maybe all the platitudes were true. I had failed
to consider, despite constant reflection,

what my being there must have conveyed.
Reflection is simply an image, a face in a mirror;

to look upon is not the same as to examine.
Perhaps there is such a thing as a neutral observer.

Each night, I had written *Here is what happened*
like a kid whose pen makes her small life exciting,

then gone on mistaking the plot for the story,
as if the point of writing were writing.

ROBERT FROST

COME IN

As I came to the edge of the woods,
Thrush music—hark!
Now if it was dusk outside,
Inside it was dark.

Too dark in the woods for a bird
By sleight of wing
To better its perch for the night,
Though it still could sing.

The last of the light of the sun
That had died in the west
Still lived for one song more
In a thrush's breast.

Far in the pillared dark
Thrush music went—
Almost like a call to come in
To the dark and lament.

But no, I was out for stars:
I would not come in.
I meant not even if asked,
And I hadn't been.

ADVENT

It's hopeless, the stars, the books
about stars, they can't help themselves
and how could you not love them for it
here in the new week with animals
burying food and everything outlined
in cold and even friends, it's hopeless,
this mess, this season, all that
is lost and tickets and strangers,
what can I say, only sitting here
on this dark bench waiting for what
I don't know, I want this world
to remain with me, this holy tumult,
which does not know it loves me
and you, friends, spectacular driveways,
an orange, the vanishing year.

MARK STRAND
SLEEPING WITH ONE EYE OPEN

Unmoved by what the wind does,
The windows
Are not rattled, nor do the various
Areas
Of the house make their usual racket—
Creak at
The joints, trusses, and studs.
Instead,
They are still. And the maples,
Able
At times to raise havoc,
Evoke
Not a sound from their branches'
Clutches.

It's my night to be rattled,
Saddled
With spooks. Even the half moon
(Half man,
Half dark), on the horizon,
Lies on
Its side, casting a fishy light,
Which alights
On my floor, lavishly lording
Its morbid
Look over me. Oh, I feel dead,
Folded
Away in my blankets for good, and
Forgotten.
My room is clammy and cold,
Moonhandled
And weird. The shivers
Wash over
Me, shaking my bones, my loose ends
Loosen,
And I lie sleeping with one eye open,
Hoping
That nothing, nothing will happen.

MICHAEL ROBBINS
COUNTRY MUSIC

God bless the midnight bus depot,
the busted guitar case.
God bless diazepam,
its dilatory grace.

God keep Carl Perkins warm
and Jesus Christ erase
my name from all the files in
the county's database.

The dog that bit my leg
the night I left the state,
Lord won't you let his
vaccines be up to date.

West Point to the south of me,
Memphis to the north.
In between is planted with
pinwheels for the Fourth.

Smokestack Lightning, Jesus Christ—
whatever your name is—
bless my fingers on these strings,
I'll make us both famous.

How about that, the new moon,
same as it ever was.
You must've been high as a kite
when you created us.

So hurry, hurry, step right up,
there's something you should see.
The sun shines on the bus depot
like a coat of Creole pink.

God keep the world this clean and bright
and easy to believe in
and let me catch my bus all right,
and then we'll call it even.

THE AUGHTS
(2000s TO EARLY 2010s)

KAY RYAN

THINGS SHOULDN'T BE SO HARD

A life should leave
deep tracks:
ruts where she
went out and back
to get the mail
or move the hose
around the yard;
where she used to
stand before the sink,
a worn-out place;
beneath her hand,
the china knobs
rubbed down to
white pastilles;
the switch she
used to feel for
in the dark
almost erased.
Her things should
keep her marks.
The passage
of a life should show;
it should abrade.
And when life stops,
a certain space
—however small—
should be left scarred
by the grand and
damaging parade.
Things shouldn't
be so hard.

EAVAN BOLAND

LINES WRITTEN FOR A THIRTIETH WEDDING ANNIVERSARY

Somewhere up in the eaves it began:
high in the roof—in a sort of vault
between the slates and gutter—a small leak.
Through it, rain which came from the east,
in from the lights and foghorns of the coast—
water with a ghost of ocean salt in it—
spilled down on the path below.
Over and over and over
years stone began to alter,
its grain searched out, worn in:
granite rounding down, giving way,
taking into its own inertia that
information water brought, of ships,
wings, fog and phosphor in the harbor.
It happened under our lives: the rain,
the stone. We hardly noticed. Now
this is the day to think of it, to wonder:
all those years, all those years together—
the stars in a frozen arc overhead,
the quick noise of a thaw in the air,
the blue stare of the hills—through it all
this constancy: what wears, what endures.

QUARANTINE

In the worst hour of the worst season
        of the worst year of a whole people
a man set out from the workhouse with his wife.
He was walking—they were both walking—north.

She was sick with famine fever and could not keep up.
        He lifted her and put her on his back.

He walked like that west and west and north.
Until at nightfall under freezing stars they arrived.

In the morning they were both found dead.
          Of cold. Of hunger. Of the toxins of a whole history.
But her feet were held against his breastbone.
The last heat of his flesh was his last gift to her.

Let no love poem ever come to this threshold.
          There is no place here for the inexact
praise of the easy graces and sensuality of the body.
There is only time for this merciless inventory:

Their death together in the winter of 1847.
          Also what they suffered. How they lived.
And what there is between a man and woman.
And in which darkness it can best be proved.

KO UN

FOUR POEMS

I'd like to buy her some toffee
but I don't have a daughter

as I pass a sidewalk store in autumn.

  •

Exhausted
the mother has fallen asleep
so her baby is listening all alone
to the sound of the night train.

  •

Frogs croaking in flooded paddies—
if there really is a world beyond,
echo far enough so my dead brother can hear.

  •

A boat whistles in the night.
For a moment I too long to sail away

but merely pull the blanket up over the kids.

> *(Translated, from the Korean, by Brother Anthony of Taizé,
> Young-moo Kim, and Gary Gach.)*

FRANZ WRIGHT

THE ONLY ANIMAL

The only animal that commits suicide
went for a walk in the park,
basked on a hard bench
in the first star,
travelled to the edge of space
in an armchair
while company quietly
talked, and abruptly
returned,
the room empty.

The only animal that cries,
that takes off its clothes
and reports to the mirror, the one
and only animal
that brushes its own teeth—

somewhere

the only animal that smokes a cigarette,
that lies down and flies backward in time,
that rises and walks to a book
and looks up a word
heard the telephone ringing
in the darkness downstairs and decided
to answer no more.

And I understand,
too well: how many times
have I made the decision to dwell
from now on
in the hour of my death
(the space I took up here
scarlessly closing like water)
and said I'm never coming back,
and yet

this morning
I stood once again
in this world, the garden
ark and vacant
tomb of what
I can't imagine,
between twin eternities,
some sort of wings,
more or less equidistantly
exiled from both,
hovering in the dreaming called
being awake, where
You gave me
in secret one thing
to perceive, the
tall blue starry
strangeness of being
here at all.

You gave us each in secret one thing to perceive.

Furless now, upright, My banished
and experimental
child

You said, though your own heart condemn you

I do not condemn you.

WHEELING MOTEL

The vast waters flow past its back yard.
You can purchase a six-pack in bars!
Tammy Wynette's on the marquee
a block down. It's twenty-five years ago:
you went to death, I to life, and
which was luckier God only knows.
There's this line in an unpublished poem of yours.
The river is like that,
a blind familiar.
The wind will die down when I say so;
the leaden and lessening light on
the current.
Then the moon will rise
like the word reconciliation,
like Walt Whitman examining the tear on a dead face.

GALWAY KINNELL

WHEN THE TOWERS FELL

From our high window we saw the towers
with their bands and blocks of light
brighten against a fading sunset,
saw them at any hour glitter and live
as if the spirits inside them sat up all night
calculating profit and loss, saw them reach up
to steep their tops in the until then invisible
yellow of sunrise, grew so used to them
often we didn't see them, and now,
not seeing them, we see them.

The banker is talking to London.
Humberto is delivering breakfast sandwiches.
The trader is already working the phone.

The mail sorter has started sorting the mail.
> . . . *povres et riches*
> . . . poor and rich

Sages et folz, prestres et laiz
Wise and foolish, priests and laymen
Nobles, villains, larges et chiches
Noblemen, serfs, generous and mean
Petiz et grans et beaulx et laiz
Short and tall and handsome and homely

The plane screamed low down lower Fifth Avenue,
lifted at the Arch, someone said, shaking the dog walkers
in Washington Square Park, drove for the north tower,
struck with a heavy thud, releasing a huge bright gush
of blackened fire, and vanished, leaving a hole
the size and shape a cartoon plane might make
if it had passed harmlessly through and were flying away now,
on the far side, back into the realm of the imaginary.

Some with torn clothing, some bloodied,
some limping at top speed like children
in a three-legged race, some half dragged,
some intact in neat suits and dresses,
they straggle out of step up the avenues,
each dusted to a ghostly whiteness,
their eyes rubbed red as the eyes of a Zahoris,
who can see the dead under the ground.

Some died while calling home to say they were O.K.
Some died after over an hour spent learning they would die.
Some died so abruptly they may have seen death from within it.
Some broke windows and leaned out and waited for rescue.
Some were asphyxiated.
Some burned, their very faces caught fire.
Some fell, letting gravity speed them through their long moment.
Some leapt hand in hand, the elasticity in last bits of love-time
> letting—I wish I could say—their vertical streaks down the sky
> happen more lightly.

At the high window, where I've often stood
to escape a nightmare, I meet
the single, unblinking eye
lighting the all-night sniffing and lifting
and sifting for bodies, pieces of bodies, anything that is not nothing,
in a search that always goes on
somewhere, now in New York and Kabul.

She stands on a corner holding up a picture
of her husband. He is smiling. In today's
wind shift few pass. Sorry sorry sorry.
She startles. Suppose, down the street, that headlong lope . . .
or, over there, that hair so black it's purple . . .
And yet, suppose some evening I forgot
The fare and transfer, yet got by that way
Without recall,—lost yet poised in traffic.
Then I might find your eyes . . .
It could happen. Sorry sorry good luck thank you.
On this side it is "amnesia," or forgetting the way home;
on the other, "invisibleness," or never in body returning.
Hard to see clearly in the metallic mist,
or through the sheet of mock reality
cast over our world, bourne that no creature ever born
pokes its way back through, and no love can tear.

The towers burn and fall, burn and fall—
in a distant shot, smokestacks spewing oily earth remnants out of the
          past.
Schwarze Milch der Frühe wir trinken sie abends
Black milk of daybreak we drink it at nightfall
wir trinken sie mittags und morgens wir trinken sie nachts
we drink it at midday at morning we drink it at night
wir trinken und trinken
we drink it and drink it
This is not a comparison but a corollary,
not a likeness but a lineage
in the twentieth-century history of violent death—
black men in the South castrated and strung up from trees,

soldiers advancing through mud at ninety thousand dead per mile,
train upon train headed eastward made up of boxcars shoved full to the
      corners with Jews and Gypsies to be enslaved or gassed,
state murder of twenty, thirty, forty million of its own,
atomic blasts wiping cities off the earth, firebombings the same,
death marches, starvations, assassinations, disappearances,
entire countries turned into rubble, minefields, mass graves.
Seeing the towers vomit these black omens, that the last century
      dumped into this one, for us to dispose of, we know
they are our futures, that is our own black milk crossing the sky: *wir*
      schaufeln ein Grab in den Lüften da liegt man nicht eng   we're
      digging a grave in the sky there'll be plenty of room to lie down there

Burst jet fuel, incinerated aluminum, steel fume, crushed marble,
      exploded granite, pulverized drywall, mashed concrete, berserked
      plastic, gasified mercury, cracked chemicals, scoria, vapor
of the vaporized—wafted here
from the burnings of the past, draped over
our island up to streets regimented
into numbers and letters, breathed across
the great bridges to Brooklyn and the waiting sea:
astringent, miasmic, empyreumatic, slick,
freighted air too foul to take in but we take it in,
too gruesome for seekers of the amnesiac beloved
to breathe but they breathe it and you breathe it.

A photograph of a woman hangs from a string
at his neck. He doesn't look up.
He stares down at the sidewalk of flagstone
slabs laid down in Whitman's century, gutter edges
rasped by iron wheels to a melted roundedness:
a conscious intelligence envying the stones.
Nie stają sie, są.
They do not become, they are.
Nic nad to, myślałem,
Nothing but that, I thought,
zbrzydziwszy sobie
now loathing within myself

wszystko co staje się
everything that becomes.

And I sat down by the waters of the Hudson,
by the North Cove Yacht Harbor, and thought
how those on the high floors must have suffered: knowing
they would burn alive, and then, burning alive.
And I wondered, Is there a mechanism of death
that so mutilates existence no one
gets over it not even the dead?
Before me I saw, in steel letters welded
to the steel railing posts, Whitman's words
written as America plunged into war with itself: *City of the world!* . . .
Proud and passionate city—mettlesome, mad, extravagant city!
—words of a time of illusions. Then I remembered
what he wrote after the war was over and Lincoln dead:
I saw the debris and debris of all the dead soldiers of the war,
But I saw they were not as was thought.
They themselves were fully at rest—they suffer'd not,
The living remain'd and suffer'd, the mother suffer'd,
And the wife and the child and the musing comrade suffer'd . . .

In our minds the glassy blocks
succumb over and over into themselves,
slam down floor by floor into themselves.

They blow up as if in reverse, exploding
downward and outward, billowing
through the streets, engulfing the fleeing.

As each tower goes down, it concentrates
into itself, transforms itself
infinitely slowly into a black hole

infinitesimally small: mass
without space, where each light,
each life, put out, lies down within us.

DEBORAH GARRISON

I SAW YOU WALKING

I saw you walking through Newark Penn Station
in your shoes of white ash. At the corner
of my nervous glance your dazed passage
first forced me away, tracing the crescent
berth you'd give a drunk, a lurcher, nuzzling
all comers with ill will and his stench, but
not this one, not today: one shirt arm's sheared
clean from the shoulder, the whole bare limb
wet with muscle and shining dimly pink,
the other full-sheathed in cotton, Brooks Bros.
type, the cuff yet buttoned at the wrist, a
parody of careful dress, preparedness—
so you had not rolled up your sleeves yet this
morning when your suit jacket (here are
the pants, dark gray, with subtle stripe, as worn
by men like you on ordinary days)
and briefcase (you've none, reverse commuter
come from the pit with nothing to carry
but your life) were torn from you, as your life
was not. Your face itself seemed to be walking,
leading your body north, though the age
of the face, blank and ashen, passing forth
and away from me, was unclear, the sandy
crown of hair powdered white like your feet, but
underneath not yet gray—forty-seven?
forty-eight? the age of someone's father—
and I trembled for your luck, for your broad,
dusted back, half shirted, walking away;
I should have dropped to my knees to thank God
you were alive, o my God, in whom I don't believe.

W. S. MERWIN

TO THE WORDS

When it happens you are not there

oh you beyond numbers
beyond recollection
passed on from breath to breath
given again
from day to day from age
to age
charged with knowledge
knowing nothing

indifferent elders
indispensable and sleepless

keepers of our names
before ever we came
to be called by them

you that were
formed to begin with
you that were cried out
you that were spoken
to begin with
to say what could not be said

ancient precious
and helpless ones

say it

MARK DOTY

IN THE SAME SPACE

The sun set early in the Square, winter afternoons,
angling over the apartments to the west, so that light would bisect

the northern row of dark houses diagonally, the grand houses
that were suddenly not of the last century but of the century before.

Then the world would seem equally divided, a while, between the
    golden
and the chill, equipoise in a bitter year. When the sun was completely
    gone

we'd turn for home, the dogs and I, and to the south, the two towers,
harshly formal by day, brusque in their authority—

at the beginning of evening they'd go a blue a little darker than the sky,
lit from top to bottom by a wavering curtain of small, welcoming
    lamps.

ANNA AKHMATOVA

THREE POEMS

Disaster has fallen on everyone, everywhere;
The presence of death is like night.
Devouring pain has swallowed everything—
Then why do we feel such delight?

Days are heavy with cherry-tree fragrance
Drifting from the orchards nearby;
Nights burn with unknown constellations
In the transparent heavens of July.

And something miraculous materializes
Among the ruins, the rubble, the grime—

Something none of us, none of us recognizes,
But has wanted for a long, long time.

     •

There were three things in life he loved:
Music at Vespers, white peacocks,
And antique maps of America.
He hated children crying
And raspberry jam for tea.
He hated women in hysterics—
And he married me.

     •

I drink to the wreck of our life together,
And the pain of living alone.
I drink to the loneliness we shared—
My dear, I drink to you.

I drink to the trick of a mouth that betrayed me,
To the eyes and the look that lied.
I drink to the terrible world we inhabit
And to God, who never replied.

      (Translated, from the Russian, by Paul Schmidt.)

GRACE PALEY

DETOUR

I had put my days behind me
almost as they happened rolling
faces streets personal dramas
into a scroll quickly
quickly sometimes my heels
were caught in the last conver-
sation so shaking to free myself
all that clutter flew
up into the air scrambled
sentences my sister's death the

name of what's his name his mouth
his fingers a heavy chunk of a
principled political statement
whose?

future was my intention now
all that detritus like sand like
dust has drifted into the eyes
of my children who after all must
continue one of my heaviest
sorrows has just tumbled at
their feet they stumble what
to do anger fear luckily their
children have imperiously
called offering their lives a
detour thank God they've all
gotten away

FATHERS

Fathers are
more fathering
these days they have
accomplished this by
being more mothering

what luck for them that
women's lib happened then
the dream of new fathering
began to shine in the eyes
for free women and was irresistible

on the New York subways
and the mass transits
of other cities one may
see fatherings of many colors
with their round babies on

their laps this may also
happen in the countryside

these scenes were brand-new
exciting for an old woman who
had watched the old fathers
gathering once again in
familiar Army camps and com-
fortable war rooms to consider
the necessary eradication of
the new fathering fathers
(who are their sons) as well
as the women and children who
will surely be in the way.

AGHA SHAHID ALI

BEYOND ENGLISH

No language is old—or young—beyond English.
So what of a common tongue beyond English?

I know some words for war, all of them sharp,
but the sharpest one is *jung*—beyond English!

If you wish to know of a king who loved his slave,
you must learn legends, often-sung, beyond English.

Baghdad is sacked and its citizens must watch
prisoners (now in miniatures) hung beyond English.

Go all the way through *jungle* from *aleph* to *zenith*
to see English, like monkeys, swung beyond English.

So never send to know for whom the bell tolled,
for across the earth it has rung beyond English.

If you want your drugs legal you must leave the States,
not just for hashish but one—*bhung*—beyond English.

Heartbroken, I tottered out "into windless snow,"
snowflakes on my lips, silence stung beyond English.

When the phrase "The Mother of all Battles" caught on,
the surprise was indeed not sprung beyond English.

Could a soul crawl away at last unshrivelled which
to its "own fusing senses" had clung beyond English?

CORNELIUS EADY

EMMETT TILL'S GLASS-TOP CASKET

By the time they cracked me open again, topside, abandoned in
a toolshed, I had become another kind of nest. Not many people
connect possums with Chicago,

but this is where the city ends, after all, and I float still, after
the footfalls fade and the roots bloom around us. The fact was,
everything that worked for my young man

worked for my new tenants. The fact was, he had been gone for
years. They lifted him from my embrace, and I was empty, ready.
That's how the possums found me, friend,

dry-docked, a tattered mercy hull. Once I held a boy who didn't
look like a boy. When they finally remembered, they peeked
through my clear top. Then their wild surprise.

PHILIP LEVINE

BURIAL RITES

Everyone comes back here to die
as I will soon. The place feels right
since it's half dead to begin with.
Even on a rare morning of rain,
like this morning, with the low sky
hoarding its riches except for
a few mock tears, the hard ground
accepts nothing. Six years ago
I buried my mother's ashes
beside a young lilac that's now
taller than I, and stuck the stub
of a rosebush into her dirt,
where like everything else not
human it thrives. The small blossoms
never unfurl; whatever they know
they keep to themselves until
a morning rain or a night wind
pares the petals down to nothing.
Even the neighbor cat who shits
daily on the paths and then hides
deep in the jungle of the weeds
refuses to purr. Whatever's here
is just here, and nowhere else,
so it's right to end up beside
the woman who bore me, to shovel
into the dirt whatever's left
and leave only a name for some-
one who wants it. Think of it,
my name, no longer a portion
of me, no longer inflated
or bruised, no longer stewing
in a rich compost of memory
or the simpler one of bone shards,
dirt, kitty litter, wood ashes,

the roots of the eucalyptus
I planted in '73,
a tiny me taking nothing,
giving nothing, and free at last.

YUSEF KOMUNYAKAA

ORPHEUS AT THE SECOND GATE OF HADES

My lyre has fallen & broken,
but I have my little tom-toms.
Look, do you see those crows
perched on the guardhouse?
I don't wish to speak of omens
but sometimes it's hard to guess.
Life has been good the past few years.
I know all seven songs of the sparrow
& I feel lucky to be alive. I woke up at 2:59
this morning, reprieved because I fought
dream-catchers & won. I'll place a stone
in my mouth & go down there again,
& if I meet myself mounting the stairs
it won't be the same man descending.
Doubt has walked me to the river's edge
before. I may be ashamed but I can't forget
how to mourn & praise on the marimba.
I shall play till the day's golden machinery
stops between the known & the unknown.
The place was a funeral pyre for the young
who died before knowing the thirst of man
or woman. Furies with snakes in their hair
wept. Tantalus ate pears & sipped wine
in a dream, as the eyes of a vulture
poised over Tityus' liver. I could see
Ixion strapped to a gyrating wheel
& Sisyphus sat on his rounded stone.
I shall stand again before Proserpine
& King Pluto. When it comes to defending love,

I can make a lyre drag down the moon & stars
but it's still hard to talk of earthly things—
ordinary men killing ordinary men,
women & children. I don't remember
exactly what I said at the ticket office
my first visit here, but I do know it grew
ugly. The classical allusions didn't
make it any easier. I played a tune
that worked its way into my muscles
& I knew I had to speak of what I'd seen
before the serpent drew back its head.
I saw a stall filled with human things, an endless
list of names, a hill of shoes, a room of suitcases
tagged to nowhere, eyeglasses, toothbrushes,
baby shoes, dentures, ads for holiday spas,
& a wide roll of thick cloth woven of living hair.
If I never possessed these reed flutes
& drums, if my shadow stops kissing me
because of what I have witnessed,
I shall holler to you through my bones,
I promise you.

MARVIN BELL

THE BOOK OF THE DEAD MAN (VERTIGO)

Live as if you were already dead.
            —Zen admonition.

I. ABOUT THE DEAD MAN AND VERTIGO

The dead man skipped stones till his arm gave out.
He showed up early to the games and stayed late, he played with
        abandon, he felt the unease in results.
His medicine is movement, the dead man alters cause and
        consequence.
The dead man shatters giddy wisdoms as if he were punching his
        pillow.
Now it comes round again, the time to rise and cook up a day.
Time to break out of one's dream shell, and here's weather.

Time to unmask the clock face.

He can feel a tremor of fresh sunlight, warm and warmer.

The first symptom was, having crossed a high bridge, he found he
could not go back.

The second, on the hotel's thirtieth floor he peeked from the
balcony and knew falling.

It was ultimate candor, it was the body's lingo, it was low tide in his
inner ear.

The third was when he looked to the constellations and grew woozy.

2. MORE ABOUT THE DEAD MAN AND VERTIGO

It wasn't bad, the new carefulness.

It was a fraction of his lifetime, after all, a shard of what he knew.

He scaled back, he dialled down, he walked more on the flats.

The dead man adjusts, he favors his good leg, he squints his best eye
to see farther.

No longer does he look down from the heights, it's simple.

He knows it's not a cinder in his eye, it just feels like it.

He remembers himself at the edge of a clam boat, working the fork.

He loves to compress the past, the good times are still at hand.

Even now, he will play catch till his whole shoulder gives out.

His happiness has been a whirl, it continues, it is dizzying.

He has to keep his feet on the ground, is all.

He has to watch the sun and moon from underneath, is all.

EDWARD HIRSCH

MY FATHER'S CHILDHOOD

I used to bring the conductor his lunch pail
on the trolley that circled Mannheim

but I can't recall now if he was my father
or my father's brother who moved to California.

Maybe if he showed me his wounds . . .

Papa guarded French prisoners in the village
where we moved after he was shot down.

He had trouble breathing after the war.

Sometimes he marched them by our house
and sneaked them in for tea. My mother
made him keep his rifle in the hall.

Otto, she said, and he put his gun away.
Selma came from Enkirch, on the Moselle.

My brother Hans had curly red hair
that looked like a burning bush,
but I was the one who stuttered.

The prisoners sang sad French songs
and gave us pieces of chewing gum
because they missed their families.

I always liked those men who lost everything.

My father had a premonition about the Nazis
and he followed his cousins to Chicago.

He was a spotter,
who never liked working in the dry cleaner's.

We lived in an Italian neighborhood
and I had to fight every day
on the way home from school.

I didn't know English at first
and we were refugees with something to prove.

Sometimes I crawled out my bedroom window
to keep the fight going.

I'd say God was a bully.

You know I can't call up one single word
of German, the bastards,

or the name of that village,

but I remember looking out a window
and seeing my mother standing in a garden.

This was before the expulsion.

I wonder if she ever liked cities.

She was barefoot.

Paradise lived under her feet.

JACK GILBERT

REFUSING HEAVEN

The old women in black at early Mass in winter
are a problem for him. He could tell by their eyes
they have seen Christ. They make the kernel
of his being and the clarity around it
seem meagre, as though he needs girders
to hold up his unusable soul. But he chooses
against the Lord. He will not abandon his life.
Not his childhood, not the ninety-two bridges
across the two rivers of his youth. Nor the mills
along the banks where he became a young man
as he worked. The mills are eaten away, and eaten
again by the sun and its rusting. He needs them
even though they are gone, to measure against.
The silver is worn down to the brass underneath
and is the better for it. He will gauge

by the smell of concrete sidewalks after night rain.
He is like an old ferry dragged on to the shore,
a home in its smashed grandeur, with the giant beams
and joists. Like a wooden ocean out of control.
A beached heart. A cauldron of cooling melt.

SOPHIE CABOT BLACK

CHEMOTHERAPY

My friend is going through the fire on his knees,
His hands, crossing the entire field of it;
Once in a while he calls out, bewildered,

The other side unclear, wanting to just
Lie down and wait among the scattered stones.
Unimaginable heat: he pants, lost in the light

Of what keeps happening—think water, think water,
And he manages to make out one nurse
Up against the bright and it takes everything

To tell her what he needs, as if he had come upon
The one tree still standing, and understood
She promises nothing, who in her uniform

Was all that was ever asked for and who
Could hold him as he has never been held.

GIVEN PORNOGRAPHY

All this work leads to holding both
At once. In the midst of the crowd
A woman services two men, serves

Might be a kinder word but we want this
Precise. Pressing a way through
To some bed or stage or platform is what

We do. And as she rises her body against
Each of them this makes the argument
Of resolution, of unlike moving into like

Until finally everything is the same.
We keep in time; this is not elsewhere.
Nowhere is the center more not the point,

What hand belongs to whom and where.
And to take turns and to bear
That someone goes first, which can never be

Exact or equal, is how faith must come
Into all that touch. Do not be astonished;
She has placed herself to be lost,

To be eaten while eating, a darkening
Bruise of too much, a guide of
Figuring which door to push against,

Already open. We watch for the ending
Not wanting it to end. What to know
That we did not before, save the ungodly

Angles. To do while being done. Polite the mirror
With anything possible; it is not about
Who wants whom more but you cannot help wondering

What happens to she who has been caught
As if between slides of glass—her body so useful.
What comes of each entrance given

Like bread to taste, to begin each day
As if starting over, considering what she has made
Of herself for herself by herself; and how

You could never have been her, until now, quiet
As a church, holy as a trinity, until just
Now the noise of trying to get it right.

ELIZA GRISWOLD

OCCUPATION

The prostitutes in Kabul tap their feet
beneath their faded burkas in the heat.
For bread or fifteen cents, they'll take a man to bed—
their husbands dead, their seven kids unfed—
and thanks to occupation, rents have risen twentyfold,
their chickens, pots, and carpets have been sold
and women's flesh now worth its weight in tin.
Two years ago, the Talibs favored boys and left the girls alone.
A woman then was worth her weight in stone.

GERALD STERN

APOCALYPSE

Of all sixty of us I am the only one who went
to the four corners though I don't say it
out of pride but more like a type of regret,
and I did it because there was no one I truly believed
in though once when I climbed the hill in Skye
and arrived at the rough tables I saw the only other
elder who was a vegetarian—in Scotland—
and visited Orwell and rode a small motorcycle
to get from place to place and I immediately
stopped eating fish and meat and lived on soups;
and we wrote each other in the middle and late fifties
though one day I got a letter from his daughter
that he had died in an accident; he was,
I'm sure of it, an angel who flew in midair
with one eternal gospel to proclaim
to those inhabiting the earth and every nation;
and now that I go through my papers every day
I search and search for his letters but to my shame
I have even forgotten his name, that messenger
who came to me with tablespoons of blue lentils.

MAJOR JACKSON
HOW TO LISTEN

I am going to cock my head tonight like a dog
in front of McGlinchey's tavern on Locust:
I am going to stand beside the man who works all day combing
his thatch of gray hair corkscrewed in every direction.
I am going to pay attention to our lives
unravelling between the forks of his fine-toothed comb.
For once, we won't talk about the end of the world
or Vietnam or his exquisite paper shoes.
For once, I am going to ignore the profanity and
the dancing and the jukebox so I can hear his head crackle
beneath the sky's stretch of faint stars.

SPENCER REECE
MY GREAT-GRANDMOTHER'S BIBLE

Faux-leather bound and thick as an onion, it flakes—
an heirloom from Iowa my dead often read.
I open the black flap to speak the "spake"s
and quickly lose track of who wed, who bred.
She taped our family register as it tore,
her hand stuttering like a sewing machine,
darning the blanks with farmers gone before—
Inez, Alvah, Delbert, Ermadean.
Our undistinguished line she pressed in the heft
between the Testaments, with spaces to spare,
smudged with mistakes or tears; her fingers left
a mounting watchfulness I find hard to bear.
When I saw the AIDS quilt, spread out in acres,
it was stitched with similar scripts by similar makers.

A. R. AMMONS

SPEAKING

There will be rains I'll need
no shelter from; cold winds
no walls need broach the chill of for me:

when fire splits seams
out of the ground, I won't
need the warmth at all: lone, ever,

when you who have given
your days to me, when you
come close, I won't sense

that last approach: not
knowing how to speak,
I'll say nothing.

CAROL MOLDAW

OF AN AGE

Less sleep but fewer tears.
Prayers pared down to tweets.
Desire scrubbed of sullenness.
A propensity for sweets—

but not truffles, truffles
I find too dense; chocolate-glazed
bacon, the idea of it, too strange.
Fads tempt less. A glass raised

in sentiment, more.
The fleet beauty of words
no longer cased unsaid.
The glass in shards.

RAE ARMANTROUT

PRAYERS

1.
We pray
and the resurrection happens.

Here are the young
again,

sniping and giggling,

tingly
as ringing phones.

2.
All we ask
is that our thinking

sustain momentum,
identify targets.

The pressure
in my lower back
rising to be recognized
as pain.

The blue triangles
on the rug
repeating.

Coming up,
a discussion
on the uses
of torture.

The fear
that all *this*
will end.

The fear
that it won't.

MARY KARR

HURT HOSPITAL'S BEST SUICIDE JOKES

In unfolded aluminum chairs the color of shit
        and set in a circle as if to corral some emptiness
                in this church basement deep in the dirt,
                        strangers sit and tell stories.
Sergei sipped wine in a hot tub. Janice
        threw back shots in a dive.
                Bob drew blinds to smoke blunts and ate nothing
                        but cake frosting bought by the case.
The first lady of someplace swiped her son's meds
        to stay slim. Craig burst through bank doors,
                machine gun in hand. John geezed heroin:
                        with a turkey baster, he says, *into a neck vein.*
A cop shoved Mark's face in the mud,
        put a shoe on his neck to cuff him and ask
                where his friends were. *I had friends,*
                        he said, *think I'd be here?*
Zola once wrote that the road from the shrine
        at Lourdes was impressively littered
                with crutches and canes but he noted
                        not one wooden leg.
In the garage, with your face through a noose,
        you kick out the ladder, but the green rope won't give,
                and when your wife clicks the garage switch and the door
                        tilts up, there you dangle on tiptoe.

Alive, all of us, on this island, where we sip only
        black liquids or clear water and face down the void
             we've shaped, and should our eyes meet
                  what howls erupt—like jackals we bawl
to find ourselves upright.

ROBERT CREELEY

THE HEART

In the construction
of the chest, there is
a heart.

A boat
upon its blood
floats past

and round or down
the stream of life,
the plummeting veins

permit its passage
to admit no gains,
no looking back.

One steps aboard,
one's off.
The ticket taker

signs the time allotted.
Seated, amorphous persons
see no scenery

but feel
a chill about their knees
and hear a fading cry

as all the many sides of life
whiz by,
a blast at best, a loss

of individual impressions.
Still I sit
with you inside me too—

and *us*,
the couple thus encoupled,
ride on into the sweetening dark.

WISŁAWA SZYMBORSKA

FIRST LOVE

They say
the first love's most important.
That's very romantic,
but not my experience.

Something was and wasn't there between us,
something went on and went away.

My hands never tremble
when I stumble on silly keepsakes
and a sheaf of letters tied with string—
not even ribbon.

Our only meeting after years:
the conversation of two chairs
at a chilly table.

Other loves
still breathe deep inside me.
This one's too short of breath even to sigh.

Yet, just exactly as it is,
it does what the others still can't manage:
unremembered,
not even seen in dreams,
it introduces me to death.

(Translated, from the Polish, by Stanislaw Baranczak and Clare Cavanagh.)

MICHAEL LONGLEY

IN NOTRE-DAME

When I go back into the cathedral to check
If the candle I lit for you is still burning,
I encounter Job squatting on his dunghill.
(Can those be cowrie-shell fossils in the stone?
No. Imagine imagining and carving turds
At eye level for our sorry edification!)
Such tiny figures make my own body feel huge
And fleshy and hopeless inside the doorway.
In my voice-box the penitents and pickpockets
Murmuring in hundreds down the aisles find room.
Each mouth is a cathedral for the God-crumbs.
Where is the holy water, the snow water for Job?
All of our eyes are broken rose windows. Look,
Your candle singes the eyelashes of morning.

MARILYN HACKER

NAMES

Be mindful of names. They'll etch themselves
like daily specials on the window glass
in a delible medium. They'll pass
transformed, erased, a cloud the wind dissolves
above the ruckus of the under-twelves

on the slide, the toddlers on the grass,
the ragged skinny guy taking a piss
in the bushes, a matron tanning her calves
on a bench, skirt tucked around her knees.
A sparrow lands in the japonica;
as if it were a signal, all at once
massed pigeons rush up from adjacent trees,
wingbeats intrusive and symphonic—a
near-total silence is the clear response.

ROBIN ROBERTSON

A SEAGULL MURMUR

is what they called it,
shaking their heads
like trawlermen;

the mewling sound of a leaking heart
        the sound
of a gull trapped in his chest.

To let it out
they ran a cut down his belly
like a fish, his open ribs

the ribs of a boat;
        and they closed him,
wired him shut.

Caulked and seaworthy now
with his new valve; its metal
tapping away:

the dull clink
        of a signal-buoy
or a beak at the bars of a cage.

MICHAEL DICKMAN

SEEING WHALES

You can go blind, waiting

Unbelievable quiet
except for their
soundings

Moving the sea around

Unbelievable quiet inside you, as they change
the face of water

The only other time I felt this still was watching Leif shoot up when
        we were twelve

Sunlight all over his face

breaking
the surface of something
I couldn't see

You can wait your
whole life

        •

The Himalayas are on the move, appearing and disappearing in the
        snow in the Himalayas

Mahler
begins to fill
the half-dead auditorium
giant step by
giant step

The Colorado
The Snake
The Salmon

My grandfather walks across the front porch
spotted with cancer, smoking
a black cigar

The whales fold themselves back and back inside the long hallways
        of salt

You have to stare back at the salt
the sliding mirrors
all day

just to see something
maybe

for the last time
        •
By now they are asleep
some are asleep
on the bottom of the world
sucking the world in
and blowing it out
in wave-
lengths

Radiant ghosts

Leif laid his head back on a pillow and waited for all the blood inside
        him to flush down a hole

After seeing whales what do you see?

The hills behind the freeway

power lines

green, green
grass

the green sea

ADONIS

WEST AND EAST

Something stretches in history's tunnel.
Something decorated and mined
carrying its oil-poisoned child
sung to in a poisoned trade.
It was an East like a child asking,
pleading,
and West was his infallible elder.

I switched this map around,
for the world is all burned up:
East and West, a heap
of ash gathered
in the self-same grave.

(*Translated, from the Arabic, by Khaled Mattawa.*)

CELEBRATING CHILDHOOD

Even the wind wishes
to become a cart
pulled by butterflies.

I remember madness:
leaning for the first time
on the mind's pillow—
I was talking to my body.

My body was an idea
I wrote in red.

Red was the sun's most beautiful throne
and all the other colors
prayed on red rugs.

Night is another candle.

In every branch an arm,
a message carried in space,
echoed by the body of the wind.

The sun insists on dressing itself in fog
when it meets me:
am I being scolded by the light?

Oh, my past days—
they used to walk in their sleep
and I used to lean on them.

Love and dreams are two parentheses.
Between them I place my body
and discover the world.

Many times
I saw the air fly with two grass feet
and the road dance with feet made of air.

My wishes are flowers
staining my body.

I was wounded early,
and early I learned
that wounds made me.

I still follow the child
who still walks inside me.

Now he stands at a stairway made of light
searching for a corner to rest in,
and to read the face of night.

If the moon were a house,
my feet would refuse to touch its doorstep.
They are taken by dust
carrying me to the air of seasons.

I walk,
one hand in the air,
the other in dreams.

A star is also
a pebble in the fields of space.

He alone
who is joined to the horizon
can build new roads.

What shall I say to the body I abandoned
in the rubble of the house
in which I was born?
No one can narrate my childhood
except those stars that flicker above it
and leave footprints
on the evening's path.

My childhood is still
being born in the cupped palms of a light
whose name I do not know
and who names me.

Out of that river he made a mirror
and asked it about his sorrow.
He made rain out of his grief
and imitated the clouds.

Your childhood is a village.
You will never cross its boundaries
no matter how far you go.

His days are lakes,
his memories floating bodies.

You who are descending
from the mountains of the past,

how can you climb them again,
and why?

Time is a door
I cannot open.
My magic is worn,
my chants asleep.

I was born in a village,
small and secretive like a womb.
I never left it.
I love the ocean, not the shores.

(*Translated, from the Arabic, by Khaled Mattawa.*)

GÜNTER GRASS
AFTER MIDNIGHT

No, this is no grim reaper,
skipping along, taking farmer and townsman,
the upright girl, the plump priest,
beggar and emperor alike,
nor is it the dancing god,
hovering over the alpine waters of Sils Maria,
pointing beyond himself as he leaps,
filling speech balloons like Superman.
It's just the two of us, paired,
when, around midnight,
war threatens yet again,
after the late news
led by the kitchen radio:
in an old-fashioned foxtrot
we draw together
all that's about to pull us apart.

Just a few measures, love,
before you see to it—

as you always do around this time—
that we get our pills:
single ones and numbered.

(Translated, from the German, by Charles Simic.)

MAURICE MANNING

ANALOGUE

The collision of three deer and a flock of martins:
fur and feathers, two kinds of flight, two exceeding
champions of grace, flutter and flash. Both possess
necessary tails, black eyes: they love their young
to pieces, peck and lick, their own kind of kisses.
Special features: iridescence and musk, split lips
and beak, gizzard and rumination, distinguishing tracks.

Beautiful bug-eaters, traipsers through the grass
and sky! Keep bobbing your heads, nip and tuck,
across the river between you! Forget the dull limits
of classification. Consider the twin trunks of the poplar tree
pointing pell-mell, divining the Great Field. Fear neither
live birth nor hatching!
                              Oh, revelation only ever comes
at sudden crossings—the heart hopping like a happy frog.

CLEOPATRA MATHIS

CANE

When the mule balked, he hit him,
sometimes with the flat of a hand
upside the head; more often
the stick he carried did its angry trick.
The mule's job was to power the press,
iron on iron that wrung the sugar
out of cane, circling under the coarse
beam attached to his shoulders and neck.

That mule of my childhood
was black, remains blackly obedient
as round and round he made himself
the splintered hand of a clock, the groan
and squeak of machinery chewing
the reedy stalks to pulp, each second
delivering another sweet thin drop
into the black pot at the center.

He hit him with a rag, old head rag,
but the animal winced only with the thrash
of a cane stalk itself—he squinted
under the rule of that bamboo.
The sun was another caning
on his black-hot flesh. He was slow
as the blackstrap syrup the boiled sugar made,
so true to the circle he dragged
we hardly saw him. We loved the rustling
house of green cane, blind in that field
of tropical grasses whose white plumes
announced the long season's wait.
We yearned for the six-foot stem, the eventual
six pieces the machete sliced
at the joints, then the woody exterior
peeled back lengthwise with a blade.
It was a black hand we waited for, his job
to lay bare the grainy fibre we chewed.
That juice on our tongues
was his sweetness at work.
Chester was his name, he kept the mule.

ROBERT HASS

THE PROBLEM OF DESCRIBING COLOR

If I said—remembering, in summer,
The cardinal's sudden smudge of red
In the bare gray winter woods—

If I said, red ribbon on the cocked straw hat
Of the girl with pooched-out lips
Dangling the wiry, black-nosed lapdog
In the painting by Renoir—

If I said fire, if I said blood welling from a cut—

Or flecks of poppy in the tar-grass-scented summer air
On a wind-struck hillside outside Fano—

If I said, her one red earring dangles from her silky lobe,

If she tells fortunes with a deck of fallen leaves
Until it comes out right—

Rouged nipple, mouth—

(how could you not love a woman
who cheats at Tarot?)

Red, I said. Sudden, red.

THE PROBLEM OF DESCRIBING TREES

The aspen glitters in the wind.
And that delights us.

The leaf flutters, turning,
Because that motion in the heat of summer
Protects its cells from drying out. Likewise the leaf
Of the cottonwood.

The gene pool threw up a wobbly stem
And the tree danced. No.
The tree capitalized.
No. There are limits to saying,
In language, what the tree did.

It is good sometimes for poetry to disenchant us.

Dance with me, dancer. Oh, I will.

Aspens doing something in the wind.

TOM SLEIGH

NOBODY

Line after line smearing off into elephantine
scrawls as she tries to recall which way
the pencil goes, my friend's wife who can't organize
her mind to spell out her name sits staring

at the bookshelf bowed under the weight
of the thousand thousand rivulets of print
she can't remember writing. Her mind keeps scabbing
over—and then she picks it and picks it

until it bleeds . . . and she's herself again,
her heart rejoicing that she's Anne and not
someone other who afflicts her like a stranger

hiding in her bedroom, whispering with affable,
red-faced jocularity that if you're nobody
and nobody's tormenting you why do you cry out?

DAN CHIASSON

TITIAN VS. ROADRUNNER

If you are made for flight, intended for it,
you had better find a pursuer, fast.
Otherwise all that fleeing is going nowhere.

This bull, he's got a bad intent, he wants
to hog the entire corner of the picture.
The girl is looking tasty to the espying putti.

This small bird crisscrossing my childhood
at enormous speed, outrunning everything,
running out of road to run down, running

out of canyon, running out of cartoon
runs out of the cartoon, never to return.
That's why this landscape looks forlorn.

The world turned upside down and shaken
like a piggybank, the one last coin
rattling around inside, just coughed it up.

MATTHEW DICKMAN

TROUBLE

Marilyn Monroe took all her sleeping pills
to bed when she was thirty-six, and Marlon Brando's daughter
hung in the Tahitian bedroom
of her mother's house,
while Stanley Adams shot himself in the head. Sometimes
you can look at the clouds or the trees
and they look nothing like clouds or trees or the sky or the ground.
The performance artist Kathy Change
set herself on fire while Bing Crosby's sons shot themselves
out of the music industry forever.
I sometimes wonder about the inner lives of polar bears. The French
philosopher Gilles Deleuze jumped
from an apartment window into the world
and then out of it. Peg Entwistle, an actress with no lead
roles, leaped off the "H" in the HOLLYWOOD sign
when everything looked black and white
and David O. Selznick was king, circa 1932. Ernest Hemingway

put a shotgun to his head in Ketchum, Idaho
while his granddaughter, a model and actress, climbed the family tree
and overdosed on phenobarbital. My brother opened
thirteen fentanyl patches and stuck them on his body
until it wasn't his body anymore. I like
the way geese sound above the river. I like
the little soaps you find in hotel bathrooms because they're beautiful.
Sarah Kane hanged herself, Harold Pinter
brought her roses when she was still alive,
and Louis Lingg, the German anarchist, lit a cap of dynamite
in his own mouth
though it took six hours for him
to die, 1887. Ludwig II of Bavaria drowned
and so did Hart Crane, John Berryman, and Virginia Woolf. If you are
travelling, you should always bring a book to read, especially
on a train. Andrew Martinez, the nude activist, died
in prison, naked, a bag
around his head, while in 1815 the Polish aristocrat and writer
Jan Potocki shot himself with a silver bullet.
Sara Teasdale swallowed a bottle of blues
after drawing a hot bath,
in which dozens of Roman senators opened their veins beneath the
    water.
Larry Walters became famous
for flying in a Sears patio chair and forty-five helium-filled
weather balloons. He reached an altitude of 16,000 feet
and then he landed. He was a man who flew.
He shot himself in the heart. In the morning I get out of bed, I brush
my teeth, I wash my face, I get dressed in the clothes I like best.
I want to be good to myself.

CARL PHILLIPS

WHITE DOG

First snow—l release her into it—
I know, released, she won't come back.
This is different from letting what,

already, we count as lost go. It is nothing
like that. Also, it is not like wanting to learn what
losing a thing we love feels like. Oh yes:

I love her.
Released, she seems for a moment as if
some part of me that, almost,

I wouldn't mind
understanding better, is that
not love? She seems a part of me,

and then she seems entirely like what she is:
a white dog,
less white suddenly, against the snow,

who won't come back. I know that; and, knowing it,
I release her. It's as if I release her
because I know.

FORECAST

Betrayal, all along, will have been the least of it.
Some fall like empire—slowly, from the wild, more
unmappable borders inward, until reduced to history,
to the nothing from which, in the end,

                         history's made;
and others, they fall with the dizzying swiftness of
one of those seized-in-the-night

                       kingdoms—chambers
awash with the blood of princelings, their spattered
crowns toys now in the conqueror's

                       fine hands . . . As for
the common choice, the rote of exile that most call a life,
days on end spent muttering about loyalty, tattooing
the word *Who?* over one nipple, *Why?* just below the other,
foraging

shirtless among the animals or, worse, only
watching them pass—blind, but for instinct—beneath
the stooped cathedrals that the trees make in a storm
that—forever, it seems—looks permanent: No. Even
slaughter will have been better, I think,

than that.

CIVILIZATION

There's an art
  to everything. How
the rain means
  April and an ongoing-ness like
  that of song until at last

it ends. A centuries-old
  set of silver handbells that
once an altar boy swung,
  processing . . . *You're the same*
  wilderness you've always

been, slashing through briars,
  the bracken
of your invasive
  self. So he said,
  in a dream. But

the rest of it—all the rest—
  was waking: more often
than not, to the next
  extravagance. Two blackamoor
  statues, each mirroring

the other, each hoisting
  forever upward his burden of

hand-painted, carved-by-hand
    peacock feathers. *Don't*
you know it, don't you know

I love you, he said. He was
    shaking. He said,
I love you. There's an art
    to everything. What I've
    done with this life,

what I'd meant not to do,
    or would have meant, maybe, had I
understood, though I have
    no regrets. Not the broken but
    still flowering dogwood. Not

the honey locust, either. Not even
    the ghost walnut with its
non-branches whose
    every shadow is memory,
    memory . . . As he said to me

once, *That's all garbage*
    down the river, now. Turning,
but as the utterly lost—
    because addicted—do:
    resigned all over again. It

only looked, it—
    It must only look
like leaving. There's an art
    to everything. Even
    turning away. How

eventually even hunger
    can become a space
to live in. How they made
    out of shamelessness something
    beautiful, for as long as they could.

DANA GOODYEAR
COUNTY LINE ROAD

Who was Father—a bandage, a mustache,
from time to time a saddening salt-and-pepper beard.
Mother? Some sort of monger—I see her with a pink fish,
my bodyweight, dill hairs clinging to her hands.
"Daddy is tired," I am said to have said,
and then I'd sing to him, sleeping.
He was an athlete, dislocated. He said to my sister, Forget Me Not.
Mother was never in the same room with any of us.
I think she was a hostess, in which case I should say,
Thank you for having me.

CATHERINE BOWMAN
THE SINK

She loves to talk on the phone
while washing the dinner dishes,
catching up long distance or
dealing with issues closer to home,
the reconnoitring with the long lost
or a recent so-and-so. She finds it
therapeutic, washing down
the aftermath. And that feeling
she gets in her stomach with a loved one's
prolonged silence. And under the sink
in the dark among the L-pipes, the confederate
socket wrenches, lost twine, wire lei,
sink funk, steel-wool lemnisci, leitmotifs
of oily sacraments, a broken compass forever
pointing southeast by east, mold codices,
ring-tailed dust motes from days well served,
a fish-shaped flyswatter with blue horns,
fermented lemures, fiery spectres,
embottled spirit vapors swirling in the crude

next to the Soft Scrub, the vinegared
and leistered sealed in tins, delicious with saltines,
gleaned spikelets, used-up votives. . . .
In the back in the corner forgotten
an old coffee can of bacon fat
from a month of sinful Sundays,
a luna moth embossed, rising—a morning star.

LES MURRAY

ELEVEN POEMS

That wasn't horses: that was
rain yawning to life in the night
on metal roofs.

Lying back so smugly
phallic, the ampersand
in the deck chair of itself.

Spirituality?
she snorted. And poetry?
They're like yellow and gold.

Being rushed through streets
at dusk, by trees and rain, the
equinoctial gales!

The best love poems are known
as such to the lovers alone.

Creek pools, grown top heavy,
are speaking silver-age verse
through their gravel beards.

Demure as a navel;
and like a cat on wet grass—
but they'll be a pair.

Tired from understanding
life, the animals approach man
to be mystified.

A spider walking
in circles is celebrating
the birthday of logic.

To win me, they told
me all my bad attitudes
but they got them wrong.

Filling in a form
the simple man asks his mother
Mum, what sex are we?

HUGH SEIDMAN

RAPUNZEL: STARBUCKS

Acquaintance's
acquaintance.

Once: young, tousled
blonde at a window.

Divorced, I heard.

Ex's third:
half her age.

First: an actual princess.

Any contract's:
cash, clout, position.

Shrink, M.D.—
grown kids, clients.

No ring—
coffee, a sandwich.

Giggles, like a girl,
at the register.

"I can't add."

Bites cake; flips
a psych journal.

Sudden ravaged face—
with normalcy.

Almost notices me.

ELAINE EQUI
PRE-RAPHAELITE PINUPS

No one is saying how it came to be this way.
Sex is and is not part of the picture.
    •
Too many people
wearing too many clothes,
thinking too few things.
    •
The wallpaper is the real center of attention,
the figures mostly background music.
    •
There is a rhythm to their eating.
One contemplates his wine,
another drinks it.
    •
I never noticed it before,
but that angel's feet are on fire!

•

It's a penitent's head
they've pasted on a voluptuous body.

•

Why, she's practically an insect herself.

•

Look how many worlds are woven
with the silly-string of the Fates.

•

The wheat field was like a drive-in movie
for the shepherd and his date.

•

The berry-boy offers his handful of red
to the gray little girl.

•

It's all in the fold,
the fertility dance of being draped over . . .

•

One could panel a library
with the grain of her hair.

•

Can't you see I'm just a poor,
blind, accordion-playing lesbian?

•

Do not disturb the visionary butterfly
at work in me.

•

The heretic wears a pretty demonic
apron and crown,

•

while Medusa's blue hairnet
tangles even the trees.

•

A squirrel, a robin;
an army of innocence
waits to molest a young girl—
asleep and unaware.

•

But isn't every story an allegory—
every house strewn with alchemical symbols like these?

•

Ach—but that rainbow is loud!
Too much beauty makes a person faint.

MATTHEA HARVEY

THE STRAIGHTFORWARD MERMAID

The straightforward mermaid starts every sentence with "Look . . ."
This comes from being raised in a sea full of hooks. She wants to
get points 1, 2, and 3 across, doesn't want to disappear like a river
into the ocean. When she's feeling despairing, she goes to eddies
at the mouth of the river and tries to comb the water apart with
her fingers. The straightforward mermaid has already said to five
sailors, "Look, I don't think this is going to work," before sinking
like a sullen stone. She's supposed to teach Rock Impersonation
to the younger mermaids, but every beach field trip devolves
into them trying to find shells to match their tail scales. They
really love braiding. "Look," says the straightforward mermaid.
"Your high ponytails make you look like fountains, not rocks."
Sometimes she feels like a third gender—preferring primary
colors to pastels, the radio to singing. At least she's all mermaid:
never gets tired of swimming, hates the thought of socks.

JENNIFER MICHAEL HECHT

GENDER BENDER

Evolution settles for a while on various stable balances.
One is that some of the girls like cute boys and some
like ugly older men and sometimes women. The difference
between them is the ones who like older men were felt up

by their fathers or uncles or older brothers, or, if he didn't
touch you, still you lived in his cauldron of curses and
urges, which could be just as worse. They grow already old,
angry and wise, they get rich, get mean, get theirs.

The untouched-uncursed others are happy never needing
to do much, and never do much more than good. They envy
their mean, rich, talented, drunk sisters. Good girls drink milk
and make milk and know they've missed out and know they're

better off. They might dance and design but won't rip out lungs
for a flag. Bad ones write books and slash red paint on canvas;
they've rage to vent, they've fault lines and will rip a toga off
a Caesar and stab a goat for the ether. It's as simple as that.

Either, deep in the dark of your history, someone showed you
that you could be used as a cash machine, as a popcorn popper,
as a rocket launch, as a coin-slot jackpot spunker, or he didn't
and you grew up unused and clueless. Either you got a clue

and spiked lunch or you got zilch but no punch. And you
never knew. It's exactly not anyone's fault. If it happened
and you don't like older men that's just because you like
them so much you won't let yourself have one. If you did

people would see. Then they would know what happened
a long time ago, with you and that original him, whose eyes
you've been avoiding for decades gone forgotten. That's why
you date men smaller than you or not at all. Or maybe you've

turned into a man. It isn't anyone's fault, it is just human
and it is what happens. Or doesn't happen. That's that. Any
questions? If you see a girl dressed to say, "No one tells me
what to do," you know someone once told her what to do.

MEGHAN O'ROURKE

MY LIFE AS A TEEN-AGER

I felt "remorse for civilization."
My nostalgia was buoyant,
fat as cartoon clouds.
I sang teen-age French, sashaying down the street:
"*Bonjour, je t'aime, comment tu t'appelles?*"
The apartment buildings leaned down at me.
I proclaimed my love for the past,
wearing fitted clothes from the forties.
I came out against pointlessness.
I drank crème de menthe like a potion.
All night boys danced in the living room,
mouthing the words to the Go-Gos,
shrugging into the night's advances,
then took their stolen kisses from girls
fat like Troy, ready for the sieging.
In the morning, the sun was a cutout in the smog.
Every window was a picture window;
the dawn grew into day, red, orange, blue,
in perfect disorder. The partygoers were outside,
building a monument out of a blowtorch
and something old and green. From where
I stood, the tree, de-leafed and nude,
appeared to bow to me,
and what had long been silent grew.

BRUCE SMITH

THE GAME

The artist is a creep with his little boxes, but the athlete is a man
who has stolen glory in all its forms, stolen honey in a cup from the
    gods
and hidden it in his insides where the bees drone. I'm always a boy
as I sit or stand in the shouting place and breathe the doses of men—

smoke and malt—as the night comes down in the exact pattern
of a diamond, a moonlit hothouse of dirt a boy knows is something
to spit on and pat into a shape. Dirt's a cure for the buried someone.
Even as it begins with its anthem, it's lost to me, the exact color
of devotion. So goodbye to the inning and other numbers on
     scoreboards
and the backs of our team, our blue and red, our lips, our business,
which is to rip into them, a boy learns, or bark at the hit or miss.
Men have skill, although I see them fail and fail again and fail to hit
the curve. I'm always a girl as I aww and ooo. What's the infield-fly
     rule?
I tried to watch the grips and tricks, the metaphysics, the spin,
the positions of fast and still, scratch and spit . . . but I thought,
in all this infinity, of the Clementes, the Mayses, and the Yogis,
of the bats of ash I would have to crack and would I have to squeeze
them home? Would I be asked to sacrifice? Would I belly-button it
or break my wrists trying not to swing? There's a box and a zone
in the air and the dirt I must own. To find my way out
or know where it is I sit, I keep my ticket stub in my fist.

C. D. WRIGHT

OBSCURITY AND REGRET

The hand without the glove screws down the lid
on the jar of caterpillars, but the apple trees
are already infested. The sun mottles
the ground. The leaves are half-dead.
A shoe stomps the larvae streaming
onto the lawn as if putting out a cigarette on a rug.
It was a stupid idea. It was a stupid thing to say
the thought belonging to the body says to its source
stomping on the bright-green grass as it spills its sweet guts.

LIKE A PRISONER OF SOFT WORDS

We walk under the wires and the birds resettle.
We know where we're going but have not made up our mind
which way we will take to get there.
If we pass by the palmist's she can read our wayward lines.
We may drop things along the way that substantiate our having been
    here.
We will not be able to transmit any of these feelings verbatim.
By the time we reach the restaurant one of us is angry.
Here a door gives in to a courtyard
overlooking a ruined pool.
We suspect someone has followed one or the other of us.
We touch the spot on our shirt where the ink has seeped.
The lonely outline of the host is discerned near an unlit sconce.
As guests we are authorized not to notice.
We drop some cash on the tablecloth.
We lack verisimilitude but we press on with intense resolve.
At the border, under a rim of rock, the footbridge.
Salt cedars have grown over the path.
The water table is down.
And we cannot see who is coming, the pollos and their pollero,
the migra, the mules, the Minutemen, the women
who wash for the other women *al otro lado*.
Or the murdered boy herding his goats after school. 6:27,
the fell of dark, not day.

PATRICIA LOCKWOOD

LOVE POEM LIKE WE USED TO WRITE IT

Says here is a girl who gets written like palms,
says here is a girl who moves paint like Tahiti.
Teeth infinite white and infinite many and with
them she infinite eat me, and mouth full of invert
and cane and coarse sugar, and her dresses all

came from across
the water, and they rode a light chop
on the sea in fast ships, and she owns twenty
pairs of the shape of her hands, and slashed silk
on her shoulder like claws of a parrot, and here
the love poem delights:
the word "parrot" will never
be replaced, and will continue meaning always
exactly what it means, as none of the words
in this sentence have done—come read me again
in a hundred years and see how I keep my shape!
Love poem back to your subject, the word "parrot"
is not the right woman for you, hard to hold
and too much red; love poem, think long arms
and flies nowhere.
I remember her now, it says, and says she is far
from me, says hear how her voice is a Western
slope, when west meant the sun it rose and set
there, and monstrous the shadows of flowers all
down it, in the days before voice meant something
you wrote with. Love poem as we used to write it
says her small brown paw is adorable, which is
to say brown as we used to use it, which is to say
just sunburned,
just monstrous the shadows of flowers all on it,
which is to say paw as we used to use it, which is
to say a human hand, and human as we used
to use it, which is to say almost no one among us.
Blond of course and blond. Blond as a coil of rope,
and someone hauled on her somewhere, and loop
after loop flew out of her helpless. The someone
was out at sea, and language on my shoulder like
claws of a parrot. I sailed the world over
to deliver one letter, one letter of even one letter,
one word, and one word as we used to use it:
in those days she was the only Lady, in those days
she wrote a small round hand,
and I hauled on it saw it fly loop by loop out of her.

CAROLYN FORCHÉ

THE LOST SUITCASE

So it was with the suitcase left in front
of the hotel—cinched, broken-locked,
papered with world ports, carrying what
mattered until then—when as you turned your back
to cup a match it was taken, and the thief,
expecting valuables, instead found books written
between wars, gold attic light, mechanical birds singing,
and the chronicle of your country's final hours.
What, by means of notes, you hoped to become:
a noun on paper, paper *dark with nouns*:
swallows darting through a basilica, your hands up
in smoke, a cloud about to open over the city, pillows
breathing shallowly where you had lain, a ghost
in a hospital gown, and *here* your voice,
principled, tender, soughing through
a fence woven with pine boughs:
Writing is older than glass but younger
than music, older than clocks or porcelain but younger than rope.
Dear one, who even in speaking are silent,
for years I have searched, usually while asleep,
when I have found the suitcase open, collecting snow,
still holding your vade mecum of the infinite,
your dictionary of the no-longer-spoken,
a commonplace of wounds casually inflicted,
and the slender ledger of truly heroic acts.
Gone is your atlas of countries unmarked by war,
absent your manual for the preservation of hours.
The incunabulum is lost—both your earliest book
and a hatching place for your mechanical birds—
but the collection of aperçus having to do
with *light laying its eggs in your eyes* was found,
along with the prophecy that *all mass murders were early omens.*
In an antique bookshop I found your catechism of atrophied faiths,
so I lay you to rest without your Psalter,
or the monograph wherein you state your most

unequivocal and hard-won proposition:
that everything must happen but to whom doesn't matter.
Here are your books, as if they were burning.
Be near now, and wake to tell me who you were.

ELIZABETH ALEXANDER

SMILE

When I see a black man smiling
like that, nodding and smiling
with both hands visible, mouthing

"Yes, officer," across the street,
I think of my father, who taught us
the words "coöperate," "officer,"

to memorize badge numbers,
who has seen black men shot at
from behind in the warm months north.

And I think of the fine line—
hairline, eyelash, fingernail paring—
the whisper that separates

obsequious from *safe*. Armstrong,
Johnson, Robinson, Mays.
A woman with a yellow head

of cotton-candy hair stumbles out
of a bar at after-lunchtime
clutching a black man's arm as if

for her life. And the brother
smiles, and his eyes are flint
as he watches all sides of the street.

WHEN

In the early nineteen-eighties, the black men
were divine, spoke French, had read everything,
made filet mignon with green-peppercorn sauce,
listened artfully to boyfriend troubles,
operatically declaimed boyfriend troubles,
had been to Bamako and Bahia,
knew how to clear bad humors from a house,
had been to Baldwin's villa in St. Paul,
drank espresso with Soyinka and Senghor,
kissed hello on both cheeks, quoted Baraka's
"Black Art": "Fuck poems/and they are useful,"
tore up the disco dance floor, were gold-lit,
photographed well, did not smoke, said "Ciao,"

then all the men's faces were spotted.

MEDBH McGUCKIAN

FILMING THE FAMINE

I
My meal of pleasure crisped like a wave
in the perfect circle of his lips,
not helped by the winds and the air:

the primal garment of his skin,
and the brush-braid on the hem of his voice,
was an answer as soft as the question.

It was an evening made of cold clouds
and the necessary flight of natural sleep,
which takes the malice of memory into the half-world.

Springs that had carried the steely dusk
only hours old into my heart
lost their coral heartbeat and were still.

The island glittered like some silver and crimson
winter fruit. The river's small leaden blue
pulse was only sad as one is in a dream.

Its whistled lament took blood from cattle
and brought down birds—its scarlet cross-stitch
roped me into grudging prayer. . . .

2
The image of peace was superimposed
on a sea of composed fragments,
fairground notes like a fragile line of surf
came from the stamens of her pearly fingers,

out of the shelter of her veil,
into the shadow of her arms.
She was all stranger, like some war
that had escaped out of a book,
all but Irish, fought according
to the code of the angels.

Mass paths and other useless roads,
devastated by street battles,
and soldiers impersonating soldiers
overlapped in a film presentation
of an island that had lived through
two famines, and still comes into my dreams.

Brickmakers and coal-heavers
and people without end
slid together in a cell of false time,
a summer of sorrow,
flat lines of darker black

in the sunken inkpots
of the brig Eliza Ann,
The Intrepid, the ship Carrick,
Hebron, Erin's Queen, Syrius,
Virginius, The Sisters,
Elizabeth and Sarah.

The springing forms of her hands
were a merciless screen against sight:
but if the notes were high and opened heaven—
they might suddenly hear something.

VIJAY SESHADRI

MEMOIR

Orwell says somewhere that no one ever writes the real story of
    their life.
The real story of a life is the story of its humiliations.
If I wrote that story now—
radioactive to the end of time—
people, I swear, your eyes would fall out, you couldn't peel
the gloves fast enough
from your hands scorched by the firestorms of that shame.
Your poor hands. Your poor eyes
to see me weeping in my room
or boring the tall blonde to death.
Once I accused the innocent.
Once I bowed and prayed to the guilty.
I still wince at what I once said to the devastated widow.
And one October afternoon, under a locust tree
whose blackened pods were falling and making
illuminating patterns on the pathway,
I was seized by joy,
and someone saw me there,
and that was the worst of all,
lacerating and unforgettable.

LINDA GREGERSON

STILL LIFE

I

His ears his mouth his
      nostrils having filled

with ash, his cheekbones
chin (all ash) and on the ash a tide

of seawrack that cannot
      be right a trail of scum or

vomit then and either
his shoulder's been crushed by the

blast or angled on the stretcher so
      oddly that raising

his arm to ward us off
he seems to be more damaged than he

is, and eyes
      that should have cracked the

camera. This was not
the current nightmare this was two

or three nightmares ago, the men
      were loading plums and

peaches onto trucks at
Qaa. And though in my lucky and

ignorant life I have never so much as
      encountered the scent

of explosives (I
had taken a different bus that day,

the city I live in is thicker with
        doctors than all of Bekaa

is thick with bombs), I've
seen those eyes before exactly.

Failures of decency closer to home.

2
(The clearing of the ghetto)

Red wool, and falsely brightened, since
        we need the help.

A child because
the chambers of the heart will hold so

little. If the filmmaker, having
        apprenticed in fables,

proposes a scale for which,
he hopes, we're apt and if

this bigger-than-a-breadbox slightly-
        smaller-than-the-microwave is

just about the vista we can
manage, let's agree to call it history, let's

imagine we had somehow seen its face
        in time. But where

in all of Kraków is
the mother who buttoned her coat?

A city steeped in harm-to-come,
        the film stock drained

to gray. The sturdy
threading-forward of a child who

might be panicked by the crowd but
        has her mind now on

a hiding place. Our
childlike conviction that she shall be

spared. Mistake that brings
        the lesson home: we lack

retention.
Chalk mark on a clouded screen.

3
But what was it like, his dying?
        It was like

a distillation.
You had morphine? We had

morphine, but he couldn't use
        the bed. *The bed?*

His lungs were so
thickened with tumors and phlegm

he had no way of breathing there.
        You'd rented the bed?

He climbed down beside it
and asked for his tools. When something

was broken he fixed it, that had
        always been the way with him.

So then . . . We left him in his
chair. But as the day went on we thought

he needed bedding so we tried to
      lift him. That's the once

he blamed us. *That's*
the look you meant. The why-

can't-you-people-just-leave-me-alone,
      the where-is-your-sense-

of-shame. I will
remember it until I die myself.

You meant well. Meaning well
      was not enough.

We meant that he
should know this wasn't lost on us.

The urn that holds his ashes does
      a better job.

4
Sister partridge, brother hare.
      The linen on the table

with its hemstitch. I
have read the books on pridefulness:

the bounty of game park and sideboard
      and loom, the ships

that brought the lemon trees,
the leisure that masters the view. But

I have come to think
        the argument-by-likeness makes

a simpler point. The lemon,
for example, where the knife has been:

the pores, the pith, the luminescent
        heart of it, each differential

boundary bound to open.
Meaning death, of course, the un-

protected flesh about to turn, but just
        before the turn, while looking

can still be an act of praise.
I see you in the mirror every morning

where you wait for me. The linen,
        Father, lemon, knife,

the pewter with its lovely
reluctance to shine. As though

the given world had given us
        a second chance.

W. S. DI PIERO

THE KISS

The mossy transom light, odors of cabbage
and ancient papers, while Father Feeney
polishes an apple on his tunic.
I tell him I want the life priests have,

not how the night sky's millions
of departing stars, erased by city lights,
terrify me toward God. That some nights
I sleepwalk, curl inside the bathtub,
and bang awake from a dream of walking through
a night where candle beams crisscross
the sky, a movie premiere somewhere.
Where am I, Father, when I visit a life
inside or outside the one I'm in?
In our wronged world I see things
accidentally good: fishy shadows thrown
by walnut leaves, summer hammerheads
whomping fireplugs, fall air that tastes
like spring water, oranges, and iron.

"What are you running from, my dear,
at morning Mass five times a week?"
He comes around the desk, its failing flowers
and Iwo Jima inkwell, holding his breviary,
its bee's hum mysteries in a Latin
whose patterned noise, like blades
on ice, became a cranky poetry

I was lost to. Beautiful dreamer,
how I love you. When he leans down,
his hands rough with chalk dust
rasp my ears. "You don't have the call,"
kissing my cheek. "Find something else."

On the subway home I found
a Golgotha air of piss and smoke,
sleepy workers, Cuban missiles drooping
in their evening papers, and black people
hosed down by cops or stretched by dogs.
What was I running from? Deity flashed
on the razor a boy beside me wagged
and stroked the hair of the nurse who waked

to kiss her rosary. I believed the wall's
filthy cracks, coming into focus
when we stopped, held stories I'd find
and tell. What are you running from,
child of what I've become?
Tell what you know now
of dreadful freshness and want,
our stunned world peopled
by shadows solidly flesh,
a silted fountain of prayer
rising in our throat.

BRENDA SHAUGHNESSY

ARTLESS

is my heart. A stranger
berry there never was,
tartless.

Gone sour in the sun,
in the sunroom or moonroof,
roofless.

No poetry. Plain. No
fresh, special recipe
to bless.

All I've ever made
with these hands
and life, less

substance, more rind.
Mostly rim and trim,
meatless

but making much smoke
in the old smokehouse,
no less.

Fatted from the day,
overripe and even
toxic at eve. Nonetheless,

in the end, if you must
know, if I must bend,
waistless,

to that excruciation.
No marvel, no harvest
left me speechless,

yet I find myself
somehow with heart,
aloneless.

With heart,
fighting fire with fire,
flightless.

That loud hub of us,
meat stub of us, beating us
senseless.

Spectacular in its way,
its way of not seeing,
congealing dayless

but in everydayness.
In that hopeful haunting,
(a lesser

way of saying
in darkness) there is
silencelessness

for the pressing question.
Heart, what art you?
War, star, part? Or less:

playing a part, staying apart
from the one who loves,
loveless.

DAHLIA RAVIKOVITCH

LYING UPON THE WATERS

Stinking Mediterranean city
stretched out over the waters
head between her knees,
her body befouled by smoke and dunghills.
Who will raise from the dunghills
a rotten Mediterranean city,
her feet scabby and galled?
Her sons requite each other
with knives.

Now the city is flooded with crates of plums and grapes,
cherries laid out in the marketplace
in the sight of every passerby,
the setting sun peachy pink.
Who could really hate
a doped-up Mediterranean city
lowing like a cow in heat,
her walls Italian marble and crumbling sand,
decked out in rags and broidered work.
But she doesn't mean it at all,
doesn't mean anything at all.
And the sea is full, brimming at her blind forehead,
and the sun pours his horn of mercy upon her
when at dusk his wrath subsides.
And the squashes and cucumbers and lemons bursting

with color and juice
waft over her the sweet savor of summer perfumes.
And she is not worthy.
Not worthy of love or pity.

Filthy Mediterranean city,
how my soul is bound up with her soul.
Because of a lifetime,
an entire lifetime.

(Translated, from the Hebrew, by Chana Bloch and Chana Kronfeld.)

MARTÍN ESPADA
CITY OF GLASS

For Pablo Neruda and Matilde Urrutia
La Chascona, Santiago, Chile

The poet's house was a city of glass:
cranberry glass, milk glass, carnival glass,
red and green goblets row after row,
black lustre of wine in bottles,
ships in bottles, zoo of bottles,
rooster, horse, monkey, fish,
heartbeat of clocks tapping against crystal,
windows illuminated by the white Andes,
observatory of glass over Santiago.

When the poet died,
they brought his coffin to the city of glass.
There was no door: the door was a thousand daggers,
beyond the door an ancient world in ruins,
glass now arrowheads, axes, pottery shards, dust.
There were no windows: fingers of air
reached for glass like a missing lover's face.
There was no zoo: the bottles were half-moons

and quarter-moons, horse and monkey
eviscerated with every clock, with every lamp.
Bootprints spun in a lunatic tango across the floor.

The poet's widow said, *We will not sweep the glass.*
His wake is here. Reporters, photographers,
intellectuals, ambassadors stepped across the glass
cracking like a frozen lake, and soldiers, too,
who sacked the city of glass,
returned to speak for their general,
three days of official mourning
announced at the end of the third day.

In Chile, a river of glass bubbled, cooled,
hardened, and rose in sheets, only to crash and rise again.
One day, years later, the soldiers wheeled around
to find themselves in a city of glass.
Their rifles turned to carnival glass;
bullets dissolved, glittering, in their hands.
From the poet's zoo they heard monkeys cry;
from the poet's observatory they heard
poem after poem like a call to prayer.
The general's tongue burned with slivers
invisible to the eye. The general's tongue
was the color of cranberry glass.

MAHMOUD DARWISH

HERE THE BIRDS' JOURNEY ENDS

Here the birds' journey ends, our journey, the journey of words,
and after us there will be a horizon for the new birds.
We are the ones who forge the sky's copper, the sky that will carve
    roads
after us and make amends with our names above the distant cloud
    slopes.

Soon we will descend the widow's descent in the memory fields
and raise our tent to the final winds: blow, for the poem to live, and
    blow
on the poem's road. After us, the plants will grow and grow
over roads only we have walked and our obstinate steps inaugurated.
And we will etch on the final rocks, "Long live life, long live life,"
and fall into ourselves. And after us there'll be a horizon for the new
    birds.

(Translated, from the Arabic, by Fady Joudah.)

ZBIGNIEW HERBERT

A PORTRAIT AT THE END OF THE CENTURY

Ravaged by narcotics strangled in a scarf of exhaust
and burnt to a blazing star the glowing Super Nova
of three evenings—chaos desire torment—
climbs onto a springboard starts from the beginning

you dwarf of our times starlet of burnt-out evenings
artist with a goat's foot who mimics the demiurge
flea-market apocalypse o prince of lunatics
hide your hateful face

while there is still time summon the Lamb waters of purification
let the true star rise Mozart's *Lacrymosa*
call for the true star the land of a hundred leaves
let the Epiphany come true the New Page is open

(Translated, from the Polish, by John and Bogdana Carpenter.)

FADY JOUDAH

THE ONION POEM

Why are there onions the size of swallows in your maple tree?
In the land of cactus wind the one-eyed dwell.
Where is the village whose name holds back the sea?
Caterpillars are for home demolitions in a globe of tents.
Autumn or spring, which is your plumage of choice?
Every empire is a return of the dead.
And Whitman, what would have become of him had you lost the war?
A rooster in rigor-mortis pose makes vultures descend.
Is that the easiest pain?
The Hittites veiled their nuclear weapon for as long as they could.
But lilies have rights, iris amendments?
And the bats for rabies are for the urban sunset.
Are you a tiger or a martyr to deforestation?
The genetic map is over the counter.
And the Black Sea is black.
And the Red Sea red.
And the leaves like waves on the pebble shore?
I rake them. My father's garden can use some ash.

C. K. WILLIAMS

PRISONERS

In the preface to a translation of a German writer,
a poet I'd never heard of, I fall on the phrase
"He was a prisoner of war in a camp in the U.S.,"

and a memory comes to me of a morning
during the second war when my parents,
on a visit to the city they'd grown up in,

took me to what had been their favorite park
and was now a barbed-wire-encircled compound,
with unpainted clapboard barracks,

where men, in sandals and shorts,
all light-haired, as I recall, and sunburned,
idled alone or in small groups.

I'm told they're German prisoners, though I know
nothing of the war, or Hitler, or the Jews—
why should I?—I only remember them

gazing back at us with a disconcerting
incuriousness, a lack of evident emotion
I'd associate now with primates in zoos,

and that my mother and father seemed unnerved,
at a loss for what to say, which I found
more disturbing than the prisoners, or the camp,

a reaction my mother must have sensed
because she took my hand and led me away—
the park had a carrousel, she took me there.

Are there still merry-go-rounds,
with their unforgettable oompah
calliope music and the brass rings?

If you caught one, you rode again free.
I never did, I was afraid to fall;
I'm not anymore, but it wouldn't matter.

I go back instead to those prisoners,
to the one especially not looking at us,
because he was shaving. Crouched on a step,

face lathered, a galvanized pail at his feet,
he held—I see it, can it be there?—
a long straight razor, glinting, slicing down.

JONI MITCHELL

BAD DREAMS ARE GOOD

The cats are in the flower beds
A red hawk rides the sky
I guess I should be happy
Just to be alive
But
We have poisoned everything
And oblivious to it all
The cell-phone zombies babble
Through the shopping malls
While condors fall from Indian skies
Whales beach and die in sand
Bad Dreams are good
In the Great Plan
And you cannot be trusted
Do you even know you are lying?
It's dangerous to kid yourself
You go deaf, dumb, and blind
You take with such entitlement
You give bad attitude
You have No grace
No empathy
No gratitude
You have no sense of consequence
Oh, my head is in my hands
Bad Dreams are good
In the Great Plan
Before that altering apple
We were one with everything
No sense of self and other
No self-consciousness
But now we have to grapple
With this man-made world backfiring
Keeping one eye on our brother's deadly selfishness
Everyone's a victim here
Nobody's hands are clean

There's so very little left of wild Eden Earth
So near the jaws of our machines
We live in these electric scabs
These lesions once were lakes
We don't know how to shoulder blame
Or learn from past mistakes
So who will come to save the day?
Mighty Mouse . . . ? Superman . . . ?
Bad Dreams are good
In the Great Plan
In the dark
A shining ray
I heard a three-year-old boy say
Bad Dreams are good
In the Great Plan

CARL DENNIS

NEW YEAR'S EVE

However busy you are, you should still reserve
One evening a year for thinking about your double,
The man who took the curve on Conway Road
Too fast, given the icy patches that night,
But no faster than you did; the man whose car
When it slid through the shoulder
Happened to strike a girl walking alone
From a neighbor's party to her parents' farm,
While your car struck nothing more notable
Than a snowbank.

One evening for recalling how soon you transformed
Your accident into a comic tale
Told first at a body shop, for comparing
That hour of pleasure with his hour of pain
At the house of the stricken parents, and his many
Long afternoons at the Lutheran graveyard.

If nobody blames you for assuming your luck
Has something to do with your character,
Don't blame him for assuming that his misfortune
Is somehow deserved, that justice would be undone
If his extra grief was balanced later
By a portion of extra joy.

Lucky you, whose personal faith has widened
To include an angel assigned to protect you
From the usual outcome of heedless moments.
But this evening consider the angel he lives with,
The stern enforcer who drives the sinners
Out of the Garden with a flaming sword
And locks the gate.

MARY RUEFLE

OPEN LETTER TO MY ANCESTORS

Sometimes I walk around the house
wearing a green clay mask
it's supposed to be for my skin
but I don't care about that
I wear it in honor of you
I am so sadly far away from you
I secretly hope someone rings the doorbell
so they cannot recognize me
Surprise! I am seasick
on my long voyage
I've left everything behind
except this valise
which I protect with my body
and God's love because I believe
in the day I will board a bus
with a bag of potatoes in my right hand
worth more than the valise
and everything in it

Thank you for that
These smoked chops are incredible
You have to look at it as one person
with a very long life
it's better that way
blood, tears, violence, hate, ashes, everything
the mad blue terror of dying
of having to learn another language
Perdurabo
it all works out in time
there is no end
I had no kids
there's a niece in Cincinnati
she's marrying a Greek next week
just so you know
I'm going to wash you off now
into the luminous depths
where even a recluse bird must fly

DALJIT NAGRA

A BLACK HISTORY OF THE ENGLISH-SPEAKING PEOPLES

I

A king's invocations at the Globe Theatre
spin me from my stand to a time when boyish
    bravado and cannonade
and plunder were enough to woo the regal seat.

That the stuff of Elizabethan art and a nation
of walled gardens in a local one-upmanship
    would tame the four-cornered
world for Empire's dominion seems inconceivable.

Between the birth and the fire and rebirth of the Globe
the visions of Albion led to a Rule Britannia

of trade-winds-and-Gulf-Stream
all-conquering fleets that aroused theatres

for lectures on Hottentots and craniology,
whilst Eden was paraded in Kew.
    Between Mayflower and Windrush
(with each necessary murder) the celebrated

embeddings of imperial gusto where jungles
were surmounted so the light of learning be spread
    to help sobbing suttees
give up the ghost of a husband's flaming pyre.

II
So much for yesterday, but today's time-honoured
televised clashes repeat the flag of a book burning
    and May Day's Mohican
Churchill and all that shock and awe

that brings me back to Mr. Wanamaker's Globe.
An American's thatched throwback to the king
    of the canon! I watch the actor
as king, from the cast of masterful Robeson.

The crowd, too, seems a hotchpotch from the pacts
and sects of our ebb and flow. My forebears played
    their part for the Empire's quid
pro quo by assisting the rule and divide of their ilk.

Did such relations bear me to this stage?
Especially with Macaulay in mind, who claimed the passing
    of the imperial sceptre would highlight
the imperishable empire of our arts . . .

So does the red of Macaulay's map run through
my blood? Am I a noble scruff who hopes a proud
    academy might canonize
his poems for their faith in canonical allusions?

Is my voice phony over these oft-heard beats?
Well if my voice feels vexatious, what can I but pray
    that it reign Bolshie
through puppetry and hypocrisy full of gung-ho fury!

III
The heyday Globe incited brave new verse
modelled on the past, where time's frictions
    courted Shakespeare's corruptions
for tongue's mastery of the pageant subject. Perhaps

the Globe should be my muse! I'm happy digging
for my England's good garden to bear again.
    My garden's only a state
of mind, where it's easy aligning myself with a "turncoat"

T. E. Lawrence and a half-naked fakir and always
the groundling. Perhaps to aid the succession
    of this language of the world,
for the poet weeding the roots, for the debate

in ourselves, now we're bound to the wheels
of global power, we should tend the manorial
    slime—that legacy
offending the outcasts who fringe our circles.

IV
Who believes a bleached yarn? Would we openly
admit the Livingstone spirit turned Kurtz, our flag
    is a union of black and blue
flapping in the anthems of haunted rain . . . ?

Coming clean would surely give us greater distance
than this king at the Globe, whose head seems cluttered
    with golden-age bumph,
whose suffering ends him agog at the stars.

V

I applaud and stroll toward Westminster,
yet softly tonight the waters of Britannia bobble
    with flotillas of tea and white gold
cotton and sugar and the sweetness-and-light

bloodlettings and ultimately red-faced Suez.
And how swiftly the tide removes from the scene
    the bagpipe clamouring
garrisons with the field-wide scarlet soldiery

and the martyr's cry: Every man die at his post!
Till what's ahead are the upbeat lovers who gaze
    from the London Eye
at multinationals lying along the sanitized Thames.

AMIT MAJMUDAR

THE AUTOBIOGRAPHY OF KHWAJA MUSTASIM

I stood for twenty years a chess piece in Córdoba, the black rook.
I was a parrot fed melon seeds by the eleventh caliph.
I sparked to life in a Damascus forge, no bigger than my own pupil.
I was the mosquito whose malarial kiss conquered Alexander.
I bound books in Bukhara, burned them in Balkh.
In my four hundred and sixteenth year I came to Qom.
I tasted Paradise early as an ant in the sugar bin of Mehmet Pasha's
    chief chef.
I was a Hindu slave stonemason who built the Blue Mosque without
    believing.
I rode as a louse under Burton's turban when he sneaked into Mecca.
I butchered halal in Jalalabad.
I had been a vulture just ten years when I looked down and saw
    Karbala set for me like a table.
I walked that lush Hafiz home and held his head while he puked.

I was one of those four palm trees smart-bomb-shaken behind the
      reporter's khaki vest.
I threw out the English-language newspaper that went on to hide
      the roadside bomb.
The nails in which were taken from my brother's coffin.
My sister's widowing sighed sand in a thousand Kalashnikovs.
I buzzed by a tube light, and three intelligence officers, magazines
      rolled, hunted me in vain.
Here I am at last, born in a city whose name, on General
      Elphinstone's 1842 map, was misspelt "Heart."
A mullah for a mauled age, a Muslim whose memory goes back
      farther than the Balfour Declaration.
You may remember me as the grandfather who guided the gaze of a
      six-year-old Omar Khayyám to the constellations.
Also maybe as the inmate of a Cairo jail who took the top bunk and
      shouted down at Sayyid Qutb to please please please shut up.

TO THE HYPHENATED POETS

Richer than mother's milk
is half-and-half.
Friends of two minds,
redouble your craft.

Our shelves our hives, our selves
a royal jelly,
may we at Benares and Boston,
Philly and Delhi

collect our birthright nectar.
No swarm our own,
we must be industrious, both
queen and drone.

Being two beings requires
a rage for rigor,
rewritable memory,
hybrid vigor.

English herself is a crossbred
mother mutt,
primly promiscuous
and hot to rut.

Oneness? Pure chimera.
Splendor is spliced.
Make your halves into something
twice your size,

your tongue a hyphen joining
nation to nation.
Recombine, become a thing
of your own creation,

a many-minded mongrel,
the line's renewal,
self-made and twofold,
soul and dual.

PAUL MULDOON

TURKEY BUZZARDS

They've been so long above it all,
        those two petals
so steeped in style they seem to stall
        in the kettle

simmering over the town dump
        or, better still,
the neon-flashed, X-rated rump
        of fresh roadkill

courtesy of the interstate
        that Eisenhower
would overtake in the home straight
        by one horsepower,

the kettle where it all boils down
        to the thick scent
of death, a scent of such renown
        it's given vent

to the idea buzzards can spot
        a deer carcass
a mile away, smelling the rot
        as, once, Marcus

Aurelius wrinkled his nose
        at a gas leak
from the Great Sewer that ran
            through Rome
        to the Tiber

then went searching out, through
            the gloam,
        one subscriber
to the other view that the rose,
        full-blown, antique,

its no-frills ruff, the six-foot shrug
        of its swing-wings,
the theologian's and the thug's
        twin triumphings

in a buzzard's shaved head
            and snood,
        buzz-buzz-buzzy,
its logic in all likelihood
        somewhat fuzzy,

would ever come into focus,
        it ever deign
to dispense its hocus-pocus
        in that same vein

as runs along an inner thigh
  to where, too right,
the buzzard vouchsafes not to shy
  away from shite,

its mission not to give a miss
  to a bête noire,
all roly-poly, full of piss
  and vinegar,

trying rather to get to grips
  with the grommet
of the gut, setting its tin snips
  to that grommet

in the spray-painted hind's hindgut
  and making a
sweeping, too right, a sweeping cut
  that's so blasé

it's hard to imagine, dear sis,
  why others shrink
from this sight of a soul in bliss,
  so in the pink

from another month in the red
  of the shambles,
like a rose in over its head
  among brambles,

unflappable in its belief
  it's Ararat
on which the Ark would come to grief,
  abjuring that

Marcus Aurelius humbug
  about what springs

from earth succumbing to the tug
      at its heartstrings,

reported to live past fifty,
      as you yet may,
dear sis, perhaps growing your hair
      in requital,

though briefly, of whatever tears
      at your vitals,
learning, perhaps, from the nifty,
      nay *thrifty*, way

these buzzards are given to stoop
      and take their ease
by letting their time-chastened poop
      fall to their knees

till they're almost as bright with lime
      as their night roost,
their poop containing an enzyme
      that's known to boost

their immune systems, should they
        prong
      themselves on small
bones in a cerebral cortex,
      at no small cost

to their well-being, sinking fast
      in a deer crypt,
buzzards getting the hang at last
      of being stripped

of their command of the vortex
      while having lost
their common touch, they've been
        so long
      above it all.

KEVIN YOUNG

BEREAVEMENT

Behind his house, my father's dogs
sleep in kennels, beautiful,
he built just for them.

They do not bark.
Do they know he is dead?
They wag their tails

& head. They beg
& are fed.
Their grief is colossal

& forgetful.
Each day they wake
seeking his voice,

their names.
By dusk they seem
to unremember everything—

to them even hunger
is a game. For that, I envy.
For that, I cannot bear to watch them

pacing their cage. I try to remember
they love best confined space
to feel safe. Each day

a saint comes by to feed the pair
& I draw closer
the shades.

I've begun to think of them
as my father's other sons,
as kin. Brothers-in-paw.

My eyes each day thaw.
One day the water cuts off.
Then back on.

They are outside dogs—
which is to say, healthy
& victorious, purposeful

& one giant muscle
like the heart. Dad taught
them not to bark, to point

out their prey. To stay.
Were they there that day?
They call me

like witnesses & will not say.
I ask for their care
& their carelessness—

wish of them forgiveness.
I must give them away.
I must find for them homes,

sleep restless in his.
All night I expect they pace
as I do, each dog like an eye

roaming with the dead
beneath an unlocked lid.

DEBORAH DIGGES

THE WIND BLOWS THROUGH THE DOORS
OF MY HEART

The wind blows
through the doors of my heart.
It scatters my sheet music
that climbs like waves from the piano, free of the keys.
Now the notes stripped, black butterflies,
flattened against the screens.
The wind through my heart
blows all my candles out.
In my heart and its rooms is dark and windy.
From the mantle smashes birds' nests, teacups
full of stars as the wind winds round,
a mist of sorts that rises and bends and blows
or is blown through the rooms of my heart
that shatters the windows,
rakes the bedsheets as though someone
had just made love. And my dresses
they are lifted like brides come to rest
on the bedstead, crucifixes,
dresses tangled in trees in the rooms
of my heart. To save them
I've thrown flowers to fields,
so that someone would pick them up
and know where they came from.
Come the bees now clinging to flowered curtains.
Off with the clothesline pinning anything, my mother's trousseau.
It is not for me to say what is this wind
or how it came to blow through the rooms of my heart.
Wing after wing, through the rooms of the dead
the wind does not blow. Nor the basement, no wheezing,
no wind choking the cobwebs in our hair.
It is cool here, quiet, a quilt spread on soil.
But we will never lie down again.

AIMÉ CÉSAIRE

EARTHQUAKE

such great stretches of dreamscape
such lines of all too familiar lines
                                   staved in
caved in so the filthy wake resounds with the notion
of the pair of us? What of the pair of us?
Pretty much the tale of the family surviving disaster:
"In the ancient serpent stink of our blood we got clear
of the valley; the village loosed stone lions roaring at our heels."
Sleep, troubled sleep, the troubled waking of the heart
yours on top of mine chipped dishes stacked in the pitching sink
of noontides.
What then of words? Grinding them together to summon up the void
as night insects grind their crazed wing cases?
Caught caught caught unequivocally caught
caught caught caught
                head over heels into the abyss
                for no good reason
except for the sudden faint steadfastness
of our own true names, our own amazing names
that had hitherto been consigned to a realm of forgetfulness
itself quite tumbledown.

   (Translated, from the French, by Paul Muldoon.)

MARY JO SALTER

PEONIES

Heart transplants my friend handed me:
four of her own peony bushes
in their fall disguise, the arteries
of truncated, dead wood protruding
from clumps of soil fine-veined with worms.

"Better get them in before the frost."
And so I did, forgetting them
until their June explosion when
it seemed at once they'd fallen in love,
had grown two dozen pink hearts each.

Extravagance, exaggeration,
each one a girl on her first date,
excess perfume, her dress too ruffled,
the words he spoke to her too sweet—
but he was young; he meant it all.

And when they could not bear the pretty
weight of so much heart, I snipped
their dew-sopped blooms; stuffed them in vases
in every room like tissue boxes
already teary with self-pity.

DEAN YOUNG

DELPHINIUMS IN A WINDOW BOX

Every sunrise, even strangers' eyes.
Not necessarily swans, even crows,
even the evening fusillade of bats.
That place where the creek goes underground,
how many weeks before I see you again?
Stacks of books, every page, characters'
rages and poets' strange contraptions
of syntax and song, every song
even when there isn't one.
Every thistle, splinter, butterfly
over the drainage ditches. Every stray.
Did you see the meteor shower?
Did it feel like something swallowed?
Every question, conversation

even with almost nothing, cricket, cloud,
because of you I'm talking to crickets, clouds,
confiding in a cat. Everyone says,
Come to your senses, and I do, of you.
Every touch electric, every taste you,
every smell, even burning sugar, every
cry and laugh. Toothpicked samples
at the farmers' market, every melon,
plum, I come undone, undone.

THE RHYTHMS PRONOUNCE THEMSELVES
THEN VANISH

After they told me the CT showed
there was nothing wrong with my stomach
but my heart was failing, I plunked
one of those weird two-dollar tea balls
I bought in Chinatown and it bobbed
and bloomed like a sea monster and tasted
like feet and I had at this huge
chocolate bar I got at Trader Joe's
and didn't answer the door even though
I could see it was UPS with the horse
medication and I thought of that picture
Patti took of me in an oval frame. Sweat
itself is odorless, composed of water,
sodium chloride, potassium salts,
and lactic acid; it's the bacteria growing
on dead skin that provides the stench.
The average life span of a human taste bud
is seven to ten days. Nerve pulses
can travel up to a hundred and seventy miles per hour.
All information is useless.
The typical lightning bolt
is one inch wide and five miles long.

JANE HIRSHFIELD

IT WAS LIKE THIS: YOU WERE HAPPY

It was like this:
you were happy, then you were sad,
then happy again, then not.

It went on.
You were innocent or you were guilty.
Actions were taken, or not.

At times you spoke, at other times you were silent.
Mostly, it seems you were silent—what could you say?

Now it is almost over.

Like a lover, your life bends down and kisses your life.

It does this not in forgiveness—
between you, there is nothing to forgive—
but with the simple nod of a baker at the moment
he sees the bread is finished with transformation.

Eating, too, is now a thing only for others.

It doesn't matter what they will make of you
or your days: they will be wrong,
they will miss the wrong woman, miss the wrong man,
all the stories they tell will be tales of their own invention.

Your story was this: you were happy, then you were sad,
you slept, you awakened.
Sometimes you ate roasted chestnuts, sometimes persimmons.

DEREK MAHON

THE THUNDER SHOWER

A blink of lightning, then
a rumor, a grumble of white rain
growing in volume, rustling over the ground,
drenching the gravel in a wash of sound.
Drops tap like timpani or shine
like quavers on a line.

It rings on exposed tin,
a suite for water, wind and bin,
plinky Poulenc or strongly groaning Brahms'
rain-strings, a whole string section that describes
the very shapes of thought in warm
self-referential vibes

and spreading ripples. Soon
the whispering roar is a recital.
Jostling rain-crowds, clamorous and vital,
struggle in runnels through the afternoon.
The rhythm becomes a regular beat;
steam rises, body heat—

and now there's city noise,
bits of recorded pop and rock,
the drums, the strident electronic shock,
a vast polyphony, the dense refrain
of wailing siren, truck and train
and incoherent cries.

All human life is there
in the unconfined, continuous crash
whose slow, diffused implosions gather up
car radios and alarms, the honk and beep,
and tiny voices in a crèche
piercing the muggy air.

Squalor and decadence,
the rackety global-franchise rush,
oil wars and water wars, the diatonic
crescendo of a cascading world economy
are audible in the hectic thrash
of this luxurious cadence.

The voice of Baal explodes,
raging and rumbling round the clouds,
frantic to crush the self-sufficient spaces
and re-impose his failed hegemony
in Canaan before moving on
to other simpler places.

At length the twining chords
run thin, a watery sun shines out,
the deluge slowly ceases, the guttural chant
subsides; a thrush sings, and discordant thirds
diminish like an exhausted concert
on the subdominant.

The angry downpour swarms
growling to far-flung fields and farms.
The drains are still alive with trickling water,
a few last drops drip from a broken gutter;
but the storm that created so much fuss
has lost interest in us.

NIGHT SONG

ARIA ABER

DIRT AND LIGHT

Last night it startled me again—I dreamed
of the corn maze through which we walked,
almost a decade ago, in the presence
of our other lovers. It was all burned down.
Purple corn glowed in the fields enveloping
the ruined maze, the woodlands washed
by October sun. Instead of you, I found in the salt-white music
of that familiar landscape an old piano, hollowed
by the draft of time, and the handle of a porcelain cup
in scorched soil. Relics of an imagined,
civil life. Today, in the lemony light by your grave,
I recited Merrill: *Why did I flinch? I loved you*, then touched
the damp and swelling mud, blue hyacinths
your mother planted there—
ants were swarming the unfinished plot of earth
like the black text of an infinite alphabet. I couldn't
read it. There was no epiphany, just dirt, the vast curtain
between this realm and the other. You never speak to me,
I thought, not even in dreams.
For hours, I sat there, mocked by the bees—
silly girl, their golden faces laughed, *she still wants
and wants*. A warm gust shook the trees,
and a pigeon settled into the dusk
of a wet pine, and then another.

FRANK BIDART

HALF-LIGHT

That crazy drunken night I
maneuvered you out into a field outside of

Coachella—I'd never seen a sky
so full of stars, as if the dirt of our lives

still were sprinkled with glistening
white shells from the ancient seabed

beneath us that receded long ago.
Parallel. We lay in parallel furrows.

—That suffocated, fearful
look on your face.

Jim, yesterday I heard your wife on the phone
tell me you died almost nine months ago.

Jim, now we cannot ever. Bitter
that we cannot ever have

the conversation that in
nature and alive we never had. Now not ever.

We have not spoken in years. I thought
perhaps at ninety or a hundred, two

broken-down old men, we wouldn't
give a damn, and find speech.

When I tell you that all the years we were
undergraduates I was madly in love with you

you say you
knew. I say I knew you

knew. You say
There was no place in nature we could meet.

You say this as if you need me to
admit something. *No place*

in nature, given our natures. Or is this
warning? I say what is happening now is

happening only because one of us is
dead. You laugh and say, Or both of us!

Our words
will be weirdly jolly.

That light I now envy
exists only on this page.

ANNE CARSON

SATURDAY NIGHT AS AN ADULT

We really want them to like us. We want it to go well. We overdress.
They are narrow people, art people, offhand, linens. It is early
summer, first hot weekend. We meet on the street, jumble about
with kisses and are we late? They had been late, we'd half-decided
to leave, now oh well. That place across the street, ever tried it?
Think we went there once, looks closed, says open, well. People
coming out. O.K. Inside is dark, cool, oaken. Turns out they know
the owner. He beams, ushers, we sit. And realize at once two things,
first, the noise is unbearable, two, neither of us knows the other
well enough to say bag it. Our hearts crumble. We order food
by pointing and break into two yell factions, one each side of the
table. He and she both look exhausted, from (I suppose) doing art
all day and then the new baby. We eat intently, as if eating were
conversation. We keep passing the bread. My fish comes unboned,
I weep pretending allergies. Finally someone pays the bill and we
escape to the street. For some reason I was expecting snow outside.
There is none. We decide not to go for ice cream and part, a little
more broken. Saturday night as an adult, so this is it. We thought
we'd be Nick and Nora, not their blurred friends in greatcoats.
We cover our ears inside our souls. But you can't stop it that way.

MATTHEW DICKMAN

FIRE

Oh, fire—you burn me! Ed is singing
behind the smoke and coals, his wife near him, the rest of us
below the stars
swimming above Washington state,
burning through themselves, he's like an Appalachian Prince
Henry with his banjo
and whiskey. The court surrounding him and the deer
off in the dark hills like the French, terrified
but in love and hungry.
I'm burning all the time. My pockets full of matches
and lighters, the blue smoke
crawling out like a skinny ghost from between my lips.
My lungs on fire, the wings
of them falling from the open sky. The tops of Michelle's long hands
looked like the beautiful coats
leopards have, covered in dark spots. All the cigarettes she would light
and then smash out, her eyes
the color of hair spray, cloudy and stingy
and gone, but beautiful! She carried her hands around
like two terrible letters of introduction. I never understood
who could have opened them, read them aloud,
and still thrown her onto a bed, still walked into the street she was,
    still
lit what little fuse she had left. Oh, fire—
you burn me. My sister and I and Southern Comfort
making us singe and spark, the family
ash all around us, the way she is beautiful to me in her singular blaze,
my brain lighting up, my tongue
like a monk in wartime, awash in orange silk and flames.
The first time I ever crushed a handful of codeine into its universe
of powdered pink, the last time
I felt the tangy aspirin drip of ecstasy down my throat,
the car losing control, the sound of momentum, this earth is not
    standing
still, oh, falling elevator—

you keep me, oh, graveyard—
you have been so patient, ticking away, smoldering—
you grenade. Oh, fire,
the first time I ever took a drink I was doused with gasoline,
that little ember perking up inside me, flashing, beginning to glow
     and climb.

RICHARD BLANCO

MY FATHER IN ENGLISH

First half of his life lived in Spanish: the long syntax
of *las montañas* that lined his village, the rhyme
of *sol* with his soul—a Cuban *alma*—that swayed
with *las palmas*, the sharp rhythm of his *machete*
cutting through *caña*, the syllables of his *canarios*
that sung into *la brisa* of the island home he left
to spell out the second half of his life in English—
the vernacular of New York City sleet, neon, glass—
and the brick factory where he learned to polish
steel twelve hours a day. Enough to save enough
to buy a used Spanish-English dictionary he kept
bedside like a bible—studied fifteen new words
after his prayers each night, then practiced them
on us the next day: *Buenos días, indeed, my family.*
Indeed más coffee. Have a good day today, indeed—
and again in the evening: *Gracias to my bella wife,*
indeed, for dinner. Hicistes tu homework, indeed?
La vida is indeed difícil. Indeed did indeed become
his favorite word, which, like the rest of his new life,
he never quite grasped: overused and misused often
to my embarrassment. Yet the word I most learned
to love and know him through: *indeed,* the exile who
tried to master the language he chose to master him,
indeed, the husband who refused to say *I love you*
in English to my mother, the man who died without
true translation. *Indeed,* meaning: in fact/*en efecto,*

meaning: in reality/*de hecho*, meaning to say now
what I always meant to tell him in both languages:
thank you/*gracias* for surrendering the past tense
of your life so that I might conjugate myself here
in the present of this country, in truth/*así es, indeed.*

GALWAY KINNELL

FEATHERING

Many heads before mine have waked
in the dark on that old pillow
and lain there, awake, wondering
at the strangeness within themselves
they had been part of, a moment ago.

She has ripped out the stitches
at one end and stands on the stone table
in the garden holding the pillow like a sack
and plunges her fingers in and extracts
a thick handful of breast feathers.

A few of them snow toward the ground,
and immediately tree swallows appear.
She raises the arm holding the down
straight up in the air,
and stands there, like a mom

at a school crossing, or a god
of seedtime about to release
a stream of bits of plenitude,
or herself, long ago at a pond, chumming
for sunfish with bread crumbs.

At the lift of a breeze, her fist
loosens and parcels out a slow
upward tumble of dozens of puffs

near zero on the scale of materiality.
More swallows loop and dive about her.

Now, with a flap, one picks up speed
and streaks in at a feather, misses, stops,
twists and streaks back and this time
snaps its beak shut on it, and soars,
and banks back to where its nest box is.

A few more flurries, and she ties off
the pillow, ending for today
the game they make of it when she's there,
the imperative to feather one's nest
come down from the Pliocene.

At the window, where I've been watching
through bird glasses, I can see
a graceful awkwardness in her walk,
as if she's tipsy, or not sure
where she's been, and yet is deeply happy.

Sometimes when we're out at dinner and a dim mood
from the day persists in me, she flies up and
disappears a moment, plucking out of the air
somewhere this or that amusement or comfort
and, back again, lays it in our dinner talk.

Once, when it was time to leave, she stood up
and, scanning about the restaurant for the restroom,
went up as if on tiptoe, like the upland plover.
In the taxi we kissed a mint from the desk
from my mouth to hers, like cedar waxwings.

Later, when I padded up to bed,
I found her dropped off, the bedside lamp
still on, an open book face down over her heart;

and though my plod felt quiet
as a cat's footfalls, her eyes at once opened.

And when I climbed into our bed and crept
toward the side of it lined with the down comforter
and the warmth and softness of herself,
she took me in her arms and sang to me
in high, soft, clear, wild notes.

HAYDEN CARRUTH

FRAGMENT OF A CONVERSATION IN BED

Then again when I saw the moon shadow
of an owl, three or four winters past,
gliding over the snow, I felt it, too,
this sense you speak of, we lying now
in our comfort, our warm, naked, loving
bodies. I knew it. Say it is the honor
of insight unexpected, such a gift! That
was far from this city of churches and
offices; it was a field in the North.
Was it the same? I think for you the moon
might have been the gift there, the sign
of further light unseeable; but I,
who could have seen the owl if I had looked
up in the brightness, somehow in that meadow,
where the vague but unmistakable form
moved over drifts of whiteness,
a perfection of movement, without force,
without sound, cared only to see the shadow.
I did not look up for the source.

DANIEL HALL

COUNTRY RADIO

It will be late (maybe too late, this worry
      keeping you from falling back to sleep)
when from around the corner or up the alley some
      convergence of bright voices
will rise to your window, cries of, what, fear
      or laughter, nothing coming clear to you

in your bed, the heart of winter, the refrigerator
      shuddering on or off.
Or they will have crested already by the time you've
      come to completely, the flow
stalled, turning outward, out from the muffle of
      bedding, the cold room, away from you,

further and further. And in their wake you'll tune
      in a signal, clearer and clearer:
midsummer, long past midnight, how the milk train
      would come dragging its dim racket out
between the farms, the passengers slumped and gently
      rocking, one man still wide-awake,

spark-lit, gazing ahead into the humid dark, a
      cool brilliance spilling over
the dry fields and cinders of the only world you
      knew. "From New York," your forbidden
transistor whispered, the audience rustling like
      grass between breezes . . . And the baton

will rise over a piece that refuses to play itself
      out as written, reworked
some nights to the point of madness, fragments
      lunging and leapfrogging in their frenzy
for resolution— Then listen, listen to me, and
      you'll hear the entire passage.

PAUL TRAN

THE THREE GRACES

Who could care about the probability of love when brought, like us,
    to this
world under endless darkness? A great mountain engulfed

by a greater ocean, we formed, ever so slowly, from tectonic plates
colliding, one mounting another, riding the way time rode

sunlight and moonlight across the icy surface of the water.
We learned, with time, to view and invent this life from the depths

where beasts, now extinct, bellowed and belted their brutal songs.
All that remains of them, and of that time, are the bones we buried,
    burnished

beneath beds of sandstone and limestone, made unknown and then
    known
when the waves and the darkness dried up. The wind whittled us

like a restless sculptor pacing around a slab of marble, imitating
God with a hammer and chisel. In the Garden of the Gods, we
    endured

the erotics of erosion. Loss. Change. What we couldn't change
and what we lost to time made us more fully ourselves

and full of ourselves. We fooled around and made a fool of God.
We, in our faulted and faultless glamour, became a brand-new home

for the bighorn sheep and lions, the canyon wrens and white-
    throated swifts
swinging low below a cloudless sky. We drank the sky and threw up

acres of wild prairie grass, piñon juniper, and ponderosa pine
from the remains of ancestral ranges and sand dunes. Maybe this
    was love

after all. We remained. We reinvented ourselves. We let the weaker
    parts of us go
and decided, despite our egos and the tests of time, to test time
    and show

how miraculous it is to exist. To live beyond survival. To be alive
twice and thrice, and countless times to find one with and within
    another.

What are the chances of that? One in a thousand. One in a million.
    One in love
proves and is living proof that anything and everything is probable

through seasons counting on rain to come down like a downpour of
    stars.
Seasons of Never This Again. Seasons of This Could Last Forever.

ROWAN RICARDO PHILLIPS

GOLDEN

For once, I slept and you watched.
I dreamed, I think.
I washed without my hands.

You watched. I moved along a scratchy plain
of dandelion, peony, wild
and luckless clover. A bee entered me.

You soothed my ache. We watched a golden sky
heckled into slate.
I will wake and say "Golden." I will wake

and say, no, nothing but that. I had become
the injurer who makes things golden,
swimming in your voice, so much deeper than mine.

WYN COOPER

I TRUST THE WIND AND DON'T KNOW WHY

I am not the girl in the picture.
I am not the smell of hyacinths.
I might be the boy.
I am off the record.

I am not a view from the island,
not the sound of waves breaking,
not parasols scattered on sand.
I am closed for the season.

I'm fingerprints on windows
that look out on rain.
I am rain that rains harder.

I'm not the new fashion, not
hands on a clock. I don't spring
forward. Cannot turn back.

I am yellow caution tape
strung from pole to pole:
Police line do not cross.

I see the sky but nothing in it,
just spots on the sun.
Then the long twilight.
Then the crackle of stars.

ROBERT PATRICK DANA

A WINTER'S TALE

It is a winter night. Fever and chill
Rummage the blind cars on Lover's Hill,
And rabbits shiver in the frozen grass.

Along the river, ice, like broken glass,
Clicks and flickers. For an hour we walk
The bank, and I half listen to your talk
Of kids and marriage. Here, piles of junk
Blaze with frost, and summer's juice is sunk
To the hidden root. But even as a bloom
Of ice melts in my hand, I think of a room
Warmed by summer moonlight. You are beside
Me on the bed. I turn. Your eyes grow wide
And darken as we kiss. Wild and sweet,
Your body whispers against me on the sheet.
But this is dream; for I have heard the west
Wind sigh down the dozing Berkshires, its past
Naming our future, the tide of its restlessness
Heaving through raw towns. It is not less
Than itself, this image. It summons me
Where breakneck houses spill toward a fresh sea.
And you, you are your father's child; your face
Tells me you will never leave this place,
His dead mills, the hope that they'll come back
To life. Downstream, they loom, crusted wrack
Jamming their floodgates, their bobbins wound
With the dust of years. Watchman and hound
Prowl the yards. But what is there to watch?
Tonight, your father warms his hopes with Scotch,
And pacing before the fireplace, stops, and turns
To stare at the *Wall Street Journal* as it burns.
Now, the town clock bells you home. But I
Draw you close. You smile a little and cry
Against my shoulder. We stand in this heavy air,
And stand, knowing all we'll ever share
Is this embrace. The sky above us palls,
And the blue snow melts about us as it falls.

ANNE SEXTON

MOON SONG

I am alive at night.
I am dead in the morning—
an old vessel who used up her oil,
bleak and pale-boned.
No miracle. No dazzle.
I'm out of repair,
but you are tall in your battle dress
and I must arrange for your journey.
I was always a virgin,
old and pitted.
Before the world was, I was.

I have been oranging and fat,
carrot-colored, gaped at,
allowing my cracked O's to drop on the sea
near Venice and Mombasa.
Over Maine I have rested.
I have fallen like a jet into the Pacific.
I have committed perjury over Japan.
I have dangled my pendulum,
my fat bag, my gold, gold,
blinkedy light
over you all.

So if you must inquire, do so.
After all, I am not artificial.
I looked long upon you,
love-bellied and empty,
flipping my endless display
for you, my cold, cold
coverall man.
You need only request
and I will grant it.
It is virtually guaranteed
that you will walk into me like a barracks.

So come cruising, come cruising,
you of the blastoff,
you of the bastion,
you of the scheme.
I will shut my fat eye down,
headquarters of an area,
house of a dream.

WILLIAM MATTHEWS

FIREWORKS

There's the whump when they're fired, the rising sigh
they climb, then the stark thump by which they blow
their safes. The fire then shinnies down the sky
like so many dark spiders on glowing
filaments. As thanks for each bright lull, we
loft, not high and not for long, a squadron
of soft, pleased cries. Also we can secede
from this to skulk, to brood sullenly on
the jingo bells, the patriotic gore,
the shattering violence these airy
filibusters flatly mimic on the lake.
Soon we'll unclump and disperse to the dark.
We're home. Lights on. We brush our teeth. Then we
douse the lights and sleep loads its projector.

BOB HICOK

VARIETIES OF COOL

A friend had a friend who winked us past rope lines,
we were enskyed for one night in hipness

it was boring

the champagne tasted no better than wonderful

the music was the same lobotomy of thump
that had been playing for years as dissent
from our Puritan roots

then we freed ourselves in a cab, something yellow
that wasn't a flower but wanted to be, sang
"Homeward Bound" passably to be happy about melancholy
and teach the driver from Sri Lanka a thing or two
about the American wistfulness for home
all the way to the Brooklyn Bridge
and walked across the night and water
that I got down on my belly and said hello to
through the wooden slats

in Brooklyn Heights we ate grapes and waved
at all the effort by the various Carnegies
and Seagrams to live forever, my friend had a cough
that became an acronym, I sat beside his missing
a man with my missing a woman in front of homes
we knew from movies but appeared less famous
than cozy at four in the morning as we tried
to decide which house wanted to adopt us

I couldn't get over the grapes

he said, *That's New York, you can get anything
as long as it's not what you really need*

he didn't say that

I'm confusing him with Mick Jagger and this poem
with a novel, he said something and I did
back and forth, it was quiet and that's how
conversation works, the grapes were good
and the night air had no idea how bad
his cough would get, I am grateful
that, on balance, the absence of stars
in Manhattan is offset by the number of lights
there's no reason to leave on but people do

YUSEF KOMUNYAKAA

THE SOUL'S SOUNDTRACK

When they call him Old School
he clears his throat, squares
his shoulders, & looks straight
into their lit eyes, saying,
"I was born by the damn river
& I've been running ever since."
An echo of Sam Cooke hangs
in bruised air, & for a minute

the silence of fate reigns over
day & night, a tilt of the earth
body & soul caught in a sway
going back to reed & goatskin,
back to trade winds locked
inside an "Amazing Grace"
that will never again sound
the same after Charleston,

South Carolina, & yes, words
follow the river through pine
& oak, muscadine & redbud,
& the extinct Lord God bird
found in an inventory of green
shadows longing for the scent
of woe & beatitude, taking root
in the mossy air of some bayou.

Now Old School can't stop
going from a sad yes to gold,
into a season's bloomy creed,
& soon he only hears Martha
& the Vandellas, their dancing
in the streets, through a before
& after. Mississippi John Hurt,
Ma Rainey, Sleepy John Estes,

Son House, Skip James, Joe
Turner, & Sweet Emma,
& he goes till what he feels
wears out his work boots
along the sidewalks, his life
a fist of coins in a coat pocket
to give to the recent homeless
up & down these city blocks.

He knows "We Shall Overcome"
& anthems of the flower children
which came after Sister Rosetta,
Big Mama Thornton, & Bo Diddley.
Now the years add up to a sharp
pain in his left side on Broadway,
but the Five Blind Boys of Alabama
call down an evening mist to soothe.

He believes to harmonize is
to reach, to ascend, to query
ego & hold a note till there's
only a quiver of blue feather
sat dawn, & a voice goes out
to return as a litany of mock
orange & sweat, as we are sewn
into what we came crying out of,

& when Old School declares,
"You can't doo-wop a cappella
& let your tongue touch an evil
while fingering a slothful doubt
beside the Church of Coltrane,"
he has traversed the lion's den
as Eric Dolphy plays a fluted
solo of birds in the pepper trees.

THOMAS SNAPP
THE ACTOR

Say you were the kid who could not sleep
In the new house in the north, with the wind
Flapping roof shingles, window banging softly
And tub humming for rain, the outside soft with moon,
And the man in the door looking into that softness—

Would you not follow? Out to the road
To hunch along the dark fringe as he walks
In a trance through the years rising like sand,
Falling back to leave him quickened
With each step, until he finds the old road
Leading to a concrete slab poured and forgot
By someone with a cottage in his head.

You crouch in fern and northern orchids.
He climbs onto the gray square,
Bows to the footweeds, and begins
A monologue. As he intones old names,
The man he was lives with his friends
In the shape of bulbs in the night
And posters curling in basements.

You are afraid for him, for yourself,
For all those players who rehearse their lines
In the trees beyond the city. As he
Storms with mad verse the indifferent air,
Something like night moves through the weeds.

FRANK X. GASPAR
NAUSICAÄ

I can see your room only with my eyes closed now—
that's how little I understand anything at all—and you
sitting up as I entered, and in one motion you throwing

off your nightgown, cornflowers and flannel, and the moment
catching your hair's wildness in an insolent shrug,
and then I was Odysseus naked before Nausicaä—but no
you were naked—I was merely doomed, and I moved
as into the twilight of a cave, like a man loving his own
ruin, happy for his wounds and happy for the wounds
to come. Maybe a spark jumped, but there is no name
for the god of fragments—there was just a fire I believed in.
And there is still a fire that I believe in. Like the nymph,
incandescent in the glade, from whom the man should have
run in terror instead of begging her to renounce her
godliness in the name of carnal love. Still, there were
old men once in their robes and togas who were wise and
famously schooled by a woman, and they told us that
everything here is a shadow of something else—like a song
plucked on strings that implies two bodies dancing in an
ecstasy beyond all earthly knowing. Where is your bed
now? Your prodigal body that whole polities might worship?
In what world? That is what I am asking, love. What world?

VIKRAM SETH

NANJING NIGHT

Full moon, the Nanjing walls, bicycle bells.
Two children huddle in the ten-o'clock movie crowd
Against the plunging cold. The air foretells
Snow, moonlit snow. Low-voiced, dog-eared, heads bowed,
Students seep out of libraries into the cold.
It is the last month—the yellow plum is in bloom.
Exams, the Spring festival; each one is to be told
His lifework by the Party. In the room
Someone grinds his teeth in his sleep and moans.
The moonlight finds two pink hot-water flasks,
Pull-up bars, a leafless ginkgo, four stones—
Either the Gang of Four or the Four Great Tasks.
I dream of the twelve full moons of the coming year:
Tilts of curved roof; branches; a stone-white sphere.

MAYA RIBAULT

SOCIETY OF FIREFLIES

When it was warm enough, you came with your nighttime
show, costing us nothing. We caught you in Mason
jars, hoping to create a new kind of bedside
lamp. Leave days rationed out by the computer,
hoarded for a vain flicker of freedom. Weekends,
I zone out on "Homeland." Sordid. I do enough
careful work to satisfy my bosses. I save
for retirement—to my bohemian eyes,
a fortune—though they say you need more
than a million. Immerse yourself in the exponential
power of dividends. And what about decorating
your rental apartment? At least put up some
curtains after fourteen years. I don't mind
the metro, eavesdropping on other people's
lives. I don't die down there every day
a little. And you rise up once more
unsolicited from the fields, with your equal
measure of appearing and disappearing.

ROBERT BLY

POEM ON SLEEP

Then the bright being disguised as a seal dove into the deep billows.
I go on loving you after we are asleep.
I know the ledges where we sit all night looking out over the briny sea,
and the open places where we coast in sleekness through the sea.

And where is the practical part of me? The practical one, who is
    cunning?
Oh, he is long since gone, dispersed among the bold grasses.
The one he does not know of remains afloat and awake all night;
he lies on luminous boulders, dives, his coat sleek, his eyes open.

MOMINA MELA

HOW TO TAKE OFF A SARI

He asks and I tell him   our bodies falling from an open window
first, unfasten the *pallu* the fall should be swift and vacant
like the backward collapse   of a moving hawk on a windscreen
wait for the bare stomach   to procure the fatigue of renewed air
                    half breath   half smoke
next, spin on one foot   the movement should be sexless   bad at love
as you fall
                    fall   let the system of the city swell in the base of your throat
drop the petticoat   walk out of its retreating puddle
this should be mildly theatrical   depending on the sun's humor
measure the distortion of reflection between collarbones   bask in the
        twisted heat
if the blouse is hooked at the back   thrust your elbows outward
in imitation of a duck stepping into water   unclasp blouse
if the blouse is hooked at the front bring your hands to your heart
as if full of gratitude   wanting to love, not knowing
exactly how   unclasp blouse like an unstitched wound.

DIANE *SEUSS*

I HAVE SLEPT IN MANY PLACES, FOR YEARS ON MATTRESSES THAT ENTERED

I have slept in many places, for years on mattresses that entered
my life via nothing but luck, as a child on wet sheets, I could not
contain myself, as a teen on the bed where my father ate his last
pomegranate, among crickets and chicken bones in ditches, in the bare
grass on the lavish grounds of a crumbling castle, in a flapping German
circus tent, in a lean-to, my head on the belly of a sick calf, in a terrible
darkness where a shrew tried to stay afloat in a bucket of well water,
in a blue belfry, on a pink couch being eaten from the inside by field mice,
on bare floorboards by TV light with Mikel on Locust Place, on an amber
throne of cockroach casings, on a carpet of needles from a cemetery pine,
in a clubhouse circled by crab-apple trees with high-school boys who are

now members of a megachurch, in a hotel bathtub in St. Augustine after
a sip from the Fountain of Youth, cold on a cliff's edge, passed out cold
on train tracks, in a hospital bed holding my lamb like an army of lilacs.

AUGUST KLEINZAHLER

SUNDAY IN NOVEMBER

And who were they all in your sleep last night
      chattering so
you'd think that when you woke
the living room would be full of friends and ghosts?

But, you see, nobody's here, no one but you
      and the room's nearly bare
except for Paddy's playstring all covered in dust
and a bottle of tinted air.

Pop and Lola, the sullen little clerk from the store,
      and eight or ten more. Now,
which were the dream ones and who did you meet that was real?
You were, for the most part, you.

Such a big room: how nice to be alone in it
      with the one lit bulb and dying plant,
the day so large and gray outside,
dogs running through it in circles, buses, shouts.

And later on where will you take her?
      Up to the rock. And what will you see there?
Roofs and the bay. Have you a song to sing her?
The wind will do and she'll think it's me.

But who were they all in your sleep last night,
      first one then the next,
with their menace, wild semaphore, and lusts?
I hardly know where you find the strength

come morning.

LOUISE GLÜCK

NIGHT SONG

Look up into the light of the lantern.
Don't you see? The calm of darkness
is the horror of Heaven.

We've been apart too long, too painfully separated.
How can you bear to dream,
to give up watching? I think you must be dreaming,
your face is full of mild expectancy.

I need to wake you, to remind you that there isn't a future.
That's why we're free. And now some weakness in me
has been cured forever, so I'm not compelled
to close my eyes, to go back, to rectify—

The beach is still; the sea, cleansed of its superfluous life,
opaque, rocklike. In mounds, in vegetal clusters,
seabirds sleep on the jetty. Terns, assassins—

You're tired; I can see that.
We're both tired; we have acted a great drama.
Even our hands are cold, that were like kindling.
Our clothes are scattered on the sand; strangely enough,
they never turned to ashes.

I have to tell you what I've learned, that I know now
what happens to the dreamers.
They don't feel it when they change. One day
they wake, they dress, they are old.

Tonight I'm not afraid
to feel the revolutions. How can you want sleep
when passion gives you that peace?
You're like me tonight, one of the lucky ones.
You'll get what you want. You'll get your oblivion.

ROBERT PINSKY

SAMURAI SONG

When I had no roof I made
Audacity my roof. When I had
No supper my eyes dined.

When I had no eyes I listened.
When I had no ears I thought.
When I had no thought I waited.

When I had no father I made
Care my father. When I had no
Mother I embraced order.

When I had no friend I made
Quiet my friend. When I had no
Enemy I opposed my body.

When I had no temple I made
My voice my temple. I have
No priest, my tongue is my choir.

When I have no means fortune
Is my means. When I have
Nothing, death will be my fortune.

Need is my tactic, detachment
Is my strategy. When I had
No lover I courted my sleep.

JERICHO BROWN

NIGHT SHIFT

When I am touched, brushed, and measured, I think of myself
As a painting. The artist works no matter the lack of sleep. I am made
Beautiful. I never eat. I once bothered with a man who called me
Snack, Midnight Snack to be exact. I'd oblige because he hurt me

With a violence I mistook for desire. I'd get left hanging
In one room of his dim house while he swept or folded laundry.
When you've been worked on for so long, you never know
You're done. Paint dries. Midnight is many colors. Black and blue
Are only two. The man who tinted me best kept me looking a little
Like a chore. How do you say prepared
In French? How do you draw a man on the night shift? Security
At the museum for the blind, he eats to stay
Awake. He's so full, he never has to eat again. And the moon goes.

JACK GILBERT

BY SMALL AND SMALL: MIDNIGHT TO 4 A.M.

For eleven years I have regretted it,
regretted that I did not do what
I wanted to do as I sat there those
four hours watching her die. I wanted
to crawl in among the machinery
and hold her in my arms, knowing
the elementary, leftover bit of her
mind would dimly recognize it was me
carrying her to where she was going.

KOFI AWOONOR

COUNTING THE YEARS

As usual, as in the earlier dreams
I come to the whistling shores
the voice of the high-domed
crab stilled
but a chorus remains of the water creatures
of earlier times, of the birth time
and the dying time, the pity,
when we resurrect the travellers
the anchorman on our singular boat
that will take us home

BARBARA HOWES
A RUNE FOR C.

Luck? I am upset. My dog is ill.
I am now in that gray shuttling trains go in for;
The sky clouds; it is hard to believe dawn will

Ever show up.—I look for omens:
Not birds broken, not Fords lashed around trees,
But some item showing that fate is open. . . .

Sometimes, far far down in the magical past
Of us all, in something that stutters, something that rises,
There is an intimation of luck just

Swinging over our way: a cat's paw loose
In the banister, a long train-run, and then,
Square and oil-shambled, blue between elms, the caboose!

MIKE NICHOLS
EXHORTATION

You have not, as I, walked
the silent sleeping streets,
with streaming eyes, running
from the women in the windows.
You have not slid, as I have slid,
under the seas to see the shells,
smiling and swimming silently.
You have not seen the moon
    running along the sky.
So shut up.

TONY HOAGLAND

THE HERO'S JOURNEY

I remember the first time I looked at the spotless marble floor
   of a giant hotel lobby
      and understood that someone had waxed and polished it all night

and that someone else had pushed his cart of cleaning supplies
   down the long air-conditioned corridors
      of the Steinberg Building across the street

and emptied all two hundred and forty-three wastebaskets
   stopping now and then to scrape up chewing gum
      with a special flat-bladed tool
                        he keeps in his back
                            pocket.

It tempered my enthusiasm for "The Collected Sonnets of Hugh
   Pembley-Witherton"
      and for Kurt von Heinzelman's "Epic of the Seekers for the
         Grail,"

Chapter 5, "The Trial," in which he describes how the
   "tall and fair-complexioned" knight, Gawain,
      makes camp one night beside a windblown cemetery

but cannot sleep for all the voices
                      rising up from underground—

Let him stay out there a hundred nights, the little wonder boy,
   with his thin blanket and his cold armor and his
                     useless sword,
until he understands exactly how
   the glory of the protagonist is always paid for
                 by a lot of secondary characters.

In the morning he will wake and gallop back to safety;
   he will hear his name embroidered into toasts and songs.

But now he knows there is a country he had not accounted for,
   and that country has its citizens:

the one-armed baker sweeping out his shop at 4 A.M.;

soldiers fitting every horse in Prague with diapers
                          before the emperor's arrival;

and that woman in the nursing home,
   who has worked there for a thousand years,

taking away the bedpans,
   lifting up and wiping off the soft heroic buttocks of Odysseus.

TOMAS TRANSTRÖMER
THE HOUSE OF HEADACHE

I woke up inside the headache. The headache is a room where I
have to stay as I cannot afford to pay rent anywhere else. Every
hair aches to the point of turning gray. There is an ache inside
that Gordian knot, the brain, which wants to do so much in so
many directions. The ache is also a half-moon hanging down in
the light-blue sky; the color disappears from my face; my nose
is pointing *downward*; the entire divining rod is turning down
toward the subterranean current. I moved into a house built in
the wrong place; there is a magnetic pole just under the bed, just
under my pillow, and when the weather chops around above the
bed I am charged. Time and again I try to imagine that a celestial
bonesetter is pinching me through a miraculous grip on my cervical
vertebrae, a grip that will put life right once and for all. But the
house of headache is not ready to be written off just yet. First I
have to live inside it for an hour, two hours, half a day. If at first I
said it was a room, change that to a house. But the question now
is this: Is it not an entire city? Traffic is unbearably slow. The
breaking news is out. And somewhere a telephone is ringing.

(Translated, from the Swedish, by John Matthias and Lars-Hakan Svensson.)

MARK WUNDERLICH

THE BATS

I share my house with a colony of bats.
They live in the roof peak,
enter through a gap.

At dusk they fly out, dip
into inverted arcs
to catch what flutters or stings,

what can only be hunted at night.
Sunlight stops their flight,
drives them into their hot chamber

to rest and nest, troll-faces
pinched shut. I hear them scratch.
In darkness they chop and hazard through the sky,

around blue outlines of pines,
pitch up over the old Dutch house
we share. They scare some

but not me. I see them
for what they seem—
timid, wee, happy or lucky,

pinned to the roof beams,
stitched up in their ammonia reek
and private as dreams.

BIANCA STONE

· WHAT'S POETRY LIKE?

Poets play the winter tarantella,
making love in the midnight hours
on a white iron bed like a dog skeleton
distinguishing the essential and unessential

moment, shared between ordinary lunatics
and screaming over a bird in an apple tree
until an elegy has to be written
to resuscitate the relation—those who look
toward the depleted wildlife of neighborhoods
with tragic relish, to see somehow ourselves
disappearing about ourselves.

Once, in New York City, years ago,
the Internet technician finally arrived.
His teen-age apprentice stood in my living room
over a Tranströmer book. He said it looked
kind of cool, and he wanted to know
what it was. "Poetry," I said.
"What's poetry like?" he asked. And
the treacherous inadequacy with which one
finds oneself explaining in a few loose
deficient words something with lungs
and no face, the immortal freak
of language you haunt and hunt
which is the original state of language
you're trying to get back to from within—
poetry, whose rare geniuses come
as bittersweet suicidal explosions
on the tongue, randomly felt during
long, tedious meals; award-winning and
already forgotten. All the emoting of the
unanalyzable fragments. All the surrender
and detonations of precision
and reckless insight
and reference to hidden wisdom and Coke cans—
conversations across time, and slips
into truth, and obscurity of thought altogether
blissful, the form itself at its best strings of dreams
in the waking life,
overlaid like unobserved clothing:
the words that sing
stillness, the silence craved

by perpetual auctioneers—that which is not
the tale of event but itself *an* event—

"You know what? Just take the book," I said finally,
pushing it into his hands—

"THANKS!" he said, and took it away, grinning a little.

But later, with snow in my head and a thunder
in my right eyelid . . . I was worried, as I was
so dangerously then, about dark, yet-unspoken things
—it frightened me: that shiny black and white book
wafting around New York City in the back
of a Time Warner Cable van, waiting to be opened,
waiting to torment him, thinking of it changing his life.

CHRISTIAN WIMAN

I DON'T WANT TO BE A SPICE STORE

I don't want to be a spice store.
I don't want to carry handcrafted Marseille soap,
or tsampa and yak butter,
or nine thousand varieties of wine.
Half the shops here don't open till noon
and even the bookstore's brined in charm.
I want to be the one store that's open all night
and has nothing but necessities.
Something to get a fire going
and something to put one out.
A place where things stay frozen
and a place where they are sweet.
I want to hold within myself the possibility
of plugging one's ears and easing one's eyes;
superglue for ruptures that are,
one would have thought, irreparable,
a whole bevy of non-toxic solutions
for everyday disasters. I want to wait

brightly lit and with the patience
I never had as a child
for my father to find me open
on Christmas morning in his last-ditch, lone-wolf drive
for gifts. "Light of the World" penlight,
bobblehead compass, fuzzy dice.
I want to hum just a little with my own emptiness
at 4 A.M. To have little bells above my door.
To have a door.

W. G. SEBALD

DARK NIGHT SALLIES FORTH

If I see before me
the nervature of past life
in one image, I always think
that this has something to do
with truth. Our brains, after all,
are always at work on some quivers
of self-organization, however faint,
and it is from this that an order
arises, in places beautiful
and comforting, though more cruel, too, ·
than the previous state of ignorance.
How far, in any case, must one go back
to find the beginning? Perhaps
to that morning of January 9, 1905,
on which Grandfather and Grandmother
in ringing cold drove in an open
landau from Kloster Lechfeld
to Obermeitingen, to be married.
Grandmother in a black taffeta dress
with a bunch of paper flowers, Grandfather
in his uniform, the brass-embellished
helmet on his head. What was in their minds
when, the horse blanket over their knees,
they sat side by side in the carriage and heard

the hoofbeats echo in the bare avenue?
What was in the minds of their children later,
one of whom stares out fearfully from a
class photograph taken in the war year 1917
at Allarzried? Forty-eight pitiable coevals,
the schoolmistress on the right,
on the left the myopic chaplain and as a
caption on the reverse of the spotted
gray cardboard mount the words
"In the future death lies at our feet,"
one of those obscure oracular sayings
one never again forgets. On another
photograph of which I possess an enlarged
copy, a swan and its reflection
on the water's black surface,
a perfect emblem of peace.
The botanical garden around the pond,
to my knowledge, is situated
on the bank of the Regnitz at Bamberg
and I believe that a road
runs through it today.
The whole leaves an impression
that is somehow un-German,
the elms, the hornbeams and densely green
conifers in the background, the small
pagoda-like building, the finely raked
gravel, the hortensias, flag iris,
aloes, ostrich-plume ferns, and
the giant-leaved ornamental rhubarb.
Astonishing, to me, the persons
also to be seen in the picture:
Mother in her open coat, with a lightness
she was later to lose; Father, a little
aside, hands in his pockets,
he, too, it seems, with no cares.
The date is August 26, 1943.
On the 27th Father's departure for Dresden,
of whose beauty his memory, as he

remarks when I question him,
retains no trace.
During the night of the 28th
582 aircraft flew in
to attack Nürnberg. Mother,
who on the next day planned
to return to her parents'
home in the Alps,
got no further than
Fürth. From there she
saw Nürnberg in flames,
but cannot recall now
what the burning town looked like
or what her feelings were
at this sight.
On the same day, she told me recently,
from Fürth she had travelled on
to Windsheim and an acquaintance
at whose house she waited until
the worst was over, and realized
that she was with child.
As for the burning city,
in the Vienna Art-Historical Museum
there hangs a painting
by Altdorfer depicting Lot
with his daughters. On the horizon
a terrible conflagration blazes
devouring a large city.
Smoke ascends from the site,
the flames rise to the sky, and
in the blood-red reflection
one sees the blackened
façades of houses.
In the middle ground there is a strip
of idyllic green landscape,
and closest to the beholder's eye
the new generation of
Moabites is conceived.

When for the first time I saw
this picture, the year before last,
I had the strange feeling
of having seen all of it
before, and a little later,
crossing to Floridsdorf
on the Bridge of Peace,
I nearly went out of my mind.

(*Translated, from the German, by Michael Hamburger.*)

SEAMUS HEANEY

ELECTRIC LIGHT

Candle grease congealed, dark-streaked with wick-soot.
Rucked alps from above. The smashed thumbnail
of that ancient mangled thumb was puckered pearl,

moonlit quartz, a bleached and littered Cumae.
In the first house where I saw electric light
she sat with her fur-lined felt slippers unzipped,

year in, year out, in the same chair, and whispered
in a voice that at its loudest did nothing else
but whisper. We were both desperate

the night I was left to stay with her and wept
under the clothes, under the waste of light
left turned on in the bedroom. "What ails you, child,

what ails you, for God's sake?" Urgent, sorrowing
ails, far-off and old. Scaresome cavern waters
lapping a boatslip. Her helplessness no help.

Lisp and relapse. Eddy of sibylline English.
Splashes between a ship and dock, to which,
animula, I would come alive in time

as ferries churned and turned down Belfast Lough
towards the brow-to-glass transport of a morning train,
the very "there-you-are-and-where-are-you?"

of poetry itself. Backs of houses
like the back of hers, meat safes and mangles
in the railway-facing yards of fleeting England,

an allotment scarecrow among patted rigs,
then a town-edge soccer pitch, the groin of distance,
fields of grain like the Field of the Cloth of Gold,

tunnel gauntlet and horizon keep. To Southwark,
too, I came, from tube mouth into sunlight,
Moyola-breath by Thames's "straunge strond."

If I stood on the bow-backed chair, I could reach
the light switch. They let me and they watched me.
A touch of the little pip would work the magic.

A turn of their wireless knob and light came on
in the dial. They let me and they watched me
as I roamed at will the stations of the world.

Then they were gone and Big Ben and the news
were over. The set had been switched off,
all quiet behind the blackout except for

knitting needles ticking, wind in the flue.
She sat with her fur-lined felt slippers unzipped,
electric light shone over us, I feared

the dirt-tracked flint and fissure of her nail,
so plectrum-hard, glit-glittery, it must still keep
among beads and vertebrae in the Derry ground.

CAROLYN FORCHÉ

THE LIGHTKEEPER

A night without ships. Foghorns called into walled cloud, and you
still alive, drawn to the light as if it were a fire kept by monks,
darkness once crusted with stars, but now death-dark as you sail
     inward.
Through wild gorse and sea wrack, through heather and torn wool
you ran, pulling me by the hand, so I might see this for once in my
     life:
the spin and spin of light, the whirring of it, light in search of the lost,
there since the era of fire, era of candles and hollow-wick lamps,
whale oil and solid wick, colza and lard, kerosene and carbide,
the signal fires lighted on this perilous coast in the Tower of Hook.
You say to me stay awake, be like the lensmaker who died with his
lungs full of glass, be the yew in blossom when bees swarm, be
their amber cathedral and even the ghosts of Cistercians will be kind
     to you.
In a certain light as after rain, in pearled clouds or the water beyond,
seen or sensed water, sea or lake, you would stop still and gaze out
for a long time. Also when fireflies opened and closed in the pines,
and a star appeared, our only heaven. You taught me to live like this.
That after death it would be as it was before we were born. Nothing
to be afraid. Nothing but happiness as unbearable as the dread
from which it comes. Go toward the light always, be without ships.

SYLVIA PLATH

THE MOON AND THE YEW TREE

This the light of the mind, cold and planetary.
The trees of the mind are black. The light is blue.
The grasses unload their griefs on my feet as if I were God,
Prickling my ankles and murmuring of their humility.
Fumey, spiritous mists inhabit this place
Separated from my house by a row of headstones.
I simply cannot see where there is to get to.

The moon is no door. It is a face in its own right,
White as a knuckle and terribly upset.
It drags the sea after it like a dark crime; it is quiet
With the O-gape of complete despair. I live here.
Twice on Sunday, the bells startle the sky—
Eight great tongues affirming the Resurrection.
At the end, they soberly bong out their names.

The yew tree points up. It has a Gothic shape.
The eyes lift after it and find the moon.
The moon is my mother. She is not sweet like Mary.
Her blue garments unloose small bats and owls.
How I would like to believe in tenderness—
The face of the effigy, gentled by candles,
Bending, on me in particular, its mild eyes.

I have fallen a long way. Clouds are flowering,
Blue and mystical over the face of the stars.
Inside the church, the saints will be all blue,
Floating on their delicate feet over the cold pews,
Their hands and faces stiff with holiness.
The moon sees nothing of this. She is bald and wild.
And the message of the yew tree is blackness—blackness and silence.

PATRICIA SPEARS JONES

SERAPHIM

Once a beauty, full figured, beloved
And then a fever, sweats, water vomited
Until the body gave out. And then,

Wings and lyres and legion of other
Angels. Singing, dancing, flying about,

But once a beauty remembers
Physical love and then its loss

Eternal life seems mundane
No conflict or need or desire.

Thus, this seraphim held melancholy
Gentle as a lull in a long conversation

But heaven allows only jubilance.
Possibly the angel needed to return

Human: with feelings, tears and laughter
Or find a way to shape the sadness into
A moment of beauty when the angel's wings
Spread and flight moves to breathing
Full of vision. There the angel's tears bond
with the visitor's fear, awe. It could be

a filmmaker's perambulating Berlin,
in search of a reason to consider
the spirit, those angels set
on top of monuments
across the handsome city.

And they love the lovers.
And one remains lovingly disinterested.

How dreams and death and a dearth
Of joy is visible. And wings spread
And wings fall. And the beloved becomes
A man who understands a woman's
Full figure. A man who fears fever.
A man who takes his lover in all
Her melancholy and lifts her up

And unto joy.

JOHNNY CASH

CALIFORNIA POEM

There's trouble on the mountain
And the valley's full of smoke
There's crying on the mountain
And again the same heart broke.

The lights are on past midnite
The curtains closed all day
There's trouble on the mountain
The valley people say.

TERRANCE HAYES

NEW YORK POEM

In New York from a rooftop in Chinatown
one can see the sci-fi bridges and aisles
of buildings where there are more miles
of shortcuts and alternative takes than
there are Miles Davis alternative takes.
There is a white girl who looks hi-
jacked with feeling in her glittering jacket
and her boots that look made of dinosaur
skin and R is saying to her *I love you*
again and again. On a Chinatown rooftop
in New York anything can happen.
Someone says "abattoir" is such a pretty word
for "slaughterhouse." Someone says
mermaids are just fish ladies. I am so
fucking vain I cannot believe anyone
is threatened by me. In New York
not everyone is forgiven. Dear New York,
dear girl with a bar code tattooed
on the side of your face, and everyone

writing poems about and inside and outside
the subways, dear people underground
in New York, on the sci-fi bridges and aisles
of New York, on the rooftops of Chinatown
where Miles Davis is pumping in,
and someone is telling me about contranyms,
how "cleave" and "cleave" are the same word
looking in opposite directions. I now know
"bolt" is to lock and "bolt" is to run away.
That's how I think of New York. Someone
jonesing for Grace Jones at the party,
and someone jonesing for grace.

THE TEENS & TWENTIES

ARTHUR SZE

FAROLITOS

We pour sand into brown lunch bags, then place
          a votive candle

inside each; at night, lined along the driveway,
          the flickering lights

form a spirit way, but what spirit? what way?
          We sight the flames

and, swaying within, know the future's fathomless;
          we grieve, yearn, joy,

pinpoints in a greater darkness, and spy sunlight
          brighten craters

on a half-lit moon; in this life, you may try, try
          to light a match, fail,

fail again and again; yet, letting go, you strike
          a tip one more time

when it bursts into flame—   now the flames
          are lights in bags again,

and we glimpse the willow tips clutch at a lunar
          promise of spring.

ROSANNA WARREN

A NEW YEAR

Was it myself I left behind? Or was
the country letting go of itself at each clackety-clack
as the train rattled northward into dusk?

Girders flashed by, the ghosts of factories.
Then frozen fields, their stubble narrowly laid out
in an ancient, foreign, indecipherable script.
New solitudes flared on the smutty pane.
As if I were aging faster than the engine's hurtle . . .
While the Hudson shoved its massive, wrinkled drowse
south, dreaming at its own pace: the drowned
river, carrying thousands of years
of sediment through torn uterus of rock.
Angry signs slashed the shadows. Wrecked cars
stacked in yards, tilting fences, sheds
pledged revenge. Then a whoosh of snow
tattered the trees and night swallowed us whole.

Till dawn, jerking me from my berth,
broke over Indiana's frostbitten furrows,
a country graveyard slotted among farms.

TADEUSZ DĄBROWSKI

BOUQUET

Paulina, the gardener's daughter, cares
about flowers doomed to die.

If I bring her a bouquet, she frees it
from the ribbons and gently places it in the hospice

of a vase. When the flowers weaken, she trims their stems
and plucks off their wilting leaves. She takes

the dead ones to the compost, from the rest
she forms a new bouquet. Thus disappear in turn:

poppies, anemones, carnations, damnations and
forget-me-nots, until finally all that's left are

gypsophila and Judas' pennies. Paulina,
the gardener's daughter, sees a bouquet in the vase

even when it's not there anymore.

(Translated, from the Polish, by Antonia Lloyd-Jones.)

MEGAN FERNANDES

SHANGHAI

I fell in love many times these months
with certain evenings,
the city awash in green Neptune light.
When I was low, I was low.
And the city welcomed it, wrestled
a steady heat from my melancholy.
To be *shanghaied* once meant
to be kidnapped against your will
during a shortage of sailors.
Some were forced to sign with guns to their temples.
Others, beat unconscious, woke
to the wide roaring sea, ready to serve.
It was violent. Today, the bright plazas
speed us into manic dream,
the kind where you know
your executioner is coming
and we all get high
on the fluorescence and doom.
This is a place where I've let people down.
But the penance is different.
Not like New York with her sad gargoyles.
Instead, Shanghai has her young, surveilling moonlight.
Outside, a wild and holy river runs full of tanks
and neon boats peppered below a bulbous skyline.
I fed a cat here. And named her.
Creaturely orange, she disappeared on Hankou Road.
It broke up my whole day. I had that small burst of fantasy

of our life together, me and her,
a new origin story that keeps repeating.
It says: here, here, here. An eternal present that keeps loss at bay.
That is the trick of this city. It looks like a weird hope,
the human species struck by a wondrous asymmetry.
There is a dimension where the cat stays.
Where I stay, too. There is a version
where the world goes uncrushed,
and instead my beloveds multiply,
and with them, their laughters.
We all wake to simultaneous dawns
breaking over Hong Kong and Nairobi,
Guatemala City and Madrid.
When one beloved says good morning,
another says, good morning.
And for another, maybe it is still night.
Here it comes again. Night.
It starts over, but this time
we have tails and survive.
We come when called.

AMANDA GORMAN

SHIP'S MANIFEST

Allegedly the worst is behind us.
Still, we crouch before the lip of tomorrow,
Halting like a headless hant in our own house,
Waiting to remember exactly
What it is we're supposed to be doing.

& what exactly are we supposed to be doing?
Penning a letter to the world as a daughter of it.
We are writing with vanishing meaning,
Our words water dragging down a windshield.
The poet's diagnosis is that what we have lived
Has already warped itself into a fever dream,
The contours of its shape stripped from the murky mind.

To be accountable we must render an account:
Not what was said, but what was meant.
Not the fact, but what was felt.
What was known, even while unnamed.
Our greatest test will be
Our testimony.
This book is a message in a bottle.
This book is a letter.
This book does not let up.
This book is awake.
This book is a wake.
For what is a record but a reckoning?
The capsule captured?
A repository.
An ark articulated?
& the poet, the preserver
Of ghosts & gains,
Our demons & dreams,
Our haunts & hopes.
Here's to the preservation
Of a light so terrible.

LUCIE BROCK-BROIDO

GIRAFFE

In another life, he was Caesar's pet, perhaps a gift from Cleopatra
When she returned to Rome   Her hair salty and sapphired
From bathing, the winged kohl around her eyes smudged
        From heat.   In another life, he was from Somalia
        Where he spent hours watching clouds
In shapes of feral acrobats tipping along their tightropes
Spun of camels' hair and jute.
        His eyes were liquid, kind.
        His lashes each as long as a hummingbird's tongue.
His fetlocks puffed from galloping, his tail curled upward
From the joy of feeling fleet across the tinted grasslands
        And the gold savannahs there.

DECLARATION

He has

        sent hither swarms of Officers to harass our people.

He has plundered our—

              ravaged our—

                    destroyed the lives of our—

taking away our—

            abolishing our most valuable—

and altering fundamentally the Forms of our—

In every stage of these Oppressions We have Petitioned for Redress in the most humble terms:

                  Our repeated

Petitions have been answered only by repeated injury.

We have reminded them of the circumstances of our emigration and settlement here.

          —taken Captive

                on the high Seas

                    to bear—

SASHA DEBEVEC-McKENNEY
KAEPERNICK

My mother is uncomfortable with my top.
She doesn't think my boobs should be
out like this. She adjusts the TV antenna and says
Isn't the TV working better now? I don't want
to watch football. I am trying to learn to do my makeup.
My mother never taught me. Should I say at this point
that my mother is white? I used to watch Pantene commercials
and think my hair could look like that if I used enough
of her product. She has one of those white-mom
haircuts now. It is thinning. She needs more volume.
She needs me to tell her I know I'm white, too.
Like I think about anything else. The football players
are kneeling because, I say, anyone could kill
your Black son. He's white, too, she says—and you
could use a little more eyeliner. She wonders
why I don't want her to help me pick out foundation.
The football players stand up. Then they play football.

HAI-DANG PHAN
OSPREY

Swelling out of the ocean like a bad feeling,
heard before seen slouching toward Miramar
over Venice Beach, it's the Bell Boeing V-22,
not sleek but versatile, able to launch
from Al Asad, fly to Mudaysis, perform pickup,
then return, all within the golden hour,
fast enough to outrun a difficult past,
the budgetary hurdles and crashes in R. & D.,
the $72-million price tag, flyaway,
its many modes, and we think moods;
you remember its namesake in another state,

fled from some outer dark, gliding above
the diamond, from left field to center,
where it made its home up in the stadium lights,
a crown of wooden swords for its nest,
hovering in the swampy air like forethought
as the crack of a bat sent a tiny moon
into orbit, a wave rippling through
the crowd, the lights on their tall stems
powered on, day powered down,
and you had no team, you did not know
whom to root for, home or away.

NICK FLYNN

THE DAY LOU REED DIED

It's not like his songs are going to simply
evaporate,

but since the news I can't stop
listening to him

on endless shuffle—familiar, yes, inside
me, yes, which means

I'm alive, or was, depending on when
you read this. Now

a song called "Sad
Song," the last one on "Berlin,"

sung now from the other side, just talk,
really, at the beginning, then

the promise
or threat, *I'm gonna stop wasting*

my time, but what else
are we made of, especially now? A chorus

sings *Sad song sad song sad song sad*

song. I
knew him better than I knew my own

father, which means
through these songs, which means

not at all. They died on the same day, O
what a perfect day, maybe

at the same moment, maybe
both their bodies are laid out now in

the freezer, maybe side by side, maybe
holding hands, waiting

for the fire or the earth or the man
or the salt—

if I could I'd let birds devour whatever's left
& carry them into the sky, but all I can do

it seems
is lie on the couch & shiver, pull a coat

over my body as if it were all I had, as if I
were the one sleeping outside, as if it were my

body something was leaving, rising up
from inside me

& the coat could hold it inside
maybe a little longer.

EILEEN MYLES
DISSOLUTION

sometimes I forget what country I'm in
I could write poems in bed
I think
have some Americans
look at your awful mov-
ie to tell you when
you're wrong
& just racist. I got this bug bite
      that could be anything.
Got no new information
to send across. I'm willing
to embrace new sorta cray-
ony tone
      scribbled version
of empty so it's kind
of full. A kid could draw this world
it
had been lived in
so long.

You forgot
to call your family
& now you're ready to write an
explicit
bible of love.

The ripple
of experience is the
only beauty here.

My coloring book
why not is so
like a movie. And I just hand you this damp
coloring book
I say there. That's my model.

Not the kind of laminate
shit you can bring
in the tub. I'm not making some
picture book of bourgeois
life. A damp
coloring book
is naturally
orange. You left
it outside   *now* you want to save
it?   It's still good
      and that's your secret.

How did a mosquito
get under these sheets. Knocking
against my calf. They
stop when I stop
thinking about them. The book
that was my very
private thing
is gone.

MARGARET ATWOOD

FLATLINE

Things wear out. Also fingers.
Gnarling sets in.
Your hands crouch in their mittens.
Forget chopsticks, and buttons.

Feet have their own agendas.
They scorn your taste in shoes
and ignore your trails, your maps.

Ears are superfluous:
What are they for,
those alien pink flaps?
Skull fungus.

The body, once your accomplice,
is now your trap.
The sunrise makes you wince:
too bright, too flamingo.

After a lifetime of tangling,
of knotted snares and lacework,
of purple headspace tornados
with their heartrace and rubble,
you crave the end of mazes

and pray for a white shore,
an ocean with its horizon;
not, so much, bliss
but a flat line you steer for.

No more hiss and slosh,
no reefs, no deeps,
no throat rattle of gravel.

It sounds like this:

ELLEN BASS
INDIGO

As I'm walking on West Cliff Drive, a man runs
toward me pushing one of those jogging strollers
with shock absorbers so the baby can keep sleeping,
which this baby is. I can just get a glimpse
of its almost translucent eyelids. The father is young,
a jungle of indigo and carnelian tattooed
from knuckle to jaw, leafy vines and blossoms,
saints and symbols. Thick wooden plugs pierce
his lobes and his sunglasses testify
to the radiance haloed around him. I'm so jealous.
As I often am. It's a kind of obsession.
I want him to have been my child's father.

I want to have married a man who wanted
to be in a body, who wanted to live in it so much
that he marked it up like a book, underlining,
highlighting, writing in the margins, I was *here*.
Not like my dead ex-husband, who was always
fighting against the flesh, who sat for hours
on his zafu chanting *om* and then went out
and broke his hand punching the car.
I imagine when this galloping man gets home
he's going to want to have sex with his wife,
who slept in late, and then he'll eat
barbecued ribs and let the baby teethe on a bone
while he drinks a cold dark beer. I can't stop
wishing my daughter had had a father like that.
I can't stop wishing I'd had that life. Oh, I know
it's a miracle to have a life. Any life at all.
It took eight years for my parents to conceive me.
First there was the war and then just waiting.
And my mother's bones so narrow, she had to be slit
and I airlifted. That anyone is born,
each precarious success from sperm and egg
to zygote, embryo, infant, is a wonder.
And here I am, alive.
Almost seventy years and nothing has killed me.
Not the car I totalled running a stop sign
or the spirochete that screwed into my blood.
Not the tree that fell in the forest exactly
where I was standing—my best friend shoving me
backward so I fell on my ass as it crashed.
I'm alive.
And I gave birth to a child.
So she didn't get a father who'd sling her
onto his shoulder. And so much else she didn't get.
I've cried most of my life over that.
And now there's everything that we can't talk about.
We love—but cannot take
too much of each other.
Yet she is the one who, when I asked her to kill me

if I no longer had my mind—
we were on our way into Ross,
shopping for dresses. That's something
she likes and they all look adorable on her—
she's the only one
who didn't hesitate or refuse
or waver or flinch.
As we strode across the parking lot
she said, O.K., but when's the cutoff?
That's what I need to know.

WHAT DID I LOVE

What did I love about killing the chickens? Let me start
with the drive to the farm as darkness
was sinking back into the earth.
The road damp and shining like the snail's silver
ribbon and the orchard
with its bony branches. I loved the yellow rubber
aprons and the way Janet knotted my broken strap.
And the stainless-steel altars
we bleached, Brian sharpening
the knives, testing the edge on his thumbnail. All eighty-eight Cornish
hens huddled in their crates. Wrapping my palms around
their white wings, lowering them into the tapered urn.
Some seemed unwitting as the world narrowed;
some cackled and fluttered; some struggled.
I gathered each one, tucked her bright feet,
drew her head through the kill cone's sharp collar,
her keratin beak and the rumpled red vascular comb
that once kept her cool as she pecked in her mansion of grass.
I didn't look into those stone eyes. I didn't ask forgiveness.
I slid the blade between the feathers
and made quick crescent cuts, severing
the arteries just under the jaw. Blood like liquor
pouring out of the bottle. When I see the nub of heart later,
it's hard to believe such a small star could flare
like that. I lifted each body, bathing it in heated water

until the scaly membrane of the shanks
sloughed off under my thumb.
And after they were tossed in the large plucking drum
I loved the newly naked birds. Sundering
the heads and feet neatly at the joints, a poor
man's riches for golden stock. Slitting a fissure
reaching into the chamber,
freeing the organs, the spill of intestines, blue-tinged gizzard,
the small purses of lungs, the royal hearts,
easing the floppy liver, carefully, from the green gall bladder,
its bitter bile. And the fascia unfurling
like a transparent fan. When I tug the esophagus
down through the neck, I love the suck and release
as it lets go. Then slicing off the anus with its gray pearl
of shit. Over and over, my hands explore
each cave, learning to see with my fingertips. Like a traveller
in a foreign country, entering church after church.
In every one the same figures of the Madonna, Christ on the Cross,
which I'd always thought was gore
until Marie said to her it was tender,
the most tender image, every saint and political prisoner,
every jailed poet and burning monk.
But though I have all the time in the world
to think thoughts like this, I don't.
I'm empty as I rinse each carcass,
and this is what I love most.
It's like when the refrigerator turns off and you hear
the silence. As the sun rose higher
we shed our sweatshirts and moved the coolers into the shade,
but, other than that, no time passed.
I didn't get hungry. I didn't want to stop.
I was breathing from some bright reserve.
We twisted each pullet into plastic, iced and loaded them in the cars.
I loved the truth. Even in just this one thing:
looking straight at the terrible,
one-sided accord we make with the living of this world.
At the end, we scoured the tables, hosed the dried blood,
the stain blossoming through the water.

JOAN MURRAY

THE EL

No one ever grabbed my ass on the stairs down to
the D. But on the stairs up to the El, it happened
all the time. I guess it was anatomically more natural,
like reaching for an apple, but the first time,
I wasn't sure how to feel. I think I felt warm,
which wasn't an emotion. It felt like a rite of passage,
though I'd never heard of rites of passage.
Disgusting is what I said when I told my friends.
A grown man. I was twelve then. It felt like flattery.

From the El, I could look into other people's windows,
but if I saw them at all, what they were doing mostly
were the same kinds of nothings we did in our own
apartment. What I usually saw were their curtains
blowing in and out, 'cause their windows were wide open.
It wasn't like the High Line, where many years later
I saw two men in a hotel room doing a performance
just for me. The High Line used to be an El. It still is in a way,
though it's covered with flowers. And I'm the train.

When I turned nineteen and got married, I went to live
up by Mt. Eden. It was cheap and noisy and the El
ran below our window and our daughter died and we were
still in school and took the D train to Manhattan now.
But coming home one night, I looked up and saw curtains
blowing in and out of someone's window. I was on an El,
I don't know where, or how I made it home. It wasn't our El,
but it's the El I dream about: I've just come down the stairs,
and now I've got to figure it out. Up on the platform
you could buy peanuts from a dispenser and either
give them to the pigeons or eat them yourself.

CHASE TWICHELL

FEATHERWEIGHT

At fourteen, I taught myself to sew
on a Singer Featherweight,

which I was an idiot to trade
years later when seduced by a Bernina.

As a child, I made clothes, costumes—
things a feral kid would wear, or Huckleberry Finn.

The only tricky part of sewing is the fitting,
making clothes that fit exactly right.

The actual sewing is easy—it's just
manual dexterity, patience, and precision.

Fitting is geometry and math.
Geometry comes to me easily,

but math is an old childhood enemy.
Its door remains locked. Why?

Because Mrs. E. was drunk, so the second grade
skipped multiplication and division in 1957?

Was that when the trouble began?
Does it date to the Summer of Catching Up?

The writhing and moaning
over the multiplication tables?

I was seven. He was my babysitter.
I wasn't injured. No one knew.

I knew. He was a friend of the family.
It had nothing to do with math.

To me, the geometry's simple.
You dismantle a body's measurements

into shapes traced on featherweight vellum:
the sleeve, the bodice, the skirt.

The parts of the body reunite
when the garment is sewn,

and the dress or the pants appear,
held together only by thread.

MARIE HOWE

REINCARNATION

Sometimes when I look at our dog Jack I think
he might be my Radical American History professor come back to
    make amends
—he gazes at me so sorrowfully.

What is it Jack, I say, why do you look like that? But Jack
doesn't answer; he lies down and rests his head on his paws.

Black hair covered nearly all of that man's body, thick
under his blue oxford shirt when I put my hand there.
Perhaps that accounted for the bow tie,
the pipe, the tweed cap.

This time I can teach him to sit and to stay.
Stay, I say to Jack, who looks at the treat in my hand
and then at me, and at the treat and then at me, and he stays.

Come, I say to Jack, but Jack does not always come.
Sometimes he sits and looks at me a long time
as when my professor would lean back in his chair
draw on his pipe and gaze at me.

But when I hold a treat Jack comes, and I remember how
the professor would lick dripping honey from the jar
lick peanut butter from the knife.

A little stubborn, our dog Jack,
shy, we thought
until the morning my daughter jumped on my bed
and Jack sprang at her growling.

And the next morning, when he rushed toward her growling
and bit her skirt and tore it, and bit her and broke her skin,
and when I went to collar him, bit me, snarling, and bit and bit.

That's when I was pretty sure he was my history professor.

The vet said this happens more often than you'd imagine.
He must always be tethered, she said, until he can be trusted.
He must learn that you and your daughter come first.
And no more couch, and no more sleeping in the bed with you, Mama,
not ever.

I finally left him so late at night it was nearly dawn—
picking up my boots by the door,
stepping down the two flights, then running toward the car.

What can I say? Jack may be my American History professor come
        back,
after all these years, to make amends,

or Jack may be actually himself—a dog.

ARIA ABER

ZELDA FITZGERALD

It's true I hate the stories about the other women,
but I love the description of their daily lives, like the scene
with twelve raspberry cakes in a French café,

or the drunkard asking for the way. A bottle of whiskey
on a heavy walnut table, my husband's hands on a glass.
No one's muses are believable, said the painter
whom I loved for twelve weeks and who would
rarely touch me. To him, the female body
was a plant: it needed to be tended and spoken
to, but too much warmth would spoil the matter.
In his paintings that I like best, women wander through cities
and notice objects. Lanterns. Hats they can't
afford. Little glasses of Pernod. I loved him
to hurt the other one, whom I loved more. And so,
most of my life, it passes like this: light touching
my skin, lying on the floor among my diaries, writing of him——
What did Proust say, months before he passed away?
I have great news. Last night, I wrote "The End,"
so now I can die. Oh! Had I known the boredom that my talents
had in store for me, I would still have asked for them.

EVIE SHOCKLEY

THE BLESSINGS

i gave mine away—
not all, but the greater portion,
some would say. i gave
away the ready claim
to goodness, to purpose. i gave
away mary, sarai,
and isis. i gave away
necessity and invention.
i gave away a whole
holiday, but i kept billie.
i gave away the chance to try
and fail to have it all. i gave
away the one thing
that makes some men
pay. i gave away the pedestal,
the bouquet. i gave away

nel wright, but i kept sula
peace. i gave away
the fine-tooth comb, but
kept the oyster knife. i gave
away the first word
the new mouth forms, the easiest
to parlay across so many
languages. escaping
the maw, i gave away
the power to hold—and be held
in—sway, but i kept
cho, parton, finney, chapman,
and tomei. i gave away the eve
who left the garden
that day, but kept the cool,
green, shady, fruitless,
fruitful stay, the evening
that did not fall
away.

JOHN LEE CLARK

A PROTACTILE VERSION OF "TINTERN ABBEY"

When I smelled the smoke, I knew
Where I was. Okay. There is water
Flowing along our flank here, and here
Near our knee is an old church.
But let us scroll up our leg
A few times. Here, inhale the smoke.
Our cold-tipped nose sniffing the back
Of our fourth hand, we hand-heel
Our lap's thick turf. Houses with pastures
That—give me an edifice—rub up
Against the very fingernails! The grass continues
Back to the brash water, and here
I need a cave. Thank you. Perhaps

Someone is holed up in there, tending
To flames that tickle your palm warm.
But never mind. Let us rove ahead
To where I found—give me tree.
Heavy with foliage. Can you feel that?
Now a claw for the knobby roots
Where I laid my head and crumbled
Clumps of dirt that I brushed off.
I had been here before, and then—

Let me think. A fist? No, no.
Give me an upturned claw, and feel
It swaying because of the rolling sun
Bumping into finger planets. . . . You were right!
We do need a fist after all.
Sliding the fire out of our palm,
We fold those thimbles into one world.
It makes perfect sense for the sun
To claim our shoulder! Our muscular star,
Our many-jointed sphere, our electric arm:
All shaking and snapping through five cycles
Of sweat and blizzard, each wobbly turn
A summons. We have indeed come back
To breathe in sweet Earth's smoky hand.

DIANE *SEUSS*

ROMANTIC POETRY

Now that the TV is gone and the music
has been hauled away,
it's just me here, and the muffling silence
a spider wraps around a living morsel.
And at times, often, the unbearable.
I bear it, though, just like you.
Long ago, I bore a suitcase filled with books,
bore it far on city streets. To sell, I guess, at some

used-books place, one of those doorways down
steps into dankness and darkness. The scent

of mildewed, dog-eared, fingered pages.
The suitcase, big and square and sharp-cornered,
covered in snakeskin, bought at Goodwill
for a dollar, knowing I had some travelling to do,
some lugging, and I was right.
What books I sold I do not know.
Maybe that's where "Modern Poetry" went.
The cover cherry-red and blossom-white.
I can see its spine in my mind's eye,
pointing downward beneath the dank

and the dark to the water tunnelling
under the city and making its way to the river.
Poems sliding down the book's spine
into water, the shock of the cold and dank,
down where my uterine lining, my blood
and cast-off ovulations, cast-off fetal
tissue swims, below the city.
The micro-dead ride modern poems
like swan boats in the park.
From the park to the river to the sea.

I'm thinking now of PJ Harvey and Nick Cave.
Balladeers. Lovers. Vita and Virginia.
Frank O'Hara and Vincent Warren. Somehow,
we ride our lost loves out to sea. Or they ride us.
It doesn't matter. Poet or poem or reader, the same
ectoplasm. The modern, in time, becomes antique,
and the stone faces of the dead convert to symbols,
ripe for smashing. Come to think of it,
symbols are terrible. As the tyrant
shouted to the masses,

part of his brainwashing campaign:
I know it, and you know it, too.

I was twenty-three when I sold off
"Modern Poetry" and sailed to Italy, seeking
Romantic poetry, which was at one time
modern, and found my way to Rome,
and Keats's death room.
His deathbed, a facsimile.
Everything he touched was burned,
to kill what killed him.

I lifted his death mask from its nail,
cradled it, closed my eyes and kissed his lips
until the plaster warmed,
and stained his face
with the lipstick on my lips. Red
as the cover of "Modern Poetry."
The color of the droplets of arterial blood
he coughed onto his sheets, and viewed
by candlelight. Then he knew he was done for.
His death warrant, he called it.

After those many kisses over his face and eyes,
and the reticulated eyelashes,
cold and tangled,
my lips were blossom-white,
my face, chalked. Like I'd caught
something from him,
and I don't just mean consumption,
though my lungs burned for years.
They still burn.
This is the danger of the ecstasy of kissing

the dead or dying poet on the mouth.
The disease you'll catch—well,
it changes you.
The tingle in the spine,
the erotic charge, will be forever married
to poetry's previous incarnations.
It's why marriage itself never worked for me.

I kept wanting to get to the part
where death parts us
and I could find myself again.

Keats made such a compact corpse.
Only five feet tall, shorter than Prince,
and intricately made. Always,
he was working it, working it out,
the meaning of suffering, the world's,
his own, the encounter with beauty,
nearly synonymous with suffering,
how empathy could extinguish him,
and he could set down the suitcase at last,
or finally deliver him to himself, distinct

as the waves in his hair and the bridge
of his nose. How auspicious,
rare, lush,
bizarre, kinky, transcendent,
romantic, to be young, just twenty-three,
and to cradle him
in my arms, as we listened
to the burbling water
of the Fontana della Barcaccia
from the open window.

KIMIKO HAHN

AFTER BEING ASKED IF I WRITE THE "OCCASIONAL POEM"

After leaving Raxruhá, after
crossing Mexico with a coyote,
after reaching at midnight
that barren New Mexico border,
a man and his daughter
looked to Antelope Wells

for asylum and were arrested. After
forms read in Spanish
to the Mayan-speaking father,
after a cookie but no water, after
the wait for the lone bus
to return for their turn, after boarding,
after the little girl's temperature spiked,
she suffered two heart attacks,
vomited, and stopped breathing. After
medics revived the seven-year-old
at Lordsburg station, after she was flown
to El Paso, where she died,
the coroner examined
the failed liver and swollen brain. Then
Jakelin's chest and head were stitched up
and she returned to Guatemala
in a short white coffin
to her mother, grandparents,
and dozens of women preparing
tamales and beans to feed the grieving.
In Q'eqchi', *w-e* means *mouth*.

VONA GROARKE

THIS POEM

This is the poem that won't open
no matter where you press.

This is the poem that cries on street corners
and plays at being lost.

This is the poem arranged at a tilt
so all the words slide off.

This is the poem with lacquered roses
closing in on themselves after dark.

This is the poem that plays itself out
in dives in the small hours.

This poem likes to fool around
in other people's cars.

This poem gives away small coins
and winks at strangers' kids.

This is the poem that understands
what it is to be a dog.

This is the poem with a teensy tattoo
you'll never get to see.

This poem has no big plans for you,
which is something, as poems go.

SANDRA CISNEROS

TEA DANCE, PROVINCETOWN, 1982

At the boy bar, no
one
danced with me.

I danced with
every
one.

The entire
room.
Every song.

That's what was so
great
about the boy bars
then.

The room vibrated.
Shook.
Convulsed.

In one
collective
zoological
frenzy.

Truthfully,
I was the
only woman
there.

Who cared?
At the Boatslip,
I was welcomed.

The girl bar
down the street?
Pfft!
Dull as Brillo.

But the tea dances shimmied,
miraculous as mercury.
Acrid stink of sweat and
chlorine tang of semen.

Slippery male energy.
Something akin to
watching horses fighting.
Something exciting.

My lover,
the final summer he was bi,
introduced me to the teas.
Often hovered out of sight,
distracted by poolside

beauties, while I danced
content/innocent
with the room of men.

He was a skittish kite, that one.
Kites swerve and swoop and whoop.
Only a matter of time, I knew.
Apropos, I called him
"my little piece of string."
And that's what kites
leave you with in the end.

There was an expiration date
to summer. Understood.
That season,
I was experimenting to be
the woman I wanted to be.

Taught myself to sun
topless at the gay beach,
where sunbathers
shouted "ranger,"
a relayed warning
announcing authority,
en route on horseback,
coming to inspect
if we were clothed.
Else fined. Fifty
dollars sans bottom.
One hundred, topless.
Fifty a tit, I joked.

It was easy to be half naked
at a gay beach. Men
didn't bother to look.
I was in training to be
a woman without shame.

Not a shameless woman,
una sinvergüenza, but
una sin vergüenza
glorious in her skin.
Flesh akin to pride.
I shed that summer
not only bikini top but
guilt-driven Eve and
self-immolating Fatima.

Was practicing for
my Minoan days ahead.
Medusa hair and breasts
spectacular as Nike of Samothrace
welcoming the salty wind.
Yes, I was a lovely thing then.

I can say this with impunity.
At twenty-eight, she was a woman
unrelated to me. I could
tell stories. Have so many to tell
and none to tell them to
except the page.
My faithful confessor.

Lover and I feuded
one night when he
wouldn't come home with me.
His secret—herpes.
Laughable in retrospect,
considering the Plague
was already decimating dances
across the globe.

But that was before
we knew it as the Plague.

We were all on the run in '82.
Jumping to Laura Branigan's "Gloria,"
the summer's theme song.
Beat thumping in our blood.
Drinks sweeter than bodies
convulsing on the floor.

DANEZ SMITH

UNDETECTABLE

soundless, it crosses a line, quiets into a seed

& then whatever makes a seed. almost like gone

but not gone. the air kept its shape. not antimatter

but the memory of matter. or of it mattering. it doesn't

cross my mind now that it whispers so soft it's almost

silence. but it's not. someone dragged the screaming boy

so deep into the woods he sounds like the trees now.

gone enough. almost never here. daily, swallowed

within a certain window, a pale-green trail on the tongue

the pale-green pill makes before it's divvied among

the ghettos of blood, dissolves & absolves

my scarlet brand. ritual & proof. surely science

& witchcraft have the same face. my mother

praises god for this & surely it is his face too.

regimen, you are my miracle. this swallowing

my muscular cult. i am not faithful to much.

i am less a genius of worship than i let on.

but the pill, emerald dialect singing the malady

away. not away. far enough. for now.

i am the most important species in my body.

but one dead boy makes the whole forest

a grave. & he's in there, in me, in the middle

of all that green. you probably thought

he was fruit.

MAX RITVO
POEM TO MY LITTER

My genes are in mice, and not in the banal way
that Man's old genes are in the Beasts.

My doctors split my tumors up and scattered them
into the bones of twelve mice. We give

the mice poisons I might, in the future, want
for myself. We watch each mouse like a crystal ball.

I wish it was perfect, but sometimes the death we see
doesn't happen when we try it again in my body.

My tumors are old, older than mice can be.
They first grew in my flank, a decade ago.

Then they went to my lungs, and down my femurs,
and into the hives in my throat that hatch white cells.

The mice only have a tumor each, in the leg.
Their tumors have never grown up. Uprooted

and moved. Learned to sleep in any bed
the vast body turns down. Before the tumors can spread,

they bust open the legs of the mice. Who bleed to death.
Next time the doctors plan to cut off the legs

in the nick of time so the tumors will spread.
But I still have both my legs. To complicate things further,

mouse bodies fight off my tumors. We have to give
the mice AIDS so they'll harbor my genes.

I want my mice to be just like me. I don't have any children.
I named them all Max. First they were Max 1, Max 2,

but now they're all just Max. No playing favorites.
They don't know they're named, of course.

They're like children you've traumatized
and tortured so they won't let you visit.

I hope, Maxes, some good in you is of me.
Even my suffering is good, in part. Sure, I swell

with rage, fear—the stuff that makes you see your tail
as a bar on the cage. But then the feelings pass.

And since I do absolutely nothing (my pride, like my fur,
all gone) nothing happens to me. And if a whole lot

of nothing happens to you, Maxes, that's peace.
Which is what we want. Trust me.

ANSELM BERRIGAN

PREGRETS

I spent a certain amount of cash at Forbidden Planet
Tower Records, the corner store on 9th & 1st, southeast
corner, the corner store on 9th & 1st southwest corner
the corner store on 7th & 1st, northwest corner, the
candy shop on 1st between 7th & 8th with the Mr. Do!
standup video game, the pizza parlor on St. Marks &
A, southwest corner with Moon Patrol, the candy shoppe
on A between 8th & 9th with Double Dragon, the corner
store on St. Marks & A, northwest corner, that preceded
Nino's Pizzeria, Oscar's newstand on St. Marks & 1st
Garibaldi's groceries with the buggy booberry cereal on
9th & 1st, northwest corner, the Yankee Stadium right
field bleachers, Gem Spa's video game alcove on the St.
Marks side, & I want, I want to be paid properly for my
childhood acting career, no powdered candy, no welcome
to golden folks as forks, roll-tap consolation, it's gonna
be really really hurt, your shot, beard at bad & gives
still can't mishandle the low strike, low helicopter
hover in the pen, aluminum dog uploads obey the love-
me principles, kick to metaphorical id, tomorrow's
probable parables charting chromophobes, the promise
of another person walking by makes an empty street
so frightening in the sketch, chase on the walk-off de-
flection, the walk-off bobble, splinter of consciousness
in the old open bowl head, don't tell the aleatories
they're being aggressive, a cabbie ran that candy shop
on 11th & 1st when it was a candy shop & he wasn't
a cabbie he told me, front to back, through his cab's slot

MEENA ALEXANDER

KOCHI BY THE SEA

The tin roof of the hospital has claw marks—
Bruised indigo

The kind you left on your thigh
That awful night when no one could come near you.

On the road from the hospital
You pass me the prescription—Same?

I peer then nod, shortsighted already.
You crane your neck, point out rain clouds

Noke—the sky has pink streaks shiny as a shell.
You always saw those things so well

You were the artistic one, keen and lovely.
I was your shadow self, strolling into water

Lying in wait for boys
So they could burn away the hurt in me

My hair black and angular
Cut into wedge shapes, flapping like sails.

At six you hid in the attic
Scrawling half-inch creatures

Scarlet word balloons jostling their lips,
Radiant ciphers no one could tell

Your imaginary friends, Susie Kali with corkscrew curls,
Mad Thoma axe in hand.

Sometimes you gathered stray cats, fed them milk
From Mama's refrigerator, bits of bread soaked in honey

You sang to them O Shenandoah
Your voice rising to the locust trees.

This road is covered with rocks and dirt
Buses with pilgrims hurtle past

You squint at a boy pedalling his cycle rickshaw
Close, far too close, drops of mud splatter us both.

You lean sideways, touch my cheek—
Let's live in Kochi by the sea

Find a house with a white balcony,
I think the angels will call on me.

LIZZIE HARRIS
LAW OF THE BODY

She who never wanted children who took pills not to have them
who took pills when she feared she would she who waited for the
right job the right partner the right moment to even open to the
idea of them she who carried them she whose organs went two-
dimensional to make space who grew a new organ whose own body
bowed to the needs of the idea of something she who vomited
every day for eleven weeks who travelled with sour candies in a
bag until her tongue bled she who bled calmly on the phone with
the doctor she who slept on the floor of an empty office she who
lowered her doses of all the medicines that made her want to live in
the first place she who fed the body that fed the body on nothing
but raw corn and vitamins she who grew forty pounds and carried
it to and from the bus to the subway to the walk to work and
back again she who took a course on labor and labored for days
she who heard the nurse say *perhaps she has a low tolerance for pain*
and thought back to when a mirror shattered her body and her
father unsure of how to stop the bleeding put her in two pairs of
sweatpants until they soaked through she who knows punishment

is always a negotiation of tolerance she who lost consciousness
when the epidural did its job too well who stomached three shots
of ephedrine to breathe again so the child inside could breathe
again she who they raced into surgery whose abdomen was sawed
through and stitched up she who held the baby covered in her own
insides who itched for days from withdrawal who loved the baby
instantly who fed the baby until she passed out who gave up sleep
and time and mind and heart she who gave so generously of her
body over and over only to have them say it was never hers to give

ANDREA COHEN

ROOSEVELT DARGON

Roosevelt Dargon, how often I have thought of you
and your leg. We were driving that last stretch
of slow road home, in snow and ice, in the blue
Vista Cruiser—what was I, five?—when your big
rig crashed. We didn't see it happen, but got there
right after, before the ambulance and cops, before
the snarl of cars that would have kept us from
reaching you. I say *us*, but what I mean is my father,
who told my brothers and me, *Stay here*, while my mother
toggled between static and Tommy Dorsey and he ran
to the jackknifed cab and found you pinned in there,
left leg mostly severed but tethered enough under
the crushed front dash to keep several bigger men
from pulling you out. There was a lot of blood you
were losing, and the tumbled lumber and concrete
blocks from the load you'd been hauling, and the smashed
glass of cling peaches in syrup from the truck you'd
swerved into, and all around you fuel was pooling,
collecting, threatening to catch fire, and I have to imagine
what you would have heard: my father's voice, calm
and measured, saying, *I'm a doctor*. He might not have
said *a psychiatrist*. What he showed you was
his Swiss Army knife, what he did was ask

permission to finish what the accident had started—
to cut the tendon, cleanly, to free you. I guess
we never know which part of ourselves we'll
have to sacrifice, or when we might need to say
to a stranger with a pocketknife, *I'd be obliged*.
And that was that. They pulled you out. Someone
may have grabbed the mangled leg as an after-
thought, but this was 1966, before the age
of reattachments. My father knelt in the snow
and wiped his knife blade clean. This was before
there would be people on the road we could
not help, before the next Christmas, and the ones
after that, when a crate of oranges would come
from Baltimore, with a card that said *Best
wishes from the leg and me*, never specifying
which leg you meant—the one you kept
or the one you let go. What the mind
keeps, it keeps. I still have my mother
humming "I Thought About You," still
have my brothers punching each other
in the wayback, still have my father,
still running with his Swiss
Army, as if he could, in some
coming blizzard, save us all.

NICK LAIRD

FEEL FREE

I

To deal with all the sensational loss I like to interface
with Earth. I like to do this in a number of ways.
I like to feel the work I am exerting being changed,

the weight of my person refigured, and I like to hang
above the ground, thus; hammocks, snorkeling, alcohol.
I also like the mind to feel a kind of neutral buoyancy

and to that end I set aside a day a week, Shabbat,
to not act. Having ceded independence to the sunset
I will not be shaving, illuminating rooms, or raising

the temperature of food. If occasionally I like to feel
the leavening of being near a much larger unnatural
tension, I walk off a Sunday through the high fields

of blanket bog, saxifrage, a few thin Belted Galloways,
rounding Lough Mallon to stand by the form of beauty
upheld in a scrubby acre at Creggandevsky, where I do

duck and enter under a capstone mapped by rival empires
of yellow feather-moss and powdery white lichen. I like
then to stop, crouched, and press my back on a housing

of actual rock, coldness which lives for a while on the skin.
And I like when I give you the nightfeed, Harvey, how you're
really concentrating on it: fists clenched, eyes shut, like *this* is bliss.

‖
I like a steady disruption. I like it when the solid mantle turns
to shingle and water rushes up it over and over, in love.
My white-noise machine from Argos is set to Crashing Wave

but I'm not averse to the presence of numerous and minute
quanta moving very fast in unison; occasions when a light
wind undulates the ears of wheat, or a hessian sack of pearl-

barley seed is sliced with a pocket knife and pours. I like
the way it sounds pattering on stone. I like how the starlings
over Monti cohere and separate their bodies into one cyclonic

symphony, and I like that the hawk of the mind catches at
their purse, pulse, caul, arc. I like the excitation passing as
a shadow-ripple back and how the bag is snatched, rolls

slack; straight, falciform; mouthing; bulbing; a pumping
heart. I like to interface with millions of colored pixels
depicting attractive people procreating on a screen itself

dependent on rare metals mined by mud-gray children
who trudge up bamboo scaffolding above a grayish-red lake
of belching mud. I like how the furnace burning earth instills

in me reflexive gestures of timidity and self-pity and deference
as I walk along the kinder surfaces, grass, say, or sand,
unable ever to meet with my eyes the gaze of the sun.

III
I can imagine that my first and fifth marriages will be
to the same human, a woman, the first marriage working
well enough that we decide to try again as soon as it's,

you know, mutually convenient. I can see that. I like the fact
that we're "supercooled star matter," even if I can't envisage you
as anything other than warm and bleating. The thing is

I can be persuaded fairly easily to initiate immune responses
by the fake safety signals of national anthems, cleavage, family
photographs, country lanes, large-eyed mammals, fireworks,

the King James Bible, Nina Simone singing "The Twelfth of Never,"
cave paintings, coffins, dolphins, dolmens. But I like it also
when the fat impasto of the canvas gets slashed by a tourist

with a claw hammer, and a glimpse is caught of what you couldn't
say. Entanglement I like, spooky action at a distance analogizing
some little thing including this long glance across the escalators

or how you know the song before you switch the station on.
When a photon of light meets a half-silvered mirror and splits
one meets the superposition of two, being twinned: and this repeats.

Tickling your back, Katherine, to get you to sleep, I like to lie here
with my eyes closed and think of my schoolfriends' houses, before
choosing one to walk through slowly, room by sunlit room.

HALA ALYAN

TOPOGRAPHY

The land is a crick in the neck. An orange grove burns
and it's sour when you burp. Whose voice is that?
There's a fable. There's a key. Every Ramadan,
the artery suffers first. A diet of heavy lamb
and checkpoint papers. Indigestion like a nightmare.
The Taurus sun burns your forehead. I mean the land.
The land looks white on the MRI images:
you call your grandfather. He's been finding the land
in his stool. His body contours the mattress like a coffin.
His hand trembles. When he drinks the land,
the urine comes out rose-colored.
The land sears the esophagus. No more lemons,
the doctor says. Two pillows at least. In July,
you lived inside your grandfather like a settlement.
You ate currant sorbet from the same cup.
Did you inherit the land in your arthritic wrist?
It makes knitting hell. On the telephone,
your grandfather tells you the land is coating his eyes.
He tells you it is worth being alive just to see that blue.
He dies and they harness his body to the dirt.
He dies and the sun is out all week.

ROBERT HAYDEN

INDIAN PIPES

Look, I said, Indian pipes,
    flowers for ghosts.
You stopped to gather a few
    of the livid blooms, then we
went on through deepening woods.
    You walk there still—
ghost flowers withering
    in your hands, long since a ghost.

TERRANCE HAYES

AMERICAN SONNET FOR MY PAST AND FUTURE ASSASSIN

The black poet would love to say his century began
With Hughes or, God forbid, Wheatley, but actually
It began with all the poetry weirdos & worriers, warriors,
Poetry whiners & winos falling from ship bows, sunset
Bridges & windows. In a second I'll tell you how little
Writing rescues. My hunch is that Sylvia Plath was not
Especially fun company. A drama queen, thin-skinned,
And skittery, she thought her poems were ordinary.
What do you call a visionary who does not recognize
Her vision? Orpheus was alone when he invented writing.
His manic drawing became a kind of writing when he sent
His beloved a sketch of an eye with an X struck through it.
He meant *I am blind without you.* She thought he meant
I never want to see you again. It is possible he meant that, too.

AMERICAN SONNET FOR MY PAST AND FUTURE ASSASSIN

Side effects include dry spells, dry coughs, dry eyes & crying,
Photosensitivity, blurred vision, trouble sleeping, trouble with gravity,

Cold feet, weight gain, weight loss, hair loss, blood lust & blood loss,
Memory loss, loss of appetite, bellyaches, headaches, heartaches,
Backaches, bruises, blueness, redness, whiteness, discoloration,
Itching, wrinkling, slouching, lying, backbiting, a taste for metal,
A taste for meddling & mixed messaging, a taste for witches'
Brews brewed by the motherfuckers who slew all the witches.
Side effects include blockages & blockades, a block-Head-of-State-
Your-business-as-usual, a block-head-strong-arm-of-the-law,
A block-head-shot-gun-point-and-shoot, down-fall-out shelters.
Side effects include nausea, dizziness, numbness, dumbness,
Dementias, deletions, leeches, letches, hexes, hoaxes, hocus-pocuses,
And, if there is justice, spiritual, moral, federal, state, & local charges.

GEORGE FLOYD

You can be a bother who dyes
his hair Dennis Rodman blue
in the face of the man kneeling in blue
in the face the music of his wrist-
watch your mouth is little more
than a door being knocked
out of the ring of fire around
the afternoon came evening's bell
of the ball and chain around the neck
of the unarmed brother ground down
to gunpowder dirt can be inhaled
like a puff the magic bullet point
of transformation both kills and fires
the life of the party like it's 1999 bottles
of beer on the wall street people
who sleep in the streets do not sleep
without counting yourself lucky
rabbit's foot of the mountain
lion do not sleep without
making your bed of the river
boat gambling there will be
no stormy weather on the water
bored to death any means of killing

time is on your side of the bed
of the truck transporting Emmett
till the break of day Emmett till
the river runs dry your face
the music of the spheres
Emmett till the end of time

CAMPBELL McGRATH

AT THE RUINS OF YANKEE STADIUM

It is that week in April when all the lions start to shine,
café tables poised for selfies, windows squeegeed
and fenceposts freshly painted around Tompkins Square,
former haven of junkies and disgraceful pigeons
today chock-full of French bulldogs and ornamental tulips
superimposed atop the old, familiar, unevictable dirt.
Lying on the couch, I am drifting with the conversation
of bees, a guttural buzz undergirding the sound
from a rusty string of wind chimes hung and forgotten
in the overgrown beech tree marooned out back,
limbs shaggy with neon-green flame-tongue leaflets
forking through a blanket of white blossoms,
long-neglected evidence of spring at its most deluxe,
pure exuberant fruitfulness run amok.
Rigorous investigation has identified two dialects
buzzing through the plunder-fall, hovering black bumblebees
and overworked honeybees neck-deep in nectar-bliss,
as the city to us, blundering against its oversaturated anthers
until the pollen coats our skin, as if sugar-dusted,
as if rolled in honey and flour to bake a cake
for the queen, yes, she is with us, it is spring and this
is her coronation, blossoming pear and crab-apple
and cherry trees, too many pinks to properly absorb,
every inch of every branch lusting after beauty.
To this riot of stimuli, this vernal bombardment
of the senses, I have capitulated without a fight.

But not the beech tree. It never falters. It is stalwart
and grounded and garlanded, a site-specific creation,
seed to rootling to this companionable giant,
tolerant and benign, how many times have I reflected
upon their superiority to our species, the trees of earth?
Reflection, self-reflection—my job is to polish the mirror,
to amplify the echoes. Even now I am hard at work,
researching the ineffable. *I loafe and invite my soul,*
for Walt Whitman is ever my companion in New York,
thronged carcass of a city in which one is never alone
and yet never un-nagged-at by loneliness, a hunger
as much for the otherness of others as for the much-sung self,
for something somewhere on the verge of realization,
for what lies around the corner, five or six blocks uptown,
hiding out in the Bronx or across the river in Jersey.
Somewhere on the streets of the city right now somebody
is meeting the love of their life for the very first time,
somebody is drinking schnapps from a paper sack
discussing Monty Python with a man impersonating a priest,
someone is waiting for the bus to South Carolina
to visit her sister in hospice, someone is teleconferencing
with the office back in Hartford, Antwerp, Osaka,
someone is dust-sweeping, throat-clearing, cart-wheeling,
knife-grinding, day-trading, paying dues, dropping a dime,
giving the hairy eyeball, pissing against a wall,
someone is snoozing, sniffling, cavorting, nibbling,
roistering, chiding, snuggling, confiding,
pub-crawling, speed-dating, pump-shining, ivy-trimming,
tap-dancing, curb-kicking, rat-catching, tale-telling,
getting lost, getting high, getting busted, breaking up,
breaking down, breaking loose, losing faith,
going broke, going green, feeling blue, seeing red,
someone is davening, busking, hobnobbing, grandstanding,
playing the ponies, feeding the pigeons, gull-watching,
wolf-whistling, badgering the witness, pulling down the grill
and locking up shop, writing a letter home in Pashto or
Xhosa, learning to play the xylophone, waiting for an Uber X,
conspiring, patrolling, transcending, bedevilling,

testifying, bloviating, absolving, kibbitzing,
kowtowing, pinky-swearing, tarring and shingling,
breaking and entering, delivering and carting away,
enwreathing lampposts with yellow ribbons,
reading Apollinaire on a bench littered with fallen petals,
waiting for an ambulance to pass before crossing First Avenue
toward home. No wonder they fear it so intensely,
the purists and isolationists in Kansas, the ideologues
in Kandahar, it is a relentless negotiation with multiplicity,
a constant engagement with the shape-shifting mob,
diversely luminous as sunlight reflecting off mirrored glass
in puzzle pieces of apostolic light. Certainly this is not
the Eternal City but it is certainly Imperial, certainly
tyrannical, democratic, demagogic, dynastic, anarchic,
hypertrophic, hyperreal. An empire of rags and photons.
An empire encoded in the bricks from which it was built,
each a stamped emblem of its labor-intensive materiality,
hundreds of millions barged down the Hudson each year
from the clay pits of Haverstraw and Kingston
after the Great Fire of 1835, a hinterland of dependencies,
quarries and factories and arterial truck farms
delivering serum to that muscular heart, a toiling collective
of Irish sandhogs and Iroquois beam walkers and Ivoirian
umbrella venders collecting kindling for the bonfire
that has lured, like moths, the entire world to its blaze.
As with my tree, the hubbub of bees its exaltation.
Apis, maker of honey, *Bombus*, the humble bumbler,
and the tree a common American beech.
It rules the yard, overawing a straggling ailanthus
hard against the wall of the Con Ed substation.
Along the fence some scraggly boxwood shrubs,
a table collapsed into rusted segments, two piles of bricks—
what's their story?—who made them, carted them,
set them as a patio, and who undid that work to create these
mundane, rain-eroded monuments to human neglect?
Why does nobody tend this little garden?
Undisciplined ivy scales the building in thick ropes
and coils of porcelain berry vine, whose fruit will ripen

to obscene brilliance come autumn, those strange berries,
turquoise, violet, azure . . . Ah, I've lost my train
of thought. Berries. The city. People, bricks, the past.
Bees in a flowering beech tree. Symbiosis. Streams and webs
and permutations, viruses replicating, mutating, evolving.
Books in a library, bricks in a wall, people in a city.
A man selling old golf clubs on the corner of Ludlow Street.
A woman on the F train carefully rubbing ointment
up and down her red, swollen arms. Acorns—
tossing them into the Hudson River from a bench as I did
when I was Peter Stuyvesant, when I was Walt Whitman,
when we were of the Lenape and Broadway our hunting trail.
Then the deer vanished, the docks decayed, the towers fell.
The African graveyard was buried beneath concrete
as the memory of slavery has been obscured by dogma
and denial. The city speaks a hundred languages,
it straddles three rivers, it holds forty islands hostage,
it is an archipelago of memory, essential and insubstantial
and evasive as the progeny of steam grates at dawn,
a gathering of apparitions. The Irish have vanished
from Washington Heights but I still see myself eating
a cold pot-roast sandwich, watching "McHale's Navy"
on black-and-white TV in my grandmother's old apartment.
I remember the parties we used to throw on Jane Street,
shots of tequila and De La Soul on the tape deck, everyone
dancing, everyone young and vibrant and vivacious—
decades later we discovered a forgotten videotape
and our sons, watching with bemused alarm, blurted out,
Mom, you were so beautiful! She was. We all were,
everyone except the city. The city was a wreck and then
it was a renovation project and now it is a playground of privilege
and soon it will be something else, liquid as a dream.
Empires come and go, ours will fade in turn, even the city
will retreat, step by step, as the Atlantic rises against it.
But water is not the end. Bricks are made of clay and sand
and when they disintegrate, when they return to silt,
new bricks will be made by hands as competent as ours.
People will live in half-flooded tenements, people will live

on houseboats moored to bank pillars along Wall Street.
It's all going under, the entire Eastern Seaboard.
The capital will move to Kansas City but nobody will mourn
for Washington. Someone will invent virtual gasoline. Someone
will write a poem called "At the Ruins of Yankee Stadium"
which will be set to a popular tune by a media impresario
and people in Ohio will sing it during the seventh-inning stretch
remembering, or imagining, the glory of what was.
Time is with us viscerally, idiomatically, time inhabits us
like a glass bowl filled with tap water at the kitchen sink,
and some little pink stones, and a sunken plastic castle
with a child's face etched in a slate-gray window.
Fish swim past, solemn as ghosts, and the child smiles sadly,
wondering, perhaps, how bees will pollinate underwater.
He seems a little melancholy. He must miss his old home,
a skin-honeyed hive of multifarious humankind,
a metropolis of stately filth doused in overrich perfume.
The castle door swings open and the boy emerges
like an astronaut stepping warily onto the moon.
When he sees us, through the warping lens of the bowl,
watching him with desperate, misfocussed passion, we are
as cartoonishly gargantuan as the past, and he as spectral
as the future, raising one small hand to wave goodbye.

MAYA PHILLIPS

BEFORE NOTRE DAME BURNED, WE WENT ON VACATION

In the grave chambers of the cathedral / we were reverent
silent // we didn't want to awaken the saints and / besides /
though votive candles and sober sermon and
venerating faithful / I had no prayers

to offer // my god was a private shame / the space between
my parents // I couldn't petition this heaven / despite

the invitation / am not so much a tourist that I'll take
another man's holy for my own / though it did

make me want to say holy / even in my godlessness / my
half-assed tourist pass through a city cramped ancient and
cobblestoned // (and yes full of lights / I wish I could've loved
such radiance) // an old world from which god

was made / and the two of us / foreign and /
together / and witness to a faith that dwarfed even what we believed
of each other // where do our heathen friends go
for forgiveness / for thinking themselves equal to

an architecture of infinite / unconditional // what I would give
for a gospel / of a life twined with mine // the word in me /taken
in vain // I've already said / I have no prayers to offer //
what holy bells toll for lack of hurt / or because // for lack of joy

/ or because // my god / I've loved / a largeness so burning brilliant //
Our Lady of love / that such fury can shatter

SANDY SOLOMON

THE BLUSH

"Two people, two baths," the boy behind the counter
said, as he checked us out of our budget room.
The hotel, which overlooked Notre-Dame,
was cheap, but charged, it seemed, for everything,
including a key to the bath. I corrected, "Two people,

one bath." Less to pay. The boy,
maybe eighteen, blushed to the tips of his ears,
smirked, then looked away. Hired for the summer,
I guessed. We paused. I couldn't not recall
me and you at either end of the large,

claw-footed, cast-iron tub
down the hall from our room. We'd sat, cramped,
but laughing; between us, the drowned pockets of our night's
pleasure and the dripping, hard-edged tap.
That blush remains—more vivid than our night,

more vivid, even, than the view across the Seine
for which we paid another, extra charge.
Opening the clanking shutters, we'd found
the scene: our own Western façade, the towers
then uncleaned, so black with soot, so fine.

THE GREAT CONFINEMENT

Year of sighs, year of planning ahead—
how to acquire food or meet friends
for afternoon talks in the outdoor air.
Of planning nothing. Whole days washed clean
in the round of known rooms, known chores.

I followed forecasts to calculate when
to walk down the alley, around the block,
the same dogs barking, recycling bins
bursting with cardboard. I envied people stuck
in the country amid trees, beside a lake
that took in sky. And people, I presume,
envied us, with our covered front porch
and back garden, its sloping tangle of leaves.
We'd thrown ourselves down wherever the music
stopped, in a place we planned to stay a season
at most, until a hidden hand could hit the volume.

Year of stories—of books, recorded voices
through the night, faces on screens: familiars
holding cocktail glasses, jam jars
into view to toast . . . what precisely?
happy hours? Of meetings, of classes: click
to speak, click to mute, click to leave.

Year of household tasks. Mold that grew
because we used the kitchen so hard:
the endless sponge-down—meal after meal,
day after day. Dust that gathered
like thoughts of Somewhere Else, Another Time,
Other People. When I set two plates for dinner,
I could imagine my mother on her daily walk—
careful, stiff-hipped, alone—to the mailbox,
silence at each elbow, around her throat.
When I searched for new ways to cook kale
or tried baking bread, as oven warmth
and savory smells revised the room in stews
or casseroles, I could imagine mothers
trying to stretch their kids' milk between
food-bank trips. Year of feeling lucky.

Year of forgetting in the days' drift. Then
abruptly remembering: sadness sensed
in a jolt, the way when I opened the kitchen bin—
just emptied, just cleaned, it seemed—
a rotten smell hit me, knocked me back.

Year of sighs, year of sighs, names
of the ones gone away, their faces appearing.
For months, as afternoon light grew long,
I thought, *Must call Mom*. Even after.

I thought of Hélène—years ago,
when we stood, she and I, before
a painting she'd made, its colors shifting
as the oil she'd rigged behind the canvas
face shifted inside its frame,
and I thought, *I like your art, your stories:*
her story's end in plastic tubes,
white edges, machine thrums
and bleeps, room mostly bleached
of color against the blue hospital
gowns that hovered then disappeared,

Hélène, inside her great struggle,
the suffocating, persistent,
solitary smell of alcohol.

Year of distance upon distance. I thought
of candles in the Hall of Mirrors when, one night,
I'd walked its length after a concert—light
echoing as lights regressed from sconce
to mirror to mirror and back in Versailles, the flames'
flicker—presence, movement—enclosed in infinite
space, each candle point insisting, *here,*
here, smaller and smaller, left and right,
as I passed through, passed among them.
What is the point? Here is the point. What
is the point? Here. Thrilling, a privileged sight
as I moved down the Hall, as down the year,
toward the night air, the dear dead
ones receding, drifting further back,
in reflected, refracted, lovely multitudes,
and then, at the end, no point, *no point at all.*

ERIKA L. SÁNCHEZ
INSTRUCTIONS FOR LIVING

It was the way summer hunted me:
a sequence of instructions
in the folds of a flower.
How do I explain the hatred of the sun,
the terrible wonder of being alive?
Fuck the fucking birds. I looked
to the sky to join the storms. I couldn't
have imagined you, swift as the lightning
I traced with my finger, a song scratched
into a back. I ached with the not-knowing.
On Mother's Day I knelt and begged
for something to help me. Is that God?

I played "Here Comes the Sun"
in the psych ward and everyone
watched as I shook. This
is not true, I said. The sun
is already here. Hope was slight
as an eyelash. How clean the sky—
a cloud that posed as a spine.
There was no container
for my despair. In your face I saw
a sequence of instructions.
When you touched me, I named
the future: Be here. Stay living.
I was running once. Did I tell you
how I wept like that? I saw a fox—
my life bound into tricks. The past
is the past is the past. An idea grown
in the name of the obvious. How
a beloved becomes a stranger
and a stranger becomes a beloved.
I can hate what is true, the thick beauty
of it. I am always in the school of the dead:
a bracket, an aside, a reordering.
I tell you language is always a failure,
a string waiting to be plucked. A song
you love and cannot resolve.
What's the difference between
rupture and rapture? Not even salt.

CRAIG MORGAN TEICHER

PEERS

I'm thinking of you beautiful
and young, of me young

and confused and maybe
beautiful. There were lots of us—

these were our twenties, when,
post-9/11, we were about to

inherit the world, and we had no idea
what to do with it. And look

what we did, and we didn't.
And now look at us, and it.

We turned away for a blip, started
whispering, kissing, had kids,

bought houses, changed bulbs,
submitted claims, changed channels,

FaceTimed, streamed, upgraded,
were two-day-shipped to, and midway

through our prime earning years
we look up again, decades groggy,

decades late. Forgive us, we thought—
but now it doesn't matter. These are our

outcomes, consequences, faults,
forties, when the hourglass

is beeping and bleak and people
like us have memories like this

and wonder if the beauty that's left
is really still beautiful, if it was.

HAGIT GROSSMAN

ON FRIENDSHIP

If a friend calls out to you late at night from beneath your window
Never send him on his way. And if you've sent him away and still
Insist on rigid rules, regain your composure after a moment
And run to the window and shout his name: "Come, Merhav!
Come back! I've got some corn cooking! Come eat something."
And he'll placidly retrace his steps and gladly accept
The key you toss down from your window,
Will come upstairs to the first floor and will be impressed
By the large pictures on the walls.
He'll sit and wait for you to slip into a clean shirt and you'll put on
The movie in the kid's room and your baby daughter
Will rush to the kitchen and come back with a red pepper for him.
He'll decline the warm corn and say he's already had dinner.
In the meantime your husband will chat with him about Tai Chi
And pour him a glass of cold sweet pineapple juice.
You'll return to the living room
And go out to the balcony and light a cigarette and sip
A cold beer. You don't yet realize
That this is a sublime moment in your life.
One of the most sublime you'll ever know.

(*Translated, from the Hebrew, by Benjamin Balint.*)

KEVIN YOUNG

LITTLE RED CORVETTE

WHEN YOU WERE MINE

Nothing passed us by. *Baby,*
you're much too fast. In 1990
we had us an early 80s party—
nostalgic already,

I dug out my best
OPs & two polos, fluorescent,
worn simultaneously—
collar up, pretend preppy.

When Blondie came on—
Rapture, be pure—
things really got going & then
the dancing got shut down

by some square.
What was sleep even for?

HOUSEQUAKE

What was sleep even for?
The year before, a freshman, I threw
a Prince party, re-screwed
the lights red & blue—

the room all purple, people
dancing everywhere—clicked
PLAY on the cassette till
we slow-sweated to "Erotic

City" or "Do Me Baby." *I'm going down
to Alphabet Street.* Did anyone
sleep alone that night? "I Feel
For You." *Shut up already, damn*—

cabbage patch, reverse running man—
get some life wherever you can.

DAVID BAKER

SIX NOTES

Come down to us. Come down with your song,
little wren. The world is in pieces.

We must not say so. In the dark hours,
in the nearest branches, I hear you thrum—

   •

The deer come to die beside the creek.
Mud the color of walnut stain. Reek and

runoff from the new development, there,
beyond the woods. Rib and skull. No jawbone—

   •

It makes a soundless scream. I hope for peace
when I walk here sometimes in the dark.

If not peace, clarity. If not clarity,
at least a place to breathe. Else I'll scream, too—

   •

Come down, little dove, far above the bay.
I hear you in a thirsty palm or up

beyond the rocks. A windy reed of song.
Blue sun, blue cloud above the sweeping bay—

   •

Sometimes we have to say so. I don't know how.
A man, a boy, an anger with no tongue

took his automatic rifle to school today.
The report we hear, discharge, echo—

   •

is the sound of sorrow, reloading.
No matter where we walk, we hear it call.

Little wing, little creek, little bay, dark hour.
Come down with your beaks of morning and blood—

JAY FIELDEN

THE MOWER

There is a grass still
grows that I once mowed,
deep green St. Augustine
I cut in patterned lines.
My father bought this ideal
family plot, a red brick ranch
with plenty of yard and a nice
swimming pool, an unusual coral blue.
The color took him
back to when they bombed the fleet,
at anchor and asleep, and how
after that they shocked his brain
and placed him in the shade
beside the box of paints
he'd hauled from ship to ship,
sketching mushroom clouds
en plein air like Gauguin
swinging in his hammock
before it became his grave.
The diagnosis was severe
depression with possible future
complications from exposure
to high levels
of nuclear radiation,
having been among the first
wave of men to stand within
the radius of the blast after
the surrender of Japan.
But they couldn't say for sure.
He did his best,
a doctor of dental surgery.
But he was never much
for beating his chest.
A father people called doctor
had a certain station that

carried with it expectations.
Our neighborhood was full
of fancy M.D. degrees, each driving
his Mercedes in dark shades
and tennis whites.
Day or night, what he liked
to do was snooze to the shrill
glow of an AM transistor radio
bleating the news while we lay awake.
All we could think about
was that there was a world outside,
but only half a man to provide.
The year I turned sixteen
and he was fifty-nine,
my mother had to get
him out of bed and dressed
to look his best,
and the lawn, which he'd kept,
grew sick with weeds and neglect.
As for the house,
my sister swept it clean,
so when our friends came by
all we had to do was leave
him in his room.
Later, we found out
that he'd seen
men and sand burned to glass.
But back then we didn't know.
We didn't know back then
how deep he'd go.
We couldn't any longer care
for him at home.
And, after that, someone
else had to mow
in lines that left
tracks in rows
that showed where

the blade had cut
one swath down
before circling back around.

JENNIFER CHANG

WE FOUND THE BODY OF A YOUNG DEER ONCE

Whitetails flicker like light in the winter woods,
where my dog and I crack open
the early morning, the ground a frozen patchwork
of leaves, the brittle ice of dirt. So much
of walking is description. Late in the year
the sun stops us cold. Or, walking is comparison,
these woods in New Jersey seem
                        (a passing thought) Ohioan,
                  then I recall that late thaw
one March in New Hampshire. Or,
                     I'm ten again wondering where
                     I last saw the deer carcass. Maybe

by the creek, maybe loose ribs, a skull
tucked into snow.
                As children
we set old logs against a middling elm,
thatched branches
into a sort of rooftop, called our dwelling
Antelope. My friend and I, we ignored the sky
cutting into our shelter and made walls
of found particleboard,
                   fragmentary, damp, worthless as kindling.
                   Her mother worshipped Zoroaster. Her father
had an Irish-American mistress. Stub of birch, first rime
graying the last moss,
the ground fascinates a spray
of blue jays.

Her father, as a university student, had dined with the Shah.
Whenever her mother polished the silver we'd joke,
"The Shah is coming to tea!"
                                    From upstairs
                              we could smell duck stewing in walnuts
and pomegranate syrup. Later, the darkest meat
fell to pieces onto bright, particulate rice.

It was like eating a secret, my mouth
stunned by acid sweetness, a terrible hunger
I could not explain to my own mother.
I wanted more, another plate of *fesenjan*, please—

instead: into the winter woods we ran
after this new world
that knew nothing of what we hid
on our tongues—other words for dusk,
revolution, and snow.
                        We dismissed our appetites. We forgot our
fathers.
        Farther, farther, I am going into the dark

of the mind, that neighbor girl, my friend—she goes
by Mrs. Bell now, so I hear, lives out west,
plants tulips every November and come spring
scythes each one mid-stem.
A crystal vase in the breakfast nook.
Cheerios in her sons' bowls, her dumb accomplished husband
nodding at the clock.
                    It was with her I found
                    the body of a young deer, fallen in a clearing,

fresh snow
powdering the deer's coat like fresh ash
fallen from a proximate fire.

Quiet,
quieter than I've ever been
with anyone, we shared the death, we stood quietly, the sky

open and gray above us.
We never said a word about the deer. I imagine that winter
as helming decay, the woods

beastly, skeletal, far reach of the trees,
the deer's bone-cage
stripped clean of flesh.
She showed me a map of Iran
in my father's world atlas. In Tehran, they had had
many servants, including a gardener and a
night nurse for her and her brother,
though she was too young
to remember any of this.

The day after solstice I note
an emerald shine to the pale sky.

On the question of origin, she explained, "Persian."
Once I described my mother as always
angry
(she was born amid a civil war), but mostly

my childhood was a quiet one. It was not
until years later that I learned
others had considered our family strange.

JANE SHORE

THE COUPLE

Jay and Linda moved to Plateau Road
and brought with them a pair of horses:
old Kahlua and his longtime mare.
When her heart failed suddenly, Kahlua—
a paint the color of the Mexican liqueur
and swaybacked like a hammock—
went on a hunger strike. Fearing
that he might die from loneliness,
Jay and Linda heard about a donkey
housed unhappily an hour north,
whose spouse likewise had died.
Donkeys are stoic, disguising their pain,
and we know grief is pain. They hauled
him home, installed him in the barn,
to see if the widowers could get along,
the Odd Couple of Central Vermont.
Nickolai, a Slavic name, means "victorious;
conqueror of the people," and, if that's so,
he's won us over, my husband and me,
Jody and David, Cathy and Eric, and other
long-marrieds of Peck Hill Road.
Driving to town for groceries and gas,
I shift my Subaru into neutral
to admire our two old bachelor uncles
free-ranging along the electric fence.
Their partnership so far so good.
Nickolai's fur, mottled gray and white
like burnout velvet, gets waterlogged
when it rains; Kahlua's is waterproof.
Nickolai's lovely floppy donkey ears
are much larger than Kahlua's,
and he has a stiffer mane; his bray
is not Kahlua's pleasant whinny—
his hee-haws, like a wheezing accordion,
reverberate off our bedroom walls.

I once saw Kahlua bare his teeth,
like Mr. Ed, the TV horse who could talk.
But they say that donkeys are more personable
than horses. More affectionate than dogs.
So it's easy to forget that he's a jackass—
confined to the barn all freezing winter,
tired of nipping at Kahlua's flanks,
he stomped Jay's pet rabbit to death.
From afar, you cannot tell which one's
the boss, albeit equal on the equine scale.
On days when it isn't thundering,
you'll find them both civilly ensconced,
silhouettes grazing against the sunset,
the moon rising over Max Gray Road.
They stand head to tail, or tail to head,
their long tails ticking metronomes,
flicking flies away from the other's eyes,
their warm sides barely touching.
Facing opposite directions, they'll
age in place, bickering, companionable—
a photo on a country calendar.

AFAA MICHAEL WEAVER

IN A BORDER TOWN

In this version of the city, no one dares read,
ragtime grows underneath Washington's obelisk,
not a monument but a threat to the clouded sky.

Next door to McCormick's, a telescope sits,
looking over the harbor, inside all of what is,
for a new constellation, *the hidden dancers*,

a joining, convergences that come only when
September moons bring heavy rains, a deluge
to sound alarms to haul in the blue crabs.

In all of this we are overgrown ants, brittle
on the tongue, held up above ourselves singing
Southern chants for spells to soften the hard.

What names us? I ask a man shuffling in bags,
a man who knows the giant ants we have become,
who knows us, but says now we have no name,

but purple iris in a golden vase over the harbor,
peace wrapping itself over the city's north border,
where horses reign over the emptied corners,

where I climb back into the old way of dancing,
wiping away the spinning-top hairdos with thick
masks over the need to be naked and breathless

so I can be freed from the one spent song.

JIM MOORE

MOTHER

My friend and I had a cat we called Mother.
I took the couch; my friend got the one bedroom
because he often had sex and needed
that private darkness. I had not yet had sex
of my own volition. No one knew
I had been raped. I was so unknowing
I barely knew it myself, how lost I was
to myself. I was maybe twenty. We loved that cat
that had wandered into our lives, rubbing our legs,
needing love and milk and a safe place
to sleep like any creature arriving on this earth
from God knows where and God knows why.
One hot August day I was sitting outside
when Mother joined me and sat on my lap,
a thing she had never done before.

And that was where she died. I called Jeff,
who had gone to a motel somewhere
with his girl of the moment. "Mother died,"
I said. There was a long silence, then
he whispered quietly, "Oh, no,"
as if he wanted to keep his sorrow to himself.
Many years later I told my actual mother
about the rape. She cried a little and was angry
on my behalf. I was calm. Relieved.
Then life went on, as it does,
without much of a pause. I was not healed
by telling her, I am sorry to say.
I am still not, at seventy-nine. The beautiful gray sky
of a rainy May day, and the lindens
coming into flower. That smell!
You and I both love it. (Did you know
all along I was writing this poem to you?)
Often at night we walk to the river
and stare down into the black current
which has reached flood stage
and carries everything before it.

FRIEDA HUGHES

SELFIE

You want to fix yourself into that event

With an image of the volcano, or street killing,

Or house fire, or fornicating bullfrogs,

Or the centaur dancing, or the unicorn

Piercing balloons over a pond with a fountain

Shaped like an oak tree from the undiscovered torts

That have scattered through office blocks and suburban homes,

And which may be uncovered one day

And be ripped from the sculpted foliage, becoming fact,

Causing this accumulation of lies to fall like leaves

Into the water below—and the unicorn to leap

Into fiction while you

Will be fixed in time to an image of crime,

Or joy, or wonder, or a unicorn,

As a commitment for life on the Internet

Repeated, retweeted,

But forever with your back to it.

KATE BAER
REASONS TO LOG OFF

The girl who said she could never eat a second slice
of pizza my senior year of college is doing really well.
My cousin posts a photo of a loaded gun. Have I ever
heard of the Second Amendment? Have I ever heard
of this new recipe? Cauliflower, a hint of lemon, some
chopped-up ginger root. Hey, do you want to lose
weight in only thirty minutes? Hey, can I have just a
moment of your time? Click here to receive a special
invitation. Click here if you want to believe in God.
Tomorrow there's a Pride walk to support the right to

marry. One comment says: I will pray for your affliction.
Another says: I hope you trip, fall down, and die.
Swipe up to find my new lip filler. Scroll down to read
why these four girls were horribly afraid. Greg is
asking for your number. Greg wants to send a
big surprise.

ERIKA MEITNER

TO GATHER TOGETHER

It is not yet after the pandemic
but most of us have bared our faces
in public. Most of us are a little haptic
though we remain somewhat wary
of strangers merging in enclosures &
what does it mean, to gather? To take up
from a resting place. We are so tired.
We are uncovered & mustering
strength. Never mind my mother's
post-stroke slurred speech & vertigo,
her ear crystals misaligned, her
neck brace. We are survivors of the
panic wars. We are reaching new
conclusions intuitively from inferences
about hugging. My radar is broken.
I'm not sure where to put all my limbs.
When they're tangled with yours it's not
a problem. Your failing configurations
of attention. My bad knees. To draw
fabric into puckers: pleated pants,
rumpled sheets, your fingers hooked
in my underpants & we bring together
all the parts of ourselves to embrace—
haul in our bodies. To harvest, like
clusters of ripened cherry tomatoes

still warm from the sun. Forget
the kale, stripped bare by bright-
green cabbage worms congregating
on thick stems. To summon everyone
back to this abundant & skeletal planet
after we've jettisoned the billionaires
into space. We celebrate the launch
with tiny coupes of champagne.
To throw open the doors & host
guests & board packed planes where
everyone is cranked & cranky about
proximity still. But look at the skyline—
clutches of buildings reaching for
billows of clouds. To assemble
in a sequence for binding, somewhere
past contact tracing. Gather is a
transitive verb.

EAVAN BOLAND

THE LOST ART OF LETTER WRITING

The ratio of daylight to handwriting
Was the same as lacemaking to eyesight.
The paper was so thin it skinned air.

The hand was fire and the page tinder.
Everything burned away except the one
Place they singled out between fingers

Held over a letter pad they set aside
For the long evenings of their leave-takings,
Always asking after what they kept losing,

Always performing—even when a shadow
Fell across the page and they knew the answer
Was not forthcoming—the same action:

First the leaning down, the pen becoming
A staff to walk fields with as they vanished
Underfoot into memory. Then the letting up,

The lighter stroke, which brought back
Cranesbill and thistle, a bicycle wheel
Rusting: an iron circle hurting the grass

Again and the hedges veiled in hawthorn
Again just in time for the May Novenas
Recited in sweet air on a road leading

To another road, then another one, widening
To a motorway with four lanes, ending in
A new town on the edge of a city

They will never see. And if we say
An art is lost when it no longer knows
How to teach a sorrow to speak, come, see

The way we lost it: stacking letters in the attic,
Going downstairs so as not to listen to
The fields stirring at night as they became

Memory and in the morning as they became
Ink; what we did so as not to hear them
Whispering the only question they knew

By heart, the only one they learned from all
Those epistles of air and unreachable distance,
How to ask: *is it still there?*

ILYA KAMINSKY

IN A TIME OF PEACE

Inhabitant of earth for fortysomething years
I once found myself in a peaceful country. I watch neighbors open

their phones to watch
a cop demanding a man's driver's license. When a man reaches for
        his wallet, the cop
shoots. In the car window. Shoots.

It is a peaceful country.

We pocket our phones and go.
To the dentist,
to pick up the kids from school,
to buy shampoo
and basil.

Ours is a country in which a boy shot by police lies on the pavement
        for hours.

We see in his open mouth
the nakedness
of the whole nation.

We watch. Watch
others watch.

The body of a boy lies on the pavement exactly like the body of
        a boy—

It is a peaceful country.

And it clips our citizens' bodies
effortlessly, the way the President's wife trims her toenails.

All of us
still have to do the hard work of dentist appointments,
of remembering to make
a summer salad: basil, tomatoes, it is a joy, tomatoes, add a little salt.

This is a time of peace.

I do not hear gunshots,
but watch birds splash over the back yards of the suburbs. How
    bright is the sky
as the avenue springs on its axis.
How bright is the sky (forgive me) how bright.

NAOMI SHIHAB NYE

WORLD OF THE FUTURE, WE THIRSTED

Stripped of a sense of well-being,
we downed our water from small disposable bottles.
Casting the plastic to streetside,
we poured high-potency energy tonics or Coke
down our throats, because this time in history
had sapped us so thoroughly and
we were desperate.
Straws, plastic caps, crushed cans,
in a three-block walk you could fill a sack.

As if we could replenish spirits quickly,
pitching containers without remorse
—who did we imagine would pick them up?
What did we really know of plastic spirals in the sea
bigger than whole countries,
we had never swirled in one ourselves,
as a fish might do, a sea urchin, a whole family of eels,
did we wish to be invincible, using what we wanted,
discarding what we didn't, as in wars,

whole cities and nations crumpled
after our tanks and big guns pull out?

How long does it take to be thirsty again?
We were so lonely in the streets though
all the small houses still had noses, mouths,
eyes from which we might peer, as our fellow-
citizens walk their dogs, pause helplessly as the dogs
circle trees, tip their heads back for a long slow slug
of water or tea, and never fear, never fear.

GREGORY PARDLO

ALLEGORY

Professional wrestler Owen Hart embodied his own
omen when he battled gravity from rafters to canvas

in a Kansas City stadium. Like a great tent collapsing,
he fell without warning, no hoverboard, no humming-

bird's finesse for the illusion of flight, no suspension
of disbelief to hammock his burden—the birth of virtue—

in its virtual reality. His angelic entrance eclipsed
when his safety harness failed. He fell out of the ersatz

like a waxwing duped by infinities conjured in a squeegee's
mirage. Spectators wilted as the creature of grief emerged

to graze on their sapling gasps and shrieks. I'd like to think
that, freed of self-hype, he realized his mask was not a shield,

and that he didn't spend his last attempting to method
Zeno's proofs. E.M.T.s like evangelicals huddled to jolt

the hub of Hart's radiating soul as fans prayed the stunt
might yet parade the emperor's threads wrestlers call *kayfabe*.

Kayfabe, a dialect of pig Latin, lingo for the promise to drop
at the laying on of hands. To take myth as history. Semblance

as creed. A grift so convincing one might easily believe
it could work without someone else pulling the strings.

MOSAB ABU TOHA

OBIT

To the shadow I had left alone before I
crossed the border, my shadow that stayed
lonely and hid in the dark of the night,
freezing where it was, never needing a visa.
To my shadow that's been waiting for my return,
homeless except when I was walking by its side
in the summer light.
To my shadow that wishes to go to school
with the children of morning, but couldn't fit
through the classroom doors.
To my shadow that has caught cold now, that's been
sneezing and coughing, no one there saying to it *God bless!*
To my shadow that's been crushed by cars and vans,
its chest pierced by shrapnel and bullets
flying with no wings,
my shadow that no one's attending to,
                    bleeding black blood
                    through its memory
                    now, and forever.

SOLMAZ SHARIF

FROM AN OTHERWISE

Downwind, I walked the wide hallways
of a great endowment.

It didn't matter if I did or didn't.
It changed only myself, the doing.

It fed down to one knuckle
then the next, this compromise.

It fed down to one frequency
and another, leaving me only a scrambled sound.

It would burn your fingertips
to walk the length of the hall

dragging them along the grass-papered walls
where they punished you

for not
wanting enough. For not wanting

to be nonbelligerent
by naming the terms

for belligerence.
The shellacked

shelves, the softly shaking
pens in their pen case.

What was given there
could be taken, and

quietly, you were reminded of this.
You were reminded all

was property of the West.
The mess of a raven's nest

built behind a donor's great bust
then gone.

The mess of bird shit on the steps
then gone. All dismantled and scrubbed

sensibility. And this was it.
This nowhere.

My school of resentment commenced.

NANCY MOREJÓN

THE DEAD

The dead are what's absent,
forgotten, inert.
A bell rings out
its loneliness swaying amid the roses.
The dead come out at night
or they come out in the afternoon
to feed from gourds,
from lecterns,
from other people's throats,
from guitar pegs,
from the key and the calabash,
from scissors blunted by use,
on the concrete of plazas,
on savage smells,
on nectar,
on bone.
In the drop of water
appears the face of the dead.
In the fragment of the sea that the passerby glimpses

lies hidden the universe of the dead.
The dead hang from the hours.
They slake the thirst of a poet friend.
The dead endure.
The dead sing.

(*Translated, from the Spanish, by Pamela Carmell.*)

FORREST GANDER

SON

It's not the mirror that is draped but
what remains unspoken between us. Why

say anything about death, how
the body comes to deploy the myriad worm

as if it were a manageable concept not
searing exquisite singularity? To serve it up like

a eulogy or a tale of my or your own
suffering. Some kind of self-abasement.

And so we continue waking to a decapitated sun and trees
continue to irk me. The heart of charity

bears its own set of genomes. You lug a bacterial swarm
in the crook of your knee, and through my guts

writhe helminth parasites. Who was ever only themselves?
At Leptis Magna, when your mother and I were young, we came
    across

statues of gods with their faces and feet cracked away by vandals. But
for the row of guardian Medusa heads. No one so brave to deface
    those.

When she spoke, when your mother spoke, even the leashed
greyhound stood transfixed. I stood transfixed.

I gave my life to strangers; I kept it from the ones I love.
Her one arterial child. It is just in you her blood runs.

GBOYEGA ODUBANJO
BREAKING

looks like it'll be a rainy week ahead thank you   now the body
of an unidentified boy aged between four and seven
was   in the river for up to ten days before a passer by
noticed   african boy's stomach included extracts
of calabar   bean and flecks of gold expert at kew gardens
     says headless   limbless boy likely to be   nigerian
growing number have spread throughout the world   coming up
goat arrested for armed robbery prime minister's response breaking
male torso   boy five or six said to be somebody's
     son boy assigned most appropriate acceptable name
after long deliberation   thought to have been in river   ten days
appeal made to family of girls' shorts boy's   body
walking man who spotted adam to be offered counselling
suspicious thames river boy behavior   should be reported
to authorities   in other news

OCEAN VUONG
SOMEDAY I'LL LOVE OCEAN VUONG

Ocean, don't be afraid.
The end of the road is so far ahead
it is already behind us.
Don't worry. Your father is only your father
until one of you forgets. Like how the spine
won't remember its wings

no matter how many times our knees
kiss the pavement. Ocean,
are you listening? The most beautiful part
of your body is wherever
your mother's shadow falls.
Here's the house with childhood
whittled down to a single red tripwire.
Don't worry. Just call it *horizon*
& you'll never reach it.
Here's today. Jump. I promise it's not
a lifeboat. Here's the man
whose arms are wide enough to gather
your leaving. & here the moment,
just after the lights go out, when you can still see
the faint torch between his legs.
How you use it again & again
to find your own hands.
You asked for a second chance
& are given a mouth to empty into.
Don't be afraid, the gunfire
is only the sound of people
trying to live a little longer. Ocean. Ocean,
get up. The most beautiful part of your body
is where it's headed. & remember,
loneliness is still time spent
with the world. Here's
the room with everyone in it.
Your dead friends passing
through you like wind
through a wind chime. Here's a desk
with the gimp leg & a brick
to make it last. Yes, here's a room
so warm & blood-close,
I swear, you will wake—
& mistake these walls
for skin.

SARAH HOLLAND-BATT

THE GIFT

In the garden, my father sits in his wheelchair
garlanded by summer hibiscus
like a saint in a seventeenth-century cartouche.
A flowering wreath buzzes around his head—
passionate red. He holds the gift of death
in his lap: small, oblong, wrapped in black.
He has been waiting seventeen years to open it
and is impatient. When I ask how he is
my father cries. His crying comes as a visitation,
the body squeezing tears from his ducts tenderly
as a nurse measuring drops of calamine
from an amber bottle, as a teen at the car wash
wringing a chamois of suds. It is a kind of miracle
to see my father weeping this freely, weeping
for what is owed him. *How are you?* I ask again
because his answer depends on an instant's microclimate,
his moods bloom and retreat like an anemone
as the cold currents whirl around him—
crying one minute, sedate the next.
But today my father is disconsolate.
I'm having a bad day, he says, and tries again.
I'm having a bad year. I'm having a bad decade.
I hate myself for noticing his poetry—the triplet
that should not be beautiful to my ear
but is. Day, year, decade—scale of awful economy.
I want to give him his present but it is not mine
to give. We sit as if mother and son on Christmas Eve
waiting for midnight to tick over, anticipating
the moment we can open his present together—
first my father holding it up to his ear and shaking it,
then me helping him peel back the paper,
the weight of his death knocking,
and once the box is unwrapped it will be mine,
I will carry the gift of his death endlessly,
every day I will know it opening in me.

MADELEINE CRAVENS

LEAVING

Not the pleasure of lovers but the pleasure of letters,
a pleasure like weather, delayed and prepared for,
not the pleasure of lessons but the pleasure of errors,
of nightmares, of actors in the black box of a theatre,
not the pleasure of present but the pleasure of later,
the pleasure of letters and weather and terror, asleep
by the lake, unable to answer, the pleasure of candles,
their wax on the table, not the pleasure of saviors
but the pleasure of errors, not the pleasure of marriage
but the pleasure of failure, the pleasure of characters
like family members, their failures and errors, their
laughter and weather, the pleasure of water, terrible
rivers, not the pleasure of empire but the pleasure
of after, our failure to keep an accurate record, not
the pleasure of tethers but the pleasure of strangers,
the terrible strangers who will become your lovers,
not the pleasure of novels but the pleasure of anger,
your failure to answer all of my letters, the pleasure
of daughters, the pleasure of daughters writing letters
in April, the failure of orchards, the terror of mothers,
not the pleasure of planners but the pleasure of errors.

RITA DOVE

PEDESTRIAN CROSSING, CHARLOTTESVILLE

A gaggle of girls giggle over the bricks
leading off Court Square. We brake

dutifully, and wait; but there's at least
twenty of these knob-kneed creatures,

blond and curly, still at an age that thinks
impudence is cute. Look how they dart

and dither, changing flanks as they lurch
along—golden gobbets of infuriating foolishness

or pure joy, depending on one's disposition.
At the moment mine's sour—this is taking

far too long; don't they have minders?
Just behind my shoulder in the city park

the Southern general still stands, stonewalling us all.
When I was their age I judged Goldilocks

nothing more than a pint-size criminal
who flounced into others' lives, then

assumed their clemency. Unfair,
I know, my aggression—to lump them

into a gaggle (silly geese!) when all
they're guilty of is being young. So far.

LAST WORDS

I don't want to die in a poem
the words burning in eulogy
the sun howling *why*
the moon sighing *why not*

I don't want to die in bed
which is a poem gone wrong
a world turned in on itself
a floating navel of dreams

I won't meet death in a field
like a dot punctuating a page
it's too vast yet too tiny
everyone will say it's a bit cinematic

I don't want to pass away in your arms
those gentle parentheses
nor expire outside of their swoon
self-propelled   determined   shouting

Let the end come
as the best parts of living have come
unsought and undeserved
inconvenient

now that's a good death

what nonsense you say
that's not even worth
writing down

GABRIELLE CALVOCORESSI

HAMMOND B3 ORGAN CISTERN

The days I don't want to kill myself
are extraordinary. Deep bass. All the people
in the streets waiting for their high fives
and leaping, I mean *leaping,*
when they see me. I am the sun-filled
god of love. Or at least an optimistic
under-secretary. There should be a word for it.
The days you wake up and do not want
to slit your throat. Money in the bank.
Enough for an iced green tea every weekday
and Saturday and Sunday! It's like being
in the armpit of a Hammond B3 organ.
Just reeks of gratitude and funk.
The funk of ages. *I am not going to ruin*
my love's life today. It's like the time I said yes

to gray sneakers but then the salesman said
Wait. And there, out of the back room,
like the bakery's first biscuits: bright-blue kicks.
Iridescent. Like a scarab! Oh, who am I kidding,
it was nothing like a scarab! It was like
bright. blue. fucking. sneakers! I did not
want to die that day. Oh, my God.
Why don't we talk about it? How good it feels.
And if you don't know then you're lucky
but also you poor thing. Bring the band out on the stoop.
Let the whole neighborhood hear. Come on, Everybody.
Say it with me nice and slow
       no pills   no cliff   no brains on the floor
Bring the bass back.   *no rope   no hose*   not today, Satan.
Every day I wake up with my good fortune
and news of my demise. Don't keep it from me.
Why don't we have a name for it?
Bring the bass back. Bring the band out on the stoop.
Hallelujah!

SAEED JONES

ALIVE AT THE END OF THE WORLD

The End of the World was a nightclub.
Drag queens with machetes and rhinestoned

machine guns guarded the red and impassable
door on Friday nights. Just a look at the crowd,

all dressed up and swaying outside, made people
want to yell the truth about themselves to anyone

who'd listen, but no one heard. The End of the World
was loud. The End of the World leaked music

like radiation, and we loved the neon echo, even
though it taunted us or maybe because it taunted us:

kids leaning out of windows hours after bedtime,
cabdrivers debating fares at the curb just for an excuse

to linger, pastors who'd pause at the corner and vow
that if they ever got inside, they'd burn it all down.

JOY HARJO

WITHOUT

The world will keep trudging through time without us

When we lift from the story contest to fly home

We will be as falling stars to those watching from the edge

Of grief and heartbreak

Maybe then we will see the design of the two-minded creature

And know why half the world fights righteously for greedy masters

And the other half is nailing it all back together

Through the smoke of cooking fires, lovers' trysts, and endless

Human industry—

Maybe then, beloved rascal

We will find each other again in the timeless weave of breathing

We will sit under the trees in the shadow of earth sorrows

Watch hyenas drink rain, and laugh.

DAWNING

JOSEPH MONCURE MARCH

GOING HOME

Below Fourteenth, at five A.M.
The taxis stopped if we looked at them:
Over streets sweet-smelling and damp
A man crisscrossed from lamp to lamp
Turning them out. The sky grew gray:
The buildings against it stood away
Knee-deep in shadows, and the air seemed
Enchanted; as though it slept, and dreamed.
We looked up as we passed the places
Where our friends were sleeping with white faces,
And noted wickedly just how many
Windows they had open, if any.
The sky widened. The shadows were gone
Below the Brevoort: you said, "It's dawn!"
And it was. From the Square, as you spoke the words
Broke out the riotous song of birds.

MARY JO SALTER

A ROUGH NIGHT

Nailed into your coffin alive, to witness
only the things seen only in the dark,
at three in the morning you turn upon the bed
you made and lie in, and gradually that witless
party last night begins to look not so bad:
those hours of bland, recyclable remarks

shared among friends were preferable at least
to this sense of spinning headlong down a hole,
unsaved because you can't cry out your fear.
Either you're sleeping alone or the wrapped-up beast
beside you snores contentedly; to be fair,
even if he were awake, your immortal soul

would be in much the same trouble. And so you rise
to warm some milk, perhaps; or pick up a book,
the worse the better; and with half a mind
to live more halfheartedly, if you can choose,
you wonder why at night you feel consigned
to fail at even that. Too early to look

hopefully out the window now, at four,
for some huge hand to screw the workaday
sun in like a bulb; or to watch it climb
as a mother mounts the stair to crack the door
of the monsterless closet. Yet by the time
light comes at last, unburdening the sky

in even-tempered gray and salmon stripes
of cloud banks (sharp as Father's brand-new tie,
and glowing with his authority), you wonder
at nothing after all, for somehow sleep's
towering wave has finally swept you under
into its viscous, lovely, odd-fished sea.

Just for an hour. Now the time to rest is over-
turned by dear life, which small birds beyond number
advertise with their cries: the call to battle,
the wolf whistle and the siren, the whispering lover,
the lullaby sung backward, the baby's rattle
shaken to tease you out of a grudging slumber.

WILLIAM STAFFORD

MONDAY

Awake, like a hippopotamus with eyes bulged
from the covers, I find Monday, improbable
as chair legs, camped around me, and God's terrible
searchlight raking down from his pillbox on Mount Hood,
while His mystic hammers reach from the alarm clock
and rain spangles on my head.

Cliff at my back all week I live, afraid
when light comes, because it has deep whirlpools
in it. I cross each day by the shallow part but
have often touched the great hole in the sky
at noon. I close my eyes and let the day
for a while wander where all things will, and then
it settles in a fold of the north.

At the end, in my last sickness, I think I will travel
north, if well-meaning friends will let me—to bush,
to rock, to snow—have nothing by me, fall
on the sky of earth in the north, and let my heart
finally understand that part of the world
I have secretly loved all my life—the rock. But now
I gradually become young, surge from the covers,
and go to work.

ELIZABETH BISHOP

LITTLE EXERCISE AT 4 A.M.

Think of the storm roaming the sky uneasily
like a dog looking for a place to sleep in,
listen to it growling.

Think how they must look now, the mangrove keys
lying out there unresponsive to the lightning,
in dark, coarse-fibred families,

where occasionally a heron may undo his head,
shake up his feathers, make an uncertain comment
when the surrounding water shines.

Think of the boulevard and the little palm trees
all stuck in rows, suddenly revealed
as fistfuls of limp fish skeletons.

It is raining there. The boulevard
and its broken sidewalks, with weeds in every crack,
are relieved to be wet, the sea to be freshened.

Now the storm goes away again in a series
of small, badly lit battle scenes,
each in "Another part of the field."

Think of someone sleeping in the bottom of a rowboat
tied to a mangrove root or the pile of a bridge;
think of him as uninjured, barely disturbed.

DONALD JUSTICE

CROSSING KANSAS BY TRAIN

The telephone poles
have been holding their
arms out
a long time now
to birds
that will not
settle there
but pass with
strange cawings
westward to
where dark trees
gather about
a waterhole. This
is Kansas. The
mountains start here
just behind
the closed eyes
of a farmer's
sons asleep
in their workclothes.

KIM ADDONIZIO

KANSAS, 4 A.M.

The train brakes to take the bend behind the grain mill.

All night, at the motel, you listen to the ice machine's cold labor.
Does it ever stop?

Thunk. No, says the vending machine as the next train goes by.

On the highway, the big rigs whine,
some carrying things that would kill you if one jackknifed off the
	overpass.

The chicken truck passes with its load of small-brained misery.

You can't hear the chickens, but you sort of think you can,
the way you can almost hear the sounds of the bar car on the train—

the bleary passengers trapped in their windows,

peering through their doppelgängers at the black
fields of wheat as they whiz past.

Childhood, did it ever exist?

What about the bar your father drank in, giving you
endless quarters for pinball . . . There it goes,

carried aloft by a maniacal wind.

Before science, a lot of wind gods
blew things around. The dead went to live on the moon.

A man might be half scorpion, a woman half fish.

An omniscient, omnipotent stranger who looked
like Santa Claus and had a throne in outer space

knew everything about you, yet still somehow loved you unreasonably.

Another chunk of ice clunks into the bin.
Under your window, an insect in the bushes scrapes out its longing.

The sounds of the world at this late hour sadden you,

but then enters the rain, hastening down, the rain that wants
to touch everything

and almost does.

KEVIN YOUNG

CROWNING

Now that knowing means nothing,
now that you are more born
than being, more awake
than awaited, since I've seen
your hair deep inside mother,
a glimpse, grass in late
winter, early spring, watching
your mother's pursed, throbbing,
purpled power, her pushing
you for one whole hour, two,
almost three, almost out,
maybe never, animal smell
and peat, breath and sweat
and mulch-matter, and at once
you descend, or drive, are driven
by mother's body, by her will
and brilliance, by bowel,
by wanting and your hair
peering as if it could see, and I saw
you storming forth,
taproot, your cap of hair half
in, half out, and wait, hold

it there, the doctors say, and
she squeezing my hand, her face
full of fire, then groaning your face
out like a flower, blood-bloom,
crocussed into air, shoulders
and the long cord still rooting
you to each other, to the other
world, into this afterlife
among us living, the cord
I cut like an iris, pulsing,
then you wet against mother's chest
still purple, not blue, not yet
red, no cry,
warming now, now opening
your eyes midnight
blue in the blue-black dawn.

ANTHONY HECHT

A LETTER

I have been wondering
What you are thinking about, and by now suppose
It is certainly not me.
But the crocus is up, and the lark, and the blundering
Blood knows what it knows.
It talks to itself all night, like a sliding, moonlit sea.

Of course, it is talking of you.
At dawn, where the ocean has netted its catch of lights,
The sun plants one lithe foot
On that spill of mirrors, but the blood goes worming through
Its warm Arabian nights,
Naming your pounding name again in the dark heartroot.

Who shall, of course, be nameless.
Anyway, I should want you to know I have done my best,

As I'm sure you have, too.
Others are bound to us, the gentle and blameless
Whose names are not confessed
In the ceaseless palaver. My dearest, the clear and bottomless blue

Of those depths is all but blinding.
You may remember that once you brought my boys
Two little woolly birds.
Yesterday the older one asked for you upon finding
Your thrush among his toys.
And the tides welled about me, and I could find no words.

There is not much else to tell.
One tries one's best to continue as before,
Doing some little good.
But I would have you know that all is not well
With a man dead set to ignore
The endless repetitions of his own murmurous blood.

HENRI COLE

FIGS

Overnight the figs got moldy and look like little brains—
or Ids without structure—that say something dark
about our species not really laying down a garden
but living out the violent myths.
An insect chorus, almost diaphanous
in a neighbor's yard, says something, too:
America began in tall ships that glowed from within,
but, for the wretched, it still wretchedeth every day.
As the bright day goes around the sun,
why do our days grow
more aggressive and difficult?
Why do the world's shadows
come so close
as its wonders beckon?

CHARLES WRIGHT

TOADSTOOLS

The toadstools are starting to come up,
                            circular and dry.
Nothing will touch them,
Gophers or chipmunks, wasps or swallows.
They glow in the twilight like rooted will-o'-the-wisps.
Nothing will touch them.
As though little roundabouts from the bunched unburiable,
Powers, dominions,
As though orphans rode herd in the short grass,
                            as though they had heard the call,
They will always be with us,
                            transcenders of the world.
Someone will try to stick his beak into their otherworldly styrofoam.
Someone may try to taste a taste of forever.
For some it's a refuge, for some a shady place to fall down.
Grief is a floating barge-boat,
                          who knows where it's going to moor?

RAY YOUNG BEAR

JOHN WHIRLWIND'S DOUBLEBEAT SONGS, 1956

I.

Menwi - yakwatoni - beskonewiani.
Kyebakewina - maneniaki
ketekattiki
ebemanemateki
ebemanemateki

    •

Good-smelling are these flowers.
As it turned out, they were milkweeds
dance-standing
as the wind passes by,
as the wind passes by.

2.

Inike - ekatai - waseyaki
netena - wasesi.
Memettine
beskattenetisono.
Memettine.

•

It is now almost daylight,
I said to the firefly.
For the last time
illuminate yourself.
For the last time.

SHARON OLDS

STAG'S LEAP

Then the creature on the label of our favorite red
looks like my husband, casting himself off a
cliff in his fervor to get free of me.
His fur is rough and cozy, his face
placid, tranced, ruminant,
the bough of each furculum reaches back
to his haunches, each tine on it grows straight up
and branches, a model of his brain, archaic,
unwieldy. He bears its bony tray
level as he soars from the precipice edge,
dreamy. When anyone escapes, my heart
leaps up. Even when it's I who am escaped from,
I am half on the side of the leaver. It's so quiet,
and empty, when he's left. I feel like a landscape,
a ground without a figure. *Sauve*
qui peut. Once I saw a drypoint of someone
tiny being crucified
on a fallow deer's antlers. I feel like his victim,
and he seems my victim, I worry that the outstretched
legs on the hart are bent the wrong way as he

throws himself off. Oh my love. I was vain of his
faithfulness, as if it was
a compliment, rather than a state
of partial sleep. And when I wrote about him, did he
feel he had to walk around
carrying my books on his head like a stack of
posture volumes, or the rack of horns
hung where a hunter washes the venison
down with the sauvignon? Oh leap,
leap! Careful of the rocks! Does true
love have to wish him happiness
in his new life, even sexual
joy? I think so. Below his shaggy
belly, in the distance, lie the even dots
of a vineyard, its vines not blasted, its roots
clean, its bottles growing at the ends of their
blowpipes as dark, green, wavering groans.

ROBERT CREELEY

THE SOUND

Early mornings, in the light still
faint, making stones, herons, marsh
grass all but indistinguishable in the muck,

one looks to the far side of the sound, the sand
side, with low growing brush and
reeds, to the long horizontal of land's edge,

where the sea is, on that
other side, that outside, place of
imagined real openness, restless, eternal ocean.

SEAMUS HEANEY

AUBADE

My children weep out the hot, foreign night.
We walk the floor, my foul mouth takes it out
On you, and we lie stiff till dawn
Attends the pillow—and the maize, and vine

That holds its filling burden to the light.
Yesterday rocks sang when we tapped
Stalactites in the great cave's dripping dark.
Our love calls tiny as a tuning fork.

JORIE GRAHAM

LATER IN LIFE

Summer heat, the first early morning
                    of it. How it lowers the pitch of the
                    cry—human—cast up
as two words by the worker street level
                    positioning the long beam on
the chain as he calls up to the one handling the pulley on
                              the seventh floor. One
                    call. They hear each other!
Perfectly! As the dry heat, the filled-out leaves thicken the surround,
        the warming
                    asphalt, & the lull in growth
                    occurs, & in it the single birdcries
                              now and again
                    are placed, &
all makes a round from which sound is sturdied-up without
        dissipation or dilation,
                              bamboo-crisp, &
                    up it goes up like a thing
                    tossed without warp of weight or
                              evidence of
                    overcome

gravity, as if space were thinned by summer now to a non-
interference. Up it goes, the
cry, all the
way up, audible and unchanging, so
the man need
not even raise his voice to be heard,
the dry warm air free to let it pass
without
loss of
any of itself along
its way . . .
I step out and suddenly notice this: summer arrives, has arrived, is
arriving. Birds grow
less than leaves although they cheep,
dip, arc. A call
across the tall fence from an invisible neighbor to his child is heard
right down to the secret mood
in it the child
also hears. One hears in the silence that follows the great
desire for approval
and love
which summer holds aloft, all damp leached from it, like a thing
floating out on a frail but
perfect twig end. Light seeming to darken in it yet
glow. *Please*, it says. But not with the eager need of
spring! Come what may, says summer. Smack in the middle I will
stand and breathe. The
future is a superfluity I do not
taste, no, there is no numbering
here, it is a gorgeous swelling, no emotion, as in this love is no
emotion, no, also no
memory—we have it all, now, & all
there ever was is
us, now, that man holding the beam by the right end and saying *go*
on his
ground from
which the word and the
cantilevered metal

rise, there is no mistake, the right minute falls harmlessly, intimate,
     overcrowded,
          without pro-
                    venance—perhaps bursting with nostalgia but
ripening so fast without growing at
     all, & what
is the structure of freedom but this, & grace, & the politics of time—
     look south, look
          north—yes—east west compile hope synthesize
exceed look look again hold fast attach speculate drift drift recognize
     forget—terrible
          gush—gash—of
          form of
outwardness, & it is your right to be so entertained, & if you are
     starting to
          feel it is hunger this
          gorgeousness, feel the heat fluctuate & say
          my
          name is day, of day, in day, I want nothing to
come back, not ever, & these words are mine, there is no angel to
     wrestle, there is no inter-
          mediary, there is something I must
tell you, you do not need existence, these words praise be they can
     for now be
          said. That is summer. Hear them.

TERRANCE HAYES

AMERICAN SONNET FOR THE NEW YEAR

things got terribly ugly incredibly quickly
things got ugly embarrassingly quickly
actually things got ugly unbelievably quickly
honestly things got ugly seemingly infrequently
initially things got ugly ironically usually
awfully carefully things got ugly unsuccessfully

occasionally things got ugly mostly painstakingly
quietly seemingly things got ugly beautifully
infrequently things got ugly sadly especially
frequently unfortunately things got ugly
increasingly obviously things got ugly suddenly
embarrassingly forcefully things got really ugly
regularly truly quickly things got really incredibly
ugly things will get less ugly inevitably hopefully

ARIEL FRANCISCO

ALONG THE EAST RIVER AND IN THE BRONX YOUNG MEN WERE SINGING

I heard them and I still hear them
above the threatening shrieks of police sirens
above the honking horns of morning traffic,
above the home-crowd cheers of Yankee Stadium
above the school bells and laughter
lighting up the afternoon
above the clamoring trudge of the 1 train
and the 2 and 4, 5, 6, the B and the D
above the ice-cream trucks' warm jingle
above the stampede of children
playing in the street,
above the rush of a popped fire hydrant
above the racket of eviction notices
above the whisper of moss and mold moving in
above the High Bridge and the 145th Street Bridge
above mothers calling those children
to come in for dinner, to come in
before it gets dark, to get your ass inside
above them calling a child who may never come home
above the creaking plunge of nightfall
and darkness settling in the deepest corners
above the Goodyear blimp circling the Stadium
above the seagulls circling the coastal trash
along the East River and in the Bronx

young men are singing and I hear them,
eastbound into eternity even
as morning destars the sky.

ROBIN COSTE LEWIS

FROM TO THE REALIZATION OF PERFECT HELPLESSNESS

Lately, every morning, after a night
   of lucid insomnia, my first thought is always
      the same: *fourteen billion years—*

our planet began fourteen billion years ago.
   I just lie there.
      Thinking.

Then I move—slowly—forward,
   millennium by millennium, trying
      to see everything

that has taken place until
   I arrive at the present moment—me
      lying in my bed.

Lately, I think about all of the other humans—
   now extinct—whose DNA spirals
      inside of our own DNA.

Then I remember
   that we will one day—soon—be extinct, too.
      Fourteen billion years.

I am terrified by the idea
   of my own death, but my cells scoff
      at the idea of four paltry *centuries.*

Sometimes, instead of going
    forward, I try to go farther back—
        beyond fourteen billion years.

I try fifteen billion, sixteen
    billion, sixty billion—long before
        our planet was ever created.

Sometimes, the small girl in me wonders
    if all of our universes are a roux roiling inside
        a large stone cauldron,

inside the warm midnight-blue
    kitchen of the infinite Black Sorceress
        alive inside my cells.

I have been
    thinking about you
        again today,

as I do—
    so often—think of you,
        wondering

if people can see the sky
    of our childhood
        the way we still see (the sky)

whenever we think
    of each other.
        Well, not see, but feel—

the way
    every feeling
        has a trillion eyes.

DEBORAH LANDAU

ECSTASIES

Catch me alive? I am today—swept through the air in a flesh,
thinky-feeling, lugging itself up the subway stairs
& now back on Spring Street again in the dazing light

pumping the marrow a breeze of breath a blood
& still the minutes accelerate & we wake backweighted
with days will we waste them all & then when we get there

we will think I wasted them all, stony before I was laid
in stone, mourning before I was mourned
& what was this velvet for? Spring didn't know—

flags of the grave? well also a jubilance not just a bawling
& off again toward whatever, drinking exalted or coughing
but still can swallow & here all your parts are warm & mostly work

& look it's luck, while not yet a word from the underworld,
the necklace of days bracelets of hours the flush of blood
present swelling the yes please of sex the abject of—

is it precarious yes exquisite *alive*, staging its trance
the hand in hand, my mouth sloshed with coffee, sugared & warm,
your silent reading this now.

ALASTAIR REID

GHOSTS

Never to see ghosts? Then to be
haunted by what is, only—to believe that glass
is for looking through, that rooms, too, can be empty,
the past past, deeds done,
that sleep, however troubled, is your own?
Do the dead lie down, then? Are blind men blind?

Is love in touch alone? Do lights go out?
And what is that shifting, shifting in the mind?
    The wind, the wind?

No, they are there. Let your ear be gentle,
At dawn or owl cry, over doorway or lintel,
theirs are the voices moving night toward morning,
the garden's grief, the river's warning.
Their curious presence in a kiss,
the past quivering in what is,
our words odd-sounding, not our own—
how can we think we sleep alone?

What do they have to tell? If we can listen,
their voices are denials of all dying,
faint, on a long bell tone, lying
beyond sound or belief, in the oblique
last reach of the sense through layers of recognition. . . .
Ghost on my desk, speak, speak.

FRANZ WRIGHT

APRIL ORCHARD

We think if we're not conscious we exist
we won't exist, but
how can that be?
Just look at the sun.
Oh, if only I could make myself
completely unafraid—once
born, we never die—
what talks we'd have, and will. It's theorized
the universe is only one
among others, infinite
others. Though
didn't Christ tell us, In my father's house
there are many rooms . . .

And I would tell you
what it's like,
real fear. And
how there are human beings for whom the sun
is never going to shine
is never going to rise again, ever, not
really—
not the real sun.
They're not exactly waking up
in radiant awareness
and celebration of their own presence these days,
who'd get rid of themselves with no more thought
(if it were possible) than you would give to
taking off a glove.
How in deep sleep sometimes even we get well.
So you can believe me, in the far deeper
sleep (these new apple leaves, maybe) we are all going
to be perfectly all right.

JANE COOPER

NO MORE ELEGIES

Today the snow crunches underfoot
and squeaks dryly like compressed sugar.
Up the road run tire ribbons,
along the paths the quick prints of rabbits.

Everyone rushed into town
right after coffee, though the icy ruts
are gray as iron, and icicles
two feet long scarcely drip.

The sun is so bright on the snow
I'm out tramping in dark beach glasses.
A clump of leafless birches
steams against a dark-blue sky.

Over there the yellow frame
of some new construction glints,
while the tips of those bushes are bloody
as if tomorrow, tomorrow would be Easter!

And a phoebe is calling, calling,
all the small birds come fluting from the pines,
"No more elegies, no more elegies!" Poor
fools, they don't know it's not spring!

SYLVIA PLATH

PHEASANT

You said you would kill it this morning.
Do not kill it. It startles me still,
The jut of that odd, dark head, pacing

Through the uncut grass on the elm's hill.
It is something to own a pheasant,
Or just to be visited at all.

I am not mystical; it isn't
As if I thought it had a spirit.
It is simply in its element.

That gives it a kingliness, a right.
The print of its big foot last winter,
The tail track, on the snow in our court—

The wonder of it, in that pallor,
Through crosshatch of sparrow and starling.
Is it its rareness, then? It is rare.

But a dozen would be worth having,
A hundred, on that hill—green and red,
Crossing and recrossing—a fine thing!

It is such a good shape, so vivid.
It's a little cornucopia.
It upclaps, brown as a leaf, and loud,

Settles in the elm, and is easy.
It was sunning in the narcissi.
I trespass stupidly. Let be, let be.

JUAN FELIPE HERRERA

BASHO & MANDELA

As Basho has said—
it is a narrow road to the Deep North—as Mandela has said
the haphazard segregation later became a well-orchestrated
    segregation
—as Basho has said the journey began with an attained
    awareness
that at any moment you can become a weather-exposed skeleton
—think of us in this manner
these are notes for your nourishment—hold them
as bowls of kindness
from journeys of bravery
the will to seek & find the sudden turning rivers & the dawn-eyed

       freedom

ANNE CARSON

EPITHALAMIUM NYC

I washed my hair the morning I got married put
on
red boots found license woke C. set off for City
Hall
had ceremony drove to Fairway got cups of tea
sat

at bench on boardwalk watched man & woman
at
next bench come almost to blows over her having
put
ketchup on his egg sandwich too bad they couldn't
just
trade hers had the sausage *Don't ever put ketchup*
on
my egg sandwich he clenched *You handed it to me*
she
cawed meanwhile their aged father paying no heed
was
pulling out bits of paper one after the other *That's not*
it
he'd say *That's one from four years ago* beautifully
mild
he searched on his wife I bet kept track of the list
when
she was alive bluish mist lifted sank on the water a
statue
(Liberty) slid us a wave from way across the bay.

BILLY COLLINS

THE FUTURE

When I finally arrive there—
and it will take many days and nights—
I would like to believe others will be waiting
and might even want to know how it was.
So I will reminisce about a particular sky
or a woman in a white bathrobe
or the time I visited a narrow strait
where a famous naval battle had taken place.
Then I will spread out on a table
a large map of my world
and explain to the people of the future

in their pale garments what it was like—
how mountains rose between the valleys
and this was called geography,
how boats loaded with cargo plied the rivers
and this was known as commerce,
how the people from this pink area
crossed over into this light-green area
and set fires and killed whoever they found
and this was called history—
and they will listen, mild-eyed and silent,
as more of them arrive to join the circle
like ripples moving toward,
not away from, a stone tossed into a pond.

PAUL ZWEIG

THE PERFECT SLEEPERS

The light flooding my chair
Is too strong at six in the morning;
It was meant for evidence of another kind—
The kind policemen use, prowling
In a room around some murderer
Whose guilt is a form of sleeplessness.

Slumped to my waist in shadow,
I squint at a landscape of horses
Motionless in a field,
Except for their tails that flick away darkness,
And their eyes blazing like angels
On a beach in hell, bruised but noble,
For they left speech behind them
On their night-long fall into the world.

Perfect sleepers,
Erect in the narrow field between thinking
And dreaming, your powerful thighs clotted with dew,

The pits of your eyes merciless but empty,
I have brought you with me into the stale gray of dawn,
Because I know that your terrors are simpler than mine:
Afraid of puddles, rabbits, and the whip,
Not of promises kept or broken, not of breathing,
Not of love's forged signature
And its costly repairs.

EAVAN BOLAND

THANKED BE FORTUNE

Did we live a double life?
            I would have said
                        we never envied
the epic glory of the star-crossed.
            I would have said
                        we learned by heart
the code marriage makes of passion—
                        duty dailyness routine.
But after dark when we went to bed
under the bitter fire
                        of constellations—
            orderly, uninterested and cold,
                        at least in our case—
in the bookshelves just above our heads,
            all through the hours of darkness,
                        men and women
wept, cursed, kept and broke faith
            and killed themselves for love.
                        Then it was dawn again.
Restored to ourselves,
            we woke early and lay together
listening to our child crying, as if to birdsong,
            with ice on the windowsills
                        and the grass eking out
            the last crooked hour of starlight.

RACHEL ELIZA GRIFFITHS

COMEDY

I am here before the nurse brings my mother breakfast.
I study her body. Try to remember if I ever caught my mother
in the dream I had the night before where the hem of her
gown flew through a silver tunnel without end. Her skin
went right through my hands whenever I was close enough
to save her. She slipped through her name, her name I could not stop
calling until I sat up alone in my crib. Embarrassed, she tells me
she remembers how she phoned me last night to let me know
she was in the morgue. She laughs as the nurse, whose feet squeak
in Minnie Mouse Crocs, arrives with tea. We watch the nurse
with eyes that will never remember her face. Thank her
for the toast that is thicker than my mother's hand.
That morphine is some powerful shit, my mother says.
I agree with her as though she has merely mentioned it is cold
outside though I have rarely had morphine &
have never made courtesy calls from a morgue. *It was late
& I didn't know where I was*, she says. *Because that wasn't death,
which means I couldn't have called you from that place.*
This is my new mother, who has finally admitted fear
into the raw ward of her heart. This is my mother who flew away
from my grasp in the tunnel without end. The woman
who could not wait for me to grab the white edge
of where she was going. *I was afraid*, she says. Looking
over the rim of her plastic cup, she shakes the world. Chipped
ice between us. *Yeah don't go & write about me like that*,
she says. *I already know you.*

D. A. POWELL

OPEN GESTURE OF AN I

I want to give more of my time
to others the less I have of it,
give it away in a will and testament,

give it to the girls' club, give it
to the friends of the urban trees.

Your life is not your own and
never was. It came to you in a box
marked fragile. It came from the
complaint department like amends
on an order you did not place with
them. Who gave me this chill life.

It came with no card. It came
without instruction. It said this
end up though I do not trust those
markings. I have worn it upside
downs. I have washed it without
separating and it did not shrink.
Take from it what you will. I will

KIRMEN URIBE

MAY

Look. May has come in.
It's strewn those blue eyes all over the harbor.
Come, I haven't had word of you in ages.
You're constantly terrified,
Like the kittens we drowned when we were little.
Come and we'll talk over all of the old same things,
The value of being pleasant,
The need to adjust to the doubts,
How to fill the holes we've got inside us.
Come, feel the morning reaching your face,
Whenever we're saddened everything looks dark,
When we're heartened, again, the world crumbles.
Every one of us keeps forever someone else's hidden side,
If it's a secret, if a mistake, if a gesture.
Come and we'll flay the winners,

Laughing at our self leapt off the bridgeway.
We'll watch the cranes at work in the port in silence,
The gift for being together in silence being
The principal proof of friendship.
Come with me, I want to change nations,
Change towns. Leave this body aside
And go into a shell with you,
With our smallness, like sea snails.
Come, I'm waiting for you,
We'll continue the story that ended a year ago,
As if inside the white birches next to the river
Not a single additional ring had grown.

(Translated, from the Basque, by Elizabeth Macklin.)

BABETTE DEUTSCH

EARLINESS AT THE CAPE

The color of silence is the oyster's color
Between the lustres of deep night and dawn.
Earth turns to absence; the sole shape's the sleeping
Light—a mollusk of mist. Remote,
A sandspit hinges the valves of that soft monster
Yawning at Portugal. Alone wakeful, lanterns
Over a dark hull to eastward mark
The tough long pull, hidden, the killing
Work, hidden, to feed a hidden world.
Muteness is all. Even the greed of the gulls
Annulled, the hush of color everywhere
The hush of motion. This is the neap of the blood,
Of memory, thought, desire; if pain visits
Such placelessness, it has phantom feet.
What's physical is lost here in ignorance
Of its own being, That solitary boat,
Out fishing, is a black stroke on vacancy.
Night, deaf and dumb as something from the deeps,

Having swallowed whole bright yesterday, replete
With radiance, is gray as abstinence now.
But in this nothingness, a knife point: pleasure
Comes pricking; the hour's pallor, too, is bladed
Like a shell, and as it opens, cuts.

C. K. WILLIAMS

LIGHT

Another drought morning after a too brief dawn downpour,
uncountable silvery glitterings on the leaves of the withering maples—

I think of a troop of the blissful blessed approaching Dante,
"a hundred spheres shining," he rhapsodizes, "the purest pearls . . ."

then of the frightening brilliant myriad gleam in my lamp
of the eyes of the vast swarm of bats I found once in a cave,

a chamber whose walls seethed with a spaceless carpet of creatures,
their cacophonous, keen, insistent, incessant squeakings and
        squealings

churning the warm, rank, cloying air, of how one,
perfectly still among all the fitfully twitching others,

was looking straight at me, gazing solemnly, thoughtfully up
from beneath the intricate furl of its leathery wings

as though it couldn't believe I was there, or were trying to place me,
to situate me in the gnarl we'd evolved from, and now,

the trees still heartrendingly asparkle, Dante again,
this time the way he'll refer to a figure he meets as "the life of . . ."

not the soul, or person, the *life*, and once more the bat, and I,
our lives in that moment together, our lives, our *lives*,

his with no vision of celestial splendor, no poem,
mine with no flight, no unblundering dash through the dark,

his without realizing it would, so soon, no longer exist,
mine having to know for us both that everything ends,

world, after-world, even their memory, steamed away
like the film of uncertain vapor of the last of the luscious rain.

ED ROBERSON

SAND

The sand sticks to me as though it had fallen
as snow   the silica's wet glitter   dry.

I am coated with a line as if I had lain
in water   floating like the boats that lie

about what they are on   in the glare—
sky and water interchanging their light.

I am uncertain what luminary
bears this sandcastle illusion upright.

This beach wasn't here before the hurricane,
houses that were here aren't here either.

The glaciation of this earth-change planes
away the known in the thin curl we feared

it was
something we brush off that could be brushed off.

MELISSA GINSBURG

SO ATTACHED YOU ARE TO LIVING IN THE WORLD

Cut off access to the feeding stream and the water will come instead
     from below. Will rise
and form puddles on the hill, even in dry weather.

The pattern of woven and knitted grasses, the plethora of knots
     worked by wind—like you,
it undoes

everything it does. Reckless skies, falling trees, horizon floating like
     algae.
You try to see yourself from the outside, where the weather

is spinning. You identify with the largest predator
because she never lets you near. Ruthless,

unabating in her shyness. Through this unseasonal flowering
the heron keeps spearing tadpoles. You can see her but you can't

get as close as you'd like. You lose track of your mind in the satellite
     photo. Are you
the solitary wood duck, its markings sleeker without the flock?
     Are you

the heron's wet legs, are you the straight-line wind?
Are you your own mistake, your own darling? Again and again you
     ocean the marsh,

lock the hurricane in the bathtub.
You walk straight into the spider's web and close its door behind
     you.

W. S. MERWIN

LOOKING FOR MUSHROOMS AT SUNRISE

When it is not yet day
I am walking on centuries of dead chestnut leaves
In a place without grief
Though the oriole
Out of another life warns me
That I am awake

In the dark while the rain fell
The gold chanterelles pushed through a sleep that was not mine
Waking me
So that I came up the mountain to find them

Where they appear it seems I have been before
I recognize their haunts as though remembering
Another life

Where else am I walking even now
Looking for me

MARK STRAND

THE CONTINUOUS LIFE

What of the neighborhood homes awash
In a silver light, of children hunched in the bushes,
Watching the grown-ups for signs of surrender,
Signs that the irregular pleasures of moving
From day to day, of being adrift on the swell of duty,
Have run their course? O parents, confess
To your little ones the night is a long way off
And your taste for the mundane grows; tell them
Your worship of household chores has barely begun;
Describe the beauty of shovels and rakes, brooms and mops;
Say there will always be cooking and cleaning to do,

That one thing leads to another, which leads to another;
Explain that you live between two great darks, the first
With an ending, the second without one, that the luckiest
Thing is having been born, that you live in a blur
Of hours and days, months and years, and believe
It has meaning, despite the occasional fear
You are slipping away with nothing completed, nothing
To prove you existed. Tell the children to come inside,
That your search goes on for something you lost—a name,
A family album that fell from its own small matter
Into another, a piece of the dark that might have been yours,
You don't really know. Say that each of you tries
To keep busy, learning to lean down close and hear
The careless breathing of earth and feel its available
Languor come over you, wave after wave, sending
Small tremors of love through your brief,
Undeniable selves, into your days, and beyond.

CAMILLE T. DUNGY

LET ME

Let me tell you, America, this one last thing.
I will never be finished dreaming about you.
I had a lover once. If you could call him that.
I drove to his apartment in a faraway town,
like the lost bear who wandered to our cul-de-sac
that summer smoke from the burning mountain
altered our air. I don't know what became of her.
I drove to so many apartments in the day.
America, this is really the very last thing.
He'd stocked up, for our weekend together,
on food he knew I would like. Vegetarian
pad Thai, some black-bean-and-sweet-potato chili,
coconut ice cream, a bag of caramel popcorn.
Loads of Malbec. He wanted to make me happy,

but he drank until I would have been a fool
not to be afraid. I'd been drinking plenty, too.
It was too late to drive myself anywhere safe.
I watched him finger a brick as if to throw it
at my head. Maybe that's a metaphor. Maybe
that's what happened. America, sometimes it's hard
to tell the difference with you. All I could do
was lock myself inside his small bedroom. I pushed
a chest against the door and listened as he threw
his body at the wood. Listened as he tore apart
the pillow I had sewn him. He'd been good to me,
but this was like waiting for the walls to ignite.
You've heard that, America? In a firestorm
some houses burn from the inside out. An ember
caught in the eaves, wormed through the chinking, will flare up
in the insulation, on the frame, until everything
in the house succumbs to the blaze. In the morning,
I found him on the couch. Legs too long, arms spilling
to the carpet, knuckles bruised in the same pattern
as a hole in the drywall. Every wine bottle
empty. Each container of food opened, eaten,
or destroyed. "I didn't want you to have this,"
he whispered. If he could not consume my body,
the food he'd given me to eat would have to do.
Have you ever seen a person walk through the ruins
of a burnt-out home? Please believe me, I am not
making light of such suffering, America.
Maybe the dream I still can't get over is that,
so far, I have made it out alive.

ADA LIMÓN

THE END OF POETRY

Enough of osseous and chickadee and sunflower
and snowshoes, maple and seeds, samara and shoot,
enough chiaroscuro, enough of thus and prophecy
and the stoic farmer and faith and our father and tis
of thee, enough of bosom and bud, skin and god
not forgetting and star bodies and frozen birds,
enough of the will to go on and not go on or how
a certain light does a certain thing, enough
of the kneeling and the rising and the looking
inward and the looking up, enough of the gun,
the drama, and the acquaintance's suicide, the long-lost
letter on the dresser, enough of the longing and
the ego and the obliteration of ego, enough
of the mother and the child and the father and the child
and enough of the pointing to the world, weary
and desperate, enough of the brutal and the border,
enough of can you see me, can you hear me, enough
I am human, enough I am alone and I am desperate,
enough of the animal saving me, enough of the high
water, enough sorrow, enough of the air and its ease,
I am asking you to touch me.

(2020)

ACKNOWLEDGMENTS

Special thanks to the individuals, estates, and publishing houses who offered gracious help in arranging permissions for many of the poems in this book, most especially: Frederick T. Courtwright of The Permissions Company; Victoria Fox at Farrar, Straus & Giroux; Peter London and Trysha Le at HarperCollins; Jeffery Corrick and the permissions team at Penguin Random House; Robert Shatzkin at W. W. Norton; the Wylie Agency.

The following poems are reprinted with permission of The Permissions Company LLC on behalf of **Alice James Books,** alicejamesbooks.org: **Jean Valentine,** "The Tractors" from *Light Me Down: The New & Collected Poems of Jean Valentine*. Originally published in *The New Yorker* as "The Suicides" (May 2, 1993). Copyright © 1993 by Jean Valentine. "The Badlands Said" from *Light Me Down: The New & Collected Poems of Jean Valentine*. Originally published in *The New Yorker* (March 25, 1990). Copyright © 1990 by Jean Valentine.

Reprinted with permission from **Beacon Press,** *Boston, Massachusetts:* "My Father in English": From *How to Love a Country: Poems* by **Richard Blanco**. Copyright © 2019 by Richard Blanco; "Vinegar Hill": From *Vinegar Hill* by **Colm Tóibín**. Copyright © 2022 by Colm Tóibín.

The following poems are reprinted with the permission of The Permissions Company on behalf of **BOA Editions Ltd.,** boaeditions.org: **Isabella Gardner,** "In the Museum" from *The Collected Poems of Isabella Gardner 7*. Copyright © 1987 by the Estate of Isabella Gardner; **Carolyn Kizer,** "The Unbelievers" from *Yin: New Poems*. Copyright © 1984 by Carolyn Kizer; **Louis Simpson,** "My Father in the Night Commanding No" from *The Owner of the House: New Collected Poems 1940–2001*. Copyright © 2003 by Louis Simpson; **Ko Un,** four poems from *Flowers of a Moment*, translated by Brother Anthony, Young-moo Kim, and Gary Gach. Translation copyright © 2006 by Brother Anthony, Young-moo Kim, and Gary Gach; **David Woo,** "Eden" from *The Eclipses*. Copyright © 2005 by David Woo.

The following poems are reprinted with the permission of The Permissions Company LLC on behalf of **Copper Canyon Press,** coppercanyonpress.org: **Ellen Bass,** "The Morning After" and "What Did I Love" from *Like a Beggar*. Copyright © 2014 by Ellen Bass; "Indigo" from *Indigo*. Copyright © 2020 by Ellen Bass; **David Bottoms,** "Under the Boathouse" from *Armored Hearts: Selected & New Poems*. Copyright © 1995 by David Bottoms; **Victoria Chang,** "Distant Morning," "That Music," "In a Clearing," "To the Hand," and "Tool" from *The Trees Witness Everything*. Copyright © 2022 by Victoria Chang; **James Galvin,** "Independence Day, 1956: A Fairy Tale" from *Resurrection Update: Collected Poems 1975–1997*. Copyright © 1995 by James Galvin; **Patricia Goedicke,** "Mahler in the Living Room" from *The Wind of Our Going*. Copyright © 1985 by Patricia Goedicke; **Deborah Landau,** "Ecstasies" from *Skeletons*. Copyright © 2023 by Deborah Landau; **W. S. Merwin,** "Another Year Come," "The Widow," "The Asians Dying," "Come Back," and "Looking for Mushrooms at Sunrise" from *Migration: New & Selected Poems*. Copyright © 1963, 1967 by W. S. Merwin; **Ruth Stone,** "Wild Asters" from *What Love Comes To: New and Selected Poems*. Copyright © 1971 by Ruth Stone; **C. D. Wright,** "Obscurity and Regret" from *ShallCross*. Copyright © 2016 by C. D. Wright; "Like a Prisoner of Soft Words" from *Rising, Falling, Hovering*. Copyright © 2008 by C. D. Wright.

The following poems are reprinted with the permission of The Permissions Company LLC on behalf of **Counterpoint Press,** counterpointpress.com: **Alfred Corn,** "Promised Land Valley, June '73" from *Stake: Selected Poems 1972–1992*. Copyright © 1973 by Alfred Corn; **Wendell Berry,** "A Speech to the Garden Club of America" (with thanks to Wes Jackson and in memory of Sir Albert Howard and Stan Rowe) from *New Collected Poems*. Copyright © 2010 by Wendell Berry.

The following poems are used by permission of **Farrar, Straus & Giroux.** *All Rights Reserved.* "At the Fishhouses," "Filling Station," "In the Waiting Room," "Large Bad Picture," "Little Exercise at 4 A.M.," "The Moose," and "Sandpiper" by Elizabeth Bishop and "Objects & Apparitions" by Octavio Paz, translated by Elizabeth Bishop, from *Poems* by **Elizabeth Bishop**. Copyright © 2011 by the Alice H. Methfessel Trust. Publisher's note and compilation copyright © 2011 by Farrar, Straus & Giroux; "Note to Wang Wei" and "A Sympathy, a Welcome" from *Collected Poems: 1937–1971* by **John Berryman**. Copyright © 1989 by Kate Donahue Berryman; "Uncollected Dream Songs" from *Henry's Fate and Other Poems: 1967–1972* by John Berryman. Copyright © 1977 by Kate Berryman. Originally published as "Posthumous Dream Songs" in *The New Yorker*; "Solitary Observation Brought Back from a Short Sojourn in Hell" and "To My Brother" from *The Blue Estuaries* by **Louise Bogan**. Copyright © 1968 by Louise Bogan. Copyright renewed 1996 by Ruth Limmer; "Elegy: For Robert Lowell" and "A Song" from *Collected Poems in English* by **Joseph Brodsky**. Copyright © 2000 by the Estate of Joseph Brodsky; "Drank a Lot" from *The Flame: Poems, Notebooks, Lyrics, Drawings* by Leonard Cohen. Copyright © 2018 by Old Ideas, LLC; "Figs" from *The*

Other Love by **Henri Cole**. Copyright © 2025 by Henri Cole; excerpt from "Visitation" from *Grand Tour* by **Elisa Gonzalez**. Copyright © 2023 by Elisa Gonzalez; "Noon" from *Poems 1962–2012* by **Louise Glück**. Copyright © 2012 by Louise Glück; "New York" from *Collected Poems* by **Thom Gunn**. Copyright © 1994 by Thom Gunn; "Rapallo," "To Another Poet" from "Jokes, etc.," "To Cupid" from *Boss Cupid* by **Thom Gunn**. Copyright © 2000 by Thom Gunn; "Casualty," "Crossings," "The Guttural Muse," "Stanza V" from "Summer Home" from *Opened Ground: Selected Poems 1966–1996* by **Seamus Heaney**. Copyright © 1998 by Seamus Heaney; "Electric Light" from *Electric Light* by **Seamus Heaney**. Copyright © 2001 by Seamus Heaney; "Among the Missing" from *Inner Voices: Selected Poems, 1963–2003* by **Richard Howard**. Copyright © 2004 by Richard Howard; "Crow Frowns" and "The Thought Fox" from *Collected Poems* by **Ted Hughes**. Copyright © 2003 by the Estate of Ted Hughes; "Freedom of Speech," "The Literary Life," and "The Fulbright Scholars" from *Birthday Letters* by **Ted Hughes**. Copyright © 1998 by Ted Hughes; "Next Day" from *The Complete Poems* by **Randall Jarrell**. Copyright © 1969, renewed 1997 by Mary von S. Jarrell; "Sunday in November" from *Sleeping It Off in Rapid City* by **August Kleinzahler**. Copyright © 2008 by August Kleinzahler; "The Soul's Soundtrack" from *Everyday Mojo Songs of the Earth: New and Selected Poems 2001–2021* by **Yusef Komunyakaa**. Copyright © 2021 by Yusef Komunyakaa; "Errata" and "Hay" from *Selected Poems 1968–2014* by **Paul Muldoon**. Copyright © 2016 by Paul Muldoon; "Turkey Buzzards" from *Horse Latitudes* by **Paul Muldoon**. Copyright © 2006 by Paul Muldoon; "The Harleys," "To a Tyrant," and "Twelve Poems" from *New Selected Poems* by **Les Murray**. Copyright © 2007, 2012, 2014 by Les Murray; "Twelve Poems" originally published under the title "Eleven Poems" in *The New Yorker*; "Father" from *Isla Negra* by **Pablo Neruda,** translated by Alastair Reid. Translation copyright © 1981 by Alastair Reid; "Postcard to the USA" from *Legacies: Selected Poems* by **Heberto Padilla**, translated by Alastair Reid and Andrew Hurley. Translation copyright © 1982 by Alastair Reid and Andrew Hurley; "Forecast" from *The Tether* by **Carl Phillips**. Copyright © 2001 by Carl Phillips; "Civilization" from *Double Shadow* by **Carl Phillips**. Copyright © 2011 by Carl Phillips; "White Dog" from *The Rest of Love* by **Carl Phillips**. Copyright © 2004 by Carl Phillips; "Samurai Song" and "Shirt" from *Selected Poems* by **Robert Pinsky**. Copyright © 2011 by Robert Pinsky; "A Monument in Utopia" from *Supernatural Love: Poems 1976–1992* by **Gjertrud Schnackenberg**. Copyright © 2000 by Gjertrud Schnackenberg; "Song" and "White Boat, Blue Boat" from *Collected Poems* by **James Schuyler**. Copyright © 1993 by the Estate of James Schuyler; "I, II, and III" from "The Bounty" and "The Season of Phantasmal Peace" from *The Poetry of Derek Walcott 1948–2013* by **Derek Walcott,** selected by Glyn Maxwell. Copyright © 2014 by Derek Walcott; "The Muse of History at Rampanalgas" from *Another Life* by **Derek Walcott**. Copyright © 1972, 1973 by Derek Walcott; "Light," "Prisoners," "Thirst," and "Toil" from *Collected Poems* by **C. K. Williams**. Copyright © 2006 by C. K. Williams; "Homage to Paul Cézanne" from *Oblivion Banjo: the Poetry of Charles Wright* by **Charles Wright**. Copyright © 2019 by Charles Wright; "Lighting a Candle for W. H. Auden," "Song," "With the Shell of a Hermit Crab," and "Yes, But" from "Four Poems" from *Above the River: The Complete Poems* by **James Wright,** introduction by Donald Hall. Copyright © 1990 by Anne Wright; "Try to Praise the Mutilated World" from *Without End: New and Selected Poems* by **Adam Zagajewski**, translated by several translators. Copyright © 2002 by Adam Zagajewski. Translation copyright © 2002 by Farrar, Straus & Giroux.

Reprinted with the permission of **George Braziller, Inc. (New York)**, *www.georgebraziller.com. All rights reserved.* **Michael Krüger,** "Footnote," translated by Richard Dove, from *Diderot's Cat: Selected Poems.* Copyright © 1993; **Charles Simic,** "Rural Delivery" from *Selected Early Poems.* Copyright © 1982 by Charles Simic.

The following poems are reprinted with the permission of The Permissions Company LLC on behalf of **Graywolf Press,** *graywolfpress.org:* **Kaveh Akbar,** "My Empire" from *Pilgrim Bell.* Copyright © 2021 by Kaveh Akbar; **Catherine Barnett,** "Son in August" from *Human Hours.* Copyright © 2018 by Catherine Barnett; **Nick Flynn,** "The Day Lou Reed Died" from *My Feelings.* Copyright © 2015 by Nick Flynn; **Tess Gallagher,** "Zero" from *Instructions to the Double.* Copyright © 1976 by Tess Gallagher; **Dana Gioia,** "In Chandler Country" from *99 Poems: New and Selected.* Copyright © 1986 by Dana Gioia; **Linda Gregg,** "Saying Goodbye to the Dead" from *Too Bright to See / Alma.* Copyright © 1985 by Linda Gregg; **Eamon Grennan,** "Sea Dog" from *Relations: New and Selected Poems.* Copyright © 1998 by Eamon Grennan; **Saskia Hamilton,** "All Souls" from *All Souls: Poems.* Copyright © 2023 by Saskia Hamilton; **Lynda Hull,** "Jackson Hotel" from *Collected Poems.* Copyright © 2006 by the Estate of Lynda Hull; **Jane Kenyon,** "Private Beach," "Heavy Summer Rain," "Prognosis," and "The Sick Wife" from *Collected Poems.* Copyright © 2005 by the Estate of Jane Kenyon. All rights reserved; **Yi Lei,** "Flame in the Cloud at Midnight" from *My Name Will Grow Wide Like a Tree: Selected Poems,* translated from the Chinese by Tracy K. Smith and

Changtai Bi. Copyright © 2010 by Yi Lei. English translation copyright © 2020 by Tracy K. Smith and Changtai Bi; **Vijay Seshadri**, "Divination in the Park" from *Wild Kingdom*. Copyright © 1996 by Vijay Seshadri; **Diane Seuss**, "Romantic Poetry" from *Modern Poetry*. Copyright © 2024 by Diane Seuss; **Solmaz Sharif**, "An Otherwise" from *Customs*. Copyright © 2022 by Solmaz Sharif; **Danez Smith**, "Undetectable" from *Homie*. Copyright © 2020 by Danez Smith; **Tracy K. Smith**, "Declaration," "We Feel Now a Largeness Coming On," and "I Sit Outside in Low Late Afternoon Light to Feel Earth Call to Me" from *Such Color: New and Selected Poems*. Copyright © 2018, 2021 by Tracy K. Smith; **William Stafford**, "Ask Me" from *Ask Me: 100 Essential Poems*. Copyright © 2014 by the Estate of William Stafford; **Mark Wunderlich**, "The Bats" from *God of Nothingness*. Copyright © 2021 by Mark Wunderlich.

*Permission is granted by **Grove/Atlantic, Inc.**, for the following:* "Blandeur": From *Say Uncle* copyright © 1991 by **Kay Ryan;** "Crustacean Island": From *Elephant Rocks* copyright © 1996 by **Kay Ryan;** "Falling": From *Selected Poems of Pablo Neruda* copyright © by **Pablo Neruda** and Fundación Pablo Neruda. Translation copyright © 1961 by Ben Belitt.

*The following poems are reprinted by permission of **HarperCollins, Inc.**, New York:* "Coastal" from *Atlantis* by **Mark Doty**. Copyright ©1995 by Mark Doty; "Night Song" from *The First Four Books of Poems* by **Louise Glück**. Copyright © 1968, 1971, 1972, 1973, 1974, 1975, 1976, 1977, 1978, 1979, 1980, 1985, 1995 by Louise Glück. "Vespers" from *The Wild Iris* by Louise Glück. Copyright © 1992 by Louise Glück. "Vita Nova" from *Vita Nota* by Louise Glück. Copyright © 1999 by Louise Glück; "Love in Place" from *Love Poems* by **Nikki Giovanni**. Copyright © 1968–1997 by Nikki Giovanni; "Notes on the Reality of Self" from *Materialism* by **Jorie Graham**. Copyright © 1993 by Jorie Graham; "The Ship Pounding" from *Without* by **Donald Hall**. Copyright © 1998 by Donald Hall; "Awaiting Winter Visitors: Jonathan Edwards, 1749" from *Saints and Strangers* by **Andrew Hudgins**. Copyright © 1985 by Andrew Hudgins; "What You Hear When You Read Silently" and "Refrigerator, 1957" from *New and Selected Poems* by **Thomas Lux**. Copyright © by Thomas Lux; "Housework," "Mood Indigo," "Sad Stories Told in Bars: The 'Reader's Digest' Version," "Fireworks," and "Poem Ending with a Line from Dante" from *Search Party: Collected Poems* by **William Matthews**. Copyright © 2004 by Sebastian Matthews and Stanley Plumly; "The Thistle, the Nettle," "America," and "Gathering Apricots" from *New and Collected Poems: 1931–2001* by **Czeslaw Milosz**. Copyright © 1988, 1991, 1995, 2001 by Czeslaw Milosz Royalties, Inc.; "Amnesiac," "Blackberrying," "The Elm Speaks," "Mirror," "The Moon and the Yew Tree," "Night Walk," and "Pheasant" from *The Collected Poems* by **Sylvia Plath**. Copyright © 1960, 1965, 1971, 1981 by the Estate of Sylvia Plath; "The Road Back," "Letter Written on a Ferry Crossing Long Island Sound," "Little Girl, My Stringbean, My Lovely Woman," "Flee on Your Donkey," "For My Lover, Returning to His Wife," and "Moon Song" from *Complete Poems* by **Anne Sexton**. Copyright © 1981 by Linda Gray Sexton and Loring Conant, Jr., executors of the will of Anne Sexton; "The Shore" from *The Last Troubadour* by **David St. John**. Copyright © 2017 by David St. John; "This Morning" from *A Wedding in Hell* by Charles Simic. Copyright © 1994 by Charles Simic; "Some Like Poetry," "Maybe All This," and "I'm Working on the World" from *Maps: Collected and Last Poems* by **Wisława Szymborska**. Copyright © by the Wisława Szymborska Foundation; "Grasse: The Olive Trees," "October, Maples," "Walking to Sleep," and "In Limbo" from *Collected Poems 1943–2004* by **Richard Wilbur**. Copyright © 2004 by Richard Wilbur and by permission of the Richard P. Wilbur Estate.

*The following poems are reprinted with the permission of The Permissions Company LLC on behalf of **Milkweed Editions**, milkweed.org:* **Carrie Fountain**, "You Belong to the World" from *You Are Here: Poetry in the Natural World*, edited by Ada Limón. Copyright © 2024 by Milkweed Editions and the Library of Congress; **Max Ritvo**, "Poem to My Litter" from *Four Reincarnations*. Copyright © 2016 by Max Ritvo.

*The following poems appear by permission of **Penguin Random House Inc. LLC**, New York:* "The Dark Hole" from *Ants on the Melon* © 1996 by **Virginia Hamilton Adair;** "Beach Wedding" and "To-Do List" from *The Unaccompanied* © 2018 by Simon Armitage; "A Curse," "Early Morning Bathing," "Fairground," and "Song [Refugee Blues]" from *Collected Poems* by W. H. Auden, © 1976, 1991 by the Estate of W. H. Auden; "Dad Poem X" from *The Study of Human Life* © 2022 by **Joshua Bennett;** "California Poem" from *Forever Words* © 2016 by John R. Cash Revocable Trust; "Walt Whitman at the Reburial of Poe" from *On Tour with Rita* © 1982 by **Nicholas Christopher;** "The Kingfisher," "In Umbria: A Snapshot," "Man Feeding Pigeons," and "What the Light Was Like" from *Collected Poems* by **Amy Clampitt** © 1997 by the Literary Estate of Amy Clampitt; "Cosmology" from *The Rain in Portugal* © 2016, "Downpour" from *Whale Day* © 2020, and "The Future" from *Aimless Love* © 2013 by **Billy Collins;** "The Birthing" and "The Wind Blows Through the Doors of My Heart" from *The Wind Blows Through the Doors of My Heart* by **Deborah Digges**, © 2010 by the

Estate of Deborah Digges; "The Kiss" from *Skirts and Slacks* © 2001 by **W. S. Di Piero;** "The Delicate, Plummeting Bodies" from *Velocities: New and Selected Poems* © 1994 by **Stephen Dobyns;** "The Firemen" and "Saying Yes to a Drink" from *A Working Girl Can't Win* © 1998, "I Saw You Walking" from *The Second Child* © 2007 by **Deborah Garrison;** "By Small and Small: Midnight to 4 A.M." and "Refusing Heaven" from *Refusing Heaven* © 2005 by **Jack Gilbert;** "Still" from *Life Among Others* © 1978 by **Daniel Halpern;** "American Sonnet for My Past and Future Assassin (7/2019)," "American Sonnet for My Past and Future Assassin (12/2019)," "American Sonnet for the New Year," and "George Floyd" from *So To Speak* © 2023, "American Sonnet for My Past and Future Assassin (2017)" from *American Sonnets for My Past and Future Assassin* © 2018, "Antebellum House Party" and "New York Poem" from *How to Be Drawn* © 2015 by **Terrance Hayes;** "A Letter" from *Collected Earlier Poems* © 1990 by **Anthony Hecht;** "Blunt Morning" and "Man on a Fire Escape" from *Earthly Measures* © 1994 and "My Father's Childhood" from *Lay Back the Darkness* © 2003 by **Edward Hirsch;** "French Novel" from *A Hundred Lovers* © 2022 by **Richie Hofmann;** "Hey-Hey Blues," "Sunday-Morning Prophecy," and "Wake" from *The Collected Poems of Langston Hughes* © 1994 by the Estate of **Langston Hughes;** "Crossing Kansas by Train," "Pantoum of the Depression Years," "School Letting Out (Fourth or Fifth Grade)," "The Small White Churches of the Small White Towns," "There Is a Gold Light in Certain Old Paintings," and "To Waken a Small Person" from *Collected Poems* © 2004 by **Donald Justice;** "To My Old Addresses," "To My Fifties," and "You Want a Social Life, with Friends" from *The Collected Poems of Kenneth Koch* © 2005 by the **Kenneth Koch** Literary Estate; "Part" from *Mercury* © 2001 by **Phillis Levin;** "Burial Rites" from *News of the World* © 2009, "The Mercy" from *The Mercy* © 1999, "Perennials" and "What Work Is" from *What Work Is* © 1991 by **Philip Levine;** "To the Realization of Perfect Helplessness" from *To the Realization of Perfect Helplessness* © 2022 by **Robin Coste Lewis;** "By the Sea" from *Alternate Means of Transport* © 1985 by **Cynthia MacDonald;** "The Autobiography of Khwaja Mustasim" and "To the Hyphenated Poets" from *Dothead* © 2016 by **Amit Majmudar;** "Journey Toward Evening" and "Ballad of Lost Objects" from *Times Three: Selected Verse from Three Decades* © 1960, "Publisher's Party" from *The Love Letters of Phyllis McGinley* © 1954 by **Phyllis McGinley;** "At the Ruins of Yankee Stadium" from *Fever of Unknown Origin* © 2023 by **Campbell McGrath;** "The Broken Home" and "Overdue Pilgrimage to Nova Scotia" from *Collected Poems* by **James Merrill,** © 2001 by the Literary Estate of James Merrill at Washington University; "The Toast" from *Poems 4 A.M.* © 2002 by **Susan Minot;** "The Arctic Ox," "Leonardo Da Vinci's," and "Tom Fool at Jamaica" from *Complete Poems* by **Marianne Moore,** © 1981 Clive E. Driver, Literary Executor of the Estate of Marianne Moore; "I Cannot Say I Did Not" from *Arias* © 2019, "Poem for My Son, Aged 10, After a High Fever" from *The Wellspring* © 1996, "The Promise" from *Blood, Tin, Straw* © 1999, "Self-Exam" from *One Secret Thing* © 2008, "Stag's Leap" from *Stag's Leap* © 2012, "Summer Solstice, New York City" from *The Gold Cell* © 1987 by **Sharon Olds;** "Allegory" from *Spectral Evidence* © 2024 by **Gregory Pardlo;** "Bohemia," "Songs Not Encumbered by Reticence: Afternoon; Healed; Superfluous Advice; To a Favorite Granddaughter," and "Swan Song" from *Complete Poems* by **Dorothy Parker;** "Prison: Poggio Reale" from *Hard Labor* © 1986 by **Cesare Pavese,** translated by William Arrowsmith; "I've Been Around; It Gets Me Nowhere" from *Collected Poems* © 2016 by **Marie Ponsot;** "Failure" from *Antarctic Traveller* © 1982 by **Katha Pollitt;** "What We Don't Know About Each Other" from *Visible Signs: New and Selected Poems* © 2003 by **Lawrence Raab;** "History: The Home Movie" from *History: The Home Movie* © 1994 by **Craig Raine;** "Meditation in Hydrotherapy," "Lines Upon Leaving a Sanitarium," and "The Tree, the Bird" by **Theodore Roethke** from *The Collected Poems of Theodore Roethke* © 1937, 1954, 1957, 1959, 1960, 1961, 1963, 1964, 1965, 1966 by Beatrice Roethke as Administratrix of the Estate of Theodore Roethke; "Argument" and "Moving" from *Sunday Skaters* © 1994 by **Mary Jo Salter;** "Dark Night Sallies Forth" from *After Nature* © 2002 by **W. G. Sebald,** translation © 2002 by Michael Hamburger; "Homage to Calder" from *Collected Poems: 1940–1978* © 1978 by **Karl Shapiro;** "Farewell" from *Dark Harbor* © 1993, "The Continuous Life," "Moontan," "The Remains," and "Sleeping with One Eye Open" from *Collected Poems* © 2014 by **Mark Strand;** "Gradations of Black" from *Collected Poems: 1953–1993* © 1993 by **John Updike;** "At Pere Lachaise" from *If It Be Not I: Collected Poems 1958–1982* © 1992 by **Mona Van Duyn;** "April Orchard" and "The Only Animal" from *Walking to Martha's Vineyard* © 2004, "Wheeling Motel" from *Wheeling Motel* © 2009 by **Franz Wright;** "Bereavement," "Crowning," and "Little Red Corvette" from *Blue Laws: Selected and Uncollected Poems, 1995–2015* © 2016 by **Kevin Young;** "Hawk-Watching" from *The Watercourse* © 2002, "Now" from *The Swordfish Tooth* © 1988 by **Cynthia Zarin.**

Reprinted with permission of **Persea Books,** New York, www.perseabooks.com. All rights reserved. **Paul Blackburn,** "The Crossing" and "The Stone" from *The Collected Poems of Paul*

Blackburn. Copyright © 1972 by Paul Blackburn; **Wayne Koestenbaum**, "The Garbo Index" from *Rhapsodies of a Repeat Offender*. Copyright © 1994 by Wayne Koestenbaum; **Rachel Wetzsteon**, "Love and Work" from *Sakura Park*. Copyright © 2006 by Rachel Wetzsteon.

*Reprinted with the permission of The Permissions Company LLC on behalf of the **University of Arkansas Press**, uapress.com:* Billy Collins, "Brooklyn Museum of Art" from *The Apple That Astonished Paris*. Copyright © 1988, 1996 by Billy Collins; **Reed Whittemore**, "Clamming" from *The Past, the Future, the Present: Poems New and Selected*. Copyright © 1990 by Reed Whittemore.

*Used with permission of the **University of Illinois Press**. All rights reserved.* "Scumbling": From *Palladium: Poems*. Copyright 1987 by **Alice Fulton**; "Kin": From *Nightmare Begins Responsibility: Poems*. Copyright 1975 by **Michael S. Harper**.

*Reprinted with permission of **University of Pittsburgh Press**:* "At the Acme Bar and Grill," from *Sleeping Preacher*, by **Julia Kasdorf**, © 1992; "Picking Grapes in an Abandoned Vineyard," from *The Selected Levis: Selected and with an Afterword by David St. John*, by **Larry Levis**, © 2003.

*The following poems are used by permission of **W. W. Norton & Company, Inc.**:* "Tree Limbs Down" Copyright © 2005 by **A. R. Ammons**, "Speaking" Copyright © 2017 by John R. Ammons, "Birthday Poem to My Wife" Copyright © 2017 by John R. Ammons, "Day Ghosts" Copyright © 1996 by A. R. Ammons, from *The Complete Poems of A. R. Ammons: Volume 2 1978–2005* by A. R. Ammons, edited by Robert M. West; "Poem on Sleep," from *Collected Poems* by **Robert Bly**. Copyright © 1985 by Robert Bly; "Quarantine," "Thanked Be Fortune," and "Lines for a Thirtieth Wedding Anniversary," from *Against Love Poetry* by **Eavan Boland**. Copyright © 2001 by Eavan Boland; "The Dolls' Museum in Dublin," from *In a Time of Violence*. Copyright © 1994 by Eavan Boland; "The Lost Art of Letter Writing," from *A Woman Without a Country* by Eavan Boland. Copyright © 2014 by Eavan Boland; "Last Words," from *Playlist for the Apocalypse* by Rita Dove. Copyright © 2021 by Rita Dove; "Incarnation in Phoenix," from *On the Bus with Rosa Parks*. Copyright © 2016 by Rita Dove; "Running," from *An American Sunrise* by **Joy Harjo**. Copyright © 2019 by Joy Harjo; "Without" Copyright © 2021 by Joy Harjo, from *Sundown in a Scarlet Light*; "Practicing," from *What the Living Do* by **Marie Howe**. Copyright © 1997 by Marie Howe; "How It Is" Copyright © 1978 by **Maxine Kumin**, from *Selected Poems 1960–1990* by Maxine Kumin; "Halley's Comet" and "My Mother's Pears" Copyright © 1995 by **Stanley Kunitz**, from *The Collected Poems of Stanley Kunitz*; "Tree with Ornaments by My Mother," from *You've Just Been Told*. Copyright © 2000 by **Elizabeth Macklin**; "All Over" and "Surface Tension," from *A Woman Kneeling in the Big City*. Copyright © 1992 by Elizabeth Macklin; "Evening Poem," from *Falling Awake* by **Alice Oswald**. Copyright © 2016 by Alice Oswald; "A Gesture," from *Cornucopia: New and Selected Poems* by **Molly Peacock**. Copyright © 2002 by Molly Peacock; "The Insomniacs" and "Living in Sin," from *Collected Poems, 1950–2012* by **Adrienne Rich**. Copyright © 2016, 2013 by the Adrienne Rich Literary Trust; "The Survivors" and "A Piece of Happiness" Copyright © by the Adrienne Rich Literary Trust; "The Influenzas," from *Teodoro Luna's Two Kisses*. Copyright © 1990 by **Alberto Rios**; "The House in Winter" Copyright © 1966 by **May Sarton**, from *Collected Poems, 1930–1993* by May Sarton; "96 Vandam," "Bee Balm," and "Little White Sister" Copyright © 1981 by Gerald Stern, from *This Time: New and Selected Poems* by **Gerald Stern**. Copyright © 1998 by Gerald Stern. "Apocalypse," from *American Sonnets*. Copyright © 2002 by Gerald Stern.

Permission granted for other poems below as indicated. All rights reserved.

"Celebrating Childhood" and "West and East," by **Adonis**, from *Selected Poems*, Copyright © 2010, translations by Khaled Mattawa. By permission of Yale University Press; "Signs, Music" © **Raymond Antrobus** reproduced with kind permission by David Higham Associates; "Flatline," by **Margaret Atwood** from *Dearly*, Copyright © 2020 by O. W. Toad, Ltd.; "now does our world descend" and "who are you, little I," Copyright © 1963, 1991 by the Trustees for the E. E. Cummings Trust, from *Complete Poems: 1904–1962* by **E. E. Cummings**, edited by George J. Firmage. Used by permission of Liveright Publishing Corporation; "Come In," by **Robert Frost** from *The Poetry of Robert Frost*, edited by Edward Connery Lathem. Copyright © 1928, 1969 by Henry Holt and Company. Copyright © 1956 by Robert Frost. Reprinted by permission of Henry Holt and Company; "Ship's Manifest" from *Call Us What We Carry*. Copyright © 2021 by **Amanda Gorman**. Used by permission of the author; **Juan Felipe Herrera**, "Basho & Mandela" from *Every Day We Get More Illegal*. Copyright © 2020 by Juan Felipe Herrera. Reprinted with the permission of The Permissions Company LLC on behalf of City Lights Books, citylights.com; "Early Sex" from *Loose Sugar*, Copyright © 1997 by **Brenda Hillman**. Published by Wesleyan University Press, Middletown, Connecticut, and used by permission; **Mark Jarman**, "The Supremes" from *Bone Fires: New and Selected Poems*. Copyright © 1985 by Mark Jarman. Reprinted with the permission of The Permissions Company LLC on behalf of Sarabande Books, sarabande books.org; **Saeed Jones,** "Alive at the End of the World" from *Alive at the End of the World*. Copyright © 2022 by Saeed Jones. Reprinted with the permission of The Permissions Company LLC on behalf of Coffee House Press, coffeehousepress.org; "Filming the Famine" from *The Soldiers of Year II*, © 2002 by **Medbh McGuckian,** by permission of Wake Forest University Press; "Burning the Bracken" by Leslie Norris, Copyright © 1970 by **Leslie Norris**. From *The Collected Poems*, Seren Books. Used by the permission of Brandt & Hochman Literary Agents, Inc.; "Mushrooms": From *American Primitive* by **Mary Oliver,** Copyright © 1983. Reprinted by permission of Little, Brown, an imprint of Hachette Book Group, Inc.; "Looking for Angels in New York" from *Looking for Angels in New York* by **Jacqueline Osherow,** Copyright © 1988. Reprinted by permission of University of Georgia Press; "Cold" from *Fusewire*, published by Chatto & Windus, 1995. Reprinted by permission of **Ruth Padel**. © 1995 by Ruth Padel; **Elise Paschen,** "Taxi" from *Infidelities*. Copyright © 1996 by Elise Paschen. Used with the permission of The Permissions Company LLC on behalf of Story Line Press, an imprint of Red Hen Press, redhen.org; Reprinted with the permission of The Permissions Company LLC on behalf of Kim Stafford: **William Stafford,** "Evening Walk" from *The New Yorker* (August 7, 1978). Copyright © 1978 by William Stafford. "A baby ten months old looks at the public domain" from *The New Yorker* (February 18, 1950). Copyright © 1950 by William Stafford. "Monday" from *The New Yorker* (December 11, 1965). Copyright © 1965 by William Stafford. "Slave on the Headland," from *Stories That Could Be True: New and Collected Poems*. Originally in *The New Yorker* (August 1, 1977). Copyright © 1977 by William Stafford; "Snow by Morning," "The Lowering," and "Staying at Ed's Place," © **May Swenson**. Used with permission of the Literary Estate of May Swenson. All rights reserved; "Notes from Underground: W. H. Auden on the Lexington Avenue IRT" by **Grace Schulman** appears in *Again the Dawn: New and Selected Poems, 1976–2022* by Grace Schulman. Copyright © 2022 by Grace Schulman. Used by permission of Turtle Point Press; **Diane Wakoski,** "Inside Out" from *Emerald Ice: Selected Poems 1962–1987*. Copyright © 1988 by Diane Wakoski. Reprinted with the permission of The Permissions Company LLC on behalf of Black Sparrow / David R Godine, Publisher, Inc., godine.com; **Susan Wheeler,** "Shanked on the Red Bed" from *Smokes*. Copyright © 1998 by Susan Wheeler. Reprinted with the permission of The Permissions Company LLC on behalf of Four Way Books, fourwaybooks.com.

Quotations used in **Galway Kinnell**'s poem "When the Towers Fell" are as follows: "The Testament," by François Villon; "For the Marriage of Faustus and Helen," by Hart Crane; "Death Fugue," by Paul Celan; "Songs of a Wanderer," by Aleksander Wat; "City of Ships" and "When Lilacs Last in the Door-yard Bloom'd," by Walt Whitman.

Poems not explicitly credited on this page should not be assumed to be in the public domain. All poems originally appeared in the pages of The New Yorker *magazine, and all rights are reserved by diverse copyright holders.*

INDEX OF POETS

INDEX OF TITLES